BROWNED OFF
AND
BLOODY-MINDED
THE BRITISH SOLDIER GOES TO WAR,
1939–1945

ALAN ALLPORT

YALE UNIVERSITY PRESS
NEW HAVEN AND LONDON

For information about this and other Yale University Press publications, please contact:
U.S. Office: sales.press@yale.edu   yalebooks.com
Europe Office: sales@yaleup.co.uk   yalebooks.co.uk

Typeset in Minion Pro by IDSUK (DataConnection) Ltd
Printed in Great Britain by Hobbs the Printers, Totton, Hampshire

Library of Congress Cataloging-in-Publication Data

Allport, Alan, 1970–
  Browned off and bloody-minded: the British soldier goes to war, 1939–1945 / Alan Allport.
    pages cm
  ISBN 978-0-300-17075-7 (cl : alk. paper)
1. Great Britain. Army—History—World War, 1939–1945. 2. World War, 1939–1945—Great Britain. I. Title.
  D759.A64 2015
  940.54'1241—dc23

                                                                        2014039438

A catalogue record for this book is available from the British Library.

ISBN 978-0-300-22638-6 (pbk)

10 9 8 7 6 5 4 3 2 1

To Barbara, Thomas, Katharine, and Lizzie

CONTENTS

ILLUSTRATIONS

ACKNOWLEDGEMENTS

Browned Off and Bloody-Minded has been a five-year project involving many trips back and forth across the Atlantic, and it was only made possible because of the kindness and generosity of a large number of people and institutions. My thanks first of all need to go to the staff of the Imperial War Museum in Lambeth where much of the primary source research was conducted. The IWM is a proud south London fixture which has recently undergone an extensive facelift in order to mark the centenary of the outbreak of the First World War; long may it continue to flourish. I would like particularly to thank Mehzebin Adam for helping me to obtain copyright clearance to quote from a number of private papers held at the IWM. Many relatives of wartime servicemen kindly allowed me to reproduce extracts from letters, diaries and memoirs, and wrote to me with encouragement about the project; my thanks to all of them. Thanks also to the staff of the National Archives in Kew, as well as the Trustees of the Liddell Hart Centre for Military Archives for granting me permission to reproduce materials from the papers of General Sir Ronald Forbes Adam. I have made every attempt to contact the copyright holders of other materials quoted in the book, but in a few cases this has proven to be impossible. I would like to extend my apologies if any individual or organisation has been overlooked, and would ask them to please supply appropriate details to the publisher, who will endeavour to correct the information in subsequent editions.

In the five years during which *Browned Off and Bloody-Minded* was researched and written I have had the opportunity of working alongside a number of wonderful colleagues and friends in New Jersey and New York. My thanks to the faculty, staff, and students of the Writing Program at Princeton

University and the History Department of the Maxwell School of Citizenship and Public Affairs at Syracuse University. Generous financial assistance was provided by Princeton's University Committee on Research in the Humanities and Social Sciences, the Maxwell School's Appleby-Mosher Research Fund, and the Syracuse History Department's travel fund. Early drafts of some of the material in the book were presented at conferences at King's College London, the Center for the Study of War and Society at the University of Southern Mississippi (thanks to Allison Abra), the Royal Military Academy Sandhurst, the annual meeting of the North American Conference on British Studies, and Chestnut Hill College in Philadelphia. An essay drawing in modified form on some of the themes of the book will shortly be appearing in *History and Poetry: Essays in Honour of Jonathan Steinberg*, edited by Harold James, Zara Steiner, and D'Maris Coffman. Several anonymous reviewers read versions of both the original book proposal and the draft manuscript, and offered invaluable suggestions for improvement. I am indebted to Diane Flanagan for assistance on some historical points, and to Andrew Newson for both obtaining some important documents for me and also for reading a draft copy of the Appendix. Jonathan Fennell kindly invited me to stay with his lovely family in Oxford during one of my trips to England, and I have enjoyed and drawn great value from our discussions about the wartime British Army. It goes without saying that all errors in this book which persist are my responsibility alone.

My thanks go for a second time to the wonderful team at Yale University Press in London, and in particular to Heather McCallum and Rachael Lonsdale for their years of advice, support, and friendship. A visit to Bedford Square has become one of the treats of my journeys across the pond. Tom and Moira Deveson are responsible for more individual kindnesses than I could possibly list here; all I will say is that while *Browned Off and Bloody-Minded* would have come into existence without them, the experience of researching and writing it would have been far more complicated and a great deal less pleasurable. Lastly, and most importantly of all, I need to thank my wife Barbara. In order to be able to complete this project over the last five years I have had to ask her to make many sacrifices above and beyond the call of duty, and she has always done so with her characteristic graciousness, generosity, and love. It is to her and to our three noisy, exasperating, wonderful children that I dedicate this book.

INTRODUCTION

I used to be a civvy, chum, so decent as can be;
I used to think a working lad had a man's right to be free;
Until one day they made a ruddy soldier out of me
And told me I had got to save democracy.

Oh, I was browned off, browned off, browned off as could be!
Browned off, browned off, an easy mark that's me;
And when this war is over and again I'm free,
There'll be no ruddy soldiering for me!

– Ewan MacColl[1]

The weather in Liverpool was glorious that morning. Men were wearing sports jackets and flannels, women bright floral summer dresses. At Anfield, the home team were playing Chelsea in the third match of the First Division season (they won 1-0).[2] Less than a mile from the famous football stadium, at 26 Vanbrugh Crescent, there was Palethorpe's sausage, mashed potatoes, thick onion and tomato sauce, steamed date pudding and custard for lunch. Saturday, 2 September 1939 was, in other words, a day much like any other. And for nineteen-year-old junior salesman Douglas Arthur, preoccupied with teenage thoughts of food and clothes and girls, there was little reason to imagine that it would end any differently.

To be sure, the morning newspapers were full of alarming headlines, at least for those who wanted to read them. Germany, in defiance of a British and French warning, had invaded Poland the previous day. In London, the Cabinet was meeting in emergency session. The Royal Navy was mobilizing. A mass evacuation of young children and mothers from Britain's major cities, Liverpool included, was in motion. This was not so much a sudden crisis as the culmination of six months of foreboding. Ever since March, when Hitler had brazenly occupied Prague in defiance of the four-power agreement signed at Munich in October 1938, a military confrontation with his Third Reich had appeared increasingly inevitable. Compulsory military service for twenty- and twenty-one-year-old men had been introduced in May. Doug himself had joined the part-time Territorial Army (TA) earlier in the year along with the rest of his mates, partly as a lark, partly as a vaguely formed act of patriotic commitment. But it is a tribute to the solipsism of youth that hardly any of these grim portents impinged on the teenager's thoughts that Saturday morning. Doug's mind was altogether elsewhere. He was thinking about the twelve shillings and sixpence raise he'd just been offered at work. The made-to-measure pinstripe suit with patent leather shoes that he'd just bought on the never-never from Rubin's the tailors. The dance at St Andrews Church. Tomorrow's ramble in North Wales with the rest of the crowd from Baxendale & Company, particularly with that nice-looking new girl who worked on the cash desk. The idea that anything as foolish as a war might intrude on any of these plans had simply not occurred to him.

It was only as he settled down in an armchair with his cup of tea that Doug noticed his mother reaching behind the mantelpiece clock for the buff-coloured envelope that had arrived with the rest of the morning's post. 'URGENT' and 'OHMS' were written across the top of it in heavy black letters. Inside was a postcard with a coat of arms. 'My stomach turned over with a mixture of excitement and trepidation when I read the terse message on the little card', Doug recalled many years later:

106th (Lancashire Yeomanry) Regiment, Royal Horse Artillery
2nd September, 1939

Gunner ARTHUR. D. Number 890650

A STATE OF EMERGENCY has been declared by His Majesty's Government and you are hereby instructed to report IMMEDIATELY to Shaw Street Barracks wearing full uniform and prepared to move without further notice.

'I swallowed carefully and could feel my Adam's apple move up and down in the dryness of my throat. I read the brief laconic message again, this time aloud. My eyes met my Mother's as I finished reading. There was no proud smile of congratulations on her face, as there had been when I received my Night School results. Her face had paled ... I said "I'd better get my things *polished and get up there then, hadn't I, Mum?"* *"Ay"*, she said, *"and I'll go and tell your Dad. . ." '*

Half an hour later, Doug was struggling into factory-stiff riding breeches and winding ankle puttees around his legs as his mother polished the buttons on his TA service jacket and his sister Jean paced up and down the hall wearing his cap and giving mock salutes. Dad had been woken from his boozy afternoon nap: 'Oh Christ, I knew that was coming' were his first words. Then: *'Doug, as an old soldier, take some good advice from me. Keep your nose clean, and never volunteer for anything. Mind your own business.'* With that there was not much left to say. They had never been a family much given to outward displays of emotion. With a 'cheerio', Doug tramped off self-consciously towards Breck Road railway station, his ammunition boots crunching on the cobblestones.

At Shaw Street Barracks, the parade ground was in bedlam. Over 600 men were milling around in confusion. Many, like Doug, were kitted out in their regulation uniforms, but others had clearly rushed straight from work; business suits, dungarees and bib-and-brace overalls punctuated the sea of khaki. One officer, who had evidently received his mobilization order while on the golf course, had arrived in an ensemble of baggy tweed plus-fours and canary-yellow stockings. No one really seemed to know what was going on. The only organized activity on the barracks square was being performed by a fatigue party which was busy scrubbing out obscene graffiti. Eventually the overwhelmed regimental staff decided to send everyone away. Having left Vanbrugh Crescent that morning not expecting to return for years, Doug found himself slinking back to his parents' house after just a few hours. It was a strange way to begin a war.

The following morning he was back, however, and he and the rest of his mates marched as one to St George's Anglican church in Heyworth Street for the Sunday service. As they were returning to Shaw Street shortly after eleven o'clock, they were met by a group of tearful women in their black Sunday shawls. *'War's been declared, lads, against the bloody Jerries'*, one of the women said. *'We'll stop the nasty bastards, though. We'll stop 'im.'* One of the beshawled 'Mary Ellens' stopped to point towards Doug, a mixture of 'indignation and concern' lighting up her face. *'Look at 'im girls. Look at that poor little bugger – he's only a boy. 'E should be at home with his mam.'* Doug's face went crimson. He knew only too well how young he looked. He also knew that he was scarcely ready to go to war. That night, on his first picket duty, he was assigned to guard the barrack-room door with a wooden broom handle. He soon fell asleep, and was woken by the sergeant, who gave him a sharp bollocking for dereliction of duty, followed by a mug of tea and a slice of bread and jam. Doug did not get to fire a rifle for two months. He could not quite shake the sense that he was just playing at being a soldier – that they were all, when it came down to it, just playing at being soldiers.[3]

This book is about a generation of young British men like Doug Arthur – boys, really, many of them – who had never expected to be soldiers, but who found themselves swept up into the violent maelstrom of the Second World War anyway. It is not a conventional military history of the war. Certainly, it touches upon many of the traditional elements of such a history – the campaigns and battles won and lost, the operations and tactics employed, the weapons and vehicles used. But they are not really its central preoccupation. And this is not a book about the decisions of the great captains of the war, the generals and field marshals and statesmen whose lives are already recorded for posterity in the *Oxford Dictionary of National Biography*. No, this book is concerned with the experience of altogether different men – the teeming masses of Freds and Franks, Georges and Archies, Bills and Dougs, the men on the bottom rungs of the military ladder, the extraordinary, ordinary men who from 1939 onwards were plucked, callow and bewildered, from peacetime life, outfitted with uniforms, weapons and kit, trained, corralled and disciplined, and sent off thousands of miles to fight and die for their King and Country against some of the most technically formidable opponents the world has ever known. It is a book about how such men, the unlikeliest of citizen-soldiers, thoroughly civilian in their habits and attitudes before the Second World War, responded to, and were shaped by, their years of encounter with the Army. And it is about how that army, however grudgingly, had to accommodate itself to *them*.

It is also a book about Britain at a transitional moment in its history – about a country which, at the mid-point of the twentieth century, was beginning to shed its fading Victorian heritage and emerge, however falteringly, into the modern world. The relationship between Britain's social history and its military history ought to be obvious enough. After all, to begin to understand what it was like to be a wartime soldier you first need to know something about the society from which he came. But even so, there has been very little attention paid to the connection between the social and military histories of the Second World War, at least so far as Britain is concerned. Accounts of the wartime 'home front' are plentiful. So are narratives of the great land, sea and air campaigns of the war – Dunkirk, the Battle of Britain, the Battle of the Atlantic, North Africa, Italy, Normandy, Burma, the strategic bombing offensive against Germany. But there has been an unfortunate lack of cross-enquiry between these two bodies of literature, little acknowledgement of how each of them could potentially inform the other. This book is an attempt to engage the two in a productive way. It is, in a sense, an extended reflection upon an observation that Richard Hoggart, author of *The Uses of Literacy* and himself a wartime subaltern, once made – that the Army he served in was 'a microcosm of British society in both its decencies and its gross imperfections'.[4]

Telling such a story has necessitated some selectivity in treatment. The wartime adjutant-general described the job of trying to capture the Army's mood as 'painting with the impressionistic brush of a Turner and not with the microscopic detail of a Canaletto'.[5] *Browned Off* has also had to be necessarily impressionistic. No single book could ever hope to capture every facet of such a vast and complex experience as the story of the wartime Army. Choices have had to be made about what to include and what to omit, some of them a matter of regret. Probably the most obvious omission is the lack of any detailed treatment of the women's Auxiliary Territorial Service (ATS). This is not because the ATS was unimportant. Far from it; by the mid-point of the war, over 210,000 'ats' were serving in 114 trade groups, from driver to draughtswoman to searchlight and anti-aircraft range-finding operator. The contribution these women made to the wartime Army's operational effectiveness is incalculable. But the story I am telling here is one of men, and the particular experience of being a young British man called into military service at a time when male life and assumptions about masculinity itself were going through important changes. The ATS has its chroniclers and will, it is to be hoped, have many more in the years to come.[6]

Like all books of its kind, *Browned Off* draws much of its testimony from the very large body of memoirs, letters and diaries of ordinary servicemen that have been published in Britain since the Second World War, as well as the voluminous collections of oral interviews and unpublished private papers maintained at national archives such as the Imperial War Museum in Lambeth, south London. Without such sources, our appreciation of what it was like to serve in the British Army from 1939 to 1945 would be immeasurably poorer. They do, however, raise some problems of method. Historians are both beholden to, and a little suspicious of, such 'ego-documents'. As sources they tend by their very nature to be unrepresentative. Men who were predisposed to keep detailed accounts of their military service were generally better educated and more articulate than their comrades, which means that they were both more likely to be officers and also, perhaps, more likely to hold idiosyncratic views about the Army. Memoirs and accounts written or recorded many years after the events they describe have to be interpreted through the distorting filter of memory – not so much because the facts are misremembered (although they sometimes are), but because as people age they inevitably come to think about the experiences of their youth in a different way than they did at the time.[7]

In recognizing these problems I have tried to take a common-sense approach to them. Government records, including the War Office's very useful materials on wartime morale, have been used wherever possible in order to test the representativeness of the claims of individual soldiers (keeping in mind, of course, that official documents were not created for the convenience of historians, and have to be interpreted carefully themselves). Particular weight has been given to accounts of the Army which were written during the war itself, when attitudes and assumptions were as yet uncontaminated by the detritus of hindsight. As for the storytellers that I have drawn upon, many of them were indeed officers, and some of them, such as the historians Sir Michael Howard and Christopher Seton-Watson, went on to distinguished public careers after the war. But other soldiers who never rose above the rank of junior NCO kept records of their wartime experiences which demonstrate remarkable attention to detail, sophistication of thought, self-reflective subtlety and literary skill. Such 'forgotten voices' provide a vital counterpoint to the view from the officer's mess.[8]

The Second World War was not just one of the two greatest military efforts ever undertaken by the United Kingdom, but also, albeit quite by chance, one of its two greatest ever sociological experiments. Between 1939 and 1945, Britain mobilized around 5.8 million men and 640,000 women for military service.[9] The former represented about one in four of the entire male population of the United Kingdom, and an even larger proportion of the young and able-bodied. Three out of every five men born between 1905 and 1927 found themselves serving in the armed forces during the Second World War; seven out of ten born between 1915 and 1927.[10] Of those 5.8 million, the majority – around 3.8 million – spent their war years in the British Army.[11] Of those 3.8 million men, all but 258,000 were civilians on the day war broke out.[12] Between the invasion of Poland and V-J Day, in other words, around 3,542,000 ordinary Britons, very few of whom had ever had any previous military experience or training, were extracted from civilian life and placed for up to seven years into the Army, an institution with practices, assumptions and an ethical code utterly different from that which the majority of them had ever known before. It was an audacious piece of social engineering.

It was not completely unprecedented. Britain had been through such an experience once before. Indeed, between 1914 and 1918, it had mobilized slightly more men for military service – 6.1 million.[13] But it is one of this book's contentions that the experiences of Army service in the two world wars were very different from one another, even though they were separated by barely a quarter of a century. Part of the reason for that bifurcation in experience was that the Second World War would take a very different course from the First, a difference that can be seen most starkly in their respective death tolls. The First World War was an exercise in mass industrialized slaughter never known before or since in British history. It cost the lives of 722,785 Britons, 673,375 of whom were soldiers.[14] By contrast, just 270,139 British servicemen as a whole, and 146,346 soldiers specifically, died between 1939 and 1945 – the Army's losses, then, only a fifth of what they had been from 1914 to 1918.[15] One in eight of the soldiers who served in the First World War never came back. Only one in 25 did not return from the Second World War. At the most basic level, the difference between joining Chamberlain's and Churchill's army rather than Asquith's and Lloyd George's was that doing so was a good deal less likely to get you killed.

But we should not conclude too readily from this that being in the Army of the Second World War was preferable in every way – or even necessarily safer – than being in the Army of the First. To be sure, the number of casualties suffered by the British Army from 1939 to 1945 was much lower than that from 1914 to 1918, making the British experience of the two world wars almost unique amongst the Great Powers; France was the only other major combatant afflicted in this way. But human loss was distributed much more unevenly in the Second World War. Most soldiers from 1914 to 1918 were front-line infantrymen. The burden of their sacrifice was heavy, but it was shared widely across the various units of the Army. Each man enjoyed, if nothing else, the consolation that his ordeal was being commonly experienced and understood. During the Second World War, barely one in five British soldiers were mustered into the infantry. But it was the 'Poor Bloody Infantry' (PBI) that continued to endure the worst and most dangerous conditions of battle. Many soldiers between 1939 and 1945 would find themselves subsisting and fighting in environments that were no less hazardous and unpleasant – indeed, in many ways rather more so – than the Western Front had been a quarter century before. The Normandy campaign chewed up lives with terrible relentlessness; the Army's monthly battle casualty rate as it fought its way out of the D-Day bridgehead from June to September 1944 was more than twice what it had averaged in France during the First World War.[16] But unlike the Tommies of the trenches, the infantrymen of Montgomery's army had to go through their ordeal without the solace of knowing that all their comrades had it at least as bad as they did. There was something particularly cruel about front-line combat service in the Second World War: for while a few suffered, the majority were merely spectators.

The burden of overseas service was also far less equitably distributed in the Second World War than it had been in the First. Most soldiers of 1914–18 would, after their initial period of recruitment and training, spend the entirety of their war in France and Belgium. In September 1939, it seemed that this pattern of deployment was going to repeat itself. Then, as in August 1914, the British Army was being sent across the Channel to take up a position on the French left flank. 'Twenty-four years to the month have gone between my first and second journeys to France to join a British Expeditionary Force', wrote war correspondent James Lansdale Hodson as he prepared to leave England with the first troops on a grey-funnelled troopship: 'My thoughts are occupied by memories: how we, that first time, marched out from Tidworth in the dark, loaded like mules, leather equipment creaking, heavy boots crunching the gravel. No music, no song on our lips.' There was, thought Hodson, a 'queer homecoming' to it all, 'a strange feeling that the intervening years have never happened'.[17] But just nine months later, the similarity between the two operational distributions came to a swift and shocking end when the BEF was harried back across the Channel in disarray. With the fall of France, the British were expelled from northwestern Europe; they would not return for four years. For most of the war, then, a posting overseas for a British soldier meant expatriation to a much more distant locale – to Egypt or Palestine, Sicily or Italy, India or Burma. You were much less likely to be sent abroad at all than you had been in the previous conflict. But if you *were* one of those chosen to go, you would probably be dispatched to a place that was utterly unfamiliar to you, to dwell alongside people you had little in common with, with little hope of home leave, much less repatriation, until the end of the war – and you might have to wait a good deal of time even then. The melancholy of homesickness would belabour British soldiers in the Second World War much more than in the First.

All the same, the minority of troops who fought at the 'sharp end' of combat or who spent long periods overseas did at least have something to distract them from the inherently disagreeable circumstances of soldiering. That was not the case for those men who spent the balance of their service in the UK itself, kept out of harm's way, but also without the gratifying sense of occupation which would have justified their having to be soldiers in the first place. Very few conscripts opposed the war in any coherent way. Their commitment to the cause was usually reliable enough – and not really so different from that of their fathers from 1914 to 1918. But being in the Army could be tremendously *inconvenient*. Even leaving aside the risk to life and limb which it entailed, soldiering meant putting aside the concerns of everyday life – education, career, marriage, children – indefinitely. 'The whole thing was so awful, it was funny', thought Anthony Cotterell when his call-up notice arrived in the post in March 1940, along with a railway voucher and a four-shilling postal order. 'Everything you had ever worked for was sent up in smoke by that halfpenny circular. Every hope, every plan.' Not, he added, that he had anything particular against the war. He accepted its justice. He was not a pacifist. 'But I was comfort-able', he confessed, 'and I didn't want to be disturbed.' He was, he supposed, 'an unconscientious objector'.[18]

Recruits like Cotterell were from a generation of young men who were peculiarly unprepared for what military service was going to be like; most of them had what journalist James Brough called a 'complete lack of under-standing of life in the Army'.[19] By 1939, Britain was in many ways a very different country from the place it had been in 1918. Its young people had, on the whole, grown up healthier, wealthier and better educated than their parents; had become more accustomed to leisure and the pleasures of personal consumption; had had far less acquaintance with the rigours of conventional discipline; had adopted a rather less class-conscious approach to life; and were a good deal more sceptical about traditional authority and the wisdom of their elders and betters. 'Times have changed. Boys have become more independent, more democratic in outlook', thought one youth organizer in 1932. They no longer lent themselves so easily to compulsion. 'The youth of today is like no other youth that our country has ever known', noted military writer Ian Hay with undisguised apprehension:

> He has been educated to consider that Jack is as good as his master – a doctrine which, though fashionable enough in civil life, cuts no ice in mili-tary society, and never can. He objects to such things as unquestioning obedience – to 'jumping to it', in other words – and artificial manifestations of respect to those above him.[20]

For millions of young Britons, life between the wars had been about radio serials and cinema matinees, dance halls and motorcycles, small families, paid holidays and indoor plumbing. None of this was a particularly good prepara-tion for soldiering and all of its Victorian assumptions. Young conscripts were going to find themselves, as one soldier put it, 'thrust into a harsh and bitter world; one of constant hardship, strict discipline, and for the first time in their lives, the feeling that they were of no importance in the larger scheme of things'.[21] It was unclear how many of them would manage the transition. Thinking of the boys who had been called up from her home village of Tadworth on the Epsom Downs, housewife Tilly Rice tried and failed to visu-alize them as soldiers. 'I wonder', she confessed to her diary, 'if this generation will make an army of like fibre to that of 1914.'[22]

Between the wars, the Army had not given much thought to Britain's rapidly changing social milieu, because the possibility that it would ever have to deal with recruits of the like of Doug Arthur or Anthony Cotterell seemed far too remote to worry about. Its leaders had been told repeatedly since the 1918 Armistice to forget about conscripts and Continental commitments entirely, and instead concentrate their efforts on imperial policing. As a tiny, anaemically financed force of *condottiere* recruiting its officers from the genteelly poor upper-middle class and its private soldiers from the half-starved slums of Mile End and Salford and the Gorbals, the Army had little need to think much about modern Britain at all, let alone the possibility of another European war, or the mass assimilation of millions of civilians into its ranks. All the institutional knowledge about man-management it had acquired between 1914 and 1918 was forgotten. From 1932 to 1935, the Staff College at Camberley, which trained officers for high command, only bothered to provide one lecture on the problems of morale in a mass citizen army.[23] The Army withered away in genteel obscurity, scattered across the frontier posts of empire, its practices 'antiquated, philistine, and . . . more appropriate to the eighteenth than to the twentieth century', according to one junior officer.[24]

So the decision to reintroduce conscription in the spring of 1939 caught its leaders totally off guard. Suddenly they had to expand their force to over ten times its pre-war size, while simultaneously reinventing it as a European-style army of heavy artillery, tanks and motor transport. And they had to figure out what to do with men from a Britain that they scarcely recognized or understood, men with skills and backgrounds unlike any that they had ever had to think about before. The novelist Eric Ambler foxed a well-meaning but bemused officer at his initial recruitment interview as the latter struggled to grasp what being a 'writer' actually meant:

'*Writer*', he said thoughtfully, as he stared at the form I had filled in. 'You don't by any chance mean underwriter or some kind of legal writer, like writer to the signet?'

'No sir, I write books, novels, detective stories mostly.' I had found that with persons who did not read much detective stories were more respectable than thrillers.

He scratched his head . . . 'but is there anything you can actually *do*?' he asked plaintively.[25]

To the more imaginative men in the War Office, in particular Sir Ronald Adam, the adjutant-general from 1941 onwards, it was clear that the Army would have to respond to the influx of such recruits with sympathy and a willingness to adapt. In Adam's view, it was going to be self-defeating to treat temporary citizen-soldiers as though they were identical to the quasi-mercenaries of the peacetime Army. Home comforts of at least a modest sort would have to be provided for them, particularly when they found themselves thousands of miles from home for the first time in their lives. Existing connections with civilian life would have to be respected. Commanders would have to cultivate (or at least fake) the 'human touch'. Discipline would have to become more explicitly a process of arbitration, with officers and NCOs seeking a fine balance between what they needed their men to do and what in practice they could get them to do. Training would have to encompass a willingness to see soldiers as more than mindless automatons. Instilling *esprit de corps* would have to go beyond an appeal to regimental tradition, imparting instead some sense of the wider political and social purpose of the war – even if such a scheme had troubling implications for the established order to which many senior officers were personally committed.

But many of Adam's fellow regulars did not see the Army's problems in the same terms at all. To senior officers disposed towards more traditional methods of discipline, what Britain was facing in the 1940s was not just a military threat from its enemies but a crisis of masculinity brought on by years of pernicious social levelling. The way to deal with Britain's 'soft' young men was to harden them, not swaddle them or pander to their discontents. The Army should apply the same model of training and assimilation that it had always used on its peacetime recruits: a ferocious regimen of parade-ground marching and spit-and-polish busywork, justified by appeals to the honour of the regiment.

Many wartime recruits baulked at this. Indeed, for some of them, the Second World War would become as much a personal struggle between the Army and themselves as a military conflict. They were caught in a collision of values, a confrontation between two very different cultures – their own and the Army's. 'I realize with convincing clarity', wrote one corporal-diarist, 'that the military machine is a graduated system for the perpetration of nonsense; that its parades, inspections and ceremonies are mostly stupid and dispensable survivals from times that are best forgotten and serve only as an excuse for men of rank to gratify their vanity and self-importance.'[26] Army life at its worst could feel like a perpetual atrocity committed against the values of privacy, self-respect and compassion. The Army, thought the poet and playwright John Atkins, 'herds random men into unwanted squads, attempts to canalise intelligence, tries to destroy independence'.[27] It treated its recruits, as one soldier put it, as a herd of 'unthinking cattle'.[28] Never in the field of conflict, thought Anthony Burgess, had so many been buggered about by so few.[29]

By 1942, in fact, the typical citizen-soldier was, in the signal phrase of the time, *Browned Off*. No one quite knows where the term originally sprang from. It may have had something to do with the colour of most Army kit (soldiers were habitually known as 'brown jobs' by men in the other services). It may originally have been a reference to the lobster-like tan that recruits acquired on overseas service. But whatever its precise etymology, in their dictionary of service slang first published in 1943, amateur lexicographers J. L. Hunt and A. G. Pringle described it as a coinage of sheer brilliance – 'the most important of all expressions' that any wartime servicemen could acquire. To be browned off meant to resemble in temperament as well as in appearance a piece of meat left cooking far too long on the stove. It was 'a kind of indifference, a state in which personal feelings and interests appear to have been suspended' in the face of the vast, anonymous, indifferent machinery of the Army.[30] The term 'browned off' encapsulated perfectly the state of mind of the jaded, underemployed squaddie three years into the war. Julian Maclaren-Ross, who in his comic short stories about Army life was to be one of the more assiduous chroniclers of Britain's reluctant warriors, described his military service as his artistic 'Brown Period'. The leaves were brown. So were the blankets. So were the soldiers.[31]

The whole story of the British Army from Dunkirk till V-J Day was, in a sense, its grappling with its own Browned-Offness. This was partly a matter of recovering self-confidence after years of humiliating defeat; of re-equipping and retraining and learning the skills that would eventually help to bring down the Axis empires. It was partly a matter of institutional change, of policies reimagined by thoughtful reformers like Adam that would better match the needs and abilities of bored and unhappy men. But it was also a matter of ordinary soldiers coming to terms with the circumstances they found themselves in, negotiating private, unspoken rapprochements with the military machine. Army service would, in the long run, change men – and in some cases, it would prove to have surprisingly powerful consolations to offer even the most resolutely unenthusiastic of them. After three years of service, the pre-war world would seem 'so unreal and detached' to artilleryman David Cooper that he could only wonder whether 'there had been a sharper cleavage than the mere signing of an enlistment form' – whether the civilian he had once imagined himself to be had actually been an entirely different man, 'a former incarnation'.[32]

The war would send millions of Britons overseas for the first time in their lives, bringing them into contact with foreigners – and often, the people of their own empire – in an unprecedented way. Some theatres of war were so ecologically hostile as to make normal life itself a challenge. Neither the sand, flies and savage fluctuations in temperature of the Western Desert, nor the stifling and malaria-ridden jungles of South East Asia were calculated to inspire much nostalgia. The Italian campaign took place not in picturesque Tuscan landscapes, but along mud-choked hill tracks in which conditions reminiscent more of Passchendaele than a modern war of movement tested the limits of British troops almost to destruction. Even the northwestern European campaign had its grim chapters, especially during the bitter winter of 1944 when British troops in southern Holland froze in the flooded polder marshes. But foreign travel also meant exposure to new sights, people and ideas. It was in Calcutta that George MacDonald Fraser, later the screenwriter and author of the *Flashman* novels set in the Victorian British Empire, first had a shoeshine, a massage and a T-bone steak.[33] For some soldiers, foreign service gave birth to a lasting romance with the exotic. It became one of the stock tropes of the war to have your photo taken astride a camel in front of the Pyramids, or to be escorted around medieval ruins in the company of some shady 'expert' guide, or to haggle for overpriced knick-knacks in a bazaar. Joining the Army was a crash course in becoming a global citizen.

For the minority who were directly exposed to combat, there were challenges of a more traumatic kind. British soldiers came from a society which regarded itself (rightly or not) as unusually gentle, a 'peaceable kingdom' in which violence was something alien and unnatural. Before the war, Geoffrey Picot considered himself to be a typical Englishman – 'unargumentative, unoffending, unquarrelsome, unaggressive, unbrave' – yet by 1944, he was commanding a mortar platoon in the bitterly contested hedgerows of Normandy.[34] There was considerable doubt amongst some in the highest positions of power as to whether such timid souls were up to the job of defeating the vastly more warrior-like professionals of Germany and Japan. To Sir Alexander Cadogan, the permanent undersecretary of state at the Foreign Office, the British Army by 1942 was 'the mockery of the world', an assemblage of 'pathetic amateurs'.[35] The sacrifices of units such as Picot's 1st Hampshires, which was effectively wiped out twice during the war without at any stage losing its operational cohesion, would offer a firm rebuke to such criticisms. But ordinary men like Picot had to come to terms not just with the fact of their own mortality, but with the moral consequences of taking the lives of others as well. The greater the sense of personal agency, the harder it was to overcome the taboo against killing. It was a burden that many men struggled with for the rest of their lives. Others, however, found that they thrived on the excitement of combat. War, with its raw, primitive energy, its sense of all artifice stripped away, its revelation of the authentic man beneath, was their natural environment. Never again would they enjoy the same emotional satisfaction that they had known in the killing fields of Normandy, Cassino and Kohima.

For most soldiers, however, the Army's consolations would come in rather more prosaic form – 'the sense of comradeship, the spirit of community, the habits of hardship borne with a cheerful grin, the sharing the burdens and division of the last cigarette'.[36] When he first walked into Caterham Barracks, Surrey, on 4 July, 1940, guardsman E. P. Danger was by his own admission 'a tall, rather weedy, and somewhat diffident insurance clerk'. Almost exactly six years later he marched out of Victoria Barracks in Windsor 'still tall, no longer weedy and certainly more self-assured'. During his time in uniform he had 'learned to be a soldier' and all that went with it:

> [I] acquired an extensive knowledge of Army procedure; marched many long, weary miles . . . and learned the art of making tea under any, and every, condition at all hours of the day or night . . . I had learned to live with all classes and types of men and to make allowances for their failings – and to see their good points. I had also learned that neither the pips on a man's shoulder, nor the stripes on his arm were a guarantee that he would stand up under pressure . . . on the whole it was a good experience and I am glad that I did not miss it. But I wouldn't like to do it again.[37]

Years of enforced masculine intimacy in the company of comrades, the daily rituals of drills and duties, the exposure to the elements, even the sight, smell and touch of khaki – all these would ultimately contribute to a close network of habits in which millions of unconscientious objectors would come to feel oddly at home, and, once the war was over, to regard their return to civilian life with apprehension as well as hope, wistfulness as well as relief. After leaving the Army in 1947, infantry platoon commander Sidney Jary went on to have a long and entirely unmilitary civilian career. Yet forty years later, he realized to his own surprise that ever since the day of his demobilization he had never stopped thinking of himself as a soldier.[38]

Peter Ustinov serves as a more unlikely, but perhaps for that reason still more illustrative, example. From the moment he arrived in Canterbury on 16 January 1942 for his basic infantry training, it was clear that Ustinov was almost preternaturally unsuited to being a soldier. A more browned-off conscript one could have hardly imagined. 'I have never in my life had such feelings of being absolutely useless as I had during my four and a half years in the service', he wrote in his 1977 memoir *Dear Me*.[39] He could not march. He could not drill. He could not apply blanco kit colouring with zeal or accomplishment. The laying out of his kit for inspection he found a particular ordeal; try as he might, it simply would not fit the prescribed geometrical patterns laid down by Army regulations. He was an aesthete, an intellectual, a wit and raconteur – someone who could find virtually no point of sympathetic engagement with the culture of the Army. 'While standing stiffly to attention, staring at nothing with the intensity of a zombie, awaiting the next primeval howl from a Neanderthal with three stripes on his shoulder ... I never had a greater impression of wasting my time and, indeed, my country's time than I did in the Army', he wrote thirty-two years after the war. 'I loathed every moment of it.'

'And', he added, 'I would not have missed it for the world.'[40]

PART ONE
REGULARS

Every reckless, wild, debauched fellow, the refuse of the beershop, the sweeping of the gaol, everyone who is too idle to work, too stupid to hold his place amongst his fellows . . . is considered by general consent to have a distinct vocation to defend his country.

Contemporary Review, 1869[1]

CHAPTER 1

COLONEL LAWRENCE AND COLONEL BLIMP

The men had eaten nothing since breakfast, and as they huddled on the darkening hilltop, almost lost to sight within a miasma of sleet, their bellies groaned in misery. Dark brown woollen shirts and Khaki Drill shorts hung from their bodies like slats of frozen cardboard. The wind, driving up the valley from the north, pummelled at their raw skin. Far beyond the breastwork of stone and the holly-oak scrub surrounding their observation point they could pick out, in dim silhouette hundreds of feet below, their comrades in the relief platoon slipping and cursing on wet rocks as they edged clumsily up the track. '*I feels like ten men*', said Private Welman, his battered face thawing briefly into a resigned grin. '*Nine dead and one in 'ospital.*'[1]

For second lieutenant John Masters, the leader of these two dozen shivering bundles – better known in official parlance as Number Seven Platoon, B Company, 1st Battalion the Duke of Cornwall's Light Infantry (DCLI) – the miseries of the moment were compounded by the fear of attack. There was, as Masters put it years later in his vivid memoir *Bugles and a Tiger*, the 'sense-sharpening chance of a sudden storm of bullets ... a rush of knifemen, a bloody hand-to-hand struggle'.[2] True, the North West Frontier had been relatively peaceful for some years. And the atrocious weather that evening surely ruled out a large, organized assault. But the local tribesmen would not miss an opportunity to cut down an isolated and incautious British soldier, especially if it meant that they could steal his Lee-Enfield rifle, a great prize to the weapon-starved natives of the area. Casualties in tribal lands were inevitable, even in periods of calm. The previous spring, a junior officer much like Masters had been shot and badly wounded not far from this very patrol route. In nine months, a regimental sergeant major of the East Yorkshire Regiment was destined to die by a sniper's bullet just a few miles away.[3]

But there were no sharpshooters lurking menacingly among the rocks that evening. The enemy confronting Masters and his soldiers – the frost and squall of central Waziristan in late winter –was vastly more indefatigable than any flesh-and-blood Pathan. Far below the platoon's gloomy eyrie 6,000 feet above sea level was the snaking path of the Sre Mela river, and beyond that the Tochi Pass, one of the great defiles connecting the Afghan plateau with the fertile Indus plain far away to the south. No matter how wretched and powerless they must have felt at that moment in February 1935, Masters's men all the same represented the leading edge of British authority on the North West Frontier – the thin Khaki Drill line that separated anarchy from imperium.

Technically, they were not within the British Empire at all, but rather in 'Tribal Territory', a sliver of mountainous wasteland dividing Afghanistan and India proper. Ever since the British advance to the Himalayas in the late nineteenth century, Waziristan had been a problem without a clear solution. It was more or less ungovernable in any conventional sense, but at the same time it was too strategically important to ignore completely. The compromise had been to administer it loosely with a corps of political officers, who maintained a coarse frontier justice through the dispensing of bribes and punishments. Bandit chiefs who were not overly belligerent were rewarded with annual tributes in cash. Persistent disturbers of the peace had their goats and sheep and camels seized. It was as part of one of those punitive expeditions from the permanent British garrison at Razmak that Masters' Number Seven Platoon now found itself trembling on a chilly Waziri hilltop.

To those serving on the North West Frontier in the mid-1930s, the twentieth century might as well never have begun. It is remarkable to think that just four years before the start of the Second World War, a war which would see the use of radar, guided missiles, jet fighters and atomic bombs, the greatest empire on the planet was being guarded, essentially, with the same rifles and bayonets that had been used at the Battle of Omdurman in 1898. The British Army garrisoning the Indian Raj had changed very little since the days of Kipling and Henry Newbolt and the uplifting boys' novelist G. A. Henty. It remained an army of mules and screw guns and walrus-moustached sergeant majors, of sola topis and puttees and swagger sticks. Grizzled veterans transported from West Ham and County Mayo still spoke in an Anglo-Hindi creole in which one carried a *bundook* rather than a rifle, slept in a *charpoy* instead of a bed, and feasted not on bread and lime juice, but *rootee* and *limbu-pani*. Masters and his men were soldiers of a particularly time-worn variety, sentries of the same vertiginous playground of Empire across which so many other Britons had marched, fought and died. They filed along narrow gullies by day, scouting trails here, reconnoitring rocky pinnacles there. By night, they crouched in scratch-built stone emplacements, drenched with sweat, drinking mugs of hot, sweet, 'gunfire' army tea under the stars. Only the electric-powered searchlights on the guard towers at Razmak and the occasional sightings of distant RAF scouting aircraft provided any dim intrusion of modernity. Being in Waziristan was, thought Masters, like returning to a 'golden age' of simple masculine pleasure, insulated from all the dreary troubles of the contemporary world.[4]

Yet all these anachronisms were, in a way, contrived. For just a few years earlier, the British Army had been at the cutting edge of military science. It had introduced the tank and the armoured personnel carrier to the battlefield. It had pioneered the use of aerial reconnaissance photographs and scrupulous ballistic calculations for artillery targeting. It had equipped its foot-soldiers with the latest in industrial-age firepower – rifle-grenades, trench mortars, machine-guns. It had been revolutionary in its employment of chemical weapons and wireless communications and combined arms tactics. Its embrace of the modern had been absolute.

Something had happened – not simply a return to the old ways, but a conscious act of renunciation, of *forgetting*, of knowingly retreating from the twentieth century back into the nineteenth. The Army had gone through an experience so profound, so terrible, that by 1935 it was talked of only with a sigh of *never again*. Masters and his men were participants in a conspiracy of silence, an unspoken agreement to pretend that the recent past had never happened. The job at hand – watch-towers to man, frontier lines to patrol, truculent natives to overawe – provided a convenient distraction. Uncomfortable memories could be smothered, for the time being anyway, beneath the reas-suring, soporific dust of tradition.

To understand what had happened to provoke this act of wilful amnesia, we need to go back nineteen years, to the early hours of a baking midsummer's morning on the first day of July 1916. The scene is the plain of Santerre in Picardy, a chalky expanse of sugar-beet fields between the River Somme and its tributary the Noye, a placid, docile landscape disturbed only by modest ridges and little valleys. The First World War has been raging across Europe for almost two years, but this little patch of France has seen little military activity as yet. Its scattered woodlands and medieval hamlets, copses and church spires are still much the same as they were centuries ago. Its placid immunity is about to disap-pear, however. For along a fifteen-mile line buckling from the village of Gommecourt in the north to Montauban in the south, thirteen divisions of the British Army and six of the French are about to leave the security of their shallow trenches and advance towards the German positions on the far side of 'no-man's land', some 500 yards or so in the distance. This will be what everyone is already calling the Big Push – the largest and most ambitious British offensive yet.

General Douglas Haig, commander-in-chief of the British Expeditionary Force (BEF) in France, is not launching the Big Push at the location or to the timeline he would ideally have liked. He would have preferred to attack much further to the north, in Flanders, and later in the summer, so as to give his inexperienced troops more opportunity to train. But the French, reeling from a massive German assault on their fortress complex at Verdun, have insisted that unless the British act now to relieve some of the pressure from their distressed army, the war will be lost by August. So Haig's operation has become, in effect, a rescue mission. Still, he is confident that his preparations have been meticulous and that his plan is fundamentally sound. If all goes according to schedule today, by dusk British troops will be 4,000 yards into enemy territory. By the end of the week, they will have punched a hole into the enemy line that the cavalry can pour through, enveloping the entire German Army in the West. It will be the long-awaited strategic breakthrough that has eluded both sides since the war began.

It is something of an accident that there is a British army in France at all. When the war broke out two years ago, the Liberal government of H. H. Asquith dispatched almost all the regular troops available in the United Kingdom – one cavalry and four infantry divisions – across the English Channel to take up position on the left flank of the French Army.[5] It was more an act of solidarity than a meaningful military decision. Britain's regular army was assumed at the time to be far too small to count for much alongside the great Continental levies of France, Germany and Russia. Besides, in August 1914 the main weight of the fighting was expected to be in Alsace and Lorraine, far to the south, not the strip of Franco-Belgian border allotted to the British.

But as it turned out, the British troops who formed up around Maubeuge on the River Sambre that summer were right in the path of the German Army's great sickle-sweep through Belgium and northeastern France. In a series of bruising encounter battles, the BEF was harried southwards to the banks of the Marne. There the German advance stuttered, halted and became a withdrawal. Allied troops pushed cautiously back, until the two sides dug in along a continuous line running several hundred miles from the Yser to Switzerland. For over twenty months the British have occupied a steadily expanding position along this vast, static battlefront.

The BEF's composition has changed utterly since 1914. Most of the old-sweat regular battalions that originally landed in France were dashed to ruin long ago. Part-time Territorial units substituted for them for a while. But at the heart of the

Army now is a levy of enthusiastic civilian amateurs. Of the 143 battalions about to attack in Picardy, ninety-seven are so-called 'New Army' units, raised during the winter of 1914–15 in a massive recruitment campaign led by the hero of the Sudan, Field Marshal Kitchener.[6] Not only is the BEF now far bigger than at the outbreak of war, but in character it is unlike any force Britain has ever fielded in battle. The men of the New Army battalions are overwhelmingly of the 'respectable' working class and the urban bourgeoisie, many of them husbands and fathers who have left behind domestic responsibilities, steady employment and good wages – men, in other words, who would never have considered military service under normal circumstances, but who in the first months of the war flocked to the colours, in some cases compelled by little more than a mystical sense of patriotism and a desire to test their manhood. Many of them are formed up in 'Pals' battalions of friends, neighbours, and co-workers who all enlisted together. There is a Newcastle Railways battalion; a Scottish Sportsmen's battalion, which includes the entire first team squad of Heart of Midlothian F.C.; the Grimsby Chums, all former pupils of the same local secondary school; the Belfast Young Citizens; and the Preston Pals, made up of volunteers from the cotton mills of the Ribble Valley. The BEF has become, quite by accident, a vast and unprecedented social experiment – the mobilization for war of the British male nation.

Very few New Army recruits have ever seen battle. Most have spent their entire military careers up to this point in damp and dreary training camps, endlessly repeating drill and bayonet practice, waiting impatiently for a crack at the enemy. Now these unlikely warriors, these city clerks and schoolteachers, barrow boys and grocers' assistants, are to get their long-sought chance to prove their mettle under fire. In truth, Haig does not have much confidence in them. As a regular soldier he knows that enthusiasm is no substitute for experience. His men have stout hearts, but they are green troops, tactically naïve. So his plan has tried to allow for this by eliminating all meaningful German opposition before the attack even begins. For a week now, British guns have pounded the enemy with over one-and-a-half million shells. In the final hours before the assault they will fire a quarter of a million more. The few Germans who survive this inundation of shrapnel and high explosive are expected to be so dazed as to offer little resistance. 'You can slope arms, light up your pipes and cigarettes, and march all the way to Pozières [two miles from the British starting point] before meeting any live Germans', one officer has reassured his men.[7]

At precisely 7.30 a.m., exactly as planned, platoon officers blow their whistles all along the front, signalling that zero hour – the time for the attack – has begun. Some of the troops ascend from their trench parapets up scaling ladders. Others, already crouching far out in no-man's land, rise up from their hiding places and rush for the German barbed wire. But everything starts to go wrong almost at once. The Germans, burrowed deep within well-fortified dugouts, have, as it turns out, survived the preliminary bombardment largely unscathed. Far from being stunned into submission by the barrage, it has provided them with ample warning of the attack about to come. Now they hurry to their rifle positions and machine-gun posts to fire on the approaching British. Some of the New Army soldiers are carrying up to 70 pounds of equipment, including timber, empty sandbags, reels of barbed wire and tools, with which they are to re-fortify the enemy positions once they are captured. Encumbered by their loads, such men make easy targets. The first wave of advancing British troops is scythed down in a hail of bullets. As their bodies fall, so other men take their place, and they in turn are killed. The few soldiers who make it as far as the German barbed wire discover that it is still mostly intact; the gaps which they have been told the artillery will have already blasted through this tangled iron barrier cannot be found. Unable to make further progress, they can only shelter in whatever shallow cover they can find and exchange desultory fire with the much better protected Germans. It is a grossly unequal contest.[8]

The fate of one New Army battalion – the 11th (Service) Battalion of the East Lancashire Regiment, known popularly (if not wholly accurately) as the 'Accrington Pals' – will, in the years to come, epitomize today's disaster.[9] For fifteen months, its 720 animated amateurs, recruited from the cotton mills, brickworks, offices and sporting clubs of the industrial Pennines, have drilled, marched, eaten, trained and slumbered together. Collectively they represent a dynamic living community on the march, a dense network of years of shared local kinships and attachments. Yet by eight o'clock, 234 of them will already be lying slaughtered in a killing zone 700 yards long by 300 wide, 'mown down like meadow grass' by enfilading German machine-guns almost as soon as they emerged from their trenches. Another 360 will be wounded, many never to recover. An entire district of young men transplanted from Lancashire to Picardy will have vanished in less than half an hour.[10]

Accrington's tragedy is just one of hundreds suffered by communities across Britain on the opening day of the Battle of the Somme. By nightfall on 1 July 1916, as stretcher bearers roam across no-man's-land attending to the cries of the wounded and dying, it is already obvious that Haig's tactical goals have not been met. In a few places some units have made it as far as the first German line of trenches, but they are in no condition to continue the advance tomorrow. Within a few days, when the final casualty figures for 1 July are tallied, it will be clear that what has taken place is not just a military setback, but a tragedy of unprecedented human proportions. Over 19,000 British soldiers have been killed. It is as though every young man in a town the size of Blackpool or Lincoln has died in the space of a few hours. It is the worst day in the history of the British Army.

The Battle of the Somme did not end on 1 July 1916. Haig continued his Big Push for the next four-and-a-half months, replacing the battalions broken on the first day with other New Army units. By the time the fighting along the Somme finally ground to a halt in November, the pretty countryside of Santerre had been reduced to a morass of shell-holes and splintered tree stumps. Over 95,000 British soldiers were dead, with almost no tangible gain to show for any of it.

In 1917, Haig finally got his offensive in Flanders. This 'Third Battle of Ypres', or Passchendaele, as it would become known to history, ranked second only to the Somme in its grisly inconclusiveness. Despite scrupulous preparations, the British artillery was again unable to deliver a knock-out blow on the first day, and after a few initial successes the whole advance was bogged down, literally, in a quagmire of mud. Passchendaele resulted in 244,000 more British casualties for only a trifling adjustment to the position of the front line. Over 54,000 of the dead simply disappeared, obliterated by artillery blast or swallowed by the waterlogged battlefield. Their only memorial would be the haunting commemorative arch unveiled at the site of the old battlefield in 1927.

In operational terms, 1 July 1916 changed nothing. But its long-term emotional significance was incalculable. What the British learned on the first day of the Battle of the Somme was a dreadful secret that in their innocence they had never previously understood: that war 'could threaten with death the young manhood of a whole nation'.[11] And its carnage was merely the worst day of four-and-a-half years of protracted butchery. By the time the fighting on the Western Front finally came to an end, in November 1918, over 722,000 British soldiers, one in eight of all who had served, were dead.[12] A country long accustomed to the trivial sacrifices of distant small wars had no psychological preparation for a holocaust of this kind. Britain after the First World War was a haunted land. Schoolboys lined up in assembly halls to pay silent homage to the martyred alumni. Family mantelpieces were shrines to 'the Fallen', with members of that lost fraternity preserved in stiff sepia poses. There was a mania for seances and paranormal communication with the ghosts of fallen loved ones.[13] Many of those men who survived brought home with them testimonies to the horrors of war. Sightless and limbless old soldiers hung around street corners selling pathetic trinkets or begging for coppers. The shell-shocked drooled and jabbered and howled in terror at their invisible demons.

No one, no matter how rich or powerful, was spared. Indeed, the fatality rate amongst the nation's elite was disproportionately high. Asquith lost a son. The Conservative leader and post-war prime minister Andrew Bonar Law lost two. Rudyard Kipling, whose martial ballads had inspired so many men to join up in the first place, lost his beloved boy John. All of the men who would be critical decision-makers during the Second World War either served on the

Western Front themselves, or else had close friends or relatives who fought and died there. Neville Chamberlain was devastated by the death of his cousin Norman in 1917.[14] Anthony Eden, who had been a captain in the King's Royal Rifle Corps, wrote afterwards that every single male member of his family had either been killed, or at some point had been wounded or captured. The war represented 'the destruction of the world as I knew it'.[15]

Still, for the first ten years or so after the war's end, the Somme was regarded as a tragic but necessary sacrifice – a battle which had extracted a terrible toll but which had been fought in the service of a noble and essential cause all the same. Haig remained a national hero to the British people, his funeral in 1928 attended by more mourners than Princess Diana's seventy years later. But after his death, the mood began slowly to change. Victory had not, after all, created the better world that people had hoped for. Sorrow transmuted into bitterness, heartache into resentment. The Somme and the war's other blood-soaked battlefields began to look less like sites of heroism and more like crime scenes. Questions, at first muffled and apologetic, then more strident, were asked. Had all the slaughter really been necessary? And if not, then who was to blame?

A new narrative of the war began to form, shaped especially by the self-exculpating memoirs of statesmen such as Winston Churchill and David Lloyd George. Churchill's account of the Somme, first published in his 1927 autobiography-cum-history *The World Crisis*, would become particularly influential. He described the plain of Santerre as 'a welter of slaughter', and the fighting there as nothing less than a British Calvary:

> [The soldiers] grudged no sacrifice however unfruitful and shrank from no ordeal however destructive ... if two or ten lives were required by their commanders to kill one German, no word of complaint ever rose from the fighting troops. No attack however forlorn, however fatal, found them without ardour. No slaughter however desolating prevented them from returning to the charge ... martyrs not less than soldiers, they fulfilled the high purpose of duty with which they were imbued.[16]

The tone of censure directed towards Haig and the other generals was undisguised. Other, still sharper attacks than Churchill's followed. Lloyd George's war memoirs were published in 1933. He described Haig witheringly as a 'second-rate commander ... not endowed with any of the elements of imagination and vision which determine the line of demarcation between genius and ordinary'. The BEF's leader had been 'incapable of planning vast campaigns on the scale demanded on so immense a battlefield'. Thanks to his bungling, hundreds of thousands of the picked young men of the nation had been slaughtered 'in the prosecution of doubtful plans or mishandled enterprises'.[17] The moral was clear: it was ultimately the British Army's own incompetent commanders, not the Germans, who had been responsible for all those deaths.

A picture began to emerge of the typical First World War British general as a chinless, haw-hawing dodderer in cavalry breeches, living miles behind the trenches in a luxurious chateau, oblivious to the sufferings of the troops in his care, incapable of coming up with anything more imaginative than (in Churchill's words) to 'fight machine-gun bullets with the breasts of gallant men and think that was waging war'.[18] In his best-selling 1936 novel *The General*, C. S. Forester, best known as the creator of Horatio Hornblower, produced one of the most famous sketches of this tragi-comic villain, in a character study perfectly calibrated to the prejudices of the times. *The General* was an account of the life of the fictional Sir Herbert Curzon, KCMG, CB, DSO, formerly of the 22nd Lancers, and supposedly one of Haig's corps commanders on the Western Front. Forester painted Curzon as a man of many virtues. His personal courage, integrity, patriotism and sense of duty were beyond reproach. But he was utterly incapable of adjusting his preconceptions to fit the modern world of war. The machine-gun, the aircraft and the tank baffled him. His offensives all ended in miserable failure, but he could not imagine any other response except to throw yet more bodies uselessly against the enemy's bullets. Forester compared Curzon's discussions of strategy with his staff officers as like eavesdropping 'on a debate of a group of savages as to how to extract a screw from a piece of wood':

Accustomed only to nails, they had made one effort to pull out the screw by main force, and now that it had failed they were devising methods of applying more force still, of obtaining more efficient pincers, of using levers and fulcrums so that more men could bring their strength to bear. They could hardly be blamed for not guessing that by rotating the screw it would come out after the exertion of far less effort; it would be a notion so different from anything they had ever encountered that they would laugh at the man who suggested it.[19]

Men like Curzon were *Blimps* – a name originally given by cartoonist David Low of the London *Evening Standard* to the irascible, bald-pated, pudding-shaped colonel, the habitué of a West End Turkish bathhouse, who would quickly become his most famous character. Low offered his audience Colonel Blimp as a stand-in for Haig and all the other First World War generals – a superannuated ignoramus, forever spouting absurd, reactionary non-sequiturs to anyone within earshot. By the mid-1930s, it was axiomatic that the British

Army was officered by such men. Their stupidity and recklessness could be taken as a given.

Was any of this fair? 1 July 1916 had been a terrible day. But it had only been one day – an exceptional day, never to be repeated – in a four-and-a-half-year long war; and a war which Britain had, after all, *won*. Horrible though the Somme and Passchendaele had been, they had all the same been critical points of inflection on the British Army's 'learning curve'. The soldiers who had fought there had begun as green troops, unused to war. Many of them had died; but those who had survived had emerged from their ordeal as veterans. Tactical failures had offered valuable lessons for the future. And by 1918, after much maladroit experimentation, the British had finally begun to understand how to use the new technologies available to them. On 8 August, the opening day of the Battle of Amiens – 'the black day of the German Army', according to the Kaiser's commander-in-chief, Erich Ludendorff – the BEF was at last able to demonstrate how much it had learned. There would be no ineffectual preparatory bombardment this time, but rather a series of precision-aimed hurricane barrages right at the moment of the attack. Advances by tanks, aircraft and infantry, some transported across the battlefield in armoured vehicles for the first time in history, would no longer be the clumsy perambulations of the past, but fast, carefully synchronized combined-arms assaults. The result was going to be dramatic. By the evening of 8 August, a fifteen-mile gap had been punched in the German line south of the old Somme battlefield. After two days, the Germans had been forced to withdraw along the whole length of their front, a retreat that would continue virtually uninterrupted until the Armistice was signed four months later.

At the moment the guns fell silent on the Western Front on 11 November, the BEF was probably the most powerful land fighting force in the world. An army that had been just 247,000 strong on the opening day of the war, dwarfed by the conscript masses of the other European powers, had expanded fourteen times over. It had grown not just in size but in operational knowledge, confidence and ability. And it had carried the principal burden of the final Allied victory. With the French Army still debilitated from the mass mutinies that had swept through it the previous year, and the United States Army still not fully mobilized, it had fallen to the men of the BEF to confront the main body of the German Army in 1918. This they had done with stunning success. In the final three months of the campaign, the British forces in France had taken 188,700 prisoners – almost half the entire Allied tally.[20] An army of unlikely citizen-soldiers, amateurs to the core, had destroyed the most feared and professional fighting machine in Europe. It had been, quite simply, the greatest victory in British military history.[21]

But by the 1930s, none of this mattered. The Army's great victories in the closing months of the war were forgotten. The casualty lists were not. Attempts to rehabilitate Haig and the other generals quickly fell to silence beneath the accusatory glare of the dead. Talk of 'learning curves' seemed obscene while tens of thousands of names were still being carved into the walls of the Menin Gate at Ypres and the Thiepval Memorial to the Missing of the Somme. The people's minds were made up. The British soldier of the Great War had been a gallant hero. He had also been the victim of a pointless, criminally orchestrated slaughter. It was never, ever to happen again.[22]

Yet if, by the 1930s, Colonel Blimp had come to stand for everything that had been wrong with the British Army during the First World War, so another colonel stood for everything that had been right about it. Just as the public needed a villain to account for its suffering, so it also needed a hero – someone to stand in moral relief to Blimp and his cronies in order to show what might have been accomplished if youth and genius had been allowed an opportunity during the war. To show, in other words, what Colonel T. E. Lawrence – 'Lawrence of Arabia' – would have been able to do if he had been given half the chance.

The story of Lawrence and his leadership of the Arab Revolt from 1917 to 1918 contrasted starkly with the grim tragedy of the Western Front. In France, Haig had relied on brute force, bludgeoning his way forward yard by yard with a seeming indifference to the human cost of his obstinacy. The Arabs under Lawrence's direction had been far smaller in number and much more ill-equipped than the forces Haig had commanded. Yet the fast-moving columns of Arab irregulars striking from the desert without warning had consistently frustrated a Turkish army many times their own size, not by fighting head on, but precisely by avoiding any direct confrontation. Lawrence had achieved victory without building a hecatomb of corpses. And his story, told through a slew of star-struck biographies as well as his first-person account, *Revolt in the Desert*, was impossibly romantic. The sober Presbyterian Haig had been stiff and (seemingly, anyway) unfeeling. Lawrence was brilliant, handsome, enigmatic, impertinent and slightly unhinged – in other words, irresistible. His defiance of convention, his unwillingness to defer to the Blimps that surrounded him, had a huge appeal to an audience for whom conventional military authority had lost much of its legitimacy. He fulfilled a model of eccentric, charismatic generalship that evoked memories of other imperial heroes such as Clive of India and Gordon of Khartoum. His sensational death in a motorcycle accident in 1935 did nothing to allay his popularity; indeed, it only added to the allure of his tragic genius.

No man did more to propagate the myth of Colonel Lawrence than his friend and biographer Captain Basil Liddell Hart, the gaunt, moustachioed writer and journalist who was Britain's best-known commentator on military affairs between the wars.[23] Liddell Hart's intellectual journey was a traumatic one. Born in 1895, the son of a Wesleyan minister, he, like so many other young men of the upper-middle-class, had joined the Army having been swept up by the wave of patriotic enthusiasm in 1914. Commissioned into a battalion of the King's Own Yorkshire Light Infantry, he had served three short tours of duty on the Western Front before being gassed on the Somme in 1916. Even before the war Liddell Hart's health had been delicate, and despite lengthy recuperation he had never fully recovered from his battlefield injuries. He spent the rest of the war engaged in staff work, and though he stayed on in the Army after the Armistice, he was effectively discharged in 1923 as a medical invalid. Needing to make a living for himself, he turned to writing. He became the military correspondent for the *Daily Telegraph*, and later *The Times*. It was from the platforms of these newspapers, as well as from a series of well-received military histories and a carefully cultivated network of senior Army contacts, that Liddell Hart was able to spend much of the 1920s and 1930s laying out his criticisms of British wartime and post-war strategy.

Temperamentally he was a man of extremes, his world composed of heroes and villains. Liddell Hart had begun the war an uncritical admirer of Haig, calling him a 'genius', and had at first described the wartime performance of British generals as 'flawless'. But during the 1920s, his opinions darkened. He became increasingly convinced that the war had been mismanaged through an ill-conceived devotion to the primacy of the head-on decisive battle, a model of war particularly associated with the nineteenth-century German strategist Carl von Clausewitz. By 1935, Liddell Hart was describing Haig as 'a man of supreme egoism . . . not merely immoral but criminal'.[24] Moreover, he now felt that it had been a ghastly error to send a large citizen army to fight in France in the first place. This was an idea he developed into a comprehensive theory, outlined in *The British Way in Warfare* in 1932. In this book Liddell Hart argued that there had been a consistent British grand strategy which had been practised from 1688 till 1914 and which had been responsible for the country's almost unbroken record of victories during those years. By eschewing the raising of large armies in the continental style, Britain had been able to use its unique geographical and commercial position to fight its enemies (usually France) obliquely – partly by blockade and the conquest of colonies, partly by subsidising other European states to raise armies on its behalf, and partly by employing its own small but well-trained army in peripheral amphibious operations. This he called Britain's 'Indirect Approach' to war. When the Asquith government had decided to hugely expand the BEF in 1914, it had abandoned the Indirect Approach and embraced Clausewitzian decisive battle with tragic consequences for the country. The result had been little more than 'futile sacrifice and national exhaustion'.[25]

Lawrence's Hejaz campaign, by contrast, had exemplified all the virtues of the Indirect Approach. The future of ground warfare, thought Liddell Hart, lay not in gigantic bloodbaths like the Somme, but in the 'super-guerrilla kind of warfare' practised by Lawrence in the desert, though with the internal combustion engine substituting for the camel.[26] It was the 'dislocation of the enemy's psychological and physical balance' through deception, surprise and speed rather than weight of numbers which would produce victory in wars to come.[27] The British Army needed to prepare for such a future by developing small, highly mobile, well-trained forces – and emphatically *not* by taking on another vast 'continental commitment' of the kind it had stumbled into so disastrously in 1914.

For massive ground armies would surely soon be obsolete anyway. Soldier though he was, Liddell Hart was intrigued by the possibilities of air power that he had glimpsed during the war. Between 1915 and 1918, London had been repeatedly attacked from the skies by German raiders who first used lighter-than-air Zeppelin airships, and later twin-engine 'Gotha' bombers. The damage these attacks had done had been negligible. Just over 1,400 British civilians had been killed, a tiny loss compared to the deaths which had been taking place at the same time on the Western Front.[28] But the British public had been terrified all the same. Men, guns and aircraft had had to be rushed back from France to defend London. Fear and fascination with bombing planes persisted after the war. As aerial technology improved, what might be possible in another great conflict? In *Paris, Or the Future of War*, published in 1925, Liddell Hart suggested that the bomber would eventually become the supreme agent of the Indirect Approach. Unlike a ground force, which was tied to one plane of movement, an air force was capable of using the third dimension of space to avoid a confrontation with the opposing side's defences entirely. Aircraft could directly threaten the enemy's government, industry and people.[29] The consequences would be swift and dramatic. 'Imagine for a moment London, Manchester, Birmingham, and half a dozen other great centres simultaneously attacked', he wrote:

> Business localities and Fleet Street wrecked, Whitehall a heap of ruins, the slum districts maddened into the impulse to break loose and maraud, the railways cut, factories destroyed. Would not the general will to resist vanish, and what use would be the still determined fractions of the nation, without organization and central direction?[30]

This would be Lawrence's 'super-guerrilla kind of warfare' perfected; indeed, the desert colonel himself had, towards the end of his life, joined the RAF and proclaimed his faith in the coming world of heroic machinery.[31] In a future dominated by the bombing plane, the rifle-armed soldier would be an anachronism – about as relevant to national defence as the beefeaters in the Tower of London.

In the years immediately following the end of the First World War, the British Army retreated back into itself. Soon, it was as though the great wartime citizen-militia which had been built up from 1914 to 1918 had never existed. Nineteen out of twenty soldiers were discharged. All the wartime divisions were dissolved, their painstakingly assembled fleets of armoured fighting vehicles and siege guns sold for scrap. New editions of the *Field Service Regulations* paid lip service to the doctrinal experience of the war. But few such recommendations percolated down to the junior officer corps. All the practical expertise in combined-arms tactics, mastered in battle after battle on the Western Front, was forgotten.[32] The documentation describing how the Army had managed its massive manpower expansion was tossed out.[33] By the time the great post-war demobilization was over, just 218,000 men remained in regular service, an even smaller number than in 1914.[34] A few wartime innovations endured. The Tank Corps survived, though reduced to just four of its original twenty-six battalions. The communications squadrons of the Royal Engineers were reformed into a new Royal Corps of Signals. But in most other respects, the process of forgetting was complete. The service that John Masters joined in 1934 was once again an essentially nineteenth-century mercenary force of riflemen, light horsemen and mule-driven screw guns.

This shrunken constabulary, scattered in piecemeal garrisons along the frontiers of the Empire, resumed its pre-war role. By 1934, the distribution of its 126 line infantry battalions differed very little from the geographical pattern that had been laid down fifty years earlier. Over one third of all the battalions were in India. Seven others were maintained in Egypt and Palestine, two of the Empire's more recent and troublesome acquisitions. Five were in China, guarding Hong Kong and the various British commercial concessions which were islands of stability in that unfortunate war-wracked shell of a state. A further eight battalions were scattered across the rest of Britain's vast littoral territory, from Gibraltar, Malta, and Cyprus to Singapore.[35] The Army's remaining sixty 'home-based' infantry battalions were acting merely as under-strength feeder units rather than viable formations in their own right – 'squeezed lemons', as they were derisively called, capable only of providing drafts of new recruits to their regimental sister formations abroad.[36]

This was the kind of Army the accountants liked: small, cheap and as far away as possible (the Treasury was particularly keen on maintaining a large military force in India; battalions stationed in the Raj were the financial responsibility of the Indian taxpayer). Cost-cutting was in vogue after years of wartime profligacy. The 'Ten-Year Rule' introduced by the Committee of Imperial Defence in 1919 on the recommendation of Winston Churchill, and renewed annually for the next twelve years, took as its guiding principle that, since no major European conflict was likely for at least another decade, the armed services could be kept at a correspondingly low level of readiness. Annual expenditure on the Army fell from £974 million in 1918 to £45.4 million in 1922. In 1932, it bottomed out at £35.8 million.[37]

Most generals accepted this diminution in the Army's size and responsibilities as permanent. 'Under existing world conditions', wrote the chief of the Imperial General Staff (CIGS) Lord Cavan to the Chiefs of Staff Committee in January, 1924, 'we require no plans of campaign except for small wars incidental to our imperial position . . . there is no need to try and justify our existence by wasting our time and energies in the compilation of elaborate plans for wars against hypothetical enemies.'[38] His successor Sir George Milne agreed. The Great War had been an 'abnormal' event. There was no likelihood of it ever recurring again. Aside from providing an occupation force in the Rhineland (which only amounted to half a dozen or so infantry battalions at any one time anyway) Britain had no continental commitment to speak of. No European power represented a sufficient threat to British interests to warrant one. Only a tiny expeditionary force of one division was maintained for emergencies. And that was largely an afterthought.[39]

So in February 1935, as John Masters and his men negotiated the rocky declines of Waziristan, it seemed unlikely that Britain would ever again create another mass citizen army. There was simply too strong a coalition of interests combined against it. It was always possible, of course, that there would be another war. But even if there was, there would be no repeat of the nation in arms, no sequel to the great military and social experiment from 1914 to 1918 that had unleashed such valour and such horror. *Never again.*

CHAPTER 2

GENTLEMEN AND OLD SWEATS

Whitehall, Friday morning, 15 October 1937: grey, chilly, unwelcoming. Victor Gregg of Holborn, eighteen years old today, unemployed, broke, bored, is killing time by watching the Changing of the Guard. As he stands in the crowd in front of Horse Guards Parade, a large uniformed man 'with a big red band over his shoulders and more stripes on his uniform than a zebra' wanders over. He has a beaming smile and an attractive offer. '*Feeling a bit cold, son? What about coming over and 'aving a nice cup of tea and a bun, all on the 'ouse?*' Hungry and curious, Gregg agrees. He walks across Whitehall to a large redbrick building in Scotland Yard. Inside, he is immediately accosted by two men in white coats who start buttonholing him with questions – name, address, date of birth, medical history. '*Good – strip off, bend over, cough, you're all right son. Send in the next one.*'

Half an hour later, a dazed Gregg emerges from the redbrick building clutching a shilling, a railway warrant and an order to report to barracks at Winchester the following afternoon. He has just enlisted in the Rifle Brigade. 'I was halfway up Drury Lane and on my way home before the enormity of what I had done began to sink in', he recalled in his memoirs. 'By the time I reached home I was shivering in my shoes. I didn't tell a soul what had happened.' He slips out of his parents' house the following morning to catch the train, leaving a note on the bed. He spends the next nine years as a rifleman. He never does get his cup of tea or his bun.[1]

Such was the typical experience of rank-and-file Army enlistment between the wars: something brusque, disquieting and vaguely illicit. When sixteen-year-old Richard Cartwright showed up at his local recruitment office in 1933 he had to be turned down because of his age. But the sergeant in charge was not done with him yet. 'Look sonny', he said, 'tomorrow, go to Oxford Recruiting Office. Do not tell them that you have been here … do not admit you are 16! Say you are 18! Even if they do not believe you, stand your ground. I am sure you will get what you want.' A few weeks later, Cartwright was at Catterick Camp in Yorkshire training as a wireless operator. Three years later he was in India.[2] Frederick Cottier, a coalminer from South Shields, spent his last ninepence on the bus fare to Durham to enlist. When he arrived in Newcastle to report for training, an orderly corporal was there to meet him at the railway platform and whisk him off to Fenham Barracks. The Army was obviously worried he was going to abscond before he got there.[3] Reporting for duty for the first time, artillery recruit J. E. Bowman was warned off by another soldier: 'For fuck's sake, go home before it's too late!'[4]

These young men had joined an army which would take whomever it could get. And those it got were usually the young, the poor and the desperate. A *Times* correspondent who was invited to a recruitment office in a large provincial town in 1937 described the experience as depressing. Of the twenty-three men who turned up that morning, at least eight or nine 'looked hungry and pinched, or weedy from an ill-tended adolescence'. Fewer than half of them could be passed as medically fit. It was impossible to escape the feeling 'that for most of them this was not so much a venture into a new career as a last resort'.[5] One in five new infantrymen at the time was functionally illiterate and incapable even of simple arithmetic.[6] Bowman noted that many of his fellow recruits looked 'as if they had been transferred from a Dr. Barnado's soup kitchen in the late nineteenth century'.[7]

Even with its unexacting standards, the Army struggled to make up the numbers. It needed to enlist at least 26,000 new men every year just to cancel out the cyclical 'wastage' of soldiers whose terms of service were expiring or who needed to be discharged for medical or disciplinary reasons. But in 1936, it was only able to recruit 22,000. Orders were given to enlistment offices that anyone 'not actually mentally deficient' could be accepted. The chief of the Imperial General Staff indicated that he had no objection to any man 'not an imbecile' being recruited – though, he added, 'I should not proclaim it loudly'.[8] Even so, this was not enough. When the Arab Revolt broke out in Palestine, over 4,700 reservists had to be recalled to the colours to strengthen the existing line infantry battalions – an expediency which was usually restricted to wartime only.[9]

But then, to join the ranks of the British Army in the 1930s was considered by the general public to be something between an embarrassment and a tragedy. 'Few British households with a son serving in the rank and file seem to be proud of the fact', bemoaned the War Office's Director of Publicity John

Beith (better known by his pen-name Ian Hay) in 1938. 'He is usually regarded as the failure of the family; he is hushed up – *he went for a soldier*.'[10] The brief exemption that soldiers had had from popular disdain during the First World War expired quickly after the Armistice. The heroic wartime Tommy, stalwart defender of hearth and home, became once again the Old Sweat, or 'swaddy' – a drunken, clodhopping lout, brave in a simple-minded way, but not fit for polite civilian company. Regulars were 'a bad lot of chaps' who were to be regarded with the deepest suspicion.[11] Robert Green, who joined the infantry in 1935, felt that he and his comrades were dismissed as 'a race apart . . . ill-educated, illiterate, foul-mouthed'. His own mother used to describe soldiers as 'the scum of the Earth': 'I used to say: *well, steady on, I'm one of them*. She said: *I can't help it. Scum of the Earth*.'[12] Driving through the Durham coalfields in a convoy of tanks, Frank Griffin recalled groups of men, their faces 'death-like', standing on the street corners gazing at them, the chill air of contempt punctuated by an occasional jeer.[13] Peacetime soldiers, thought Griffin, were regarded by typical civilians as 'pariahs, baby-killers, rapers of women, outcasts from society':

> In buses, trams, and trains, civilians edge hastily away from the nearness of khaki; in the streets the people make a clear throughway for troops walking on the pavement; in cafés and restaurants, if soldiers sit at a table with civilians, the latter finish their meal in a rush and ask for the bill; in public houses in towns and villages where troops are seen rarely, the men turn their backs on the soldiers, scorning to say even a word of greeting; in 'superior' cinemas the girl in the cash-box says *I'm sorry* . . . when a soldier asks for a rather expensive seat.[14]

If the soldier was regarded as loathsome, the Army itself was held up for ridicule. To the typical young Briton, soldering was all 'marching back and forth like automatons, offering jerky salutes to officers, and occasionally running about and firing blank ammunition at an imaginary foe', lamented Hay. 'It all seems like a lot of make-believe, rather petty and ridiculous.'[15] 'Much of what the Army does is laughed at by the man in the street', thought another officer. 'It is all an out-of-date joke.'[16] The only thing soldiers seemed to do between the wars which was worth taking at all seriously was to intervene in strike action, and this was not calculated to endear them to the working-class public. In August 1919, troops with fixed bayonets charged a crowd of rioters in Liverpool, shooting dead one man and injuring dozens more.[17] During the 1926 General Strike, thirty-six infantry battalions were deployed across Britain to escort food convoys and guard government buildings and railway stations.[18]

As for the Army officer: 'It has for many years been almost axiomatic in England that he is a fool – the fool of the family', wrote a retired major-general to *The Times* in 1937.[19] To Liddell Hart, it seemed that the public took it largely for granted that an Army commission was a symptom of idiocy. Schoolmasters would only recommend boys with 'more brawn than brain' for the Royal Military College at Sandhurst, and only if it would be 'quite impossible' for them to succeed in any other walk of life. Any pupil of talent who expressed interest in a military career was hurriedly warned off with 'pained surprise' by his masters. Public schoolboys preparing for the Sandhurst entrance exams were assumed to be the dimwits of their class, Colonel Blimps in embryo.[20]

Given this less than flattering portrait, the Army had almost as much difficulty finding enough officer candidates between the wars as it did ordinary recruits. Whilst in Germany's Weimar Republic every boy of good family, it was said, was 'burning to become' an officer, the British Army could never find enough suitable candidates. In 1937, only 550 of the 650 open subaltern positions were filled.[21] Those young men who did go to Sandhurst often did so in a fatalistic mood. John Masters had originally considered a career in law, but found himself drawn to military service in the Empire partly by the weight of family tradition – his father was a retired lieutenant-colonel in the Indian Army – and partly by a lack of other options. 'No-one tried to force me to go to India when my time came', Masters reflected years later. 'But where else was there to go? What else was there to do?'[22] David Hunt, who later became a colonel attached to Field Marshal Alexander's staff, summed up the feelings of many of his generation. 'To join one of the services in peacetime could obviously not be contemplated except by someone cursed with inborn blood lust', he wrote. 'It helped also, I believed, to be rather stupid.'[23]

In fact, there was scarcely such a thing as the 'British Army' at all in the 1930s, in the sense of a single, coherent, unitary institution. What existed instead was a collection of several dozen regiments, each of which enjoyed an effectively independent corporate existence that was only occasionally and weakly disturbed by the intrusions of the War Office in London. The unique constitutional character of the British Army between the wars cannot be overstated. Other armies had units they called regiments too. But for the most part, those were simply tactical formations with no peculiar privileges, rights of self-governance or special claims on the allegiance of their men. Only the British Army regarded the regiment as the essential building block of its organization and identity. Subtract the regiments from the Army, and what remained? The War Office; the military colleges; a smattering of departments and depots. That was all. The junior officers of the Grenadier Guards did not regard 'the Army' as something they belonged to at all, but rather an alien and contemptible thing – 'a vague, remote, enormously incompetent authority quite outside ourselves'.[24] The regiment mattered. The Army did not.

This had not always been the case. While some regiments could trace their origins back as far as the Restoration, the modern regimental system had really only been created in the 1870s. It had been the product of a late Victorian reorganization of the Army led by two successive secretaries-of-state for war, Edward Cardwell and Hugh Childers. Before the Cardwell-Childers reforms, most British infantry regiments had been made up of one battalion and were identified primarily by a number rather than a name. They claimed no particular recruitment district within the United Kingdom, or attachment to any particular county or borough.[25] Their men were enlisted under terms of 'General Service' which meant that they could, if necessary, be drafted en masse from one regiment to another if the War Office deemed it necessary. Officers, who continued to purchase their ranks just as they had done in the Duke of Wellington's day, were highly promiscuous in their regimental allegiance, moving to and fro as opportunities for promotion came up.[26]

The Cardwell-Childers reforms brought all this to an end by abolishing purchase, reducing the length of service of the rank and file, and compulsorily amalgamating all the single-battalion regiments into two-battalion 'localized' regiments with specific depots and geographically defined recruiting districts. The 30th and 59th Regiments of Foot became the East Lancashire Regiment, for instance, with an administrative depot in Burnley. Some of these unions were made rather arbitrarily. There was no obvious reason for adding the 108th Madras Infantry to the Royal Inniskilling Fusiliers, for instance.[27] Veterans grumbled that the new regiments were bastard progeny, unnatural products of unsought marriages. Nothing good would come of them.[28]

The two reforming secretaries of state hoped that by associating the new regiments with particular geographical areas, and simultaneously reducing the length of rank-and-file enlistment, military service would become a more popular and respectable prospect for civilians of a broader social background. The 'youth of every class, whether in town or country, whether artisan, mechanic or peasant' might be persuaded to consider a few years in his local regiment, as Childers put it.[29] The plan did not work. There was really no way of getting around the Army's least attractive quality: the disagreeable conditions of service that were inherent in its mission of far-flung imperial defence. Soldiers were required to spend many years continuously overseas, often in parts of the world with unhealthy tropical climates. Their working life was often severe and monastic. Pay was not good. Prospects for advancement within the Army were usually modest at best. Prospects outside of it upon mustering out were a good deal worse. Soldiering was ill-suited to the conventional rites of manhood, especially marriage and paternity. Gambling, liquor and the sordid pleasures of the garrison town brothel were poor substitutes for a normal family life. Localization did little to alter the cockeyed patriotism of the typical Briton. Civilians cheered on soldier-boys during rumours of war and despised them to their faces once the crisis was over. The peacetime army remained a dumping ground for the indigent and disgraced.

The newfangled regiments did, however, endure. After some initial hesitancy and an ameliorating passage of time, their men took to them. Indeed, regimental identity now became more important than ever, because there was far less cross-regimental movement of officers and ORs than before. Transfers only took place now *within* regiments, usually between their 1st and 2nd battalions. By the 1930s, it had become most unusual for a soldier ever to leave his regiment of enlistment during his time in the service. Only by promotion to the rank of brigadier or above did an officer depart his regiment, and often then with a good deal of regret.

The Duke of Cornwall's Light Infantry, to which John Masters was temporarily attached in 1935, was like most English county regiments a product of the Cardwell-Childers reform project, and the way in which it had forged a particular identity for itself since its creation in 1881 was typical.[30] Each of its constituent battalions, the 32nd Cornwall Light Infantry and the 46th South Devonshires, had brought with them to the marriage a set of battle honours and customs to be shared across the new regiment. The South Devonshires, first raised in 1741, contributed their tradition of wearing a red feather or patch behind the cap badge, a practice which dated back to the Battle of Paoli Tavern during the American War of Independence. In the aftermath of that battle, the Continental Army had accused the 46th's Light Company of murdering American prisoners, and though the charge had in fact been groundless the vengeful Pennsylvanians had pledged that henceforth they would single out men of the South Devonshires for special retribution. It was a threat to which the 46th's men had responded with dry hauteur by adopting their unusual headgear so as to be more distinctive than ever in the face of the enemy.

The 32nd, first raised in 1702, had an even grander pedigree. Its men had stood at the centre of the Duke of Wellington's infantry line at Waterloo in 1815 and had remained under almost continual French artillery and musket fire throughout the whole day, absorbing the greatest proportionate losses of any British Army regiment of foot during the battle. Their most celebrated feat, however, was their defence of the Lucknow Residency during the Indian Mutiny of 1857, a 148-day ordeal that was to become one of the signal epics of the British Raj. During the protracted investment of the Residency, crated pieces of regimental mess silver had been used to plug gaps in the crumbling defensive walls, and when Masters was seconded to the 1st Battalion of the DCLI in 1934 these battered relics – including a soup tureen with the musket ball which had punctured it seventy-seven years earlier still rattling inside – were proudly displayed in glass cases. The various regimental colours, cased and capped and crossed, and looking, Masters thought, like 'huge black rockets', sat behind the president of the mess each evening at dinner. On special guest nights they were unfurled, lighting the room in embroidered majesty with the accompaniment of 'silver trumpets of the past'. 'In their silken richness', Masters wondered, 'I saw all that glory, and those muskets buried in the mud of forgotten fields.'[31]

Other regiments rejoiced in their own traditions. Soldiers of the Glosters wore badges on the front and rear of their caps to commemorate the all-round defence of their regiment's position at the Battle of Alexandria in 1801. The band of the Leicestershire Regiment played *Wolfe's Lament* before the National Anthem in tribute to their part in the taking of Quebec. Certain days of the calendar had sacred status, marking some peculiar feat of arms: for the Somerset Light Infantry it was 7 April (Jellalabad Day), for the Gordon Highlanders 20 October (Dargai Day), whilst for the Green Howards 20 September, the anniversary of the Battle of Alma, was a hallowed occasion on which the captured drums of the Tsar's Vladimir and Minsk Regiments were solemnly trooped. Some traditions seemed to have been invented simply out of a desire not to conform. Worcestershire green was a subtly different shade from the grass green worn by other regiments. The 11th Hussars insisted on sounding last post ten minutes earlier than everyone else. The marching pace of the Rifle Brigade was slightly faster than that of any other regiment, often throwing parades into confusion.

Not all of these distinctions were particularly sensible or constructive. Regimental culture was passionately divisive. The pecking order of prestige across the Army was enforced in a spirit of withering snobbery. The line cavalry regiments looked down on the infantry as their poor relations. The Royal Tank Corps, proud of their modern-mindedness, thought of the cavalry as oafish and obsolete. The Household Division and the elite rifle regiments looked down on everyone. Everyone looked down on the non-combat branches, the so-called 'tail' corps. English and Welsh regiments disliked Scottish regiments, and the feeling was reciprocated. Hatreds fuelled by ancient and obscure slights could sometimes lead to bloodshed. The Coldstream Guards detested the Royal Scots. A detachment of the Royal Welch Fusiliers could not be safely bivouacked next to men of the Highland Light Infantry. The cult of the regiment produced a passionate *esprit de corps* within the ranks. But it also produced soldiers solipsistically obsessed with the fortunes of their own regiment and indifferent to any other concern. Loyalty to the Army as a unitary institution scarcely existed at all. Whenever a question of reform came up, the first – really the only – question anyone asked was: *is it good for my regiment?* If it was, they were in favour of it. If it was not, they were against it. This did not create an intellectual environment in which tough decisions could be made. The regimental system had its virtues, noted Captain J.R. Kennedy in 1935. But it also 'deified bombast' and perpetuated an attitude of mind 'not consistent with modern tolerance, modesty, and intelligence'.[32]

Take, for instance, the question of mechanization, the signature military controversy of the period between the wars. In 1933, the Army was still heavily invested in the horse as a weapon of war. It possessed fifty-seven mounted cavalry regiments, while the Royal Tank Corps was just four battalions strong.[33] Although the process of converting these units to tanks and armoured cars had been under discussion since the end of the First World War, it did not properly get under way until 1935, and progress was uneven. At the outbreak of war in September 1939, two cavalry regiments were still mounted. To Liddell Hart and his fellow military correspondent J.F.C. Fuller, 'a phalanx of reactionary Blimps' sentimentally fixated on the horse had been responsible for this lacka-daisical conversion process.[34] Fuller described the interwar cavalry corps as an 'equine Tammany Hall' which preferred to contemplate losing a battle rather than abandon its traditional mounts.[35]

The horse certainly played an important symbolic role in the life of the Army. Elite regiments such as the Life Guards continued to inhabit a pre-industrial world of chaff and oats and steaming manure, of wet cobblestone floors and the gleam of sword and breastplate, a world of snow-white pipe-clayed leather shimmering on the drill square in the morning.[36] The day-to-day life of guardsmen while on ceremonial duties was organized around meticu-lous attention to the visual, the self-indulgent display of obsolete splendour. Uniforms and tack were expected to dazzle unnaturally, the coats of the horses to shine in the sun. Whenever trooper Tim Bishop watched his comrades ride through Hyde Park during the warm summer months, or listened to the trum-peters sounding the last post in the darkness above Knightsbridge, he was transported by the romance of it all: 'At such times I would think: *Who would be a civilian?*'[37] His was the respectable, chocolate-box British Army, its bear-skins and brass bands still much-admired by a public that otherwise thought little of soldiers and took scant interest in military matters.

Equestrianism was central to the self-image of the gentleman-officer. Much of a subaltern's free time was organized around the field sports which were said to be essential to the moral education of a fighting man. In 1935, a War Office committee on the Value of the Horse in the Training of Officers concluded with only one dissent (from its sole civilian member) that it was vital to keep instructing subalterns in the art of horse riding in order to attract the 'right sort of people' to the Army. Archibald Montgomery-Massingberd, the Lincolnshire squire who served as CIGS from 1933 to 1936, thought that the Army needed more than ever 'the class of boy who from his early days has been imbued with a love of the horse . . . we cannot do without him'.[38] Many of the students who attended the Army's Staff College at Camberley between the wars seem to have been more interested in its drag hunt than by its lessons in military strategy. In 1937 the Army was still spending six times as much per pupil on horse-riding lessons than on tank training.[39] It was regarded as a great compliment to say of an artillery officer that he was more interested in the horses that pulled his guns than the guns themselves.[40]

But too much can be made of this. Reactionary cavalry officers cannot be solely blamed for the slow pace of mechanization. More prosaic forces were at work too. The Army was starved of funds between the wars; there was simply never enough money to re-equip and retrain in any comprehensive way. In no single year between 1926 and 1934 did the Treasury ever grant the Master-General of the Ordnance more than £1 million to spend on new weapons.[41] Only in the final years before the outbreak of the Second World War did the financial spigots ease open to some extent.

Rapid earlier mechanization would not in any case have made much sense, given the Army's predominantly imperial mission in the 1920s and 1930s. Units posted across the Empire were expected to be able to operate in ecologically marginal areas in which there were no extensive road networks. Their soldiers had to be capable of carrying with them all of the supplies and equipment they needed, rather than relying on a long and burdensome logistics train. The vehicles available to the Army at the time were not capable of meeting such requirements. The thinly armed and armoured Vickers Medium Tank, the mainstay of the Tank Corps from 1923 to 1933, was so clumsy and fragile that it could barely make a journey of fifty miles even under good conditions without its steel plating shaking itself loose, its brakes failing, or some other mechanical disaster taking place.[42] In 1925, two Vickers Mediums were sent to India for field trials. Even though they had been fitted with special air-cooling fans to compensate for the fierce tropical heat, one of them caught fire before it had even reached the training depot.[43]

In fact, given the Army's lack of money and the unreliability of much of the hardware that was available to it, it is surprising just how far the mechanization process progressed in the final years before the outbreak of the Second World War. The Army in India may have been left to rely on animal power, but the

Army back in the UK was becoming petrol-driven. By 1937, just 6,544 horses and mules remained in service, compared to 28,244 in 1913. The Royal Artillery had mostly retired its horse teams and was in the process of converting to motorized gun tractors. Infantry platoons were being issued with lorries to transport their kit and weapons. Troop-carrying companies had been created at the divisional level to move large numbers of soldiers by road. The Vickers Universal Carrier, a pioneering model of an armoured personnel carrier, was coming into general service. By the time of the invasion of Poland, the British Army in Europe was rather more motorized than the German Army.

Many soldiers embraced the change. The disappearance of the horse was a bittersweet moment, to be sure; it meant, amongst other things, the end of an important emotional outlet within an all-male institution that did not provide many other opportunities for the expression of kindness or compassion. It was hard to feel the same way about a tank or a gun tractor as one had about a living, breathing creature.[44] But mechanization offered important practical compensations. Men were relieved of the dirty and irksome tasks of mucking-out and cutting chaff. The conversion to motor vehicles also meant an opportunity to acquire trade skills which would be useful later in civilian life. Ultimately, whatever their private regrets, most soldiers came to terms with the inevitability of it all. When the men of the 17th/21st Lancers heard their colonel announce in January 1938 that their horses were soon to be replaced by armoured cars, subaltern Robert 'Val' ffrench Blake remembered 'a great sort of gasp, followed by a cheer out of the soldiers . . . we were all relieved this had finally come'.[45] The conversion to armour did not produce the exodus of embittered Blimps from the cavalry that some critics had predicted. Of the thirty-two officers serving in the 11th Hussars on the eve of its mechanization in 1928, only two resigned their commissions. Most officers were actually reassured rather than distressed, because, as their regimental journal reminded them, 'Now we know our position as a regiment is secure for a great number of years.'[46]

And there was the rub. So long as mechanization meant the survival of the cavalry regiments, the cavalrymen themselves were happy, indeed eager, to embrace it. But did maintaining the institution of the cavalry, rather than transferring its officers and men to newly created battalions of the Royal Tank Corps, make sense for the Army as a whole? In 1939, the War Office announced the creation of a new umbrella formation, the Royal Armoured Corps (RAC), in which the mechanized cavalry regiments and the Tank Corps (renamed as part of the process the Royal Tank Regiment) would now coexist. It was an awkward marriage between two branches of the service which had little regard for one another. But more dangerously, it also encouraged the cavalry regiments to think that nothing had really changed – that substituting armour plate for flesh was a mere technical detail, and that cavalry tactics on the battlefield needed no alteration. It would take many deadly encounters with the anti-tank guns of Rommel's Afrika Korps to disabuse the cavalrymen of that particular delusion.

So if the British Army of the 1930s was out of date, this was not simply because it was technologically obsolescent; because in many ways, it wasn't. The issue was rather one of *world view*; or, to be more exact, what the Army believed the proper order of society and the relationship between its officers and men should be. Its attitude towards the social order remained that of the world before 1914. One regular described the Army's atmosphere in the 1930s as that of a 'large, well-run country estate'.[47] It was committed to a model of social and moral hierarchy that was becoming more and more anachronistic with each passing day, a model imbued with a set of assumptions about class, authority and power which no longer commanded nearly as much respect outside the barrack gates. It was little wonder that soldiers and civilians regarded one another with a mixture of incomprehension and suspicion. Mentally, they had come to occupy different worlds.

Essential to this growing lack of understanding was the fact that the peace-time Army recruited most of its soldiers from the margins of society. What is striking about the accounts of the young men who joined up between the wars is the miserable life that so many of them were fleeing. Douglas Wright, who grew up as one of nine children in the depressed pit town of Poynton, Cheshire, joined the Grenadier Guards in 1938 largely to escape the Dickensian conditions he had known as a boy. His family lived in a damp and cockroach-infested two-up-two-down, with one cold tap, the lavatory in a foetid outside shed, no electricity or gas service, and only a couple of paraffin lamps for lighting. Wright and his brothers and sisters subsisted largely on a diet of bread and potatoes. With their mother broken by endless physical toil and the casual cruelty of her husband, the children spent most of their day trying to come up with reasons not to be at home.[48] Young men such as Wright saw little of the rising affluence and democratization of mid-century Britain. Theirs was a very different country, a land of rust-red squalor and immiserating poverty, haunted by the spectre of the dole queue. One in ten of the poorest Britons still suffered from chronic undernourishment between the wars.[49] In the slum districts of London's East End and the putrid tenements of cities such as Liverpool, Hull and Glasgow, families with young children were crammed into two or three damp, insect-ridden rooms, lacking even the most basic sanitary and washing facilities. It was from such crevices of despair that the Army drew its rank and file.

In their own way, too, most officers were also from the social margins. By the 1930s, the Army no longer drew the majority of its subalterns from the country gentry. The abolition of purchase in 1871 and the introduction of competitive entrance examinations at Sandhurst and the Royal Military Academy at Woolwich had caused a slow but inexorable decline in the dominance of the landed squire-archy within the officer corps.[50] In 1860, over half of all incoming Sandhurst cadets had listed their fathers' occupation as 'gentleman'. By 1930, only one in ten did so (this at a time, incidentally, when almost one-quarter of German Army officers were noblemen).[51] The choicest regiments – the Household Cavalry, the Brigade of Guards, the elite rifle regiments and the cavalry of the line – continued to attract young men of title and breeding. The two regular battalions of the Coldstream Guards were graced between the wars by the presence of such gran-dees as the Earl of Cottenham, Sir John Gwen Carew-Pole, Sir Walter de Stopham Barttelot and the Honourable George William Lawies Jackson, heir to the Barony of Allerton.[52] Such regiments maintained their social exclusivity by a system of punitively high mess bills and expenses, making it impossible for an officer without independent means to pay his way.[53]

But the majority of officers were not authentic gentlemen. Rather, they were scions of the 'service' dynasties which had sprung up during the Georgian and Victorian eras – those families which for over two centuries had supplied the Empire's needs for civil servants, churchmen, teachers, sailors and soldiers. The sons of service families grew up not on elegant country estates, but instead in rented rooms in seaside retirement ghettos such as Eastbourne and Lytham St Annes, or in shabby terraces of the likes of Kensington and Earl's Court. They had little claim to any real gentility. Few of them could trace more than the feeblest of blood-links to the squirearchy. Hardly any of them owned any land. Their financial circumstances were usually perilous. But their identifica-tion with the traditional elite was absolute all the same.[54] George Orwell, the son of a petty functionary in the Indian Civil Service and one of the most famous products of an Edwardian service dynasty, described his background as 'lower-upper-middle-class'. He remembered as a young man how his patri-cian status was drummed into him by his parents and teachers, even though it was almost purely notional:

Theoretically you knew all about servants and how to tip them, although in practice you had one, at most, two resident servants. Theoretically you knew how to wear your clothes and how to order a dinner, although in practice you could never afford to go to a decent tailor or a decent restau-rant. Theoretically you knew how to shoot and ride, although in practice you had no horses to ride and not an inch of ground to shoot over.[55]

Many of Britain's great captains of the Second World War were born into such threadbare gentility. Claude Auchinleck's father, who had been a lieutenant-colonel in the Royal Horse Artillery, died of a pernicious anaemic complaint contracted in the tropics when his son was just eight. His widow raised Claude and her three other children single-handedly, eking out a miserable Army pension by serving as an invalid's companion in a Hampshire coastal resort.[56] One of Bernard Montgomery's grandfathers had been lieutenant-general of the Punjab; another, the headmaster of Marlborough College and Dean of Canterbury. But the Montgomery family's fortunes went into a steep decline during the late nineteenth century, and when in 1887 his father Henry, an Anglican vicar, inherited a destitute family property in County Donegal, he had no choice but to move half-way across the world and take a position as Bishop of Tasmania just to prevent the estate's foreclosure. When Bernard arrived at Sandhurst in 1907 he was required to live on a weekly allowance of nine shillings, which meant that every penny had to be carefully accounted for. Even the luxury of a wrist-watch was beyond his means.[57]

It was not that becoming an officer promised a release from this life of continual penny-pinching, nor much in the way of future opportunity. A second lieutenant received ten shillings a day, less than a bricklayer or a bus driver.[58] 'His life', as one captain of the time put it, 'is one long struggle from the day he is first gazetted.'[59] Promotion even for the ablest subalterns was sclerotically slow, and usually based on seniority rather than merit. The actor David Niven, who joined the Highland Light Infantry (HLI) in 1930, dated the collapse of his military ambitions to watching fellow officers trace with weary resignation the pages of the fawn-coloured *Army List* devoted to the HLI.[60] 'Slowly, like the damp of a disused house [the] deadening frustration' of it all bored into him.[61]

The Army's lack of any pressing mission between the wars, however, left plenty of time for gentlemanly recreation. Officers enjoyed unparalleled opportunities for sport, especially riding. As a Winchester schoolboy, David Scourfield yearned to devote his life to equestrianism. But as a younger son with no great financial prospects ahead of him, he seemed fated instead for an office job in London. Then, one day, he saw two beautiful horses being ridden by a couple of subalterns. 'I thought to myself: *that's the life for me. Exactly what I've been looking for.*'[62] John Watson spent most of his time in the Royal Leicestershire Regiment between the wars riding and playing bridge and chess. 'I just joined the Army to enjoy myself', he admitted later. He ended up enjoying himself rather too much, and had to take an overseas secondment to the King's African Rifles because he was £600 overdrawn.[63] A foreign posting offered not just cost savings, but also rich opportunities for sport. In India, three days a week were typically devoted to hunting. Officers could spend their generous leaves on such manly adventures as tiger-stalking in the Himalayan foothills.[64] While stationed with the Ceylon garrison in the mid-1930s, E. B. Thornhill spent much of his day riding and playing tennis at his club. 'I only had to be in the office between breakfast and lunch.'[65]

And here was where the appeal of Army life lay: for it offered a space in which men of limited prospects could pretend that they were to the manor born. The key thing about many service families, as Orwell recognized, was that the modern world was a riddle to them. The growing democratization of British society after 1918 and the spread of mass consumer culture was some-thing which had completely passed them by. Commerce and industry they looked down on as 'trade', a mysterious and vulgar way of making money. Their mental world view was at least a century out of date. Many of their sons did not grow up aspiring for worldly success in a modern sense; they yearned, rather, to be leisured country gentlemen. And that was precisely the fantasy which the Army could deliver. The regiment – with its silver plate and commissioned portraiture, its richly decorated mess and endowed chapel, its avuncular colonel and devoted retainers – had a quasi-aristocratic atmosphere which made up for any deficiencies in pay and prospects.[66] The Army was a world within which the shabby-genteel without money or pedigree could play at being toffs.

The life of the ordinary soldier between the wars offered no such fantasies, of course. Most ORs were housed in Victorian dormitory barracks which had been superficially modernized with electric lighting and hot and cold bath houses, but which still retained a grim prison-like atmosphere. Some 'tempo-rary' barracks hastily assembled during the First World War, such as the leaky wooden huts that dotted the windy plain of Catterick Camp in North Yorkshire, still remained in use years after they were supposed to have been replaced.[67] The barrack room at the Artillery Depot at Woolwich was likened to a cowshed, albeit a clean one.[68] Soldiers slept on heavy solid iron beds lined up at tight intervals, with mattresses built from coif-filled rectangles known as biscuits. The food they got was, according to Richard Cartwright, 'repugnant and revolting'; plates of greasy porridge and rissoles complemented by hunks of dry bread and mugs of unsweetened cocoa, with perhaps the occasional spoonful of jam or sliver of butter.[69] Pay was risibly low, and actually worse than it had been in the Duke of Wellington's day. The two shillings per diem of a private soldier in the 1930s only had half the real purchasing power of the single shilling which a Waterloo redcoat had received.[70] 'Everything is bare, hard, rough, and uncouth in the extreme', observed Frank Griffin of his life as a recruit in the 1930s:

There is not the slightest atom of privacy or comfort; not the faintest thing resembling a home which can help one adapt oneself to a new life among strangers of all types. The sense of desolation which filled us new recruits often brought me near to tears. I saw some men actually crying in the quiet of their beds during the night.[71]

Yet the drop-out rate was low. In 1934, fewer than seven in a hundred recruits had left the Army by the end of their first three months of service.[72] Military conditions, even at their bleakest, rarely broke such men. Most of them were, after all, inured to austere circumstances, habituated to want. The Army could scarcely dish out anything worse than they had known as civilians.

And soldiering came with its own rewards. The regiment pushed and cajoled and harried you and forced you to do all sorts of absurd and disagreeable things. But it looked after you in return. It taught you how to take care of yourself. Slum recruits often lacked the most rudimentary notions of hygiene. Some had no idea what a toothbrush was.[73] Until he joined the Guards, Douglas Wright had never worn underwear.[74] The regiment offered you an education. By the 1930s, the Army was operating what amounted to a shadow schooling system for the functionally illiterate male children of the underclass, providing them with rudimentary but solid instruction in reading, writing and arithmetic. The regiment offered you a helping hand when you needed it. Its NCOs were not all bawling tyrants. The sergeant who put you on a charge for some petty lapse during kit inspection, or who screamed at you for hours on the parade ground, might also turn out to be a thoughtful and kindly father figure. Sam Small, who had enlisted in the Northamptonshire Regiment partly to get away from his hectoring siblings, was discovered by his squad sergeant sobbing quietly in the lavatory on the eve of his first Christmas leave. After coaxing the problem out of him, the sergeant made arrangements for Small to stay in barracks over the holiday, and wrote to the young man's family sternly warning them to leave their brother alone.[75]

Most of all, the regiment provided you, often for the first time in your life, with a sense of identity – of belonging to something bigger and more important than yourself. Most recruits did not enter the Army with much pre-existing social capital, much notion of membership in a meaningful community. The regiment offered them a purpose that had hitherto been missing from their lives, a haven from the 'undisciplined chaos' of the civilian world that had largely neglected and ignored them.[76] It invested in its men a feeling of inclusion, of participation in a stable social order that would take responsibility for them, would bring order to their formerly confused and unhappy lives, would instil in them pride and self-confidence. The regiment initiated them into a close-knit family with its own private rites, languages and traditions. It was a fraternity stretching across time and space in which all members, past, present and future, belonged – the sort of sacred union which political scientists call an 'imagined community'.[77]

There was a price. The Army expected its men to accept its internal rules, its formal and informal hierarchies, without question. The officer's role was unashamedly paternalistic. 'I played football and ran cross-country with my platoon', recalled John Masters. 'I inspected its smelly feet and noisome socks and sat up late listening to its involved stories of domestic betrayal. I congratulated it, admonished it, put it under arrest, and admired its snapshots.'[78] Officers were expected – in theory, anyway – to behave as good parents towards their children, to put the comforts of their men above their own. They were encouraged to demonstrate many admirable personal qualities: compassion, humility and self-sacrifice not the least amongst them. But the Army also assumed that there was a natural and unchangeable condition of human inequality, an unbridgeable gap between the leaders and the led, founded on class distinction and blood. As William Graham of the Cameron Highlanders, put it, officers and men were expected to regard one another as 'two different kinds of human beings'.[79] Subalterns were encouraged to treat the rank and file much as they would treat domestic servants. Philip Pardoe was advised to speak to his men as he would to his chauffeur.[80] It was the ordinary British soldier's job to do as he was told; to exhibit, as the 1932 training manual put it, 'a cheerful and unhesitating obedience to orders'.[81] He was not expected to think.

The regiment also brooked no rivals for its loyalty. It took in young men whose connections to the civilian world were weak to begin with, and made them weaker still. In return for its protection and support, it expected its members to separate themselves as far as possible from all other emotional attachments. It did not encourage the creation of family ties. Most soldiers were forbidden to marry 'on the strength', which meant that if they proceeded to take a wife without permission they received no marriage allowance or assistance with housing. Few did. Marriage was regarded as destructive to *esprit de corps*: 'an Army is not a stud farm', wrote Ian Hay in 1938. Allowing wives to intrude into the corporate life of the regiment would be a 'blighting influence' which would cause morale to crumble.[82] Life for the typical young soldier was, as Richard Cartwright put it, 'monastic . . . the only time we saw a member of the opposite sex was behind a canteen counter'.[83] 'Respectable' women were difficult for soldiers to court because of their low pay and status. Sexual urges were expected to be dealt with by discreet encounters with prostitutes, so long as the proper hygienic precautions were taken. Frustration and resentment were a result. Frank Griffin and his comrades in the Tank Corps would get fighting drunk every weekend and head into town to pick quarrels with townspeople. Women, he recalled, 'we hated intensely, and every civilian was in our opinion a swine'.[84]

It was not easy for a soldier to forge a stable long-term relationship with a potential marriage partner in any case, because the Army physically removed him from Britain for so much of his service. Of the 687 Army units operational in 1934, 246 of them were overseas, 126 of them in India.[85] The rank and file recruit between the wars could expect to spend up to six uninterrupted years in the Raj.[86] Given such a long exile, it is not surprising that some men found little point in maintaining family connections back in Britain. Arthur Jeffrey, who joined the Devonshire Regiment as a boy soldier, spent five years in Malta, during which time he sent no more than a dozen letters home. Even his commanding officer finally admonished him for his lack of consideration when his parents wrote in anguish to the War Office to find out if their son was still alive.[87] Albert Chapman, who had gone to India as a teenager, did not see his mother again until she lay on her deathbed twelve years later. She scarcely remembered him: ' "You're Teddy from India, aren't you?", she said. I said, "Yes, Mum." And the book closed on that chapter.'[88] One ageing Irish Warrant Officer, who had spent twenty-eight years east of Suez, was bewildered when he returned home to his native Dublin. Shanghai felt far more familiar.[89]

Soldiers were encouraged to adopt the mental outlook of their regiment, a world view that was closed in on itself, sullenly defensive, suspicious of everything beyond the barrack gates. 'Your values, your standards – everything was different' from civilian life, thought Robert Green:

> You could on pay day take your money out of your pocket, chuck it on your bed and go to dinner and come back and there wouldn't be a halfpenny missing. But two blokes wouldn't think twice about going down town and bashing somebody with a good wallet behind the ear and taking it. But they wouldn't have dreamed of robbing their mates . . . the outside world thought they were absolute louses and so they just behaved like it in lots of cases.[90]

Many young officers rejoiced in this insularity. For them, the regiment served as a useful site of internal exile, happily detached from the realities of a world which they found alien and unappealing. The more closed-minded the Army was, the better.[91] This was an attitude which the retiring commander-in-chief of the British Army in India, Field-Marshal Sir Philip Chetwode, complained about at his farewell address in October 1934. Many of his junior officers, he felt, had sunk into a 'state of complete mental slackness', their narrow interests 'bounded by the morning parade, the game they happen to play, and purely local and unimportant matters'. Many officers scarcely even bothered to read the newspapers, let alone pay attention to political developments in India.[92] According to Harold Macmillan, the typical regular British staff officer somehow managed to travel all over his country's Empire without learning a thing about it. His entire experience of the world was confined to the walls of the military mess at Aldershot or Poona. By the end of his career, he was just about sophisticated enough to be the secretary of a golf club.[93]

Not that the Army really encouraged its officers to take their job seriously. The training programme at RMC Sandhurst, with its relentless emphasis on drill and spit-and-polish, seemed more interested in producing perfect private soldiers than thoughtful, well-rounded leaders.[94] Interwar proposals to develop Sandhurst into a full-fledged university on the model of West Point, a move which would have helped to expand the mental horizons of its cadets, were abandoned because of lack of money.[95] Training for the Army's artillerymen and engineers at the ostensibly more 'scientific' Royal Military Academy in Woolwich was little more sophisticated than that at Sandhurst. The Woolwich cadet did not enjoy 'a scintilla of independence of action of thought', being taught simply 'to accept what he was told without argument'.[96]

Nor did things improve once the young officer arrived at his regiment. Many colonels took no interest in the professional development of their subalterns, leaving the running of their battalions to the adjutant and the regimental sergeant major and packing off their lieutenants to the playing field.[97] Junior officers who actually wanted to learn their trade were left bored and frustrated, complained Captain J. R. J. MacNamara in 1937: 'Subalterns tumble over each other in their company offices, making themselves some little job here or there, usually having nothing better to do for many hours than to slap their calves with the irritating Army cane.'[98] Most infantry battalions were in any case so under strength that there was little opportunity for an ambitious young officer to learn his trade even if he had wanted to. When David Niven arrived to inspect his first platoon, only seven men out of a nominal strength of forty appeared on parade.[99] During the nine months leading up to the outbreak of war, Philip Pardoe did not once have his whole platoon together for a single continuous twenty-four-hour period. 'We never really got to know one another', he confessed.[100] A subaltern with the Manchester Regiment acknowledged that he wasn't really a professional soldier before the war: 'My mind wasn't wrapped up in the job at all really.'[101]

There were important exceptions to all this, of course, some of whom would later rise to great prominence within the Army – sober, dedicated young professionals who took their careers seriously. But they were the exceptional few. Taking too much of an interest in military affairs, being seen to try too hard, was regarded as insufferably bad form – a gauche departure from the tradition of effortless gentlemanly amateurism. On joining the Grenadier Guards, Peter Carrington was told by his new commanding officer that there were only two things he really needed to remember. These were not to marry until he was twenty-five, and to hunt in Leicestershire at least two days a week. This was January 1939, with war just a few months away. 'I wondered if there might be, perhaps, something more' to the job, thought Carrington. There was, as it turned out. He was also told never to wear a grey top hat before the June race meeting at Epsom.

'We reckoned we were very good', Carrington reflected later about his fellow Grenadiers. But it was, he came to see later, a misplaced self-confidence:

> We were, in fact, not well trained ... there was, despite all the fun, the loyalty, the pride of Regiment, a certain complacent lethargy ... there was a certain infectious self-indulgence in the atmosphere which led to softness of fibre.[102]

Did this matter? So long as the Army was never asked to be anything more again than a tiny imperial gendarmerie, perhaps not. But what if one day it was expected to be a great deal more?

CHAPTER 3

STRANGE DEFEAT

'A lovely summer day, and almost a lovely war', noted Corporal E. J. Manley of the 92nd Field Regiment, Royal Artillery, as he sat writing letters home beneath the cool evening shade of an old apple tree in a village cemetery in Picardy. It was 7 May 1940, and Manley and his mates were billeted in a barn near the hamlet of Lihus – a 'small old fashioned dreamy village', with two tiny cafés, a water tower, half a dozen or so ponds thick with green weeds, and a church with a rickety slate roof. 'We are slack, as usual', he noted, 'and the day is spent mainly lounging about on the grass amongst the chickens.' The other lads had adopted a stray puppy whom they had named Adolph. It was a glorious spring, with nothing to disrupt the tranquil bucolic mood. If a war had to be fought, it was a very pleasant way to go about it.[1]

For Manley and his comrades *were* at war, all the rustic calm of their surroundings notwithstanding. For over seven months, thirteen divisions of British soldiers – almost 400,000 men, all told – had been assembling across northeastern France, readying themselves to fight the Germans. This was countryside long familiar to British troops, the 'blood-stained cockpit' of Europe over which their predecessors had fought so many times.[2] Evidence of the most recent episode of violence, the war of 1914 to 1918, was everywhere. In many places only saplings stood, the ancient woodlands having been scythed flat a generation earlier. Commonwealth War Graves cemeteries, meticulously attended by British gardeners, dotted the landscape. Weathered trench lines remained visibly etched into the wet clay soil. As the troops arrived and dug in, so the ground surrendered the detritus of the past; steel helmets, shells cases, spent cartridges, gas masks. Soldiers trudged along newly constructed trenches already flooded to the knees. On an inspection of the Aubers-Fournelles ridge,

General Alan Brooke, commander of II Corps, rediscovered the billet he had inhabited as a junior officer in 1914. It set off a 'mass of memories', he wrote that night in his diary, 'which were given a bitter tinge through the fact that I was back again starting what I thought at the time I was finishing for good'.[3] In cosy *estaminets* behind the lines, soldiers self-consciously sang 'Tipperary' and 'Pack up your Troubles'. All the conditions were in place for the kind of brutal clash of arms which had taken place a generation before. Only one thing was still missing on 7 May 1940, in fact: an enemy to fight.

But how had the British Army ended up back in France anyway? For years, the mantra had been repeated over and over: *never again*. No more Continental commitments; no more Sommes; no more Passchendaeles. And yet here were Manley and his mates, and almost every other serving British soldier besides, preparing to re-fight, over the same ground, much the same kind of war as their fathers had endured. What had happened to cause the British government to do such a complete volte-face, to allow the unthinkable – another great land war against the Germans in Europe – to become thinkable again?

About the last thing that Neville Chamberlain, a man with no natural sympathy for soldiering whatsoever, had ever expected to do as prime minister was to revive the Continental commitment. Like the no-nonsense Birmingham businessman he was, Chamberlain saw all military spending as inherently wasteful.[4] Armed conflict he regarded as an exercise in tragic futility: 'In war, there are no winners. But all are losers.'[5] He came into office with a firm conviction that all diplomatic problems could be resolved peacefully, and that most foreign statesmen were fundamentally level-headed, liberally minded men like him who abhorred violence and preferred compromise to conflict – something that Hitler was cruelly to expose as a naive hope.

All that being said, however, Chamberlain did not consciously neglect the defence of the British Empire after he came into office in May 1937. He was not the complacent dove that his popular reputation nowadays would suggest. Indeed, one of his first decisions after becoming Prime Minister was rapidly to accelerate the scale of Britain's military rearmament. In two years, the annual defence budget rose from £186 to £384 million.[6] During his time in Downing Street, the 'Chain Home' early-warning radar system was constructed and the Hurricane and Spitfire came into operational service with the RAF. These were the weapons which were to win the Battle of Britain in the summer of 1940. Much abuse would later be heaped upon Chamberlain, some of it by men who had supported him at the time. But he was no woolly-minded naïf. He never disputed that Britain had to prepare, however deplorably, for the possibility of war.

But the prospect of another Continental commitment, another mass citizen army sustaining hundreds of thousands of casualties in France or Belgium, utterly appalled him. He believed, as Liddell Hart (his 'principal strategic mentor') did, that it would be disastrous to repeat the strategy of the Great War should another conflict break out in Europe.[7] He also believed – and he was probably correct about this – that the ordinary voter in 1937 shared his view. The British people, Chamberlain wrote at the time, were 'strongly opposed to continental adventures', and would be 'suspicious of any preparation made in peacetime with a view to large scale military operations' in Europe.[8] 'We shall never again send to the Continent an army on the scale of that which we put into the field in the last war', he told his Cabinet colleagues.[9] So far as the prime minister was concerned in 1937, the British Army would maintain its strictly limited mission of imperial defence.

It is worth noting here that even Winston Churchill, the archest of all the anti-appeasers, was no more interested in building another large British Army or undertaking a Continental commitment than Chamberlain. In Churchill's mind, it was the *French* Army – in which he had an entirely unwarranted confidence – which was to be the bulwark of Allied land power in any future war with Germany. It was the French people, not the British, who would undergo the holocaust of casualties that would result from any repeat performances of the Somme or Passchendaele – though whether the French people would be happy to go along with this plan was not something Churchill seems to have given a lot of thought to in the 1930s.[10]

So how should Britain fight another war, if one came about? On this point, Churchill and Chamberlain were in agreement: through air power. By 1937, the experience of terror bombing of towns and cities such as Guernica, Chungking and Shanghai suggested that Liddell Hart's prophecy twelve years earlier was coming true: that in any future European war the decisive blows would be launched not by traditional land armies but by duelling fleets of aircraft. The priority for Chamberlain's government, then, was to build up the Royal Air Force to such a strength that it could threaten any aggressor with a devastating 'knock-out blow' from above. A war fought by bombers, waged largely against unarmed civilians, was horrible to contemplate. But then so was another war of mass armies. And the very speed and decisive character of a knock-out aerial blow might well cause less suffering on aggregate. As Liddell Hart had argued in 1925, 'the ethical objection to this form of war is at least not greater than to the cannon-fodder wars of the past . . . a swift and sudden blow of this nature inflicts a total of injury far less than when spread over a number of years.'[11] To the liberal mind, it could be argued that bombing was actually the better and more humanitarian option of the two.

So it was the Royal Air Force which received the lion's share of Chamberlain's new rearmament funds. Its share of total military spending quickly increased from 15 to 35 per cent. By 1938, the RAF had risen to *primus inter pares* within the armed forces. As for the Army, it was the Cinderella service, the after-thought, pushed to the back of the appropriations queue.[12] The prime minister's new secretary of state for war, the industrious but scheming gadfly Leslie Hore-Belisha, spelled it out to the House of Commons. In composition the Army would be 'high-quality', but its mission would have strictly 'limited dimensions'.[13] If there was to be any kind of expeditionary force at all, it would be equipped and trained exclusively for operations in what he called a colonial 'Eastern theatre' – perhaps to protect Egypt from an Italian invasion. It would certainly not go to France. If war were to break out against Germany, the only task the Army would be expected to perform would be to man searchlight and anti-aircraft batteries to defend against enemy air raids. The nation's soldiers were to dig in around the perimeters of Bomber Command's aerodromes and passively observe the war taking place above them.[14]

The events that were to bring this policy to ruin began to unfold with a dreadful inexorability in the spring of 1938. On 24 April, leaders of the German-speaking community in the Czech Sudetenland, prodded by orders from Berlin, demanded regional autonomy from the government in Prague. Their intention was to use these new powers to secede from the Czech state entirely. Hitler voiced his support for his ethnic compatriots and threatened military intervention if their ultimatum was not met. The Czechs sought assistance from Britain and France. Mediation dragged on throughout the summer without result. Then, on 13 September, the Sudeten leaders broke off negotiations. The Czechs girded themselves for invasion. On 15 September, Chamberlain flew personally to Hitler's private retreat at Berchtesgaden to try to strike a deal. They met again in Bad Godesberg on 22 September, but that summit ended in confusion and anger as Hitler ratcheted up his demands. Now, he insisted, nothing short of the immediate annexation of the Sudetenland by Germany would satisfy him. Chamberlain returned to Britain with war apparently just days away. Armageddon was only averted at the last minute by Mussolini's suggestion that there should be a four-power conference in Munich. The leaders met on 29 September. Germany, Italy, Britain and France signed an agreement surrendering the Sudetenland to Hitler. The Czechs, who were not invited to a conference deciding the fate of their own country, were left with a choice: solitary resistance to the Germans or surrender. They capitulated in despair. Chamberlain flew back to London the following day to be met at

Heston aerodrome by an exultant crowd which listened in gratitude and relief as the prime minister promised 'peace for our time'.

For a few days, Britain was euphoric. Then the mood began to change. The temporary respite from war that had been salvaged at Munich did little to compensate for the patently shabby treatment that Czechoslovakia had received from its supposed friends. Hitler had been bought off, but there was little reason to suppose that the German dictator's appetite for territory had been satiated permanently. Most humiliating of all for the British was the realization that without a large army equipped for European operations, their bargaining position at Munich had been feeble. The spectre of air attack had not chastened Hitler at all.[15] In Cabinet, the foreign secretary Lord Halifax now wondered aloud whether France would 'cease to be enthusiastic' about its cross-Channel partnership if Britain continued to show such unwillingness to accept a share of the military burden on land.[16] The French commander-in-chief's deputy put the issue bluntly to the British liaison officer in Paris. 'France', he said, 'does not intend England to fight her battles with French soldiers.'[17]

Back in Britain, the public attitude towards national service turned more hawkish. Much to its own surprise, the Army began to exceed its recruitment targets.[18] Conscription, for so long an utterly taboo proposal, reappeared on the spectrum of political possibility. A *Daily Express* opinion poll commissioned in June 1938 had suggested that 57 per cent of the British people were opposed to a mandatory call-up. A similar poll in the *Daily Mail* after Munich showed a majority now favouring conscription.[19] The shadow of Hitler and his limitless ambitions had made even a mass army imaginable once again.[20]

Any lingering confidence in the Munich settlement was swept away on 15 March 1939, when German troops marched into what remained of Czechoslovakia. The Führer dissolved the government in Prague and formally disavowed the agreement he had made with Britain and France the previous September. For Chamberlain it was a bitter personal humiliation, and the clearest possible indication that his policy of appeasing Hitler had failed. War now seemed more or less inevitable. With his foreign policy in ruins, the prime minister did a total about-turn on the role of the Army. On 25 April, universal male conscription was announced. The Military Training Act – the first bill in British history ever to authorize a peacetime call-up – was read to the House the following day. Despite some token opposition from the Labour benches, it passed quickly. Discussions began with the French for a second British Expeditionary Force to cross the Channel if and when war with Germany broke out.

In the space of a few weeks, the prime minister had entirely abandoned a position he had held with obdurate tenacity for years. More remarkable still, he had done so without consulting any professional source of advice, and with no consideration of what the practical short-term consequences for the Army would be. When the deputy chief of the Imperial General Staff, Sir Ronald Adam, heard the news, he gave a look of 'almost incredulous bewilderment'.[21] For twenty years, the War Office had been told that it would never again be expected to fight another large war in Europe. Now it was being ordered to prepare for precisely such a war within a matter of months – and, at the same time, to absorb hundreds of thousands of raw civilian recruits. It was, grumbled Henry Pownall, the Director of Military Operations and Intelligence at the War Office, 'a proper granny's knitting' to be unravelled'.[22]

By mid-July, the first conscripts – officially known as 'militiamen' – began arriving at Army camps for their basic training. But the time for pre-war preparations was almost over. On Friday, 1 September, Germany invaded Poland. Chamberlain, who had extended a territorial guarantee to the Poles after the seizure of Czechoslovakia, demanded that the Germans immediately withdraw. Hitler ignored him. On Sunday, 3 September 1939, at 11 o'clock in the morning, Great Britain declared war on Germany.

And so soldiers like E. J. Manley went off to war. For some, it was a moment of trepidation; for others, one of curiosity and excitement. Just as one expeditionary force of grinning, callow-faced youths had departed for Picardy and Artois in 1914, so now their sons embarked for the same eerily recognizable destinations – Amiens, Armentieres, Cambrai. Long-dormant recollections stirred of events half a lifetime ago: of *vin blanc* mixed with grenadine syrup; of plum and apple jam and illicit barrack-room games of Crown and Anchor; of sweltering forced-marches across Degas landscapes; of the black clinging mud and the corpses hanging on the old barbed wire. Donald Callander, commander of an anti-tank gun platoon, could not help but reflect on the fate of his uncle, killed at his own age in 1915. 'One was trained for war', he recalled later. 'One was trained to the thought that it was one's job. But I must say that having been brought up on the fact that the life of a second lieutenant was 24–48 hours in the First World War – and I was a second lieutenant – it did leave a slightly cold feeling in my heart.' But he reconciled himself to his fate: '*Oh well, this is it; I'll get on with it.*'[23]

Among the soldiers of the 1st Royal Irish Fusiliers – 'the Faughs' – there was no such gloom, or at least no public evidence of it. 'The troops love the thought of a war', wrote subaltern John Horsfall to his father. 'They think it means vast hoards of booty.' After years of dull garrison duty and thankless marking-time for the regulars, now there was a chance for glory and promotion. At the *Spread Eagle* hotel in Thame, Oxfordshire, the officers of the Faughs spent the first night of the war in boozy exuberance.[24] Over the days that followed, Horsfall and his fellow junior officers snatched opportunities here and there to buy the kit they thought they might need in the trenches – shooting sticks, balaclavas, shaving brushes. Chaplains busied themselves performing marriages. Bandsmen packed up their instruments along with the regimental plate and colours, and began studying first aid drill.

Within six days of the outbreak of war, the first troopships taking the British Expeditionary Force (BEF) to France had left Southampton and the Bristol Channel ports for Cherbourg, Nantes and St Nazaire. By the end of the month, five divisions – over 152,000 officers and men, 21,000 vehicles and 36,000 tons of ammunition – had crossed without a single loss of life. On 3 October, I Corps began taking over French positions along the Belgian border. The sector of front allocated to the British stretched eastwards of Lille across the grim industrial landscape of the Nord *département*, from the towns of Maulde to Halluin, and then along the River Lys. The BEF set up its headquarters in Arras – another name from history, another reminder of battles fought not so many years before.[25]

The new BEF even had an authentic hero of the First World War to lead it: John Vereker, 6th Viscount Gort, released from his position as CIGS – to his and Hore-Belisha's enormous relief, given that the two men could hardly stand being in the same room together. Gort was in many ways the paradigmatic regimental officer, resembling C. S. Forester's Sir Herbert Curzon to an eerie and worrying degree. His reputation for physical courage was unmatched. As a young man in Flanders he had won the Victoria Cross, the Military Cross and the Distinguished Service Order with two bars. The prospect of battle delighted him. 'Here we go again, marching to war', was his first gleeful comment on arriving at his new headquarters. 'I can't expect everybody to be as thrilled as I am.' Gort was conscientious, self-denying, resolute, loyal, well-liked and much admired amongst his peers: 'a great gentleman', according to Henry Pownall. But like so many regular officers of his generation, the parameters of Gort's mental outlook were severely restricted. He had never held high field command before being appointed to the BEF. He was to spend much of his time in France fussing like a regimental adjutant over trifling details of administration, rather than reflecting deeply on the strategic problems that faced his troops. The peacetime British Army had trained him to be a superlative regimental commander – but no more than that. In the view of some of his colleagues, Gort was clearly out of his depth. Alan Brooke felt he had the brain of a 'glorified boy scout'.[26]

If Gort had hoped for a rapid opportunity to test his generalship, he was to be disappointed. The Germans, fully engaged in their campaign in Poland in the autumn of 1939, were in no hurry to mount any repeat of the Schlieffen Plan.

The British and French had no desire to go on the attack themselves. So instead there was a curiously bloodless re-enactment of the Great War in northern France – faithful in every point of detail apart from the killing. Not until 9 December, when Corporal William Priday stepped on a French mine after his night patrol lost its way in the dark, was a British soldier killed in action. Priday's burial was a great novelty, attended with full military ceremony.

December 1939 also brought the coldest winter in living memory. On one day alone 49 degrees of frost were recorded in northern France. In some places the telephone lines hung so thick with rime that they sank to only a foot above ground.[27] 'The straight, unhedged roads seemed to reflect the frost back at us, and the very air seemed frozen', thought signaller Wilfrid Saunders. 'The cold went straight through overcoat, battle dress, scarves, pullovers, and vests, striking us as if with a sharp knife, into our very bones.' Vehicle radiators had to be drained each night to prevent the water freezing. Soldiers' caps froze to their heads. Greatcoats and socks froze solid as boards. Bread froze on plates. Hair froze.[28] Heavy falls of snow were punctuated by thaws and driving rain, bringing fresh miseries as trenches crumbled and infantrymen scrambled to dig fresh drainage schemes in mud halfway to their knees for up to six hours a day.[29] The inactivity became demoralizing. 'Drama gave way to farce', thought Horsfall: 'ardour dampened like the wet clouds above us.' Reservists, recalled to the Army from well-paid and comfortable civilian jobs, seethed at their apparently pointless exile from home. 'Many of them thought they were swindled and were here, in France and in some discomfort, under false pretences', noted Horsfall. 'And there were overtones of ignominy.'[30] The most significant casualty of this most 'boring, uncomfortable and vexatious' of winters was the secretary of state for war, sacked by Chamberlain after he became embroiled in a squabble about the time it was taking Gort's troops to construct pillboxes.[31] It was a sad and silly end for Hore-Belisha, a man who would be quickly forgotten in the drama of subsequent events, but who in his brief time at the War Office had been an energetic, if erratic, military reformer.[32]

So 1939 became 1940. The weather slowly got warmer. Soldiers began to explore their new home. The industrial mining villages of the *Nord* were far from the picture-postcard image of bucolic France. Vast pyramids of pit spoil dominated the horizon; the sky was frequently shrouded by a haze of inky dust. British troops watched the black-faced local miners, miniature wine-barrels swinging from their belts, walking to and from the collieries. What caught the attention of many new arrivals were the cheap and potent local liquors. For drinkers who had been brought up on British beer at fourpence a pint, the idea of twopence for a half-pint of brandy or three shillings for a bottle of champagne was a dangerous temptation. On one of his first nights in France, Wilfred

Saunders went on a mammoth bender with his comrades, consuming twenty-three drinks of eleven different varieties and spending most of the early hours of the following morning vomiting it all up.[33] Some of Donald Callander's Highlanders became such persistent fighting drunks that they had to be tied to stakes as field punishment.[34] Men who sought a different soldierly recreation were enticed to Lille's famous red-light district. The more discerning or romantic of them enjoyed Sunday evening dances with respectable village girls, though any hopes they nursed of a passionate display of Anglo-French *concorde* afterwards were usually dashed by the interference of some hawkish chaperone. Other men ingratiated themselves with local families, getting their 'feet under the table' and home-cooked meals in their bellies in the time-honoured manner of all British soldiers overseas. After all, they reasoned, we could be here for years: might as well make ourselves comfortable.[35]

The war drifted on in its phantasmal way. Occasionally, a British unit would be selected to go on patrol along the Maginot Line. During once such night-time encounter, Robert Green shot at a group of distant Germans. When he returned to his own lines, his platoon sergeant major insisted that Green hand in every spent cartridge he had fired so as to keep the battalion's ammunition figures balanced. 'You think I go around collecting bloody empties, counting them, with a German patrol on our hands?' Green shouted back at him. 'But that was typical', he reflected years later. 'This business of checking everything was so ingrained in everybody . . . it was just sheer habit. A throw-back to the old peacetime army.'[36] War was not being allowed to interfere with proper soldiering.

The army in France grew – slowly. Back in Britain, the process of calling up and training civilian conscripts which had begun a few months before the outbreak of war with the Military Training Act continued, though at a sluggish pace – the government, complained journalist Douglas Reed, was prosecuting the war with all the pace of an elephant trying to compete in the Derby.[37] From January onwards, eight Territorial Army (TA) divisions of part-time auxiliaries arrived to join the regular battalions of the BEF. Even so, the Expeditionary Force remained modest in size compared to the much bigger French and German armies. And in character, it was still much the same imperial gendarmerie that John Masters had known in Waziristan in 1935 – the army of gentlemen and Old Sweats. This worried senior commanders such as Brooke. His corps had arrived in France 'quite unfit for war, practically in every aspect'. His anti-tank gunners had not had proper training. Many of the artillerymen had never even fired their weapons before. After a visit to a Territorial battalion of the Gordon Highlanders, Brooke judged them 'totally unfit for war in every respect' and thundered in his diary: 'It would be sheer massacre to commit it to action in its present state in addition to endangering the lives of others.'[38] On inspecting a Black Watch battalion, he found the troops 'very ragged' and in dire need of additional training. The exercises of one of his divisions left him 'very disappointed'.[39] 'To send untrained troops into modern war is courting disaster such as befell the Poles', he ruminated to himself.[40]

The embarrassing truth was that Britain simply did not have the military supplies on hand – the weapons, stores or facilities – properly to outfit and equip even its regular troops, let alone its conscripts. Twenty years of indifference had withered away the defence industry's manufacturing base. It would take many months to ramp up production to full wartime levels. Even then, the Army would have to compete with the equally pressing demands of the RAF and the Navy. Much progress had been made in motorizing the Army in the final two years of peace, but a lot remained unfinished. Many infantry units had never been issued their organic transportation and had to requisition civilian trucks of uncertain vintage before they sailed for the continent. The countryside of northern France was soon strewn with broken-down and abandoned cars and lorries.[41] Donald Callander was given a bright red post office van to use as his platoon administrative vehicle.[42] Of the 240 heavy anti-aircraft guns the BEF was supposed to possess, it arrived in France with only 72 of them, and with less than one-third of its approved scale of ammunition. Four in ten of its anti-tank guns had yet to be issued. None of its field artillery regiments had received any of their new 25-pounder guns.[43] In September 1939, the Royal Tank Regiment was in the process of re-equipping itself with an excellent new armoured fighting vehicle, the Infantry Tank Mark II (the 'Matilda'), a potent weapon arguably superior to anything the Germans possessed at the time. But only two Matildas had been delivered from the factory when war was declared. Most other British tanks in service were obsolete light models, armed only with machine-guns. Many lacked essential modern equipment such as radios and armour-piercing ammunition.[44]

Territorial units were if anything even worse off than the regulars. The TA had long been the Army's stepchildren, last to receive modern weapons and equipment. Some of their peacetime uniforms would have 'lowered a tramp's self-respect', lamented *The Times*.[45] Few Territorials had ever experienced realistic instruction. Exercises between the wars had had to be carried out with flags representing non-existent troops and broomsticks taking the place of anti-tank weapons and machine-guns. Shortly before the passage of the Military Training Act, it had been decided to double the size of the TA from 170,000 to 340,000 men. But no preparation had been made for how this was actually going to work in practice.[46] Each existing battalion was ordered to create a second-line duplicate of itself, which meant surrendering half of its precious reserve of experienced officers and NCOs. Unit cohesion inevitably suffered. By November, 1939, only half of all Territorials had been serving in their units for more than six months.[47] 'We were just ploughing about in mud, in wellington boots with only one uniform and puttees', recalled Francis Docketty, who had served as a Territorial since 1937. 'We felt like broomstick soldiers.'[48] On average, TA divisions arriving in France in spring 1940 had only one quarter of the equipment they were supposed to possess.[49] Officers in Bill Cheall's infantry company who had not had the foresight to purchase their own revolvers, binoculars or compasses privately before they left England had to do without.[50]

But perhaps none of this would ultimately matter; for perhaps the BEF would never actually have to fight. After all, the 1939 campaigning season had come to a close without incident. The Germans had not rushed to assault the Western Front as they did in 1914. Perhaps they would not attack in the spring either. Perhaps, as the new secretary of state for war Oliver Stanley privately predicted, they would not attack at all in 1940.[51] Perhaps they would never attack. Perhaps Hitler would sue for peace, or his generals would assassinate him. No one could tell for sure what the future held. But the longer the great clash in the West was deferred, the greater the chance was that it would never take place at all. Chamberlain had been forced to accept a second Continental commitment, but perhaps new Sommes and Passchendaeles could still be avoided. If so, the BEF's unpreparedness was not so very dangerous. It was a humane bit of optimism. But it depended, fatally, on the Germans being willing to remain idle indefinitely. On 9 April 1940, they stirred into action.

The fighting began not, as everyone had expected, in the sooty villages of the *Nord*, but hundreds of miles to the north, in Denmark and Norway. The Danes capitulated to the German invaders with only token resistance after a few hours. Norway was a different matter. By 10 April, King Haakon VII and his government had fled Oslo and the Germans had seized most of his country's major towns, but the mountainous hinterland remained unconquered. This opened up the possibility, if the Allies were fast enough, of an intervention to save Norway. The British were still stumbling to catch up, however. They had been mulling over some rather inchoate plans for a military occupation of Norway themselves, but they had not anticipated that the Germans would beat them to it. Their response was correspondingly a work of improvisation. With almost all of the regular army in France, only four infantry brigades, two of them Territorial, and five hastily mustered Territorial 'Independent Companies' were available for dispatch to Norway. Some of the battalions sent across the North Sea had been on ceremonial duty at Buckingham Palace a few days before.

The infantry units sent to Norway in April 1940 arrived with virtually no artillery or anti-aircraft support. Each soldier was outfitted with three kitbags of clothing apiece, including a 15-pound lambskin coat. But no motor transport had been provided to move this cumbersome baggage around. Unlike the German troops, who were trained and equipped with snowshoes and skis, the British were unable to operate in Norway's waist-deep snow; their movements were exclusively confined to the road network. This meant that whenever they encountered German ground forces, they were swiftly and easily outflanked. Few of the Territorials were sufficiently familiar with their own mortars or light machine-guns.[52] The Independent Companies, forerunners of the later Commando units, were made up of picked volunteers who were supposed to operate as hit-and-run troops in the Norwegian hinterland. They were brave and enthusiastic men. But quite aside from the fact that their units had been thrown together at the last minute, with little special equipment or training, no thought had apparently been given to whether the kind of guerrilla tactics they were supposed to practise were really feasible in the harsh climatic conditions of northern Scandinavia.[53]

Indeed, most of the British troops who arrived in Norway were utterly bewildered by the environment they found themselves in. Many had never even seen a mountain before, let alone been instructed in the special problems of alpine warfare. Some commanders had been issued with the wrong maps.[54] The Norwegians were not impressed. One officer described the newly arrived British Territorials as 'very young lads who appear to have come from the slums of London . . . they have taken a very strong interest in the [local] women and engaged in wholesale looting of stores and houses.' They would, he forecast, 'run like hares' at the first sound of the enemy.[55]

The fate of SICKLEFORCE, which made up half of the British expedition to Norway in April 1940, says much about the Army's preparedness for war that spring. One of SICKLEFORCE's two brigades, the 148th (Territorial), embarked at Rosyth on 14 April on a large transport vessel with orders to sail for Namsos. But after two-and-a-half days of waiting at anchor in the Firth of Forth, new instructions arrived from London; its men were to disembark, re-embark on a different ship, and proceed to Åndalsnes instead. When the 148th finally reached Norway on 18 April, the brigade's commanders discovered that in their scramble to leave Rosyth they had left behind all their vehicles and most of their anti-aircraft guns, ammunition and food.[56] In the confusion most of the headquarter's wireless equipment and mortar shells had also been mislaid.[57] Reduced to infantry small arms, the troops were ordered to take up a defensive line south of Lillehammer on 20 April. The following evening they encountered an enemy *Kampfgruppe* pushing northwards. This was to be the first major engagement between British and German troops in the Second World War. The outcome was not encouraging. After some brief resistance, the brigade was outflanked and it was forced to retreat back to a position further north, known as Tretten Gorge. There, on the morning of 23 April, the Germans appeared again, this time launching a full-scale assault supported by artillery, engineers, light tanks and aircraft. The men of the 148th had had no sleep for three days. They had been under almost constant air bombardment since they had arrived in Norway. Exhausted, ill-equipped and demoralized, they broke in confusion. Fleeing troops sped northwards in commandeered lorries, strafed by German bombers along the way. A Danish officer serving as a volunteer in the Norwegian forces observed the chaos: 'Truck after truck of hysterical British soldiers drove past me . . . there was wild confusion. British officers managed to stop the trucks and tried unsuccessfully to restore order. [But the men] refused to follow orders and drove on, yelling and screaming.'[58] Only nine officers and 450 men out of the 1,000 who had originally arrived in Norway as part of the brigade escaped death or capture.

The Army's first campaign of the war would end with 1,869 men killed, wounded or taken prisoner. The experience in Norway had been marked from start to finish by what the official history would later call 'slowness and vacillation . . . confusion, hasty planning, and unsatisfactory improvisation.'[59] Winston Churchill, in his memoirs, described how depressing it was to see some of the finest regiments of the regular British Army 'baffled' by the sheer 'vigour, enterprise, and training' of the Germans.[60]

By the time the last British soldier left Scandinavia, however, the fiasco there had already been overshadowed by an even greater calamity to the south.

The sound of an ululating air-raid siren woke second lieutenant J. P. Whitehead at first light on the morning of Friday, 10 May 1940. He looked at his watch and sighed: another reconnaissance plane, no doubt. He rolled over and went back to sleep. A little later, his mind filled only with thoughts of breakfast, he got up and strolled from his billet to the company mess. On the streets of Bapaume, the small town close to the Franco-Belgian border in which he and his troop of artillerymen were stationed, little could be heard aside from the eerie droning of the siren. At the steps of the mess he met his colleague Captain Lamont. 'Have you heard?' asked Lamont. 'The *Bosch* have bombed Grevillers aerodrome.' 'I was incredulous', Whitehead recalled. By noon, his unit had received its orders to move. Excited but composed, they advanced along a wooded avenue leading towards Brussels. Already, the crackle of machine-gun fire could be heard in the distance ahead.[61]

All across northwestern Europe at that moment, hundreds of thousands of soldiers and airmen were in motion. The Germans had invaded the Netherlands, Belgium and Luxembourg. Enemy paratroopers were landing outside The Hague and Rotterdam. Glider assault teams had already descended on to the Eben-Emael fortress, at the critical juncture of the River Meuse and the Albert Canal, and disabled its main gun cupolas, allowing German tanks and infantry to race across the Belgian frontier without serious resistance. The sky over the Low Countries was thick with Luftwaffe fighters and bombers. The day – *Der Tag* – had come at last. There was other shocking news that Friday too, but in the rush to action many British troops would not hear of it for many days. Back in London, Neville Chamberlain, having lost the confidence of his own party in the wake of the Norwegian disaster, had just resigned the premiership. The king had asked the first lord of the admiralty, Winston Churchill, to form a new government.

For the BEF, the news of the German attack meant the abandonment of the entrenchments they had spent so much energy building during the winter. Back in November, Gort had agreed to a French plan that when the Germans invaded Belgium, his three corps, along with the French First and Seventh Armies, would cross the frontier and advance to meet the enemy as far eastwards as possible, digging in ideally along the River Dyle. Christopher Seton-Watson spent 10 May leading his troop of guns out of the industrial squalor of the Lille suburbs into the pastoral hillsides of Flanders. The Belgian locals greeted them with '*Bravo les Tommies!*' at every village.[62] John Horsfall's Faughs, encamped in the grounds of a chateau in Picardy, drew up in parade formation on the gravel drive, the creases in their trousers knife-edged, to be marched to the tune of the regimental piper through the Amiens countryside for entrainment to the border. The weather was crisp and cloudless, the mood tense but confident.[63] E. J. Manley and the rest of the 92nd Field Regiment received their marching orders on 14 May. They left Lihus and moved right up to the Belgian border, billeting finally in the church hall of Hersin Coupigny, a mining town about twenty miles from the old First World War battlefield at Vimy Ridge. There, in the scorching sun, the troops blistered their hands digging trenches and listened to the German air raids getting closer and closer. Manley found the time to court a local girl, Jeanne, from whom he departed with many tears when his unit finally crossed the frontier on 16 May (he promised to write; he never did).

The three weeks which followed were destined to become hard-coded deep into the British national memory. The BEF and the French advanced into Belgium, digging in amongst the lilac trees and the copses filled with bright yellow flowers, secure in their assumption that they could hold and press back the oncoming Germans. But the enemy assault on the Low Countries was a ruse. The true centre of gravity of the German attack was much further south, along the forested banks of the River Meuse near the French town of Sedan. By nightfall on 12 May, German combat engineers had crossed to the far side of the river, overcome the feeble local defences and begun the assembly of the first of a series of pontoon bridges which would allow the seven armoured divisions waiting within the Ardennes woodlands behind them to pour into the French interior. By 15 May, a fifty-mile gap had been punched through the front line at Sedan. German tanks were streaming northwestwards towards the Channel coast in an attempt to surround and isolate the entire Allied force in Belgium. Although most of the French Army was as yet unbloodied, its high command had already psychologically conceded the fight after the collapse along the Meuse. On 21 May, German tanks reached the mouth of the River Somme near Abbeville. The trap was snapped closed.

Few of the BEF's soldiers, engaged with other German forces along the River Scheldt many miles to the northeast, were as yet aware of their dire predicament. On 18 May, Manley's diary records his artillery regiment somewhere on the main road between Lille and Brussels, having fought its way for two days through thousands of Belgian refugees streaming in the opposite direction. At three o'clock in the afternoon, his troop fired the first rounds of its 25-pounder field guns in anger. 'We must be butchering the Germans', Manley proclaimed afterwards, 'they have no guns firing.' However, by the following morning he and his comrades had retreated twenty kilometres westwards and were resting in the grounds of a large deserted mansion, amongst piles of furniture, books, crockery and silver scattered and abandoned. At noon that day his diary records a 'frantic order to move. Jerry has broken through and we are surrounded by all accounts. We tear off.' The Royal Engineers began blowing up the bridges behind them. By 20 May, the 92nd Field Regiment was entrenched literally in the shadows of the Canadian war memorial on Vimy Ridge, its gunners living on cold bully beef and biscuits. 'The air is thick with planes coming over every few minutes', wrote Manley:

> Don't recognize any RAF. German planes fly over unmolested, the only response an occasional feeble burst of machine gun fire, totally ineffectual ... a huge column of smoke goes up. Perhaps a petrol dump ... we feel that this is futile and most of us are cursing England for such a humiliating situation ... lie in the grass [hiding from enemy aircraft] and feel absolutely abandoned. Surely this can't be what was expected of us?

Even Lord Gort had little idea of what was going on. Caught up in the enthusiasm of the initial advance, he had exacerbated the muddle of information by abandoning his own headquarters and moving to a forward command post near Lille, at which he could only receive a fraction of the battlefield intelligence he really needed. Not until 21 May was the severity of the situation the BEF was in fully appreciated.[64] Gort ordered a counterattack towards Arras, led by a small force of Matilda tanks, to try to re-establish contact with the main French force to the south. Initially this looked as if it might work. The armour of the Matildas was so thick that most German anti-tank shells just bounced off them. But a lack of reinforcements prevented the British from making anything of their early advantage at Arras. The German envelopment remained complete. On 25 May, Gort abandoned any further attempts at breaking out southwards. Instead his men began a fighting withdrawal towards the Channel ports, especially the key harbour of Dunkirk.

By then, E. J. Manley's troop, having lost contact with the rest of the 92nd Field Regiment in the general confusion, had been drifting through the French countryside for some days, spending several hours in the little *ville* of Lens, a town 'blasted to hell', its streets strewn with machine-gunned bodies and the swollen and stinking corpses of horses. By 25 May, however, his troop having regained contact with its parent formation in Armentières, Manley's diary records a curious moment of calm, even confidence. Being able to wash and undress and eat his first hot meal for several days had left the young artilleryman 'oddly content'. He spent that evening reading an Evelyn Waugh comic novel. On 27 May, his mood lightened still more with news of the battle. 'We are doing well and the Germans are retiring steadily from French soil', Manley wrote. 'Rumours of a big Allied push through the Siegfried Line.'

All of which made the discovery on 29 May that the BEF was totally surrounded, and that the Belgian Army on its flank was throwing down its arms in surrender, all the more bewildering. At 6.30 that evening, the 92nd Field Regiment was ordered to fall back to the sea. 'Route an unbelievable shambles', Manley wrote. 'Hundreds and hundreds of new lorries ditched and burning. Tanks and stores abandoned. Guns spiked. A calamitous retreat.' On the night of 1 June his troop, now just outside Dunkirk, managed to get a little fitful sleep, though the men were still 'expecting to be blown sky high any minute'. After destroying their vehicles and spiking their 25-pounders they marched the last six miles into the town. 'What a sight . . . wagons literally by the thousand, wounded, dead, black oily craters, kit, suntanned men, boats of all shapes and sizes . . . Nazi planes buzz as we cross the beach . . . a flaming inferno. Sky thick with palls of black smoke.' They were taken to one of the harbour's 'moles', or wooden jetties, for immediate embarkation. After three and a half hours of tense waiting, their rescue ship cast off. Manley was back in Dover at three o'clock the following morning.[65]

Of his own arrival at the outskirts of Dunkirk a few days earlier, John Horsfall recalled seeing military policemen and sappers carefully martialling all incoming vehicles, guns and tanks into long neat rows, which were then promptly set ablaze. 'Mile upon mile this grim scene met us', he wrote later, 'an infinity of destruction and the immolation of an army . . . [it was] a scene of utter military shambles.' The panorama around the town provided an image of 'absolute catastrophe':

> Everywhere in front and around us raging fires erupted, flaring skywards and shooting through with orange streaks the dense palls of pitch black smoke which drifted idly in the slight breeze . . . [the Luftwaffe] was hard at work pounding the town and docks, wheeling and plunging, the howls of sirens in perfect orchestration with the scream of descending bombs. The sky was thick with [dive bombers] coming in crossing and criss-crossing from all directions, like teal packs driving in on a wild evening's flighting.[66]

On 2 June, the last BEF units embarked from Dunkirk. Over 186,000 British and 171,000 troops of other nationalities had been rescued.[67] The remnants of the French First and Seventh Armies, which had served as a rearguard for the departing British, fought on valiantly alone for another 48 hours until they were overwhelmed. Dunkirk's fall did not mean the end of the British ordeal, however. A Territorial infantry division, the 51st (Highland), had been cut off from the rest of the BEF following the German breakthrough. After drifting helplessly westwards towards Saint-Valery-en-Caux in Upper Normandy, two of its three brigades finally surrendered on 12 June. Meanwhile Churchill, his mind apparently stimulated by thoughts of the defensive lines of Torres Vedras built by the Duke of Wellington outside Lisbon during the Peninsular War, was insistent that the scattered remnants of the British forces still in France should retire to Brittany to be reformed into a new BEF. As late as 13 June, the day before the Germans entered Paris, elements of the 1st Canadian Infantry Division, the last fully established division the British possessed, were still arriving in Cherbourg to join this expedition. Alan Brooke, who had only just been extracted from the beaches of Dunkirk, was sent back to France to command the new expedition. He arrived at Le Mans on 14 June and at once appreciated the folly of Churchill's plan. Most of his putative force was made up of abandoned line-of-communications troops, tradesmen with little military training or equipment, and certainly with no inclination to continue any serious fighting. After a blunt telephone conversation with the prime minister (the first time the two men had ever spoken), Brooke received Churchill's reluctant permission to abandon Brittany. By 25 June, the final 144,000 British troops south of the River Somme had left France.[68] The sinking of the Cunard liner *Lancastria* off St Nazaire on 17 June, with at least 1,500 British military personnel among the dead, was a grim epilogue to a campaign which had been characterized by one disaster after another.[69]

What was to be made of those three weeks of 'jangled mess of talk and noise and movement'? Writing to his brother from Lyme Regis a few days after returning from Dunkirk, Christopher Seton-Watson was still struggling to work out what had just happened to him and hundreds of thousands of other British soldiers. His sense-impressions were still too 'blurred and without any relation or proportion' to provide a coherent narrative, he confessed:

> They were three weeks of little sleep and constant moving. We travelled just over 1,000 miles in all. I was always furiously busy, sometimes very fright-ened and often very angry – with myself for not being more competent, with the exasperating nuisances (mostly human) which crop up in a battle, but chiefly with the stupid sense of helplessness with which we had to watch the green countryside and those clean, prosperous towns and villages so swiftly pounded into mangled remnants of terror, suffering, and desolation.

For all of the disasters he had witnessed, however, he was not disheartened. 'We must be prepared for the loss of Paris and many more trials, but we will win through.'[70]

Certainly, bravery had been abundant. Five Victoria Crosses were awarded to men of the BEF for acts of valour during the 1940 campaign, two of them posthumous. All of them went to regular soldiers, but displays of courage were not confined to the professionals. Many of the Territorial battalions put up a much harder fight than anyone expected, given their inadequate training and weaponry. The 1st Bucks Battalion mounted a valiant if doomed defence of the town of Hazebrouck for two critical days during the height of the evacuation, delaying the advance of a German armoured division despite being heavily outnumbered. The 1st Queen Victoria's Rifles, which had been rushed over to France with neither proper equipment nor preparation, helped to defend Calais for four days until the town was totally overwhelmed.[71] Overall, discipline held up remarkably well throughout the campaign considering the scale of the calamity. Brooke's II Corps was able to hold up the German 6th Army at the Ypres-Comines canal long enough to allow most of the British Expeditionary Force to escape to Dunkirk.[72] Not everyone in the BEF behaved heroically, particularly in the desperate final days on the beaches. Incidents of

drunkenness, looting, insubordination and cowardice, including officers abandoning their own men, were reported.[73] But there was no mass panic.
Phlegmatic and world-weary, the typical BEF soldier responded to the catastrophe unfolding about him with remarkable composure. Enemy records
discovered at the end of the war confirmed that this was the *Wehrmacht*'s
somewhat puzzled verdict too. British POWs had discussed their defeat with
their captors with 'complete equanimity', their conviction that their country
would win in the end apparently 'unshakable'.[74]

For the press back home, the lesson of the campaign was clear: 'When it
comes to scrapping the British have proved themselves supreme', claimed the
Daily Mirror immediately after Dunkirk. The BEF had given 'a complete answer
to the jeering Nazi and Italian publicists who have been proclaiming for years
that Britain is decadent'.[75] Against 'a million German soldiers, outnumbered in
tanks by four or five to one, beneath sky thick with bombers, and beset on three
sides', Britain's tiny army had fought 'as no man thought men could fight'.[76] The
battle had simply been unequal because of the disparity in numbers and equipment on the two sides. 'Give men such as these the weapons they need', vowed
the *Mirror*, and 'they will then be unconquerable'.[77]

But not everyone was in a mood to stiffen their upper lip. While smashing
up vehicles and equipment on the approach to Dunkirk, infantryman Robert
Green's main emotion had been one of 'absolute shame'. He said to his mate
Stan, 'You know, it's going to take us 50 years to live this thing down'.[78] Basil
Dean, the director of the Forces entertainment service ENSA, who was sent
down to the southeast coast to try to buoy up the morale of the evacuated
troops, recalled meeting 'dismayed men, savagely wounded in their pride ...
seeking relief in bitter criticism of those set over them'.[79] What the press had
described as a magnificent British accomplishment seemed to one London
doctor attending to the evacuated wounded to have been 'nothing better than
a defeated and defeatist rout. Men swarmed into the hospital, some raging
mutinously at their officers ... others swearing that they would never fight
again.'[80] Lionel Baylis, a 48th Division signaller who spent the last sixteen days
of the 'ghastly tangle' in France foraging from farms for food, and who hauled
his soaked frame into a boat at Dunkirk, put the whole matter succinctly in a
letter to his brother afterwards. 'I think the Army is a shower of shit.'[81]

John Horsfall, though expressing himself more delicately than this, agreed
that the British Army's failure in France had been too obvious for even the
most self-assured Tommy to pretend otherwise:

> I think it has to be admitted that our soldiers were conscious of a lapse
> of management ... one could not fail to be aware of the loss of grip

somewhere. Our men knew it soon enough, and it became the task of the officers to stifle the subject or laugh at it when we could no longer ignore it.[82]

For a defeat it had been, without question. Overall, 11,104 members of the BEF were killed during the campaign itself, or subsequently died of their injuries. Over 14,000 men were wounded. More than 41,300 would spend the rest of the war in captivity.[83] Though the majority of troops were successfully evacuated, they left behind in France almost all of their heavy weapons and modern equipment. Of 2,794 guns that had originally been sent to the Continent, only 322 came back. All but 4,739 of 68,618 vehicles were lost. More than 70 per cent of the BEF's 109,000 tons of ammunition, and 96 per cent of its 449,000 tons of supplies and stores were abandoned. Just twenty-two tanks made it back to Britain, none of them Matildas.[84] Hundreds of thousands of soldiers escaped the Germans, but as an exhausted, disarmed mob, not an army. Whole battalions, brigades, even divisions, were swallowed up in the chaos. In the whole of the UK, only 54 anti-tank guns, 420 field guns and 163 heavy guns were left. Enough equipment existed to supply just three divisions.[85] The pre-war regular British Army, for all intents and purposes, had ceased to exist.

Two decades of benignly neglecting Britain's land forces, of pretending that a European state with Great Power pretensions could manage perfectly well without an army, had reached their bitter fruition. 'For 20 years [we have] thought little about how to win big campaigns on land', lamented Colonel Ian Jacobs of the War Cabinet Secretariat, as Gort's army fell to pieces across the Channel. 'We have been immersed in our day-to-day imperial police activities.'[86] There would no longer be the luxury of such indifference. A new, bigger, better army would have to be hurriedly reassembled from the wreckage of the old. What would it look like? How could it be best organized, trained and led so as to avoid another catastrophe? Could it ever beat the Germans? Nobody knew.

PART TWO
CIVVIES

I am a louse, a nothing, a miserable flea,
I am a private in the RAOC.
Less than the dust, a remnant of the damned,
Despised, unwanted, shunned by all,
Vermin, carrion, answer to my country's call.

I did not know, I could not tell,
To be a private is eternal Hell,
This holocaust of dumb despair
Shrivels my soul and tears my heart,
Leaving a shell, an empty broken part.

Never more I'll hear the mavis sing,
Nor see again the swallow on the wing,
This vale of tears, this wilderness,
This yawning chasm of impenetrable dark
Has left me bereft of life and hope.

Tonight I buy myself a piece of rope.

Anonymous, An Ode to Happiness[1]

CHAPTER 4

ARMY OF SHOPKEEPERS

'R-oi-oi-oight mahr-kha-a-ahr!'
'Ohn . . . p'ae'd!'
'Dress b'th'roight, dress b'th'roight . . . Dress b'th'ROIGHT, thart dozy marn there.'
'Squaa-a' . . .'
'Hon the wordsacommand brace y'self ready for the followin' or sub-sequent wordsacommand . . .'
'Squaa-a . . . SHUN!'

Staff Sergeant MacAllcane – bull-necked, bushy-moustached, eyes bulging, thick, sneering lips gaping – barks the drill commands for falling-in on parade to his newest squad of recruits. As his face contorts from side to side beneath the black japanned peak of his cap, he gives the impression of 'a savage wild animal, half-blinded with rage or pain':

'Suffering Chroist, whaat have they sent us this toime?'
'Oi'll tell ye' what ye' are, all of ye'. Look at ye'! Look at ye'! Who said ye' were soldiers? What crayzy man ever sent ye' to these camp. What crayzy man ever supposed I could make soldiers of ye'?'
'Ye're a bahd oidle show-er!'

His accent is 'pure Aldershottish' – neither truly Irish nor Scots, but a mongrel barrack-room blend of the two, whispered in mock pity or bellowed in staccato fits of feral rage. During pauses, he taps his feet and clenches and unclenches his fists in anticipation of his next bestial roar:

'Deed ye' muthers love ye? Ye're no gud t'me.'
'Starnd up that marn whoile I'm haddressin' ye'!'
'Oi'll send ye' back t'ye muthers afore I've dun with ye' crying, cry-IN',
I weel!'

The place is Longmoor in 1942 – but it could just as easily be Catterick, or Fulford, or Larkhill, or one of dozens of the other regimental depots and training camps in which luckless Army recruits found themselves rudely dumped during the Second World War. Staff Sergeant MacAllcane is the particular bête noire of 'Paul Grimmer', the lightly fictionalized protagonist in David Holbrook's autobiographical novel about his war service in the Royal Armoured Corps, *Flesh Wounds*. But in his vein-throbbing ferocity, MacAllcane could easily stand in for every other warrant officer or NCO who bullied, badgered, wheedled and otherwise terrorized new soldiers 'on the square' during their six weeks of basic training. MacAllcane has a genius for sadistic improvisation, an uncanny knack for calibrating exactly how to maximize a recruit's torment at any given moment. A few days after their first encounter at Longmoor, he drills Grimmer through an hour's punishment parade for some trifling offence, quick-marching the young man futilely round and round a few square yards of tarmac in full kit until his uniform is sodden with sweat, his face twisted in suffering, and only agonized yelps capable of making it past his swollen tongue. MacAllcane utters no words of abuse on this occasion: he is clever enough to realize that a 'cunningly monotonous regular series of maddening orders . . . to no purpose but humiliation' is the most effective way of stripping Grimmer of his dignity. Paul cannot help but admire the sheer devilry of it. By the end of their six weeks, MacAllcane will have reduced a squad of grown men, some of them respectable middle-aged husbands and fathers, pillars of their communities, into a gaggle of 'tyrannized children.'[1]

Of course, as any regular could have told Grimmer, this was how the Army did things. Pre-war soldiers had long grown used to such treatment. Fifteen years or so before Paul's ordeal at Longmoor, Royal Dragoons recruit Spike Mays had stood to attention on much the same parade ground, perspiring madly as the sun beat down on his head. 'Sweat rolled from our faces and cascaded down our forearms', he recalled years later:

And our legs were slimy and sweat-tortured where the thick folds of grey flannel shirts rucked up over-intimately inside our thick Bedford-cord riding breeches. Our legs were imprisoned in puttees; our feet incarcerated in great ammunition boots shod with iron tips at heel and toe. The great red railings at the south end of Beaumont Barracks made us think we were prisoners, shut off from what friendliness and humanity existed in the world; and that our instructors were not human beings like ourselves, but gaolers and torturers.

Mays' drill-sergeant, like MacAllcane, was a skilled wordsmith, with an equally inventive machine-gun repertoire of provocations:

You look like a lot of blue arsed apes skulking behind telegraph poles. You're supposed to chuck those bundooks about like matchsticks, not go sneaking and hiding behind 'em. No strength, no guts, no fire in your bellies, and I know why. Out every night with them NAAFI girls with your fly buttons at the quick release. No sense of balance, no idea of timing, and the only bloody drill you ever think about is blanket drill, knife and fork drill, sleeping, eating, and shagging![2]

But men of Mays' background were far more used to being bawled at than men of Grimmer's. Many had spent their formative years in forbidding and often loveless homes and institutions; discipline was all that such foundlings had ever known. It tended to be very different for temporary wartime soldiers. They had rarely undergone such treatment before. They had never been screamed at, over and over again, day after day, for offences which they scarcely even understood. They were about to discover, as the novelist and wartime conscript Kingsley Amis did, that the Army was an institution with its own unique standards of reason, 'a world much like our own in general appearance', as he put it, 'but with some of the rules changed or removed, a logic only partly coinciding with that of our own world, and some unpredictable areas where logic seemed missing altogether or to point opposite ways at once'.[3] To Rupert Croft-Cooke, joining the wartime Army was like 'having entered a strange world in which the old values counted for nothing ... like passing through the looking-glass or down the rabbit-hole for Alice, and though one sought as she did for some logic or sense of proportion, one had to conclude that although these had to exist one would never find them by the standards of civilian life'.[4] John Guest described becoming a soldier as like walking across a long bridge and watching the arches crumble and collapse behind you. Once you began crossing, there was no going back.[5]

It could be said that there were three British Armies during the Second World War, each metamorphosing into the next as the conflict went on. The first of these Armies was the tiny imperial gendarmerie which travelled to France in September 1939 and which stumbled back to England, shaken and bewildered, nine months later. The third and final Army was the one which returned overseas from around mid-1942 onwards, though this was not really a single Army so much as a set of individual expeditionary forces which departed the UK at punctuated intervals and then went their separate ways – one to North Africa, and then (after merging with the forces already *in situ* in the Western Desert) to Sicily and Italy; one to India and Burma; and one, the largest of all, back to France on D-Day.

But it was the second of the wartime British Armies that men like Paul Grimmer joined in 1942 – the home-based, mass citizen militia of stock clerks and shopkeepers, draughtsmen and delivery boys hurriedly assembled between Dunkirk and El Alamein. *This* was the Army that the majority of officers and men first encountered during the Second World War. It was an Army without victories to its credit; still struggling to absorb its strange new charges; uncertain as to what to do with them; uncertain, indeed, as to what its further role in Britain's grand strategy would be; and, above all, deeply apprehensive as to whether it would ever really be up to the task of defeating the German *Wehrmacht* or the forces of Imperial Japan. It is the least remembered of the three wartime Armies today. But arguably it was the most important of all of them, because within it were trained the officers and men who would go on to achieve final victory.

Its foundations were laid on the day that the war broke out by Parliament's passage of the National Service (Armed Forces) Act. With the introduction of the Act, all male British nationals aged between eighteen and forty-one and normally resident in Great Britain became liable, if and when called upon, to serve in His Majesty's Forces.[6] Conscription was organized by birth cohort. At an appointed date, all men of a particular cohort received a letter telling them to report to their local Ministry of Labour employment exchange. There their personal information was taken. Each man's name and professional qualifications were checked against a 'Schedule of Reserved Occupations' to see if he was in a line of work deemed vital to national importance; if he was, he was barred from enlisting – even voluntarily. If he was not, then a few weeks or months later he received a letter summoning him to a medical board examination. Special arrangements were on hand for registrants who wished to apply for deferment or exemption on grounds of economic hardship or conscientious objection. This was a mobilization that was sober, efficient and compulsory. Its signature experience was of hanging around, waiting nervously but resignedly for something to happen – waiting, above all, for the machinery of state to finally take notice of you.

Much was made at the outbreak of war, and has been made since, of how different the mood of the recruits in 1939 was from 1914. Tilly Rice, a thirty-six-year-old mother evacuated from Surrey to Cornwall, detected only 'solemn resignation' in the eyes of the khaki-clad youngsters she met. 'Maybe they are more selfish, maybe they are more thinking, but whatever it is, I have yet to meet a young man who is burning with the old patriotic zeal', she wrote in her diary.[7] A February 1940 *Mass-Observation* report suggested that 'the mass of conscripts are joining up in a mixture of readiness and reluctance, relief and negative interest . . . there is nothing comparable to the fervour and energy shown by those who bore the brunt of the last war.'[8] The magnificent intensity of August 1914 seemed to have vanished. This was a war of diffidence and knowing glances and shrugs, rather than thunderclap excitement. Men were slouching to their call-up in 1939 accompanied by the ominous drones of air-raid sirens rather than the cheers of well-wishers.[9]

Some of this was to be expected. Confidence in the verities of traditional patriotism had been shaken between the wars. The institutions of state – Church, Crown, Parliament – had consistently failed to live up to expectations. The Church of England's mild reassurances about a better world to come seemed pitifully inadequate consolation for the catastrophes of the Somme and Passchendaele. The Abdication crisis had seen His Britannic Majesty shirk his duty to the nation in the pursuit of private pleasure. Successive Westminster administrations had been powerless in the face of economic calamity at home and political crisis abroad. It had been, as Robert Graves put it, a 'confused and inglorious' period.[10] Some conservative writers in the 1930s worried that if and when another war broke out, young men would refuse to take up arms at all, having been taught, as historian Arthur Bryant put it, 'the wickedness of fighting' at school and university.[11] 'The present generation have been sedulously inoculated . . . with the belief that war is a crime' warned Ian Hay in 1938.[12] In 1933, members of the Oxford Union debating society had voted that they would '*in no circumstances fight for King and Country*'. An 11.5 million-strong 'Peace Ballot' in 1935 organized by the League of Nations Union registered strong support for international arms control. The Peace Pledge Union (PPU) founded by Canon Dick Sheppard in 1936 went even further, persuading 118,000 young men to swear an oath formally refusing to participate in any future wars.[13]

There was enough popular ambivalence about Britain's war aims in 1939 – and indeed throughout the conflict – to deflate the enthusiasm of even the most callow, Rupert Brooke-adoring young subaltern. It is hard to know what to make of the jumble of answers given to the question *what are we fighting for* offered up to an Education Corps lecturer by soldiers in 1943:

I do not know (very common);
For my wife and kiddies (rarely);
Freedom, liberty, King and Country (common, but never with any
follow-up explanation);

Because I like our way of life better than the German way (ditto);
For the bastard capitalists;
Because Jewish international financiers wanted a war;
Because I've got to (very common);
To get a better world (no follow-up);
For six foot of earth or the dole;
To defeat the Nazis (common);
Nothing – it makes no difference who wins (only one instance);
Freedom of speech/vote/worship/organized labour (common).[14]

'Soldiers don't fight for something', insisted subaltern Andrew Wilson. 'War is something that catches them up. After that it is a closed arena, in which you struggle with yourself and your fear.'[15] Still, another soldier, Richard Terrell, believed that much military cynicism was cultivated and affected. He recalled one aggrieved private in his dormitory saying loudly: '*Fuck! I've a good mind to get an interview with the CO. I'll tell him I've become a conscientious objector on political grounds. We'd be better off under the fucking Germans.*' A few other men muttered *hear hear!* on cue. But, of course, the soldier did nothing of the sort; and he never really intended to.[16] Scorning war aims was a way of blowing off steam, not making a seriously articulated statement of belief. Most soldiers would have been far too embarrassed ever openly to embrace the principles of King and Country in front of their mates. But this does not mean that traditional British values, however hazily conceived, had no meaning for them at all. The moral contrast between Britain and its enemies in the Second World War was just too self-evident to be ignored.[17]

Interwar pacifism proved, in the end, to have made far less impression on the young than men like Arthur Bryant had feared and that Dick Sheppard had hoped.[18] Anti-war books such as *All Quiet on the Western Front* had sold well in the 1930s. But then so had works like R. C. Sherriff's *Journey's End* and Ernest Raymond's *Tell England*, which both described the First World War in unapologetically moral terms as a test of Christian selflessness.[19] Popular children's adventure stories lauded the conflict as a heroic quest.[20] A great deal has been written about the 59,000 Britons who registered as conscientious objectors (COs) during the Second World War.[21] But what's arguably most significant about them is how unimportant they were in the end. At the peak of the CO 'surge' in 1939, just 2 per cent of those young men eligible for call-up requested a hearing on such grounds. And their numbers dwindled thereafter to a rounding error. The government was willing to treat conscientious objectors with relative indulgence precisely because they mattered so little.[22]

Individual responses to the outbreak of war varied hugely. For some recruits, the arrival of a letter informing them of their call-up seemed more like a notice of execution than a call to arms. Summoned to the colours of the Queens Own Royal West Kents, R. F. Songhurst felt as though someone had kicked him in the bowels. 'In a mood of deepest misery, I went indoors and changed into my uniform', he wrote. 'All that I could foresee was a sudden and painful death in front of me.'[23] Anthony Babington walked across Chelsea Bridge on the night he was recalled to his TA regiment in a fit of gloom. 'I fought to overcome the depression which had overwhelmed me. I did not want to be a soldier and I had no wish to fight a war ... wherever I turned my mind I seemed to be confronted by the mournful spectre of finality.'[24] But others were elated by the news. Herbert Parker-Jones, who loathed his job in the City of London, regarded the call-up of his Territorial Army unit as his liberation from slavery. 'It was a wonderful experience', he recalled. 'I ran down Lime Street vowing never to return.'[25] Indeed, the outbreak of war in September 1939 was accompanied by scenes outside some recruitment offices straight out of Larkin's poem 'MCMXIV', with 'long uneven lines' of eager volunteers 'grinning as if it were all an August Bank Holiday lark'.[26] The Army's Central London depot at New Scotland Yard had to be closed on the Monday following the declaration of war because the rush of volunteers was so great. At the Drill Hall in Acton, overwhelmed clerks worked till midnight to try to clear the backlog of applications.[27]

Enthusiasm could come from the most unexpected quarters. Given his High Tory principles, it is not surprising to learn that Enoch Powell quit his position as Professor of Greek at Sydney University on 4 September 1939 and sailed immediately for Britain to join the Army (though once he got back to the UK, he found His Majesty's Government frustratingly uninterested in his services; the only way he could eventually persuade the War Office to let him enlist at all was by getting a note from the Australian High Commissioner's office claiming that he was a Dominion subject).[28] Less predictable was nineteen-year-old Oxford undergraduate Frank Thompson's decision – much to the chagrin of his parents – to join the Royal Artillery on the day before the war broke out.[29] Thompson was a card-carrying member of the Communist Party who just a few months earlier had marched through London in a protest against the introduction of conscription. There was scarcely anyone in Britain less convinced of the merits of the Chamberlain administration. But Thompson's detestation of fascism was so intense that he was willing to make no end of short-term compromises in order to fight Hitler. As he wrote to fellow undergraduate and Party member Iris Murdoch after she pointed out that the official Communist line was that this was an 'imperialist' war,

Sure, lady, I know the party line is better;
I know what Marx would have said. I know you're right. . .
Somehow today I simply want to fight.
That's heresy? Okay. But I'm past caring.
There's blood about my eyes and mist and hate. . .
Now's not the time you say? But I can't wait.[30]

The eagerness of many Irishmen to volunteer is also an interesting wrinkle in the conventional picture of disenchantment in 1939. Traditionally the British Army had regarded Ireland as one of its principal recruiting bases, and around 20,000 Irishmen from both north and south of the 1922 treaty line were already serving as regulars at the outbreak of war.[31] Family tradition may have played some part in the decision of these men to enlist in the 1930s, though the parlous state of the Irish economy at the time must also have been a powerful spur. At the Royal Ulster Rifles depot in Armagh, recruiters waited patiently each morning during the autumn of 1939 as five or six boys crossed the border, 'some of them, literally, in their bare feet . . . small, undernourished, with a hint of desperation'.[32] But poverty alone cannot explain the decision of around 43,000 citizens of the Irish Free State voluntarily to enlist in the British armed forces during the war.[33] Some of these men gave up good jobs and risked the opprobrium of the Irish state – and, in the case of the 5,000 or more soldiers who deserted the Defence Forces, subsequent arrest and imprisonment – in order to follow their convictions.[34]

What sort of convictions these were varied, of course. Few Catholic Irishmen had much love for an overseas king or the empire their new nation had so recently sloughed off. But, like Frank Thompson, their hatred for fascism was such that they were willing to assent to the most unlikely of allegiances in order to help destroy it. Dubliner Desmond Fenning regarded himself as 'very nationalist' by inclination. But as he said later, 'I didn't like the Germans, the Nazis, and I saw no reason why not to go in and help to get rid of them.' Other volunteers maintained a lingering attachment to Britain despite all that had happened in the recent past: Irish identity in 1939 was by no means straightforwardly two-dimensional. 'I suppose I was pro-British, you know – against the Germans, anyway', recalled William Gannon from County Meath. John Coyle, originally from Rosemount in County Westmeath, was working at an oil company in London when the war broke out. His brother, who was also in Britain employed at an aircraft factory, suggested that they both return to Ireland to avoid possible conscription. But Coyle decided to stay. 'This country gave me a job', he reasoned, 'and I'll fight for it if it wants me to.'[35]

Most young Britons did not have such complicated issues of class or national identity or ideology to mull over. Indeed, the majority of them probably did not think of themselves as 'political' or even patriotic in any conscious way at all. High-blown displays of King-and-Country nationalism were more likely to discomfit than inspire them. But they were nonetheless moved by a gentle, intimately conceived love of place – especially of the local and the familiar. 'I am not a flag-waving patriot, nor have I ever professed to be', insisted Private Rowbery in a letter to his mother in 1944, shortly before his death in combat:

> England's a great little country – the best there is – but I cannot honestly and sincerely say that it is worth fighting for. Nor can I fancy myself in the role of a gallant crusader fighting for the liberation of Europe. It would be a nice thought, but I would only be kidding myself. No, mum, my little world is centred around you and includes Dad, everyone at home, and my friends – that is worth fighting for.[36]

Perhaps, in the end, many men joined the Army because they could think of no good reason not to. Richard Buckle had always been repelled by everything to do with militarism. Yet in October 1939, he found himself to his own amazement enlisting as an ensign in the Scots Guards. Why did he do it? He could give no answer. 'Did I join up out of herd instinct, from an inherited sense of duty, because I knew I should be conscripted sooner or later anyway, or for fear of offending my mother and grandparents?' he wondered. He knew only one thing for sure. 'It certainly never occurred to me not to.'[37]

For the first nine months of the war the Army expanded, albeit sluggishly. The decision to introduce conscription immediately (or, more precisely, to continue and enlarge the conscription programme which had already begun in spring 1939) was not made because the government feared having to coerce young people into fighting. If anything, it was worried about the opposite. The appeal for volunteers in 1914 had been inspiring, but it had wrought chaos because little thought had been given to the needs of the war economy back in the UK. Hundreds of thousands of skilled men from trades vital to industry had had to be identified and returned from France to the home front. Chamberlain's administration wanted to avoid any such disruption. Instead of all the 'fuss' and 'surface turmoil' which had characterized 1914, what would take place this time (noted *The Times* approvingly) was a 'quiet unostentatious rally' of the nation.[38] It was still possible to jump the queue and volunteer for the Army, as 153,000 men had done by Christmas 1939.[39] But the government was ambivalent at best about this. Volunteering out of turn interfered with the smooth operation of the call-up machine. Men were gently encouraged not to rush things. Their turn would come soon enough.[40]

Then in spring 1940, the storm broke in the West: Norway, then France and Flanders, then Dunkirk. The evacuated regulars disembarked from their rescue boats in Dover, weary and confused, clutching their rifles but little else. The prospect of invasion loomed. The call-up notices suddenly began to stream out of Whitehall. The Army doubled in size.[41] Tented encampments sprang up from the Hebrides to Cornwall. The streets of garrison towns such as Caterham and Aldershot began to teem with men in uniform. 'At the beginning of the war, one turned round to look at a soldier', wrote a civilian in Stepney. 'Now they are seen too often to cause much comment.'[42] The story of our 'Finest Hour' in 1940 is usually told in terms of air power: of the RAF's valiant Few battling against the Luftwaffe over the skies of Kent, and the stoic heroism of the people of London, Coventry and other industrial cities blitzed by Hitler's bombers. But the event which touched the greatest number of lives that year was the rapid expansion of the Army. By December, one in three British men aged between twenty and twenty-four was wearing khaki. For every regular who had been serving at the beginning of the war, there were now six conscripts and volunteers.[43] Suddenly, a million civilians who had hardly given a thought to soldiering a year earlier were having rifles thrust into their hands and being posted to quiet south coast beaches and lonely country lanes to await Hitler's panzers.

On paper, it was all very impressive. 'Never before in the last war – or in this – have we had on this island an Army comparable in quality, equipment or numbers to that which stands here on guard tonight', Winston Churchill reassured his BBC radio listeners on 14 July 1940. 'Every week has seen their organisation, their defences, and their striking power advance by leaps and bounds.'[44] The truth was more sobering. The call-up had been accelerated more for political than for military reasons.[45] Churchill felt he needed to demonstrate to parliamentary backbenchers and the press that his new administration was taking the war seriously. Conscripting more soldiers was a tangible way for him to contrast his management of the war with that of his languorous predecessor, Chamberlain.[46] Whether it really made any sense from an operational point of view was quite a different matter. The Army's training system was overwhelmed by the rush of recruits. Superannuated veterans of the Great War had to be recalled from the Army Officer Emergency Reserve as instructors, though their knowledge of modern weapons was scarcely any better than that of the trainees themselves.[47] The BEF had lost the equivalent of up to ten divisions' worth of weapons and kit in France, and all that materiel would have to be replaced before the needs of fresh units could even be considered.[48] So the new men would have to make do with what was available, which was not much. Even rifles were difficult to get hold of at first.[49]

General Alan Brooke, who had impressed Churchill with his forthright manner when they had clashed on the telephone back in June, was the man now appointed by the prime minister to lead this half-trained militia into battle should the Germans invade. The prospect, Brooke admitted, was an 'almost unbearable' burden to him.[50] As the new commander-in-chief of Home Forces toured the country throughout the summer of 1940 he confided in his diary that the 'nakedness' of Britain's defences was terrifying. 'The more I see of conditions at home the more bewildered I am as to what has been going on in this country since the war started!' Brooke wrote on 1 July. 'It is now 10 months and yet the shortage of trained men and of equipment is appalling!'[51]

Amongst the men themselves there was a mood of quiet if nervous deter-mination, leavened by occasional episodes of comic opera, and an amused nonchalance at the sheer brazen hopelessness of it all. Thomas Howarth, a former assistant master at Winchester exiled to Formby to serve as a junior officer in a battalion of the King's Liverpool Regiment, mused that he and his men were preparing to fight anything from 'flying tanks playing military music from their exhaust-pipes to Lutheran pastors descending from a clear sky armed with explosive *blutwurst*'.[52] For gunner John Guest, serving in a light anti-aircraft battery on the Stour estuary, the most memorable night of the invasion summer of 1940 was spent hunkered in a bramble bush as he and his comrades awaited what they were told was an imminent German parachute attack. For hours, Guest stared into the inky sky, imagining the fearsome Nazi warriors about to descend on Essex – 'nightmare figures in Wellsian garments, strange helmets and goggles, floating silently down clutching machine guns.' His battery commander kept running around in circuits from one gun emplace-ment to the next, his revolver pointed dramatically at the sky, hissing in a fierce stage whisper: '*Airborne invasion! Keep quiet! O damn . . . where's the sergeant?*' The whereabouts of the sergeant was a matter of no small importance, because he was in charge of the Lewis gun, the only weapon the battery possessed which had any ammunition. Quite defenceless, Guest tried to get comfortable amongst the brambles and hoped that he wouldn't be visible when the para-chutists landed. Suddenly, there was a tremendous clatter of *rack-a-tac-tac-tac-tac-tac* as a torrent of red tracer bullets sped through the night air. Everyone buried their heads in the ground and waited for the Germans to finish them off. Silence fell. Finally, the sergeant gave an apologetic yell. '*It's only me, sir. I was just moving the Lewis gun, and it went off.*'[53]

In the end, the Germans did not come. By the winter of 1940, thanks to the victory of the RAF in the Battle of Britain, it was clear that there could be no invasion until at least the spring. And even then, the prospect of a successful amphibious assault had clearly diminished. The Royal Air Force and Royal

Navy had established a powerful defensive cordon around the British Isles. At night the Luftwaffe's bombers continued to raid, largely unopposed. But this was a nuisance, not an existential threat. The danger of strategic isolation – of the U-Boat fleet cutting off Britain's lines of maritime communication to the rest of the world – was more serious. A great battle was still to be fought in the Atlantic. But the Army would play no part in that. All immediate fears of invasion vanished in any case on 22 June 1941, when the German Army suddenly turned eastwards, invading the USSR. Hitler had evidently abandoned the strategy of directly attacking Britain. He had gambled instead on a swift and decisive victory in the East, presumably hoping that by defeating the Soviets he could force the demoralized British to the negotiating table.

With the diminishing of the invasion threat, the great expansion of the British Army also came to an end. By early 1941, it was becoming apparent that if the furious rate of intake of the previous six months was maintained, Britain would soon start running short of war workers. The other two armed services were making equally grasping demands on personnel. Something would have to give. In March 1941, Churchill's Cabinet issued a Directive in Army Scales which imposed a fixed manpower ceiling on the Army of 2,195,000. This was to nudge steadily upwards throughout the war, until by V-E Day the Army's size reached just short of three million. But by December 1942, the War Office had most of the men it was going to get. Of the roughly three million male civilians who became soldiers between the outbreak of war and the German surrender, half of them entered the ranks before the end of 1940 and three-quarters before the end of 1942.[54] If you were a former civilian who served in the British Army during the Second World War, the likelihood is that you joined it sometime between Dunkirk and Alamein. The period which, as it turned out, would be the Army's greatest time of troubles.

'Acres of concrete and tarmac enclosed by high stone walls, surmounted by barbed wire': Richard Holborow's initial glimpse of Horfield Infantry Training Centre on his first day as a new Army recruit was not, to say the least, encouraging. 'No prison could have presented a more dreary sight', he despaired:

> No tree or patch of green grass was allowed to intrude on the view of acres of black tarmac decorated with white painted bollards and a profusion of warning signs. All around you was the unrelieved ugliness of the Victorian architecture.

Holborow had originally hoped to join the Navy, but his application had been turned down, his dream of serving under the White Ensign as a smartly dressed able seaman disappearing into a future that would never be. Now, to his sorrow, he had arrived at Horfield in the northern suburbs of Bristol, 'destined by some wretched trick of fate to serve my King and Country in that nasty brown colour'.[55] Such feelings were not untypical. Up to the point of his call-up, A. G. Herbert dreamed of flying a Spitfire. He had been provisionally accepted into the RAF, and had been trying to attend night classes to learn the Morse code and maths skills he would need as a pilot or navigator. But because his long hours working in a gyro compass factory interfered with the school's schedule, he had to drop out. The RAF lost interest in him. One month later, he was conscripted into the Gloucestershire Regiment. 'I felt angry and insulted', he remembered. 'I was down to earth with a bump.'[56] His war had barely begun. And already it seemed like a defeat.

It is not that men such as Holborow and Herbert were reluctant to serve their country; they just did not want to serve it as soldiers. This lack of enthusiasm can be seen in the wartime enlistment figures. By 1941, the Army was attracting only one out of every four volunteers. It was the only one of the three armed services that relied for most of its wartime manpower on conscripts – and it did not even receive the best of those. When registering for call-up, you were allowed to express a preference to serve in the Navy or the Air Force if a slot could be found for you. The number of registrants who did this always far exceeded the number of applicants those two services actually needed. In 1941, for instance, 327,520 out of 2.2 million annual registrants expressed an interest in joining the Navy, and 824,417 the RAF – yet that year those two services only absorbed 92,600 and 174,400 conscripts respectively. By mid-1942, the RAF had a waiting list of 47,500 men (the equivalent of two and a half infantry divisions) hoping to train as aircrew.[57] Both the Navy and the Air Force were spoiled for choice; they could cherry-pick the best and brightest of the bunch. The Army had to be content with whomever was left over – often 'the unwilling, the least intelligent, and the least desirable'.[58] 'Nobody wanted to have anything to do with the old-fashioned footslogger', as Guardsman Gerald Kersh put it.[59]

The Army had always been the wooden spoon service so far as the public was concerned. The Navy had centuries of victorious tradition to play on: Jack Tar – that 'apogee of national virility' – had always been regarded by civilians as a more wholesome fellow than his disreputable cousin Tommy Atkins.[60] As for the RAF, before the war the newest of the three service branches had cleverly fostered a 'highly self-conscious aura of modernity' about itself which gave it a special glamour and sophistication.[61] Its officer-pilots were known for their noisy, swaggering braggadocio and well-cut azure uniforms. Its ground crewmen received higher wages, smarter kit and better prospects for post-service employment than soldiers. The RAF seemed to embrace an altogether more democratic attitude towards promotion and reward than the Army, one in which mechanical competence mattered a lot more than the school you had gone to or whether you could recite a litany of regimental honours.[62] To the modern-minded young man in the 1930s, the Air Force represented the kind of country Britain was becoming, not the country it had once been. An RAF corporal summed up the feelings of his fellow aircraftmen in 1937. Soldiering to them meant 'drill and firing and heaps of cleaning', whereas in the Air Force 'we can work with tools and engines, and see things happen from what we do'.[63] Servicing Hurricane fighters at a comfortable aerodrome somewhere in the United Kingdom was rather more appealing to the young and ambitious than peeling potatoes in Peshawar.

But by 1942, there were other factors at play too. The Navy and RAF were having rather good wars. The bluejackets had rescued the troops from Dunkirk, sunk the battleship *Bismarck* and were engaged in a heroic life-or-death struggle against the U-Boats in the North Atlantic. The Royal Air Force, for its part, had saved the nation in the Battle of Britain; and its bomber aircraft now made up the only real offensive force being employed against Germany. To be sure, Bomber Command's early attacks on the Reich's cities were not really having much effect on the enemy's production and morale (the great and terrible firestorm raids were to come later). But the public was not to know that. And at least the RAF was visibly doing *something*. Both services enjoyed high public esteem as a result. The Navy commanded the 'unqualified respect' of civilians according to Mass-Observation. The RAF was regarded as 'a brilliant set of individuals'.

As for the Army – Mass-Observation was hard-pressed to find anyone in Britain with anything particularly encouraging to say about it. 'Not our strongest point'; 'Shortage of brains at the top'; 'Can't imagine them indulging in a blitzkrieg'.[64] The Army's record by 1942 was not good. Most of its men were not engaged in any fighting at all. They were billeted in tented encampments strung across the British countryside, attending to what Arthur Kellas called the 'domestic avocations' of the soldiering life – checking kits, holding lectures on orienteering and fieldcraft, weeding gardens, holding courts of inquiry into lost bayonets and other petty misdemeanours.[65] The typical British soldier was following the course of the fighting not by poking his head out of a trench, but by reading about it in a newspaper: 'In joining the Army', Rupert Croft-Cooke realized following his call-up, 'I had escaped the war.'[66]

So when a recruit such as Richard Holborow or A. G. Herbert showed up at his training depot, all he knew was that he was joining the service with the lowest pay, the worst uniforms and weapons, the most tedious and demeaning discipline and (apparently) the stupidest leaders. He was joining the service which, unlike the Navy and the Air Force, seemed to be doing little of any real military value in the service of the nation, and which was anyway incapable of fighting its enemies. He was joining the ranks of what one soldier called 'the unknown men of the war, the forgotten men . . . nearly three million of them, all sucked out of their useful civilian jobs; all swallowed, swamped, and disheartened in that vast bog of bungledom, that drain of drowned hope and talent'.[67] In short he was joining the British Army.

The first night in barracks was always the worst. Cosy childhood bedrooms with pyjamas and dressing-gowns neatly tagged with names and school houses, and bound volumes of the *Model Railway Magazine* on the bookshelves, had not prepared new recruits well for iron beds and hard biscuit mattresses, chafing boots, freezing concrete floors and itchy prison-like smocks.[68] For Maurice Merritt, his new dormitory was a 'chamber of horrors minus the chamber . . . odious smells, fetid air, sweaty bodies, tobacco fumes, poor ventilation'. The noise was incessant: snoring, belching, farting, pissing, the tramp of studded ammunition boots in the hallway.[69] S. C. Procter cried himself to sleep thinking of his parents as he tried to settle on his 'bed of nails'.[70] Henry Novy, a twenty-one-year-old clerk sent to a Royal Army Medical Corps depot in Leeds, settled back on his straw palliasse, tired, depressed, his teeth aching, and tried unsuccessfully to sleep. 'I kept thinking of home, and all I had left went round and round in my head, ceaselessly, persistently . . . I felt so depressed that I wanted to cry, but I couldn't.' It was, he thought, simply 'hell'.[71]

Military service was going mean exposure to all sorts of new, often unpleasant, and certainly disorientating tactile and mental experiences: to unfamiliar foods, clothes and belongings; to extremes of filth and cleanliness; to long stretches of tedium, punctuated by bursts of panic; to prying eyes and poking fingers; and to peculiar laws, customs, routines. For some recruits, the prospect was simply horrifying. R. H. Lloyd-Jones watched a conscript intake being received at his regimental depot in early 1940. 'Many seemed to be under strain', he noted. 'They had to be asked details of their families; some could not remember their children's names, one or two could not even remember their own names.' One broke down in tears and had to be consoled on the company commander's shoulder.[72] When journalist Anthony Cotterell arrived at his Infantry Training Centre, he and 200 other nervous, well-scrubbed adolescents were led shambling away from the railway station with the other passengers watching them 'with the same fascinated horror that people watch convicts'.[73] Cotterell's brother Geoffrey, who had been called up earlier in the war, recalled 'white faced, round shouldered young men with spotty skins and no confidence' stumbling through his own camp gates, all with the self-assurance of Christians about to be fed to the lions.[74] The future actor Dirk Bogarde kept a diary of his first days of military service. 'Today I start life in the Army', it began in May 1941:

> Feel sick ... train crowded – soldiers, old women, conscripts like self. Journey awful – gaze out at receding country – wonder if I'll die and never see London again ... arrive Richmond Yorks at 6.45. Bundled into Army lorry with 22 others. Arrive at camp – bleak, barren and horrible – have awful supper – sausages. Get shown into bunk room – sleep on floor on straw biscuits – 4 blankets – lights out at 10.30. 25 of us here, all homesick dead tired – feel life has ceased forever – weep four bitter tears under my blankets. Feel much better when find my neighbours doing same.[75]

The wartime citizen Army was a reflection of the society it defended, and every bit as diverse. Soldiers were English, Scottish, Welsh and Irish; British only by descent, and not British at all. They were Protestants, Catholics, Jews, Hindus, Muslims, freethinkers and, at least in one case, a druid; Liberals, Conservatives, Socialists; fascists and communists; men who were ideologically driven; men who were wholly apathetic about politics.[76] Some soldiers supported the war effort with passionate gusto. Others were appalled by violence and unconvinced of its merits. Most were sexually straight, though a significant number of them – perhaps as many as several hundred thousand – were not.[77] Lots were virginal, a few debauched. Some were bright; some foolish; some conscientious; some lazy; some compassionate; some mean-spirited; some heroic; some cowardly. In terms of class and education, they ran the entire spectrum from barrister to borstal runaway, Old Etonian to charity school illiterate.

All members of the national community were represented; but not equally represented. For if the Army was a reflection of society, it was a partial, distorted reflection. Vast numbers of the industrial labour force – at first, almost five million men out of a total pool of 14.6 million – were excluded from military recruitment due to their indispensability to the war economy by the Schedule of Reserved Occupations.[78] The number of 'reserved' workers changed throughout the war according to the needs of military production. But broadly speaking, those most likely to be reserved were skilled craftsmen involved in the manufacture of weapons, munitions, aircraft, ships and motor vehicles. The reserved were typically mechanics, machinists, tool and pattern-makers, boilermakers, riveters, draughtsmen and other artisans needed in the metal, chemical, electrical and engineering trades. Miners, dockers and agricultural workers also received special dispensation from the call-up. Victorian Britain, the Britain of steam and iron, of smoky factories and shipyards and pitheads, was on the whole kept out of the wartime Army.

Those least likely to be reserved were men who had worked in Britain's pre-war construction, retail, processed food, textile, finance and education sectors, all of which contracted drastically between 1939 and 1945. The wartime Army was an army of shopkeepers, bricklayers, bank clerks, confectioners, bespoke tailors, accountants, schoolteachers, painters, undergraduates and travelling salesmen – men whose civilian skills were often highly respected and remunerated in time of peace, but who were poorly suited to the needs of war. By the end of August 1944, there were 152,000 former van and lorry drivers serving in the ranks of the British Army; 79,000 grocer's assistants; 51,000 decorators and paperhangers; 26,000 porters; 13,500 chauffeurs and taxi drivers; 12,000 insurance canvassers; 10,500 barbers and wigmakers; 6,200 cinema projectionists and ushers. 2,030 artists were in khaki. So were 2,712 journalists and 1,482 actors. 225 novelists and poets had exchanged the pen for the sword.[79] Richard Terrell, a bookish thirty-year-old husband and father of two living in a nice block of flats in Wandsworth in September 1939, was one such recruit. The author of two novels, and an assiduous book reviewer for newspapers and magazines, it had never crossed his mind that he of all people would one day be expected 'to dress up as a soldier and learn about the parts of a Bren gun or an anti-tank rifle'.[80]

Men like Terrell were not the kind of soldiers who the Army traditionally relied on in peacetime at all – the eighteen- or nineteen-year-old semi-literate boys from the social margins, habituated to institutional discipline, pathetically loyal to anyone who showed them the slightest kindness or affection, long inured to hardship.[81] These new soldiers were altogether older, worldlier, less rough-edged men. Even though the RAF and the Navy took the pick of the choicest recruits, wartime Army volunteers and conscripts were still generally far better educated and from more socially respectable backgrounds than regulars. One in four of them was aged thirty or over.[82] One in four had progressed at least as far as secondary school. One in twenty had been to university.[83] Half were married, many of them with young children.[84] Prior to his call-up, Rupert Croft-Cooke had expected his fellow soldiers to be like the 'blasphemously grumbling' hard cases and down-and-outs he had met while pea- and hop-picking on summer holidays before the war. But instead he found himself surrounded by a most unmartial collection of 'bourgeois intellectuals, schoolmasters, graduates, bank-clerks, professional misfits, unsuccessful actors and journalists, tourists' couriers and the like', none of whom had any military experience (though all of whom were convinced they should rightfully be officers.)[85] Anthony Cotterell's platoon of twenty recruits turned out to include a tobacconist, a grocer's assistant, a lorry driver, a waiter, a baker, a dyer, a wireless mechanic, a butcher, a loom worker, a chauffeur, a printer, two clerks and six labourers.[86] Norman Craig found himself billeted with a university under-graduate like himself, a Jew who had once worked at the Coney Island fun fair, and a soccer-playing ex-grocer from Cardiff.[87] Aitch-dropping corporals turned out to be former car salesmen.[88] One wartime major with the breezy, self-assured manner and immaculate pencil-thin moustache of a regular Blimp was an ex-bus conductor.[89]

The men whom former public school master Thomas Howarth encoun-tered at his officer cadet school in Bulford in early 1940 were a typically implau-sible bunch of temporary warriors:

Williams: 19 years old. Insurance clerk.

Mandy: Ex-actor and schoolmaster. A face I shall never forget with its humorous but hyper-strained sensitivity.

Seymour: Radley and Christchurch, horses and hounds.

Taylor: 'ersatz' gentleman and car salesman.

Winckles: Handsome, worrying, incredibly dull, with his fiancée and account-ancy his only interests.

Ashby: Slick, vigorous – Cockney vulgarianism at its most complacent, but altogether memorable.

Rodgers: Fascist and Munchausen.

Watson: Pretty, spotty, ineffectual little clerk.

Hanks: Hobbledehoy farmer's lad.

Knight & Ogden-Smith: [Territorial] by branch-line from Ealing.

Cracroft: Operatic singer with a feather in his hat.

Blythe: A glorious contentious Scots engineer. The best product of the hydroelectric age.

Everett: Chocolate-eating youngster with a pink face and evanescent moustache.

Kent: Rough and regular – genial, blasphemous anarchist.

Woodward: African backwoodsman.

Ashmore: Pocket Captain Blood, five-foot-four of military bristle.[90]

These were the soldiers – many of them well established in civilian life, self-possessed, but also completely unused to roughing it – of a new and very different kind of army. As Ian Hay put it (and not with approval), they were 'accustomed to a certain standard of living', had more 'active and intelligent minds', rebelled instinctively against 'unimaginative handling by authority' and were 'irked by monotonous repetition of routine duties, and especially by the emptiness and boredom of hours of leisure'. The customary diversions of the peacetime soldier were not going to be for *them*.[91]

They were not just different from the peacetime regulars. They were also very different from the citizen-soldiers of their fathers' generation, the men who had fought the First World War. For one thing, twenty-five years of better diet, sanitation, exercise and subsidized medical care had produced in them a much physically healthier recruiting class.[92] This would have come as a surprise to the public health commentators who had gone to great lengths between the wars to bewail the physical deterioration of Britain's young manhood.[93] Old eugenic anxieties about the enfeebled condition of the urban working class still lingered. The typical recruit from the cities was a physical wreck, insisted Anthony Cotterell in 1941. 'His chest is flat, his stomach unhealthily swollen. There is dandruff lurking in the brilliantine and he carries himself as if he has no shape.' The explanation, thought Cotterell, was simple:

> He has lived badly and fed badly. Never at any time in his life has he under-
> gone a regular week-in-week-out regime of simple food, regular hours and
> exercise . . . he has been brought up in a poky, frowsty-smelling little house
> where he slept with the windows closed. When he was a baby his mother fed
> him anything he fancied in the way of cheesecakes and cheap sweets and
> fish and chips.[94]

This was mostly nonsense. Young British men were, on the whole, healthier in 1941 than they had ever been. By the 1930s, the typical sixteen-year-old boy applying for a job with the Post Office was sixteen pounds heavier and one-and-a-half inches taller than his 1914 predecessor.[95] The per capita consumption of vegetables in Britain rose by 64 per cent between the wars, fruit by 88 per cent.[96] This is not to say that all was well within British bodies. National dental care was still totally inadequate. Nine in ten of all Army recruits needed the attention of a dentist on entering the Forces. Two-fifths of them had to undergo extensive reconstructive work on their teeth.[97] Around 12,000 men suffering from under-nourishment, scoliosis, poor posture and flat feet had to be directed to Physical Development Depots before their basic training in order to build up their physiques.[98] But far fewer men in the Second World War had to be rejected on grounds of physical incapacity than in the First.[99] In the final twelve months before the 1918 Armistice, only about one-third of potential recruits were graded as fully fit, and 42 per cent were judged incapable of combat service entirely.[100] By contrast, between 1939 and 1945 80 per cent of men were accepted at intake, and 65 per cent of them placed in the highest physical category possible.[101] One elderly doctor who had inspected troops in the earlier conflict remarked in 1940 on the 'immense improvement in the health and muscular development' of the men he now saw joining the Army.[102]

So their cavities and bleeding gums aside, physically these men were much readier for war than their fathers had been. What about their mental preparation, however? It was hard to be so certain about that. Britain, unlike the nations of Continental Europe, had no tradition of peacetime conscription. The French *poilu* and German *Landser* had often spent some time in the pre-war ranks before being called up to fight; life in uniform was not wholly unfamiliar to him.[103] Few British citizens in 1939 had ever done the same. Had the Military Training Act passed some years earlier, then many more young men at the outset of the Second World War would have had some idea of what to expect once they were called up. But the 1939 Act was rushed through so late that its practical consequences were minimal. Fewer than 35,000 'militiamen' had been enlisted by the time Germany invaded Poland, and even they had only been in the Army a few weeks. The Territorial Army went through a rapid expansion in the final months of peace, but most of its recruits had barely received their uniforms by the time full mobilization was announced. They were almost as green as the conscripts.[104]

Of course, the men of 1914 had had no previous military training either. Nonetheless, they had arguably been better prepared for what soldiering was going to be like. For one thing, before the First World War Britain's youth clubs and organizations had focused heavily on paramilitary instruction. Groups such as the Boys' Brigade and the Boy Scouts, the latter of which had been formed by Lord Baden-Powell explicitly to teach young men soldiering skills, had offered lessons in field-craft, dispatch-running, signalling, tracking and rifle shooting. After 1918, these groups had adapted to changing tastes by 'civilianizing' their activities. Paramilitary training had been de-emphasized in favour of dancing, gymnastics and whist drives.[105] Church youth groups' drill parades and Bible classes had given way to billiards, table tennis and film shows. Organizations that had not reformed had withered. Manchester's Jewish Lads' Brigade, which required its boys to wear khaki uniforms and attend summer Army-style camps, had been seriously in debt by the late 1930s because of its declining enrolment.[106] The semi-official Army Cadet Force lost 100,000 of its 120,000 members between the wars.[107]

But still more important than that, the character of ordinary life for the working class in 1914 – and it was the working class which supplied the majority of the Army's recruits during the First World War, even if white-collar workers were disproportionately represented in the ranks – had shared many similarities with military service: austere, physically demanding, subordinated, hierarchical.[108] The soldiers of Haig's army had grown up in a world in which children (according to one 1911 account) were reduced 'to a state of mental and moral serfdom'. There were 1.5 million domestic servants in Britain in

1914, men and women whose very lives revolved around the prompt demonstration of obedience.[109] One Salford-born Edwardian described his working day as made up of a 'multitude of petty tyrannies and humiliations'. Employers liked their workers 'round-shouldered, servile and abject', as the foreman in a large Swindon railway workshop put it.[110] Many of the Tommies of the First World War had become used to the tedium and subservience which would characterize military life long before they ever reached the Western Front. 'They were inured to a certain degree of physical discomfort and material deprivation', as historian John Bourne has put it. 'They had quite low levels of expectation. They could put up with a lot . . . there was nothing new [to them] about poverty, hardship, disruptive and unpredictable outside authority with an alien agenda.'[111]

To be sure, for some Britons life in the 1930s was not so very different from this. In the slums of Lancashire and Clydeside, the interwar decades were years of squalor and want. In 1939, 15 per cent of all insured workers in Tyne and Wear were out of work. In Wales, it was one in five; in Northern Ireland, one in four.[112] Journeying to the broken shipyard town of Jarrow in 1933, in which two-thirds of insured workers were unemployed, J. B. Priestley described the thick air 'heavy with enforced idleness, poverty, and misery', the men, wearing 'the drawn masks of prisoners of war', engaged in what he called a 'perpetual penniless bleak Sabbath'.[113] Many comparatively well-off working-class people in the 1930s still lived in conditions that would, by twenty-first century standards, be considered austere. 'It is difficult for anyone [today] to imagine that kind of life', thought Roy Close of his pre-war childhood in north London:

Small coal fires in one room; no fires in the bedroom unless you were ill; draughts; chilblains; gas mantles for lighting; radio only if you made your own 'wireless set' until you could afford to buy one, and parents sitting at the kitchen table with available money before them planning the weekends' purchases. Sometimes there was a joint of meat for Sunday lunch, but chicken was a rarity, a great luxury, a 'special treat'.[114]

Even so, the number of Britons living in poverty more than halved between 1914 and 1935.[115] Urban blight of the kind that haunted Tyneside was increasingly becoming a regional rather than a national problem. During his travels in 1933, Priestley saw signs of an emerging British society very different from the 'distressed areas' of the north, especially when he visited the thriving light-industrial regions of the English Midlands and the Home Counties. If Jarrow represented the dying heart of one civilization, so the Somerdale chocolate factory near Bristol and the Morris Motors plant at Cowley outside

Oxford represented the thriving hub of another – a civilization of cheap retail goods, of 'arterial and by-pass roads ... giant cinemas and dance halls and cafés, bungalows with tiny garages, cocktail bars, Woolworths, motor-coaches, wireless, hiking, factory girls looking like actresses'.[116]

Young people fortunate enough to be part of this new Britain were, by the 1930s, enjoying an unprecedented level of mass privilege.[117] Many were growing up in the four million new houses built between the wars, houses that often boasted electricity, gardens and indoor plumbing.[118] Families were smaller now than ever before, the working-class home by the 1930s only having on average 2.5 dependent children, compared to 3.9 in 1900.[119] Mothers and fathers now had more time, energy and money to devote to their individual sons and daughters. Young people were getting used to greater privacy and material comfort. It was becoming increasingly common for a child to have a bedroom of his or her own. Exposure to adult life was now delayed thanks to the 1918 Education Act, which had raised the school leaving age from twelve to four-teen. Independent spending power was growing fast.[120] Whole industries were emerging to cater to the new consumer culture of young people with cash to spend. By the 1930s, a vast 'hobbies' literature of books and magazines had come into being, feeding young people's interest in motorcycles, radio and gramophone records.[121] Movie palaces were thrilling audiences with the spectacles of Hollywood. By 1938, two million adolescents were going dancing every week, with young men preening themselves on the dance-floors in their trilby hats and 30-shilling suits.[122] If dancing was not to their taste, then there was speedway racing, football pools, hiking. For the daring, there were summer holidays in Blackpool or Brighton, the erotically charged Ibizas of their day.

What was emerging was (in the words of historian Selina Todd) 'a new, modern working class' never seen before in Britain, one 'no longer fractured by unemployment but united by a commercialized leisure culture that spoke of reasonable wages and time in which to enjoy them'.[123] Or as George Orwell put it at the time, a 'general softening of manners' was taking place as the 'tastes, habits, manners and outlook' of the working and middle classes converged. 'Many workers in the light industries', suggested Orwell, 'are less truly manual labourers than is a doctor or a grocer.'[124] Imagine, then, how baffling and painful it was going to be for young men of this privileged genera-tion to be transported by the Army to a Dickensian milieu they had never known before – a world of workhouse dormitories, Victorian grotesques and peremptory deference.

At dawn reveille, the routine of Army life began. The new soldier was stripped of his civilian clothing, his civilian haircut, his civilian identity. He was pumped full of vaccines, often with painful side-effects (future prime minister Edward Heath had such a violent allergic reaction to the vaccination jabs he received during his first week in the Army that he was hospitalized).[125] The soldier was outfitted in battledress (BD), the standard-issue uniform modelled on work-men's overalls, which was known to give off a peculiar camphorated odour due to an obscure chemical treatment during its manufacture, and which made its wearer look, as one soldier put it, like 'a sack of potatoes tied in the middle'.[126] The short woollen BD blouse gave no protection to the loins, and if, as frequently happened, the buttons flew off at the back, the soldier was left with a chilling gap at his backside. Because the blouse buttoned up to the neck, it did not allow the wearer to display a collared shirt and tie underneath – an impor-tant 'badge of respectability' in the 1940s, as the War Office belatedly acknowl-edged, and one that was specifically provided for in the version of BD issued to all ranks of the RAF.[127] The khaki BD side cap offered no protection from the rain or sun and was guaranteed to fall off in front of the regimental sergeant major at an embarrassing moment.[128] Why, asked Reginald Crimp in 1943, did the British soldier have to be decked out in such unprepossessing garb? 'One thing about the Hun, he looks every inch a fighting man', griped Crimp:

> His belt and jackboots, close-fitting jacket and trousers and aggressive steel helmet all add up to a tough proposition . . . our battledress looks almost comic in comparison. If ever attire was designed to accentuate quirks of figures it was surely BD. And for the worst part of the ensemble – the 'blouse' – there's only word: Blowzy.[129]

With the new soldier's uniform came other labels, categories, grades. All the information that mattered about him was now reduced to a series of barely decipherable pencil scribbles on his AB64 Service and Pay Book and charge sheet – his name, rank, seven-figure identification number (pressed also into the two tags strung around his neck), official religion, boot size and list of mili-tary crimes. Batteries of doctors appraised his naked flesh to determine where to slot him on the scale of usefulness, from A1 ('only minor, remediable disa-bilities; without defects of locomotion; can undergo severe strain') to E (perma-nently unfit and disposable).[130] Military psychologists calculated his level of intelligence, his propensity for certain types of trade, his emotional stability, his willingness to kill. He was now an anonymous tooth on a great whirring cog.

Having categorized him, the Army put him to work. His mornings and afternoons were spent tramping the square – up and down, round and round, working the arcane minutiae of drill into his muscle memory. *Quick march! Slow march! Turn on the march! Incline on the march! Salute on the march! Right*

wheel! Left wheel! Slope arms! Order arms! Port arms! Present arms! Trail arms!
Evenings were the time for 'bullshit', or meticulous spit-and-polish. The
fragrances of heated boot black and the sweet glueish odours of liquid cleaner
wafted along barrack block corridors, as soldiers were caught up in a 'feverish
activity of housewifery'. Floors were polished until they had the surface of a
glassy rink (and were far too dangerous to actually walk on). Stoves were
meticulously black-leaded, fire-buckets glossed a dazzling pillar-box red.
Soldiers dyed webbing with watery Blanco colouring compound, polished
hollow brass buttons to a glistening sheen, pressed the creases of khaki trousers
to a knife-like edge, and smoothed the surfaces of boots with warm spoons.[131]
Buttons, Blanco, but most of all boots: these, thought one wartime serviceman,
were the 'absorbing interest' of the Army. 'There is such simple satisfaction', he
admitted, 'such a thrill of definite, undeniable achievement, in coaxing a twinkling ebony smile from the face of stubborn black leather.'[132] In early 1941,
officer cadet John Guest commented in his diary on his section's increasingly
fanatical attempts to outshine – literally – every other barrack room at
Shrivenham Officer Cadet Training Unit (OCTU):

> We have spent every evening of the last fortnight on our hands and knees
> scraping our bedroom floor with razor blades until it is absolutely white!
> Why? Partly because we were told that the floors were not clean enough . . .
> We now have to take our shoes off outside the room and walk about inside it
> in our socks. We are provided with floor-polishers called 'bumpers'. The
> handle of ours has been scraped with a razor blade till it looks like a bleached
> bone, and a special pair of woollen gloves has to be worn by anyone who
> touches it. We have a bucket in our room for rubbish; it has now been
> burnished so brightly that if you even put cigarette ash into it everyone
> screams. We unscrew all the handles and latches on the windows before
> polishing them, also the bit of metal round the key-hole and the door-knob.
> I have really wondered sometimes if I'm not going mad.[133]

Soldiers preened and fussed over one another before inspection, tugging at
one another's blouses and belts and berets, trying to fine-tune their shapeless
BD ensembles to the correct angle of adjustment, 'titivating themselves like
actresses'.[134] This was high-stakes work. A carelessly laid-out kit, an irregularly
draped uniform, an inattentively dusted windowsill, could mean a charge and
consequent loss of privileges. Soldiers hoping to leave camp on a pass had to
subject themselves to examination at the guardhouse. Grown men could be
reduced to impotent weeping fury if their leave was delayed or cancelled for the
crime of being 'improperly dressed', which, depending on how sadistically

pedantic the inspecting officer or NCO was feeling at that moment, could mean anything from the discovery of a speck of dust on an epaulette to the tiniest drop of oil blemishing a rifle muzzle.

Spit-and-polish was not necessarily correlated with cleanliness or healthiness. While the Army was obsessive about the superficial appearance of its men, it seemed far less interested in what they looked like underneath their uniforms – never mind what they smelled like. As Stan Scott put it, 'You could go ten weeks without having a bath, but if you had a nicely Blancoed belt with the brasses polished, you were all right.'[135] By September 1940, troops crowded into hurriedly constructed camps were complaining about the lack of basic laundry facilities and the unavailability of hot running water. Three weeks might pass before a man could take a proper wash; epidemics of lice and scabies broke out. 'What I have to put up with', a RASC private wrote home from Craigmillar camp in the Orkney Islands,

> bad grub, wet clothes and blankets, no beds to sleep in, a wet tent that leaks like a sieve, bad sanitation, no lavatory . . . I tell you that they have broke my spirit so that when I go to bed at nights I could sob my heart out. I have started getting rheumatism already. The first chance I get I shall desert, never fear.[136]

For the first five weeks of his basic training in the RAMC (its motto at the time: *mens sana in corpore sano* – a healthy mind in a healthy body), Anthony Burgess did not bathe, shaved in cold water and became chronically constipated. His PT exercises were done to the sound of his infirm comrades' coughing and wheezing as they all shivered in the cold December dawn. 'This seemed', he thought, 'no way to run an army.'[137]

But then the Army ran entirely according to its own rules and principles. It was, as Anthony Cotterell put it, 'a nation within the nation, with different laws, different clothes, different standards of conduct'.[138] Nothing in civilian life quite compared to it. You were not hired: you were summoned. You could not quit, though generally speaking you could not be fired either, no matter how badly you behaved. You lived at the workplace. There was no clocking on or off; your employer decided when your duty ended, and if indeed it ended at all. You could be relocated without consultation or warning, thousands of miles from everything you knew, often for years at a time. Your fate was decided seemingly at random, soldiers possessing all the agency of 'a shuffled pack of cards in a conjuror's hands'.[139] The Army's rules sometimes contradicted everything that peacetime life had taught you about good conduct and manners. Actions that would have been praiseworthy in the past – dropping everything to go the bedside of a sick relative, say – were now regarded as serious crimes. Behaviour that would have been illegal and immoral in peacetime – assaulting perfect strangers, blowing up other people's property – were now regarded not just as part of your job, but as positively meritorious. The Army explained nothing, apologized for nothing. Being a soldier meant having little or no idea of what was happening to you or why, where you were going next, or what you were going to do once you got there. Rumour, often baseless, but all the same addictive, was all you had to go on. 'We would stop [on the march] about lunch time and were hungry. Was there time to cook something? Nobody knew,' noted Richard Terrell:

> If the column stopped in the evening, perhaps because of a broken bridge, how long would the sappers take to mend it? Or, should we settle down for the night? Nobody knew. When at some stage we were ordered to sleep, we covered ourselves in groundsheets (often wet) and tried to snooze . . . just as were dozing off we would hear a word of command: *Prepare to move.* We responded with a stream of expletives.[140]

The uniforms, the improving talks, the gossip, the Out-of-Bounds signs, the Saturday detentions, the physical jerks on cold winter mornings, the erotic fumblings in the dark – for recruits of at least two kinds, anyway, there was something oddly familiar about it all. 'I have never been in prison', noted Australian-born soldier Alan Wood, 'but friends of mine who have been assure me that life in the Army constantly reminds them of the old days in Dartmoor.' Soldiering possessed all the 'totalitarian flavour' of the Victorian penitentiaries they had known before the war:

> Something about the atmosphere is indefinably the same. As we marched up and down the parade ground in the murky light of early morning, wearing our drab khaki pullovers and our shapeless khaki forage caps, the scene brought back vividly to their minds the period for exercises in the prison square. As we laboured with picks and shovels and wheelbarrows to lay down brick and rubble roads on our gunsite, they instinctively recalled the road gangs on cheerless Devon moors.[141]

Former public schoolboys shared with ex-convicts this sense of the familiar. V. M. Sissons's days in his school Officer Training Corps (OTC) had provided an excellent foundation in drill, spit-and-polish and musketry, and he was well accustomed to 'being chivvied about with no chance of answering back'. Indeed, the only real difference between the Royal Corps of Signals and his alma mater, so far as he could see, was that the Army's food was better, and officers and NCOs were much more pleasant than his schoolmasters and prefects had ever been.[142] As soon as Rupert Croft-Cooke walked through the gates of the Field Security training depot at Winchester in 1940, he felt immediately transported back to his youth. 'I half expected' he wrote, 'to be asked by one of the old hands in khaki what my father did for a living.' The longer he spent in the Army, the more Croft-Cooke realized that its mental atmosphere was indistinguishable from that of Eton or Harrow. He found himself editing a depot newspaper which ran exactly the same stale in-jokes and sporting results as a school magazine. He received a note from a grown-up (his commanding officer) excusing his absence when one of his relatives visited. New boys arrived in the middle of term, as they had done in school; 'frightful rows' went on behind the scenes:

> [There were] football matches against rival establishments, favouritism, whispered confidences, and if not tuck-boxes at least pocket-money to spend in the canteen. Instead of school walks we had motor-cycling, instead of end-of-term examinations we had tests, instead of popular or unpopular masters we had sergeant instructors, instead of a Head we had the Commandant, and we did PT, wrote letters home, grumbled at the food, quarrelled amongst ourselves, and tried to pass the Common Entrance Examination to go to [advanced training at] Matlock.[143]

Strangeways or Shrewsbury, Wormwood Scrubs or Wellington: if you were an alumnus of one of those highly selective British institutions, then military life held no particular surprises for you. For everyone else, there was much to learn.

CHAPTER 5

BRITAIN BLANCOES WHILE RUSSIA BLEEDS

15 February 1942. The skies above Singapore Island are choked with clouds of satin-coloured smoke pouring from the burning oil tanks in the harbour. All around is the chaos of military collapse, already depressingly familiar to the British Army from Norway and Dunkirk: wrecked vehicles lying overturned in shell craters; the flotsam of fleeing civilians – clothing, furniture, bicycles, prams – abandoned in the streets; corpses flung into gutters and ditches, festering in the heat unattended. An eighteen-year-old Chinese student watches one column of the more than 70,000 British troops captured on the island marching into Japanese imprisonment, 'an endless stream of bewildered men' who seem to have no idea what has happened to them, or why they are even in Singapore in the first place. One of their conquerors, Colonel Masanobu Tsuji, remarks later of the British POWs placed under his men's guard that they were discovered 'squatting on the road smoking, talking, and shouting in rather loud voices'. Their main response to their predicament had not seemed to be one of anger or hostility, but of mere resignation: they looked, thought a puzzled Tsuji, like 'like men who had finished their work by contract at a suitable salary, and were now taking a rest free from the anxiety of the battlefield'.[1]

This disaster was supposed to be unthinkable. Singapore was the 'Gibraltar of the East', the British Empire's great fortress-base east of Suez, said to be unconquerable. Confidence in its ability to withstand a siege was therefore high when the Japanese began advancing down the Malay peninsula in January 1942.[2] But the island's defences had been designed to repulse a naval assault from the South China Sea, not an amphibious landing across the narrow Johore Strait separating Singapore from the mainland. The city's garrison was large, over twice the size of the Japanese force that came to besiege it. But few of the defending troops were experienced. An entire British infantry division (the 18th) had only just arrived, and its men had not even had time to acclimatize to the tropical weather. There was little in the way of food and water to sustain such a large force over the length of a long siege. By 15 February, the Japanese were on the verge of overrunning the island completely. Churchill sent General Percival, the British commander, a telegram urging that 'there must be no thought of saving the troops . . . the battle must be fought to the bitter end'.[3] But Percival saw little point in a glorious but futile mass martyrdom. He raised the white flag.

One man who escaped the chaos in Singapore was the editor of the city's main newspaper, the *Straits Times*. After the surrender, he was asked by the British government to compile a report on what he had seen. The collapse at Singapore, he wrote, had not been caused by materiel disadvantage. The opposite was the case. The Japanese were far less well militarily accoutred than the island's defenders. What doomed Singapore was the 'almost complete demoralisation of the defending troops; the striking lack of any offensive spirit; the widespread acceptance of the view that the battle was a forlorn hope; and, in isolated cases, an actual refusal to fight'. Though some individual British battalions had done well – he singled out the performance of the Argylls, the East Surreys and the Leicesters – most had been thoroughly outfought by the enemy. A key problem, he suggested, was an overemphasis on 'kit' at the expense of basic fighting skills. 'We were not underequipped; we were over-equipped. Our men were over-burdened', he argued:

> [They] seemed to expect transport to carry them immediately they withdrew from an actual fighting area. The infantry had lost the art of marching . . . we were bogged down with the weight of stuff which could have been dispensed with, and men and materials were used to provide transport for presentation to the enemy because we were not sufficiently mobile to prevent him getting behind it.[4]

Another survivor, a soldier who eventually made his way to Indonesia after a gruelling three-week odyssey by sampan and steamboat, wrote to his mother afterwards of the doomed fortress: 'I am ashamed to have taken part in this disastrous campaign. Still, I now know what war is really like.'[5]

Perhaps if Singapore's fate had simply been a one-off disaster in February 1942, its loss, though serious, would not have been felt so keenly back in London. But Percival's surrender was merely the latest episode in what, by the third year of the war, was becoming a depressingly predictable story of defeat after defeat on land. Whenever the British Army found itself on a battlefield, it seemed to spend the majority of its time retreating and surrendering. Its only real accomplishment up to this point in the war, chided one civilian, had been the mastery of 'victorious withdrawals'.[6]

It was not that the Army had lost *all* its battles. Indeed, in January 1941, it had enjoyed its first great triumph of the war when it had routed an Italian force which, in a great show of bluster and incaution, had crossed over from Libya a few months earlier and invaded Egypt.[7] For a few weeks, as the British Western Desert Force (WDF) had pursued the disintegrating Italian forces falling back on Tripoli, it had looked as though the enemy might be expelled from North Africa entirely. But in February the Germans sent a relief force to Libya led by General Erwin Rommel, who had already proved himself to be a master of armoured warfare in the campaign in France. Rommel quickly threw the British back across the frontier into Egypt. Even before Rommel's attack, the WDF had been badly weakened by Churchill's decision to send 60,000 troops to Greece to defend against an expected German invasion. The Germans did indeed attack Greece shortly afterwards, but the hasty British intervention made no difference to the outcome of the campaign. The British expeditionary force had to withdraw to Crete, and was then thrown off that island when it was attacked by seaborne and airborne forces.

In June, on the southern shore of the Mediterranean, the British counterattacked against Rommel in what was dubbed Operation BATTLEAXE. The WDF's strength had been more than made up by a large reinforcement of fresh troops and tanks from the UK, so its prospects seemed good; the Germans and Italians in Libya were outnumbered almost two to one. But after just three days of fighting, BATTLEAXE had to be called off. The attack had stalled badly. British armoured units charging cavalry-style into the German positions, unsupported by any infantry or artillery, had been mauled by anti-tank guns. Eight British tanks had been destroyed for every one German tank lost.[8] General Archibald Wavell, who had won fame for the WDF's victory against the Italians, was packed off to India and replaced by General Claude Auchinleck.

In November 1941, Auchinleck's desert force – now renamed the British Eighth Army – tried again.[9] Operation CRUSADER, the new offensive, lasted for over seven weeks. It was victory of a kind. Rommel's outnumbered army, worn down by losses, had to retreat back into Libya. The British garrison in the Cyrenaican port of Tobruk, which had been under siege since April, was relieved. But the Army's performance on the battlefield had once again been deeply unsatisfactory. Badly choreographed British tank attacks had generated the same disproportionally high losses. Auchinleck was forced to concede to his superiors in a confidential post-mortem on the battle that 'our armoured forces are incapable of meeting the enemy in the open, even when superior to him in numbers'.[10]

Any reassurance the Army was able to extract from the partial success of CRUSADER was dispelled almost immediately when news arrived of disaster thousands of miles to the east. On 8 December 1941, Japanese troops attacked British, Dutch and American colonies throughout East and South East Asia. Hong Kong fell on Christmas Day, Singapore fifty-two days later. But Britain's humiliation in the Far East did not end there. Japanese forces in Thailand poured across the border into Burma. On 7 March 1942, the colony's capital Rangoon had to be abandoned. Its garrison, accompanied by over half a million British and Indian civilians, was forced to flee northwards towards the Indian frontier – a 900-mile trek through mountainous, malarial jungle in monsoon season. More than 50,000 men, women and children died on the way.[11] India itself now stood on the front line, poorly defended and ripe for invasion. 'Cannot work out why our troops are not fighting better,' General Alan Brooke, the new chief of the Imperial General Staff, wrote in his diary as news reached him in Britain of the growing disaster in Burma. 'If the Army cannot fight better than it is doing at present we shall deserve to lose our Empire!'[12]

On 26 May 1942, just as the scale of this defeat in the East was being absorbed, Rommel reopened the fighting in North Africa by launching a surprise attack on the Eighth Army's defensive line at Gazala in Cyrenaica. Despite Rommel's forces being outnumbered both in soldiers and tanks, they swiftly outflanked the British. By 14 June, Auchinleck had no choice but to order his men to pull back. It was a withdrawal which quickly turned into a 'vast cattle stampede' of soldiers and vehicles, an eleven-day, 320-mile race along the coastal road to Alexandria, during which the British had to abandon vast dumps of petrol, food, water and ammunition to the enemy. Over 25,000 British and Commonwealth soldiers slipped away unaccounted for from their units, some returning after a few days, others disappearing for weeks or months.[13] A South African division was ordered to hold fast in Tobruk, but the port's defences had been neglected since the end of the siege six months earlier. On 21 June, the garrison of 35,000 men in Tobruk surrendered. Churchill received the news in the White House Oval Office where he was meeting President Roosevelt. When the telegram was handed to him, the prime minister visibly winced – the first time his military attaché General Ismay had ever seen him do such a thing. It was, admitted Brooke in his diary, a 'staggering blow'.[14] From a strictly operational point of view, Tobruk's fall was not so very important. But the Libyan port had acquired a symbolic value far exceeding its military significance. To lose it after all the effort and sacrifice made in holding it the previous year was deeply humiliating. It was Singapore all over again.

The crisis reached its height on Wednesday, 1 July 1942, twenty-six years to the day since Haig's New Army had been slaughtered on the Somme. Rommel's men were now just sixty miles from Alexandria. Auchinleck's troops dug in at a coastal railway junction just short of the Nile Delta called El Alamein, in expectation of making a desperate last stand. At the British Embassy and Army General Headquarters in Cairo, preparations began to abandon the Nile base entirely. Clerks set alight massive heaps of classified documents; the day later became known as 'Ash Wednesday', in memory of the clouds of smouldering paper fragments which had drifted across Cairo like black snow. Gleeful Egyptian civilians excited to see their British occupiers on the verge of total defeat prepared red, white and black bunting to greet Rommel's troops. Italian and German flags were openly displayed in shops.[15] Mussolini himself, it was said, had flown from Rome to Libya, bringing with him a white horse on which he planned to ride in the victory parade through Egypt's capital.

Mussolini never got his parade. Rommel's advance to El Alamein represented the high-watermark of German and Italian success in North Africa.[16] In Burma, too, the Japanese paused along the River Chindwin, unable to maintain the momentum of their progress westwards. The war in both theatres was, in fact, at a crucial turning point, beyond which Allied fortunes were going to dramatically improve. With hindsight, we can see that things in autumn 1942 were not really as bleak as they looked. But *at the time*, the British Army appeared, quite simply, to be a lost cause – an army incapable of defeating the Germans or the Japanese, even from a position of numerical superiority. Minor victories against the weaker Axis satellites, the Italians and the Vichy French, were little compensation for the humiliations of Singapore and Tobruk. Cyril Joly and his men in the Western Desert felt 'baffled by the monotonous sequence of our disasters . . . our pride bruised, our confidence battered, we were all sensitive about our defeats and a little hurt by the feeling that perhaps our worth was in dispute.'[17] At home, the press was losing patience. 'After the French debacle the public surveyed the scene and accepted the explanation that we lost because our equipment was inferior to that of the Nazis', wrote *Tribune*'s military critic shortly after Singapore's fall in early 1942. 'I doubt whether these early explanations will satisfy in future.' The root problem, he thought, was that:

> The training prescribed for the British Army has been, and continues to be,
> utterly inadequate for the tasks it has to face . . . we have not only prepared
> weapons for the wrong war, we have not only developed a strategy for the
> wrong war, but we have also prepared our soldiers for a war which has not
> happened.[18]

After all, by 1942 the Army had had almost two years to recover from Dunkirk. If its equipment was still inferior, *why* was it inferior? If its training was inadequate, *why* was it inadequate? 'The Germans still have the better all-purpose gun; the better tank; the better plane', complained war correspondent Alan Moorehead after the surrender of Tobruk. 'The Germans always mass their fire-power . . . they have more training than we have', he continued. 'Quick decision men – that's what we lack most of all.'[19] The *Daily Mirror* blamed an 'absence of control' at the top. 'We have been content to sit and let the enemy make every move. When we did move it was too late.'[20] There was, thought Arthur Kellas, a worrying mismatch between the amiable 'picnic warfare' being practised by his own side and the 'alarming lesson in efficiency in violence and destruction' that the Germans were offering.[21] 'The strength and efficiency of the enemy were becoming evident and our own insufficiency and indolence already appalling to me.'[22]

As for the Army back in Britain, it was facing a crisis of its own in 1942, albeit of a less imminently catastrophic kind. An epidemic of absenteeism had broken out. Desertion and Absence without Leave (AWL) – the distinction between the two offences is largely a matter of interpretation – had reached unprecedented proportions.[23] In almost every unit, there were, as the Army's official history of wartime morale later put it, a 'constant, and by no means negligible, proportion' of men disappearing from camps and bases.[24] An average of 1,650 soldiers were having to be struck off the active duty rolls each month because they had been missing for over twenty-one days. Even though eight out of ten of these men would ultimately return to their units (either of their own volition or because they had been caught and arrested), their temporary absences were all the same causing a serious headache for their commanding officers.[25]

And there were other indications that morale in the ranks was in a perilously fragile state. Prolonged inactivity on dull anti-invasion tasks had worn down patience, inducing what John Guest called an 'awful mental constipation', borne of the tediousness of day-to-day ritual. 'To do the smallest thing outside the routine of mere living is an intolerable effort', he wrote in his diary. 'It is as though one's whole energy is absorbed in mere endurance – making one's bed, keeping clean, washing mess-tins, cleaning the camp, fetching water, polishing buttons and badges.'[26] When he subsequently became a junior officer in a Lancashire battalion, Guest saw much the same resigned despair in the faces of the men he now commanded. They were, it seemed, 'little better than prisoners', serving without purpose or any hope of release:

> If we were abroad it would be better, but here, seeing the buses and the trains that could take them to their homes . . . never have I felt so acutely what is broadly referred to as 'the pity of war'. I have always been inclined to

think of it in terms of violence, loss of life, rather than this inconspicuous sadness.[27]

The War Office's quarterly morale reports for 1942 made for sobering reading. The typical British soldier, they warned, felt unappreciated and underemployed.[28] According to a private in the Black Watch, conscripts had become mentally conditioned to see themselves as 'inferior beings'.[29] 'The Army today is grumbling and mumbling, murmuring and muttering, simmering with tales of discontent', thought journalist Frank Owen. 'I can scarcely find a man who does not profess his burning desire to be in mufti. The man who admits he is glad to be a soldier is regarded as a crank.'[30] Tommy Atkins, in short, was thoroughly Browned Off.

An Australian journalist-turned-soldier, Alan Wood (writing under the *nom de guerre* of 'Boomerang'), laid out his own thoughts on the Army's condition that spring in a brilliant, scathing critique called *Bless 'Em All*. The book was considered so inflammatory that the *Spectator*'s reviewer accused its author of 'doing Hitler's work for him'.[31] But Wood's argument clearly struck a chord. *Bless 'Em All* sold 37,000 copies in its first fifteen months of publication. Even the secretary of state for war, Sir P. J. Grigg, was forced to admit that he had read it.[32]

According to Wood, the Army in 1942 was being run by men with an obsession with drill and spit-and-polish to the neglect of all other duties; by COs with a 'childish delight in arranging [troops] in regular patterns', moving them like clockwork toys in 'a rigid, mechanical motion', rather than doing anything with them more immediately relevant to the conditions of modern warfare. Bullshit had become an end in itself, rather than a means to discipline and good order; a way to fill up time in the least imaginative, most useless way possible. There was, thought Wood, something perverse about hundreds of thousands of fighting men spending their days cleaning, scrubbing, washing, cooking and darning rather than training for battle. He wondered aloud why an entire generation of young men had been called into military service simply (it seemed, anyway) in order to release large numbers of unskilled labourers, kitchen maids and charwomen for highly remunerated work in armament factories. As these barbs suggest, there was a touch of wounded masculine pride to *Bless 'Em All*, a suggestion that the Army, far from making men of its soldiers, was symbolically neutering them. It was hardly gratifying to the male ego, Wood complained, to know that the war wound you were likeliest to receive as a British soldier in 1942 was housemaid's knee. The Army, he concluded, had settled on a 'tailor's dummy, clothes-horse conception' of the military life, one dangerously divorced from the blitzkrieg spirit of the age.[33]

Drill and spit-and-polish were hardly military innovations in 1942; and they had always been defended on the grounds that even though they might seem irrelevant to modern warfare, they all the same inculcated in the soldier qualities which remained vital to his trade even in the twentieth century – an unhesitating obedience to orders, and the habit of paying close attention to small details which (in a different context) might make the difference between life and death. Drill, so the argument went, encouraged a diverse group of men not just to march together, but to work and fight together. Spit-and-polish taught self-respect and made you a precise, proud, efficient, dutiful member of a military unit. It was necessary that the soldier, as Ian Hay put it in a radio broadcast in 1940, be 'clean, sober, punctual . . . and perpetually, as it were, on his toes', because 'the more perfectly trained and disciplined the unit as a whole, the greater the individual safety of each member of that unit.'[34]

Many soldiers would later attest to the truth of this. Dunkirk veteran Roy Close felt it was brought home to him by the behaviour of BEF troops disembarking at Dover. The men who had clearly lost heart shuffled along in unbuttoned tunics, while those who despite everything still held on to their pride and composure formed threes and marched smartly away from the quayside.[35] Peter Carrington, who as a regular Guards subaltern saw more than his fair share of military drill and bullshit, reflected after the war that its purpose was respectable enough – in principle, at least. 'I don't think attention to detail, insistence on correctitude in small observances, is contemptible,' he wrote:

> But it should be kept in proportion, and by some the proportions were in those days unhealthily exaggerated. The theory . . . was that officers and men who had been trained and disciplined to get every small personal detail right, whether in drill, dress, cleanliness or whatever, would similarly expect and observe the highest possible standards in every duty they were called upon to perform. *If it's worth doing, it's worth doing properly* was often heard . . . the trouble was that a lot of things were also worth doing which we didn't do at all.[36]

Professor C. W. Valentine of the University of Birmingham came to a similar conclusion in a guide for Army instructors published in 1943. It was all very well to assume, he wrote, that 'the repeated performance of boring obnoxious things' would set up a 'general habit of obedience'. But it seemed more likely to Valentine that a man asked to do flagrantly futile things would come to suspect that other things he was asked to do were futile as well – even if they were not. The importance of 'general neatness, cleanliness and pride in appearance' was, he thought, accepted by most British troops. But what they did not accept was the lack of proportionality in the time spent doing such things.[37] As one brigadier put it in his morale report to the War Office in 1940, it was not that conscripts wanted to avoid bullshit and drill simply because they were lazy. It was rather that they were wartime soldiers, and therefore much quicker than peacetime regulars 'to differentiate between war efficiency and "spit-and-polish" efficiency'.[38]

Attitudes towards bullshit and drill tended to highlight a broader difference in outlook between regular and wartime soldiers. It was not just that peacetime recruits were more habituated to spit-and-polish than conscripts, though, of course, they were. It was also that conscripts had a greater personal interest in getting the war over with as quickly as possible. The expansion of the Army after 1940 had meant rapid promotion for many regulars. Those amongst them who wanted to squirrel themselves away in comfortable depot jobs were able to do so with little difficulty. A quick and victorious end to the war would, for such men, be disastrous: it would mean the loss of pay, rank and personal comforts. One of Harry Wilson's company sergeant majors made no secret of the fact that he wanted the war to go on for ever.[39] This is not to deny the courage and steadfastness of many regulars serving in front-line units. They had 'an austerity which is useful for war', thought John Mulgan, 'and you thanked God when you met them – the straight-backed, humourless, reliable men, without imagination but also without temperament, who did what they said they would do and often got killed in the process'.[40] But other Old Sweats were less impressive. 'They pretended they knew all there was to know about everything but actually didn't know a great deal at all', thought Bill Cheall of the peacetime ex-regulars recalled to his battalion of the Green Howards in 1939. 'We got the impression that they were only a pack of scroungers . . . they were not very reliable and gradually crawled their way into jobs where they felt sure they would not take part in any battles.'[41] There was, thought Reg Crimp, a 'pretty clannish, closed-shop trade-union' attitude amongst the regulars of his unit. Years of civilian condescension towards the licentious soldiery were not going to be forgiven overnight.[42]

Weapons instruction and tactical training, geared towards relatively unedu-cated peacetime soldiers, were a widespread source of frustration during the war. The teaching system, complained one conscript soldier, had been designed for the needs of 'rural ploughmen' rather than intelligent modern citizens.[43] Rote memorization and the repetitive 'naming of parts' (a process immortal-ized in Henry Reed's 1942 poem of the same name) were as much as many regular NCO instructors could manage. Such men paid far more attention to the unvarying repetition of the textbook training language itself than any meaning it might possess. 'I got the impression', noted Peter Ustinov of his time in basic training, 'that most of the noncommissioned officers had a vocabulary of 10 words, used in an infinity of different ungrammatical patterns.' The conscripts, he thought, 'came armed with words and even sentences, but they had nowhere to put them, nowhere to practise them.'[44] Valentine remarked on a tendency by some NCOs to regard the exact duplication of training verbiage as superseding any other consideration. Too many corporals and sergeants treated the names of weapons parts 'with the same awe as a child regards his catechism.[45] When Norman Craig was seconded to teach a weapons' instruction class, he was told to begin every lesson with the words, '*What we're going on with now is . . .*' One day he decided to exercise a little variation by beginning, 'Now, the lesson I propose to take this morning is . . .' He found himself sharply rebuked by the presiding NCO for this 'presumptuous originality.'[46]

Weapons training seemed, in any case, to be something the Army hurried through as fast as possible in order to make more time for what really interested it – more drill and spit-and-polish. Dennis Newland, who was called up from his job at the Midland Bank to become an electrical repairman in the Royal Corps of Signals, did not resent hours spent learning weapons skills and technical information about his job. What he did resent was what he called 'pointless polishing and unnecessarily imposed discipline, such as saluting officers when off-duty.'[47] Men such as Newland were all too aware that massive battles that were going to settle the fate of mankind were being fought on the Eastern Front at the precise same moment that they were busy polishing their boots. 'Britain blancoes while Russia bleeds', one commando was heard to grumble as he dyed his webbing for the umpteenth time.[48]

To journalist Frank Owen, who provided Wood with a preface for *Bless 'Em All*, the basic mistake the Army was making in 1942 was its belief that it could train worldlier and better-educated wartime conscripts in the same way that it had always trained its peacetime regulars. These men were no longer 'the dregs of the community', he insisted, but 'grown-up, fit citizens' who needed to be handled very differently. 'In two years' struggle', noted Owen, 'the Army has grown enormously. But 'it still has all the old merits and the old defects, without conforming to the new realities around it.'[49]

One of those old defects which was being particularly resistant to the realities of the age was the Army officer selection process. The service's need for junior leaders during the Second World War was insatiable. In September 1939, it had just 14,000 regular and 19,000 Territorial officers, far too few to command a conscript army.[50] By the beginning of 1941, 54,000 emergency commissions had already been granted, and by the end of the war over 210,500 men had been elevated into the officer corps.[51] There were never enough. Demand far outstripped supply.[52] The War Office had no choice in the end but to ask the Australian and Canadian armies to loan it some of their excess regimental officers to make up the numbers.[53]

Army policy on officer selection in 1939 was founded, somewhat uneasily, on the experience of the First World War. As the BEF had haemorrhaged junior officers in the battles of that war, so the War Office had had no choice but to commission men from the ranks en masse rather than simply relying, as it had done before 1914, on the county squirearchy and upper-middle class service families to provide candidates. By 1916 it had gone even further, announcing that future wartime commissions would be given only to men who had served a period in the ranks (though time in a public school or university Officer Training Corps was allowed to count towards this).[54] Overall, three in five officers during the First World War came from non-traditional backgrounds.[55] Over 1,000 of them were former coalminers, 168 ex-navvies.[56]

After the 1918 Armistice, the broad democratizing trends that had begun to sweep Britain made it difficult to abandon this experiment in upward social mobility completely. In 1924, a commission chaired by the former secretary of state for war, Lord Haldane, concluded that in the future it would be neither 'necessary nor desirable to confine the selection of officers to any one class of the community'.[57] The 'Y' Scheme, introduced in 1922, allowed junior NCOs to apply for a cadetship to Sandhurst or Woolwich with an exemption from the usual tuition costs.[58] But its impact, in the end, was slight. Most of the ex-rankers who availed themselves of the Y Scheme ended up in unglamorous positions in the Army's 'tail' branches, notorious as promotional dead-ends. The principal teeth arms – the infantry, cavalry and artillery – went back to being officered by men of the old elite. Over eight in ten officer cadets between 1918 and 1939 were ex-public schoolboys. A third of them had gone to just ten schools.[59]

The majority of senior officers regarded this return to the old ways with equanimity, if not relief. To most of them, the creation of non-traditional officers during the war had been a regrettable emergency measure only. Although a few of the new subalterns had excelled, most had been 'poor in quality' because they lacked the necessary breeding to lead troops in battle.[60] Selfless qualities of leadership could not be acquired by training, went the argument, but only by absorption from birth in the culture of *noblesse oblige*. The 'temporary gentleman' of the trenches was remembered in the Britain of the 1920s and 1930s largely as a literary trope, and a tragic one at that – the man of humble origins, unnaturally raised above his station, only to have his genteel pretensions cruelly stripped from him on his return to civvy street.[61] In any case, the likelihood of ever needing so many officers again seemed so remote that it was a problem the Army scarcely thought worth worrying about.

So the outbreak of the Second World War caught it both off guard and unsure as to how to proceed. Clearly, its need for officers would be at least as great as it had been in the trenches (in fact, it would turn out to be greater; the ratio of officers to ORs, which had been 1:25 in the First World War, had fallen to just 1:15 by 1943.)[62] Such a large number of vacancies would require a broad approach to candidate selection. Leslie Hore-Belisha, who had little sympathy for the Blimpish domination of the officer corps in any case, rejoiced at this. 'In this Army', he announced to the public in October 1939, 'the star is within every private soldier's reach. No-one, however humble or exalted his birth, need be afraid that his military virtues will remain unrecognized.'[63] Others remained unconvinced. John Dill (educated at Cheltenham College), who served as Churchill's second wartime CIGS, worried that only public school-boys really possessed the social *gravitas* to lead working-class soldiers effectively. 'Men will follow and work better for some lad who is a gentleman', he insisted, 'it has always been so.' Anthony Eden (an Eton old boy) agreed. Promotion without reference to social background might be all very well in the RAF, where officers were primarily technicians, he mused. But the main role of an Army subaltern was to be a leader. And leaders did not hail from board schools.[64]

In practice, for all the War Office's talk of meritocracy, officer selection in the early years of the war continued to favour traditional candidates. Possession of a 'Certificate B' confirming attendance at a university Officer Training Corps (OTC) programme made you eligible for immediate commissioning. Men who had earned the less advanced 'Certificate A' from a public school OTC were expected to serve some time in the ranks before being referred to an OCTU, but they were earmarked from the beginning as potential officers, and placed in special platoons with their own barracks which were often excused fatigues and other mundane duties. Such favouritism provoked much resentment amongst those who were excluded. 'Open-minded and intelligent men just arrived from civil life who have accepted the pontifical statements in the press that the Army is democratic' would not take kindly to being so obviously left out of the chosen few almost from the day they first wore uniform, warned a 1940 morale report.[65] Moreover, sequestering potential officers away from ordinary soldiers rather negated the whole point of them spending time in the ranks in the first place – they were hardly likely to get much sense of the rank-and-file soldier's point of view if they never had any contact with him.[66]

Men with neither Certificate A nor B who nonetheless aspired to a commission could only bide their time and hope for a personal recommendation from their commanding officer, to be followed if successful by a one-on-one interview with their divisional or district commander, or from September 1940 onwards, a three-man Command Interview Board. It was a system rife with inconsistencies and abuses. By mid-1941, the secretary of state for war was being harried by dozens of parliamentary questions on the alleged horrors of the Command Interview Board system every week.[67] Men who had attended such boards complained that their interlocutors had been far more concerned with calculating their wealth and social status than in discovering whether they possessed any more objective evidence of leadership qualities. The only thing Eric Ambler's Board members wanted to know was how much money a writer of thrillers could make (he plucked the figure of £1,500 a year out of the air, drawing appreciative murmurs. 'Nothing long haired or scruffy about fifteen-hundred a year' was practically etched on their brows.)[68] Norman Craig was asked if his father was wealthy enough to loan him £5 if he ever 'got into a scrape'. The Boards were also keen to ferret out any signs of suspect intellectualism. Craig's admission that he enjoyed reading poetry in his spare time almost sank his initial application, which was only salvaged by the hasty addition that he also played rugger for his battalion.[69] Gerald Kersh was confronted with a scarlet-faced colonel who demanded to know if he read The Times, if he was a Bolshevik, and what he would do if he were given £50 and a fortnight's holiday (Kersh had memorized the right answer: 'Take a nice long walking tour in Wales.')[70] Julian Maclaren-Ross knew of a corporal with a splendid physique and spotless military record who was turned down by a Scottish Board because he could not tell them what the length of the Forth Bridge was – though the real reason, thought Maclaren-Ross, was the man's pronounced cockney accent.[71] By contrast, Leslie Philips sailed through his pre-OCTU interview, even though he was a Tottenham factory worker's son, because stage school elocution lessons had equipped him with a pitch-perfect simulacrum of a patrician accent. 'Nobody would have guessed that I had never been at Radley, Harrow, or Wellington.'[72]

Even those aspirants fortunate enough to negotiate the Command Interview Board still had to pass through a three- or four-month OCTU course; and there they might be subject to still more withering snobbery. Jack Garnham-Wright and his fellow cadets were summoned to see their commanding officer because he was unhappy with the way they were buttering their bread in the dining hall. As 'every good person of breeding' was supposed to know – and they, apparently, did not – a piece of bread was only to be buttered at the moment before it was eaten. Another of his tests was to ask what a covey of partridges suddenly taking off from a small wood might indicate. Any cadet whose answer had some immediate military bearing – for example, that the disturbance of the birds might indicate enemy movement in the wood – was sharply rebuked. '*There is a fox in the coppice!*' he would explain. '*As any gentleman worthy of the name would know.*' The inference throughout his time at OCTU, thought Garnham-Wright, was undisguised: 'Cadets from nameless suburbs, and from nondescript state grammar schools could not expect to be admitted to the ranks of the elite.'[73] Under the Command Interview Board system, an ex-public schoolboy was fourteen times more likely to become an infantry officer than a soldier who had attended a state school.[74] The British Army was fighting for democracy; but its commitment to equality seemed shaky at best.

Stories like those of Garnham-Wright's had by spring 1942 provoked left-leaning newspapers such as the *Daily Mirror* into Blimp-hunting. 'WEED THEM OUT!' it thundered in one leader column. The Army was being led by 'brass-buttoned boneheads, socially prejudiced, arrogant and fussy', with a profound knowledge of 'the last war but two'.[75] Britain's soldiers themselves were blameless for their recent spate of defeats, insisted the *Mirror*: 'No men ever fought more courageously or more doggedly.'[76] The Army's misfortunes since the outbreak of war were the result of decisions over which the ordinary Tommy had had no control.

For some of those brass-buttoned boneheads, however, the problem was very different. From their point of view, the Army's mid-war malaise was not being caused by its disdain for democracy, but by its hasty and unwise embrace of it. Even before the disasters of 1942, complaints were already being voiced at high rank that the officer corps was being hollowed out. 'Our new armies are being officered by classes of society who are new to the job', suggested OCTU commanding officer Lieutenant-Colonel R. C. Bingham in a letter to *The Times* in January 1941. 'These classes, unlike the old aristocratic and feudal (almost) classes who led the old Army, have never had "their people" to consider', he proposed:

> They have never had anyone to think of but themselves . . . they have been reared in an atmosphere in which the State spoon feeds everybody from cradle to grave, and no-one feels any responsibility for his fellow men.[77]

Bingham's imprudent sally was to cost him his command; the Army could not be seen publicly to underwrite such blatant snobbery. But his views were certainly held by other senior officers, even if they were more cautious in how they expressed them. By spring 1942, fears of a breakdown in Army man-management at home were growing – that there existed, as a War Office morale report put it, 'a deplorably large proportion of officers who fail to care properly

for their men's welfare and to inspire their men's respect'.[78] To the traditional-
ists, this crisis was being caused by the commissioning of the products of
obscure secondary schools and nameless concrete suburbs. What you got for
all your democratizing of the officer corps were 'cute and brainy' subalterns
rather than those with old-fashioned character – men epitomized by second
lieutenant Hooper in Evelyn Waugh's *Brideshead Revisited* (1945), junior
officers who were overly familiar with the ORs yet insufficiently considerate
of their real needs.[79] The commander of one training brigade remarked
upon the 'cynical indifference to responsibility' characteristic of subalterns
hailing from what he called 'the smaller universities'.[80] Could such milksop
grammar school boys ever be expected to lead soldiers to victory against the
Wehrmacht?

But the problem of officer selection was only the start of it. To the tradition-
alists, the mass of ordinary soldiers themselves had become corrupted by
hand-outs and easy living. They had, it was suggested, lost the stoicism and
instinctive confidence in authority which had maintained the Army throughout
the gruelling years of the First World War. Haig's soldiers, wrote Major R. A. C.
Radcliffe in an essay for *Army Quarterly*, had been of a generation which had
been content, on the whole, to receive orders and to obey them without much
questioning:

> They showed very little inclination to write to the popular press about their
> grievances and frustrations (a then unknown word), and they were compar-
> atively content with such simple pleasures as concerts, comforts and canteens,
> with an occasional hot bath. And although they might on occasion get fed
> up, it did not enter their simple heads that they were more or less entitled to
> get periodically 'browned off' when things were not to their liking.

Two decades of social improvements, 'spoon-fed amusement' and expanded
public education – producing men with 'the doubtful advantage of being able
to repeat the thoughts and sayings of others ... without giving them the
compensating power of intelligent criticism' – had produced an army of
conscripts that was simply not willing to do what it was told.[81]

This was a refrain that pre-dated the war. Social critics had long been
warning that the sons of the Empire were becoming weak, pampered, unmanly.
It was disturbing, wrote youth organizer Sidney Hatton in 1931, to see 'soft-
faced, mealy-mouthed, pomaded puppets' giving themselves over to the 'softer
delights of the cinema and dance hall' rather than those vigorous pursuits of
boxing and football that stouter-hearted British boys had once enjoyed.[82] The
state's spoon-feeding of benefits from cradle to grave had created 'a fool's para-

dise of youth', as one lieutenant-colonel put it in 1938: the demand for amusement and pleasure had driven out any sense of self-sacrifice from within the young. '*Strew my path with roses and give me a good time*' was all that the modern boy wanted to hear.[83] The journal of the National Association of Boys' Clubs compared with alarm the 'shadowy and shiftless manhood' of Britain's spoiled brats with the 'men of heroic mould' being produced by the *Hitler Jugend* movement in Germany – full of youngsters with 'concrete ideals' and 'martial values'.[84]

This was a critique with a specifically class dimension. The blurring of social status since 1918, the democratization of leisure, the decline in the culture of hierarchical deference, the ever-greater opportunities open to those in Britain without wealth or status – all those things which made the citizen soldier of the 1940s very different from the man his father had been a quarter century before – were said to be precisely the problem. A generation had grown up that had never had to strive. To Herbert Moran, president of the Medical Board at Colchester Military Hospital in 1941, there had been far too much of a tendency since the Armistice 'to put the emphasis on intelligence rather than character' in Britain, to think about rights and comforts rather than duties and burdens, to disseminate within the young working-class male in particular 'an aggressive selfishness' that had whittled away at his self-discipline. There had, Moran thought, been 'quite definitely a decrease in the spirit of pugnacity' in the youth of the nation. Something had happened to British soldiers; they had become moral pygmies, stunted by the easy life and security that they had enjoyed as civilians. 'The old spirit of adventure' had died out in them; 'their capacity for endurance had shrivelled. They were 'oppressed, harassed, fretted by the new conditions' of military service, distressed by their separation from loved ones and troubled by a communal life few of them had ever known before. Even sleeping on a single mattress on the floor of a requisitioned hotel was an intolerable burden to many of them. They wore their uniforms not with pride, but as a 'garb of shame'.[85]

Some generals saw a direct link between the sort of generational decline highlighted by Moran and the Army's military failures. In his confidential dossier for the War Cabinet on the lessons of the failed Norway expedition in 1940, General Auchinleck complained (in a section later excised from the published version of the report) that:

> By comparison with the French, or the Germans, for that matter, our men for the most part seemed distressingly young, not so much in years as in self-reliance and manliness generally. They give an impression of being callow and undeveloped, which is not reassuring for the future, unless our

methods of man-mastership and training for war can be made more realistic and less effeminate.[86]

General Edmund Ironside, chief of the Imperial General Staff in the opening
months of the war, fretted after Dunkirk that 'the namby-pamby people that
have grown up in late years are not to be trusted in this emergency'.[87] Henry
Pownall, Gort's chief of staff during the campaign in France, went further. 'As a
nation we have got fat and lazy', he wrote in his diary. 'Hitlerism has at least
inspired the spirit of self-sacrifice in his nation – with us there is no such spirit
of service. People have thought only of what they could get from the State, not
what they can give.'[88] He continued on this theme after the defeat at Singapore
two years later: 'The temper of an army is bound to be largely the reflex of the
temper of a Nation. And the Nation has grown soft this 20 years.' There had
been too much 'fat living . . . self-interest; amusement'.[89] Secretary of state for
war Sir P. J. Grigg felt, too, that a 'general pansydom' had afflicted Britain's
youth, a sapping of masculine character which was undermining the troops'
willingness to endure.[90] An anonymous rant included in Grigg's files and dating
from early 1942 sums up the Blimpish position in uncompromising language:

> The Army is <u>LISTLESS</u> and <u>LAZY</u>. It is too conscious of the absence of
> luxury its soldiers engaged in in peacetime . . . it must be explained that all
> <u>BLAME, SHAME lies on every individual</u>; that they didn't want conscrip-
> tion in peacetime; that they allowed Baldwin to do nix – and liked it; that
> they enjoyed and enjoy a high standard of living; that they are soft; they
> have been found wanting. They must bow their head in shame until their
> exertion wins the war.[91]

Not everyone who held such a view was necessarily blind to the Army's other
problems. British troops, complained Alan Brooke to Grigg in March 1942,
were being 'called upon to fight despite deficiencies in nearly all types of
weapons'.[92] Brooke was not sparing of his own generals either. 'Half our Corps
and Divisional commanders are totally unfit for their appointments', he
lamented in his diary. 'And yet if I were to sack them I could find no better!
They lack character, imagination, drive and powers of leadership.'[93] But in his
darker moods, the CIGS was also known to expound to his deputies on the
'low quality of our people, the lack of ideas, the sloppy thinking encouraged at
the universities' and the 'general softness and pleasure-seeking of the pre-war
years'.[94] Writing to the Indian viceroy Archibald Wavell in the wake of the
disasters in Singapore and Burma, Brooke argued that 'we are not anything like
as tough as we were in the last war. There has been far too much luxury, safety

first, red triangle etc. in this country. Our one idea is to look after our comforts and avoid being hurt in any way.'[95] Wavell agreed, blaming 'softness in education and living' for the collapse in the Far East.[96]

Churchill was even more vociferous in his criticism of the high command. At a dinner party at Chequers in April 1941, the prime minister threatened that if Egypt fell he would have all the commanders in the Middle East shot.[97] The following year, at a particularly disputatious War Cabinet meeting, Churchill peppered his angry comments about the Army's failures with asides to Brooke such as '*Have you not got a single general in that army who can win battles, have none of them any ideas, must we continually lose battles in this way?*'[98] The prime minister bewailed the Army's unimaginative handling by its leaders, its shoddy equipment, its obsolete training methods. Yet Churchill also suspected that something was lacking in the common British soldier. 'In 1915', he told his old friend Violet Bonham-Carter after the fall of Singapore, 'our men fought on even when they only had one shell and were under a fierce barrage. Now they cannot resist dive bombers.'[99] 'I don't know what we can do', Churchill said of the Eighth Army in the wake of the Gazala disaster later that year. 'All our efforts to help them seem to be in vain.'[100] The surrender of Tobruk hit him just as hard as Singapore. 'I am ashamed', he confessed. 'More than thirty thousand of our men put up their hands. If they won't fight . . .'[101]

It comes as a shock to us today, after years of hearing of the hardscrabble origins and stoic toughness of Britain's wartime 'Greatest Generation', to hear such views – and from Churchill, no less. But the prime minister in 1942 was simply expressing the feelings of many of his own age and background. He was a member of the patrician class which had reached adulthood before the First World War. To men such as Churchill, there was little to admire about the young people of the 1940s. The new civilization of dance halls and motor-coaches and cheap retail goods that J. B. Priestley had written about so approvingly in 1934 left them unmoved. Such things were not signs of progress, but of decay, of everything that had been going wrong with Britain since 1918. Now, in 1942, deficits in character caused by years of spoon-feeding and soft living and the facile benefits of universal education were threatening to bring Britain to destruction. Perhaps the Navy and the Air Force, which had the luxury of choosing the best of those who remained of Britain's youth, would be all right. But what of the Army? Where, now, were those gritty, imperturbable Britons who had beaten the Kaiser's troops so soundly on the Western Front? What had happened to such myrmidons? The British soldier's regimental insignia, even his uniform and weapons, were much the same as they had been a quarter of a century before. But what of the man inside that uniform? Would he ever be able to measure up to his father?[102]

CHAPTER 6

GET SOME SERVICE IN

On the night of 30 May 1940, a small group of men crossed the beach adjoining the little Flanders sea coast town of La Panne, climbed into a collapsible canvas boat they found among the dunes, and pushed off into the English Channel. They were an unlikely group of nocturnal sailors. At the oars were Brigadier Frederick Lawson, Royal Artillery commander of the British 48th Infantry Division, and several of his staff officers. Serving as coxswain was General Sir Ronald Forbes Adam, the commander (until a few hours before, anyway) of the rearguard forces which at that moment were defending the shrinking perimeter of the British Expeditionary Force along a perilously thin line stretching northwards to Nieuport and down to the main evacuation point at the harbour of Dunkirk. Earlier in the day, Adam had received orders from the BEF's commander-in-chief, Lord Gort, to return to Britain. Now, like everyone else in Gort's disintegrating army, he was improvising his escape from France as best he could.

The boat made some distance from the beach on what was fortunately a glass-still sea. After a little while, Adam's party saw a British destroyer anchored offshore, on to which they were hoisted. They were not the Royal Navy's only guests on board that night. To his great pleasure, Adam discovered that his old friend Alan Brooke, commander of the BEF's now-defunct II Corps, had also been ordered back to Britain and was making his way in the same vessel. The destroyer's captain gave the two generals his cabin to rest in. Brooke, who had scarcely slept more than a few hours all week, dozed off almost immediately in the main bunk. Adam sat in a chair, browsing by invitation through Brooke's diary until he too fell asleep. By nightfall, the destroyer had weighed anchor and was making its way back across the Channel. Its exhausted passengers scarcely even heard the sounds of falling bombs or the rattle of the anti-aircraft guns firing just a few yards away from where they slept. When they got back to Dover the following morning, Adam and Brooke drove together to Whitehall to brief the CIGS, General Dill, on the rapidly deteriorating situation in France. They had much to report, little of it good.[1]

Though it was simply an accident of war that Adam and 'Brookie' happened to accompany one another back to England from Dunkirk, there was all the same something nicely fitting about the coincidence. For these were the two men who, within eighteen months of the BEF's disaster, would be the most senior military figures on the Army Council: Brooke from December 1941 the chief of the Imperial General Staff, and thus Churchill's most senior military advisor; Adam his adjutant-general (AG), responsible for all matters of Army personnel, administration and welfare. It would fall to Brooke and Adam to take the shattered BEF and combine it with the conscript militia being raised at home to create a new force, perhaps capable one day of returning to France. The two men complemented one another's character and virtues. They had been subalterns together in the Royal Horse Artillery before the First World War, and had also served as fellow instructors at the Staff College at Camberley in the 1930s. They knew and trusted one another completely. Throughout the remainder of the war, they would dine together regularly whenever they were both in London. The CIGS was, in Adam's view, 'one of the most forward looking men that I have ever known, and with the soundest judgement'.[2] Brooke, for his part, would say of Adam in 1944, 'In spite of all the criticisms I have heard during the past year, and there have been many, I could not imagine anybody in the Army more capable than him to carry out the duties of AG'.[3] Too often the story of British high command during the Second World War was one of rivalries and intrigue: Dowding feuding with Leigh-Mallory, Slim with Wingate, Montgomery with, well, everybody. Brooke and Adam were the rare and agreeable exception: two intelligent, talented men who were able to work together smoothly and effectively.

Though Adam did not realize at it at the time, his trip across the Channel on the night of 30 May marked not just the end of his time with the BEF, but also the end of his short operational military career. For just a few months, he had been in command of Gort's reserve corps in France. His only real taste of action had come with his appointment as leader of the ad hoc defensive perimeter forces around Dunkirk; Adam's cool, well-organized handling of that task was later said to have extended the lifetime of the evacuation pocket by several days, saving tens of thousands of Allied troops from capture.[4] But he would never lead soldiers on the field of battle again. For a year after Dunkirk, Adam served as the General Officer Commanding (GOC) of Northern Command, responsible for the defence of the east coast of England from the Wash to the

Scottish border. Then in June 1941, he was appointed to the War Office as adjutant-general. This was a pressing and difficult assignment. It was Adam's job as AG to address the malaise in the mid-war Army, to adjudicate between the Blimps lamenting the pansification of British manhood and the grumblers in the lower ranks complaining of an Army obsessed with ramrod-stiff backs and immaculately sheened buttons.

'It was clear . . . that the morale of the Army at home was not as good as it should be', he wrote in his memoirs after the war:

> The war was not going well; the men had been inactive for some time except for those in the Air Defences of Great Britain; many were employed on guarding vulnerable points; they could not get home and see their families even when stationed quite close. Officers with little experience were not paying sufficient attention to their men's troubles, and often men were prevented from seeing their officers by senior NCOs, and this at a time when air raids were occurring, and the official announcement of vague areas of attack only increased the anxiety of the men.[5]

Yet, as Adam discovered on arriving in Whitehall in 1941, the Army did not even have any method of monitoring and assessing overall service morale. The War Office's traditional obsequiousness to the regiments, and its assumption that 'man-management' came naturally to gentleman-officers anyway, meant that the temper of the Army was not measured in any objective way at all. Whether or not this inattention had been acceptable when past AGs had had to deal merely with a small all-volunteer peacetime force, it made no sense at a time when the Army had become a mass levee of citizen-conscripts. One of Adam's early acts as adjutant-general, then, was to assemble the machinery for a comprehensive assessment of Army mood. A permanent Morale Committee was created. John H. Sparrow, a barrister, former fellow (later Warden) of All Souls, and literary polymath, was assigned to compile quarterly summaries on the morale situation at home and overseas by drawing on a variety of sources, including commanding officers' reports, the home intelligence surveys compiled by the Ministry of Information, disciplinary statistics, and excerpts from soldiers' letters which caught the eye of the official postal censors.[6] In a letter to his mother, Sparrow described the remit of his new job:

> You could not make a bigger mistake than to suppose that morale in battle is what the War Office is concerned about . . . the problem is exactly the reverse – to keep up the morale of the Army during long periods of boring inactivity . . . reports and enquiries are being made about pay,

entertainment, leave, food, accommodation, relations of officers and men, wrong men in wrong jobs etc. etc. – all the 1,001 things which go to make the Army contented or discontented. *That's* the present morale problem, which touches every side of Amy life. *Not* whether men run away in battle.[7]

Anyone judging the new adjutant-general by his appearance and pedigree might have been surprised at this new approach. A hereditary baronet, an Old Etonian and the physical embodiment of the stiff-upper-lipped regular officer – tall, handsome, square-jawed, impeccably groomed – Adam seemed, on the surface, the archetypal Blimp. But beneath that conventional exterior was a man of rare sympathy and intelligence, animated, as *The Times* would say in his obituary in 1983, 'by a passionate desire to extend the benefits of knowledge and social progress as widely as possible.'[8] He appreciated from the start of his tenure as adjutant-general that he was not simply going to be able to reverse a quarter-century of sweeping social change. The conscript of 1941 was the man his country had made him, for good or ill, and there was little that the War Office could do about it either way. For the duration of the war, then, the Army was going to have to come to terms with this peculiar interloper who now made up its ranks – to work out how to engage his best qualities and ameliorate his worst. The result would be a slew of reforms sponsored by Adam to shake up Army personnel selection, promotion, welfare arrangements and current affairs education.

In the eyes of some of his peers, these reforms made Adam the architect of a dangerously radical enterprise. Sparrow's early reports on the mood of the Army were regarded by P. J. Grigg as far too inflammatory, and the secretary of state for war threatened to have the whole Morale Committee broken up unless a more 'balanced' tone was introduced.[9] Churchill, an old soldier of the more traditional school, never warmed to the adjutant-general's methods (the modern Army, he complained, seemed more interested in 'dental chairs and YMCA institutions' than winning battles). Indeed, the prime minister tried on more than one occasion to remove the AG to some distantly impotent sinecure such as the governorship of Gibraltar. Only Brooke's firm backing saved him.[10] Though in later life he seems to have maintained a moderately left-of-centre political outlook, Adam's wartime critics probably exaggerated the extent of his radicalism. Not all of his views were necessarily progressive or indulgent. Up till the end of 1942 Adam continued to push without success, for instance, for the reintroduction of the death penalty for desertion in the face of battle.[11] The AG saw his reforms not as doctrinaire radicalism, but as simple, practical common-sense. The world had moved on from 1914. The Army was going to have to recognize that stubborn fact if it wanted to win the war. And he would do his best to make it do so.

* * *

It was only days after eighteen-year-old accounting clerk John Bain enlisted in the Argyll and Sutherland Highlanders that he realized he had made a big mistake. 'I found nothing in my temperament fitted me for the part of soldier', Bain (better known in later life as the poet Vernon Scannell) wrote. 'I was unpractical, any kind of mechanical apparatus threw me into a panic.' Elementary tasks such as cleaning his kit and appearing smartly on parade were beyond him. Even his uniform did not fit:

> I was fairly tall but at that time quite lean, so that trousers of suitable length were far too slack at the waist and the seat hung low and baggy like a Muslim's pantaloons. When I wore battle-order my small pack, which was supposed to sit high between the shoulder blades, would sag miserably near the small of my back *like a bloody parachute*, as one disgusted sergeant remarked.[12]

William Lucas, too, 'hated the army' from the moment he joined. 'I didn't get on,' he told an investigating criminologist in 1950. 'I didn't like discipline. I had always done whatever I wanted all my life and I couldn't change. I was too wild. I didn't like the company forced upon me in barracks. I wanted to be alone and to do as I liked. I was no asset to the army. I know that.'[13] Lucas, like Scannell, would end up deserting twice. Both men were caught and would do time in military prison for their offences. Some deserters were even more audacious serial offenders. Hughie MacIver, a stocky Glaswegian whom Scannell met while awaiting his own trial, spent more time in military detention during the war than he did with his unit. Eight times, the Army attempted to send him overseas. Eight times, he absconded. His closest call was when he was led in handcuffs to a troopship bound for North Africa:

> They thought they'd got me that time. They wouldna take off the cuffs till they'd got me on the big boat at Greenock. Rommel must have been aye worried when he heard I was on my way. I was a wee bit worried myself. But as soon as it got dark I was over the side like a flash and I had a mile's swim to the shore ... seven months it was before they caught up with me and they wouldn't have got me but I went and got drunk.[14]

Wartime desertion is usually framed today as a problem of *battlefield* trauma – of the shell-shocked soldier, distressed by his nightmarish experiences in combat, fleeing his unit in despair.[15] But three in five of all British troops who were convicted of deserting their units during the Second World War absconded while they were stationed in the United Kingdom, far away from the front line. The number of desertions amongst troops stationed overseas did not exceed those stationed at home until the final year of the war.[16] Absenteeism and desertion between 1939 and 1945 were primarily home service problems.

What to do with men such as Scannell, Lucas and MacIver – whether to punish, rehabilitate, or simply get rid of them – was one of the first challenges Adam faced as adjutant-general. As it happened, even before the war he had been interested in modern theories of personnel selection and how they might assist military discipline. He had read with approval the research of the National Institute of Industrial Psychology (which he would chair after the war), an organization co-founded by the psychologist Charles Myers, who had done some of the earliest work on shell shock during the First World War. He also knew that the American and German armies had invested much time in psychological theories of manpower selection.[17] Adam's interest in what was still widely held (as he complained in an open letter to all commands in December 1943) as 'a species of black magic' was unusual for a man of his rank.[18] But his penchant for 'trick-cyclists' would have great influence on the Army's wartime treatment of desertion. Although no two psychologists or psychiatrists ever agreed completely about the causes of 'problem soldiers' during the Second World War, one theme that ran consistently through their theories was *predisposition*. That is, men like Scannell were said to be innately prone to rejecting military discipline, either because of low intelligence, or due to some subconscious neurosis stemming from a traumatic childhood or adolescent experience. Enthusiasm for both 'constitutional' and Freudian explanations for human behaviour was at its height in the 1940s.[19] Examination of individual desertion cases seemed to bear out the claims of the predispositionists that mental backwardness or 'inadequate personality' could explain the decision of most men to abscond. In one late-war study, for instance, over half of the convicted deserters scrutinized were said to display signs of psychiatric instability. One in three had a pre-war history of difficulty adjusting to normal conditions at school or work.[20]

The starting point for reducing incidences of desertion, then, was to identify 'useless soldiers' in advance and to discharge them as quickly as possible from the service – and, ideally, to keep them out of the Army in the first place. Such pre-screening had only ever been cursorily attempted by the regular force, which had never been in a position to be especially picky about the men it took on, and which had always been ambivalent about whether stupidity in the soldier was really such a bad thing anyway. Such quality control as existed had been almost entirely abandoned during the frantic rush to absorb conscripts after Dunkirk, when a few minutes' conversation with a recruiting officer and a check of educational qualifications had been about as much of a vetting as most recruits had received. So within just a few weeks of arriving at the War Office in June 1941, Adam established a fully staffed Directorate for the Selection of Personnel (DSP). New recruits would now undertake pattern-identification testing to give a rough-and-ready sense of their innate intelligence, making it easier to spot 'dullards' at an early stage. Such DSP testing from 1942 onwards caused about one in fifty new recruits to be rejected outright for reasons of mental instability. Another one in twelve was flagged as showing signs of being so 'dull and backward' that he would need special training to be of any use to the Army.[21] During the first six months of Adam's tenure in the War Office, 7,800 soldiers diagnosed as neurotics were discharged from the Army.[22]

Mental predisposition could not explain all cases of absenteeism, however. By 1941, too many men who had otherwise shown themselves to be intelligent and well-balanced soldiers were also deserting or going AWL. The reasons for their unhappiness had to be identified. Investigation suggested that many absentees were abandoning their units because of concerns back at home. Some soldiers were worried about how their families were managing in the absence of the male breadwinner. Others were seeking information about parents, wives and children who lived in towns and cities that had been subjected to air raids. A disturbingly large number had received news, malicious or well founded, that their wives or girlfriends had been unfaithful to them, and had gone home either to try to save their tottering relationships, or, in a few cases, to enact revenge. The Army had made little allowance for such problems at the start of the war. Peacetime regulars had never been encouraged to maintain strong links with home. Most of them had left civilian life behind without so much as a backwards glance when they joined the service. But wartime conscripts who had enlisted in the Army strictly for the duration could not be expected to set aside their pre-war lives so readily.

The existing apparatus for dealing with family troubles was totally inadequate. Many soldiers were not even allowed to discuss their concerns with their own officers, leaving them (in their own minds anyway) with little option but to go AWL. To try to reduce this sense of desperation, Adam doubled the length of privilege leave for home troops in summer 1941 from two weeks to four, and made more flexible provision for the issuing of special compassionate leave. Junior officers were expected to offer 'request hours' each week in which soldiers could approach them confidentially with their concerns. Hundreds of Local Area Welfare Officers (LAWOs) were recruited to work in liaison with existing organizations such as the Soldiers' Sailors' and Airmen's Help Society and the Women's Voluntary Service to assist servicemen's wives with financial difficulties, and to help negotiate a reconciliation between husbands and wives suffering matrimonial problems caused by the strain of separation.[23]

Adam also sought to eliminate, or at least shorten, some of the more irksome features of the soldier's day-to-day life. Pay and sick parades, regarded by many men as a huge waste of time, were simplified. Unnecessary fatigue duties were truncated. Army Council Instructions (ACIs) were issued to all commands discouraging COs from excessive drill and spit-and-polish. Attempts were made to make instructional training less tedious by the dissemination of more imaginative teaching techniques and the use of films. Army food, a traditional source of complaint within the ranks ('one didn't expect cordon bleu cooking', recalled a sapper of the Royal Engineers training camp near Chester, 'but this was ghastly ... thick greasy stew in which wallowed huge lumps of fat, presumably masquerading as dumplings') was improved by the creation of a specially trained Army Catering Corps.[24] A Directorate of Welfare was established to coordinate better entertainment and recreation for off-duty men.[25]

One of the biggest sources of unhappiness within the mid-war Army was the placement of men in jobs to which they were poorly suited. As with the problem of 'useless soldiers', pre-war policies that had been exacerbated by the chaotic circumstances of 1940 were to blame. Each regiment and service corps of the regular peacetime Army had competed with the others for recruits, and had jealously hoarded the men it had got, regardless of whether it could usefully employ them. Parochial rivalries had been allowed to trump the common good. Two years into the war, absurdities abounded, picked up by the press and MPs, of sheet metal workers sweeping barrack-room floors, skilled mechanics working as cooks. Anthony Burgess saw 'men of great academic distinction ... clearing parade grounds of scraps of paper and specialising in the disposal of kitchen swill'.[26] Failure rates in trade training were unacceptably high – up to 27 per cent in some cases. A parliamentary committee appointed to investigate the issue estimated that fewer than half the engineers inducted into the Army since the outbreak of war had been allocated to any suitable technical job. The situation was regarded as so serious that the War Cabinet banned any further intake of engineers into the Army until it got its house in order.[27]

Adam sympathized with the critics. The War Office, he complained, was 'wasting its manpower in this war as badly as it did in the last', posting each man to a corps of service 'almost entirely on the need of the moment and without any effort to determine his fitness' for the job in question.[28] His answer, announced in January 1942 and first implemented that July, was the General Service Corps (GSC). This was a clearing house in which all new recruits would do their six weeks of basic training before allocation to a specific branch of the Army. During their time in the GSC, soldiers would be given intelligence and aptitude testing by DSP evaluators, whose job would be to assess what trades they were best fitted for, and to recommend them for eventual posting based on their particular skill-set. Only once they got to their new parent corps would they undergo specific vocational training – sixteen weeks for the infantry, and up to thirty weeks for a more technically demanding job as, say, a signaller.[29]

The GSC reform also afforded a way to improve the efficiency of officer training, for it, like trade selection, was perceived to be in crisis by 1941. The problem was not just one of discrimination against non-public school candidates, though that was certainly part of it. The more fundamental dilemma was that the Command Interview Board system was simply not working. Up to half of the cadets being recommended to OCTUs were subsequently failing their courses and having to be 'RTU'd' – Returned to Unit. This was a huge waste of Army time and resources.[30] Board members, who had received no training in personnel selection and who often spoke to candidates for barely twenty minutes, were evidently not as good at spotting suitable officer material as they thought they were. Plus, it was suspected that some commands were deliberately withholding the names of excellent NCOs because they did not wish to lose them, and passing along 'duds' instead – this at a time when the Army was estimated to be short of around 18,000 officers.[31] So in early 1942, Adam created the War Office Selection Board (WOSB) programme. New recruits deemed by their GSC evaluators to have leadership potential were sent to one of seventeen WOSB units around the country. There, along with thirty to forty fellow candidates, they underwent a two- or three-day programme of tests, interviews and evaluations drawn up by military psychiatrists which were designed to assess their intelligence, initiative and charismatic authority. Those who passed were forwarded to fully fledged OCTUs for several months of intensive officer training. DSP officers also conducted periodic 'comb-outs' in Britain and overseas to find potential officers in the ranks whom commanding officers might have tried to squirrel away.[32]

The results were dramatic. Almost two-fifths of the officer candidates previously sent on to OCTUs by the Command Interview Boards had been graded as 'below average' in quality when they got there. That proportion now fell to one in four under the WOSB system. The number of candidates rated as 'above average' rose from 22 to 35 per cent. And this improvement in quality was being accomplished while at the same time broadening the social pool of candidates. By winter 1942, public schoolboys made up only 15 per cent of successful OCTU graduates. One in four new officers had never even been to as much as a secondary school.[33] The perception that the WOSB system had made the whole process of officer selection fairer was encouraging more potential candidates to step forward from the ranks. The number of men attending OCTUs rose by 65 per cent during summer 1942.[34]

Adam's reforms from 1941 onwards were the main institutional basis for how military life began to change in the second half of the war. Some of their effects were impressive. Training failure rates in key trades fell to as little as one in twenty men.[35] The OCTU failure rate fell to just eight per cent.[36] In all, of the more than 125,000 potential officers who attended a WOSB in the United Kingdom during the war, almost half were ultimately deemed suitable for full training at an OCTU.[37] By 1945, the desertion rate was only three-fifths of what it had been in 1941, even though the Army was engaged in much fiercer fighting than it had been four years earlier.[38]

Some of Adam's initiatives were stymied, however. There were definite limits to what even an energetic adjutant-general could do to stamp his influence on an Army as decentralized as Britain's. Army Council Initiatives could be sent out, stern pronouncements made, but so long as an individual commanding officer kept up 'a reasonable façade', as one junior officer put it, then his battalion remained 'an absolutely watertight compartment', free from the War Office's observation or interference.[39] Some COs continued to defy Adam's entreaties concerning excessive drill and bullshit even as they were being posted on the noticeboards of their own bases. The men of the Ordnance Corps depot in Donnington, Shropshire were quietly elated in spring 1942 that their commanding officer had just had 'the biggest bollocking of his life' after his scrupulous edicts on polishing brasses and shoes had been found out by the AG's office. But they knew it would be only a temporary victory. 'The CO is down, but he's not yet out', noted one of his men. 'We have already had a long lecture on smartness and the like. He wants the NCOs to discover more petty crimes . . . and hut floors must be scrubbed white (an impossibility).'[40] Within such commands, bullshit remained the central preoccupation of the soldier's working life from the first day of the war to the last.

But change and adaptation within the Army was not just a story of diktats handed down from Whitehall. Adam's work was certainly important, and it provided the broad context in which change at the micro-level took place. But it was only part of what was going on. Ordinary soldiers were not just passive spectators, watching their own lives unfold; they too had agency. It was traditional for the Army's old lags to tell opinionated new recruits to *get some service in!* before trying to throw their weight about in barracks. In the months and years that followed Dunkirk, Britain's wartime soldiers got some service in. They became accustomed to the Army's peculiar internal culture, its 'ways'. And each of them responded in his own idiosyncratic manner to what he found – usually by negotiating some tacit agreement or compromise with those placed in command above him. Every soldier had to decide on what terms he was willing to make peace with his life in khaki. A few never could manage it, and they either fled or sought some means of 'working their ticket' by acquiring a discharge. One teenage recruit in the Suffolk Regiment spent his time in barracks drinking metal polish to try to give himself stomach ulcers. Another deliberately wet the bed and refused to bathe.[41] But such uncompromising acts of resistance were unusual. Most men, in the end, achieved some sort of accommodation, however grudging, with their lot. The typical wartime soldier rarely absorbed the Army's world view entirely, and never ceased to find some aspects of it perverse or objectionable. But all the same, he was able to discover some tolerable middle ground, some point of compromise, which made his day-to-day life in uniform bearable. His place in his own story needs to be emphasized as much as that of Adam's.

Admittedly, it didn't always seem to new recruits that they *had* any agency. Few British institutions were as blatantly, unapologetically hierarchical as the Army. From the moment he put on his uniform for the first time, the soldier was no longer a member of the democratic community, but rather a link within a Great Khaki Chain of Being which stretched from the cells at the Aldershot glasshouse to the office of the chief of the Imperial General Staff in Whitehall. Every duty and privilege he possessed depended on where exactly he was situated along that chain. For those occupying the lowest, most subordinate positions, discipline was liable to be enforced swiftly and ferociously. A private soldier's superiors could scream at him, insult him, detain him by force. They could punish him for delinquencies which would not even have ranked as minor social solecisms in civvy street – being bareheaded outdoors ('improperly dressed'), say, or walking across the barrack square with hands in pockets ('idle on parade'). He could be charged for literally doing nothing at all – the crime of 'dumb insolence', or failing to have a sufficiently obsequious look on his face. If all else failed, the reliably vague Section 40 of the Army Act – *action to the prejudice of good order and military discipline* – could always be invoked by a censorious NCO. The purpose of military law was to enforce compliance, not justice. 'One feels the scales weighted against one from the word go,' complained Reg Crimp about the punishments that were doled out in the company commander's office:

> What a farce . . . the parade of miscreants waiting to be taken singly inside; the '*hats off!*' command from the sergeant-major, whereat one has to fling one's cap (bearing the regimental badge) to the ground, which seems to suggest presumption of guilt even before trial; the quickstep hustling and bustling under escort into the presence of the presiding officer, which has the effect (probably designed) of reducing one to a condition of abject indignity; then, facing the officer, seated inquisitorially at his table, escort

on either side, the sergeant-major prodding one menacingly in the ribs from behind, listening to the conventional bellowing of the NCO stating the case and giving evidence, which always seems so unnecessarily malevolent and damning.

Most officers, he admitted, tried to be reasonable and impartial. But authority always had to be seen to be vindicated, even in cases where the original charge was transparently unfair.[42]

Confronted by the apparently overwhelming power of the Army, treated as 'numbered parcels', commodities to be passed around as the War Office saw fit, some soldiers retreated into a sort of blissful mental surrender.[43] There was a 'cowish imperturbability' to being in uniform, thought Anthony Cotterell, a pleasing state of dumb but happy resignation to your fate.[44] Grown-up civilian life had been full of difficult choices – what should I do? Where should I live? Whom should I marry? Joining the Army was, as Alan Wood put it, 'the nearest possible approach to obeying the biblical injunction to be born again', a way of living which had all the comforting simplicity of infancy:

> Everything is arranged for you. The time you get up; the clothes you wear; the hours you work and the hours you play; the time you are sent to bed at night, tired out by simple bodily fatigue, to sink into the sweet, sodden slumber of childhood . . . you enjoy simple excitements like riding on lorries, or paddling round a muddy gun-site with great big gum boots on. You revel in schoolboy jokes about sex. You feel your mental age falling lower and lower. Your brain shrinks. The cares of the years, the worries of a grown-up man with a wife and family to support, slip from your shoulders . . .[45]

Yet the more they paid attention, the more they realized that they *did* have some control over their own fate – so long as they learned how the Army worked. Being a soldier was a performative act, and the trick was to work out your part: to memorize your lines, outwardly conform, appear to take the rules seriously and implement them scrupulously, while all the time quietly gaming the system to your own advantage. The regulars were masters of such panto-mime obedience – all 'bogus boot-stamping and spuriously smart salutes', supplemented by secret dodges and ways of avoiding any unnecessary exer-tion. You could learn much by mimicking them.[46] One of the 'golden rules for raw recruits' which Arthur Calder-Marshall suggested in a 1941 article for *Horizon* was 'do everything which you can't avoid briskly, smartly, and efficiently, remembering that the majority of fatigues are given to those who look as if they don't want to do them'; and to 'pretend to punctiliousness of procedure, even to the point of idiocy. The man who appears over-careful not to transgress any of the Army rules can get away with twice as much as the man who doesn't give a damn.'[47] Or, as one of David Cooper's mates put it less decorously, '*In the fucking Army you can't call your fucking soul your own, and you get on best if you fucking well don't say nuffin.*'[48] Wise soldiers never argued; but, at the same time, they never did any more work than they absolutely had to. It was different on the battlefield, of course; there you were expected to muck in and do your share without prompting or complaint. But in barracks, 'malingering with style' – giving off the appearance of earnest busyness without actually doing anything – was considered both perfectly acceptable and even something of an art form.[49] At Henry Novy's camp, a third of the men would quietly disappear after breakfast each morning, slip off to the barber's shop, wait in the medical inspection room 'for treatment' or simply hide amongst the grass banks surrounding the depot. 'In this place you learn to be an artful bloody dodger', said Novy. 'Are you going to be a mug? I know I'm not.'[50]

It was useful, too, to learn about, and exploit, the Army's obsession with red tape – particularly its belief that if something did not exist on paper, and preferably in triplicate, it did not exist at all. Much of the tragi-comedy in Julian Maclaren-Ross's wartime short stories about military life revolves around bureaucratic absurdities set off by misplaced paperwork: of soldiers finding themselves stranded in administrative limbo through the inattention of some distant, anonymous clerk. In Maclaren-Ross's most famous story, 'I Had to Go Sick', a luckless recruit who cannot quite raise one of his legs properly on the march due to a childhood accident is passed from one officious but negligent medical officer after another over a period of several months, during which his leg steadily gets worse as he is put through a series of humiliating and useless treatments. This thralldom to form-filling could be the soldier's ruin. It could also work in his favour. In his early weeks at the RAMC training depot at Newbattle Abbey, near Edinburgh, John Wilson (later better known as the author Anthony Burgess) noticed that the non-existent 'Private F. L. Wilson', and not the very real Private J. Wilson, kept being listed on company work rosters. So he stopped showing up for duty. When summoned to see his commanding officer to explain his absenteeism, Burgess performed a masterclass in the 'quasi-cynical tone of suave, impersonal obedience' long practised by regulars when speaking to their superiors:[51]

'*You admit you are Wilson?*'
'*Yes, but not F. L.*'
'*You are the only Wilson in B Company. It was your duty to assume a typing error and obey an obvious order.*'

'It is not my duty to assume that my superiors make errors. Almost by definition they are incapable of errors.'
'You will say sir!'
'Sir.'
'All right. Dismissed.'

It took another week for F. L. Wilson to disappear finally from the duty roster.[52]

Under the right circumstances, it was even possible (if risky) to get away with outright defiance. At one of their first meals at Shaw Street Barracks, Doug Arthur and the rest of the newly mobilized gunners of the 424th Battery, 106th Lancashire Hussars broke into spontaneous mutiny when they returned from a day of training only to find 'two small pieces of cold boiled potato, a sorrowful looking piece of greyish boiled beef about two inches square, and a spoonful of peas' waiting for them at the cookhouse. 'Big Hammy', a reliable barracks-room troublemaker – and someone who bore more than a passing resemblance to Mussolini – jumped on to one of the wooden trestle tables and began bellowing mutinous entreaties to his comrades below, egging them on. 'We don't have to put up with this shit! If everybody sticks together and refuses to eat they'll have to make the robbin' bastards in the cookhouse give us a decent meal.' Within moments of Big Hammy's outburst, the spirit of revolution had overtaken the whole battery. The men began chanting the lyrics to 'The Red Flag' and the Irish rebel song 'The Wearing of the Green' – both strictly proscribed by Army regulations – while beating out the rhythms with their cutlery on the bare trestle tables.[53]

The local military authorities had to be careful about how they responded to outbursts like this. In principle, they could apply all the fierce injunctions of King's Regulations against troublemakers, with the ultimate threat of death by firing squad or (more realistically) the 'glasshouse' – military prison. But a commanding officer who immediately fell back on the severest measures of discipline risked acquiring a reputation amongst his own superiors for not being able to control his men. British soldiers had to be handled with caution. Theirs was no Pharaoh's slave army to be whipped into submission, but rather an army of democratically aware citizens, self-conscious about their 'rights', often schooled in the trade union culture of collective action, and well aware that a persistent lack of cooperation on their part could quickly bring the military machine grinding to a halt.

Plus, overreacting to acts of indiscipline generally missed the point of why they had broken out in the first place. Disobedience was rarely a *cri de coeur* against the Army as a whole, but more often a bargaining tool, albeit one that was to be used only with extreme caution, and usually only after the severest provocation. It was a way of sending a message to the powers that be that they had exceeded what could be reasonably expected, and that some compromise had to be offered. Most wartime 'mutinies' were fits of passion rather than serious challenges to authority, emotional responses to some grievance (real or imagined) that usually ran their course when the likely consequence of continued resistance was made clear to those involved. The dinnertime rebellion of the Lancashire Hussars fizzled out peacefully when the battery commander appeared at the cookhouse door and, civilly but firmly, told the men that if they did not present themselves on parade immediately, then he would summon an infantry company with fixed bayonets at the ready to arrest them all. His warning broke the spell; despite Big Hammy's entreaties, the Hussars trudged meekly out one by one on to the snowy drill square. That was not quite the end of the story, however. The battery had backed down, but no attempt was made to punish them for their misbehaviour – and, more to the point, there was a marginal improvement in the cookhouse food afterwards. Organized acts of indiscipline were performances with a set of unwritten rules which were usually acknowledged and respected by both sides. So long as the commanding officer in question was sensible enough not to play the self-important fool, and so long as the men were wise enough not to push their luck, things did not get out of hand. Soldiers may have occasionally mumbled exasperated threats to throw down their weapons or to 'do' some particularly tyrannical sergeant major or unsympathetic officer, but these were fantasies. Very rarely did they ever come to anything.

Soldiering was not just about confrontation and submission. There were comforts to it as well if you learned where to look for them. To thrive, as Rupert Croft-Cooke put it, on 'a few encouraging words from an unthinking oaf in authority, to delight in a cup of bad tea and a cigarette snatched between parades, to laugh inordinately at clumsy humour or be moved almost to tears by another's misfortune' – these were the 'small compensations' of Army life which made it bearable.[54] After a few months in uniform, John Guest discovered how much he enjoyed sentry duty on warm starlit nights, watching the sun rise and listening to the birds' chorus in splendid isolation.[55] Dennis Argent found it thrilling to ride in the back of an Army truck as it sped along an ancient country road like Watling Street on a misty autumn morning.[56] The Army offered boyish excitements. It provided playgrounds and sports. It taught you to ride motorcycles and drive trucks. You got to handle weapons and destroy things. Harry Wilson recalled with glee the first time he was issued a rifle: 'For a long time I couldn't let it alone. It was a thrill to handle it and a reassuring pleasure to see it recline, powerfully and gracefully, against the garret wall.'[57]

Even spit-and-polish could have its satisfactions, for there was a simple Zen-like enjoyment to polishing boots immaculately for hours at a time, gently circling the leather with the bone handle of a toothbrush lubricated with polish, water and spit – not very relevant to the war effort, perhaps, but pleasant enough in its own way.[58] When all else failed, there was the thought of the next leave to focus on – 'a week's peace, privacy, out of uniform, lying in bed, saluting nobody, forgetting to do up a button.'[59]

There was as well the primitive communism of the barrack room, its lack of privacy both claustrophobic and liberating. Soldiers slept together, dressed and bathed together, paraded together, ate together, panted and sweated around obstacle courses together, showered together, bared their genitals for inspection together.[60] Their entertainment was collective: the shared radio, the newspapers and books and magazines passed from one set of hands to another, the interminable evening debates over hands of cards, the boozy sessions in the wet canteen. Your comrades' lives became your own. Such mates formed the innermost of what Arthur Calder-Marshall called the 'structure of greater alliances' you needed to survive as a soldier – the series of concentric loyalties from which you drew strength, of platoon against platoon, regiment against regiment, rankers against NCOs and officers.[61] The dormitory was, as Norman Craig put it, 'a haven of camaraderie' in the midst of the Army's horrors, with its warm and smoky fug, profusion of blankets and everlasting dixie of luke-warm tea. After the day's last parade was over, he and his mates lounged on their beds, polishing their boots and writing letters, joking and arguing about everything:

> The barrack room was perhaps the most complete democracy in the world. Inside ours, freedom of expression was absolute . . . chores and other activities were arranged on a cooperative basis of scrupulous equality. We were always broke, and even the shameless importunity with which we cadged cigarettes from each other and raided one another's food parcels served to underline our essential unity and interdependence. From the common will and sympathy there sprang a deep fellow feeling and corporate identity.[62]

The Army offered no place for shyness or inhibition. Confidences were expected to be pooled within the primary group of the barrack room, sexual histories chronicled at length and in graphic detail. No blushes were spared. 'Smutty stories go around quite a lot', wrote one recruit about his new unit. 'Swearing is terrific. Everyone swears, from the company sergeant major to the scruffiest private, or most babyish face. Dozens have told me that they never swore in civil life, but that it just caught on here.'[63] The word *fuck* peppered so much of Army speech that it slowed down even the simplest of communications.[64] For men who had grown up in particularly inhibited households, this was scandalous – and exhilarating. Brian Aldiss, brought up in respectable lower-middle class suburbs, discovered that all the social taboos he had acquired through childhood, all the codes 'designed to hide what one was really hoping, feeling, enjoying, suffering', had suddenly vanished now he was in the Army. 'You could be your own awful self . . . all the hypocrisies of home-life dissolved.'[65] He was shocked, and also thrilled, to learn about depravities far beyond the imaginings of his own buttoned-up West Midlands childhood:

> Wally had actually fucked girls behind the sofa in his own home. His parents were often drunk – his mother had once set light to the net curtain and the house had nearly burnt down. His sister used to let the old man from next door feel her in the outside bog, in exchange for sweets. And his father! – Page senior, from Wally's account, was an embodiment of lusty lower-class life, a factory hand who fought people in boozers and at football matches, had shaken his fist at their Member of Parliament, had driven a car over a cliff, and, having been caught by Wally fucking a neighbour's daughter up against the wall of a boozer after closing time, had uttered this immortal piece of advice: *Don't you 'ang round 'ere sniffing at my crumpet – you're old enough to sniff out your own crumpet!*[66]

These barrack-room confessionals may have helped the more sheltered recruits puzzle out lingering questions they had about sexual anatomy and method.[67] If they did not, then the Army's graphic lectures on the perils of syphilis and gonorrhoea certainly did. One of Geoffrey Picot's comrades was so shocked by a film show about VD treatment that he fainted.[68]

Army service opened up not just greater knowledge about sex but also unique opportunities for erotic exploration. Many young soldiers were beyond their parents' (or wives' or girlfriends') supervision for the first time, encamped in strange towns, often with little to do, and tempted by the 'anonymity and lack of self-consciousness' of wartime, with the blackout being a great facilitator of discreet intimacy.[69] Often, members of the female Auxiliary Territorial Service (ATS) were stationed nearby. In mixed anti-aircraft units, soldiers even found themselves working the guns alongside ATS personnel; these sites soon became notorious for their rampant licentiousness, though the evidence suggests that this was mostly just lurid gossip.[70] Soldiering often brought men out of themselves, burnishing their self-confidence, particularly with regard to the other sex. One of Len England's new comrades surprised himself by flirting with a girl behind the counter of the YMCA kiosk: 'I've only been in the Army five days! And now look what I'm doing!'[71] The sex-obsessed milieu of the barrack room made virgins discomfited by their condition, and eager to relieve themselves of it. Norman Smith became obsessed with the idea that he might be killed before making love, and ended up having an affair with an older, married (and vastly more experienced) woman.[72] At many Army camps 'passion wagons' ferried men with passes to local towns each evening. It was a timeless and popular military pastime to spend your off-duty hours trying to pick up a 'tart' on a street corner or at a dance hall – though while some soldiers had effortless success at this, for others it could be a frustrating waste of time. Where the affectionate consent of a girl could not be had, a young man in a hurry could always fall back on a cold cash transaction. One of the soldiers in Geoffrey Picot's section declared that he was going to seek out a prostitute on his first leave in London in order 'to find out all about it'. He returned to his camp successful, though with a bad case of buyer's remorse. In retrospect, £1 for five minutes of awkward fumbling in a Soho alleyway seemed like a poor return on an investment which could have bought forty bars of cream chocolate.[73]

Other men had a rather different sexual awakening in the Army. During a talk of 'exceptional frankness' given to some RAOC recruits in Lincolnshire, the instructor wrapped things up by offering a bit of matter-of-fact advice: if you *had* to have sex with a stranger, it was safer to do it with another man than with a prostitute.[74] Many new soldiers had never even realized that that was an option. Life in an all-male barracks was to reveal a hitherto unknown dimension to human sexuality. One signaller stationed at Ordnance Hill in northwest London had never understood what the word 'homosexual' meant until a tall, well-dressed young man tried to pick him up one night on the walk back to barracks from St John's Wood station.[75] Another was initiated into the same mystery when two soldiers in his dormitory began sleeping together in the same bed. Nobody else in the unit, he noted, found anything particularly unusual or shocking about this.[76]

How much homosexual activity actually took place between British soldiers during the war is unknown. A few cases made press headlines because of their bizarre or scandalous details. In September 1941, for example, Sir Paul Latham, a wealthy, one-legged, Conservative MP who was serving as a captain in the Royal Artillery, tried to kill himself by driving his motorcycle into a tree when his sexual liaisons with three of his own gunners were discovered by the Army authorities. Latham survived to be cashiered for 'disgraceful conduct' and was sentenced to two years in prison.[77] In all, 790 ORs and 103 officers were convicted at courts-martial for crimes of 'indecency' between 1939 and 1945. But these men must have only represented a fraction of the Army's actual gay and bisexual soldiery.[78] Years spent in an almost exclusively male environment, often thousands of miles away from home, surely encouraged sexual experimentation, whether out of boredom, curiosity or desperation. 'It is a quite well-recognized fact that such activities do occur, and that those who participate will frequently admit to them', noted a RAMC private in Essex in a report to Mass-Observation in 1941. Most gay solders behaved with discretion: they had learned by necessity how to pass as straight. A few, though, flaunted their sexual predilections openly, proudly adopting female nicknames ('Sheila', 'Nora') and making themselves up with rouge and lipstick when off duty.[79]

Considering that homosexuality remained a criminal, as well as a military, offence during the Second World War, punishable by a long prison term, it is surprising how much even the indiscreet could get away with. Whether or not they condoned homosexual behaviour, few straight soldiers seem to have been especially perturbed by the presence of their gay comrades in the ranks. John Sparrow's sexual predilections were only lightly concealed, but during his brief stint as a private soldier in the Ox and Bucks Light Infantry he got on very well with the other men of his platoon; indeed, he enjoyed life as a private so much that it took considerable lobbying by family and friends to persuade him to accept a commission.[80] As for commanding officers, most took a cautious line on the matter. Homosexuality had always been a fact of life in an all-male institution such as the Army.[81] Front-line comradeship involved a level of physical intimacy and affection that was often difficult to categorize sexually. C. Macdonald Hull's autobiographical novel *A Man from Alamein* includes a scene in which a platoon commander complains to the colonel about the supposedly immoral behaviour of two of his men. The colonel will have none of it: both soldiers are exemplary members of the battalion, and one of them has won the Military Medal. 'This business of men sharing blankets; well Christ man, this [goes] on all the time under active service conditions', he explains to his prurient lieutenant:

> Each man only has one blanket and in the cold nights they share the bloody things. And each man usually has his special 'mucker'. They share their cigarettes, they share everything; they do what they used to call 'mucking in deadly' ... you don't realize the two chunks of human gold you've got there![82]

What mattered to most COs was military efficiency, not what took place between consenting adults after dark. If a gay soldier did his job poorly, his sexual behaviour could be used as an excuse to get rid of him. But if he was in all other respects a capable man, valuable to his unit, then what he got up to in private was none of the Army's business. Indeed, men who were known to be one another's long-standing partners were often billeted and posted together as an informal military 'couple'.[83] Only those with the primmest comrades or the least forbearing commanding officers were ever really at risk of being caught.[84] For those who had suffered persecution for their sexuality before the war as civilians – and who would suffer it again in the prudish post-war years, as anti-sodomy laws were more strictly enforced and Britain became what one historian has called a 'heterosexual dictatorship' – the Army represented an unexpected haven of tolerance.[85]

That was the thing about soldiering. However much you hated it at first, you inevitably came to find something about it that you enjoyed. You might even discover that being a soldier suited you, that you were good at it – better, perhaps, than at anything you'd ever tried your hand at before. The Army could bring out qualities in you that you didn't know existed, qualities which you found you liked. Before entering the Royal Engineers, J. B. Tomlinson had been a trainee architect, a profession he had never found easy because of his lack of skill in drawing and freehand expression. Being a soldier, however, he took to 'like a duck to water'. 'I was a natural', he realized, a peg which had found its right hole at last. Suddenly, his pre-war middle-class life in a provincial town seemed 'synthetic, shallow, insignificant, unimportant' when set against the exciting new world which the Army had opened up for him.[86] Private Dirk Bogarde began his military service in May 1941 crying himself to sleep in a miserable bunk in Yorkshire. Yet four years later, Captain Bogarde would write to his father from northern Germany that 'I think I'll have a serious try at staying on in the Army . . . I've enjoyed the companionship and the unexpected lack of responsibility. The Army, as far as it can, DOES take care of you, and I'm not at all certain now that I would ever be able to settle down among civilians again.'[87]

Bill Makins, business manager for Cyril Connolly's wartime literary journal *Horizon*, was, like Bogarde, about as unlikely a candidate for the role of happy soldier that one could imagine. He was bearded, bookish, bacchanalian, politically left-wing and without any emotional engagement with the war effort at all. The prospect of joining the Army appalled him. He tried every dodge he could think of to avoid being called-up. On the day he finally left for his basic training, he sent his friend, the novelist Julian Maclaren-Ross, a farewell note 'such as one might receive from a lamb on its way to the slaughter'. But within a few months, Makins was writing excited letters back to London describing the top marks he'd received in his training course. He'd given up drink and tobacco (*'must keep fit, you know'*), and couldn't understand what anyone had against discipline and regulations – without which you couldn't run an army, after all. A promotion to sergeant soon followed. His beard disappeared, forgotten, unmourned. Makins had become a soldier. And he loved every minute of it.[88]

It could be addictive, the theatricality of Army routine – the drill, the dressing-up, the saluting, the guard duty. The literally regimented life it offered, disciplined, predictable, very different from the unstructured meandering of civvy street. The faces of soldiers praised for smart turnout on inspection were said to 'glow and become moist-eyed with joy'.[89] There was much pleasure to be had in 'plain bodily exercise in the open air' after years of sitting on an office stool, admitted even that trenchant critic of bullshit, Alan Wood; a 'strange secret pleasure in acquiring the power to perform complicated marching movements with rhythm and precision'.[90] Henry Novy confessed with a certain shamefacedness that he had come to feel pride in being a soldier, being 'well-disciplined, in step, doing hard work'.[91] Norman Craig and his mates, who began by despising all manifestations of Army authority, eventually sought out officers just so they could demonstrate the beauty of their own salutes. 'We would stride brazenly past', he recalled, 'feigning to ignore them, until the final second when, with a stiffening of the frame and a sharp "eyes right" we would flash out a copy-book salute of quivering rectitude.'[92]

For a few soldiers, there was even the discovery of the pleasure of obedience, of complete submission to a superior's will. Enoch Powell found 'the framework of discipline, the exactitude of rank, the precision of duty' as a private soldier in the Royal Warwickshire Regiment 'almost restful and attractive' compared to anything he had previously known in academia or would later know in politics.[93] By the end of his basic training, David Holbrook ('Paul Grimmer') had forgotten all about Staff Sergeant MacAllcane's persecution. He had become fit and wiry. He could delight self-consciously in his mastery of Army skills. He felt 'tremendously alive . . . no other experience in his youth had made him feel so full of animal energy'. He had begun to feel contempt for anyone whose existence was softer and less disciplined than his own, who did not wear khaki, who could not drill, whose trousers were uncreased.[94] All of the screaming and bullying and bullshit had done its job after all. There was, thought Norman Craig, 'an element of ecstasy, a strangely joyous satisfaction' in being assimilated by the military machine. The war was revealing something which was either reassuring or disturbing, depending on your point of view: that even within the meekest, mildest, most modern-minded British boy, the product of twenty years of civilian pampering, there squatted 'something of the Nazi' for the Army to bring out.[95]

In mid-1944, Two Cities Films, in cooperation with the Ministry of Information, released *The Way Ahead*, a story of Army life written by (Lieutenant) Eric Ambler and (Private) Peter Ustinov, directed by (Captain) Carol Reed and starring (Major) David Niven, who had returned to Britain from Hollywood at the outbreak of war and had been gazetted into the Rifle Brigade. *The Way Ahead* was conceived by Niven two years earlier as an attempt to do for the Army's public image what Nöel Coward's highly successful *In Which We Serve* had done for the Royal Navy's. As a propaganda exercise it was something of a flop because it was released so late: by the summer of 1944, the mid-war issues it addressed – of how to stimulate *esprit de corps* in an army of bored and bemused conscripts on home service – no longer seemed nearly so urgent. But what remains interesting about *The Way Ahead* is how it chronicles, in a surprisingly accurate way for a public relations piece, the problems that the Army faced in 1942, and how it ultimately overcame them.[96]

The film uses a clever continuity device: two ageing Chelsea Pensioners, veterans of the fictional Duke of Glendon's Light Infantry ('the DOGs'), ruminating on the inadequacies of the young people now being called on to defend Britain. '*These young fellows nowadays, they haven't got the stomach for it . . . it's all this education and machinery and going to the pictures.*' Anxiety about what the film's marketing materials called the 'pampered generation' with 'untrained bodies' going off to fight was familiar enough to the cinema-going public in 1942 to need little explanation. Sure enough, the new platoon which joins a battalion of the DOGs and which is the focus of *The Way Ahead* begins its Army service as a thoroughly unprepossessing bunch of mid-century Everymen. Car salesmen and travel agents, rent collectors and retail clerks: all of them prissy, whingeing wet blankets, determined to make the worst of their military experience. '*You wouldn't think we was human beings!*' moans Private Brewer after being bawled out by the platoon sergeant for walking across the parade ground with his hands in his pockets. These are much the same spoonfed idlers whom Churchill had suspected of giving up Singapore and Tobruk without a fight.

All the same, they have the makings of a good platoon. But they need sound, progressive leadership. Sergeant Fletcher (future Doctor Who William Hartnell) is the archetype of the tough-but-fair NCO: hard on slackers, but equally quick to offer the recruits praise when appropriate, believing in them more than they believe in themselves. Lieutenant Perry (Niven), meanwhile, is the adjutant-general's idea of the modern citizen-subaltern. He is free of pomposity and class-condescension; demanding of his men, but sympathetic towards their problems; solicitous of their welfare without seeking superficial popularity; and willing to base his right to command from quiet-spoken authority and leading by example rather than an appeal to rank. Such paragons of man-management were hardly ubiquitous throughout the real-life Army of

1942, of course. *The Way Ahead* is a fantasy of best-practices, not a documentary. But Adam's recognition that conscript civilians had to be led by a different type of officer would, from the mid-point of the war onwards, make a slow but perceptible impression on subaltern selection and training. 'The Army tries to turn us into professional soldiers,' complained Arthur Calder-Marshall in 1941: 'but the formulas based on training mercenaries fail with us.' Potentially, he argued, conscripts might be better soldiers than regulars:

> But only if methods are devised to use our full powers, our initiative, invention, resourcefulness. To the regular there may be comfort in the attitude, *Theirs not to reason why, theirs but to do and die.* But the reason why is very important to us, if we have to do and die.[97]

If Army morale was a good deal better by the time *The Way Ahead* was released, then this was in part because men of influence such as Adam had heeded Calder-Marshall's call to take more seriously the special needs and talents of wartime recruits.

The Way Ahead also anticipates another change: in the men themselves. Fletcher and Perry's soldiers grow up. They stop acting so self-pityingly, come to recognize the point of their punishing training schedule and begin to appreciate some of the previously dormant qualities that the Army has stimulated within them. Grousers become leaders. Loafers transform into doers. It's a rebirth, though, which can only take place because the Army is willing to grant its men a certain level of ironic detachment from their soldiering. No film sanctioned by the War Office in 1942 was ever going to portray outright scrimshanking in a good light. But *The Way Ahead* does suggest a way for soldiers and the Army to agree to meet each other halfway – with each member of the fictional platoon coming to accept, as most real-life conscripts did, some of the battalion's demands on his privacy, personal comfort and dignity, even if he never fully identifies with the Army as an institution. *The Way Ahead* articulates a new post-heroic philosophy of morale. Eric Ambler summed it up as: '*Yes, we know how you feel. We understand. Everyone feels the same at first. But if we don't feel too sorry for ourselves we can just about make the job worth doing.*'[98] Fletcher and Perry's men remain, even at their most inspired, civilians temporarily in uniform only: soldiers of a kind, but soldiers who are in no way willing to surrender their personalities wholly to the military machine. This was not a message that every senior officer wanted to hear in 1942. The verdict of some of the more truculent amongst them on *The Way Ahead* was pithy: 'Tripe.'[99] But the adjutant-general liked it. And the wartime Army was willing, in the end, to settle for it.

The real turning point in *The Way Ahead* does not come through some parade-ground epiphany, however. It comes by way of a set of marching orders. The platoon is sent to take part in Operation TORCH, and in the final reel it finds itself in the thick of the fighting in Algeria. It is through close-combat overseas that the tedium of home service is finally banished. And indeed, if any one thing did change the mood of the real-life Army from the mid-point of the war onwards, it was the fact that it had begun *doing something*. Brooke and Adam had inherited a force that was mostly cooped up in cheerless depots and camps scattered across the United Kingdom, its men in little physical danger, but also, given their inactivity, at a loss to understand why it had been necessary to take their civilian freedoms away in the first place. As more and more of them began to depart Britain's shores from the end of 1942 – to North Africa at first, then Italy, India and Burma, and eventually France, Belgium, the Netherlands and Germany – so their brooding ceased. Norman Craig, who had found military life in England 'more and more of a sham' as he read stories of the fighting raging in Libya, was relieved when his battalion finally got its orders to ship out, regardless of the additional dangers and discomforts he knew this was going to mean for him personally.[100] Overseas service would involve no end of privations, regrets, terrors. But at least it felt like real soldiering.

PART THREE
CRUSADERS

Roll on the ship that takes me for a trip,
Far from this land of pox and fever:
Mosquitoes, bugs and flies
Tear out your fucking eyes:
Roll on the boat that takes me home.

Anonymous[1]

CHAPTER 7

INTO THE BLUE

'A ray of sunshine shafted through the smoky air from a roof-light and illumi-
nated the silent ranks. We humped our kit and shuffled out onto the wharf.
Suddenly it was all bustle and light. Sunshine sparkled across the waters of the
Mersey, boats fussed about the river, horns tooted, dockworkers shouted and
there, towering above us, reared the sheer sides of our ship RMS *Highland
Brigade*.' In a thin drizzle, second lieutenant John Hudson and the rest of his
draft of Royal Engineers staggered up the troopship's ribbed gangway, knees
buckling under the weight of their kitbags. As they reached the promenade
deck, Hudson looked back towards the Liverpool skyline. 'Would I ever see
those old Liver Birds again?' he wondered. He and his fellow soldiers were
heading into what amounted to foreign exile – 'cut out of the herd to be shooed
towards the slaughterhouse door' – in a mood of bland official indifference.
How long would they be gone? Would they ever return? No man, not even
Churchill himself, could say for sure. Yet as the ponderous vessel slipped into
the Mersey estuary, her bow rising in the water, Hudson's mood began to lift
along with it. 'I gloried in the throbbing power of the diesels roaring defiance
to all U-Boats from the funnel above me', he remembered 'This had to be the
experience of a lifetime.' The adventure was on. The *Highland Brigade* and her
human cargo were leaving the twilight shores of England. Within a few hours
they had vanished from sight into the vast black ocean.[1]

By the end of the Second World War, over 2.6 million British troops, around
seven in ten of all soldiers, had undergone at least one voyage like Hudson's.[2]
The length of their foreign service varied enormously, however. A quarter of a
million servicemen were stationed overseas continuously for more than five
years.[3] But hundreds of thousands of others went abroad for just a year or two.

Many never left Britain at all. Severe limitations on shipping space encouraged the War Office to reuse troops already *in situ* overseas whenever new operational needs arose, rather than sending replacements from home. Those who ended up overseas, stayed there for a long time. No home leave, even on compassionate grounds, was allowed until the end of 1944. A system for rotating men with long overseas service back to Britain known as PYTHON was introduced towards the end of the war, but the initial qualification for inclusion was stiff – six years of continuous foreign duty. Few men were eligible until the end of the fighting allowed some relaxation in the standards.[4]

There was little obvious rhyme or reason to the way that the burden of expatriation was distributed during the Second World War. The role that sheer chance played in it is illustrated by the wartime histories of two largely identical regular county battalions: the 2nd Lincolnshires and the 2nd Wiltshires. The war began for both of them in much the same way. Each was sent to France in 1939 as a unit of the BEF. Each took part in the retreat from Belgium in May 1940. Each was evacuated from Dunkirk. But from that point onwards, their experiences were completely different. The 2nd Wilts spent only twenty-two months in the UK re-equipping and retraining before being sent to southern Africa to take part in Operation IRONCLAD, the invasion of Vichy French Madagascar. From there it was posted to India, then Iraq, and then Persia. It was one of the infantry battalions to invade Sicily in July 1943. It landed in southern Italy that September, participated in yet another amphibious operation at Anzio the following March, did a short period of garrison duty in Palestine before returning to Italy, and finally was sent to Germany as part of mopping-up operations in spring 1945, ending the war in Schleswig-Holstein. By contrast, the men of the 2nd Lincs remained in the United Kingdom for almost exactly four years, preparing for their role in what was ultimately to become the British Second Army. Theirs was one of the first battalions to land on SWORD Beach on D-Day, and for the next nine months they fought their way across France, the Low Countries and Germany, finishing the war in Bremen. Both battalions saw fierce combat and suffered heavy casualties. But the men of the 2nd Wiltshires endured the additional trial of long-term absence from home, three-and-a-half years of exile in a series of strange foreign lands, separated from everything they knew or cared about. There were wartime ordeals other than just death and injury. Separation anxiety was said by Army psychiatrists to be at the heart of all forms of war neurosis, its 'only single symptom . . . its great common measure.'[5]

Few issues generated as much strife within the wartime ranks as the inequitable distribution of long overseas service. Visiting India and Burma in the summer of 1945 to assess morale, the War Office's John Sparrow found the mood 'strikingly bitter'. Officers and men were united in their obsession with repatriation and their belief that they were being ignored back home. A 'barrier of mistrust and even hostility towards authority' had grown up which transcended rank: the troops, he wrote, 'have succeeded in persuading themselves that "they" could perfectly well improve the conditions and shorten the period of service overseas if they wished, and that it is lack of interest and selfishness that prevents them from doing so'. Churchill was booed whenever he appeared on a newsreel.[6] It is the troops in Burma who have gone down in history as Britain's wartime 'Forgotten Army'. But such sentiments were common elsewhere too. Most soldiers overseas, whether they were in Italy or Egypt, Persia or India, also considered themselves unjustly forgotten by the public back home. Middle East Force unofficially renamed itself the 'Men England Forgot'.[7] Soldiers constantly complained that their service was being marginalized in the newspapers or on radio; Army morale reports were filled with gripes that some or other corps or division was not receiving the publicity it rightly deserved ('You don't realize how well you're doing until the *Daily Mail* tells you', as one gunnery officer put it).[8] Unflattering media coverage set off howls of complaints.[9] Troops who were regarded as the spoiled darlings of the press, the hoggers of the limelight, were particularly resented. It greatly irked First Army units that their exploits as part of Operation TORCH were as nothing at home compared to the fame of Montgomery's Eighth Army. As one disgruntled eulogist (prompted by a remark he overheard that '*you are no bloody hero unless you've been in the Monty mob*') wrote of a fellow First Army soldier killed in Tunisia:

He lies quiet in the desert.
Sun-bronzed legs shot through with lead;
The battle sounds still linger
But he does not hear – he's dead. . .

But Praise's voice is muted,
Seeks no record of his fame –
The poor boy died at Medjez
And not at Alamein.[10]

Though in their turn, the Eighth Army men in Italy would come to resent all the attention that the men of 21st Army Group got following D-Day.[11] Meanwhile, the soldiers in Burma begrudged the 'jammy buggers' in Italy, whom they imagined were spending the entire war drinking *vino* and copulating with olive-skinned *signorinas*: 'They get fags flown out from England, and Yank rations and Yank beer. No wonder they are stuck where they are – they're too pissed to fight!'[12] As for soldiers back in the UK, their main role in the People's War seemed to consist of defending Blackpool from the Canadians.[13] If there was one thing that all wartime soldiers could agree about, it was that someone else, in some other distant place, was doing less to win the war than *they* were.

Expatriation was not all misery, however. Going overseas did at least offer you the possibility of doing something more consequential with your time than blancoing webbing and painting stones white on the parade ground for the thousandth time. Contemplating his dispatch to Libya, the protagonist of Dan Billany's autobiographical novel *The Trap* finds himself unexpectedly excited by the prospect. 'I had not been out of Britain before', he reflects,

> And now I was to go far, into incredible tropical waters, to see things which I knew only as phrases in geography books, and to take part in real war, not the hedge-scrambling, blank-cartridge-firing shadow-boxing of our 'exercises'. If there is anything more soul-killing than real war, it is imitation war.[14]

Plus, by the final years of the war, the Army abroad had entered into the soldier-tourist entertainment business on a big scale. Early welfare arrangements for overseas troops had been rudimentary – a mobile NAAFI canteen selling tea and buns here, a sprinkling of footballs and dart boards and wirelesses there. Individual regimental associations and private charities such as the YMCA and the Salvation Army were expected to pick up much of the burden. By the time of the Italian campaign, however, the War Office was funding elaborate rest camps which were a kind of nascent Club 18–30 for bored Tommies on leave.[15] 'A year or so ago NAAFIs like this were undreamt of', wrote Harry Wilson in March 1944, after visiting the palatial seafront rest centre for soldiers at Bari, with its palm trees and orchestra.[16] The rest-and-leave centre outside Rome was 'a real snorter', thought Reg Crimp:

> You could have a marvellous time without stirring a foot beyond the gate. Everything's perfectly organized and the whole set-up designed purely for the comfort and amusement of the troops in residence. The food is excellent – plentiful, varied, expertly cooked and dashingly served by Italian waiters under titillating frescoes of females in *dishabille* on the restaurant walls. There's a theatre-cinema, with afternoon and evening shows, a large Naafi with booze and snouts galore; a football pitch, tennis courts and an open-air swimming pool. The Recreation Wing comprises lounges for reading and writing, a library, billiard and ping-pong rooms, a gift shop, a

photographer's studio and a hairdressing establishment. Also a super bath-room, with hot and cold showers.[17]

A foreign posting represented an opportunity to see something of the rest of the world, usually for the first time. Very few young British men had ever been outside the United Kingdom at the beginning of the Second World War. They came from a country which was far less cosmopolitan, far more parochial and inward-looking, than it is today. The package holiday jaunt to Torremolinos was still thirty years away. Margate and Rhyl were most people's idea of exotic getaway destinations. The war, however briefly, disrupted such solipsism. A. M. Bell MacDonald found himself getting 'increasingly Empire-minded' as his troopship docked at one British seaport after another en route for India.[18] Robert Lees, a medical officer specializing in the treatment of venereal disease, found his services in demand in virtually every garrison post between Siena and Swaziland, and after the war he tallied up the glamorous sights that he had had the opportunity to visit courtesy of the Army:

> The absolute quiet of the moonlit desert: the stench and heat and noise of Baghdad; the beauty of Tehran; the heavy perfume of the Palestinian orange groves; the historical miracle of Jerusalem; the incredible beauty of spring flowers in the Jordan Valley; the bazaars of Damascus and Aleppo; the beat of drums at night in Khartoum at the feast of the Prophet; trout fishing on the slopes of Mount Kenya; Pretoria smothered in jaracanda blossom; the beauty of Capetown seen from Table Mountain; Vesuvius in eruption; Rome; Florence.

'All these, and a thousand more, were worth the fatigue and frustration, the heat and smells and flies', he reflected.[19]

Not many soldiers had a travel schedule quite as generous as *that*. Still, the great military cantonments of the war – Cairo, Rome, Calcutta – were places of great historical or cultural interest in their own right. Whole indigenous industries sprang up to service the needs of bored and curious Tommies on local leave. Many soldiers were intimately familiar with the religious and historical significance of the places they had been sent to defend, even though they had never visited them before. Biblical and classical literacy were far more pronounced in the 1940s than they are today. Egypt was not just a dustbowl of sand and *wadis*, but sacred ground: the land of Joseph and Potiphar, Moses and Pharaoh, and the Holy Family's flight from Herod. It was the place where the Israelites and the early Christians had striven and prayed and beseeched the Lord, where Caesar had pursued Pompey and been seduced by Cleopatra.

Palestine, which just a few years earlier had been in the midst of a violent insurgency, was comparatively placid during the war years, and so became a popular destination for troops on leave from Egypt. Native guides facilitated tours of the holy sites for visiting soldier-tourists, taking them around the Mount of Olives, the Garden of Gethsemane, the Wailing Wall and the various Stations of the Cross. Evidence of the ancient past was littered across North Africa and the Levant. At Sufetula, one of the best-preserved classical sites in North Africa, Tim Bishop stood in wonder before the remains of the Forum and the public baths and the 'moon-washed crumbling archways' of a city which had thrived thousands of years before.[20] Others travelled to see the painted frieze on the cornice of the Ptolemaic shrine at Siwa where Alexander the Great had once worshipped.[21] At the El Hamma oasis in southeastern Tunisia, where soldiers could wash their clothes in the hot stream, some of the pavement still in use had clearly been laid by Roman sappers.[22] For a few piastres Tommies could tour the subterranean catacombs carved out beneath Alexandria twenty-four centuries earlier.[23]

The locals, too, seemed to have stepped right out of the pages of Herodotus or the Gospels. Watching Egyptian peasants tossing ground grain into the air to separate out the chaff as their womenfolk filled clay vessels at the banks of the Nile, Christopher Seton-Watson mused that he was seeing a pattern of life that had remained essentially unaltered for centuries: 'I suppose the Pharaohs watched just the same work being done in just the same way.'[24] In Tunisia, John Guest had the feeling of viewing an Old Testament tableau come to life, 'the men in their long *bernouses* tending the sheep, the women drawing water at the wells', scenes familiar to him from Sunday School storybooks.[25] To Doug Arthur, who before his call-up had been no further away from Liverpool than Llandudno, it was a thrilling prospect to see in front of him the Sphinx that had graced the cover of his school geography book, and to pick with his own hands the same dates he had bought in packets at the Co-Op.[26] The Second World War represented a little foretaste of the coming age of jet-setting mass tourism.

Men were affected by their overseas experiences in different ways. Some would stubbornly insist on their British otherness throughout. Others would demonstrate a 'chameleon-like genius' for absorbing the language and culture of the local milieu.[27] John Hudson admired the way in which men in the Far East could make themselves understood by 'rattling off a mouthful of execrable slang' mixed with a few foreign, mostly French, phrases:

Beaming in the friendliest way, a Tommy might say: '*Nah then! You big black whiskered ape, what abaht it then? Fancy a cuppa char or un more-so de choc-o-latt?*' And back came the Punjabi reply, with a cordial flash of white teeth: *'That's good, you red-arsed monkey, try some of our curried goat – it'll make a man of you!'*[28]

The typical soldier went overseas with plenty of preconceptions about 'foreigners' already lodged in his mind, few of them flattering. The Frenchman was comic and excitable; the Arab sinister and treacherous; the Italian some combination of all these things, complemented with ice-cream, a barrel organ and perhaps a concealed stiletto.[29] The soldier's encounter with the real-life versions of these caricatures – as a comrade, an enemy, a liberator, an occupier, a friend, a paramour, a client and a persecutor – would challenge some of his prejudices and reinforce others.

The war would expose a generation of Britons to a world that was not made up exclusively of pink faces. In 1939, Great Britain might have been at the centre of the greatest multi-ethnic empire in history, but very few people of colour lived in the UK itself. Only about 7,000 blacks and Asians were permanent residents, most of them clustered in the slum ghettos of seaports such as Liverpool and Cardiff.[30] The vast majority of Britons had never set eyes on a non-European. There were so few people of colour resident in Britain that the Army did not quite know what to do about them when conscription was introduced in 1939. Unlike in the United States, where there was an unambiguous policy of military racial segregation, HM Forces had never established clearcut rules on the matter.[31] In the 1930s, the War Office had tended towards the view that people of non-European descent could not, by definition, be British, and thus they could not serve in the regular Army. But at least a handful of 'coloured' recruits had enlisted in the peacetime ranks without objection.[32] In October 1939, under pressure from the Colonial Office, the War Office reversed this earlier ruling and announced that not only were all Crown subjects from the colonies eligible to serve in the Army if resident in Great Britain, but that non-Europeans could also seek a wartime King's Commission if they wished. In April 1940, 'Joe' Moody, son of the influential Dr Harold Moody, leader of the League of Coloured Peoples, became a subaltern in the Queen's Own Royal West Kent Regiment, only the second black Briton ever to command white soldiers.[33]

Men such as Moody were highly unusual, however. The overwhelming majority of British troops heading overseas had never known anything other than a world of whiteness. To thrust them into the midst of a frantic, polyglot city like Alexandria or Bombay, in which theirs might be the only white face in a crowd of thousands, represented a culture shock of the highest order. As they soon discovered, 'abroad' was a place where the normal rules of good conduct did not necessarily apply. In colonies such as Egypt and India, the expectations about how men of their race and occupation should behave were vastly different from those they were used to in Britain. Soldiers realized that they could comport themselves in ways that would have provoked withering disapproval back home – whether that meant cheating a native street vendor of his money, or openly propositioning a woman for sex ('*here there is nobody to watch what you do or where you go!*' a dipsomaniacal subaltern with a mistress and a borrowed motor-car gloried in Bombay).[34] Even in Italy, France and Germany, where the majority population shared the white complexion of the British soldiers who now occupied their lands, civil society had been so smashed up by the war that the normal standards of behaviour had given way to an all-consuming struggle for survival in which anything was potentially imaginable.

The unwritten maxim that 'what happens in Naples stays in Naples' (or Brussels or Cairo or Calcutta) did not necessarily bring out the best in the British soldier. Whether because of his whiteness, his relative wealth, or his privileged legal status as a member of an occupying army, he enjoyed what was often an unhealthy power advantage over the resident population. Some men were cognizant of this and showed admirable self-restraint. Others greedily took advantage of everything and everyone they could. The effervescent fizz of liberation could last only so long; even friendly civilians soon discovered how destructive the presence of an army could be – to physical property, to the rule of law, to moral standards.[35] In some places and at some times, soldiers cosied up to the locals – 'getting your feet under the table', as it was known – and showed a fine-tuned 'homing instinct for finding themselves a family who would wash their socks, cook them fried potatoes and listen admiringly to their conversations', headed by 'an alien version of Mum, the dispenser of cups of tea and uncritical kindness'.[36] Elsewhere and at other times they treated civilians with bullying contempt. '*It serves the bastards right; they are a defeated nation and should stay like it . . . they're black outside and yellow in*' was the old soldier's view of Indians, according to an exasperated Communist sergeant, Clive Branson. 'No argument will change these idiots', he wearied.[37] Such men lived up to all the worst stereotypes of the bumptious Briton abroad – 'nasty, brutish, and in shorts'.[38]

'We're there!'

After six weeks or more rounding the Cape of Good Hope in the sweltering hold of a 'Winston Special' troopship, even the sight of Port Tewfik's grimy oil-tanks and chimney stacks and warehouses must have been a welcome relief. Reg Crimp arrived with the rest of his reinforcement draft on the SS *Franconia* on the morning of 23 July 1941. Within a few hours of disembarking, they were encamped at Geneifa Infantry Base Depot, a sprawling flat vista of oblong tents extending across the desert for miles in neat ranks and files. 'The scenery here is certainly stark,' he wrote in his diary,

> Sand, of course, everywhere, stretching great distances on all sides to the low horizon: making eye and mind alike ache with its arid, uncompromising harshness. Then all this monotonous, sun-strident expanse sealed over by the equally monotonous and even more blatantly glaring sky . . . a military camp is an ugly enough thing. But when its drabness is superimposed on such stark desolation, the result is grim.[39]

Until mid-1943, this is what 'overseas' meant for most British troops. At the height of the struggle for the North African shoreline, more than 1,000 Commonwealth soldiers and 5,000 tonnes of supplies were arriving in Egypt every day.[40] Depots such as Geneifa and the equally massive and sprawling military facilities at Hilmiya and Almaza near Cairo expanded to become cities of canvas and stone in the midst of the wilderness, with offices and mess kitchens, storerooms and lecture huts, open-air cinemas and football pitches, canteens selling Stella beer from refrigerated chests, and bathing pools for the men to escape the worst of the corrosive afternoon heat. The road from Cairo to Alexandria was one continuous flood of traffic – troop carriers, staff cars, tanks on transporters, ration and ammunition lorries, crated aircraft – with a constabulary of military policemen stretched along its length, struggling to keep the whole writhing procession from coming to a standstill. And finally, beyond Alexandria and the snaking coastal road, was the Western Desert itself – 'the Blue', a 1,000-mile swathe of sand and scrub extending from the Nile Delta to the Libyan capital Tripoli. A world as utterly different from Britain as it would be possible to imagine. And, for two-and-a-half years, the Army's central preoccupation.

The Western Desert campaign meant different things to the nations which fought it. To the Germans, focused above all on the Russian front, it was a sideshow – an exotic, but ultimately minor distraction from the real battle that was taking place far away on the Ukrainian steppe. The British, however, saw the desert war very differently. No other episode of the Second World War would impress itself with the same Homeric permanence upon their national memory. They would remember their victory at El Alamein in October 1942 as the war's quintessential triumph, and the all-conquering Bernard Montgomery as its greatest general. Elegiac pride had much to do with this. Alamein was not just a beginning, but an ending too: the Army's first major battlefield success of the war, but also the last time the British would win a campaign against the Germans unassisted by the Americans. It was Britannia's final hurrah as an independent Great Power.

The Western Desert was also distinctive because of the army that fought there. The Eighth Army was (aside perhaps from the Fourteenth Army in Burma) the only wartime British field formation to develop a unique identity. The desert soldier, thought Australian journalist Alan Moorehead, looked 'like no other soldier in the world':

> He looks at first sight like a rather rakish and dishevelled boy scout, the effect, I suppose, of his bleached khaki shorts and shirt and the parapher-nalia of blackened pots and pans and oddments he carries around in his vehicle which is his home. He practically never wears a helmet, and he has a careless loose-limbed way of walking which comes from living on the open plains.[41]

The desert war made its mark upon the body. The Eighth Army veteran could be spotted without difficulty from the tell-tale characteristics on his skin: the henna-red complexion; the suppurating sores on arms and legs caused by persistent exposure to the desert wind; the thick adhesive sand-sweat paste that crumbled off him in dry flakes.[42] Reinforcements newly arriving from Britain, 'their knees not yet brown', were painfully aware of the physical difference between themselves and the old-timers. 'We were raw. We were rookies', wrote Neil McCallum of his own unit of callow replacements in Suez. 'Nothing could disguise our palsied pasty faces, our blanched innocence. Nothing could hide our inelegant tropical clothing, unstarched and limp, or the way our puttees came undone because we wound them inexpertly . . . like young schoolboys, we were filled with the shameful naked feeling of those outside the elite.'[43] Norman Craig did not feel confident about stepping out in Alexandria until his uniform had acquired the crumpled and bleached look of the 'real desert type'.[44]

There was a distinct Eighth Army style too, a 'puckish, casual manner' that became particularly associated with the Western Desert soldier – a product, ultimately, of the stark practicality imposed on day-to-day behaviour by an environment as hostile as the Blue. There was little room in the desert for Army bullshit or concern for the perquisites of rank.[45] This informality expressed itself in the strange ensembles worn by officers and men, the corduroys and sheepskin jackets and silk scarves accessorizing standard-issue Khaki Drill (KD). It expressed itself too in Eighth Army's unusually cosmopolitan atmos-phere. Until the closing stages of the campaign, the British Army in the Western Desert was scarcely British at all. In October 1941, 73 per cent of its divisions had been raised outside the United Kingdom.[46] The presence within its ranks of large numbers of Australians, New Zealanders, South Africans, Indians, Poles and Free Frenchmen gave it a diverse, pan-imperial character which the bulk of the British Army back home never shared. Added to this was the jumble of Italian and Nile Delta Arabic adopted by the troops as their private creole, some of which was unknown even in other parts of North Africa. When the British reached Tunisia, the locals assumed that the Eighth Army veterans who greeted them with the Egyptian phrase 'sayeeda' were speaking English.[47] Not for nothing did Eighth Army men refer to the First Army soldiers whom they met in early 1943 as 'those bloody Inglese'.[48]

Long separation from home bred a certain bloody-minded hostility towards interlopers. 'Still finding it hard graft fitting in with the new mob', complained Reg Crimp after he was transferred to a new battalion in March 1945. 'The trouble is they're not regulars, they're not Desert Rats, and they've never got their knees brown. Cairo and Alex, Benghazi and Tripoli are merely names to them; Msus, Mechili they've never even heard of. What do they know of desert brews and pawny rations, burgoos and Berka bints, desert sores and the khamsin? Of sandblown trucks, full of jumbled kit, with brewcans bobbing on the side?'[49] Eighth Army veterans who had fought throughout the whole North African campaign were contemptuous of the 'luxury parade-ground' uniforms and equipment of First Army troops whom they met for the first time in Tunisia in early 1943.[50] For their part, the First Army men – who had endured much hard fighting themselves – thought the Desert Rats a little too pleased with their own myth, too 'noisy and overconfident', altogether too keen on 'sunning themselves in publicity'.[51] But behind this conceit lay insecurity. By the time they linked up with First Army, many desert soldiers had been over-seas for three years. They felt isolated, neglected, forgotten in a strange and hostile land. If We'll Meet Again and The White Cliffs of Dover came to symbolize the spirit of the civilian war effort, then it was no accident that a song from the Blue, the syrupy German ballad Lily Marlene, came to represent the lonely pathos of the British soldier far away from home.

It was the heat that everyone noticed at first, of course. A heat which could sun-toast bread, turn dishes and utensils into scalding hot plates, deliquesce butter at the touch of a knife. A glancing touch of flesh against metal left throbbing blisters in its wake. Warm tea gushed out of swollen sweat-pores almost as soon as it was drunk.[52] The temperature in the Western Desert could reach as much as 120 degrees on a June day; in some parts of the Middle East it got even hotter.[53] During the inferno of summer in Iraq, Harry Gaunt felt a 'continuous fight to keep awake' as his body was slowly cooked. 'It was just as though a tremendous weight was bearing down on the top of my head and one found it difficult to fight the ensuing drowsiness . . . the only way I found it possible to rouse myself to carry on working was to take my *chagul* (canvas water carrier) outside and pour the contents over my head and face to revive my senses.'[54] All life in the desert, including the fighting, was conditioned and organized by the sun's course across the daily sky. By noon in the worst months of the year, the earth was a furnace-void, the heat 'a solid wall', as Reginald Crimp put it; 'the middle distance disintegrated into incessant sizzling' as mirages formed and vision itself became distorted, objects stretching along surreal angles.[55] Men had to abandon the shade of their tents in mid-afternoon to avoid being parboiled.[56] Yet at night the thermometer plunged, and thin Khaki Drill shirts and shorts were hurriedly supplemented with woollen sweaters and corduroys as soldiers shivered on sentry duty and watched frost form on truck casings.[57]

Then there was the wind – mournful, shrill, hot enough to braise exposed skin, carrying with it all the sand and grit and detritus of hundreds of miles of wasteland, seeping through tent partitions, soiling kits and uniforms.[58] The Blue's habitual sandstorms were made much worse by the breaking up of the desert's hard crust under the tracks and wheels of thousands of vehicles. Loose dust hung in the air, waiting to be funnelled into the vicious spring squalls from the south known as the khamsin winds.[59] Discarded tins, old petrol cans and loose camel-scrub were flung at great speed across the desert surface, smashing into anything they encountered.[60] As for the sand, it was simply everywhere – in food, hair, engines, ears, guns. Sand, wrote Neil McCallum, was 'the foundation of the visible world' when out in the Blue:

> Particles of friable rock, blown by the wind, drift like smoke on the horizon. Close-packed underfoot the sand is the shifting insecure ground. When a mug of tea is finished there is the sediment of sand at the bottom. There is sand in the food, no matter how recently it has been taken out of a sealed tin. The hairs of the body are individually outlined by a coating of fine powdered sand . . . rub your hands on a handkerchief . . . the grains are still there, golden, minute, invincible, a grey-gold dust.[61]

It was a permanent impediment to movement, or indeed activity of any kind. One of the commonest sights when driving in Egypt was to see a squad of grunting, sweating soldiers at the roadside, straining to release their bogged-down truck from the sandy furrow it had got stuck in.[62]

To men whose expectations about the desert had been shaped by P. C. Wren's *Beau Geste* or the sets of Ramon Navarro movies, seeing the Blue for the first time could be disenchanting. After two years of back-and-forth fighting, much of it was a rubbish heap, defaced with the cumulative junk of both armies. Instead of 'the palm trees and camels and sand dunes and Pyramids and ever-present sunshine in clear blues skies' promised by Wren and Hollywood, what newcomers more often encountered was a forlorn landfill of rusty cans, tyres, boxes, worn track ruts and abandoned trenches half silted up.[63] Even stretches unspoiled by man were often naturally brutal and ugly. On his visit to Libya in late 1942, Cecil Beaton described a 'featureless forlorn desolation . . . a scrubland without interest . . . impure and drab as a dump'.[64] South of the Gulf of Sirte in the inhospitable Fezzan region, Christopher Seton-Watson remembered nothing but 'an undulating waste of waterless, glaring sand and stones' in which not even camel-scrub could grow: 'I never want to travel such a penitential route again', he declared after two days of stumbling over its 'raw ribs' in an Army lorry.[65]

The war for the Western Desert lasted twenty-seven months, but only six of them involved any major fighting. Most of the combat was confined to a narrow strip of land along the coast barely 100 miles from end to end. For much of the time and across most of its extent, then, it was the Blue itself that was the British soldier's enemy, not the unseen Afrika Korps. It could be an evil place – a land of conscious malevolence, seething in its hatred for the presence of man, engaged in a continual battle of attrition with him, steadily whittling down his wits and his health. After three months in the desert, Harry Wilson recorded that his engineering section was starting to fall apart through dysentery, boils, sores and eyestrain. 'Some have crumpled up together and have been sent home', he wrote, 'others are thinner, weaker, and more listless. A few seem to have degenerated morally.'[66] Wounds would not heal properly under the withering sun. Whole battalions were laid low by jaundice.[67] Then there were the desert vermin – the cloth-destroying 'woolly bear' worms that would get into metal uniform cases and eat clothes; the insects that snuck into mattresses and bed frames which could only be expelled by dousing them with kerosene.[68] But worst of all was the desert fly, *Musca sorbens*, far larger and more aggressive than his docile European cousin, his numbers vastly multiplied through fattening on the refuse of war. During the worst of the fly season, men were draped in iridescent clouds of them, shimmering like 'black suits of chain mail'.[69] They were the 'curse of the desert . . . responsible for three quarters of the exasperation, short tempers, and genuine hardship' of life in the Blue, according to Seton-Watson. 'One puts down a mug on a rock, and in ten seconds twenty flies will have settled around it, on the rim, on the sides, in the tea itself. They follow the food into one's mouth. They are hungry, persistent, and merciless.'[70]

The desert was a place of absence, a void, a blank slate, a land without past or future, a terra incognita in which 'the outside world had for practical purposes ceased to exist'.[71] Navigation had to be conducted in essentially naval terms, for with few landmarks or visible points of reference to rely upon other than a ribbon of rutted tyre marks or the occasional *bir* (well), a driver hoping to get from one place to another could only take his compass and aim at a set of map coordinates, trying to maintain a roughly straight line at an even speed for what might be seven or eight hours of uninterrupted monotony.[72] Getting lost could portend death. All the essentials of life, let alone war, had to be imported into the Blue – food, tobacco, fuel and, above all, water. Men in forward positions sometimes had to survive on as little as a gallon of water a day, supplementing their ration by drinking from their vehicle radiators if necessary. During the battle for Gazala, a few forward units were reduced to half a pint per man.[73] Endless cups of 'desert char', tea brewed in large cauldrons or cut-off petrol cans over a blazing gasoline fire, kept the Eighth Army going. A single battalion might get through 100 gallons of fuel a day just in brewing-up, and accidental petrol burns occupied a large amount of the Royal Army Medical Corps' time.[74] Between mugs of tea, soldiers ate bacon and fried bread, bully beef from the tin, sometimes cooked with onions and potatoes, and herrings in tomato sauce.[75] If all the bread was gone, then broken-up army biscuits could be soaked in water in a mess tin to make porridge ('burgoo'), toad-in-the-hole or jam pudding.[76]

The existential bleakness of living this same existence day after day, going through the same mundane routines, eating the same food against the same sterile backdrop, ate away at lively minds, robbing men of their curiosity and animation. Time itself became imprecise ('*Is it Monday or Tuesday?*' asked one soldier of another. '*It's Saturday.*' '*Yes, but Saturday of this week or last?*')[77] The result could be a desert weariness described by Reg Crimp as an 'extreme mental sluggishness, sheer physical apathy, and a vast aversion to exertion'. Even the simplest of menial tasks – cleaning, brewing tea, moving to a new patch of shade – became unbearable ordeals, demanding spiritual resources exhausted in the unremitting heat. 'It's only now that you realize how much you live through the senses', reflected Crimp as he prepared for another dreary day in the Blue:

> Here there's nothing for them. Nothing in the landscape to rest or distract the eye; nothing to hear but roaring truck-engines; and nothing to smell but carbon exhaust-fumes and the reek of petrol. Even food tastes insipid, because of the heat, which stultifies appetite. The sexual urge, with nothing to stir it, is completely dormant . . . for weeks more, probably months, we shall have to go on bearing an unbroken succession of empty, ugly, insipid days.[78]

Yet not everyone found the Blue's barrenness entirely disheartening. Christopher Seton-Watson needed no reminding about the discomforts of life in the desert. 'There is no scenery', he readily admitted, 'there is practically no visible life except the flies, travelling is uncomfortable . . . endless miles of wicked rough stones and sharp knobbly boulders.' But all the same, there was a certain stark beauty to its emptiness, especially once the heat had waned and the flies had dispersed at the end of the day. At sunset, he wrote, 'the sand turns to pink, the horizon is yellow and gold and greenish white, and the camp's white tents glow with red.' Once the wind had subsided, the night-time silence was 'weird and rather thrilling'.[79] Animals might emerge from their daytime slumbers to wander and hunt: hyenas, wild dogs, foxes, kites, even gazelles in some places. There was a primitive authenticity to it all, thought Cecil Beaton, a sense of calm and simplicity very different from the 'horrible restlessness' of teeming Cairo: 'Life is smooth, on an even keel, nearer to realities.'[80] To camp out in the middle of the Blue, knowing that you might be the only human being for twenty miles or more, that your entire world had condensed to a campfire and a few cans of food and water and petrol in the back of a lorry, that your connection to civilization was, for the time being anyway, severed – there was a primordial satisfaction to it, a sense that 'nature at her worst' was in the process of being mastered and subjugated. 'I suppose', thought Seton-Watson, 'that Kipling would call it a man's life.'[81]

Cairo, 12 August 1944. The city is in uproar. Hundreds of British soldiers of the 78th Division, recently arrived after long service in Italy, are rioting. Cars are being overturned, windows broken, cafés and bars smashed up. Pitched battles are taking place through the streets. What exactly has set off the trouble will remain disputed for many months to follow. Some soldiers will insist that a Captain Swing-like agitator has planned the whole thing with staff college meticulousness. Others will simply put it down to spontaneous passions. Either way, the principal targets of the rioters' anger are clear enough: Arab vendors, whom, the soldiers insist, have been overcharging the men of the 78th since they arrived in Egypt. By the end of the night, shops will have been raided and their contents destroyed or looted, peddlers and shoeshine boys beaten up or terrified into submission. The Military Police will not fully restore order until the morning of 13 August, by which time 100 men of the 78th will be in prison across Cairo. But many others will have been spirited away back to their barracks by the sympathetic Divisional Provost Marshal, and the whole affair will be quickly hushed up. Having blotted its copybook, the division will be hurriedly packed off back to Italy weeks ahead of schedule.[82]

The events of 12 August would come to represent the lowest point in the intimate but antagonistic wartime Anglo-Egyptian relationship, a meeting of two societies central to the experience of soldiering in the Western Desert. It has often been said that the campaign in North Africa was a war without civilians. This is true only in the limited sense that the fighting took place mostly in empty desert space. The fellahin peasants worked the land far from any site of battle, while the wandering Berber nomads of the desert kept a low profile, waiting until the armies had passed by before descending on the wreckage and the corpses to scavenge. But Egypt was a country with a population of almost seventeen million people in 1940, and relations between the British and the locals were inevitable, and indeed necessary, for the functioning of daily life. Most interaction took place in the bustling 'dragoman-tourist-pavement atmosphere' of Cairo and Alexandria.[83] The British Army relied upon the local Egyptian workforce almost entirely for its labouring, provisioning and recreational needs during the war. British troops in Cairo and Alexandria interacted with ordinary Egyptians every day, employing them as porters, waiters, laundrymen, vendors, guides, pimps and prostitutes. It was a relationship which did not make for one of the happier or more edifying chapters of the war. It can be summarized by a single word – 'wog': 'a word of reference and a word of contempt', a word which distilled into one, ugly syllable the entirety of British disdain for the Arab.[84]

Cairo was a place where you went to forget the war. After months in the Blue living off brackish water, bully beef and tomato paste, men arriving in the Egyptian capital on leave wanted to enjoy themselves to the full. For officers, that might mean the Gezira Sporting Club, where you could watch girls in bathing costumes frolic by the pool as you sat under a shady veranda, with a Sudanese waiter in a red tarboosh topping up your ice-cold beer from time to time; or there was the bar lounge in Shepheard's Hotel, with its enormous domed ceiling, tapestries and stained-glass windows.[85] For ORs, Cairo meant epicurean excess after the austerity of the desert – omelettes and tomatoes, ice-cream and fruit-salad and milkshakes, greasy-spoon restaurants such as *Cafe-Bar Old England* and *Home Sweet Home*, where you could stuff yourself with water-buffalo steak, egg and chips.[86]

Cairo was also 'the oriental city par excellence', its very name evoking fantastical visions of mystery, danger and corruption – 'dark streets with deep secrets, and all the violent extremes of Eastern life . . . depths of depravity and perversion unimagined in the West'.[87] Its carnivalesque atmosphere invited misbehaviour, its labyrinth of streets opportunities for release from the stifling restrictions of Army discipline. Cairo meant, above all, sex. Officers were shepherded into discreet, tidily run brothels where an assistant provost marshal would stand at the front door like a polite English publican keeping order.[88] The ORs instead made for Cairo's central red-light district, the Sharia-el-Berka, a city of sin notorious across the Middle East. At one point during the war, it was estimated that as many as 45,000 military clients were being serviced by the Berka's working girls every month.[89] With its smell and its decay, its filth-ridden gutters and its grimy three-storied tenement whorehouses, the Berka was an unprepossessing destination for vice. But for young men who had not so much as seen a woman for months, and who knew that they might well not return from their next trip to the Blue, its allure was irresistible. Prim warnings from medical officers about the perils of VD did little to diminish the Berka's glamour in the minds of virgin soldiers. The Army, aware that Cairo's prostitutes played an important role in stiffening troop morale, was more concerned about the cleanliness of the men's bodies than their souls. It set up Prophylactic Ablution Centres, at which Berka-bound Tommies could receive condoms and squirts of permanganate potash crystals over their penises to minimize the risk of infection.[90]

The actual experience of the Berka was invariably disappointing. Doug Arthur, who had imagined beforehand 'slim beautiful girls clad in diaphanous night-gowns, smelling of jasmine', was deflated to discover that the typical Cairo brothel was less an Oriental House of Pleasure from a Victorian print than a dismal slum smelling of urine and tobacco. The *bints* whose enticing names – Suzette, Mimi, Fatima – were chalked on the signboard outside were not dark-eyed young beauties, but 'bored, blowsy looking whores of indeterminate age', lolling on a grimy sofa.[91] Harry Wilson, who went on a 'scientific' visit to the Berka in May 1941, found the girls 'fat and ugly, bored and indifferent, exhausted and all of them (I regret to say) utterly repulsive . . . the whole business was nauseating.' Yet there were plenty of soldiers willing to part with fifteen piastres to enjoy their sweaty, hurried favours.[92]

With the cockeyed logic of imperial masculinity, the British Tommy took the very willingness of the Egyptians to gratify his sexual desires as proof that they were a disgusting people. He already thought of them as physically dirty: 'I cannot possibly describe the filth of the Arabs', wrote John Guest: 'They live in what look like hollowed-out dung hills . . . the rags they dress in are beyond description – hundreds of small pieces crudely stitched together, and displaying horrible sores on their legs, arms, and chests.'[93] Cairo's 'peculiar, spicy, aromatic pong' reminded Doug Arthur of the 'subtle whiff of a broken sewer pipe'.[94] The depravities of the Berka – the whorehouses, the backstreet sex-shows, the urchins with packs of pornographic postcards who offered to pimp their sisters – just reinforced how morally unclean they were as well. Before arriving in Egypt, Spike Mays was officially briefed that the primary racial characteristics of Egyptians were 'drug and dope peddling, white slavery, pimping, prostitution, homosexuality and VD'.[95]

The Egyptian wog, as every British soldier knew, was an inveterate layabout and thief. 'What a bunch they are!' wrote Harry Wilson after being placed on 'wog chasing' duty at his unit's supply dump:

> Most of them come from the squalid villages round about and a weirder assortment of humanity can hardly be imagined. Filthy, illiterate, stupid (except for low cunning) and very often infected with disease, they look less like men than animals which have degenerated in captivity. They have to be treated like slaves, not out of cruelty but because they have the slave mentality. They are bone lazy.[96]

Wog indolence and dishonesty were cited as justifications for the treatment meted out to them. Wogs had to be kicked to get them to work. When they were mistreated, it was only just deserts for their past crimes. A. J. Mills was shocked when he first saw his comrades rob an Arab street merchant, but he was reassured that such behaviour was fine because *the wogs steal anything*.[97] Such violence was usually on a petty scale. But there was always a simmering sense of mutual antagonism between the British and their Egyptian hosts, played out in small deceits and cruelties. At camp cinemas, troops would throw four-acker beer bottles at the projectionist. If the film got boring, they might smash up the seats and terrify the cashier.[98] For their part, Arab boys would run alongside tram cars and snatch exposed wrist watches.[99] 'Johnny Wog of Cairo, diseased and avaricious . . . steals from us, stabs us on occasion, and on occasion we shoot him', noted Neil McCallum ruefully. 'And the British Tommy mutters to his swaddy, *Kick him in the arse, Charlie. He's only a bloody wog*.'[100]

Appalling as this behaviour often was, it has to be said that the ordinary soldier was only copying the lead of his superiors. The Army regarded wog lives as cheap. Patrick Hynes's company was told by its commander that if they ever accidentally injured an Arab, it was better to finish him off than try to save him: that way, the British taxpayer would have to pay for a burial blanket rather than a disability pension.[101] One brigadier, annoyed by a spate of petty thefts from his camps, arranged for a posse of Bren carriers to scour the desert at night, with a bounty of £5 per head (dead or alive) for any Arab caught with stolen goods. The manhunt was only abandoned when the disposal of bodies in the Egyptian heat became more problematic than the thefts themselves.[102] Even King Farouk, nominally an independent sovereign ruler, was treated with barely disguised scorn by the generals at GHQ Cairo. When he showed insufficient willingness to appoint a new prime minister on British orders in 1942, troops and tanks immediately surrounded his royal residence and ordered him to submit at gunpoint. The fact that even the country's monarch could be pushed about with such open contempt hardly encouraged the Army's lower ranks to treat Farouk's subjects with any more courtesy.

And for all their condescension, some ordinary soldiers were thoughtful enough to sense the underlying economic exploitation that kept the mass of Egyptians in their squalid state. While 'only a saint could refrain from kicking' them, thought Harry Wilson, he nonetheless pitied their condition. 'Poor creatures!' he wrote in his diary. 'How I loathe the Egyptian ruling class ... the dirtiest pack of scoundrels any side of Suez.'[103] Christopher Seton-Watson was far more scornful of Cairo's sleek, wealthy native businessmen than its gutter orphans. 'They are hardly lifting a finger to help us in our struggle', he noted of the 'revolting' Egyptians who frequented Gezira's fashionable bars. 'They must be making a nice pile of money out of us ... and all the time they enjoy themselves in their clubs and at the races, flaunting their wealth and most enthusiastically wishing us success in the Western Desert.'[104] It was the 'native vampire and the foreign one', thought Dan Billany, who daily ate away at the health and dignity of the peasant masses, reducing them to 'withered wretches'. Their persecutors – both British and indigenous – 'destroyed them, mocked them', and, worse, blamed them for their own miserable condition:

They called them 'dirty wogs': starved them till their ribs showed white, and their children's shins were no thicker than a stick of celery – so that they *prayed* for even a crust – then 'all wogs are beggars': kicked them till they flinched at a shadow – 'shifty wogs': robbed them till there was nothing but their breath to steal, then 'every wog is a thief': and remember always – it is the glory of our civilisation – that it's all free contract and legitimate trading. There's no hint of slavery about it. A man doesn't *have* to work the land for a *piastre* a day. He can always starve.[105]

Still, such pointed self-criticism was the exception. It is hard to read the story of Britain's presence in wartime Egypt today without a sense of embarrassment. British soldiers during the Second World War often behaved with remarkable humility, kindness and courage. But they were flawed human beings, not plaster saints, and if we are to acknowledge their best conduct we also need to be clear-eyed about their worst. The British arrived in wartime Egypt with all the racial baggage of their native land. Most of them had a firm and unchallengeable belief in their own superiority as white people.[106] The result was an attitude towards non-Europeans which was patronizing at its best, ugly and vindictive at its worst, a crude intolerance which degraded the persecutors as much as it did the persecuted. And in the long run it was self-defeating. 'I feel

that someday Europe, and the white races, may pay sorely for their contemptuous arrogance to nearly all coloured peoples', reflected Neil McCallum in
1943. He was speaking prophetically. Twelve years after the 78th Division's riot,
Anthony Eden's government would stumble into a humiliating defeat at Suez,
its precipitate actions encouraged by the old canard that Johnny Wog of Cairo,
that supine and cringing oaf, could never stand up to British power.

CHAPTER 8

COME TO SUNNY ITALY

So there it was, a great high hunk of rock emerging in the distance from the green waters of the Ionian Sea: Italy. The war correspondent Alan Moorehead, sweat-soaked from his morning's climb, stood at the cliff edge and gazed in admiration. 'One was hardly prepared for its nearness', he wrote afterwards. 'It was so close that you could discern the roads and the occasional house among the olive groves.' It was mid-August 1943, and Moorehead and three of his comrades had just single-handedly liberated the Sicilian coastal town of Taormina (no great military feat; at the first sight of British soldiers, Taormina's handful of grubby and terrified defenders had thrown their guns into the sea). A few miles behind Moorehead, tens of thousands of other British and American troops were advancing rapidly, mopping up the few remaining pockets of Axis resistance on the island. Many of them had spent the past ten months fighting the 1,500 miles from Alamein to Tunis. With the crossing of the Strait of Sicily five weeks earlier, they had begun the process of shedding their North African identities, exchanging flies and *khamsin* grit for marsala wine and olive oil. Already the soldierly patois of the Blue was giving way to the language of Verdi: as one man noted, '*Quoisketier, bardin, stanna, swire* and *said bint* have well-nigh surrendered to *molto bono, presto poco, un'momento* and *come state signorina*.'[1] Now there was the prospect of returning to the European mainland itself. 'This', wrote Moorehead, 'was the country towards which the Eighth Army had been fighting for three years . . . all of us had many times lost hope, or at least the immediate sense of hope; and now that we had arrived in sight of Italy it was an unaffected joy merely to stand and look and look.'[2]

Italy offered a return to green fields after years of desert sores and Bedouin tents. Russet-hued, sun-scorched Sicily was not, admittedly, all that distinguishable from Tunisia. Much of Calabria, too, would turn out to be 'not really a change from the Middle East', as Harry Wilson complained – the same 'stone and earth mounds, the same kinds of lizards; and up above, the unclouded sun just as warm'.[3] But as Eighth Army soldiers travelled further and further up the Italian spine, they were struck by the increasing greenness of everything. The 'graceful hills, villages crested with rich valleys of vine and corn, white roads edged with flowers, and dazzling fields of yellow daisies' of the Plain of Foggia were enough to 'jerk throbs from sand-parched throats', wrote Reg Crimp.[4] This was lush countryside of a recognizably European kind. Apulia, with its stone terraces and cone-roofed cottages and tiered vineyards, looked to be 'the Kent of Italy'.[5] Dense clumps of farmhouses in the river valleys disgorged succulent peaches, pears and plums.[6] If Egypt had reminded soldiers of the Bible, the cultural frames of reference were now the Middle Ages and the Renaissance as transmitted through art. 'Do you remember those fantastic little stone towns perched on the tops of hills in backgrounds of paintings by so many Italian masters?' wrote John Guest in a letter home. 'The winding, shining little rivers, and the rocks, and those slender black trees with round bunches of foliage that are so often silhouetted against skies of infinite depth and clarity? All these are actually here and can be seen.'[7] The 'piercingly beautiful' cypress-strewn hills around Luco di Mugello in Tuscany might have been aspects of a landscape by Leonardo, Perugino, Raphael or Gozzoli.[8] Scots Guards officer Walter Elliott was also reminded of da Vinci as he wandered a mountain goat track above Capua, watching the setting sun illuminate the town's ancient domes, listening to the bells calling the peasants to vespers as they had done every evening for centuries.[9] 'One was back in Europe, in Western civilization', wrote Richard Hoggart. 'It was a heady homecoming.'[10]

Mount Vesuvius, which in spring 1944 had begun its first major eruption for forty years, added an infernal majesty to the already splendid scene. Norman Lewis, a British intelligence officer whose diary describing life in post-liberation Naples is one of the most enlightening and thoughtful documents of the campaign, watched the lava stream trickle down the mountain's slopes as the sun faded behind the Tyrrhenian Sea. 'By day the spectacle was calm', he noted,

> But now the eruption showed a terrible vivacity. Fiery symbols were scrawled across the water of the bay, and periodically the crater discharged mines of serpents into a sky which was the deepest of blood reds and pulsating everywhere with lightning reflections.[11]

As for the Italians themselves, they too were reassuringly European-looking. Life in their cities was recognizably modern; Richard Hoggart called Naples

'Leeds in technicolour', while one of his soldiers remarked of the huge pasta meals at his local girlfriend's parents' house that 'the atmosphere was much like Sunday dinner with a roast and two veg at his own home'.[12] And they were much friendlier than the Arabs, despite having been enemies so recently. Most Italians seemed more relieved than dismayed at their defeat by the Allies. Advancing through Sicily, Hugh Samwell's Highlanders were mobbed with uproarious children calling for *caramello!* (sweets).[13] Neil McCallum's platoon was cheered and clapped wildly at every town they arrived in. In Scordia 'the people were hysterical', he wrote:

> It was an emotional jag for the civilians, a rag-time of tears and laughter. Girls offered military favours in the nearest houses. Some of our men vanished and came back ten minutes later, flushed and stupefied and grin-ning. No skin-scouring desert sand about this war, but soft flesh.[14]

Travelling with the first Allied column to enter Naples on 1 October 1943, Alan Moorehead noted that as the troops approached the outskirts of the city the crowd, which had begun slowly accruing along the roadside in Castellamare and Pompeii, suddenly swelled into a 'tumultuous mob of screaming, hyster-ical people' on all sides. 'They stood on the pavement and leaned out of their balcony windows screaming at the Allied soldiers and the passing trucks', he wrote:

> They screamed in relief and in pure hysteria. In tens of thousands the dirty ragged children kept crying for biscuits and sweets. When we stopped the jeep we were immediately surrounded and overwhelmed. Thrusting hands plucked at our clothing. *Pane. Biscotti. Sigarette.* In every direction there was a wall of emaciated, hungry, dirty faces.
>
> I had had the notion that the people would be hostile, or resentful, or perhaps reserved. I had expected that they would indicate in some way the feelings they had had as enemies in the past three years. But there was no question of war or enmity here. Hunger governed all. There were some who in their need fawned and grovelled. They thrust their dribbling children forward to whine and plead. When a soldier threw out a handful of sweets there was a mad rush to the pavement, and women and men and children beat at each other as they scrambled on the cobblestones.[15]

'Wine and grapes. Vermouth and champagne, six shillings a bottle – grand stuff! But damn all else; no food, no nothing! Bags of women, though! Just the job! Fifty-four brothels here, all of them in bounds.' A non-stop flow of booze and tarts – if

this precis given by a passing Tommy at Taranto harbour was anything to go by, then it seemed that Italy had much to commend it.[16] A new infantry replacement fresh out of England was heard to say out loud: '*It's halfway to Heaven here already. I wouldn't mind dying in a place like this.*' Six weeks later he got his wish. His comrades found his body lying in a cornfield, riddled with German machine-gun bullets.[17]

The decision to cross the Mediterranean and invade Italy was made in a heady mood. After putting up a stubborn six-month resistance in Tunisia, the final 230,000 German and Italian troops on the southern shore of the Mediterranean finally surrendered in May 1943. Mussolini's fascist regime in Rome, humiliated by its defeat, was now clearly tottering. An intriguing possibility seemed to present itself. If the Allies could deliver another swift blow to fascist prestige, say by invading Sicily, then not only could the Gibraltar-Malta-Alexandria supply route be restored, but Italy might drop out of the war entirely. That would rip open a gaping hole on Germany's southern flank. Top-secret ULTRA signals intelligence suggested that in such an eventuality the Germans planned to deploy their defences no further south than a line from Pisa to Ravenna. If the British and Americans showed enough dash, then, they could seize Rome without resistance and begin pressing on the German defences along the River Arno by the end of 1943. The British Chiefs of Staff calculated that the Germans' need to redeploy their garrisons in Yugoslavia and Greece to protect against this new threat would leave their position in the Balkans 'disastrously weak'. The Third Reich would be dealt 'a military disaster of the first magnitude'.

The Americans were not so sure. Focused above all things on a cross-Channel invasion, they were suspicious of any Mediterranean distractions. In selling the plan to them, then, Churchill and Brooke emphasized that an Italian campaign would simply be a way of drawing German strength from France and of further ensuring the success of Operation OVERLORD, due to proceed in 1944. Privately, the two men may have hoped that conquering Italy would render OVERLORD unnecessary. Success in Italy might mean that the much-feared assault on the Western Front need never take place.[18]

On 10 July 1943, four British Commonwealth and three American assault divisions landed in Sicily. By 17 August, the last Axis defenders had abandoned the island, withdrawing to Calabria. On the face of it, the operation was a complete success. Yet a German force of just 50,000 men with little assistance from the Italians had been able to hold off almost half a million invading troops for five weeks. Most of the Germans had escaped across the Strait of Messina without difficulty, taking their weapons, vehicles and supplies with them. A more careful examination of what had happened might have introduced a note of caution into Allied plans. But hubris was in the air.[19] On 25 July Mussolini had, after all, fallen from power as hoped. The new government in Rome was secretly negotiating terms of surrender with the Allies. The Italian mainland looked ripe for conquest.

On 3 September, Eighth Army troops made landfall in Calabria on the tip of the Italian boot. They met only light resistance. On 9 September, as the news of the formal Italian surrender was being broadcast by radio to the world, the British 1st Airborne division landed at Taranto, while 150 miles to the west on the Tyrrhenian coast a much larger force of one British and one American corps prepared to disembark on the beaches below the city of Salerno. Both forces, it was hoped, would encounter only light opposition. J. H. Rehill, waiting a few miles offshore of Salerno in a landing craft, heard the news of Italy's capitulation and was energized by a 'surge of euphoria' that swept across the ranks. Many of his fellow soldiers had had a fairly easy time of it in Sicily, he noted later. They assumed that this invasion would go as smoothly as the last. 'This landing will be easy', they thought. 'Each landing would be easier than the last one!'[20]

But the Germans were lying in wait at Salerno. Assumptions about Axis strategy based on ULTRA would turn out to be calamitously wrong. Hitler, guessing correctly that his Italian allies were on the verge of abandoning him, had changed his mind about his defensive deployments. Instead of leaving his troops in the north of the peninsular, he had ordered six divisions under the highly able General Albert Kesselring to take up positions south of Naples. The Allied troops disembarking at Salerno would not be met with white flags or bottles of vino, but with a withering hail of artillery, tank, mortar and machine-gun fire. For eight days, the fate of the embattled bridgehead hung in the balance. Only the superiority in Allied naval and air power finally tipped the scales against the Germans. But even in defeat they were able to break off from the battle in good order, and retreat towards a solid defensive line on the River Volturno.

The ordeal at Salerno, as it turned out, was just a foretaste of what the next twenty months of fighting in Italy were going to be like. If, as General Eisenhower dubbed it, the D-Day campaign across France and Germany was the 'Great Crusade', then the Italian campaign – which was to last twice as long, and progress at half the speed – might have been called the Great Dismay. The British and Americans soon found that their material advantages in man- and firepower were neutralized by Italy's ideal defensive conditions. Encouraged by the success of their delaying action at Salerno, the Germans dug in along a series of short but unflankable defensive lines that took advantage of the Italian peninsula's narrow oblong shape, its corrugated interior, and its succession of wide, fast-flowing rivers – the Volturno, the Rapido, the Liri, the Garigliano, the Biferno, the Trigno, the Moro, the Sangro (lyrical names that were soon to mean only pain and despair to British and American troops). The Allies, it turned out, had grossly underestimated the difficulty of negotiating Italy's mountainous spine, and of moving large numbers of mechanized troops and vehicles along its primitive road network. As the *Wehrmacht* steadily retreated it took with it every scrap of food and head of livestock it could get its hands on. What it could not take it methodically blocked or destroyed – bridges, railways, viaducts, hill passes. The Pontine marshes south of Rome, drained by Mussolini's engineers in the 1920s, were reflooded with brackish water, turning much of Lazio into a malarial swamp. Roads and fields were mined, buildings booby-trapped with malicious ingenuity. Allied progress was reduced to a crawl. Every successful battle 'seemed merely to open up new obstacles ahead. A few more Germans killed. But then – nothing.'[21] 'Though we didn't always go forward in the African campaign', lamented John Guest in his diary, 'it was nearly always exciting, and one kept oneself fully wound up. But now . . . we sit and wait and wait.'[22]

The verdant clutter of the countryside made it beautiful but also deadly. In the open desert, ambush had been almost impossible. The enemy could be seen approaching from miles away. In Italy, woodlands and hedges and hillsides offered endless opportunities for cover. Clear lines of fire were reduced to a few dozen yards. Tanks, once the masters of the battlefield, were now deathtraps, ponderous easy targets for camouflaged anti-tank guns. Eighth Army soldiers found that all the tactical tradecraft they had mastered in Africa had to be forgotten as they learned about confined close-country fighting for the first time. 'Compared with the old desert warfare this Italian sort is much more costly, owing to closer contact with the enemy', noted Reg Crimp in spring 1944. 'On the Blue we rarely got within sight of him, there was so much space and visibility. But the thick and tortuous country here stacks all the cards for concealment and surprise.'[23] Whereas in the desert engagements had taken place at hundreds or thousands of yards' range, now the two armies were locked in brutal intimacy, often within shouting or throwing distance of one another's positions.

This close-quarter trench warfare reached its apogee at Anzio from January to June 1944, when the two sides were at times barely fifteen yards apart. The battle for Anzio began as an attempt to outflank the German 'Gustav Line' by landing two Allied divisions forty miles to the south of Rome. Like the Italian campaign itself it was an ingenious idea, perhaps too clever for its own good. Either because of the American commander's tardiness or because he was given insufficient resources for the job – the controversy remains unsettled – the beachhead was soon surrounded by enemy troops. Instead of the Anzio attacking force trapping the Germans along the Gustav Line, it soon found itself bottled up in its tiny landing zone, in danger of being totally annihilated. With German guns deployed on the enveloping high ground and able to observe all movement beneath, the British and Americans had to entrench as close to the enemy as possible to escape their artillery fire. Raleigh Trevelyan, a Rifle Brigade subaltern attached to the Green Howards, led a platoon dug in at the extreme northernmost point of the line in March 1944. His men could hear the Germans opposite talking, laughing and singing, even coming to recognize the voices of individual enemy soldiers – Leo, 'Moupi'. The smell of cooked German food and hot German coffee wafted across the lines, tormenting them as they lay in their own cheerless trenches hardly daring to move. Occasionally a luckless *Landser* on his way to pick up his rations would lose his way and wander oblivious right into the British company HQ, still clutching his greasy mess-tin.[24] At another place along the line the Germans were only six paces away, and they could roll hand-grenades into the British firing pits.[25]

It was disorientating to find such menace amongst such loveliness. 'There was a bewilderment in my mind', thought artillery signaller Tom Roe as he gazed at a patch of celandines at Anzio:

Sunshine and blossoming flowers proclaimed a message of life; the constant threat was death. Budding trees and bushes hinted at a beauty to come; the shell-holes and the charred branches, abounding, cast a shadow of foreboding and frustration. The thought of death seemed normal enough when the days were dark, rain-swept, cold, and slimy . . . but who wanted to die in a land of spring sunshine?[26]

By the end of 1943, the twenty-five Anglo-American divisions of 15th Army Group were still well south of Rome, pressing with frustratingly slow effect against just eighteen German divisions.[27] An expedition which had been intended to tie up enemy resources was arguably becoming as much of a drain on the Allies as it was on the Germans. The Americans grumbled that they had predicted this all along, and pushed forward with their plans for OVERLORD. Almost forgotten in the midst of everything were the Italians themselves, nominally now on the Allied side, though condescended to and exploited by their friends as much as they had been by their foes – fugitives in their own country, abject in the ruin that their former *Duce*'s belligerence had visited upon them.

On 5 June 1944, after a gruelling four-month battle to break the German line at Cassino, the Allies at last entered Rome. The first Axis capital of the war had fallen! But the triumph held the world's attention for barely twenty-four hours until it was trumped by the far more consequential news of the invasion of France. It was a cruel coincidence which in many ways encapsulated the whole experience of soldiering in Italy. For the former Desert Rats, who had got accustomed to being the darlings of the British press on the 'highlight front', to be stranded in such an obvious backwater of the war – every bit as miserable and dangerous as North Africa, but without any of the compensating glory – was a bitter fate.[28] 'We were spoilt darlings, the only British Army in action', recalled Reg Crimp. 'Now we're merely outsiders, also-rans. The Second Front is hogging the huzzahs.'[29] The story that the Conservative MP Lady Astor dismissed the troops in Italy as 'D-Day Dodgers' grew out of a misunderstanding.[30] But the very fact that the legend became so pervasive says much about the depth of unhappiness in Eighth Army in the final months of the war.

By the winter of 1944, with the Allied offensive once again having run out of momentum in the flooded plain of Romagna, it was becoming obvious to everyone that no decisive breakthrough would ever take place in Italy. The misery was now accentuated by mud – a creamy *café au lait*-coloured slime that coated everyone and everything, soaking through boots and socks, rotting away exposed skin and causing the trench-foot which, along with frostbite, dysentery and malaria, debilitated more Allied troops in Italy than enemy action. The peninsula's climate had turned out to be cruelly fickle. Days of roasting, breezeless sun could suddenly give way to a week of thunderous downpours that the built environment was totally inadequate to absorb. The only really good roads in Italy were the two coastal highways, one on the Tyrrhenian side and the other on the Adriatic. Beyond these, in the hinterland, most travel had to take place on dirt tracks which had never before had to bear the weight and volume of an Allied mechanized army. In dry spells they threw up clouds of dust, coating all the grass and trees for fifty yards on either side with fine choking silt.[31] With the coming of the rain, they became mudslides. 'The cumulative psychological effect of mud is an experience which cannot be described', wrote John Guest in December 1944, in the midst of the worst weather in Italy for twenty years:

> Vehicles grind along the road beneath in low gear. Either side of the road is a bank of mud, thigh-deep. The sides of the roads collapse frequently and the huge trucks, like weary prehistoric animals, slide helplessly down into the ditches and stick there until dragged out by recovery teams. All the traffic gets held up and people sit in the vehicles

clapping their gloved hands to keep warm, smoking, and making wan facetious remarks to the pedestrians who go slopping and slithering past in their gum boots. My men stand in the gun pits stamping their feet in the wet, their heads sunk in the collapse of their greatcoats. When they speak to you they roll their eyes up because it makes their necks clod to raise their heads. Everyone walks with their arms out to help them keep their balance.[32]

All movement turned to a crawl in mud season. In Minturno on the banks of the Garigliano, slit trenches became so silted up with mud that soldiers had to sit on tree branches.[33] Brigades which had won a reputation for speed in the desert were forced to abandon their lorries and Bren carriers, reduced to commandeering mules to shuffle along mountain passes. Ambulances could not negotiate the washed-out trails; half a dozen casualties might require a whole platoon to become temporary stretcher-bearers for a night. Wounded soldiers died needlessly on the way to a field dressing station for want of a vehicle to carry them.[34]

The desertion rate in Eighth Army in the winter of 1944 was the worst of any Allied army in the whole war.[35] Over 1,000 British troops absconded every month.[36] Many of them had fought from Alamein to Tunis to Cassino with hardly a rest: their 'capital of courage', as one infantry platoon commander put it, had finally been exhausted.[37] The fact that even their own leaders seemed to think the campaign had become futile was hardly an encouragement to the troops to risk their lives any longer. By the final winter of the war the battle for Italy had become a half-forgotten leftover, a bright idea that had long lost its lustre. The fighting was as grisly as ever, but its results were increasingly irrelevant to the outcome of the conflict. 15th Army Group's units were peeled away to be used in Greece and France. Drafts of reinforcements and supplies dwindled. Ambitious commanders disappeared for more promising jobs elsewhere. *'Ike and Monty left us'*, the men sang bitterly:

Jumbo's gone away; gone to reign in glory in the USA.
Even Alexander's left the sinking barque;
AAI is left with General fucking Clark![38]

'It was as unpleasant a campaign as any in modern history', thought David Hunt, a senior intelligence officer on General Alexander's staff.[39] By its end, 18,737 British troops had died for the sake of an 'expensive, slow, and unpunctual' slogging-match across waterlogged valleys and mud-soaked terraced hills. Sunny Italy, the land of grapes and poplars and truffles, had turned out to be a Mediterranean Passchendaele.[40]

'This country is full of weird contrasts', wrote artilleryman Christopher Seton-Watson in summer 1944 as his unit occupied a position near Lake Trasimene:

> One can spend the morning at an artillery observation post, looking out over the enemy lines, probably sitting in a shattered house surrounded by mines and shell craters and all the usual desolation of battle ... then a 20-minute drive and one is in the centre of a lovely old town, almost untouched by war, full of civilians strolling as if there had never been a German within thousands of miles ... the narrow streets and alleys, the squares and piazzas full of statues and surrounded by noble Renaissance facades, the lovely doorways, the towers and churches and archways transport one to an entirely different world.[41]

Italy was jumbled with artefacts of the past like this. Antique castles and fortresses were a reminder of all the armies since classical Greece which had trodden exactly the same path the Eighth Army was now on.[42] The country's surfeit of history greatly complicated the process of fighting itself. The German retreat in 1944 ran right through some of the greatest sites of artistic importance in the world – Florence, Siena, Pisa. The Allies were cognizant of the need to exercise restraint in the use of force, to be seen as liberators, not vandals. Commanders who had grown accustomed to the barren, intrinsically valueless expanse of the North African battlefield, a wasteland that they could happily blast to smithereens without consequence or protest, now had to accommodate cultural sensitivity into their planning. Bombing targets were graded according to their artistic as well as their strategic value. 'Monuments officers' declared which locations could be shelled and which could not.[43] 'It is not the Art of War any more but the War of Art', complained French general de Montsabert to the British war correspondent Wynford Vaughan-Thomas. How you approached an assault on a town depended as much on the charm and uniqueness of its architecture as the dispositions of the enemy:

> The fifteenth century? I must not attack but must make an outflanking movement. The sixteenth? Then I permit myself a little machine-gun fire. The seventeenth? Ah! Now we can have artillery support. The eighteenth means tanks and for the nineteenth, *monsieur*, I have no hesitation in calling in the air. If only Italy had all been built in the twentieth century we should be on the Alps by now.[44]

It was jumbled with people, too. Italian civilians were a feature of the battlefield in a way they had never been in North Africa. Peasants wandered back and forth across the lines, some watching firefights as though they were spectators at a Cup Final match, others, with their bundles of clothes and their donkeys, clinging to the routines of day-to-day life even as their worlds disintegrated around them.[45] Alan Moorehead watched one farmer continue to plough his fields while mortar shells fell around him in a 'curiously human and pathetic' ritual of normality:

> The people could never get used to the sudden arrival of death in a village street they had known for forty years or more. They never accepted it, never comprehended it. They were unable to drag their minds out of the lazy, easy-going past to the violent present. And when a child was killed, perhaps in front of the local tavern, they cried over it with a nameless uncomprehending anguish, blaming no human agency, attributing everything to the implacable will of God.[46]

To Leonard Melling, these unworldly Italians were a 'gaunt, ragged people . . . amongst the most simple I have ever met. Their poverty was more dire, collectively both in the rudeness of their dwellings and the paucity of the chattels which they contained than that of any Europeans I have encountered.' Yet the very fact that they were so 'credulous and simple' gave them an attractive peasant authenticity that had been lost in more civilized places:

> Warm-hearted and hospitable, rooted to their beloved soil, unpretentious and industrious, [they] were some of the most refreshing people I have met. Few could read and write. They knew little or nothing of politics, but their illiteracy does not prescribe them as lacking in intelligence. Perhaps with their not imbibing in large quantities the literary trash which is so profusely disseminated today permits them to enjoy a clearer understanding of the real things in life.[47]

To others, though, the fantastic poverty and ignorance that existed outside the cities was not charming but shocking. It seemed as though time had stood still in the Italian countryside for 500 years.[48] It was not just the sight of the rustic little stone towns that evoked the Middle Ages; it was the behaviour of their inhabitants too. A well-to-do family of three or four peasants might live in a one-room hut, with a pig tethered to the door jamb and chickens pecking at the ground. Women would spend long days at local streams washing clothes by scrubbing them against rocks.[49] Peasants would 'listen with breathless interest' to descriptions of an outside world they had never glimpsed.[50] Norman Lewis was astonished at the medieval atmosphere of magic and cruelty that still seemed to pervade much of rural Campania. Fervent parishioners prayed to talking crucifixes and relics which bled and sweated. The miseries of the war had aggravated peasant fanaticism: women were being accused of witchcraft, penitents beating themselves with wooden boards to ward off evil spirits. Revellers danced to ward off typhoid and smallpox.[51] The British expected such barbarism of the Wogs back in Egypt. But it was far more disturbing to see it being carried out by people who, cleaned up and dressed for the part, would not have looked out of place on the Walworth Road.

So perhaps the Italians were not so much like the British as they superficially seemed. And as the exuberance of liberation began to wear off, the cities also revealed a more disturbing pattern of life. Italy represented the first great humanitarian crisis that the advancing Allied armies had to deal with. They did not handle it well. The British and Americans who arrived in Naples in October 1943 were almost totally unprepared for the responsibilities of civil administration. The record of the Allied Military Government (AMGOT) in Italy has been described by one historian as a 'saga of incompetence, mismanagement, and missed opportunities'.[52] By the time Naples fell to the British and Americans, the thick web of graft and thuggery which had constituted civil society under the fascists was snapping apart. Southern Italy's infrastructure, its roads and railways and bridges and viaducts and electric sub-stations and telegraph lines – all the apparatus necessary for sustaining day-to-day life in a great urban centre such as Naples – were either already in ruins, or being systematically destroyed by Allied bombers and retreating German sappers. Already people did not have enough to eat. Soon they would have nothing to wear either, and nothing to keep them warm. They would fall ill with typhus, smallpox, malaria. And then they would die, some quietly in their homes, others in the streets, their bodies sometimes unattended for days. Most of the 400,000 tons of food which the Allies hurriedly imported into southern Italy in the wake of their arrival immediately disappeared on to the black market. Starvation loomed. Thousands of Neapolitans gathered on the roadsides to hunt for edible plants. Children prised limpets off rocks to boil into broth.[53] Proud *intellettuali* with 'scarecrow shoulders and turnip-coloured faces' sold their last possessions on street corners for a pittance. Respectable women prostituted themselves for a few tins of food or some packets of Lucky Strikes.[54] 'It is impossible not to pity starving people', wrote Harry Wilson:

> Especially when they herd together near the cookhouse and watch us eat with longing eyes and watered mouths, intercepting us when we go to throw away our leavings and entreating us to let them have them. It's downright embarrassing. Instead of dumping our scraps we now throw them into a

large bowl, and this revolting mixture, often covered with grease and gravy is eagerly shared out amongst the crowd.[55]

But suffering was not ennobling. By the end of 1943, the city of Naples' entire economy seemed to have been recast on principles of theft, vice and graft. Everything was available for the right price – including sex, of course: one third of the nubile female population was estimated to be on the game.[56] But also tobacco, nylons, brandy, chocolates, silk stockings, gloves, perfume and all manner of other luxury items at grotesquely inflated prices. Shops sold sweets and cakes while children starved in the gutters outside.[57] Alan Moorehead watched with appalled fascination as more and more pimps and black market-eers appeared along the Via Roma with each passing day after liberation:

You want nice girl? Biftek, spaghetti. Verra cheap. Good brandy. Only fife hundred lire. Beautiful signorina. Every ten yards down the street a dark little man would slide up to you and pluck you by the sleeve. Children of ten and twelve were being offered in the brothels. Raw spirit mixed with flavouring was sold in dirty bottles with fake labels. Every form of imitation jewellery came out on the pavements. Six-year-old boys were pressed into the business of selling obscene postcards; of selling their sisters, themselves, anything . . .

In the whole list of sordid human vices none I think were overlooked in Naples during those first few months. What we were witnessing in fact was the moral collapse of a people. They had no pride any more, or any dignity. The animal struggle for existence governed everything. Food. That was the only thing that mattered. Food for the children. Food for yourself. Food at the cost of any abasement and depravity. And after food a little warmth and shelter.[58]

The Army's property seemed to be regarded by the locals as an inexhaustible treasure hoard that was there to be taken at will. Anything not guarded or nailed down disappeared almost immediately. Feral gangs of urchins roamed the streets, expertly pickpocketing soldiers. 'Almost everyone thieved or fiddled', noted Richard Hoggart.[59] The only way to prevent an Army lorry being purloined while parked on the street was to remove the rotor arm from the engine, and even then the driver might return from a brief errand to find his wheels gone, his petrol siphoned off, and the goods he had been carrying stolen.[60] 'A kind of jungle law' operated throughout the city – 'the survival of the most cunning, or the least scrupulous. You are expected to know that you will be cheated, and if you cheat in return you will be esteemed the more for it.'[61] Norman Lewis thought that the Neapolitans regarded the occupying British as easy marks, 'only one degree better than cuckolds', from whom they could take with contemptuous ease.[62]

Perhaps, then, behind all the artless grins and the cheery embraces, there was something less than innocent about the Italians – a moral shallowness, a refusal to accept the normal rules of decent behaviour? 'Difficult not to feel sorry for many of them, but difficult to keep up my sympathy after the hundredth hard-luck story. You just have to spread it thin', thought intelligence officer B. F. Spiller.[63] This extended to politics too. Pleasant though it was to be received so enthusiastically in a nation which until recently you had been at war with, there was, all the same, something a little maddening about the way in which the Italians seemed to want instantly to forget twenty years of fascism. They 'pulled solemn faces and made dramatic gestures at any mention of *Tedeschi* [Germans]', thought Norman Craig, but 'somehow their colourful and exaggerated tales never quite rang true'.[64] There was a 'complete lack of any sense of responsibility or shame or regret for Italy's part in the war', according to Alan Moorehead. 'Everything was blamed upon the Fascists, especially by those who had hidden their uniforms and ceased to be Fascists overnight.'[65] As Christopher Seton-Watson's artillery unit travelled up the spine of Italy he noticed the same scene re-enacted every time they liberated a new town:

> The main square fills with people, of all ages and classes and sexes; red flags are produced, speeches made, the band parades up and down, the local Fascist's windows are broken (he himself has usually fled), walls are covered with slogans (*Viva Matteotti* is the favourite) and any English soldier who appears on the scene is carried shoulder high to the nearest cafe and plied with *vino* . . . youths appear in gleaming red shirts and scarves and silly little 'partisan' caps like paper hats out of a Christmas cracker, with a star set in the middle of the peak. Long stories are told of heroic deeds in the face of vast German armies. The gullible are persuaded that every mountain in Italy was for three long years covered with Italian soldiers refusing to fight for Musso.

'What children the Italians are. It's impossible to hate them', he conceded. And yet, he couldn't help wondering: how many of the beaming, guileless youths now cheering on the Tommies had been enthusiastically parading in black shirts just a few weeks before?[66]

Perhaps the Allies had no right to expect anything else. The conflict in Italy exposed, as no other campaign of the war would quite so starkly, the moral ambiguities of war. By 1943, the British were feeling rather pleased with themselves, rather more convinced of their own moral rectitude than was good for them. Italy chipped away at a little of that complacent self-admiration. The Allies had landed on the peninsular claiming to be the peasant's friend. And what had they accomplished? They had smashed homes, burned crops, reduced children to alms-begging, women to prostitution. Friendships, family alliances, local customs and courtship arrangements had been broken up by their clumsy, brutal intrusion into the delicate patterns of traditional life. Plenty of liberators were colluding in Italian thievery. The Special Investigations Branch of the Corps of Military Police established thirteen sections across the country, chasing groups of armed deserters like the 'Tiger Gang', which specialized in highway robbery and shop-breaking.[67] But even some regimental policemen were on the take. By the end of the war, they were running the black market trade in cigarettes, tyres and Army blankets in Lombardy.[68] The British had not behaved at all well in Egypt, although that had been at the expense of a people with whom they felt little racial identification or sympathy. The Italians were just too similar in complexion and habits to be so easily dismissed. It was hard for thoughtful Tommies not to feel a sense of shame as well as pity for the chaos and destruction they had wrought up and down a land that had seemed to them, at first, such a garden of delights.

In William Woodruff's autobiographical novel *Vessel of Sadness*, about his experiences at Anzio, he imagines an encounter between an *Inglese* soldier and a 'wrinkled, dark-clad' Italian matron which could easily serve as an epitaph for the entire campaign. Woodruff's soldier upbraids the woman for her keening and the accusatory glances she sends in his direction. 'Is this the way to greet those who would free you?' he demands. He is here in her homeland as a redeemer, risking his own life to defend hers. The Germans, he points out, would not permit her insolence to go so unpunished. She is unmoved. How much more could she possibly be punished anyway? Her home lies in ruins about her. Her sons are buried in Tobruk. Her daughters have been killed by an artillery shell fired by one side or the other – it scarcely matters which. Her husband's body lies in a nearby field. Even her sow and her dappled-grey mare are dead. Suffering is hardly new to this woman. But the war has taken away from her the few things she possessed that made her life of ceaseless toil and penury otherwise endurable.

'On the plain of Latium they had scratched peace', Woodruff concludes. 'And inserted the harrow of Hell.'[69]

CHAPTER 9

FIGHTING BLOODY NATURE

'Imagine dense thick jungle . . .'

'Black night, men in Indian file, each hearing but hardly seeing the man in front and the man behind, the column a quarter of a mile long from front to rear; the creak of mule harness, clink of metal on metal.' The ground beneath your boots pliant, squelching under the weight of your 60 pounds of kit. The air damp, foetid, steaming with the evaporating heat of the day. Mosquitoes and fat flying beetles tracing wide parabolic arcs around you, buzzing and whirring. Jackals and pie-dogs barking somewhere, far off. And beyond the curtain of trees, other animal noises, deep-throated, primitive, prehistoric; a brontosaurus might raise its head above the canopy any moment and give off an antediluvian roar. Then, suddenly, explosions – *'brief flashes of fire, the man in front jerking back, falling, knocking you down, something hot and wet pouring over your head, a voice you recognize, calling, cut off to a meaningless wail of agony.'* More clamour, confusion, the smell of cordite in the air. Your heart in your throat, your breathing fast and laboured, briny perspiration gathering on your lips. *'The mules jerking, tugging, one broken loose from its leader, perhaps it's dead, crashing away through the trees. Roars of Bren guns from close, very close, the bullets seeming to come straight at you . . .'*[1]

Burma, 1943. Over 260,000 square miles of lush river valley and rugged highland and sun-baked plain, teak forest, mangrove swamp, rice paddy shrouded in morning mist. One thousand two hundred continuous miles of coastline, stretching lazily along the Bay of Bengal from Chittagong in India to Thailand's Tenasserim Hills. Twenty degrees of latitude, equivalent to travelling from the

Shetlands to Barcelona. To the north, the Himalayas; to the south, the Strait of Malacca and the East Indies. Twelve thousand feet of elevation. Seven thousand species of plant life. Monkeys, water buffalo, elephants, rhinoceros, tigers; more poisonous snakes than anywhere else in the world. Fifteen million human inhabitants, most of them crammed into the Irrawaddy Plain, a fraction of them still leading a largely uninterrupted Palaeolithic existence, scattered amongst the forested uplands. Most of the hinterland still undisturbed by modernity: few metalled roads or railways, travel in many places by sampan or dirt track or jungle trail. It might take a party of fit men twelve-and-a-half hours to march fifteen miles.[2] Burma: until a year ago a colonial dependency of the British Raj swallowed up in three Victorian wars. Governed by inattentive mandarins with neither wisdom nor efficiency. Now lost to the Japanese, and awaiting reconquest.

Of all the strange and disorientating places British soldiers were sent to during the Second World War, Burma was amongst the most alien of the lot – as weird and unnatural in its own way as the North African Blue. Its climate, its landscape and its peoples were utterly unlike anything the vast majority of soldiers had ever encountered. The novelist George MacDonald Fraser, who served as a lance-corporal in a Border Regiment section, was disconcerted to find himself dumped in the middle of a country 'where you could get dinner off a tree . . . wake in the morning to find your carelessly neglected mess-tin occupied by a spider the size of a soup-plate, and watch your skin go white and puffy in ceaseless rain'. Cumberland was just four days away by mail, yet for Fraser and his mates it might as well have been on another planet.[3] The Burmese jungle conjured up childhood nightmares of being lost within a vast gloomy labyrinth of monster lairs. It teemed with life, but was every bit as hostile to the intrusion of man as the Western Desert. It was full of unnerving noises – howls, screams, angrily buzzing insects that sounded like a thousand telegraph wires in perpetual hum.[4] It was especially terrifying at night. Few British soldiers had ever been in such all-consuming darkness. The temptation to blast away at flickering shadows and far-off sounds was constant.[5] Swarms of black flies consumed everything. The jungle's smell was 'stomach-churning'.[6] 'This ain't fighting bloody Japs; it's fighting bloody nature!' one of Robin Painter's men grunted after slogging through the Burmese interior. Painter conceded that:

> when a man had to put up with being perpetually wet through with festering jungle sores, with the unpleasantness of leeches attaching themselves to any part of his body, with ticks and fleas, exhaustion, the stink of rotting corpses, with marching over indescribable country, with mosquitoes, snakes, and steamy jungle, is it to be wondered at that the ever-present danger of the Japanese became sometimes a secondary consideration?[7]

Throughout the war, a reassignment to the Far East was regarded by most British soldiers as the worst of all possible fates, the one posting they dreaded above every other. The unpopularity of being sent there was such that in February 1944 the War Office toyed with the idea of sending all convicted deserters to Burma – or merely spreading a rumour that it might do this; for just the possibility of being packed off east of Suez might be enough to keep soldiers in Europe on the straight and level.[8] 'I loathe the idea of Burma', Reg Crimp confessed to his diary when rumours that his battalion would be sent there began circulating in October 1943:

> It's further from home. I'm browned off with eastern peoples and countries, feel a yen for something European, with familiar customs and culture. Burma means getting involved with the Jap war, which is obviously only in its infancy and will probably last years after the whistle goes in Europe. With nearly two-and-a-half years' foreign service behind me, this prospect is lethal. Don't like the Japs. Germans are at least human.[9]

Quite apart from the horror of having to fight an enemy as detested as the Japanese, by late 1943 the conflict in the East seemed to have lost all synchronicity with the rest of the war. In Europe, the tide was clearly turning against the Germans; if they were not yet beaten, they were at least in full retreat. It had become possible, just possible, to imagine an end to Hitler and his regime. In Burma, the Japanese seemed as solidly ensconced as they had been since they first invaded. How long would it take the British to march the 800 miles from the Indian frontier to the Irrawaddy Delta? Months? Years? Would they ever even get there?

Early attempts to operate in Burma's hinterland were not encouraging. In the winter of 1942–3, an Anglo-Indian army marched out from Chittagong to advance along the Arakan coastal peninsular and seize the island of Aykab, which lay at the confluence of the Mayu and Kaladan rivers. Control of Aykab's airfield would be a necessary precondition for any assault on Rangoon. At first, optimism was high. Nine brigades were involved. British and Indian forces were reckoned to outnumber the Japanese in the area by at least five to three. But the operation was a disaster. Even though the British had ruled Burma since the nineteenth century, they would in the early years of the Second World War demonstrate an embarrassing lack of basic knowledge about its environment.[10] The army that invaded the Arakan was totally unprepared for the daunting logistical difficulties of manoeuvring and fighting in dense mountainous jungle, mangrove swamps and leech-infested creeks. In the absence of a proper road network connecting Chittagong with the battlefield, supplies had to be ferried fifty miles by water and dirt tracks using river boats and mule trains. The Japanese were formidably dug in at the tip of the peninsular that led to Aykab, having built timber and earth bunkers so resistant to artillery rounds that the attackers at first thought they were made of concrete. Not only were the clumsy British assaults repelled, but a Japanese retaliatory action overran the headquarters of one of the attacking brigades and briefly captured its commanding officer until he was killed by a shell from one of his own guns.

With the arrival of the monsoon rains in early May, the offensive had to be called off. The imperial forces stole ignominiously back across the border into India, having achieved little other than some (admittedly useful) jungle-craft training and a renewed lesson in humility. 'I have rarely been so unhappy on a battlefield', said General William 'Bill' Slim, future leader of the 14th Army in Burma. 'Things had gone terribly, terribly wrong.'[11] Back in London, Churchill was apoplectic. 'This campaign goes from bad to worse ... we are being completely outfought and outmanoeuvred by the Japanese.' It was fortunate, thought the prime minister, that the happier news coming from North Africa in spring 1943 – Tunis had just fallen – had distracted the public from the 'lamentable scene' being played out along the Bay of Bengal.[12] Once again, the British Empire had shown itself incapable of performing military operations east of Suez with any conviction or competence. This was bungle, not jungle warfare.[13]

The defeat in the Arakan only confirmed Churchill's view that a land war in Burma was a waste of lives and resources. Direct recovery of the lost colony was unnecessary. So long, he argued, as the Japanese remained on the east bank of the Chindwin, they were a military irrelevance to the campaign as a whole; let them 'rot away', ignored.[14] He saw little point in a protracted land battle in the Burmese hinterland itself. 'You might as well', he told Alan Brooke, 'eat a porcupine one quill at a time.'[15] To Churchill, the only thing that mattered was to reconquer Singapore as quickly as possible and thus restore some of Britain's battered prestige east of Suez. Burma fitted into that scheme only tangentially. Rangoon might provide a useful base for an amphibious leapfrog to Malaya. And the fastest route to Rangoon was by sea, not by land.

But the prime minister did not get his way. For one thing, the landing craft that would have been necessary to seize first Rangoon and then Singapore by amphibious assault were simply not available, having been diverted to the Mediterranean. For another, the Americans, who were otherwise indifferent to the fate of the British Empire in the East, were insistent that some attempt must be made to reconquer north Burma and so restore the land supply link with their client state, Republican China. And most important of all, in March 1944 the Japanese crossed the Chindwin and invaded India's Manipur province. This attack drew the campaign's centre of gravity far inland from the coast. Once Slim had successfully defended Manipur's capital Imphal after a four-month siege, it was only logical for the army he had assembled there to pursue the retreating Japanese back across the Chindwin and to make for Mandalay and the Irrawaddy plain. This Slim was to accomplish in one of the most brilliantly fought campaigns of the entire war. His 14th Army was less than forty miles north of Rangoon when the city fell without opposition to a belated seaborne assault on 2 May 1945 (the Japanese having fled a few days earlier).[16]

Slim's victory came about because he was able successfully to negotiate the three most daunting obstacles facing any European army in Burma – malaria, monsoon and morale.[17] Malaria took far more British lives during the war than the Japanese ever managed. One brigade in the first Arakan campaign lost half its total strength from the disease in just eight weeks, three-and-a-half times as many casualties as it suffered from combat.[18] Slim could not eradicate every mosquito in Burma, but with better prophylactic treatment, his army became less susceptible to their ravages. By 1945, hospitals were admitting 40 per cent fewer malaria cases than they had dealt with three years earlier.[19] Then there was the problem of Burma's four-month summer monsoon season, during which ground communications slowed to a crawl. Slim was able to militate against its effects by having his troops shed much of their hefty and burdensome equipment, allowing them to move faster. He also utilized Allied control of the skies over Burma by improved methods of dropping food, arms and ammunition by air, freeing troops on the ground from the difficulties of conventional resupply.

His greatest challenge, however, was to turn an army of misfits into a coherent fighting force. In manpower terms, Burma sat very low on the priority list. Slim had to make do with 'the scrapings of the barrel'.[20] His 14th Army was a mongrel blend of Britons, Indians, Nepalese and West and East Africans, half a million miscellaneous troops assembled more because they happened to be available than because they were especially suited to the mission. Slim's predecessor General Noel Irwin, who had commanded the failed Arakan campaign, was scathing about his army's low quality. 'I can say', he wrote to the commander-in-chief in India, General Wavell, 'that [my] troops practically without exception are not worth 50 per cent of Jap infantrymen in jungle country.' He was not alone in this opinion. 'The British soldier is a rotten and gutless fighter', asserted another of Irwin's officers. 'The men who come here to fight come hating the powers that send them . . . and they come praying that they may not have to fight.' A third officer reported that British troops seemed 'exhausted, browned off, or both'. They feared the jungle, hated Burma itself, and had 'the strong feeling that they are taking part in a forgotten campaign in which no-one in authority is taking any real interest'. Though impressive in numbers, they were, compared with the seasoned Japanese veterans, little better than a 'rather unwilling band of levies'.[21]

It was Slim's genius to instil in these unpromising jungle soldiers a belief that they were not beaten – that they could take on the enemy and defeat him. Doctrinal manuals were updated to reflect the hard lessons that had already been learned about jungle warfare. Combat schools were established to teach soldiers vital skills for living and fighting in the Burmese interior: how to cross rivers quickly without drawing enemy attention, how to travel fast and silently at night, how to live off Burma's indigenous flora and fauna.[22] The new confidence and professionalism of 14th Army was confirmed when the Japanese were thrown back, first in the Arakan in February 1944, and then four months later at Imphal and Kohima. Slim slowly improved the conditions of day-to-day life for his soldiers. By the final year of the war, welfare provisions in Burma were much better than they had ever been before. Regular beer and cigarette rations were distributed to the ranks – the latter being especially important; in the front line, only ammunition had a higher supply priority than tobacco. Care packages were circulated which included soap, writing paper, handkerchiefs and towels.[23] Men could send and receive letters more frequently than before using microfilmed airgraphs. Links with the outside world were also reinforced with BBC radio broadcasts, mobile cinema units, a dedicated SEAC newspaper and visits by ENSA concert parties. The Forgotten Army started to feel a little less forgotten.[24]

What Slim had managed to do was remarkable – to inculcate within a thoroughly defeated army a sense of stubborn professional pride that would carry it all the way from Manipur to Rangoon. What he could not do, for all the confidence and affection he inspired in his men, was to make the reconquest of Burma seem really worth the cost. The campaign was ferocious, but it never possessed much moral urgency. As Slim's troops were well aware, few people back in Britain were following the 14th Army's exploits with anything other than tepid half-attention. The Japanese never represented a convincing existential threat to Britain itself. Compared to the Blitz or the Battle of the Atlantic, the fate of Burma, or for that matter India itself, seemed immaterial to most civilians. Few of them had ever been east of Suez. Fewer cared especially what happened there. The only meaningful purpose to the war in Asia was to get the whole thing over and done with and bring the boys of the 14th Army back home as quickly as possible. What happened to Burma after that was of little concern. It is striking that when, in 1948, the colony was abandoned to its nationalist leaders after all the expense and sacrifice of recapturing it just three years previously, the British people responded with something between a yawn and a sigh of relief.[25] '*For your tomorrow, we gave our today*', the memorial at the Kohima war cemetery reads, in majestic, haunting commemoration of the 1,420 Commonwealth soldiers buried there. But for whose tomorrow did they die, in the end?

'If I had thought of India at all in more peaceful days', mused Brian Aldiss after he arrived in Bombay in October 1943, 'I had regarded it as a place where people were miserable and starved to death.' Now he was confronted for the first time with the country itself in all its gut-wrenching sensuality – 'noisy, unregulated, full of colour and stink' – a land of laughter and wild gesticula-tions and agonies unimaginable in cosy middle England. 'There was nothing familiar. It took your breath away. It swarmed, rippled, stewed, with people . . .'

> Jungly music blared from many of the ramshackle little shops. Guajarati signs were everywhere. Tangled overhead cables festooned every street. Half naked beggars paraded on every sidewalk. Over everything lay the heat . . . people were washing and spitting at every street corner, and hump-backed cows were allowed to wander where they would, even into build-ings . . .
>
> The most alarming deformities were presented to our eyes: a child with both arms severed at the elbows, beggars ashake with alien palsies, men with blind sockets of gristle turned imploringly to heaven, skeletal women with fetus-shaped babies at their breasts, scarecrows with fly-specked limbs, deformed countenances, nightmare bodies – all aimed at us with a malign urgency.

'Knowing absolutely nothing of the culture, caring nothing for it, we saw it all as barbarous.' Aldiss and his comrades quickly acquired what was to be their 'first and most important word' of military Urdu – '*Fuck off! Jao! Jao, you bastards, jao!*'[26]

India was the great receiving station of British troops bound for Burma, the place where men fresh from the UK acclimatized themselves to the ferocious tropical humidity before being dispatched to the front line. For regular soldiers between the wars, a posting to the Raj had been one of the signal experiences of Army life; most men had spent at least four years there, often under condi-tions which were an agreeable change from the prison-like severity of home service. Old Sweats spoke fondly of 'the Shiny', as it was known, with its commodious barrack rooms and cool, white cotton sheets, its native wallahs who cleaned kits and washed laundry, and the pine-scented hill stations where fortunate battalions could shelter from the worst of the summer heat.[27] 'The food was superb', recalled Richard Cartwright of his time at Cambridge Barracks, Rawalpindi, in the 1930s: 'We were waited upon by Indian bearers. It seemed unbelievable that we who were just about the lowest of the low in rank could enjoy a standard so high in our catering.'[28]

For conscript soldiers, this pre-war sumptuousness had given way by 1943 to the rather more rudimentary conditions of places like Gaya transit camp in Bihar province, a flyblown plain of tents, mosquito nets and barbed wire which possessed 'an evil reputation for unpleasantness, bureaucratic chaos and suffering.'[29] But in military cantonments such as Poona and the Staff College at Quetta, regular officers still enjoyed their morning squash and polo, sipped on their gins-and-lime, indulged in 'poodle-faking' (obsequious flirtation) with the memsahibs, and generally pretended as though the war was just a vague and unpleasant rumour from far-off. 'England was being bombed, men were dying on two continents', noted John Masters, 'but the girls and wives and grass widows here in Quetta still wore long dresses to the club dances, and all of us changed into mess kit for dinner, and into dinner jackets to go to the club, and we organized picnics up the Hanna Valley, and games of charades, and sardines.'[30] At the Officer Training School in Bangalore, cadets were still being taught how to hand out calling cards and sign visitor's books in the proper-Sahib manner.[31] For men who had just arrived straight from blacked-out, austerity Britain, there was something rather indecent about all this excess. For their part, the India old hands regarded 'Bloody ECOs' (Emergency Commissioned Officers) like John Hudson as distasteful intruders, cuckoos who would be tolerated with thinly disguised contempt until such time as they could be shunted along the conveyor belt to Burma. 'If they found us intrusive, we found them incomprehensible.'[32]

'I don't think the troops were ever prepared to like India,' suggested Raymond Cooper.[33] Most soldiers knew very little about the Raj other than the few scraps of information they might have picked up from Kipling or *The Lives of a Bengal Lancer* or history lessons at school about the Black Hole of Calcutta. 'India' meant elephants and maharajahs, tiger-stalking, widows burned on funeral pyres, and picturesque rural poverty.[34] The reality did not impress. It was unbearably hot and sticky. The food was too rich and gave you the runs. The water was not safe to drink. Dangerous animals and insects lurked every-where. The people had disgusting personal habits – Calcutta was, to the young George MacDonald Fraser, a 'vast, proliferating Augean stable'.[35] Imperial enthusiasts had always wanted ordinary Britons to take more of an interest in their own empire. Now hundreds of thousands of them were seeing it for the first time, but the results were not at all what the imperial boosters had hoped for. The attitude of the typical British soldier towards the Raj could be summed

up in 'a brief but expressive phrase', thought John Sparrow: '*India stinks*.' The
men hated the climate, the squalor and the civilian 'riff-raff' with whom they
came into habitual contact (they made an exception for the Indian Army's
sepoys, whose martial courage they admired).[36] 'Everything was terrible to us
because it was strange', recalled Aldiss:

> We laughed and pointed in horror at anything you would find in different
> form in Exeter or Bradford. The bright posters for native films, ointments,
> or magazines; the amazing script which flowed over shops and placards
> like a renegade parasitic plant; the unlikely *beobabs* and *deodars* that shaded
> the road; and particularly the smells and foreign tongues and wailing
> musics – all so closely related that they might have poured from one
> steaming orifice – these things seemed like the stigmata of some sleazy and
> probably malevolent god.[37]

India was, quite simply, 'the arse of the world.'[38]

The problem, according to Rupert Croft-Cooke, who arrived as a field
security sergeant in 1943 and came to adore the land and its people, was that
the typical private soldier's encounter with India was almost calculated to frus-
trate him. Stuck in some dusty encampment, sustained by tins of watery bully
beef and hot beer, his engagement with the locals largely confined to being
ripped off by rapacious camp-followers and brothel madams, it was hardly any
wonder that India appeared to him merely 'a place of flies, unbearable heat, and
exasperating *dhobi wallahs* . . . it had little to show which could be recollected
fondly afterwards'. It was a place of banishment from which the soldier brooded
'with angry impatience' on his own lost country.[39] What British troops wanted
above all was to get back to a world of 'football, fish and chips, and women',
thought Richard Terrell. 'They were not afraid of India, but fed up with it.'[40]

Then, of course, there was the politics. India in 1942 was seething with
discontent. Its nationalist Congress movement had declared a state of mass
civil disobedience to protest Britain's continuing presence. Many troops
arriving in the subcontinent found themselves seconded to internal security
duties. These policing responsibilities – patrolling city streets, guarding official
buildings, breaking up demonstrations – were sordid and thankless work. It is
not that most British troops had any sympathy with the nationalists, so much
as they were utterly indifferent to India's fate. '*Dear Mother*', wrote one
soldier home, '*it says in this book I'm reading that India is the Crown Jewel of the
British Empire. If so, take it from me, they ought to pawn the bloody thing.*'[41] India
could 'stew in its own juice' so far as most soldiers were concerned; and if it
should fall apart in their absence, so much the better.[42] Internal security duties

were vexing because they were not what citizen soldiers had signed up to do. They had not come all this way 'to act as policemen to a lot of natives'.[43]

In its reconquest of Burma the 14th Army would discover, as the Eighth Army had already done in Egypt, how discomfiting it was for the locals to despise *you* almost as much as the enemy. Though Burma's scattered hill tribes had remained mostly loyal to the British during the Japanese occupation, it was well known that the ethnic Burmese majority had openly greeted the Japanese as liberators. By 1945, three years of clumsy and brutal Japanese administration had squandered most of that good will. But all the same, there was little enthusiasm about a British return. The British had done precious little for Burma during their long years of colonial rule, and to many Burmese it seemed that they were returning with only destructive impulses in mind. Wandering around the hamlet of Tiddim in the Chin Hills, Raymond Cooper reflected sadly on what the locals must be thinking of him and the other foreign intruders who had come to disturb their bucolic isolation with 'gas masks and swinging scabbards and clumsy boots and sputtering engines'. For generations, 'the cattle bells had sounded on these hills and the rice had grown and withered in the valleys', wrote Cooper. But now, 'like a nut between crackers', it was Tiddim's misfortune to lie between two armies which had suddenly come to care about the place's existence. Less than a year after his visit, the British would burn Tiddim to the ground to deny it to the Japanese, making its bewildered people refugees. 'How could we explain', thought Cooper as he gazed sadly at the tiny mission church, 'that ours too was a Christian path which led us to take from these people their fields and homes ... and to lord it over their lives and deaths?'[44]

If India's cities represented the infinite variety of human experience, then the jungle was nature's realm – amoral, aloof, resolutely indifferent to man's presence. This was countryside that devoured armies whole. 'Only when you stood in that landscape, with your boots firm on the ground, could you understand why advances by either side were so slow', remarked Aldiss, gazing on the scenery around Imphal for the first time:

> Whatever the country looked like from the air, from the ground it was baffling. To the confusion of whatever prehistoric calamity had thrown up this maze of small mountains and valleys, nature had added entangling forest. Every hill, valley, re-entrant, and salient was covered with vegetation which, although from a distance it looked little more than knee-high scrub – so large were the Assamese perspectives – on closer acquaintance proved to be a riot of thorn, bamboo, and towering trees. Every minor

feature, nothing on a map, proved capable in actuality of swallowing a battalion. Every hillside mopped up men as a sponge mops up beer.[45]

Once under the tree cover, soldiers vanished within mazes of dips and ravines, gullies and mountain spurs. 'You might get a glimpse through the thickets of the crest, cloud drifting over it, and think, *Thank fuck, we're there at last!* You'd reach it, and it would prove to be just another false crest, and more thicket and another crest looming above you. Those bastard and everlasting hills!'[46] Whereas in Europe places of military interest might be identified by the names of towns or villages, in Burma there were usually only milestone or altitude markers to act as reference points, so feeble was the human impression on the land. At one point during the second Chindit expedition, John Masters mapped out a defensive position in the jungle as a cricket field – *Cover Point, Midwicket, Deep* – in order to try to give his men some greater sense of ownership of the terrain, in the same way that desert soldiers years before had named lonely cairn-marked crossroads in the Libyan wasteland as Knightsbridge, Piccadilly Circus and Leicester Square.[47] Engulfed by the blackness of the tropical forest, Leo de Filippis drew comfort from the luminous face and mechanical ticking of his wristwatch, a reminder of the civilization he had left behind. 'It was 9.30. That meant that in England it was three o'clock in the afternoon ... people back home were either finishing lunch or having tea, or perhaps in cinemas or crowding the high street; whilst here was I, wrapped in my blanket and lying among the decayed vegetation of a Burmese jungle.'[48] But ultimately, any attempt to impose human control on such an immense and forbidding landscape was futile. Raymond Cooper felt as though he was trying to defend the Alps with a platoon.[49] The front line scarcely existed. British and Japanese patrols might pass within a few yards of one another, completely oblivious of each other's existence. Neither side controlled Burma. It merely tolerated their temporary presence.

The soldier's central preoccupation in the jungle was not fighting the enemy, but making forward progress. 'Everything is hostile', complained Eric Murrell. 'Huge brittle dry leaves prick and cut one, great grass blades are as sharp as knives – nothing is soft or pleasant.'[50] Brian Aldiss recalled 'the eternal climbing, slipping back, the possibility of losing your footing and falling on to the man behind, or the man in front falling on to you. It was like madness, your leg muscles threatening to seize up, your heart threatening to burst.'[51] Every step in thickly overgrown country meant slashing with machetes through trailing vines and creepers. A soldier on jungle patrol was estimated to expend 6,000 calories a day, though his rations only refurbished him with 4,000.[52] To newcomers with soft feet and bodies, this meant an unpleasant process of 'hardening' to the rigours of march discipline. Sweat poured in 'great salty streams' from the forehead, across the face, and down the chin, as Richard Rhodes James described it:

> All the aches and pains of yesterday appear again, to be joined by the partic- ular discomforts of today. The ill-adjusted pack, the rubbing of the water- bottle or haversack, that place where the belt fails to coincide with the contours of the body ... and then the boots, pinching, slipping, rubbing, the socks sliding down the foot and collecting in an abrasive bundle at the heel.[53]

Climbing through steep bamboo jungle with a carpet of smooth, wet branches underfoot was particularly torturous. 'You'd put a foot down and began to transfer weight to it', wrote Masters,

> [But then] you slid back on the bamboo stems, which might have been greased and specially placed there for the purpose. You made a net upward gain of three inches. Now the other foot – another three inches. You slid back five inches ... time and again I clung to a bamboo, head bowed and sweat dripping, shaking with exhaustion and helpless anger, no breath to swear at the trees, no strength to shake them, cut them down, jump on them, burn them.[54]

All the while there was the torment of the insects. There were plenty of large and dangerous animals in Burma – man-eating tigers, crocodiles, pythons, a snake (the krait) with such a lethal bite that it was known as the 'two-step' because after being attacked by it that was as far as you would get before drop- ping dead – but by and large these creatures had the sense to keep out of the way of large numbers of men carrying guns.[55] The mosquitoes, however, had no fear of soldiers. They whizzed and hummed all day, turning men's faces into masks of great red blotches. Leeches were even worse – 'bloated, squashy, red monsters' which fattened up like purple plums, and which had to be carefully removed (sometimes from the crotch) by the application of salt or a hot ciga- rette end, lest their heads remained buried in the skin to cause ulcerations that could eat away fat and muscle. One of the grim comic spectacles at the end of a day's march, noted Masters, was to watch the leeches advancing on him and his exhausted men. 'From far and near, in front, behind, left and right, they arched towards us, along the ground, along the boughs of the trees, smelling blood.'[56]

Not all of Burma was jungle. Above the timber line, the hills were covered only in a thin skein of brushwood. In other places, elephant grass grew six feet high, sharp enough to rip fabric and slice flesh. Much of the central plain in dry season had no tree cover at all, its rice paddies and parched scrub broken up instead by sandy gullies and desiccated river beds (*chaungs*). That is, until the monsoon burst around late May. The arrival of the four-month-long monsoon rains was another reminder to the soldier (as if he needed one) of his power-lessness in the face of nature. Some parts of Burma received 140 inches of monsoon rain every year.[57] Dusty *chaungs* suddenly metamorphosed into raging creeks. 'If you haven't seen the monsoon burst, it's difficult to imagine', explained George MacDonald Fraser:

> There are the first huge drops, growing heavier and heavier, and then God opens the sluices and the jets of a million high-pressure hoses are being directed straight down, and the deluge comes with a great roar, crashing against the leaves and rebounding from the earth for perhaps a minute – after that the earth is under a skin of water which looks as though it's being churned up by buckshot. Before you know it you are sodden and streaming, the fire's out, the level in the brew tin is rising visibly, and the whole clearing is a welter of soaked blaspheming men trying to snatch arms and equip-ment from the streams coursing underfoot.[58]

The monsoon rain brought new miseries – not just the difficulties of marching, eating and sleeping in what amounted to a perpetual six-inch-deep lukewarm bath, but also its effect on soaking skin. John Hudson's men were often so wet their entire bodies became creamy and wrinkled, 'like an old washerwoman's hands'.[59] 'You couldn't do a thing', complained Aldiss. 'You could hardly breathe. The air was water. Every man had prickly heat, which the rain stung and soothed by turns. I could feel my toes rotting off in my boots.'[60] Men developed trench foot, sores, carbuncles, boils, swollen and weeping gums. Soldiering in Burma was so inimical to life that after just eighty days in the jungle men would start to become anaemic from exhaustion, malnutrition and stress. Their wounds would not heal properly. They could die from a cut finger.[61] By the end of the second Chindit campaign, only 188 men out of 2,200 survivors of 111th Indian Infantry Brigade were still medically fit for duty.[62] At the time he left Burma, six-foot tall signals officer Robin Painter had been reduced to just eight stone in weight by leg ulcers, dysentery and jaundice.[63] The Second World War was, on the whole, a triumph of military medicine. Only one British soldier died of disease for every four that were killed by the enemy.[64] Burma was the great exception to that story of iatric progress, the one theatre of the war that modern pharmacology never mastered. For all of the achievements Slim's army made in the battle against malaria, Burma remained a deadly place for human beings to traverse in large numbers.[65] It was a country that chewed men up and spat them out again.

The Jungle is your Friend, the 14th Army slogan went – a bit of wishful thinking conjured up by the top brass that convinced no one. The jungle was no one's friend.[66] Yet for all its horrors, all its inhumanity, it could be a profoundly beautiful place too – one impossible to love, perhaps, but impossible to forget as well. Eric Murrell described the gorgeous scene as the monsoon paused for the first time over Assam in July 1942. 'A great belt of mist was wreathing up from the valley between us and the sun', he wrote:

> All the lower part was grey-white, like the smoke of an immense fire blotting out the valley, but the upper part of the mist was transformed by the sun behind it into flaming orange and gold; it was ever moving, ever changing, wafting and eddying upwards into the blue sky just like spires of flame or a woman's gold tresses blowing upwards into the wind – one thought of a vast funeral pyre of a Brunhilde, filling the whole sky, burning before one's eyes.[67]

John Hudson found an almost spiritual majesty to the jungle landscape even in the midst of the dreadful fighting in Manipur. When the clouds lifted and the curtain of mist retreated from the battlefield, he could see 'remote glints of water, rice paddy, tree-shrouded villages and forests cloaking the slopes' of the distant mountains. It was, he thought, 'an Arcadian paradise', at least when seen from afar. 'In those brief interludes we lifted out eyes from the filth of our lives, imbibed clean air and glimpsed beauty.' He remembered the church in his hometown, where as a boy he had sat and listened to the young girls of the choir sing *Stay, Master, stay upon this heavenly hill*. What a place to rediscover such thoughts! And yet 'the sweet music of that hymn still conjures up for me those frontier ranges swept by gunfire and monsoon rain'.[68]

CHAPTER 10

SECOND FRONT

'Life', complained Lieutenant Jack Swaab, as he watched the white-flecked waves off Southend Sands on the afternoon of 5 June 1944, 'is as stagnant as a tin of syrup.'[1] For two days, he and the rest of the men of his artillery troop had been cooped up on an American Liberty Ship, dossing down in wet corridors, eating cold bacon and sausage washed down with lukewarm tea, waiting for the abatement of the vicious spring squall that had churned up the Channel. All of southern England at that moment was, as another soldier, Jocelyn Pereira, put it, 'a waiting room on a gigantic scale'.[2] For months, the peace of the Home Counties had been disturbed by 'sundry bangs, the rumble of engines and the clatter of tracks' as lorryloads of troops, stores and rations, accompanied in convoy by thousands of tanks, jeeps and armoured cars, had assembled at ports of embarkation along the south coast.[3] Solders such as Swaab and Pereira were kitted out with all the accoutrements of invasion – lifebelt and vomit bags, 800 cigarettes, three-pound slabs of chocolate, tea and milk, 1,200 francs, soap, waders, morphine, OXO cubes, chewing gum, guidebooks to France; the only thing the Army had forgotten to hand out, Pereira drolly noted, was a pamphlet from the Chaplain's branch on *How to Behave When Dead*.[4] Now they had to loll patiently on the transports and hope for something to happen to break the boredom. It was hard fully to appreciate, wrote Swaab in his diary, 'that soon I may be hearing the waves on a real beach, and the sound of gunfire, flares by night, the crunching crash of bombs and the moan of the dying'.[5]

This would not be Swaab's first battle. He had joined the 51st (Highland) Infantry Division in Benghazi on New Year's Eve, 1942, and for five months he had served as a forward observation officer during the Eighth Army's sanguine and protracted reduction of the Afrika Korps in the Tunisian hills.[6] He had then landed at Pachino at the southeastern tip of Sicily in July 1943, and at the end of that six-week campaign had crossed the Strait of Messina into Campania with the rest of his division. But the Highlanders had not lingered in Italy for long. In November 1943, Montgomery had decided that they, along with the men of two other battle-hardened Eighth Army divisions, the 50th (Northumbrian) Infantry and 7th Armoured, would accompany him back to Britain. There they would enjoy a few months of rest and recuperation on home soil, but only until the spring. For then they were to be used as the vanguard troops in Monty's last and toughest campaign: Operation OVERLORD, the long-awaited Allied invasion of France.[7]

The news that they were going to be sent into action once more did not exactly thrill the Mediterranean veterans. Many of them had already served over 300 continuous days in the front line. By their own reckoning they had more than 'done their bit' in this war. Now, they thought, it was time for other, fresher soldiers to take their place in the fighting.[8] When it became clear that they were to be part of the D-Day invasion force, the result was a desertion crisis. As the 50th moved into sealed camps along the south coast in preparation for OVERLORD, some of its men used blast grenades and Bangalore torpedoes to blow holes in the fences and liberate themselves.[9] Soldiers of the 3rd Royal Tank Regiment who had fought at El Alamein were 'virtually mutinous', according to one of their officers, painting the walls of their barracks at Aldershot with 'No Second Front'.[10] Jack Swaab himself was not a party to such insubordination. Like the majority of Eighth Army veterans, he accepted, however grudgingly, the need to go wherever he was sent. He would continue to fight the war 'till either it or I shall end'. Still, he felt 'no ardour or enthusiasm for the future' as he waited for D-Day. 'I can hardly remember peace as a coherent entity now', he wrote. 'I hope very deeply that the war will end this year. I am genuinely tired of the Army, weary of the war.'[11]

Most of the British troops waiting in the Channel on 5 June 1944 felt rather differently, because unlike Swaab or the other men of the 51st, they had never been in action. On the eve of the invasion of France, twenty of the twenty-five divisions stationed in the British Isles had seen no service abroad since the war's outbreak.[12] D-Day represented for the troops in such divisions the end of three or more years of humdrum home service routine – of incessant training, pedantic spit-and-polish bullshit, and also, perhaps, the nagging suspicion that they were not really soldiers at all, but frauds in elaborate fancy-dress. At last, all the finicky obsessions of the parade ground that had preoccupied them for so long would fade into irrelevance: 'such kindergartens, such play-places, with their artificial enthusiasms', thought David Holbrook on the eve of the invasion, 'the foolish lingo – wordsacommand! SCHO! Uup! Toop! Threep! Animal noises! What use would all that be tomorrow?'[13] 'Here was the Second Front', exulted Robert Woollcombe, a junior officer with the 6th King's Own Scottish Borderers. 'We were upon the rostrum of the world. At last, after the months and years of waiting whilst others went out, we too were out, to take part of deeds. Now all was justified.'[14] 'I was almost ashamed how much I was enjoying myself', admitted Pereira, a Coldstream Guards subaltern, of the preparations for OVERLORD. 'From the moment that the first envelopes arrived in the Orderly Room with the inscription "Top Secret" and their huge blobs of red sealing wax, a distinctive atmosphere seemed to engulf one's life, giving it an air of indefinable adventure, so that the brief summer days before the invasion were an experience all of their own.'[15] All of Sherman tank gunner Ken Tout's hopes since joining the Army 'had simmered slowly up to this boiling, spilling delight of foreign adventure . . .'

> The schooling, and training, and drilling, and stamping of steel-rimmed boots . . . all for the moment of truth. These beaches, the grimy sunshine, the gun-metal surf, the chill of imminent battle, the pageant of massing vehicles: Normandy![16]

As his landing craft approached the French shoreline on the morning of 6 June, trooper John Smith watched with pleasure as the straps on his webbing stiffened in the salty spray of the Channel and their coating of green blanco began to smear with rust. At last, none of that mattered any more. 'I was enjoying myself more than ever in the Army.'[17]

With hindsight, the invasion of France in June 1944 has a feeling of inevitability to it. But for some years after Dunkirk, it was far from clear whether the British Army would ever be sent to fight in northwestern Europe again. For a long time Churchill, who had been unimpressed by the BEF's performance in 1940, was flatly dismissive of the idea.[18] It was 'impossible', he insisted in a memo in March 1941, ever again 'for the Army, except in resisting invasion, to play a primary role in the defeat of the enemy'.[19] After all, it had been one thing to disembark a small force across the Channel with the cooperation of the French. It would be quite another to launch one against a hostile coastline defended by tens or even hundreds of German divisions. A landing on the European Continent could have only one outcome, Churchill confided to his assistant private secretary John Colville: 'The War Office would not do the job properly; indeed, it was unfair to ask them to pit themselves against German organization, experience, and resources. They had neither the means nor the intelligence.'[20] To defeat the Third Reich, the prime minister concluded that the

British must trust to the time-honoured Indirect Approach – economic blockade, the sponsoring of resistance activities amongst the occupied peoples of Europe, and, most important of all, bombing. Ideally, as a Chiefs of Staff Committee strategy paper drawn up for the Anglo-American conference at Placentia Bay in August 1941 argued, 'The [future] role of a British Army on the Continent will be limited to that of an Army of Occupation.'[21] The soldier's only job would be to disarm the exhausted, bombed-out Germans and herd them into POW camps.

In the end, though, the Indirect Approach was not enough by itself. Bombing brought terror and destruction to Germany's cities, but it could not by itself break the Reich's war economy. The pinprick irritations of Commando raids on the European mainland were useful as propaganda exercises, but they did little seriously to reduce the *Wehrmacht*'s strength. Brave groups of resistance fighters, many armed and assisted by British agents, took up arms across the Continent. But their value was more symbolic than real. By the end of 1943, it was clear that without a cross-Channel invasion, the war in the west could only end in two possible ways. Either Hitler was going to be left in control of France and the Low Countries, or Stalin was. Neither prospect was palatable.

So on D-Day, 6 June 1944, the British Army, accompanied by US and Canadian forces, returned to France for the first time in four years. The eleven-month expedition it was setting out on would be the shortest of the Army's four major campaigns between Dunkirk and V-J Day. But it would be the biggest. By September, 714,000 of the 1.7 million British troops outside the UK were with Montgomery's Anglo-Canadian 21st Army Group in France and Belgium, compared to just 499,000 in Italy and 242,000 in India and Burma.[22] And it would also be the bloodiest. Approximately 30,280 British troops would lose their lives in the campaign to liberate northwestern Europe – one in four of all the soldiers who died fighting against the Germans and the Italians during the Second World War.[23]

What became known after OVERLORD as the British Liberation Army (BLA) was the first field force to fight within a short travelling distance of the UK since Dunkirk. As a result, its soldiers enjoyed perks that their comrades in far-flung theatres such as North Africa, Italy and Burma did not. Welfare arrangements in 21st Army Group were generally excellent. John Sparrow, the War Office's morale expert, visited the troops in the field in early 1945. Montgomery's men, he reported back, were being 'thoroughly well looked after, and felt [themselves] to be so'. Basic amenities were easily available through NAAFI stores. Soldiers had plentiful access to laundry and shower facilities. Food was generally good, and liberally supplemented by produce and livestock 'liberated' from German farms. Brussels, just a short distance from the front since its liberation in September 1944, offered the weary soldier plenty of rest and recreation. The contrast Sparrow saw between the morale of the men in Germany and those he had visited in Italy the previous year was striking. Soldiers in the Mediterranean had formed 'an army of exiles, among whom every deprivation was apt to give rise to a grievance, and every grievance to become a bugbear'. Many of them had been absent from Britain for four-and-a-half consecutive years. Home leave was impossible. Letters took at least a week to arrive. In Germany, on the other hand:

> [The men] feel themselves to be fighting within a stone's throw of their homes. Letters and newspapers reach them within two or three days; home leave is in operation, and every man knows that, since compassionate leave is subject to no quota, that if there is serious trouble in his family he will get home within a day or two.[24]

Walter Elliott, a Scots Guards officer who had served in 15th Army Group before being transferred to northwestern Europe, found soldiering in Germany far more agreeable than it had ever been in Italy. Now he was able to stay warm and dry at night with a good supply of blankets and greatcoats, something he had never been able to do in the Appenines. Casualties in his unit could be transferred rapidly out of the battle line and air-transported back to hospital in England within a matter of hours if necessary, a vast improvement on the rudimentary medical facilities available on the front line in the Mediterranean.[25]

But the BLA paid for its privileges in blood. The army it fought in Normandy was the single largest German force the British had confronted since Dunkirk. El Alamein had been an important victory, but the eleven British Commonwealth divisions which had won it had only been facing four German divisions. In the Normandy campaign, Montgomery's fourteen Anglo-Canadian divisions found themselves pitted against a roughly equal number of *Wehrmacht* and SS divisions – still small beer by the standards of the Eastern Front (twenty German divisions had fought at Stalingrad alone), but a far more substantial force than anything Rommel had ever commanded in the Western Desert. At El Alamein, the British had been opposed by about 250 light and medium German tanks. In Normandy, they faced 600 – half of which were of the much-feared heavy Panther and Tiger class.[26] This was combat of a continental scale against the most formidable of enemies, and the results were correspondingly savage. During the six weeks that followed D-Day, 11,910 of 21st Army Group's men were killed, an average daily death toll of 270 (it had been just 146 at El Alamein).[27] By the end of August 1944, all the British infantry divisions in

Normandy had lost three-quarters of their initial fighting strength.[28] A whole new category of casualty rate – 'double intense' – had to be invented by the statisticians to account for the losses.[29]

The death rate within infantry battalions was especially appalling. The 4th Somerset Light Infantry, which landed in Normandy on 23 June 1944 with an establishment of thirty-six officers and 700 ORs, lost sixty-five men in its first two weeks of action. By 18 July, the battalion had received twelve officer and 479 OR replacements, yet it was still below full strength. All told, by the end of the war forty-seven of its officers and 1,266 of its men had been either killed or wounded – a casualty rate of 178 per cent. An infantryman serving with the 1st Royal Norfolk Regiment had a two-in-three chance of becoming a casualty before the end of the war, and a one-in-six chance of being killed.[30] By January 1945, Private Stanley Whitehouse was one of just ten survivors from the forty members of his platoon who had landed in France on D-Day.[31] These were butcher's bills to rival infantry battalion losses on the Somme.

In truth, the British Army which Montgomery took with him to Normandy in June 1944 was not really big enough for the momentous task it was being asked to take on. For years, Churchill had looked to the Indirect Approach to beat the Germans. He had orchestrated a long campaign in North Africa. He had tried to gut the Axis through the so-called 'soft underbelly' of Italy. He had approved the creation of a massive strategic bombing force, which at its greatest extent was more than 225,000 personnel strong.[32] But all these stratagems were ultimately a distraction from the only thing that was really going to defeat the *Wehrmacht*, which was to fight it in open battle in northwestern Europe. By the spring of 1944, that had become clear. But it was too late to reverse years of fundamental manpower decisions. Montgomery was only going to have half the British troops at his disposal in France that Haig had had in 1918. A smaller army meant fewer casualties overall. But it also meant that the beleaguered minority of British soldiers at the 'sharp end' would bear an especially punishing burden.

'The soul of Normandy', wrote one of them later, 'was in the gusts of the guns':

It was in the Haut de Bosq … where we found men torn apart by tank tracks and crushed into every mockery of the human form. It was in a fear that you could hardly believe. In the damp odour of the dead. The frightening corn. A woman's corpse half-buried in the rubble of a cottage, and the dazed little strings of civilians, with their bundles, fleeing towards Caumont, and the droning bombers like legions of ogres, black in the midsummer skies.

'There was no hope in it', he thought – 'only dread, and the cold inhumanity of battle.'[33]

In the other major theatres of the war, what had struck British soldiers was the sense of entering a place distant from their homeland, and not just in space, but in time also. The landscape and peoples of North Africa had imitated the pages of the Old Testament. Italy was one Renaissance Old Master after another. Burma was a Mesozoic dream-nightmare. But Normandy? Normandy was ... England. 'It might have been Somerset', thought Jocelyn Pereira of the rustic countryside that he and his men encountered as they trundled off the invasion beaches.[34] 'The orchard-dotted hills and the winding hedge-lined roads looked exactly like the country around Stone Street in Kent', agreed John Foley. 'Every minute we expected to round a corner and find a board proclaiming *Teas, Light Refreshments and Minerals*, or come in sight of a swinging sign saying *The Ship and Shovel*.'[35] Geoff Jones was reminded of Burneside in the Lake District, Ken Tout of Hertfordshire. Normandy's 'gnarled, ancient, prolific trees' had the disconcertingly familiar look of old English forests. 'This is a place for chickens to peck and pigs to chunter and horses to champ', thought Tout.[36] And Normandy was not just England, but pre-1939, pre-austerity England to boot: a fat, sedate country, seemingly as yet untouched by war. Trevor Greenwood was struck by the magnificent crops of fresh-grown corn and beans in the gently undulating fields, the large, apparently prosperous farms.[37] Normandy in June 1944 seemed to Pereira to be a land of peace, of 'cream, butter, camembert cheese, artichokes, cider, Calvados' – a place of flourishing innocence about to become 'startlingly and horrifyingly different'.[38]

For the Germans had determined to fight for Normandy to the bitter end. This made little sense strategically; once it was clear that it could not throw the D-Day invading forces on the beaches immediately back into the Channel, the *Wehrmacht* would have been much better advised to withdraw from the region entirely and defend the line of the Seine, out of range of Allied naval bombardment and fighter-bomber cover. By the time the eleven-week OVERLORD campaign was over, twenty-five of the thirty-eight German divisions which had been committed to defending Normandy had been effectively destroyed. Of one million *Wehrmacht* and *Waffen-SS* troops, 240,000 had been killed or wounded, another 200,000 captured. These were irreplaceable losses, sacrificed in a mission that was doomed from its inception.[39]

But that was little comfort to the Allied soldiers who had literally to enact the Axis defeat in Normandy yard by bloody yard. Strategically, the campaign was lost for the Germans from the beginning. But tactically, Lower Normandy offered them excellent short-term defensive opportunities. Inland from the

Bay of the Seine, much of the hinterland of Calvados through which the Allied forces would have to progress if they wanted to break out of their invasion bridgehead was *bocage* country – a patchwork of small fields and stoutly built farmhouses separated by massive overgrown hedgerows and narrow sunken lanes. Charming in peacetime, this ancient landscape was the perfect site for what the Germans came to call *schmutziger Buschkrieg*, or 'dirty bush war'.[40] Hidden behind almost impenetrable earth banks up to eight feet high and ten feet wide, *Wehrmacht* troops could open fire on advancing Allied infantry and tanks at point-blank range with their heavy machine-guns and anti-armour projectiles, then withdraw to the next field (leaving mines and booby-traps behind them) before the shaken victims of their ambush had time to mount a counterattack. Beyond the southern boundary of the *bocage* there was 'Swiss Normandy', a region of steep parallel ridges and gullies dominated by a few key high points that offered the side which held them superb artillery observation posts and anti-tank lodgements. David Holbrook marvelled that so peaceful and innocent a landscape, with its oak and elm forests, its rustic place-names – Cresserons, Plumetot, Cazelle, Périers-sur-le-Dan – could harbour such menace. A delightful vista might suddenly reveal a concrete and earth-covered fortification manned by veteran German *Panzergrenadiere*; the silence would be broken by the spit of tracer bullets, 'spreading in the fields and hedges the confusion of corpses, burning vehicles, and the blackened relics of broken machines of war'.[41]

It was this uninviting battlefield which was to be the home of eight British infantry divisions, four armoured divisions and seven independent armoured brigades throughout the early summer of 1944. Collectively they were responsible, along with the Canadian troops of 21st Army Group, for a front line which, until the climactic breakout from the bridgehead in late July, stretched approximately from Ouistreham at the mouth of the River Orne to the left flank of the American forces west of Caumont. The troops soon despaired of their lot. 'It wasn't like this in Sicily or Italy', the soldiers of the 1st Hampshires were complaining after a few weeks:

> There we fought a battle and the Germans pulled out. We got on the road
> and travelled 90 miles one day before we saw the enemy again. But here you
> fight a battle and nothing happens, except you fight another one later on,
> and nothing happens then either.

That a drawn-out quagmire like the Italian campaign could look like a rapid gallop in comparison to Normandy says much about the depths of frustration that were being felt by British soldiers after weeks trapped in the Calvados *bocage*. Mortar platoon officer Geoffrey Picot could see no good end to it. 'It had taken the invasion forces seven or eight weeks to gain a little strip of coast, perhaps about 20 miles deep', he reflected gloomily. 'At the present rate of casualties we would not have an army left by the time we reached the battlefields of the First World War; and even if we could find an army from somewhere it would take decades to reach Berlin.'[42]

In the end the breakthrough did come, but only through the application of such massive ground, air and naval firepower that much of the pretty Normandy countryside was reduced to smoke and ashes. 'The destruction is heartbreaking', thought tank commander Trevor Greenwood of the once-lovely little hamlets he and his men drove through. 'There is a peculiar ghastliness about the countryside . . . the smell of dead cattle, and their grotesque shapes in the fields: the roads lined with derelict vehicles; the wrecked homesteads; ruined villages.'[43] Jocelyn Pereira had assumed that he was desensitized to war damage after four years of the London Blitz. But nothing had prepared him for Normandy. 'Everything still lay in an extreme of disorder', he wrote of the first smashed village he encountered:

> Household goods, doors, window frames, furniture, rubble and burnt-out
> vehicles were all mixed up . . . every house was shell-torn, every roof a sort
> of crazy lacework of holes and collapse, and the pounded mortar formed a
> thick, white dust that lay over everything like a mantle of snow.[44]

A distinctive and horrible feature of the Normandy battlefield was the huge number of animals left lying dead and mortally injured in the fields. Kingsley Amis found the sight of lifeless horses 'almost more pitiful' than that of German corpses, their upper lips drawn above their teeth in a death-grimace of pain.[45] Dead cows could be seen, or rather smelled, everywhere amongst the wild roses and the peonies; lying with their legs pointing to the sky, swathed in maggots, their stomachs bloated with noxious gases, the sour milk in their udders giving off a foetid stink.[46] Theirs was one of the central fragrances of the 'Normandy smell', according to John Smith, along with 'the sickening odour of burned and decaying flesh, the bitter stench from the blackened shell of buildings'. Then there were the other tell-tale leftovers of a battle recently fought – the dead Germans slumped in verges, still clasping their weapons to their breasts; the burned-out vehicles; the abandoned kit of both sides; and the rifles planted into the ground, muzzle first, marking some ad hoc grave, surmounted now and again by a helmet and a name scrawled in chinagraph pencil.[47]

Given the extraordinary breadth of destruction visited upon their province, it is hardly surprising that the Norman peasants were as ambivalent about the arrival of the Allies in June 1944 as the Campanians and Neapolitans had been a year earlier. 'It was a strange kind of liberation we brought them', admitted Geoffrey Picot, 'wrecked farmsteads, damaged villages, obliterated towns . . . for many, caught inescapably in a battle, it was the liberation of death.'[48] John Smith got the impression from the local people he met that while they were pleased that France was being freed from the Germans, they would have greatly preferred it if the Allied invasion had happened somewhere else. The Normans had hardly been touched by the fighting in 1940, and they had been little disturbed by the enemy occupiers ever since. Now their homes were being bombed, their crops crushed underfoot and their cows shot.[49] Almost 20,000 French civilians died in the battle for Normandy, in addition to the 15,000 who had already perished in the Allies' preparatory 'softening-up' bombing in the spring.[50] Caen, Lower Normandy's greatest city, and one of the architectural treasure-houses of northwestern Europe, was laid waste (pointlessly, some felt) by aerial bombardment in late July.[51] Countless other smaller, ancient communities across the Calvados region were smashed in now-forgotten skirmishes throughout the high summer of 1944.

It was hard, acknowledged Woodrow Wyatt, for ordinary Normans to look upon such destruction and not conclude that it was personally directed against them. The Germans naturally took every opportunity to insinuate exactly that: a Nazi poster of Joan of Arc distributed widely across the region showed her burning at the stake, the flames of Rouen Cathedral behind her, with the caption 'The Assassins always return to the scene of their crime.'[52] For the first few weeks of the invasion there was also the fear that OVERLORD would simply turn out to be a Dieppe-style raid, after which the Allies would depart and the Germans would return to enact revenge on civilians who had greeted them too enthusiastically.[53] Not all the French were hostile. British troops marching into newly liberated Norman villes often found themselves greeted with grins and embraces, victory-V signs and bottles of the robust local apple brandy. But they also had to get used to suspicious stares through shuttered windows, peasants complaining bitterly about broken fences and stolen potatoes, and reproachful glances from the bereaved. By midsummer 1944, few Norman residents were upset to see the armies of both sides move on as the Germans began their frantic retreat eastwards towards the Reich.

The Wehrmacht had lingered too long in Normandy. Instead of withdrawing to the Seine once the Americans broke out of the bridgehead in late July, Hitler ordered the bulk of his remaining armoured units to counterattack – a futile effort which only drew them deeper into a fragile pocket centred on the town of Falaise. Even after finding themselves surrounded, the German forces did not receive permission to retreat until 16 August, allowing them only five days in which to flee before the salient was finally pinched closed by Allied pincer thrusts. Perhaps 20,000 German troops escaped, leaving all their vehicles and heavy equipment behind them. As many as 10,000 were killed, another 50,000 taken prisoner.[54] The German Army in the West had, for the moment anyway, ceased to exist. Much to their own surprise, British, Canadians and Americans found themselves advancing across France without opposition. Soldiers who had become habituated to a fortnight's gruelling battle over a couple of hundred yards of no-man's land now drove along country roads for dozens, sometimes hundreds of miles a day without encountering a single German. The roads were suddenly thick with Allied vehicles advancing eastwards, churning up clouds of dust as they went (the dust in France in summer 1944 was said to be even worse than in the Western Desert two years before).[55] Geoffrey Picot had never dared dream that victory in Normandy 'was going to pay such a rich dividend ... the nature of the advance astonished us. Our wonder grew with every kilometre we travelled, every town we entered, every frontier we crossed.'[56] 'An unbelievable change had come over the battlefield', as Alan Moorehead put it:

> The road blocks had vanished. The guns were silent. Everything was in movement, and that claustrophobic feeling we had had in the narrow bridgehead was now suddenly and completely dissipated ... the whole army had gathered itself into an irrepressible momentum, and it stretched back along the roads for 200 miles, gargantuan, frightening, thunderous, forever renewing itself and rearing forward.[57]

On 19 August, American troops reached the Seine. On the 25th, the German garrison in Paris surrendered. On 3 September, the fifth anniversary of the war's outbreak, units of the Welsh Guards reached Brussels. The following day, Antwerp was captured. On 9 September, the first Allied troops entered the Netherlands. The Normandy gloom had been suddenly replaced by the effervescence of painless liberation. In the Belgian capital, frenzied crowds deluged British troops with wine, cakes and flowers; they scrawled their names on tanks and lorries, poured champagne on passers-by, danced in the streets.[58] Colin MacInnes described the scene in Brussels on the day after the first British troops arrived: 'They were so glad to see you. The kids took hold of your hands and the women wouldn't even leave you alone at all. I thought it was just they were a bit excited, but it was more than that, it was like as if they'd been waiting for us all their lives ... they were buying you drinks all the time, offering you

meals and hot baths.'[59] Belgium struck most Tommies as a distinct improvement over Normandy (that its people had not suffered the depredations of the
OVERLORD battle had much to do with this, of course). The houses were
'neater, tidier, more modern', thought Trevor Greenwood. 'The air of dilapida-
tion, so evident in France, was far less noticeable.' Brussels had 'well-dressed
civilians, fine shops, cleanliness, order – and intelligent looking people. And
the girls!'[60] The Dutch too were impressive in their scrupulous tidiness and
their high educational standards, especially their fluency in English. Holland
looked as though 'someone with a modernist and slightly cosmopolitan view of
life had taken Welwyn Garden City very seriously to heart, then applied an
improved version to an entire country'.[61]

It seemed as though the end of the war itself might be just a few days away.
On 5 September, a rumour spread through Geoffrey Picot's battalion that the
BBC had announced Germany's surrender, causing great confusion all afternoon until the story was exposed as a bit of wishful thinking gone accidentally
viral.[62] All the same, some commanding officers in the BLA were taking bets
that the end would come by October.[63] 'Hope we're not all being too optimistic',
wrote Jack Swaab in his diary.[64] They were. The Germans were already reas-
sembling their shattered army. On 17 September, the blow which was supposed
to finish off the *Wehrmacht* once and for all was launched when three Allied
airborne divisions landed in southern Holland, in an attempt to seize the
seventy-eight-mile road from the Belgian border to the city of Arnhem on
the lower Rhine and secure a path of advance for Montgomery's tanks on to
the North German Plain. Despite valiant efforts, the final and most crucial
bridge at Arnhem could not be reached before the paratroopers there were
smothered in an unexpectedly vigorous German counterattack. Montgomery's
'dagger-like thrust' into Germany became a thin salient pointing nowhere.

With the failure of the Arnhem gamble, it soon became clear that the war
would not in fact be over in 1944 after all. The front line stabilized along the
German border as the weather deteriorated and the Allies paused to gather
supplies. 'The days of great achievement seemed to be over', thought Jocelyn
Pereira. 'Every prospect ahead was uninviting.'[65] What followed were four
months of static attritional warfare across the flat flooded polders of northern
Flanders, a war of cold sludge and slate skies every bit as unpleasant and spirit-
sapping as the worst days of the Ypres battle in 1917. Troops had to wash their
feet twice daily and apply camphorated powder in an attempt (only partly
successful) to avoid an epidemic of trench foot.[66] In Limburg, Pereira saw the
November roads become coated in a 'thick, brown sauce' of autumnal mud as
bad as in Italy. 'Mud was spattered all over the leafless, war-scarred trees', he
recalled:

It coated the soiled minefield tapes by the roadside; it clung like toffee to the signal wires draped along the telegraph poles; it seemed to have been sprayed over everything like a coat of paint; and the whole dismal landscape of waterlogged heaths was of the same dreary colour ... a sort of forlorn resignation hung over the place, as though it had been set aside from the world as a showground for desolation.[67]

After the mud came the snow. For the handful of remaining BEF men who had frozen along the Franco-Belgian frontier during the winter of 1939–40, this second phoney war had a depressing familiarity to it. The graphite grease in personal weapons froze up, forcing soldiers to cock their rifles by hammering the bolts with stones or pieces of wood. Water froze in cans. Bedding rolls tied on to vehicles could not be unattached or unfurled. The touch of a metal surface was painful. Jeeps and lorries spun on road surfaces glassy with ice. Sentries had to be relieved after twenty minutes on duty to prevent them collapsing or hallucinating in the cold. Teeth chattered, feet throbbed with chilblains, knees and elbows ached rheumatically.[68] The sun reflecting on the dazzling white landscape was blinding. 'I shan't forget for a long time the red blood on the white snow', wrote Jack Swaab of the miseries of Belgium in December 1944, of the days spent in frozen inactivity, punctuated by minutes of terrifying ferocity as patrols exchanged gunfire or artillery bursts shattered the overhanging pine trees:

> The numbness and pain of the feet, the drenching tiredness, the twinges of fear, and the night sky lit by flashes, and the whistle of shells nearby as one crouched in the snowy ditch, soaked, and tired beyond belief.[69]

'*You are now in Germany: Behave Like Conquerers!*' the sign read as John Smith and the rest of the 141st Regiment, Royal Armoured Corps, crossed the frontier from Holland in early 1945. Smith was not sure what to make of such instructions. Conquering 'seemed a bit un-English', he thought. No one from up high had offered much advice on the matter.[70] Certainly, Smith's first sight of German civilians – three old men, clad in clogs and old overcoats, stumbling down the road looking for stray cigarette butts – did not inspire feelings of Genghis Khan-like wrath. 'They looked frightened and touched their hats to me', he wrote afterwards. Could these miserable specimens really be members of the *Herrenvolk*, the Aryan Master Race?[71]

The British Army's encounter with Germany had, strictly speaking, begun back on the afternoon of 20 September 1944, when a troop of self-propelled anti-tank guns commanded by Captain Aubrey Beaty had crossed the border at Wyler Meer, between Nijmegen and Cleves, for a couple of hours to shell some enemy farmhouses.[72] But aside from a few such tentative expeditions, the vast majority of British troops had remained on the west bank of the River Maas, just inside the Netherlands, throughout 1944. The Third Reich proper began a few miles away – a shadowy and sinister prospect on which to brood during the winter months. The invasion of Germany was held up for about six weeks by the Axis counterattack on the American lines in the Ardennes in December (the so-called 'Battle of the Bulge'). It was another precipitate operation by the *Wehrmacht* which only hastened its defeat in the long run, but all the same the Ardennes campaign forced the Anglo-US-Canadian armies to push back their own offensive timetable. Not until 8 February 1945 did troops of the BLA finally advance into the Reichswald forest across the Maas. They captured Cleves and Goch in an exhausting month-long campaign, before moving on to the rolling grassland of Rhenish Prussia and the banks of the great River Rhine itself.

The invasion of Germany was the beginning not just of a military operation, but what Alan Moorehead called 'an immensely complicated relationship between ourselves and the defeated', one that would continue long after the war itself had ended.[73] In every other previous campaign in Europe, British troops had fought in friendly territory, either as defenders or as liberators (technically the Sicilians had been an enemy people when Eighth Army had landed at Pachino in July 1943, but their enthusiastic greeting made a nonsense of this). By entering Germany, the British Army was finally fighting on the soil of an indisputably hostile nation. A nation, moreover, which provoked in the minds of most soldiers a mixture of fascination, fear, mystery and hatred. For years, 'the Germans' had, for the majority of British troops, been a horror-show abstraction with little connection to living, breathing people. Now they would be finally observable at close hand.[74] Few Britons, Moorehead believed, could think clearly about their German enemies any longer. Even those soldiers who spoke the language and had visited the country before the war were entering it this time armed with 'a mass of prejudices and a profound ignorance' of what had taken place there since 1939.[75]

The country they were invading would turn out to be a study in staggering contrasts. Much of urban Germany had been reduced to charred ruins by British and American strategic bombers and ground artillery fire. Cleves and Goch had been almost entirely demolished before the ground forces arrived, and 21st Army Group would progress further along this trail of tears and destruction as it crossed the Rhine in March and entered the North German Plain. Wesel, Osnabrück, Münster, Hanover, Bremen, Hamburg – all were heaps of smoking rubble. Even soldiers who had experienced the Blitz in 1940 and 1941 were shocked by what they found on reaching northern Germany's devastated cities. Driving through the remains of Bremen, Peter White's column had to pause repeatedly to negotiate enormous bomb craters in the middle of the road. 'Falling tram wires, shot and blasted from their poles, trailed in profusion over our route and gathered thickly like brambles' he recalled:

> Here and there groups of houses were still blazing fiercely on either side . . . pathetic, frantic figures and shouting drew attention to some old people and children staggering frenziedly about in the smoke-filled, flame-lit half-light in a snowstorm of swirling sparks. It made one's heart sick to see them attempting such a hopeless task of saving their homes from the flames with only pots and pans and buckets of water filled from the broken water main in a crater.[76]

'I was stunned by the totality of it', said Bill Bellamy.[77]

Yet outside the bombed cities, the affluence of the western German countryside – fat with the spoils of a plundered continent – was equally shocking. Much of the Third Reich in spring 1945 was a country undamaged by war, thought Scots Guards officer Walter Elliott. Oxen and horses could be seen ploughing in 'fields aflame with yellow cowslips' adjoining beech woods 'tinged with green'.[78] A thick layer of 'solid bourgeois comfort' still girdled Germany's unbombed towns and villages. The shops sold radio sets and vacuum cleaners, French liqueurs and silk stockings. The pantries of respectable *Hausfrauen* were stocked with eggs, bacon, hams, butter, cheeses.[79] Martin Lindsay's men found the farmyards around Goch packed with poultry, livestock and fodder, and though the town's houses were badly damaged their cellars still boasted row upon row of jars of preserved fruit and vegetables. 'The linen cupboards and pantries would have been the envy of any British housewife', he thought. 'Such Germans as were now beginning to appear had good clothing and shoes.'[80]

For front-line troops living on the tinned meat, sardines, dry hard-tack biscuits and dehydrated porridge of 'compo' food crates and twenty-four-hour ration packs, such plenty was irresistibly tempting. And they were not in the mood for self-denial. Throughout the earlier campaigns of the war, British soldiers had been continually chided by their superiors for 'winning' provisions and equipment that did not rightfully belong to them. In a random inspection of eighteen units in the Middle East in late 1942, £19,000 worth of unauthorized kit had been discovered.[81] Officers of the King's Dragoon Guards, the first unit to enter Naples, were later accused of having cut down paintings from their frames in the Princess Palace, and making off with a valuable collection of antique *Capodimonte* porcelain.[82] In Normandy, this process of 'winning' continued. A Civil Affairs Unit in Ouistreham near Caen noted that looting by British troops was 'pretty general', and that the prestige of the Allied forces amongst the local civilians had suffered a severe blow because of a spate of brazen thefts.[83] By October 1944, the Army's Claims and Hirings Directorate had had to pay out over £60,000 in compensation to Norman residents for looting by British troops. Hundreds more claims for such *réquisitions irrégulières* remained to be investigated (though the French, it has to be said, had not been shy about appropriating Allied military tyres and petrol themselves).[84] Holland would also suffer depredation at the hands of some of its more cold-hearted liberators. At the end of the war the British and Americans had to make a joint settlement of £220,000 to the Dutch authorities for looting carried out in the Nijmegen area alone.[85] Martin Lindsay was shocked at the way the men of one British infantry battalion methodically sacked a Belgian village after capturing it from the Germans. Every house was plundered room by room, with the contents of drawers and cupboards flung in a pile to be picked through for the choicest spoils.[86]

Still, most British soldiers remained cognizant of the fact that they were amongst allies whilst in France and the Low Countries, and their officers restrained them from the worst excesses of theft and destruction. Once they entered Germany, however, such moral reservations largely disappeared. 'We thought we would have what we liked and live where we liked, and we looked forward to travelling on forever, skimming the cream of goods and sensations from all the places that awaited us', recalled Colin MacInnes of the mood of his unit as they waited to advance into the Reich. Looting, he believed, had an irresistible attraction to it:

> The opportunities are enormous, and there is no risk during the first few days of the fall of a town, when the old authority is overthrown and the new one not yet established. Even for those who are not thieves by nature, the attraction of what seems at first a delightful game, is overwhelming.[87]

Some units observed an informal moral economy of plunder, balancing discipline and self-respect against operational needs. The officers of the 12th King's Royal Rifle Corps, for instance, accepted that their men were at liberty to enter German homes and take whatever they needed for the prosecution of the war. If they happened to find the odd bottle of schnapps or a suckling pig on these expeditions, then no awkward questions would be asked afterwards. But there was to be no wanton defiling or sacking of German property.[88] Not all soldiers observed even these highly qualified niceties, however. Once safely across the

German border, many of them decided that the ethical constraints that had previously curtailed their behaviour no longer applied. Soldiers began 'indulging quite indiscriminately in whatever fancies entered their heads', an appalled major in the Royal Artillery recalled. Men could be seen wheeling prams and barrows down the streets, piled high with swag. What could not be stolen was smashed or burned.[89] For several weeks in the late spring of 1945, until the military authorities finally began cracking down, almost anything of value in Germany was fair game. 'German cars by the hundred were dragged out of garages and hiding-places under the straw in the barns, painted khaki and driven away', noted Alan Moorehead. 'Cameras and watches and revolvers were taken automatically from prisoners and frequently from civilians. Wine was fair booty for everybody. In nearly every town the shops were broached, the distilleries emptied.'[90] In Cleves' medieval cathedral, already smashed by bombs, soldiers ripped down ancient tapestries with knives, rolled them up and stuffed them in their kit.[91]

It was not a very edifying scene. But then, by March and April 1945 the men of the BLA were tired, world-weary and cynical. Frightened, too; for death remained their constant companion, even as the Third Reich crumbled to pieces around them. The battle for the Reichswald, fought across muddy fields and woodlands in persistent rain, was ferocious. One infantry division alone suffered 2,445 casualties.[92] East of the Rhine, organized *Wehrmacht* resistance was beginning to fall apart. But there always remained the danger of ambush by groups of die-hard Nazi soldiers, militiamen and Hitler Youth fanatics. Every soldier was conscious of the fact that the war was coming to an end. No one wanted to be the last Tommy to die for his King and Country. The troops became trigger-happy, blasting away at houses and out-buildings where once they might have cautiously reconnoitred on foot. It is not surprising, then, that they were less than fastidious about German private property rights.

They were aware, too, that much of the property that the Germans claimed as their own might have once belonged to some luckless French, Belgian or Dutch family. The official guidebook to Germany issued to British troops by the Foreign Office's Political Warfare Executive warned that while there would be some 'pitiful sights' in the Third Reich, the Germans only had themselves to blame for their plight:

Hard luck stories may somehow reach you. Some of them may be true, at least in part, but most will be hypocritical attempts to win sympathy. For, taken as a whole, the German is brutal when he is winning, and is sorry for himself and whines for sympathy when he is beaten.[93]

The enemy, it continued, might superficially look like Britons (except for being bigger, fleshier and blonder), 'but they are not really so much like us as they look'. Their thoroughness and erudition were accompanied by a cringing taste for obedience. There was an unstable mixture of 'sentimentality and callousness' in the Teutonic soul that made them prone to hysterical outbursts and irrational mood swings.[94] And as conquerors they had behaved monstrously. Evidence of grotesque German cruelties was accumulating rapidly by spring 1945. Even men who had not seen for themselves the charnel house at Bergen-Belsen, liberated on 15 April, were soon hearing about mass graves and starving slave-labourers. There was something almost distasteful, then, about the willingness of German civilians to acquiesce so completely with the wishes of their conquerors, to abandon their own moral agency so glibly. Martin Lindsay was struck by the abject compliance of the Germans he met: 'They obeyed all orders, however unpleasant, with an appearance of willingness ... [they] appeared to revel in obedient cooperation.'[95] Jack Swaab found German servility almost as disagreeable as German arrogance. 'I hate the sight of them', he wrote of the groups of ragged, doe-eyed children who approached his gunners begging for food. 'Their nasty little blonde heads seem to typify these false racial creeds which have brought us to such a pretty pass.' But he acknowledged that non-fraternization was probably a doomed policy from the start. 'The men are so incredibly stupid; already one or two have been caught feeding chocolate to German children. We never seem to learn.'[96]

Even some hard-faced, clear-eyed soldiers could not help but be moved by the suffering they observed. Peter White had no illusions about the Germans and their wartime behaviour. He had seen for himself the torture tables and vivisection slabs at the concentration camp at Vught in the Netherlands, organized with scrupulous Teutonic care and chromium-plated modernity. He had felt the grey ash under his boots in the camp crematorium. 'We were staggered to think that such monsters could exist to staff and run such a place', he wrote.[97] Yet on 7 May 1945 he found himself billeted at a farmhouse north of Bremen alongside an elderly German couple with four school-aged children. All that day, rumours of the war's end had been circulating throughout White's battalion. After the official announcement of the German surrender from the BBC, some adjacent British units began firing red, green and white Verey flares into the Saxon skies. The farmer and his wife, prematurely wizened from a life of backbreaking toil, their faces 'weather-beaten and sun-tanned ... like a couple of wrinkled walnuts', could tell that something important had happened, but were not sure what. They looked at White inquisitively.

'*Der Krieg ist kaput, be-ended*', he strung together from his smattering of German vocabulary.

'*Zo . . . allus kaput, allus kaput. Keine zieg, Hitler! Verdamt schwein!*' the
farmer answered slowly, wearily. And, '*Zo . . . Engelandt keine zieg, Deutschland
keine zieg . . . der verdamdt Nazis.*' And with that, he turned to embrace his
wife, who stood, sobbing, holding with whitening knuckles a small picture
frame. It fell to the table as she buried her head in her arms, revealing a black-
banded photograph of a young man in Luftwaffe uniform. 'Nothing could have
so eloquently summed up the utter waste and stupidity of the war', wrote White
years later. There were no real winners. Everyone had lost.[98]

What difference did it make in the end, the British soldier's brief but intense
wartime encounter with the world beyond his own national borders?

Every summer throughout the 1950s, Alf Smith, the transport manager for
the Armstrong Whitworth Company's aircraft and missile plants near Coventry,
led a procession of low-loaders across the Channel to the Paris Air Show. It was
a complex three-week undertaking, involving the movement of vast articulated
lorries with fragile and expensive cargoes along narrow, winding French roadways, and no-less delicate negotiations with policemen, customs officials and
other agents of the Fourth Republic's ponderous bureaucracy. But as his son
Adrian wrote years later: 'For men like my father, travelling abroad in peacetime held no fears. To go to the continent in the 1950s was to revive old memories and revisit old haunts in less trying circumstances.' Smith had first landed
in France on 17 June 1944 as a subaltern in the Royal Warwickshire Regiment,
and had actually managed (by a mixture of bravado and misadventure) to be
present in the French capital on the day of its liberation two months later. Paris
was to become *his* city, a place that he would return to annually for many years
with complete confidence that he knew exactly where he was going and what
he wanted to do there. For Alf Smith, the war made 'Abroad' a place where he
felt entirely at home.[99]

Other suburban horizons were also permanently expanded by the war – by
the sights of Provencal sunshine glinting off the Mediterranean at dusk, the
North African *khamsin* in full bellow, or the black-and-white tiled floors of a
Flemish interior plucked straight from the canvas of a Vermeer or a De Hooch.
For Rupert Croft-Cooke, a wartime posting to India as a field security sergeant
was the beginning of a love affair with the subcontinent that would last his
whole life.[100] Three years with the Intelligence Corps in North Africa and Italy
severed Norman Lewis permanently from his middle-class North London
upbringing, launching him instead on a successful career as a travel writer and
journalist. Tastes for Normandy apple brandy, Indonesian *nasi goreng* and
early Italian chamber music would trickle back to post-war Dudley and
Nuneaton and Kirkcudbright. Denis Healey described a shaft of sunlight that

he saw illuminating Botticelli's *Primavera* in a storage closet in Montegufoni as one of the most exciting moments of his life.[101]

Healey, as it happened, had been planning to return to Merton College after his demob to complete an art history senior scholarship. But the war deflected him into a political career by the interest in international affairs that it had awoken in him. Other men of his parliamentary cohort also found that their wartime encounter with Abroad had sharpened their political beliefs. A young Royal Artillery officer called Edward Heath was convinced of the vital need for European reconciliation after witnessing the trial of the Nuremberg suspects in late 1945. In Normandy the year before Heath had met for the first time Maurice Schumann, then one of General de Gaulle's Free French tank commanders, later France's Foreign Minister, and the man with whom Prime Minister Heath would eventually negotiate Britain's entry into the EEC in 1973.

For other soldiers, however, Abroad had been eye-opening in an altogether different way. Travel can narrow as well as broaden the mind. The cultural insularity of British life in the years after the Second World War, that broadly held sense that foreign institutions and values were things to be distrusted, not admired, may have had quite a lot to do with ex-servicemen turning their back on a world which had, to them, seemed unruly and miserable.[102] After all, the societies through which they had travelled during the war had been, almost without exception, poorer and more backward than their own. There seemed little that the peasants of Calabria could possibly teach the British about sound economic management.[103] Starving refugees were there to be pitied, not emulated. The grasping Italians, the suspicious French, the pathetic, self-pitying Germans – these were poor advertisements for a possible United States of Europe. As for the Empire: its poverty and chaos looked too permanently entrenched to ever possibly change. Those ungrateful natives had not shown much enthusiasm for the presence of the long-suffering British anyway. So why not let them stew in their own juices? To hell with Europe. To hell with the Empire. *That* was the lesson that many soldiers took home with them from the war. Britain – 'alone, self-contained, redoubtable' – had beaten back the evils of Continental fascism and Asiatic fanaticism by relying on its own values and virtues.[104] Its people had nothing to learn from quarrelsome and mendacious foreigners. Decades of national psychic isolation – splendid or otherwise – would follow V-E Day and V-J Day.

PART FOUR
KILLERS

How easy it is to make a ghost.

> Keith Douglas, 'How to Kill'[1]

CHAPTER 11

TEETH AND TAIL

The first Japanese soldier William Cochrane ever saw lay splayed out, stomach exposed, in a jungle clearing. He wore no boots, just a strange-looking pair of shoes. His trousers were pulled up unnaturally high, so that the bottom of his legs were oddly, vulnerably bare. Cochrane's platoon sergeant pointed distract-edly towards the body: *'Make sure he's dead.'* The young soldier raised his rifle hesitantly and shot from a distance of about five feet. The prostrate target went into 'the most terrible jerking convulsions and contortions' as the bullet struck home. The sergeant was not impressed. He gestured to Cochrane and led him forward until the two men were both standing right over the recumbent body of the Japanese soldier. He gave it a sharp kick.

'See this frigger?' the sergeant barked:

'You think this is a man! This ain't no man, this is a friggin' insect see! This only wants two things, to kill you an' to die for its boss in Tokyo! Your job is to stay alive an' to fulfil its second wish, right? You shoot it, an' make sure it stays down, savvy?'

'Aye!'

'If it's down an' not out, finish it off, better to waste a bullet than take a chance.'

'Aye!'

'If you're unsure about yer clip, do it wi' yer pig sticker. Go for the soft parts, the belly or even better the neck. In! Twist it! Out! Now, you!'

'Right! Aim through the target, don't ponce about! Use yer friggin' body weight! In! Twist out! Friggin' good, again! In! Twist! Out! Enough! Okay, have a blow for a minute.'

Cochrane slung his bayoneted rifle and cupped a cigarette in his shaking hands as other men from the section came over to congratulate him. '*Friggin*' *hell Cocky, you did a good job on 'im!*' they laughed. He felt a dizzying mixture of emotions: 'curiosity, elation, disgust, triumph'. He was a twenty-year-old boy from a small Scottish village, who had scarcely ever been away from home before. Now it was 1944, and he was in a Chindit column in the middle of the Burmese jungle, skewering the guts of a man he had never so much as laid eyes on until today. It was a moment both shocking and, in a way, reassuring. The praise of his mates helped to attenuate the feelings of shame that were welling up inside him. It was a dreadful thing to have a man's life on your conscience. But this was not Britain; this was Burma. Burma was a place in which the dreadful was to be expected. 'The acceptance of terrible things as normal', Cochrane wrote in his memoirs after the war, 'gave me a strength that I vowed to myself I would get through this.'[1]

A few months later, five thousand miles away, another young Briton of about the same age as Cochrane lay on a bunk on a transport vessel sailing across the English Channel, trying to imagine what the following day – D-Day, 6 June, 1944 – would be like. 'Here I am', wondered tank officer David Holbrook. 'This is what I asked for, after all.' He thought about how he might behave in combat. It was hard thing to picture:

> In his mind's eye he recalled newsreels of men walking with bayonets in smoke, the Dunkirk beaches palled with black clouds, men's fraught faces as they clung to clattering machine-guns. Something like that. The regiment would wade through waves and beach debris and come together, the tanks assembling in French fields. But what happened after that . . .?
>
> As he sank to sleep he thought of the other young men of his generation, each young man alone, like him, thoughtful and apprehensive in his place in the flotilla, on deck or below deck . . . a hundred thousand others, a myriad young, were lying in this darkness, ready, their hearts beating with nervous anxiety, on the water, in airplanes, in gliders, concealing their anxiety with hard clowning chatter.[2]

The twin prospects of killing and of being killed frightened and fascinated soldiers above all other things during the Second World War. How, they wondered to themselves, would they respond to the traumatic demands of battle? Would they rise to the occasion as Cochrane had managed to do when the moment came – stifle their fears and their moral qualms, maintain their self-composure, make themselves useful to their comrades, act with courage and dignity? Or would they blanch, stumble, collapse shivering and tearful, soil themselves, let down their mates, shame their families? Would they survive unscathed or be blown to pieces – or worse, be horribly maimed, blinded, crippled? In his autobiographical novel *From the City, From the Plough*, Alexander Baron imagined a junior officer on the brink of going into combat for the first time weighing up just these questions. The young subaltern had always previously thought of war in a blandly self-congratulatory way, picturing himself winning medals, or perhaps at worst being sent back to hospital with a minor and painless wound. Now, as he prepared to find out at last what battle was really like, he was beset by altogether darker possibilities:

> Being delivered home to his mother like a helpless package, handless or armless or legless . . . his mother weeping over his smashed and frightful face . . . sprawling dead, faced downwards by the roadside, with the battalion plodding by as he if had never existed.[3]

Throughout the war the Army's Directorate for the Selection of Personnel sought a way to introduce some predictive scientific measure of battle temperament, to gauge beforehand how men would behave in combat. The shortage of major land engagements with the Germans between Dunkirk and D-Day made the selection of combat soldiers especially difficult. 'In the fourth year of the last war, men were streaming home from France to become officer cadets', pointed out journalist James Lansdale Hodson in an article for *The Spectator*. 'They knew, and their officers knew, their behaviour under stress of war.' But no such practical trial was available for the mass of servicemen stationed in mid-war Britain. 'Very few of them have been in battle, or even under fire . . . [yet] the choice of men for commissions must still be made.'[4] In the absence of any widely available empirical test, then, the Army fell back on psychological evaluation. All new soldiers after 1942 were rated on their supposed suitability for the fighting arms as part of their General Service Corps assessment. But in the majority of cases the results were simply too vague to be of any use. Five per cent of recruits were rated by the DSP as 'highly suited' to the rigours of combat. Three per cent were 'poorly suited'. As for the rest – who knew?[5] Psychiatrists, in the end, were not fortune-tellers. 'No adequate test of courage' existed, as one of them conceded.[6] Only battle itself would ever reveal the truth.

When the moment of truth did arrive, some men did not behave the way anyone had expected them to. The best boxer in Dudley Anderson's battalion, a soldier of apparently limitless courage, deserted in a panic on the eve of D-Day. Yet one of the battalion's worst soldiers – scruffy, inattentive to orders, the sort of man who would reliably fall asleep on sentry duty – won the Military

Medal for single-handedly destroying a German tank.[7] It was 'the quiet unspectacular members of the platoon' who always turned out best, thought Raleigh Trevelyan. 'The flamboyant ones, always boasting and out to impress, invariably let us down.'[8] One of the corporals in Stanley Whitehouse's company had done a great job of playing the hero in battle exercises back in Britain, leading charges with yells and curses with his steel helmet propped back at a fashionably rakish angle. But as soon as he arrived in Normandy, he began scheming to get sent back home. Eventually he was reduced to rubbing dirt into mosquito bites in an attempt to infect them.[9]

While all British soldiers wondered how they would behave if they were tested in battle, in practice few of them ever actually found out. Promotion and overseas service were two of the ways in which wartime experiences fissured and went off along different paths. But the most important experiential divide was whether or not you were one of the handful of men regularly exposed to combat. No other factor would have such a profound effect on your fate as a soldier, or the kind of war that you were going to have. To Colin MacInnes, combat troops seemed to have accessed 'a greater reality' than he and other rear-area soldiers could ever know. They were witnesses to an essential truth about the war which would always be lost on those who merely looked on. 'If we drove up among them to the forward areas they were quite friendly', he wrote,

> but they made us feel that there were secrets which could be known only to those who shared their existence. As we looked at them from the comfort of our soft vehicles and clean clothing, their eyes returned our glances and said: '*we don't hold it against you that you're not here with us, it's all a matter of how you're posted and it might have happened to you. But since it hasn't, don't try to understand what you can't.*' Most of us admired them, and even envied them; but this, half-heartedly. They, at any rate, knew the German Army in an intimate, physical way, while to us it remained an unknown juggernaut.[10]

To infantryman Rex Wingfield, 'base wallahs' such as MacInnes were 'creatures from a civilized, strange, unreal world, the world outside the slit-trench, outside home, looking in.'[11] They seemed to gaze on combat troops with a 'funereal sympathy and awe'.[12]

Of all the Great Powers that fought in the Second World War, only the United States distributed the hazards of battle amongst its soldiers as unequally as Britain did. In October 1937, nine in ten of the officers and men of the British Army were serving in its combat or 'teeth' arms.[13] But by autumn 1944,

that ratio had fallen to just six in ten. The remainder could be found instead in
the Army's 'tail', the shadow force of tradesmen, specialists, clerks and labourers
who toiled in the vast rear-area system of bases, depots and camps across
Britain and the overseas theatres of the war.[14] In seven years, the Royal Army
Service Corps (RASC), responsible for the transport and supply of men, stores
and equipment, expanded forty-five times over, from 6,675 officers and ORs
to 303,862. The Royal Army Ordnance Corps (RAOC), which handled the
replacement and repair of equipment and vehicles, took on so many responsibilities that by 1942 it had been split up, with a separate Corps of Royal
Electrical and Mechanical Engineers (REME) being created which by 1944 had
itself grown in size to over 151,000 men. 'We carry a civilisation with us through
this waste land', wrote Neil McCallum of the Western Desert in 1943:

> When the infantryman stops his marching with a final curse and lets his
> pack fall to the ground there unfolds behind him a network of uniformed
> bankers, bakers, smiths, storekeepers, sanitary officials, doctors, nurses,
> transport men, newsmen, communications men, entertainers . . . there are
> hospitals, radio stations, airports, brothels, holiday camps . . .[15]

On his tour of Italy and the Middle East in the summer of 1944, the War Office's
morale expert John Sparrow visited base and training depots, transit camps,
convalescent depots, rest camps, leave camps, education and information
centres, ordnance depots, signals units, workshops and detention barracks.[16]
Amongst the more baroque components of the Army's tail were its Mobile Tent
Repair Teams, its Psychological Warfare Language Units, its X-Ray and
Physiotherapy Repair Sections, its Flour Milling Units, its Sheet Metal
Container Sections (with their associated Petrol Tin Factory Detachments), its
Bitumen Roads Companies and its Pest Destruction Advisory Units.[17] The
appetite of the tail for manpower was insatiable.

Some teeth arms grew to great size during the war as well. By 1944, the
Corps of Royal Engineers had expanded from a pre-war strength of just over
7,900 officers and men to 254,182. At the war's end, the Royal Artillery was
bigger than the Royal Navy. New teeth arms – the Reconnaissance Corps, the
Army Air Corps – were created between 1939 and 1945 to satisfy the innova-
tive technical demands of mid-twentieth-century battle.[18] But not all the men
of the teeth arms were equally exposed to combat. Some had very dangerous
wars. Sappers in Royal Engineers field companies who cleared enemy mine-
fields and built pontoon bridges under fire were at much at risk as any soldier.
So too were Royal Armoured Corps crewmen, expected to lead assaults against
German positions teeming with anti-tank guns. But other teeth soldiers, either

by accident or design, saw almost as little of the war as their comrades in the tail. The men of Kingsley Amis's Royal Corps of Signals unit had spent weeks before OVERLORD in preparatory battlefield training involving live-fire artillery barrages. Yet in the event, they drove all the way from the D-Day beaches to Germany without a single one of them ever needing to use a weapon.[19]

Of all the teeth arms, it was the infantry that continued to shoulder the greatest burden of risk in this war; and it was the Poor Bloody Infantryman (PBI) with his tin hat, rifle and bayonet who had to advance, take and hold enemy positions in all weathers and conditions. His was the most physically arduous, unsafe, unglamorous, uncelebrated, underpaid and indispensable job in the wartime Army. The risks run by infantrymen were much greater than those undertaken by any other group of soldiers. Of the 114,736 British officers and ORs who died as a direct result of enemy action during the Second World War, 68,401 of them – three out of five – were serving in one of the line infantry or Foot Guards regiments, even though these made up less than 20 per cent of the Army's total strength.[20] Junior infantry officers lived especially unhealthy lives. Of the fifty-five subalterns who served in the twelve rifle platoons of the 1st Gordon Highlanders between D-Day and the German surrender, one in four died. Of the survivors, only three came out of the campaign completely unscathed.[21]

Dangerous as service in the other teeth arms could sometimes be, the infantryman was twice as likely to be killed in action as any other soldier at the 'sharp end'.[22] The 2nd Scots Guards infantry battalion did not arrive in Germany until mid-March 1945, just six weeks before the German surrender, when the worst of the campaign was already over and the job of the infantry had become largely a mopping-up operation against the last vestiges of the *Wehrmacht*. But in those six weeks alone, twenty-six of the battalion's men were killed, including nine officers, while another 265 were wounded. By contrast the regiment's 3rd battalion, which was serving as a tank formation on the same front, lost just one officer and seven ORs during those same six weeks.[23]

It was for this reason that relations between the PBI and the other teeth arms were sometimes fraught. 'There was something maddening about men who travelled into battle in vehicles', thought infantryman Norman Craig. 'They always had their blankets, their overcoats, their rations and their water cans to hand. They didn't really know what war was like.'[24] British artillerymen were highly regarded by the infantry for their technical skill and the inestimable firepower that they could bring down upon the enemy. But gunners were nonetheless resented for their detachment from the physical consequences of what they did.[25] While Robert Woollcombe admitted to being awed by the power of British barrages, it troubled him that such 'dispassionate acts of mechanical precision employed in killing' were set into motion by men who, moments after unleashing their murderous fire on the enemy infantry, would be calmly 'lifting mugs of tea and lighting cigarettes' in their dugouts miles behind the front.[26] Infantrymen also complained that there were far too many 'rubberneckers and Bright Ideas Boys' leading tank and artillery units – officers who liked to show up for an hour or two in the front line, rile up the enemy with a demonstration of firepower, and then disappear before the inevitable retaliatory barrage.[27] Some armoured commanders were disliked for appearing to treat the infantry merely as 'a convenient expendable mass' which could be thrown against anti-tank guns.[28] When the peace of Rex Wingfield's platoon started to be disturbed every morning by the arrival of a 25-pounder field gun which would fire ten rounds at the opposing lines and then flee to the safety of the rear-area zone before the German response could begin, he and his mates plotted revenge. One day, one of Wingfield's comrades removed the rotor arm from the engine of the artillery tractor, so that the gunners had to sit through the German counter-barrage their actions had provoked. They never showed up again.[29]

But this tension between teeth arms paled into insignificance compared with the resentment that all front-line troops nurtured towards the men of the rear-area zones – the Line of Communications (L of C) wallahs, the B-Echelon boys, the men of 'the other Army', as Trevor Greenwood called them without affection.[30] Today we tend to lump together all veterans of the Second World War as an undifferentiated mass of heroes who deserve equal approbation, no matter what job they performed. Such a lack of discrimination would have infuriated the men of the teeth in 1944. So far as they were concerned, the troops behind the lines, with their dry uniforms and freshly cooked rations, were scarcely soldiers at all. The tail, to them, was an entirely different organization, operating according to its own, vastly more preferable conditions of service. An infantryman was *fourteen* times more likely to die in action than a soldier in the support arms.[31] 'The truth of the matter', thought Coldstream Guards officer Jocelyn Pereira, was that there was 'a good deal of odium towards the L of C, who indispensable and magnificent as their contribution was, seemed in comparison to live such a happy life while the PBI bore the heat of the day'.[32] 'They talk about their long service, whine about going home', seethes a less polite infantryman in Guthrie Wilson's autobiographical novel *Brave Company*. 'Service! Why God damn me! It's one long picnic for them':

> Bloody little small-town nobodies doing the big shot act all over Italy, it makes you cry . . . and when you talk to 'em, they don't look you right in the eye, most of 'em. But you know what they're thinking; oh yes, you know all

right: *'Here's another of the bloody fools, one of the thick-head tribe that wasn't clever enough to get a soft job like me!'*[33]

A dislike of staff officers is usually associated with the Western Front from 1914 to 1918. But 'teeth' soldiers in the Second World War also resented those brass-hats ensconced in comfortable sinecures in the rear-area zone. To Jack Swaab and his comrades, the identifying badge of General Eisenhower's SHAEF headquarters was *The Cross of Shame*, or *The Red Badge of Courage*.[34] On leave in Cairo, Reg Crimp mocked the 'well groomed resident clerks' of the city in his diary. 'How immaculately laundered they look', he wrote, 'in their spotless shirts and well-pressed slacks with tailored wasp-waists and bell-bottoms to give an impression of civilian elegance!'[35] Equally despised were Cairo's Military Police – 'sadistic thugs whose only virtue is a brutality which is counterpart to the cowardice which keeps them out of the front line'.[36] All rear-echelon types were pursuing much the same war aim, thought Neil McCallum: to 'be respectably accepted by wearing uniform, and safe by wearing it in a cushy job'.[37] For every man in the Blue, there were another twenty back in Cairo 'bludging and skiving in wine bars and restaurants, night clubs and brothels'.[38] Christopher Seton-Watson was bitter about the 'inanities and nonentities with no knowledge and no sympathy for their work' who infested the Egyptian capital in 1942, 'occupying jobs on which thousands of lives depend, eating and drinking well, sleeping in the afternoons, spending their lives trying to get away with it and avoid being bothered'.[39] These were the 'Gaberdine Swine' of GHQ Middle East, also known as 'Groppi's Light Horse' after Cairo's most fashionable restaurant, the crisply tailored, lotus-eating staff officers whose anthem was said to be:

We never went west of Gezira,
We never went north of the Nile,
We never went past the Pyramids
Out of sight of the Sphinx's smile.
We fought the war in Shepheard's and the Continental Bar,
We reserved our punch for the Turf Club lunch
And they gave us the Africa Star.[40]

As the last line suggests, the issuing of campaign medals to non-combat troops was a source of considerable anger to many in the teeth arms who felt that they alone deserved such a distinction. 'All the base-wallahs have [the Africa Star], as well as people who've only been here nine months and seen no action', noted Crimp acerbically in the winter of 1943. 'They say the ATS in Cairo have it too and that soon the wogs will be getting theirs.'[41] 'Anybody who has been anywhere between Suez and Casablanca can have it', complained one soldier in a letter home in December 1943.[42] Campaign medals were 'debased', thought Norman Smith, by granting them to NAAFI staff.[43] To troops in the Far East in 1945, the Burma Star was the derisory 'Chowringhee medal', because all it seemed you had to do to earn one was to take a stroll along Calcutta's main high street.[44] The men of John Hudson's unit saw the Burma Star as a trinket for 'the safely ensconced base-wallahs, the *babus* and the staff officers . . . to be awarded for Gluttony Beyond the Call of Duty'.[45] It says something about the indiscriminate way in which such awards were distributed that by 1949 only one in three of the ex-soldiers who were eligible to receive a campaign medal had actually bothered to apply for it.[46]

This disdain by the teeth for the tail was not particularly fair. Support troops performed vital tasks. Many of them worked long, monotonous, often thankless hours repairing vehicles and keeping the front-line formations supplied with food and ammunition. It was difficult, tiring, but also boring and inglorious work, without any of the psychological consolation of seeing a spectacular military effect from it. 'It is easy enough for a man making a shell or digging men from under debris or bringing a convoy over safely to see how his actions are helping to win the war', pointed out one RAOC soldier. 'But imagine a man packing a stack of cases, or recording a string of numbers on endless sheets of papers . . .'[47] The troops of the Royal Army Service Corps were said to put up with 'more bullshit, more aimless routine, more blind-alley effort and more browned-offness' than any other group of soldiers.[48] The mental toll could be heavy. Two out of three soldiers who were treated for psychiatric illness in the Middle East had never been in battle, but rather had fallen victim to homesickness, melancholy and depression while serving in tail units.[49] And rear-echelon jobs were not invariably safe. Over 6,800 officers and men of the main support corps died as a result of enemy action during the war.[50] The driver of a ration truck who visited Geoffrey Picot's platoon in Normandy one evening was killed by an artillery burst that left the fighting soldiers surrounding him completely unscathed.[51] In emergency situations, men of the tail were expected to pick up their rifles and fight the enemy just like any other soldiers.

Still, all the infantryman knew as he crouched in his muddy slit trench somewhere in Tuscany or Zeeland or Assam, his clothes filthy and sodden, his food cold and tasteless, his peace of mind continually disturbed by the crack of shellfire and the cries of the wounded, was that somewhere to the rear of his position were other soldiers who at that moment were lots of things he was not – clean and warm and well-fed and out of harm's way, for a start. Was that their fault? No. But it still did not seem fair that they – the great mass of the Army – were living in 'comparative luxury' while a tiny handful at the cutting edge were being methodically slaughtered.[52] It would have taken the sweet reasonableness of a saint not to be vexed by this. And the British infantryman was no saint.

Indeed, in the mind of a soldier sheltering from the fusillade of a German MG-42, *anyone* not being fired upon by a heavy machine-gun at that precise instant was a non-combatant, no matter who they were. The hazards of battle were infuriatingly uneven. There was, thought George MacDonald Fraser, something inherently unjust about the way in which two infantry sections of ten men apiece could go into battle in Burma, and while 'one wouldn't even see a Jap all day, the other lost half its strength clearing bunkers not far away'.[53] Jocelyn Pereira remembered one engagement in Normandy in which he was able to sit in a ditch eating sardines and biscuits in relative comfort while just over the brow of a nearby hill a neighbouring infantry company was being plastered with German artillery fire.[54] From the infantryman's point of view, anyone whose life was fractionally safer than his own, even for just a few minutes, was a shirker. The length of a football pitch could represent the difference between life and death. Stanley Whitehouse's comrades regarded the 'rear-area zone' as beginning just a hundred yards behind the front.[55] One of the section commanders in Norman Craig's battalion was pickier still: he referred to the men at platoon headquarters as 'base-wallahs' because their position was fifty yards behind the leading troops.[56] Even the tiniest, most incremental scrap of security was an envied – and resented – privilege.

What was particularly vexing to the infantryman was that even though he was performing the single most vital task in the entire Army – if he faltered, everyone else came shuddering to a halt behind him – he and his comrades nonetheless seemed to have been dumped into their battalions almost as an afterthought. It was not an imaginary grievance. Throughout the war, the adjutant-general often spoke of his concern that infantry units always seemed to get 'the rejects from other arms of the services'.[57] When General Noel Irwin griped at a press conference after the failed Arakan campaign of 1943 that the British put their 'worst men' into the infantry, he was sacked – not because what he said was untrue (Slim, who was no admirer of Irwin, agreed with him) but because of his tactlessness in publicly discussing the issue.[58] General Harold Freeman-Attwood, who commanded the 46th Infantry Division in North Africa, protested to the War Office that his infantry replacements had 'insufficient brains'.[59] A study of wartime Scottish soldiers who had taken intelligence tests at school in the early 1930s suggests that, on average, infantry privates had an IQ ten points lower than that of rank-and-file tradesmen.[60] The PBI were well aware that their branch of the service was regarded as a discard pile by the rest of the Army. The effect this had on morale is not hard to imagine. Leslie Phillips was compulsorily transferred to the infantry from the Royal Artillery in November 1943 along with 2,000 other junior officers who had been deemed surplus to requirements by their original regiments. 'They were all as bitter as I was about what had happened', he recalled. 'There was constant muttering about resignation, stifled only by the certainty that this would lead to being called up again as a private.' The sense that such a transfer was a demotion was universally shared.[61] Psychiatrist S. A. MacKeith warned the War Office in 1944 that the low status of the infantry in Italy was causing more discontent than any other single morale factor. 'Infantrymen felt that they were subjected to greater degrees of danger and discomfort than were soldiers in other arms', he wrote:

> Yet they found themselves regarded with 'semi-affectionate contempt' by civilians and others, they received the lowest pay in the Army – with no 'hard-lying money' or 'combat pay' – and they were provided with no badge or flash indicative of their combatant role and their efficiency therein.

'It was difficult', he thought, 'to imagine a situation more destructive to morale.'[62]

Concern about the poor quality of the men entering the infantry had been one of the reasons for Adam's overhaul of personnel selection in 1941 and 1942. Yet the introduction of psychological testing and the creation of the General Service Corps may have actually made things worse. Part of the problem was that it was never easy to define precisely the qualities that an infantryman should have. There was no clear occupational parallel to infantry soldiering in civilian life. The 1937 edition of the Army's *Infantry Training Manual* described the ideal infantryman in flattering terms as an 'expert hunter ... confident and expert in the use of weapons, skilled in the use of ground and able to stand fatigue without undue loss of efficiency. He must be determined, inquisitive and self-dependent'.[63] This was all very well in theory, but it was much harder for an overworked DSP official to put into concrete terms than, say, the skill-set that was required to be a clerk or a driver. Plus, the traditional military canard that intelligence was actually more of a burden than an asset in foot soldiering may have influenced even the most even-handed evaluator. Infantrymen in Britain were often loaned out as general-purpose labourers to perform tedious manual tasks – clearing bomb damage, bringing in the harvest and guarding factories, aerodromes and beaches. Treating them as a pool of cheap manpower to be sent hither and thither did not exactly encourage anyone in authority to think of infantry soldiering as a skilled trade in its own right.[64]

The result was that the needs of the other services and the other branches of the Army were consistently prioritized over the PBI. Recruits were only allotted to the infantry regiments once everyone else had had their choice – which meant that infantrymen tended to be the soldiers no one else wanted. The RAF received first pick of all; then the Navy; then the Army's technical corps; then the armoured units; and only then the infantry, who too often were left with the barrel scrapings.[65] Some military trades had dozens of grades, the infantry, it seemed, only two: 'Cannon Fodder, Classes I and II.'[66] All it seemed you needed to get in was a trigger finger and a pulse.

Part of the reason for this was that for several years after Dunkirk, politicians and generals were hypnotized by the spectacle of mechanized combat. The Axis victory in spring 1940 had awed them. Germany's use of tanks and aeroplanes seemed to represent the future of warfare. Foot-slogging infantry, it appeared, were now defenceless against armoured vehicles supported by ground-attack aircraft.[67] If the British Army was ever going to fight the *Wehrmacht* again with any chance of success, it would, so the theory went, have to reinvent itself as a tank-centred force lavishly equipped with anti-aircraft (AA) and anti-tank (AT) weapons. So once war production began to ramp up in early 1941, many of the infantry battalions, which had been hurriedly thrown together in the invasion panic of the previous summer, were converted with equal haste into AT, AA, armoured and armoured reconnaissance formations. Between January 1941 and December 1942, around 100 of the Army's approximately 500 infantry battalions, with about 80,000 men in them, were disbanded entirely or reorganized and retrained.[68] Churchill was particularly insistent about the need for tanks, tanks and more tanks. As early as the autumn of 1940, he had ordered the creation of ten armoured divisions.[69] By September 1944, the War Office had met this target; indeed, it had more than met it. With the equivalent of twelve armoured divisions, the British Army was, relative to its size, the most tank-heavy fighting force in the world.[70]

Not all of these conversions were necessarily well thought out. Take, for instance, the story of the Guards Armoured Division (GAD), formed in June 1941 by the re-equipping of seven Foot Guards battalions with tanks and reconnaissance vehicles. In all, over 8,500 Guardsmen exchanged their rifles for coveralls as a result of the transition.[71] Little discussion took place within the War Office as to whether or not this was really a good idea.[72] Grenadier Guards officer Peter Carrington, who crossed Europe in a GAD Sherman in 1944 and 1945, was never persuaded that it was. Not only was it difficult to cram tall Guardsmen into the cramped confines of a tank turret, but the change in combat role also did not play to the natural strength of the Guards as soldiers. Guardsmen were punctilious in their obedience to orders, a quality that was far less valuable in an armoured unit, where 'speed and imagination and initiative' were at a higher premium. Guards Warrant Officers and NCOs were 'admirable men', thought Carrington:

> But they were executants of pretty rigid orders, custodians of a fairly inflexible scheme. They knew their basic infantry soldiering inside out. To find their Guardsmen separated from them by the steel walls of an armoured vehicle was disconcerting.

The Army, in his view, got 'the worst of two worlds' when it created the GAD. It traded in thousands of superb infantrymen, which it needed desperately, and in return got thousands of mediocre tankmen, which it didn't.[73]

In any case, by D-Day it was becoming clear that many of the assumptions that the Army had based its post-Dunkirk reconstruction on had been greatly exaggerated. In 1944, the Luftwaffe was no longer the terror it had once seemed. Indeed, German planes had largely disappeared from the skies over Italy and France. The Army's prodigious number of anti-aircraft units had little to shoot at. Montgomery's 21st Army Group also found itself with more towed anti-tank guns than it knew what to do with, because such powerful but clumsy weapons were turning out to be less useful than expected for an army on the offensive.[74] And the tank was no longer the unstoppable killing machine it had once appeared to be. Thanks to the promiscuous distribution of landmines and the development of cheap, potent hand-held bomb projectors such as the German *Panzerfaust* – an 'outsized bassoon' which could blow a tank's turret from its chassis at fifty yards – armoured vehicles were now just as often prey as they were predators. Before D-Day, Sherman gunner Ken Tout's preoccupying anxiety had been the mighty German 'eighty-eight' anti-tank gun. But in the *bocage* hedgerows of Normandy, he and his comrades came to fear still more the 'solitary field-grey hero' lurking in the shadows with his portable bazooka.[75] Infantrymen, conscious of their own naked vulnerability to gun and shell fire, sometimes thought of the tank as an 'overpowering leviathan'.[76] The reality by 1944 was anything but.

What the fighting in Italy and later Normandy confirmed was that for all of the war's technical advances, the infantry were still the lords of battle. Mechanized firepower could only do so much. Ultimately, foot soldiers still had to advance into contact with the enemy. But this very indispensability made the PBI dreadfully vulnerable. Although the overall casualty figures in the OVERLORD operation proved to be lower than originally forecast, the *infantry* losses specifically were far higher.[77] And by mid-1944, the Army simply did not have enough replacement infantrymen to handle such a rapid wastage rate. Too late, the consequences of treating infantry manpower selection so casually became clear. Men had to be hurriedly reassigned from other arms and services en masse. Large numbers of redundant AT and AA personnel were retrained for infantry duties. In Italy, 18,000 such soldiers were compulsorily reposted to rifle battalions. Over 35,000 sailors and airmen were transferred to the Army.[78] Still it was not enough. The War Office had no choice but to take the drastic step of breaking up existing units just to keep the others in the field. In France, one infantry division (the 59th) was dissolved completely, and another (the 50th) reduced to cadre strength. Three reserve divisions in Britain (the 76th, 77th and 9th Armoured) were cannibalized for replacements. In the Mediterranean, two armoured divisions (the 1st and 10th) were disbanded, and each infantry battalion in Italy reduced in strength by one company. The situation was worst of all in India and Burma, where manpower problems were exacerbated by the need to repatriate men who had been serving in the East for many years. By October 1944, the Allied commander-in-chief in South East Asia, Lord Mountbatten, was warning London that he was already 30,000 men short, and that the gap between the troops which he needed and those which he had available was likely to grow even larger in the upcoming campaign season. In the closing months of the war in the East, the last two exclusively British infantry divisions in the theatre (the 2nd and 36th) had to be withdrawn from operations because of lack of replacements. If the conflict against the Japanese had not ended in August 1945, it is not clear whether Mountbatten's army could have kept fighting at all without a massive – and politically controversial – resupply of troops from Europe.[79]

Riflemen were in such short supply by the end of the war that there was little chance of withdrawing them from the front line for any extended period of rest and recuperation. Instead, they found themselves sent back into combat again and again. Many infantrymen came to feel that their only chance of escape would be through death, incapacitation or desertion; and of the three, the last was the least frightening. By 1944, soldiers with previously fine combat records were coming to the conclusion that, as a report from Italy put it, 'It would be better to spend the time in the safety and comparative comfort of a military prison rather than to return to the line to so little hope of final relief.'[80]

Churchill blamed the War Office. To his mind, he had been warning about the infantry shortage ever since he became prime minister. In December 1940, he complained to his first secretary of state for war, Anthony Eden, that too few soldiers were fighting men. A mass of what he called 'statics', or the 'fluff and flummery' of the Army, were living well on the government dole while accomplishing very little. 'We are not doing our duty in letting these great numbers be taken from our civil life and kept at the public expense to make such inconceivably small results in the fighting line', he griped.[81] In January 1941, Churchill protested to General Wavell that Middle East Command needed 'less fat and more muscle'. The commander-in-chief in Cairo was enjoined to 'continually comb, scrub, and purge' all the rear echelons until every soldier possible was playing a combat role. 'It is distressing', added the prime minister, 'to see convoys sent by the heart's blood of the nation's effort consisting so largely of rearward services of all kinds.'[82] On 4 January 1943, Churchill wrote to Eden's successor, Sir P. J. Grigg, demanding to know why only 27,000 out of 211,000 British troops in the British First Army fighting in Algeria were infantrymen. 'I am well aware of, and I sympathize with, the modern tendency which has led the great development of specialist arms of all kinds', acknowledged Churchill. But 'it would seem that this tendency has been carried too far when the infantry, who bear the brunt of the fighting, are reduced to such extremely small proportions'.[83] The prime minister took up the theme again in November 1944 at news that the 50th Infantry Division was to be dismantled. 'It is a painful reflection', he complained, 'that probably not one in four or five men who wear the King's uniform ever hear a bullet whistle, or are likely to hear one . . . one set of men are sent back again and again to the front, while the great majority are kept out of all fighting.'[84]

But as Brooke patiently had to reiterate over and over to Churchill after such tirades, you could hardly have the mechanized army the prime minister was *also* constantly demanding if you were not prepared to set aside the troops to keep it fuelled and repaired. An armoured division in Normandy in 1944 required 1,000 gallons of petrol to move just one mile.[85] Someone had to transport that petrol from tankers to depots to the field. And those petrol trucks themselves had to be kept fuelled and repaired, and so on. There was a cascading effect across the Army every time you introduced a new resource-guzzling, high-maintenance tank, gun and vehicle. It was the inexorable logic of mass industrial warfare, not simply the idleness of the fluff and flummery, which was driving the growth of the Army's tail.

And Churchill had not improved the situation by promoting so aggressively the creation of elite light infantry formations – 'special forces' troops, as many of them would now be known. Britain was in a class of its own when it came to the creation of such private armies during the Second World War. By D-Day, there were something in the region of eight equivalent-divisions of them scattered around the world, in an Army which had only twenty-two conventional infantry and armoured divisions to begin with.[86] No other Great Power devoted as large a share of its combat troops to such elite forces. Why was this? The

British Army's tradition of using makeshift columns to fight irregular 'small wars' on the colonial frontier may have had something to do with it. It also reflected the experience of 1940. The War Office had been much impressed by the Germans' use of paratroopers, covert special forces detachments, and 'fifth columnists' in the conquest of France and the Low Countries, and gave their exploits rather more credit for the outcome of the campaign than was really warranted.[87] But Churchill's peculiar attitude towards war was critical too. The prime minister was fascinated by elite light troops. They excited his memories of the rugged, fast-moving Boer horsemen of the South African War. Dash, cunning and heroic individualism seemed to him essential qualities of military genius.[88] He was naturally drawn to soldiers such as Orde Wingate, the truculent maverick of the Burma campaign who created the Long Range Penetration or 'Chindit' Force to execute hit-and-run operations behind enemy lines.[89] To Churchill, long an initiate of the Colonel Lawrence school of generalship, men such as Wingate ('a man of genius and audacity ... the Clive of Burma', the prime minister rhapsodized to Brooke) were the real answer to the Germans and Japanese.[90] By relying on rapier-fast dexterity rather than dull mass, they could win the war without the need for cruel infantry-slogging matches.[91]

The actual record of Britain's wartime special forces was mixed at best, however. There were, for instance, the four Special Service or 'Commando' brigades, each of about 2,000 men, which were formed on Churchill's instigation in 1940 to perform 'butcher and bolt' raids against the German-occupied European shoreline.[92] The Commandos attracted thousands of the British Army's best troops, and became emblematic of a cold-blooded toughness, both during and after the war.[93] But for much of their existence, the War Office regarded them more as a nuisance than an asset. An otherwise sympathetic recent history of the wartime commandos' exploits is honest enough to concede that strategically speaking, most of their missions were of 'questionable value'.[94] Commando raids had some utility as morale-boosting exercises in the bleak mid-war years when small-scale sabotage attacks were all that the Army could realistically hope to mount against the *Werhmacht* in France. But by the end of the war, the Commandos had racked up a 'lengthy and bloody list of failures', and many of the tasks that they had successfully accomplished could have been performed equally well, and at less expense, by regular line infantry battalions.[95]

Then there was the record of the airborne troops – the 28,345 soldiers of the wartime British Army's two parachute divisions and one independent parachute brigade.[96] The heroism that these men displayed during the D-Day landings, and later in the doomed offensive at Arnhem, is not in question. What *is* questionable is whether all their courage was ever put to any really worthwhile use. Of the four large-scale missions the airborne forces performed during the war, only one, the D-Day drop, can really be said to have been a success. Their other three drops – in Sicily, the Netherlands and the Rhineland – were, respectively, a tragic fiasco, a noble failure and an expensive sideshow.[97] The 1st Airborne Division only spent nine days in action during the whole of the northwest European campaign. As its survivors marched away from Arnhem after the failure of Operation MARKET-GARDEN, they were jeered by British tank crews: '*Some people have all the fucking luck – one battle and home to England*.'[98] This was not, to put it mildly, a very generous reception given what the paratroopers had just been through. But it does demonstrate some of the frustration felt by regular line troops towards what seemed to them to be an idle (and comparatively well-paid) elite.

It was Wingate's Chindits, however, who were the single greatest waste of British Army manpower in the Second World War. Chindit Force performed two major operations against the Japanese. The first, Operation LONGCLOTH, was a 1,000-mile expedition across the enemy-occupied Burmese interior from February to May 1943. The Chindits blew up railway bridges, ambushed road convoys and attacked isolated Japanese posts, resupplying themselves by airdrops into jungle clearings. LONGCLOTH resulted in extremely high casualties – of the 3,000 soldiers who took part, over 800 did not return across the Chindwin, and of those who did, 600 were too debilitated by their experiences to ever serve in combat again. The expedition's practical results were marginal: 'It seemed that all we had done was to kill a small number of the enemy, blow up the railway in a few places (damage which could be repaired in a matter of weeks), and cock a snook at the Japanese', thought subaltern Robin Painter, who had lost three stone in weight during the campaign and had to be hospitalized for seven weeks afterwards. 'I began to ask myself whether it was worthwhile.'[99]

Still, LONGCLOTH was a relatively small endeavour, and if nothing else it had demonstrated a crucial lesson that the Army in Burma badly needed to learn in 1943 – that the Japanese were not, after all, unbeatable.[100] It is much harder to make a case for the following year's Operation THURSDAY, a six-month expedition which involved more than three times as many troops, resulted in even more casualties (over 1,400 dead or missing, 2,400 wounded, over half the survivors bedridden through tropical illness), and with just as little strategic result. The need to find troops for THURSDAY required the dissolution of an entire regular infantry division (the 70th) which had fought with distinction in the Western Desert campaign. John Masters, who was chief of staff in one of Wingate's six brigades, and later assumed its de facto command, thought that by THURSDAY the Chindit Force had become much too large for its own good. Its twenty-four battalions were the equivalent of two-and-a-half divisions, yet because it had no artillery or engineering support it was not even as powerful as a single regular division. He was embarrassed to be thought of as one of the 'spoiled darlings of a maniacal publicity seeker'.[101]

Major John Randle of the 10th Baluch Regiment said of the two Chindit expeditions that they were 'an epic of human courage ... but strategically a waste of time'.[102] The same could be said about many of the missions of Britain's wartime special forces. They demanded extraordinary reserves of bravery and fortitude. They were romantic echoes of a very different kind of war from the gruelling slogging matches of Anzio or Kohima. But they were ultimately products of the same fallacy of the Indirect Approach which was also responsible for the strategic bombing campaign – the belief that costly head-on land battles with the main force of the enemy could be postponed indefinitely by guile and ingenuity. Special forces came at a high opportunity cost. Every soldier who was recruited as a commando or a paratrooper was a soldier lost to the regular line infantry. The airborne forces alone represented the equivalent of twenty standard infantry battalions.[103] And the men who were attracted to special forces were exactly the soldiers that the infantry desperately needed. The leader of one parachute battalion is said to have boasted that there was not a private soldier under his command who would not have been at least an NCO had he been in a regular rifle unit.[104] If he had paused for a moment to consider what the consequences of this were for the Army as a whole, he might not have been quite so pleased with himself. Britain's private armies had their small victories, but by their very existence they denied the infantry a vital pool of leaders, men whose talents would have been far more usefully (if less glamorously) employed if they had been placed in command of other soldiers.[105] They were magnificent. But perhaps, as a December 1943 War Office report warned, they were 'a frivolity that this nation is not in a strong position to sustain'.[106]

CHAPTER 12

THE GRAMMAR OF WAR

Imagine driving a car at high speed down a road. Except this particular car has all its windows painted black, so all you have to peer through to see where you are going is a 10-inch slit of clear glass in the front windshield. Now imagine the same car hitting a grass bank so steep that it tilts the whole vehicle at a 30-degree angle, and then toppling over a hillock and crashing down almost perpendicularly on the other side. And imagine people shooting at you all the while. That, thought Norman Smith, was a little what it was like to be inside a tank careening into battle.[1] Encased in a steel enclosure, you were, thought one trooper, in 'a little world of your own' once the hatch closed up – sealed off from all the noise and confusion of things taking place just yards away from you, but also deafened by the recoil and choked by the noxious gas discharges of your own weapons.[2]

Confinement within a tank was reassuring if you had become habituated to it, claustrophobic if you had not. Engineer John Hudson, who occasionally had to travel in armoured vehicles during battle, never felt anything other than oppressed and suffocated inside a tank, 'as though I was under the lid of a roasting dish waiting for the oven to come off. But for their regular crew members, these tough steel boxes were as comforting as his shell was to a hermit crab'.[3] After dropping into the 'tight little den' of the gunner's compart-ment inside his Sherman, Ken Tout felt like a Victorian chimney-sweep trapped inside a narrow flue – there was something almost reassuringly foetal about it, 'a sealed-off-wrapped-about, doubled-up feeling'.[4] The innards of tanks were a 'substitute for home', thought David Holbrook, with their cooking stoves and shelves of tinned food, their crevices for storing cigarettes and biscuits and letters from the wife. They offered 'chattering comradeship, offers of chocolate and tea, gossip and chaff', with a community of four or five men working and eating and sleeping within a few feet of one another.[5] No other fighting unit was as intimately organized as a tank crew. The mood of each man was a 'delicately adjusted thing, like a tuned musical instrument,' as Peter Elstob put it. 'Confidence and an attacking spirit were transmitted to all . . . uncertainty and a preoccupation with defence ran through [them] like a shiver.'[6]

To be inside a tank in battle was, above all, *confusing*. You were a subterranean dweller, a 'death-beetle inside a steel wall', a 'mobile troglodyte'. Through the vehicle's telescopic periscope, war was reduced to 'a small oblong of dust cloud, penetrated only by a feeble tail light' of the tank in front – a grey haze that might suddenly become a 'blazing world' of colours as the landscape exploded in flame.[7] It was not just that you had little idea of what part your individual vehicle was performing in the overall plan of attack, little sense of the grand strategy being played out all around you. It was also that you had little idea of where you even were, or what was going on just a few yards to your front or rear. Trevor Greenwood's first experience of combat, during an assault in Lower Normandy in summer 1944, left him quite bewildered. He watched from his tank, stationed on a crest of high ground, as an accompanying body of infantry disappeared into the woods below, enveloped by a curtain of smokescreen. He waited for an hour, then two, as nothing seemed to happen, except for an occasional burst of machine-gun fire in the distance. Then he noticed that the tank next to him had caught fire. There was no sign of an enemy. '*What on earth was happening?*' he wondered. Then there was the sound of a high-velocity shell rocketing towards him:

> Hells bells! My tank was being fired at. Two misses! Darned if I could see any gun flashes or tanks. I peered frantically through the telescope: there seemed to be at least one more tank in difficulties, and several smaller vehicles on fire. And then the major's voice – he wanted help . . . smoke. He got smoke . . . all of us poured it out as fast as we could . . . I noticed one or two nearby vehicles moving away, but where to? Soon I couldn't see a thing but smoke, but gave the driver orders to advance: better go anywhere than stay and be shot up. Eventually I found my way back to lower ground away from the danger zone . . . but I was still hazy about the situation.

Afterwards, he discovered that his own squadron had lost two tanks in the engagement, and a neighbouring squadron had been almost wiped out. He had been 'in battle'; he was now a combat veteran. But what had actually happened? He still had almost no idea. The whole thing had lacked any sense of form, of logically organized narrative: battle, it seemed, was simply a flicker of dissonant images taking place without any obvious causal connection to one another.[8]

It was little better for the infantry. All was 'stupefying, brutalising ignorance'.[9] Neil McCallum, who arrived in North Africa too late to take part in the Battle of Alamein, asked another veteran soldier what it had been like. All the man could remember was that '*everyone was shouting, screaming, swearing, shouting for their father, shouting for their mother. I didn't know whether to look at the ground or at the sky, someone said look at the ground for the spider-mines, someone said look at the sky for the flashes, shells were coming all ways, the man next to me got hit through the shoulder, he fell down, I looked at him and said Christ and then ran on, I didn't know whether to be sick or dirty my trousers.*'[10] When William Cochrane's platoon stumbled into an ambush in Burma, the result was equally chaotic. At the first sound of automatic fire, everyone started running to left and right; section careened into section, men shouted and fell down and did not get up. 'I was lying in the grass frightened to move, but I could see the rest of my mates scattered round me,' recalled Cochrane:

> I could see the fear in other men's faces as we looked at each other through the grass and I'm sure that they could see the fear in mine. What really frightened me was that I didn't know what to do. There were clouds of smoke and the flash of explosions very close by to where I was firing. I was just firing in the general direction that I thought we had been fired upon and I desperately needed someone in command to tell me what to do.[11]

It was, thought one soldier, 'a bloody miracle we won the war when nobody knew where the hell anybody was half the time'.[12]

Battle engaged as well as inhibited the senses, sometimes fantastically so. There was the sensation of heat blasted down the back of your neck from a sizzling artillery airburst, accompanied by a cloud of sulphurous smoke.[13] There was the cacophony of sounds – the fabric-tearing *Brrrrrrp! Brrrrrrp! Brrrrrrp!* of German machine-guns; the 'brain-splitting shock wave' of shells landing close by; the vicious crack of field artillery at close hand; the 'soft siffle, high in the air, like a distant lark, or a small penny whistle' of mortar shells in flight, culminating in their ferocious slap to the ground and the whine of shrapnel in the air.[14] A Seaforth Highlander, Alastair Bothwick, compared being an infantryman in an artillery battle to being a fly trapped inside a banging drum.[15] Barrages produced a 'sustained, muffled hammering . . . like rolls of thunder' echoing without respite.[16] Christopher Seton-Watson differentiated the 'sharp bark' of the 25-pounders from the 'deeper loud bang' of the medium pieces.[17] At El Alamein, the sound of hundreds of guns 'all bucking and recoiling, spitting fire and snapping like a pack of vicious terriers all at once' loosened teeth and bowels.[18] And mixed in with the din of small arms fire and the growl of tank engines and the churn of caterpillar tracks on mud, one might also hear the oddly banal, conversational chatter of the wireless net, as matter-of-fact as a BBC weather forecast.[19]

There was, too, the curious silence that descended on the battlefield once the crashing and the roaring had stilled – 'the quietness of death', Raleigh Trevelyan called it, broken only perhaps by birdsong in the smoky darkness. After being at the receiving end of one sustained artillery assault, Trevelyan remembered hearing 'a cry of the most intense agony, but also of despair and loneliness' somewhere in the distance:

> It was so shrill and so short that I thought it must be some sort of hallucina-tion . . . another cry followed, the same voice and more drawn out; and another, and gradually fading into sobs, which became articulate: '*Darling, darling, oh darling, darling, darling . . .*' each word more and more faint until the last was smothered by a further volley of grenades.[20]

War had a smell – 'thick, clinging, tainting the palate as with a sour scum', thought Neil McCallum, 'the smell of high explosive mingled with the smell of human guts. It is a smell of death, brassy, metallic, with a loathsome sweetness in it.'[21] John Smith described it as 'the sickening odour of burned and decaying flesh, the bitter stench from the blackened shell of buildings.'[22] To David Holbrook it was the scent of burned gunpowder, to Ken Tout a smell of 'open latrines spiced with lilies and rotting oranges – sweet but abominably putrid'.[23] For John Foley, combat was aromatically defined by the whiff of hot gun oil intermingled with the cordite fumes that gathered in the cramped confines of his Churchill tank, an acrid composite that made everyone's eyes flood with tears.[24] The smell of war might be the distinctive odour of the enemy soldier too – the 'strange, pungent' scent of *Wehrmacht* tobacco, rifle oil, disinfectant soap, stale sweat, synthetic petrol and bad cologne.[25] The fragrance of the Japanese, insisted George MacDonald Fraser, was equally unmistakable – 'stale cooked rice and sweat and human waste and . . . Jap'.[26]

Visually, battle had a breathtaking, savage majesty to it. During the night-time artillery barrage at El Alamein, the sky was lit with 'flash after flash, like sheet lightning, illuminating the sand with a ghostly yellow incandescence; the western horizon became suffused with the brick-red glow of exploding shells'.[27] The tracer from heavy anti-aircraft guns produced pulsating scarlet orbs in the sky, complemented by the ruddy spray of cannon-fire and 'necklaces of white flak'.[28] A fusillade of rifle bullets across an orchard left the air 'thick as if with bees, but with red fires streaking' through the trees: rods of light sparked and cracked on the stone walls and the roadways, throwing up dust and sending loose fragments of masonry careening off, ripping through foliage.[29] Battle after dark was like a 'flaming tartan pattern fed into a giant kaleidoscope and then run through a high-speed cine camera', thought Ken Tout. 'All the fire-work displays that ever happened, laid one over the other and interspersing, frantically changing, blooming, and disappearing.'[30] To William Cochrane, the flash that exuded from the Cutts compensator of a Tommy gun had a strobe effect that made a firefight at night look curiously like an old silent movie.[31] Watching infantrymen advance into the Reichswald in February 1945, John Foley was also struck by childhood memories of the cinema. 'Khaki-clad figures with fixed bayonets charging ... one or two of them throwing their hands into the air and dropping dramatically to the ground, while others quietly folded up as if their bones had suddenly turned to water.' It was all very much like a sepia newsreel of the Somme.[32]

Sometimes the film ran at the wrong speed or jammed completely. Time was subject to strange spasmodic distortions during combat, accelerating in a blur, then braking to a halt. A confused melee that might in reality have lasted sixty seconds could seem to drag on for hours.[33] A minute under a barrage was 'forever'.[34] When a mortar bomb exploded six feet away from Alex Bowlby, he could recall in detail afterwards the split second between the blast and his body's response – seeing the 'dark red of disintegrating metal and the funnel of flame opening round it' as two sharply contrasting hues in his vision. It was all his eyes could take in for several moments. 'This, plus the blast, plus the fact that we couldn't dig in, reduced me to jelly', he remembered thinking. '*Desert. Desert. Desert. The next time I will*, I promised myself.'[35]

Of all war's phrases, it seemed to Jocelyn Pereira that none was quite so apt as 'baptism of fire'. 'An undefinable something', he wrote, seemed to separate the veteran soldier from the man who had never personally seen battle, 'almost as though a knowledge of war were some secret rite'.[36] Soldiers who had experienced combat, even of the briefest kind, were highly conscious of their initiation into this exclusive club, and could act with 'pompous superiority' towards those only a fraction greener than themselves.[37] Trevor Greenwood remembered meeting a group of discomfited American infantry reinforcements in Holland who begged for as many scraps of information about the Germans as they could get. 'How easy it was for me to understand their feelings', wrote Greenwood later. 'Their eager questioning: their thirst for even the minutest detail ... their drawn and serious faces – revealing that dreadful anxiety about the future' that he had once shared too.[38]

Young British men such as Greenwood had been thinking about war all their lives. They had, after all, grown up in a country haunted by the myths, legends, horrors and glories of the trenches. 'We had never outgrown the shadow of that earlier war which our fathers had fought', thought John Mulgan. 'It brooded over our thoughts and emotions . . . as children we had heard men's stories, coming home, had stood silent in parades of remembrance, knew the names of old battles and heroes as part of our lives.'[39] The paraphernalia of the trenches – the brass cartridge cases and greatcoats and serge puttees, liberated Lugers and spiked Prussian helmets – had cluttered Britain's parlours and attics. Boys had listened to fireside tales of Loos and Thiepval and the Hindenburg Line, of 'sergeant majors who really did dock the rum ration, of the French and their peculiarities, of bombardments and mines, of friends who never returned'.[40]

Much of it had been terrifying. John Hudson recalled 'scarred men, grim, gassed, and afraid of laughter' chanting the same sardonic, monotonous refrain: '*Little do you know, Son! Little do you know!*'[41] Richard Holborow's uncle Harry had died of appalling injuries in the Dardanelles campaign in 1915, and an image of the war's 'terrible blood-letting' was permanently fixed in his consciousness by the stories of his youth.[42] George Meddemmen's vision of war, courtesy of his uncle, was 'a horrid picture of mud and slime and death and brutality'.[43] But even veterans who had experienced the ghastliness of the Western Front had sometimes been ambivalent about what the Great War had meant to them. George Orwell, who had been slightly too young to serve in the trenches, remembered boys a little older than himself talking of their military experiences in the 1920s unceasingly, 'with horror, of course, but also with a steadily growing nostalgia'.[44] The war had been horrific. But it had also been exciting. Army life, for all its cruelty and violence, had provided spiritual satisfaction through its shared ordeals. Some veterans romanticized their accounts without even realizing they were doing so. Although Ronald Elliott's father was 'basically a pacifist', he looked back on his Army service with unabashed sentimentality. 'The old man glamorized it', recalled Elliott years later. 'He'd seen the atrocities and desolation, but at the same time it was something that had been quite an experience for him . . . he tended to take a very rosy view.'[45] A. J. Mills was struck more by the wistfulness of his father's memories than their horror. 'I knew all about war – or thought I did', he wrote later:

Hadn't I sat round that old kitchen range on cold winter evenings and listened to the Old Chap's stories of the last lot? How could it be so dodgy when I was so comfortable being told about it? . . . Oh! I knew you could get hurt in a war. But even that couldn't be too bad. The Old Chap reckoned the first time he hadn't even realized that he had been hit. Just fallen over. It was only when he tried to get up and found he couldn't use his left arm that it dawned on him he was wounded . . . so it couldn't be too bad.[46]

War was terrible, to be sure, but it was also a test – perhaps the only real test – of masculinity.[47] Orwell suspected that his whole life since the age of ten had been spent in mental preparation for a particular kind of war closely resembling the Western Front, 'a war in which the guns rise to a frantic orgasm of sound, and at the appointed moment you clamber out of the trench, breaking your nails on the sandbags, and stumble across mud and wire into the machine-gun barrage'.[48] Commando subaltern Arthur Kellas felt that he shared with many of his peers a neurotic obsession with war, 'a complex of terror and longing' about an experience they had only heard about second-hand as children, but which seemed in some way the only appropriate measure of manhood.[49] Bill Bellamy, whose father had fought in France in 1918, longed to continue the family tradition: 'My constant prayer was that the war would not finish before I was old enough to fight.'[50] 'I suppose deep down if I really analyse my feelings', reflected Alfred Baldwin years later, 'my father had served in the Army. My grandfather had served in the Army. I felt that I wanted to be as good or equal to them.'[51]

But very few young men of Baldwin's age had any idea how they would actually fare if and when the moment came. They had, after all, grown up in a country which by historical standards was extraordinarily gentle and secure, a 'peaceable kingdom' in which violence was something that most people rarely experienced any longer.[52] The national homicide rate was amongst the lowest in the world.[53] The casual drunkenness and domestic abuse which had once characterized British working-class life was no longer nearly so tolerated by law or public sentiment. Corporal punishment in schools lingered on, but it was employed much less often, and less savagely, than it had been by the Victorians. Between 1914 and 1939, the number of birchings issued by magistrates declined from 2,000 a year to just 170.[54] To say that violence was un-British was not just a statement about values; it was, for most people anyway, a simple fact.

But would this mean that British citizen-soldiers would be burdened on the battlefield by their own civility?[55] In a December 1943 report on the fighting in Italy, the War Office's Director of Military Training worried that the young men being recruited into the Army had been so 'brought up from the cradle . . . to look upon wars and battle as beyond human endurance and something not to be even contemplated' that as soon as they heard their first mortar shell or artillery round, they immediately went to ground and could not be persuaded to continue fighting.[56] Was the trouble that, as Montgomery put it in a letter to Brooke, 'our British lads . . . are not killers by nature'?[57]

Generals were not alone in worrying about this. Ordinary soldiers also agonized about whether they were really up to the task of overcoming enemies as fearsome as the Germans and the Japanese. When it came down to it, could they ever be the warriors their enemies seemed to be? Watching his commando trainees pant and stumble their way around the hills near Lochaber in the Scottish Highlands, Arthur Kellas could not help but compare them unfavourably with the German troops who had just conquered France and the Low Countries, 'who cover thirty miles a day with a kind of crusading zeal in the name of the Third Reich'. Could the products of Liverpool slums and Midlands mills and offices ever do the same? 'Their spirit was keen enough', Kellas acknowledged. 'They asked nothing more than to "have a crack at Jerry". But I was beset by doubts whether they were any match for Jerry. I wondered whether some of us had the stomach to be serious.'[58] Later, as he saw a column of pale-faced teenagers pouring up the gangway en route to North Africa in 1942, Kellas was struck by the 'miserable aspect' so many of them seemed to offer. 'I was distressed, and dismayed to think that these little men were supposed to reconquer Europe.'[59]

By contrast, the German soldier 'looked the part', thought Colin MacInnes:

A real warrior. Not like our friendly, scruffy squaddies . . . you can see it in [his] face and whole bearing. It makes you feel he was born to wear that uniform, and look how well he wears it, how sure and successful he looks. For them, being a soldier isn't a job, it's a vocation . . . it's a fulfilment, something so many of them do so well instinctively.[60]

Observing his first German POWs, Tim Bishop noted how they all looked to be 'well-fed, surly looking youths of grand physique . . . desperadoes, yet having the unmistakably attractive atmosphere about them of good soldiers'.[61] To another Briton the Germans seemed 'horribly tough . . . all looking about eight feet tall and twice as bloodthirsty'.[62] Their coalscuttle helmets gave them such a sinister aspect that they were sometimes stripped of them on capture to seem less intimidating.[63] Even Teutonic corpses compared favourably with British ones. Inspecting a group of *Wehrmacht* dead in Normandy in summer 1944, Andrew Wilson was struck by their lordly uniformity:

All young, all with strong white teeth in mouths where the flies were gathering, all the same golden sun-tan, now like a mask on the bloodless faces beneath. I couldn't help comparing them with the usual British infantry platoon – the tall and short, bandy-legged and lanky, heavy-limbed countrymen and scruffy, swarthy Brummagem boys with eternally undone gaiters. Even in death, I found something frightening about such fine German manhood.[64]

The Japanese, to western eyes anyway, had none of the imposing physicality of the blond Aryan beasts of the *Herrenvolk*. But they seemed to Robin Painter's and Brian Aldiss's comrades all the same 'veritable supermen', fanatically brave, cruel and devious opponents, ideally suited to the hostile environment of Burma, members of 'fearsome yellow tribes who survived in jungles where nobody else could'.[65] They were, acknowledged John Masters, 'the bravest people I have ever met . . . they believed in something and they were willing to die for it, for any smallest detail that would help to achieve it. What else is bravery?' They were 'frugal and bestial, barbarous and brave, artistic and brutal', the authors of exquisite little sonnets which they wrote up in their diaries, and also the torturers of unarmed prisoners. They were monstrous by British standards. But there was something *martial* about them all the same which it was difficult not to admire – and to compare unflatteringly with the sapless products of modern western civilization.[66]

It did not help that British soldiers entering close combat with the Germans were encumbered with a more practical doubt as well – that the enemy were not only better soldiers, but better armed to boot. This was one of the great paradoxes of the mid to late war. By El Alamein, the Allied armies in the west could depend on overwhelming air and naval superiority wherever they went. Their access to supplies, machinery, vehicles and artillery support was vastly greater than anything the Germans could manage. And yet the *Wehrmacht* always seemed to have better, more powerful front-line weapons. 'Jerry has been "one jump ahead", the same old pattern all through the war', complained Reg Crimp in January 1945. 'These superior weapons and the victories they've given him have boosted his morale.'[67] The British infantryman, once he had advanced too far to rely any longer on the protective fire of his own artillery, just did not carry as formidable a set of personal weapons with him as his enemy.[68]

It was not so much the gun he carried; both he and his *Wehrmacht* opponent were issued much the same bolt-action rifle that their fathers had used a quarter of a century before – the Short Magazine Lee-Enfield in the British case, the Karabiner 98k in the German. Neither rifle had any inherent advantage over the other. But German infantrymen were able to call on a far greater reserve of squad-level automatic firepower. The magazine-loaded Bren light machine-gun issued to British infantry sections was reliable, accurate, and well liked by many soldiers. But it 'sounded like a pop-gun' compared to the much faster belt-fed MG-34 and MG-42 'Spandau' fielded by the Germans.[69] 'It's depressing to compare their respective firing rates', thought Crimp. While the Spandau unleashed a 'breakneck splutter', all that the Bren was capable of in response was a 'stutter, merely perfunctory'.[70] Denis Forman believed the British gun to be a 'fragile and hysterical creature' compared to its German rival.[71] Even the Spandau's appearance was far more 'vicious and purposeful' than that of the homely Bren.[72] Time and again, advancing British troops found themselves pinned down in no-man's-land by the ceaseless ministrations of a Spandau they could not hope to match in firepower. It 'dominated the battle-field with a brilliant and lordly defiance'.[73]

In other respects too, the German infantry were better equipped. The German MP-40 'Schmeisser' sub-machine gun was considered by some British troops 'the best of its kind ever made'; captured examples were jealously guarded by their owners.[74] The British equivalent to the MP-40, the Sten, was dismissed as 'a wretched weapon' – crudely made, clumsy to handle, inaccurate beyond 50 yards, and constantly jamming and misfiring.[75] While the standard sidearm issued to German officers, the Luger, was renowned for its accuracy even in novice hands, the equivalent British pistol, the Enfield No. 2, managed to combine (as one of its bearers complained) 'total mechanical reliability with complete ineffectiveness'.[76] 'You could barely hit the sea from a dinghy' with it, as another soldier put it.[77] Comparative War Office tests of the German 8-cm and British 3-inch heavy mortars in 1943 suggested that the *Wehrmacht's* weapon was the more accurate of the two (a conclusion which many shaken British infantrymen had already arrived at for themselves).[78] The Boys anti-tank rifle, an ungainly elephant gun widely distributed at the beginning of the war, had a terrific recoil and muzzle blast but was useless against all but the thinnest German or Italian armour. 'For all the effect it had I might have been a little girl trying to hurt a heavyweight boxer', complained Tim Bishop after firing one against an advancing panzer in 1940. '[The tank] did not retaliate. Perhaps its crew had not even noticed.'[79] Its replacement, the PIAT (Projector, Infantry, Anti-Tank) spigot mortar, was a much more potent weapon which acted as a 'superb morale destroyer' in Raleigh Trevelyan's words because of the great noise and clouds of smoke it gave off.[80] But it lacked the penetrative capa-bility of the German Panzerfaust.[81]

These vulnerabilities in small arms, however, were minor compared to the seemingly vast disparity in power between British and German tanks from 1941 onwards. To this day, furious debate continues as to whether such a disparity really existed or not. But that it was *perceived* to exist at the time is undeniable. By 1944, British tank crews were nursing 'a definite inferiority complex' towards the Germans.[82] 'I remember the first time we were going to get a tank as good as Jerry's', complains one of the members of the Sherman crew in Peter Elstob's autobiographical novel, *Warriors for the Working Day*:

> And you know what it was? A Honey with a pop-gun. Then we had Crusaders. They were supposed to be as good as Panthers, but he could still knock us out before we could get near enough to have a go, so they took away the Crusaders and gave us these bloody Shermans –Tommy Cookers – Ronsons – 'always light first time.' Don't talk to me about smashing new tanks.[83]

The monstrous German 'heavies' of the final years of the war – the Panther and the Tiger – inspired a fear amongst British troops far out of proportion to their actual numbers on the battlefield. In Normandy, a sardonic rule of thumb was said to be used by tank commanders: if one Tiger was reported in the vicinity, they should send four Shermans or Churchills to deal with it – and expect to lose three of them.[84] The very names of the big cats were a stroke of psychological genius, thought Richard Holbrook. 'The legend of their invulnerability was paralysing . . . tired men in terror sought with red and painful eyes the threatening shape in the smoke, the shape of the irresistible monster.'[85] The merest rumour that a Panther or Tiger was approaching could send veteran troops into a panic. Even after being knocked out, the German tanks somehow managed to look more formidable than any Allied fighting vehicle. The Tiger's long gun, tipped with a massive muzzle brake, appeared vicious and menacing even in death. The Sherman's stubby gun, cocked skywards, seemed 'pathetic' by contrast, 'surprise, pain and bewilderment' etched into its every subordinate line.[86]

The myth of the Tiger's supposedly impenetrable armour and invincible gun grew with every encounter. John Foley's crew met one for the first time on the evening of 7 August 1944, as their Churchill tank, *Avenger*, stood guard in the hamlet of Brieux on the eastern bank of the River Orne, about a dozen miles south of Caen. A Tiger suddenly loomed into view, trundling along the other side of a thick stone wall. *Avenger*, as yet unseen by its approaching rival, slunk into a position between two cottages overlooking the road, a perfect spot from which to stage an ambush. Foley and his crew felt the ground shake as the 57-tonne Tiger rolled into sight once again, now just 40 yards away from them. *Avenger* fired – once, twice, three times. It was point-blank range. And yet, through the brick-dust and smoke, Foley watched with gathering despair and fear as each of the 75-mm rounds went ricocheting harmlessly off the Tiger's front armour. Then it was the Germans' turn. The Tiger's 88-mm muzzle flashed. *Avenger* reared back on its front sprockets as the enemy shell penetrated the Churchill's front mantlet, bounced around the crew compartment, and then smashed into the rear engine block, sending up a gush of flame and smoke. *Avenger*'s driver was instantly decapitated. The rest of its crew bailed out, fortunately hidden from the Tiger's view by the thick charcoal clouds now bellowing from the Churchill's ruined interior. They were able to make their escape, stunned but unharmed.

Afterwards, the recriminations flew thick and fast:

'Bouncing off, they were. Bouncing off like peas off a flippin' drum!'
'Next time we meet the bastards I'm going to bail out and climb into their turret with a bayonet. Do a damn sight more good!'

Foley tried to put a brave face on things. 'Some of our tanks are better in some respects than some of the German tanks, and vice versa.' 'And what have we got that will keep out an eighty-eight, in the same way that they can keep out our seventy-fives?' spat back one disgusted crewman. 'I racked my brains but couldn't think of anything off hand', admitted Foley. 'I wished I had one of those clever articles from the *Army Quarterly* in which ballistic experts proved by numbers that we had better tanks and guns than the enemy.'[87]

If he had had the information to hand, Foley might have been able to console his men with the fact that only about one in twenty German tanks in Normandy was a Tiger. The majority of armoured vehicles the defending Germans were equipped with were Panzer IVs – tough workhorses, to be sure, but possessing no innate advantages over the British Army's Shermans, Churchills and Cromwells. And in any case, even the big cats were not undefeatable. They were plagued with mechanical problems, and often had to be abandoned in the midst of battle because of their engines overheating or their tracks jamming (panzer crews in northwestern Europe may not have been impressed by the firepower of Allied tanks, but they did envy their reliability). Rocket-firing RAF Typhoon fighter-bombers decimated any slow-moving German Heavy Tank Company that dared cross the Normandy countryside in daylight. And the British did have a few tanks of their own that could measure up to the big cats. The 'Firefly', a modified Sherman up-gunned with a 17-pounder anti-tank weapon, could (on a good day, anyway) take out a Tiger from the front at 1,000 yards.[88]

The Spandau was not an all-conquering weapon of the battlefield either. Sidney Jary thought that the German use of it was unnecessarily 'protracted and discordant'. *Wehrmacht* infantry sections were too reliant on their machine-guns, hardly bothering to use their own rifles. When they were denuded of the Spandau's defensive firepower, they were left clumsy and ineffective.[89] German troops were said to be particularly lumbering and nervous during night operations, during which they regularly blazed away with their Spandaus at nothing in particular – a foolish act of bravado which simply gave away their own position and telegraphed how jumpy they were.[90]

Still, all of these qualifications were immaterial if *you* were the one crouching in a ditch with Spandau bullets ripping through the air a few inches from your head, or watching the tank alongside you 'vomiting up the life within it in black gouts' after the impact of an 88-mm armour-piercing round.[91] There was, the War Office was forced to concede, a 'feeling of inequality – almost of injustice' shared by many British troops when it came to the weapons issued to the two sides.[92] They already went into battle with the nagging suspicion that the Germans were better soldiers than they were. It was doubly discouraging to find out that their firearms and tanks were superior too.

So far as artillery and air support went, the balance of firepower from 1942 onwards was quite different. The RAF's heavy four-engine bombers and single-engine fighter-bombers ('Jabos', as the Germans called them) were capable of delivering timely, accurate and overwhelming destruction on demand.[93] Peter White's men watched an 800-aircraft daylight raid on Bremen in spring 1945 with a mixture of awe and shock. 'An abrupt and terrifying wall of billowing black cloud erupted and continued to spatter and spread', White wrote of the doomed city. 'Suddenly the sound of the explosions reached us in an apparent pressure wave of crump-crump-crumping rumblings which swept around us like a rising tide.'[94] The Royal Artillery was no less menacing. Norman Craig recalled a breathless sensation as he saw the 'spectacular and deliberate savagery' of the preliminary artillery barrage at Alamein: it was, he thought, 'a thrilling and disturbing moment'.[95] Walter Elliott and his men watched 'stupefied and delighted as schoolboys' as massed British field guns pummelled the far bank of the Volturno River in Italy.[96] Robert Woollcombe was left tingling with excitement as he saw British guns, their 'thunder angry, violent and death-dealing', open up before a company assault in France:

> [The barrage hurled] itself over strong points, enemy gun areas, forming-up places, tank laagers, and above all concentrated into the creeping mass of shells that raked ahead of our own infantrymen, as thousands of gunners bent to their task. Little rashes of goose-flesh over the skin. All this 'stuff' in support of us! Every single gun at maximum effort to kill; to help us.[97]

Being caught in a British artillery barrage was one of the most terrible experiences of the war. At critical moments during the campaign in northwestern Europe, a Royal Artillery battery might fire 1,000 rounds per gun per day;

barrels would grow so hot that cold water had to be poured on to them to prevent them from starting to melt.[98] A lance-corporal at Arnhem watched mesmerized as 120 German paratroopers, 'the cream of the German Army, the most stubborn defensive fighters in the world', simply abandoned their positions after a ferocious artillery bombardment and walked over to the British lines, hands in the air, some bellowing *Kamerad!* with all their might, others 'crying like babies'.[99]

But air and artillery firepower, for all their destructiveness, could only do so much. There was no getting around the battlefield's 'final 200-yards' problem – the fact that no matter how shattering the preliminary bombardment, there was still a point at which the bombs and the shells had to stop, and the tanks and infantry had to advance across no-man's land to take the enemy's position. It was in that final 200-yard dash that the attack would either succeed or fail, and it required frail human beings to see it through.

Relatively little thought had been given to this problem between the wars. Training regulations in the 1930s paid lip service to the ideal of the fit, independent-minded, confident infantryman, but the actual implementation of his training was left to the individual regiments, and so was discordant and often ineffective. No infantry tactical school existed until 1939.[100] It was only after the humiliations of Dunkirk, Greece, Crete and North Africa that serious thought began to be applied to modern infantry and combined-arms training. The breakthrough came in July 1941, when the Army opened its first divisional battle school, commanded by Captain Lionel Wigram. Training would now be based around the simulation of tough and realistic combat conditions. Recruits were to be exposed to the sensory experiences they would encounter on the battlefield – live ammunition, authentic artillery barrages – so as to make the real thing less frightening. Soldiers would learn simple prearranged drills which they could perform whenever a particular offensive or defensive action was required. The 'Battle Drill' idea soon caught on.[101] By mid-1943, it had, as one infantry officer put it, 'assumed the proportion of Holy Writ' across the Army.[102]

In adopting Battle Drill methods, the Army was moving towards the model of combat training that is still used to great effect by NATO's professional volunteer armed forces today.[103] Wigram's major insight was that troops needed to be *preconditioned* to the disorientating physical environment of the modern front line; and that the best way of overcoming the inherently stressful circumstances of battle was for them to learn meticulously prescribed rote actions that they could repeat as ordered almost without thinking.[104] In principle, all the components of modern infantry training were there. But the wartime British Army of seventy years ago did not have anything like the time and resources to devote to training as it does now. Battle school instructors had to rush their charges through their programmes as quickly as possible. No settled body of doctrine that had been definitely proven to work in the field could as yet be applied. Methods were inevitably rudimentary. Drills were too often rigid and overcomplicated.[105]

The result, then, was that in practice many British soldiers – perhaps even the majority – quickly forgot everything they had learned in training as soon as the bullets started flying. Wigram himself acknowledged the problem after he had had the chance to observe troops in action in Sicily in 1943. The typical infantry battle, he wrote in a report for Montgomery, followed very different rules from the exercises that had been laid down so carefully back in Britain:

> Enemy MGs open fire. The whole platoon lie down except the platoon commander and three or four gutful men. Five or six men start making tracks for home. Meanwhile, the gutful men under the platoon commander dash straight in to the enemy position without any covering fire and always succeed in taking the position. In some instances some positions are taken by as few as two men, and every battalion commander will confirm that it is always the same group of nine or 10 who are there first, and on whom the battle depends.

Though the attack might succeed, in other words, its accomplishment would rarely have much to do with battle drill one way or the other. Too many soldiers were simply forgetting all that they had been taught as soon as they heard the first shot. 'There is nothing wrong with Battle Drill in theory', Wigram insisted. 'But it presupposes that you have an [infantry platoon] in which every individual knows his job and his place, and in which every man is brave enough and experienced enough to do as he is told. Of course in practice you have no such thing.'[106]

Other commentators besides Wigram came to much the same conclusion. 'On an average, in a platoon of 25, five will do their best to fight', suggested the commanding officer of a British infantry battalion. 'Fifteen will follow a lead. The rest will be useless.'[107] In his book *Men Against Fire*, published shortly after the war, the American combat historian S. L. A. Marshall argued that only one in four of his own army's soldiers had ever actually fired their weapons once they entered close combat. Marshall's methodology remains controversial to this day.[108] But it is interesting how closely his one-in-four figure parallels Wigram's observation that out of a platoon of twenty-four soldiers, 'six gutful men will go anywhere and do anything. Twelve "sheep" will follow a short distance behind if they are well-led . . . four to six will run away.'[109]

Tough, realistic training had its virtues, particularly when troops were confronted with a battlefield such as Burma or the Western Desert, so environmentally hostile to their presence that simply operating in it needed special skills.[110] But while you could familiarize infantrymen with the sensory confusion of battle all you liked – aim machine-gun bullets inches from their faces on the exercise field, until they grew so weary and contemptuous of the noise and the smell that they scarcely noticed them – the fact was that as soon as a real-life Messerschmitt-109 flew over their heads for the first time, a good proportion of them would invariably forget everything they had been taught about fire discipline and begin blazing away so randomly that their officers would have to dive for cover to avoid being accidentally killed.[111] A single enemy sniper encountered for the first time could cause a whole platoon of soldiers to fall to the ground in terror, drill be damned.[112] You could try to enforce what David Holbrook called 'the reassuring grammar of war', the idea, encapsulated within battle school doctrine, that combat could be made to follow a precise, coherent and predictable set of rules, that men would habitually follow clear pre-planned instructions. But it was never really like that, at least for the ill-prepared citizen-soldiers of a mass army. 'In the field there was always chaos, confusion, squalor', the novice inevitably discovered:

Each man was lost in the impersonal hell, where metal chased flesh, in one great melee. No individual made effective decisions, but reacted for the most part blindly to stimuli, and fought wild. One's greatest enemy was chance, and the complex and elusive laws governing odds, where metal was flying fast and bodies of flesh were among it. The guns babble and thump, men shout and yell, smoke drifts between, there are lights, howls, explosions . . .[113]

Holbrook's own first experience of being under fire was an apt demonstration of this. It lasted barely three minutes. But in that time he felt himself being stripped of every facade of his own self-respect. He lost 'every conviction, political, moral, human . . . all trust in the regiment, in comradeship'. He would have bowed to any god at that moment, surrendered to any enemy, just to make the explosions around him stop. The only way he was able to control his panic was to disassociate himself from his own body entirely, to imagine that he was looking down with detached curiosity on his squadron as they huddled in raw terror in the Normandy soil.[114] Fear could swiftly overwhelm reason, dignity, good character. Listening to the 'vicious hiss' of an unseen anti-tank gun firing at his vehicle, Trevor Greenwood found it impossible to think straight: 'Every single fibre and nerve [was] too occupied in trying to see from where the shots were fired.' He had to suppress a powerful instinct to abandon his tank and flee for cover.[115] When a red-hot lump of shrapnel glanced his hand, Ken Tout was suddenly, horribly reminded of 'all the ways in which a human body can be ripped apart, butchered, squashed, spattered, spread-eagled, grilled, racked with a million agonies'. '*Lord*', he prayed, '*let me be a tree . . . let me be a mole or a grass snake, able to squirm into the safe recesses of the earth.*'[116] While trapped in a barrage, Michael Howard was struck by a 'blind personal paralysis' such that 'all thought and feeling, even fear' was frozen. 'The shutter descended and reduced me to something out of all semblance of a man.'[117]

So what, beside drill, *did* matter? What ultimately decided whether an attack succeeded or failed, whether a platoon or troop followed its orders or instead became (as the parlance of the time had it) 'windy' or 'sticky', reluctant to advance and even to return fire? In his observations of combat in Sicily, Wigram noticed the effect that herd instinct played in battle. Though a minority of soldiers could always be relied upon to follow orders without hesitation, and a similar small number would panic and flee no matter what, the majority would generally do whatever they saw the rest of their comrades doing. Much has been made since the Second World War of soldiers' loyalty to the so-called 'primary group' of their immediate comrades as the fundamental source of their combat motivation. That is, soldiers risk their lives not for abstract concepts like patriotism or ideological allegiance to a cause, but rather for fidelity to the mates with whom they live day in, day out, in embattled intimacy.[118] That there was a lot to be said for the importance of the primary group is attested in the accounts of many wartime soldiers. Courage, thought Norman Craig, was 'essentially competitive and imitative'. What counted was the example being set by those around you. But this could work against combat discipline, as well as for it.[119] The primary group could exacerbate as well as dampen individual soldiers' fears, undermine as well as buttress their collective nerve.[120] If enough of your mates stood firm under fire, their example would shame you into compliance. But if enough of them decided to run, their behaviour offered you a moral licence to do the same. 'What a small degree there was between sticking it and breaking down, when going forward under fire', thought Norman Lindsay. 'It only needed one man to shout *this is murder, I'm getting out* and he would take half a dozen with him.'[121] Ken Tout noticed that whenever his troop was shelled, men always watched one another's reactions for a prompt before deciding whether to dive to the floor or remain standing. 'Panic and un-panic are very similar in their causes, if not their effects', he came to believe.[122]

What the primary group needed above all was someone to lead it – someone to provide the right behavioural cues at moments of stress. This might be a trusted and experienced NCO. But the man whom soldiers instinctively looked to above all for guidance was their officer. The subaltern set the moral bench-mark for everyone else in the primary group. It was his job to maintain a 'grip' over the rest of the men – for if grip was lost, they would quickly become unre-sponsive to orders, unable to move forward, or indeed do anything aside from cower.[123] It was he who needed to provide a 'certainty of salvation' to which they could cling when their own confidence had collapsed.[124] The subaltern could draw on all the disciplinary authority of the Army if he had to; junior officers would, if necessary, browbeat their men with the power of King's Regulations. Threats of violence were not out of the question. During the Battle for Normandy, at least one officer of the 1st Hampshires had to threaten to shoot a fleeing soldier if he did not turn round.[125] The colonel of a particularly windy infantry battalion was required to draw his revolver on his men several times in the fighting after D-Day.[126] But no officer could do this continually. Indeed, battlefield leadership meant acknowledging that the normal discipli-nary protocol of the barracks ceased to apply once the firing started. 'When you are walking hand in hand with death all day', as John Hudson put it, 'repri-mands no longer matter.'[127] Prudent officers learned to overlook what in other circumstances would have been astonishing breaches of discipline. One of the subalterns in Alex Bowlby's battalion went on an advance patrol accompanied by a corporal and an OR called Private Sadler. During the patrol, the officer, peering over a trench parapet, was fired upon by a German sharpshooter. 'Get that sniper, Sadler!' he demanded. '*Get him your fucking self!*' was the response. The officer's face flushed, but he did nothing. Eventually, as the unreasonable-ness of the order sank in, he turned to his NCO: 'Perhaps we should go home, corporal.' '*Yes, sir, I think we should.*' No further action was taken.[128] Prudent subalterns let such infractions pass without comment so long as they did not get out of hand. What mattered was the following of sensible commands, not meek acquiescence to some pointless and clearly suicidal whim.

The officer's job on the battlefield was both therapeutic and exemplary. 'Grip' was better maintained by a mixture of persuasion and representative courage than by threats or appeals to rank. The subaltern, faced with a cowering soldier, had to cajole him back into the line by playing on some quality that might overcome his panic – reason, or embarrassment, or his love of his comrades. When Geoffrey Picot found a stretcher-bearer lying sobbing on the ground, he calmed the man down by gently reminding him of all the men further forward who were relying on him to help them. 'They had had to stick all the shelling', he pointed out, 'they had had to contend with a lot of small-arms fire.' The stretcher-bearer was shamed into recovering his wits.[129] Sometimes appealing to soldiers' innate competitiveness did the trick. Raleigh

Trevelyan found that sneering at the alleged failings of other platoons in the company – *'just what you'd expect from them!'* – helped his own men to keep their nerve at moments of crisis.[130]

The most important way in which the subaltern got his men to stand and fight, however, was simply by doing it himself – and preferably in the most dramatic way possible. Strome Galloway's first test of battlefield leadership was as a junior officer in command of two sections of the London Irish Rifles in North Africa. His company, caught in the middle of a German mortar attack, and already suffering numerous casualties, was ordered to charge the enemy. Galloway gave the command to fix bayonets. He heard the click of bayonet handles snapping closed on rifle lugs. He yelled *'charge!'* 'But nobody budged', he remembered later:

> They just lay there, shuddering as each successive bomb hit the ground near them, scattering its fragments. There was no safety for any of us lying in the open ground. I stood up and began to move forward, red streaks of machine-gun tracer flying over my head. Almost instantly my two sections rose as one man, and followed me as I broke into a trot towards our objective.
>
> When one will lead, most men will follow – of that there is no doubt.[131]

The officer's job was 'essentially histrionic', thought Norman Craig. The trick was to 'feign a casual and cheerful optimism to create the illusion of normality and make it seem as if there were nothing in the least strange about the outrageous things one was asked to do. Only in this way could he ease the tension, quell any panic and convince his men that everything would come out right in the end.' Most private soldiers, Craig thought, had 'a touching faith in anything an officer told them' in battle.[132] If a subaltern insisted that an enemy position could be taken, and that it was safer to stand up and advance than huddle in the dirt and wait to be killed, then as often as not his men would believe him – though usually the only way he could really hammer the point home was to stand up himself and risk being killed. On one occasion when Alex Bowlby and his comrades could not be roused to move under German artillery and machine-gun fire, their company commander walked slowly back and forth along the line of crouching soldiers, calmly repeating to them *'Look at me . . . they can't hit me. Look at me.'* 'The Germans didn't hit him', noted Bowlby. 'His courage hit us.'[133] William Cochrane's platoon had a similar experience when it was caught in a jungle depression with Japanese bullets flying just over the men's heads. Their lieutenant told them to stand up and charge the enemy machine-guns. At his first command, only one man, the platoon sergeant, did so – and he was immediately and gruesomely cut down, the lower part of his face destroyed in a spray of blood, saliva and skin. The lieutenant spoke to them again, calmly but firmly:

> *When I give the order you must all get up and go forward and when I say all,*
> *I mean all! If you don't do it now, you are all going to end up like him!*

Somehow it got the platoon's wind up. 'I was like most private soldiers', admitted Cochrane later. 'I needed to be directed.' At the lieutenant's second command he recalled jumping up and running with the rest of his mates towards the Japanese bunkers, 'screaming like a maniac'. The enemy position was taken.[134]

A good officer had to be self-consciously blasé about the risks he was taking and asking others to take. Jack Swaab recorded in his diary that as shells screamed down on his position, he knew how important it was to remark out loud, as nonchalantly as he could, *Hm, fairly close* ... and hope that no one noticed the slight tremble in his voice.[135] For some subalterns, the fact that they were, so to speak, on stage helped them feign an indifference to danger. 'Dicky' Buckle – who, as fellow officer Michael Howard observed, was regarded as utterly fearless by the rest of the men of his battalion in Italy – thought that courage came much more easily to an officer than to an OR, because the former had more to lose by not showing it.[136] Buckle's case was all the more extraordinary because, aside from the remarkable aplomb he showed day after day in the face of danger, he was also an unapologetic, indeed outrageously camp, homosexual. He was known to wander through the German lines in daylight idly rummaging about for interesting things to purloin; once he found a wedding dress, and after carrying it back to the British trenches he wore it to dinner that night in the mess. On another occasion he walked in on his fellow officers and announced, '*My dears, I've just slept with a Cardinal's nephew.*' Howard thought that Buckle was either going to win the Victoria Cross or be court-martialled for gross indecency, or perhaps both. None of his men cared. They enjoyed his eccentricity. And he was brave, which was all that ultimately mattered.[137]

To conduct such confidence-building exercises in battle after battle was extremely hazardous. The typical platoon commander in northwestern Europe in 1944 served for about two months in the front line before becoming a casualty; his company commander, about three. When such men were wounded, their subsequent chance of survival was about three to one against.[138] Reg Crimp, serving in the Middle East, was not at all surprised when most of the men in his unit who had been identified as potential OCTU candidates declined to have their names put forward for training. They knew all too well that infantry subalterns were being 'skittled like ninepins' by the Germans at that precise moment.[139]

The War Office, conscious of these unacceptably high loss rates, tried to teach junior infantry officers training in Britain to lead from the centre of their platoon, rather than from the front – a position that was both less likely to lead to them being hit, and which also allowed them to 'read the battle' more effectively.[140] Their job, it was drummed into them in battle drill exercises, was to kill the enemy, not to get themselves killed. The problem was that, while this might have been perfectly sensible in theory, it flouted the unwritten Army rule that soldiers needed to see their officer ahead of them, charging into battle with pistol drawn – a position which was at once suicidally dangerous and also essential to the maintenance of grip. Briefing his platoon before their first attack, Michael Howard informed everyone that he would be following, not commanding, the first section up the hill, just as he had been taught back in Britain. His senior NCO, Sergeant Hurst, turned to him with 'a look of combined protest, resignation, and – yes, it has to be said – contempt that I shall never forget', Howard recalled in his memoirs, '*Won't you be leading us, sir?*' he asked. 'That', Howard realized, 'was what young officers were supposed to be for, especially young Guards officers. That is why they died like flies.'[141] The War Office's instructions were perfectly rational. But they defied the contract implicit between officers and men on the battlefield – that the latter would do whatever the former asked of them so long as the officer took on the greatest burden of risk himself. Many subalterns, realizing this, disregarded their instructions; some, inevitably, at the cost of their own lives.

But aloofness towards danger could be pushed too far as well. A successful subaltern had to maintain a fine balance between showing inspirational confidence and coming across as a 'death or glory boy' or an 'MC wallah' – someone more concerned about winning medals than keeping his men alive.[142] Some new officers flaunted too openly the map boards, binoculars and other paraphernalia of rank which they knew made them potential targets for snipers. 'Their bravery was never in question', thought Stanley Whitehouse, 'but it was seldom tempered with prudence or circumspection. Some might just as well have strolled about in pink pyjamas.'[143] More to the point, their ardour could come across as an insufficient respect for the need to keep casualties low. 'By now most of us are beginning to feel a bit uneasy about him', wrote diarist Reg Crimp of his replacement company commander in July 1944. 'He certainly seems bent on doing something spectacular, regardless of cost.' When the captain was killed a few weeks later by a mortar bomb, the general verdict amongst his men was '*keen sod, but a bit too keen*'.[144]

In his first weeks in Normandy with 18 Platoon, D Company, 4th Somerset Light Infantry, Lieutenant Sidney Jary acquired a reputation for being an MC wallah. 'It was obvious that he was sincere and caring', one of his corporals wrote later, 'but that in itself was not enough.' During an early reconnaissance patrol, Jary darted ahead into an enemy-held village and disappeared for some time before returning to the platoon with a big grin on his face to announce that the place was deserted. The men were not pleased. 'It suddenly dawned on me that our young friend was thoroughly enjoying his war', noted Corporal Proctor disapprovingly. '*Don't ever do that to us again!*' Proctor shouted. As Jary grew in experience, he learned to behave less recklessly, not so much for his own sake as for that of his troops. 'I discovered', he wrote, 'just how much soldiers resent and fear a young officer who sees battle as a means to win his spurs, possibly at the cost of their lives.' Bravery was essential for grip, but it was not sufficient. What the men also needed to see in their leader was a 'serious attitude' to the profession of soldiering – a sense that, at the end of the day, their survival was more important to him than winning a Mention in Dispatches.[145]

There was no getting away from the inherent moral ambiguity of the junior officer's place in the front-line unit. 'An infantry subaltern', reflected Jary after the war, 'is faced with a conflict which cannot be resolved':

> One gets emotionally involved with those under one's command. Without this bond few men will respond and, consequently, little can be achieved. However, to win battles decisions have to be taken and orders given which, at times, may seem to be a betrayal of this trust.[146]

In order to lead the soldiers under his command effectively, he had to become the protective father figure, the patriarch, of the primary group. But sometimes that meant getting his children killed. Parent and predator, guardian and traitor; Judas-like, the young officer charged into battle, making promises he knew he could not keep, to men whose loyalty he had both rightfully earned and might wilfully have to sell out at any moment. It was a lot to place at the feet of a teenage second lieutenant scarcely old enough to shave.

CHAPTER 13

CATEGORIES OF COURAGE

'*The whole company went quite berserk.*' That was the only way that Walter Elliott could explain afterwards what happened that night in the autumn of 1943 on a barren hill above Rocchetta e Croce in Campania. All that previous day, his Scots Guards company had slogged up steep muddy tracks towards the forward positions from which they were to begin their attack, sustaining heavy casualties from German artillery and machine-gun fire along the way. The likelihood of their planned uphill assault being successful looked bleak. But somehow, when the moment came, their very misery was turned against the enemy in the form of a primitive battle-fury. 'We started charging around the flank of the hill swearing like madmen and almost artificially furious with the enemy above who made us feel so frightened', recalled Elliott:

> Then our courage soared as we closed in on the summit . . . surmounting the crest we leaped on those terrified Germans who stood their ground. There was no withstanding the company once its blood was up. Our shouts of *come on out and fight you bastards!* to the surrounding trenches and dug-outs could be heard even by battalion headquarters; but any Germans who did so were promptly bayoneted . . . it was as if all the pent-up fury at the shelling, the casualties and not being able to get one's own back was at last to have its vengeance.[1]

Being under fire provoked a wide range of responses – surprise, confusion, catatonic terror. But under the right circumstances, a soldier's fear could stimulate rather than paralyse his mind. Violence, if provoked by enough panic and frustration, was not so difficult to mete out. 'Given the advantage of surprise and murderous tools . . . anybody can do it', thought Arthur Kellas.[2] Combat could intoxicate even the mildest of men. At moments of crisis in battle, Stanley Whitehouse found himself dripping with sweat, clenching his teeth and swearing hysterically, 'buoyed up as though on drugs', as fears for his own safety were converted into blind rage.[3] Facing an imminent assault on a Japanese strongpoint, Frank Baines was amazed at the 'unnatural feeling of exultation' within himself, so strong that he had to restrain himself from leaping up and charging suicidally at the enemy guns. *'So this is the beserk madness of Nordic Vikings!* I thought sententiously to myself. I never knew I was capable of it.'[4] All of his middle-class sensibilities had for that moment disappeared.[5]

After the war, Geoffrey Picot defined what he thought were four different 'categories of fear' that he had experienced at one time or another during his service as a subaltern with the 1st Hampshire infantry battalion. Categories one and two had been provoked by various forms of artillery bombardment, while category three was the gut-wrenching dread Picot had felt every time he had been about to go into action; these were fears associated with some specific, imminent personal danger, and all of them had come and gone relatively quickly. But category four was an altogether different fear. It was the chronic anxiety produced by cumulative exposure to battle, the gathering certainty in the soldier's mind that his luck could not hold out for ever, and that the longer the war went on, the greater the likelihood he would be killed or crippled. It was that last kind of fear, Picot thought, that did you most harm in the long run – the horror that would not go away even in the war's quietest moments, but which instead festered inside your mind, incrementally breaking down your composure.[6]

Inverting Picot's taxonomy, it might also be useful to think of distinct categories of courage that were all tested under different circumstances during the war, and which soldiers possessed to widely fluctuating degrees. There was the courage displayed in the heat of the moment – the adrenaline-fuelled, almost impudent boldness which briefly took hold of the Scots Guards at Rocchetta e Croce. Such valour could occasionally propel men to conduct actions of the most astonishing fearlessness (or, if you prefer, foolhardiness). During the Tunisian campaign in 1943, Irish Guardsman John Kenneally twice charged a large body of German troops almost single-handedly. Reflecting on what he had done years later, he was self-effacing about his motives, admitting that on each occasion he had acted merely out of 'a strange don't-give-a-damn feeling' which had momentarily possessed him.[7] This was what another Guardsman called the 'sheer effrontery' of youth and inexperience, the instinctive courage of soldiers, often quite green, who had yet fully to realize how treacherous the battlefield could be.[8] It was also just the type of courage which often won you a medal. Kenneally was awarded the Victoria Cross for his actions, making him only the fifth member of his regiment ever to receive the highest British decoration for bravery in combat. But then, charging the enemy with a Bren gun as Kenneally had done was just the kind of anecdotally compelling, easy-to-visualise act that best appealed to a committee of senior officers reviewing recommendations for gallantry awards. A medal-winner needed more than just courage. He also needed a good story.

The Army was very good at rewarding the 'tremendous dash' of young men such as Kenneally caught up in the excitement of battle.[9] What it was not so good at was recognizing a second, altogether different category of courage – the unglamorous but more fundamental courage of the long haul. This was the courage of soldiers who risked their lives day after day without faltering or complaint, who never did anything particularly dramatic, but whose calm competence was often a good deal more valuable to their comrades than the occasional rush of blood to the head. Such 'steady bravery and good work' was vital to unit performance, but grossly undervalued in the military reward system.[10] After returning from the Chindit THURSDAY expedition in 1944, John Masters was infuriated when the Victoria Cross that he had recommended for his brigade doctor Desmond Whyte was downgraded to a lesser Distinguished Service Order. 'Desmond has not dashed out and rescued one wounded man under fire', conceded Masters. But over 100 days he had saved the lives of 200 men of the brigade, all the while remaining 'calm and efficient and cheerful while shells blast the bodies to pieces under his hands'. So far as Masters was concerned, Whyte had done more to keep the brigade from falling apart in Burma than any other soldier. But the Army authorities were unmoved. Only a specific and colourful feat of bravery could secure a VC.[11]

This was unfortunate, because during campaigns which might last for months or even years, it was the degree to which soldiers possessed the second rather than the first category of courage – the courage of stoic endurance, rather than intemperate daring – which determined whether or not they remained useful members of their units. 'There were those who were foolhardy . . . and there were those who did their jobs come what may. It was the latter whom one preferred to have on one's side', thought E. P. Danger.[12] And it was in the quiet aftermath of battle, when the distracting sights and smells and sounds of combat had at last receded, that the more substantive form of courage really began to be tested. Stanley Whitehouse always felt 'too terrified to be frightened' when he was actually being fired upon. Much worse was the period after the battle, when his surge of adrenaline had ebbed away, and he was once again free to reflect upon the dreadfulness of war and the grotesque vulnerability of

his own body.[13] Soldiers responded to this dangerous freeing up of their imag-
inations in different ways. Some became gregarious; some bad-tempered;
others disappeared for a time, wanting to be alone.[14] Norman Craig found that
reading *Jane Eyre* after a battle helped discharge the nervous emotions that had
accumulated inside him. It was a cathartic release. 'The tears', he remembered,
'trickled down my gritty cheeks on to the pages.'[15]

It was at lunchtime, while Christopher Seton-Watson was sitting in a truck
talking to his Regimental Signals Officer, that he heard a tremendous bang
about fifteen yards away – a clamour quickly followed by the clatter of metal
fragments through his vehicle's canvas canopy and, a few seconds later, by a
succession of shouts and groans. Seton-Watson hurried out to see what had
happened. A single 75-mm German shell had landed without warning right
where his clerk Gunter was sitting brewing tea. Gunter 'never had a chance',
Seton-Watson wrote of the incident in his diary. 'His stomach and back had
been torn away and he was lying in pools of blood.' The clerk died on an ambulance stretcher on his way to hospital.[16] Even for men who had seen much
battle action, Gunter's death was of a particularly distressing kind. It was bad
enough to see your comrades die in combat – charging an enemy machine-gun
position, say. But those were circumstances in which death was being overtly
courted, and its appearance, though never welcome, was at least to be expected.
When death interrupted a scene of quiet domestic intimacy – eating, chatting,
sleeping, boiling a kettle – it was far harder for the soldier to take in. It was too
stark a reminder that his life could be plucked away from him with capricious
ease at any moment.

The fighting man encountered the dead everywhere he went, of course.
Dead bodies on the battlefield were very different from the corpses that he
might have occasionally seen in civilian life. These were not the creased,
mottled, desiccated remains of aged relatives, carefully embalmed and respect-
fully laid out in some funeral parlour; these were young bodies, their spirits
choked out of them with obscene prematurity. Michael Howard was struck by
his first view of German corpses in southern Italy, 'shrunken pathetic dolls
lying stiff and twisted, with glazed blue eyes'. Not one of them seemed more
than a teenager. Some were practically children.[17] Richard Hoggart found the
'fragile broken bodies' of lifeless enemy troops, all looking around fifteen years
old, a horrible sight – but also, in some strange, lost way, a beautiful one too.[18]
Dead soldiers could seem incredulous, outraged even, by their own predicament. Walking across a field of battle just ended, Robert Woollcombe was able
to trace the course of an infantry platoon attack by the distribution and posture
of the bodies that had been left behind. In one corner was the lieutenant who

had led the charge, still looking 'faintly surprised' by what had happened to him, his neck slightly twisted, and with scarcely a mark on him except for a congealed stain close to his kidneys. Nearby, one of his corporals lay grasping a machine-gun, 'his face pudding-like, and boiled sweets still in his pocket'. Still another soldier, fair-skinned, tow-headed, was unblemished except for a small bullet hole puncturing his forehead. His bright blue eyes continued to stare out in 'sightless astonishment' over his fate.[19] In Burma, John Hudson encountered the corpse of a Japanese officer whose pebble eyes stared out at him in silent rebuke. 'Each black whisker on his parchment jowls stood out as though magnified', recalled Hudson. 'His red lips pouted wetly beneath his black moustache, as though he were expecting a kiss.'[20] Peter Cochrane was never quite able to get over the lack of dignity with which most bodies crumpled up in death at distorted angles. It was one thing to expire in a noble and sentimental pose – doubled back over a gun barrel with your sweetheart's photo jutting from your breast pocket, say. It was quite another to be splayed out in some absurd and demeaning composition. 'It seemed in a muddled way', he thought, 'that if one had to be killed, one had the right to die decently and not left lying about in a posture that too often could only be described as ludicrous.'[21]

But death by high-explosive could be even less decorous than that. As a chaplain in the 6th Armoured Division, it was one of Geoffrey Druitt's more gruesome tasks after a battle to climb inside burned-out tanks to assist with the removal of bodies. Sometimes all that remained within the hull was dust and a charred hip bone sitting on the driver's seat. Other times a charcoal-grey skull, a set of shoulders, ribs rapidly turning to powder, or a pair of disintegrating arms and legs would have to be extracted.[22] In Italy, Norman Lewis encountered a knocked-out German tank in which the trapped crew had been broiled so thoroughly that a great puddle of fat had seeped out on to the ground beneath the hull, 'quilted with brilliant flies of all descriptions and colours'.[23] Andrew Wilson, who served in a Churchill 'Crocodile' flamethrower unit, saw the results of his handiwork for the first time in Normandy when he inspected the remains of a German anti-tank crew he and his crewmates had just incinerated. The dead Germans seemed 'to have been blown back by the force of the flame and lay in naked, blackened heaps', he recalled:

Their clothes had burned away. Only their helmets and boots remained, ridiculous and horrible . . . one of them had been caught by the flame as he ran away, splashed with the liquid which couldn't be shaken off. His helmet had fallen off and now he lay with black eyeballs, naked and charred and obscene.

It was, Wilson noted laconically, all very different from the neat working diagrams with which the operation of the Crocodile's flamethrower had been explained in training back in England.[24]

Few soldiers, even the most battle-hardened, could look upon such scenes without reflecting upon their own fragile mortality and the alarming lack of agency that they possessed over their own destiny.[25] We are used to thinking of the civilian fatalities of the Second World War as the passive victims of external forces. But soldiers had equally little control over their own fate. By far the largest number of British battlefield wounds were caused by artillery fire, a form of attack to which the ordinary soldier had no effective response other than to look for shelter wherever he could find it and to hope for the best.[26] An explosion was no respecter of skill, experience, virtue, character. It killed without regard for the personal qualities of its victims. They, in turn, could do nothing to lessen their chances of being hit, other than to take cover. This help-lessness – this inability either to hit back, or even to improve your odds of survival in any meaningful way – was a cruelly disempowering thing to have to live through day after day in the front line.[27] One Scots Guards officer said that he would rather face 1,000 bullets than a single day of shelling.[28] A War Office investigation showed a stark divergence between the psychological efficacy of certain enemy weapons such as bombing aircraft and mortars and their actual likelihood of causing casualties. Even though soldiers had relatively little chance of being killed by, say, a Stuka dive-bomber, it was the fact that they could do little to influence its chances of hitting them which made the German plane so frightening (artillery was an unusual case, being both terrifying *and* objectively deadly).[29] One series of weapons in particular – the German Nebelwerfer rocket launchers – made such a disturbing sound when they were fired (described by one soldier as a 'rusty gramophone handle being wound') that the British Army considered introducing a version of its own, even though it was known that Nebelwerfer attacks rarely resulted in many casualties.[30]

The presence of the dead reminded soldiers that the odds of their indi-vidual survival were getting worse every day they remained in the front line. After all, a single battle was usually just one episode in a much longer campaign. From its landing in Normandy till V-E Day, the 1st Gordon Highlanders fought thirty-six major actions, in all but two of which the battalion was required to assume the burden of attack.[31] Every time such a unit went into combat, its men had to risk their lives anew. It was all very well to be brave *once*. 'Any fool can be brave in his first action' confessed Michael Howard, who received the Military Cross (MC) for valour in Italy. He had only behaved so boldly on that first occasion because he knew that he was being watched by his superiors and he was keen to impress them. 'It was not to happen again.'[32] Michael Carver, commander of 4th Armoured Brigade in Normandy, felt that 21st Army Group's collective confidence and aggression diminished perceptibly in the weeks following D-Day as soldiers began to appreciate how dangerous their situation really was. 'In the early days in the beachhead it was fairly easy to get people to take exceptional risks, whether they were old sweats or keen young chaps, eager to win their spurs', he wrote. But disillusion quickly sank in. 'One was so often being told that the coming battle was the one that was going to break through and that no losses would deter one. Then the whole thing would come to a grinding halt.'[33] As Martin Lindsay put it, 'for an officer to go into a dozen actions without being killed or badly wounded was like a coin coming down head six times running. He knew that his luck could not possibly last.'[34] After six months of 'narrow shaves' at the front, Lindsay found that his tolerance for risk had declined markedly. 'When one has ridden in a number of steeplechases without a mishap it does one's nerve good to have a harmless fall. But now I had seen too much and had too great a respect for the law of averages.'[35] 'As one gained in experience', agreed Jocelyn Pereira, 'one's nerves seemed gradually to become less resilient under the strain.'[36] Eventually, the strain might prove too much.

Bravery, as Churchill's doctor Lord Moran (himself the recipient of an MC in the First World War) put it in his 1945 classic *The Anatomy of Courage*, was like capital accumulated in a mental bank account. No two soldiers had exactly the same starting amount. Some would draw on their balance faster than others during the course of a campaign. But every soldier, ultimately, would exhaust his supply in the end. There was no such thing as 'getting used to combat'. Men, he thought, 'wear out in war like clothes'.[37] The signs that a soldier had reached the limits of his courage could vary. Some men who had previously appeared to be models of fortitude might snap, suddenly and dramatically, perhaps for no obvious reason. One of Rex Wingfield's comrades, who had survived weeks in the front line without demur, suddenly broke down in tears when he saw a flush toilet. 'The sight of an ordinary domestic thing like a lavatory pan reminded him suddenly of his home, his wife and two kids', thought Wingfield. 'Fatigue and battle exhaustion did the rest.'[38] A stretcher bearer in Anthony Babington's infantry company, a man known to have 'nerves of iron', was found one day lying in a trench sobbing like a child. Other men would enter a slow but inexorable decline. Giving up habits of personal cleanliness was a worrying indicator, as was a tremor to the hand or a haunted look to the eyes.[39] Alexander Baron suggested that the tell-tale symptoms were 'a twitching in the calves, a fluttering of the muscles in the cheeks, breath like a block of expanding ice in the lungs, the stomach contracting, sickness rising in the throat'.[40] An excessive nervousness might take hold, known as being 'bomb-happy'. One private in

Italy described seeing bomb-happy men duck when a bee buzzed by. An entire platoon might fall to the ground in fear because a man nearby had started gargling.[41] Sometimes nervous exhaustion would express itself in a quite different way through a fatalistic insouciance. When one of his comrades stopped crouching under fire and instead shambled about with a ramrod-stiff back and a gaunt stare in the eyes, Stanley Whitehouse called it the 'deathwish walk' – a sign that the man had lost the will to live.[42] David Holbrook described the same gaze as 'the blankness of psychic withdrawal', the look of a man 'beyond horror . . . expressionless, like those of the dead'.[43]

Robert Woollcombe saw such symptoms take hold of his batman, 'Jamie', during the OVERLORD campaign. As the weeks passed during the hot summer of 1944 and the Normandy *bocage* fighting dragged on without apparent hope of any conclusion, the formerly obliging and efficient soldier's willpower steadily drained away. Jamie's 'eyes grew unhappy. The smile vanished . . . his features became pinched, and periodically he would heave vast sighs.' His conversation dwindled to a series of monotone grunts. When he was not sleeping, Jamie occupied himself by chewing on army biscuits incessantly. He lost interest in his work. 'Withdrawn in mute misery', he even stopped writing to his wife. Jamie's personality had been 'bludgeoned out by the guns'. Eventually, he was wounded and shipped back to Britain – as much a relief to Woollcombe and his other comrades as it was to Jamie himself.[44]

So what could broken soldiers such as Jamie do once their capital of courage was exhausted? They could ask to go sick, and trust that their unit doctor and commanding officer were sympathetic to their plight. This might result in treatment, or at the very least, a chance to sit out the next action. As Lionel Wigram pointed out in his report on the Sicilian campaign in 1943, it was an open secret that many regimental colonels deliberately left out of battle twenty or so men in their battalion whom they knew would run in terror if they were placed under fire. Wigram had originally disapproved of such exceptions when he learned of them, feeling that nervous soldiers should 'take their medicine like everyone else'. But he had come to see the wisdom of the practice. All that the presence of 'windy' men in the battle line did was depress unit morale. It was better to keep them out of the fighting completely than to have them flee in panic once the bullets started flying.[45]

If a traumatized soldier had no luck going sick, he could hope for the 'Blighty wound' that Woollcombe's batman Jamie eventually received – an injury serious enough to have him returned to Britain without actually killing him. Such wounds could be surreptitiously manufactured. During the fighting in Normandy in July 1944, one infantry company alone lost fifteen men due to suspected self-inflicted wounds (SIW).[46] In their despair, some of Stanley Whitehouse's comrades began sticking their hands out of their slit trenches during artillery bombardments in the hope that they would receive shrapnel injuries. Others rubbed dust into open sores in order to infect them, or smashed their trigger fingers with mess-tins full of sand. Whitehouse himself, in a particular moment of anguish, thought about shooting himself in the hand with a Sten gun, a useful weapon from the point of view of the SIW-minded because of its notorious tendency to misfire. He only changed his mind because he was interrupted during his final preparations.[47]

Soldiers could also go 'on the trot' – desert. Desertion, as we've seen, was overall more a problem of the home front than the front line. Nonetheless, thousands of British soldiers absconded from their units in northwest Europe, the Mediterranean and North Africa during the war. (Burma was the only theatre in which desertion was not a major problem, and the reason for that had nothing to do with the unpleasantness of the fighting: there was simply nowhere to desert to.) As casualty figures rose, so did incidences of desertion. During the final twelve months of the war, there were 8,425 convictions for desertion in overseas commands – a fourfold increase on the previous year. And these cases represented only those men who were caught or who turned themselves in and were subsequently found guilty at court martial.[48] General Adam, visiting Italy early in 1945, found that the problem of desertion had come to 'obsess most commanders' minds'.[49]

The desertion problem presented the Army with three questions. First, was it ultimately a moral or a medical issue – in other words, was there a meaningful distinction to be made between 'deserving' and 'undeserving' deserters, between otherwise good soldiers who had succumbed to the tremendous mental pressures of war through no fault of their own, and men who were simply gutless? Next, if such a distinction *could* theoretically be made, was there any reliable test by which you could categorize each individual case of desertion? And lastly, what types of punishment or treatment were appropriate for deserters? These questions had implications not just for the practice of military law but also for the Army's approach more generally to the problem of psychiatric injury. But the War Office was never able to arrive at a definitive answer to any of them – not only because of genuine uncertainty about where the truth lay but also because of the irreconcilable demands of discipline, manpower supply, and political accountability. All the Army was ultimately able to do was to muddle through with a set of policies that were conceptually messy, but manageable.

During the Great War, the British Army had sentenced 3,080 of its soldiers to death, and had actually executed 346 of them, 266 for the crime of desertion.[50]

But in 1930, Parliament had abolished all capital crimes under military law except for mutiny and treachery. It was not a decision that sat well with many Second World War generals. As early as spring 1940, Lord Gort had already begun to request that the death penalty be reintroduced as a possible punishment for desertion on active service. The Eighth Army's commander General Auchinleck made the same proposal in spring 1942, and it was taken up again in 1944 by General Alexander during the Italian campaign. Gort's, Auchinleck's and Alexander's arguments were all much the same. They believed that the typical sentence for desertion of two to three years in military prison had no deterrent effect. Indeed, for soldiers who wished to avoid the rigours of combat, detention in an Army stockade was a good deal more preferable than front-line service. It was 'false sentimentality', insisted Auchinleck, to assume that all deserters were the victims of battlefield trauma, and he suggested that this was the widespread view within the Army too. 'I do not believe', he said,

> the great majority of soldiers of ordinary courage, resolution, and sense of duty will resent the idea that dangers which they themselves face without flinching should also lie in wait, in circumstances of dishonour, for those who shirk their duty and abandon their comrades.[51]

Whatever the disciplinary case for the resumption of the death penalty, however, it never stood a chance. It was simply a political non-starter. It would set off a parliamentary furore that no member of the coalition government was willing to tackle. Besides, reinstating capital punishment might make it look as though the Army's morale was faltering; it would seem too much like an act of desperation. Yet there was not much else the War Office could offer its frustrated theatre commanders. Even giving deserters longer prison terms was not a realistic option because of the desperate need for manpower in the teeth arms; soldiers who had been convicted of many years in military gaol were already having their sentences suspended after just a few months so that they could be returned to their units.[52] All the Army could ultimately do was offer a statement in January 1945 that when demobilization began any man who had previously deserted would be pushed to the back of the release queue. Even this modest deterrent fell short of ruling out a possible post-war amnesty for deserters – which was eventually enacted, as many soldiers always suspected it would be, in 1953.[53]

But it was not just fear of a political backlash or the need for infantry replacements that prevented a wartime resumption of the death penalty for desertion. There were sincere ethical issues at stake, too. In summer 1944, John Sparrow, the adjutant-general's morale expert, visited Eighth Army in Italy and spoke with a number of staff and regimental officers, military psychiatrists, court-martial presidents and commandants of detention barracks about the desertion problem. Sparrow concluded that 'undeserving' deserters certainly existed in Italy: some men were leaving their units as a 'soft option' and with the confident expectation that, even if they were caught, they would not only be able to live out the war in 'comparative ease and safety' in military prison, but that they would probably receive a pardon for their behaviour one day. The only threat that would ultimately deter such men was the possibility of execution, and Sparrow knew as well as anyone else that that was not going to happen.

But such displays of brazen funk only represented a small proportion of all desertion cases. Far more common were 'deserving' soldiers – Sparrow called them 'involuntary' deserters. Some were men with the kinds of constitutionally weak characters which were the obsession of Adam's Directorate of Service Personnel back in Britain. By rights, they should never have been allowed to reach the front line in the first place. But there were other involuntary deserters for whom such a congenital explanation made less sense. Some were soldiers with excellent records of service who had broken, Sparrow felt, 'simply because they had had all they could take'. The balance of their courage had been spent. Punishing such men was not only unjust, but also wasteful of valuable manpower. 'Many such cases could have been prevented from ever becoming court-martial cases if the men had been rightly diagnosed as needing medical treatment at an early stage.'[54]

What did ordinary soldiers themselves think of all this? Every man who absconded from the front line placed an extra burden on his comrades who stayed behind. By the winter of 1944, some infantry platoons in Italy were so denuded of replacements that a rifle section which was supposed to have a complement of nine soldiers might be reduced to five or six. If just two men of such a section deserted, it would be down to one third of its establishment strength.[55] It's hardly surprising, then, that cases of 'involuntary' desertion were often viewed with a good deal of scepticism by the other men in the ranks. 'Two chaps who disappeared on the eve of our recent dabble have returned to the fold', noted Reg Crimp in his diary in July 1944. 'They claim, of course, to be bomb-happy, hoping perhaps for a grading as unfit for service in the front line. Even the chance of a court-martial doesn't daunt them. A military nick breaks no bones and a term inside has the edge, I suppose, on getting squashed like flies under an iron flail.'[56] There was no worse crime than letting down your mates. Scrimshanking was a pardonable, even admirable sin when away from the front line; but it was unforgiveable once the bullets started flying.

Some men who were initially extended the benefit of the doubt squandered it. One of Alex Bowlby's fellow platoon members, Private Coke, fled before his first action in Italy. After giving himself up, Coke was let off with a warning from the commanding officer and returned to his platoon so shamefaced that none of his comrades felt like berating him. '*I wrote 'ome and told me girl I'm no good*', said Coke self-pityingly: '*told 'er I was yellow.*' Bowlby was touched by this display of humility. 'You'll be alright, Cokey', he reassured him.[57] But the mask soon slipped. Coke quickly deserted again; and this time he had to be apprehended by the Military Police. On his return to the platoon, instead of offering up another show of self-reproach, he congratulated himself on his cleverness in securing a court martial and removal from the front line. As Coke was driven away by MPs for the last time, he sneered at his former mates: '*I'll be alive when you're all fucking dead!*'[58]

Cases like Coke's discouraged soldierly compassion. Britain in the 1940s did not have a culture in which there was much tolerance for the expression of private fears or doubts amongst men. Public exhibitions of trauma that today might be viewed as healthy and cathartic were regarded then as perverse and shameful.[59] Nonetheless, there was all the same a tacit understanding within the Army that soldiers who had 'done their time' with credit should not be pushed beyond a reasonable limit. One night during the battle for Tunisia in 1943, as his company was being shelled, one of Neil McCallum's men suddenly collapsed on his stomach and began to sob uncontrollably. How, McCallum wondered, was he supposed to explain to such a soldier in the middle of battle that he needed to pull himself together?

> That he should be up on his feet with his rifle in his hand – 'aggressively tough' – and not spend his glorious patriotic hour lying on the ground moaning for his wife and his family in his suburban home?

After a little while, the soldier recovered his composure. No one spoke about it afterwards.[60]

By the end of the war, the Army had concluded that nervous breakdown in combat was neither purely a problem of moral failure nor one of weeding out the mentally weak. It was too simplistic to suggest, as two leading psychiatrists had put it, that only 'the psychopathic, the damaged, defective or constitution-ally unstable' were vulnerable to bomb-happiness.[61] Any soldier could suffer from a nervous breakdown under the prolonged stress of combat, and effective treatment in the field was best handled by the swift application of commonsen-sical care. The first indication of this came during the 241-day investment of Tobruk from April to November 1941, when it was impossible to evacuate any but the most seriously wounded casualties. RAMC doctors in the besieged port had nothing to offer their patients suffering from psychoneurotic symptoms other than a chance to eat and drink and sleep in peace. Rather to everyone's surprise, such rudimentary treatments proved highly effective. The Tobruk experience suggested that many bomb-happy soldiers were not congenitally useless soldiers at all. They just needed a few days of compassionate care to pull themselves together.[62]

What the RAMC had stumbled on was the principle known as PIE – *proximity, immediacy, expectancy* – which lies at the heart of forward military psychiatry today.[63] Using the PIE principle, traumatized soldiers were to be treated as close to the front line as possible, so as not to give them a sense of total psychological withdrawal from the battlefront. They were to be dealt with promptly rather than being shunted to waiting areas while the 'real' wounded were attended to. Most important of all, they were never to be allowed to form the impression that their medical confinement was anything other than a temporary rest that would naturally end with their return to their units. The phrase 'shell shock' was banished from the lexicon. These men were said to be suffering, rather, from 'exhaustion', a word which legitimized their condition (there was nothing shameful about being tired out) while also emphasizing its transient nature.[64] Treatment was to be kept simple. The soldier would be given a chance to eat, to shower, to change into clean pyjamas and (perhaps assisted by a dose of barbiturates) to sleep for one or two days. Then, after a further day or so to 'sort himself out', he would have his freshly laundered uniform returned to him and would be encouraged to resume some light military duties such as morning parade. Two or three days after that, he would, ideally, return to his unit.[65]

From 1942 onwards, 'Exhaustion Centres' following the PIE principle were established behind the lines in all of the Army's major theatres of war. PIE embodied something which many soldiers seem to have intuitively understood: the role that even quite simple improvements in human comfort and dignity could play in improving cheerfulness and self-confidence. Sidney Jary was always far less bothered by physical danger when he was in the front line (which was at least exhilarating) than by dirt, hunger and lack of sleep. 'In the small hours of the morning, with boot laces cutting into swollen feet, a foul-tasting mouth and an aching stomach, life had little to commend it.' An issue of clean shirts, socks and underwear was a tremendous fillip to unit morale; a chance to bathe, even better.[66] Norman Craig noticed the same thing. A good meal, a wash and a sound night's sleep often did wonders for men who had previously seemed finished.[67] The Army's policy of trying, whenever possible, to pull its soldiers out of the line every two weeks or so for a four-day break provided a vital opportunity for tired and grimy men to get hot food, clean clothes and some uninterrupted rest. British soldiers were luckier in this respect than American GIs, who were expected to remain continuously at the front for anything up to eighty days. That difference in policy is said to have given British infantry units greater battle endurance.[68]

Overall, the RAMC did a much better job of treating psychiatric casualties in the Second World War than it had done in the First. But its statistics, particularly the rates at which bomb-happy soldiers were returned to duty, have to be treated with some caution. There is some evidence that Army doctors in the field deliberately exaggerated their number of success stories in order to please the War Office. Most fighting men who attended an Exhaustion Centre were subsequently returned to non-combat duties; few ever went back to their original units. Relapses were common. Once a soldier had used up the balance of his courage, replenishing it was a painfully slow process – usually too slow for the Army's needs.[69]

Most fighting soldiers never reached the stage of total exhaustion. They endured, even in circumstances which must have seemed at times unendurable. Indeed, the story of the British Army in the Second World War is one of remarkably good behaviour under what were often severely testing conditions. During the final twelve months of the war, there were 32,543 court-martial convictions of British ORs overseas.[70] Given that the average strength of the Army outside the UK during that period was about 1,800,000 men, this means that there were approximately eighteen court-martial convictions for every 1,000 soldiers serving overseas – and this during twelve months which saw some of the most desperate fighting of the whole war.[71] Of course, not all disciplinary offences were tried in front of a court martial. But that figure still suggests a very low rate of indiscipline, especially given the absence of a capital deterrent.[72] Perhaps, then, the real question we ought to ask is not why a small minority of British troops failed to withstand the test of war, but rather why the great majority passed it. Why, despite the low opinion that many of their own commanders had of them, did British soldiers raised in the 'spoon-fed' 1930s rarely exhaust their finite reserves of courage? What motivated them to stick it out no matter what?

Religious belief, like patriotism, laboured under the burden of being an officially prescribed Army virtue, and was therefore automatically suspect in the eyes of many soldiers. Britain by the mid-twentieth century was no longer the self-consciously Protestant nation it had once been. Church attendance across all denominations had been in decline for decades. But the War Office still mandated religious observance whenever practical in the form of Sunday Church Parade, an experience described by Harry Wilson as a 'long, drawn-out display of bull' from first to last. It was 'patently obvious', he thought, 'that we were paying our respects, not to God, but to the colonel of the battalion and to the abstract, powerful deity called Discipline'. The typical padre's address was 'mainly a colourless succession of truisms delivered without any air of conviction'.[73] Compulsory religious attendance, a 300-year-old Army tradition, would in fact be one of the earliest victims of post-war military reform, abandoned in 1946 as even the Chaplain-General's office was forced to concede that it might be doing more harm than good to the troops' spiritual welfare.[74] The harrowing experience of war robbed some men of any confidence they might have once held in a just and benevolent deity. After enduring the traumas of Dunkirk and the assault on the Gustav Line in Italy, J. E. Bowman could no longer take the idea of God seriously. 'Suffering, carnage, betrayal and heartbreak stalked abroad unchecked in my grim world.'[75] Spike Milligan insisted that the closest a man in uniform ever got to being religious was if he dropped a shell on his foot and yelled *Jesus Christ!*[76]

For all that, however, the majority of British people in the 1940s, in and out of the Army, remained thoroughly, if inarticulately, Christian in their moral outlook. Few of them took much interest in questions of dogma, but their idea of the good life was still framed by the values of the New Testament. Some traditional church practices endured even when observance of the sacraments did not. A knowledge of, and enjoyment in, hymn-singing remained surprisingly popular across mid-century Britain, as did the practice of private prayer. As late as the 1950s, one in three Englishmen still prayed at least once a day.[77] Even J. E. Bowman acknowledged that while his own faith had collapsed in the face of war's horror, some of his comrades had been fortified by their own religious convictions.[78] The consolations of the Christian afterlife cannot be dismissed as one factor in keeping soldiers going.

The Army paid lip service to religion, but its bedrock conviction was that soldiers fought, in the end, for their regiments rather than for God. Men, it believed, were willing to die for the honour of those peculiar sacred brotherhoods to which they had been initiated. Regimental *esprit de corps* was the 'priceless possession' of the British Army, as one former adjutant-general put it. 'It makes every man from the colonel to the last joined drummer feel that it is far better to lose his life than do anything to discredit his regiment.'[79] Regimental loyalty had certainly been at the moral centre of the peacetime volunteer army, and it continued to exert a powerful influence on regulars who served in the Second World War. In September 1939, the NCOs of the 1st Royal Irish Fusiliers had already all served for at least fourteen continuous years with the battalion. Some had been there for over twenty-one. 'There was not one of them', thought John Horsfall, 'that was not fully identified with the regiment. It was their whole life, and love too.'[80] It was Sidney Jary's view that if 21st Army

Group's infantry battalions had had the 'numbered anonymity' of most foreign armies, then many of his men would not have survived the ordeal of protracted combat because their officers and NCOs would not have cared enough about the reputation of their regiment to look after them properly.[81] It was because of their acute self-consciousness of being subalterns and tradition-bearers of the Somerset Light Infantry and not, say, the Lancashire Fusiliers, or the Queen's Own Cameron Highlanders, that they were motivated to do their utmost.

Some senior officers were devotees of regimental purity to a preposterous degree. In 1943, Neil McCallum, who had been formally commissioned into a Scottish Lowland regiment, was seconded to a battalion of the Gordon Highlanders in Tunisia, despite the ferocious objections of its colonel (who spoke with a clipped Mayfair accent). 'In the past few months Australians, Greeks, Canadians, English, South Africans, French, had been fighting together in this country', reflected McCallum drily. 'Yet we were now bumping against a clan system which had been nominally destroyed by Butcher Cumberland in 1746.'[82] Some officers seemed to regard the defence of their regiment's immaculate condition from any threat of external pollution as more important than military efficiency. Though he was eventually (and with great reluctance) accepted by the Gordon Highlanders as a replacement, McCallum was left in no doubt as to his status as an interloper. When the battalion was invited to take part in the Army's victory parade through Tripoli, he was told that he would not be allowed to march with the rest of the men – the news being delivered to McCallum by a 'real' Highlander. Who came from Plymouth.[83]

That last detail suggests something of the absurdity of the situation: because by 1943, the fight for regimental purity was clearly lost. Whatever geographical logic the system had once possessed was long gone. Replacement drafts were being assembled out of whoever was available, regardless of their place of origin. Fewer than half of the soldiers who served in a British infantry battalion during the Second World War had a close territorial connection to the regiment they served in.[84] As the war went on and casualties mounted, so the mongrel character of the regiments became more pronounced still. By mid-1943, only three of the thirty-two original officers of the 5th East Yorkshire Regiment were still serving, and most of the men who had replaced them wore different regimental cap badges entirely.[85] Cockneys were being fitted with kilts, Geordies the flash of the Royal Welch Fusiliers. During the Italian campaign, one battalion preparing for an assault received a draft of odds-and-sods from fourteen different other regiments; its exasperated colonel wrote to his superiors requesting that the new men ought at least to be supplied with the insignia of the regiment for which they might be about to die.[86] The infantry, as Anthony Burgess put it, was becoming 'a stew in which the meats of proud battle history were [being] reduced to a neutered fibre'.[87] General Adam, who as a former artilleryman had little personal attachment to the Cardwell-Childers system, would have liked to have gone still further to create a general 'Corps of Infantry' within which all officers and men could be moved around as needed. The old regimental scheme, he insisted, had become 'unworkable and almost a farce'.[88] But the idea would have provoked far too much parliamentary opposition, and he had to give it up quietly.

The total investment of identity in the regiment which regular soldiers took for granted was not something that most conscripts ever found particularly attractive. Their primary mental associations lay outside the Army entirely – in family, community, workplace, class. The particularistic loyalties of the regiment they happened to find themselves in held comparatively little meaning. This is not to say that unit loyalty played no part at all in sustaining wartime soldiers; far from it. But it operated at several levels, including those which were organizationally higher and lower than the regiment. Many soldiers identified far more with their division or field army than their regiment. They felt more conscious and proud of being a member of the 7th Armoured Division (the original Desert Rats), the 51st (Highland) Infantry Division, Slim's 14th 'Forgotten' Army or the downtrodden 'D-Day Dodgers' than the East Surrey Regiment or the 13th/18th Royal Hussars.[89]

In the same way, the individual company, platoon and section to which an infantryman belonged generally meant far more to him than the ghostly abstraction that was the regiment. Raleigh Trevelyan, who was nominally a subaltern of the Rifle Brigade but who spent his time at Anzio attached to the Green Howards, felt that the 'nebulous loyalty' he was supposed to have to his parent regiment meant little compared with his 'ties with the blokes' of his adopted platoon.[90] The primary group could have a powerful hold on a soldier's allegiance in times of stress – though once again we should be careful not to regard it as the be all and end all of combat endurance. Fidelity to your friends could mean ducking out of danger alongside them as well as withstanding it together.[91] When Vernon Scannell returned to his platoon after serving time in a detention barracks for desertion, his best friend Hughie was angry at him – not for deserting, but for forgetting to take anyone else with him when he did. '*I thought we were pals. I couldna believe it when I looked around and you wasna there . . . if you make up your mind to take a walk* [again] *let me know this time and I'll take a walk with you. OK?*'[92]

What of the role of the great charismatic generals of the war? Bernard Montgomery's appointment as commander of Eighth Army in August 1942 has often been cited as the turning point in the Western Desert war (and thus in many ways Britain's entire ground war in the west) because of his revivifying effect on the morale of the troops fighting against Rommel.[93] The great general himself was in no doubt as to his own indispensability. 'It seemed to me that to command such men [as the Eighth Army's soldiers] demanded not only a guiding hand but also a point of focus. And I deliberately set about fulfilling this second requirement', he wrote in his *Memoirs* of the period before Alamein. 'It helped, I felt sure, for them to recognize as a person – as an individual – the man who was putting them into battle.'[94] To be sure, by October 1942, morale reports from Egypt were speaking of the popularity of Monty's 'confident and attacking attitude' and his willingness to meet soldiers personally and to take them into his confidence.[95]

Monty's style of leadership was a self-conscious reaction to the generalship of the First World War. Fairly or not, Haig and the other brass-hats of the Western Front were remembered as aloof and distant figures, cocooned in their luxurious headquarters miles behind the front lines and demonstrating little curiosity about the men in the trenches.[96] Monty, like many of his fellow commanders in the Second World War, was determined to be an anti-Haig. Patrician disdain was out; down-to-earth approachability was in. 'Everyone was aware of how sparsely he lived', recalled one soldier, 'how he hated the "careerists" who infested most headquarters; how he couldn't bear pomposity. We all knew that he ran his operations from close behind the lines, not from some sumptuous chateau many miles to the rear.'[97] To Sidney Jary, Monty's 'mischievous humour and utter lack of pomposity coupled with his single-minded professionalism extended his personal influence to the most junior soldier . . . we felt we knew him and that he knew us.'[98] Anthony Powell, who served on Montgomery's staff in northwestern Europe, felt that the field marshal inspired 'confidence rather than admiration or devotion', but that 'his instinct for what was required in our age for the army he was to command, the war to be fought, was substantially a sound one.'[99]

All that being said, however, Monty's personal touch had its limits. Some soldiers were less than charmed by him. His style could be grating and affected, his visits to individual units overly theatrical and too obviously stage-managed. During the pursuit of Rommel's forces after Alamein, Montgomery circulated a message to his troops promising them 'good hunting'. To Norman Craig, 'communications of this kind always sounded totally artificial and irrelevant . . . how could any activity as revolting as war possibly be presented in sporting terms?'[100] Visiting Norman Smith's Royal Tank Regiment unit before D-Day, Montgomery (an officer of the Royal Warwickshire Regiment) managed to annoy the troops by presumptuously wearing the RTR badge on his beret. His delivery of a half-baked rousing speech 'only served to increase our suspicions', complained Smith. 'We were ready to fight, and we were not chicken, but we would rather have had someone just tell it straight. Three cheers were called for, and to a barely audible response the great man got back into his Rolls and departed.' He was, as an old desert hand put it, '*a bit of a bull-shitter*'.[101] Montgomery's self-puffery could kindle resentment. Many of the men of the 50th Infantry Division never forgave him for what they felt was his disastrous mishandling of the Battle of the Mareth Line in spring 1943. When Monty visited a battalion of the Durham Light Infantry after the battle and scattered packs of cigarettes on the ground as gifts, the battalion's officers hissed to the ranks that any soldier who tried to pick one up would be punished. No one did. When he visited the division before D-Day, he was booed.[102]

William 'Bill' Slim never held as prestigious a wartime command as Montgomery, but the 14th Army's leader seems to have been rather more successful at managing his performance as a soldier's general. 'His appearance was plain enough', thought George MacDonald Fraser: 'large, heavily built, grim-faced with that hard mouth and bulldog chin; the rakish Gurkha hat at odds with his slung carbine and untidy trouser bottoms.' Slim's oratorical style was unadorned, even banal; there were no jokes, no heavy-handed attempts to adopt the colloquial patois of the rank and file (one of Churchill's mistakes when addressing the troops), no ringing phrases. Yet, thought Fraser, that was precisely why he was so admired: 'It was that sense of being close to us, as though he were chatting off-hand to an understanding nephew (not for nothing was he "Uncle Bill") . . . that was his great gift.'[103] Some of Montgomery's men adored him, others loathed him, and many respected his abilities while finding his personal foibles irritating. No such qualifications seem to have attended Slim's reputation. He enjoyed almost universal admiration amongst the soldiers of the 14th Army.[104]

But not every charismatic commander played the Everyman. Even in a people's war, there was still room for a general with old-fashioned swank. To Guards officers, at least, the really inspirational commander of the war was someone far less well remembered today than either Montgomery or Slim – Harold Alexander, Monty's commander-in-chief in the Western Desert and Italian campaigns. 'Alex was essentially a soldier's soldier and he was the one general that most of the troops knew by sight', thought E. P. Danger. 'He had style, he had panache, he was unmistakable, and he had an Irish Guards "set up" to his cap even when in full dress uniform. But he never went around surrounded by a crowd of hangers-on and bodyguards.'[105] Coldstreamer Michael Howard agreed. 'Montgomery's military virtues were reluctantly recognized, but he would not have been welcome in the mess.'[106] The man the Coldstreamers idolized was the 'gentle and patrician' Alex – 'small, polite, intelligent, [who] asked shrewd questions about the welfare of the men, and made an excellent impression.'[107]

One reason why soldiers could endure the horrors of the front line does not sit very well with the liberal values of twenty-first-century Britain: because some of them enjoyed it. Battle freed life from all its petty complexities. Spit-and-polish bullshit ended when the bullets began to fly. The nearer you were to the enemy, the fewer base-wallahs and other detested rear-echelon types you had to concern yourself with. 'What a clarity and a simplicity it really had!' as one soldier put it.[108] Plus, there was the sheer thrill of the hunt and the kill. Some men thrived on the adrenaline rush of danger. Robert Woollcombe, whose batman Jamie succumbed to battle exhaustion in Normandy, had a platoon sergeant called Whitemark who underwent a transformation after D-Day of a very different kind. Whitemark, a man who had previously been an unruly and persistent defaulter, was revealed, to everyone's surprise, to be a natural leader. He seemingly had no sense of fear, and was able to communicate his own cool serenity to the other soldiers around him, even under the worst of fire. He volunteered for patrols, carried them out without fuss, and was soon known for killing the enemy with a calm efficiency. He expressed no interest in life after the war, or any particular desire to see it come to an end. The battlefield was his element. When asked why he enjoyed life on the front line so much, Whitemark could only grin and reply enigmatically, '*Ah, sir. I'm the nomadic type.*'[109]

Raleigh Trevelyan's first experience of killing in cold blood was one of unalloyed pleasure. As the German he had shot through the head collapsed from sight, Trevelyan felt a swell of ecstasy inside himself, the same raw thrill he had experienced as a boy when he stalked roosting pigeons and wild rabbits on expeditions in the woods. 'I was triumphant . . . before long I was pouring out the story to an audience, flatteringly impressed.'[110] The equation of killing enemy soldiers with game hunting was not uncommon. During the Battle of El Alamein, Reg Crimp saw the regimental colonel and the adjutant standing in a trench alongside one another, each with a borrowed rifle, calmly picking off German tank crewmen as they bailed out of their damaged vehicles with the 'mock-emulative gusto' of two rival sportsmen on a grouse shoot.[111] Shooting a Japanese officer for the first time felt, for Frank Baines, little different from bagging a sparrow with an air rifle as a ten-year-old. 'I felt a cool, wary character taking over inside me – someone who confronted his adversary with detachment and an indifference to committing violent acts.'[112] The first man Corporal Harry 'Smudger' Smith of the Royal Engineers killed in Normandy was a German sniper he stabbed in the back with a bayonet. 'He gave a little grunt, and then he was down, dead at once', he recalled later. 'I saw he was SS. So it seemed a great thing to me, something I'd never done before. It was interesting, I'd enjoyed doing it, and although it was murder, I'd no regrets.'[113]

The idea that the conflict between the British Army and the *Wehrmacht* was (as Rommel put it) a *Krieg ohne Hass* – a war without hate – needs to be carefully qualified. Unarmed prisoners were sometimes cut down in cold blood by both sides. Tank crews trapped in their knocked-out vehicles were killed by vengeful infantrymen.[114] 'Any German who tries to surrender nowadays is a brave man; we just shoot them there and then, with their hands up', admitted one private of the 15th (Scottish) Division in Normandy. 'There's nothing to choose between the British and the Germans as regards atrocities.'[115] There was little sentimentality on either side. On the evening of 25 December 1944, a few picked members of Robert Woollcombe's battalion pretended to host a Yuletide party while the rest of its riflemen lay in wait with fingers on their triggers, hoping to tempt the Germans into crossing no-man's-land – a 'Christmas Truce' of an altogether grislier kind than the one in 1914.[116] The dismembering of enemy corpses is something we associate more with the Pacific island campaigns fought between the Americans and the Japanese than the western European theatre, but it happened there too. One of Stanley Whitehouse's comrades briskly hacked at the fingers of any dead Germans he found in order to remove their rings.[117] Dudley Anderson saw British troops extracting gold teeth from the mouths of dead *Landsers*. 'Had there been concentration camps in Britain, there would have been no shortage of volunteers to staff them', he thought. 'I had seen some of them at work.'[118]

Yet hatred of the other side tended to be the product of raw, nerve-rattled emotions rather than cold calculation. Where it existed, it was usually directed at particular enemy formations out of a sense of moral outrage – usually from a belief, real or imagined, that they had 'broken the rules' first, and so had forfeited the right to any sympathy. The Waffen SS were regarded (with good reason) as troops who gave no quarter, and therefore could expect none in return. Soldiers of the Black Watch in Normandy were disinclined to accept German surrenders because of allegations that Scottish medics had been fired upon while attending to the wounded in battle.[119] Particular enemy tactics were regarded as contemptible, even if one's own side used them too. Snipers were loathed by regular infantrymen and rarely had their surrenders accepted. Sniping, even when conducted by the British, was 'sordid', thought Sidney Jary, 'as unprofessional as it was unnecessary . . . a cold and calculated way of killing which achieved no military advantage.'[120] Fury at enemy sniper activity was sometimes released by the murder of prisoners unlucky enough to be in the vicinity at the time.

Complicating this moral outrage, however, was a countercurrent of compassion for enemy troops – the recognition that they, too, were front-line soldiers going through hardships and indignities no less than the British themselves.

'They did what they had to do just as we did', thought John Kenneally. 'They stuck their faces into the same ground as we did; they were covered in the same filth and rubble as we were.'[121] Norman Craig thought that infantrymen of all nations shared a strange friendship for one another in the face of the 'common indiscriminating slaughter' that threatened them all.[122] 'We received them as comrades', wrote Rex Wingfield of one group of Germans his platoon captured:

> These blokes had been going through it just like us, only they'd had our artillery thrown in as well. We knew what that meant. We'd had some. Regardless of race or uniform, we 'flatties' were a people apart from, and superior to, other human beings . . . we passed them food and cigarettes.

'It wasn't charity or pity, but understanding and comradeship', he explained. 'They understood too.'[123] It was difficult not to feel empathy for men who, stripped of their uniforms, could as easily have been from Durham or Deptford as from Dusseldorf. One of Stanley Whitehouse's comrades broke down in tears when he inspected the body of a German he had just killed in Holland and found photos of the man's wife and children inside his pocket. It was the response, at once self-reproaching and angry, of a 'kind and thoughtful and sensitive' man to a situation he had never asked to be in and which he found utterly hateful – the fact that he had been forced to take the life of a husband and father whom he had never even met before.[124]

Even the British relationship with the Japanese, soured though it was by differences of race and the – well-deserved – reputation of the Imperial Japanese Army for acts of systematic brutality, did not always amount to simple blind hatred. On one occasion as Frank Baines and the rest of his Chindit platoon looked down on a group of Japanese soldiers about to be ambushed, he found it impossible not to identify and sympathize with the 'poor benighted bastards' who were about to die.[125] Chivalric considerations could sometimes interfere even with the fighting in Burma. John Shipster recalled a young subaltern who, while out on patrol, spotted two Japanese soldiers fishing with little bamboo rods. Although they were a perfect unsuspecting target, he could not bring himself to gun them down without warning, especially whilst they were in the midst of such a peaceful bucolic activity. The alternative plan he came up with was to creep up on them, shout '*Boo, you bastards!*' and only then open fire with his Sten gun. Unfortunately, the subaltern's chivalric manners cost him dearly. His Sten jammed at the moment he revealed himself, and before they were killed the Japanese soldiers had enough time to throw a clutch of hand-grenades which took off one of his legs. After this incident Baines's commanding officer issued a special Order of the Day to prevent such further displays of gallantry: '*Remember that the Japanese are not pheasants. You can shoot them on the ground.*'[126]

Most British soldiers seem to have concurred with Neil McCallum that you 'cannot hate the bastard who is trying to kill you'.[127] Tank commander Bill Bellamy had more reason to detest the Germans than most: while he was on active service, his mother lost her life in one of the first V-2 attacks on London. Yet he gained no personal satisfaction from the act of killing, and acted 'more in the spirit of self-preservation than in a determined effort to kill the enemy', he reflected in his memoirs. 'In a way I felt apologetic when I either pressed the trigger or caused it to be pressed.'[128] Any pleasure derived from killing usually receded quickly enough. Raleigh Trevelyan's self-satisfaction at bagging his German victim was knocked out of him quickly enough when one of his fellow officers dubbed him 'Killer' sarcastically. '*So you're in your element at last!*' 'In a flash', remembered Trevelyan, 'all my defences had been irretrievably demolished. I could never go there again.'[129] The first German Anthony Babington killed was a young officer, 'slender, fair-haired, and boyish', and not at all like the image of the Beastly Hun that had been conjured up by his training sergeant back in Britain. Babington fired a bullet into the man's chest and the *Wehrmacht* officer died instantly, falling back with a look of 'pain and surprise' on his face. It was all done 'compulsively, without forethought' or hesitation. Yet afterwards, Babington had a powerful urge which he needed to suppress to go back to the site and pray over the dead man's body. He consoled himself with the thought that the bullet might have been fired by one of his comrades, even though he knew this wasn't really plausible.[130]

The Army worried that its citizen-soldiers had been drained of their natural belligerence by the etiolating comforts of modern civilization, but its efforts to do something about this were clumsy and half-hearted. The War Office committee assigned to investigate the Dunkirk campaign in 1940 recommended that a 'fiercer, aggressive spirit' had to be inculcated within the common soldier; it had to be 'constantly and persistently rubbed into all ranks' that their duty was to 'seize every opportunity of killing the enemy'.[131] Partly as a consequence of this, in early 1942 some battle schools in Britain experimented with 'hate training' techniques intended to stir up a violent emotional response towards Axis soldiers. Trainees were doused with animal blood while on exercises, shown photographs of atrocities committed by the Germans and Japanese, lectured on the perfidiousness of the enemy, and harangued during bayonet practice by instructors with loudspeakers intoning '*hate, hate, hate*'. But the experiment was abandoned after a few months after a BBC radio report describing the programme 'in vivid and lurid detail' provoked complaints from politicians, churchmen and members of the psychiatric profession.[132] 'Toughening' was one thing; deliberately inculcating hatred was held to be un-Christian and un-British. Plus, it fitted poorly into the Army's own apolitical conception of its mission. Regimental culture eschewed hatred as vulgar and unprofessional. The King's enemies were there to be killed, not despised. Personal rancour only complicated the job. Hatred, thought John Masters, warped judgement. Amongst his Gurkhas, the Germans and the Japanese were simply the 'dushman' – the enemy. 'Once you had said *dushman* you had said all that was necessary.'[133] Better, thought many officers, to rely on cool, rational Anglo-Saxon level-headedness than to try to emulate the frenetic and unstable passions of foreigners.

In fact, it was untheatrical, gentle men who often made the best soldiers. John Horsfall had no time for the 'noisy and the flamboyant . . . [who] time and time again caved in from fear, or stress, or both'. Far more reliable were the modest, quietly spoken soldiers of his battalion who were habitually revealed to be 'made of teak'.[134] Sidney Jary agreed. It was not aggressiveness, physical stamina, a 'hunting mentality' or a taste for blood which made a good infantryman, but rather 'sufferance . . . a quiet mind . . . [and] a sense of the ridiculous.'[135] A 'mature compassion' was what you looked for in a reliable rifleman, not bloodthirstiness.[136] Courage could be found in the unlikeliest of soldiers. One of Jary's platoon members was a private called Charles Raven, a clerk from north London 'so out of place on the battlefield' that it was far from clear how he had ever been put into the infantry in the first place. There was not a single day throughout the campaign in which Raven was not scared stiff, a fact that he shared without hesitation or embarrassment with the other members of the platoon. By November 1944, after four months in the front line, Raven was feeling his nerve starting to falter. He approached Jary one evening and asked permission to report sick the following day. Jary reluctantly agreed – attendance at sick parade was one of the unwritten rights of every British soldier – but he asked Raven to think it over during the night, and then talk to him again in the morning if he still felt the same way. When the morning came, Raven carried on with his duties as though the conversation had never happened. The incident was never mentioned again.

'I can only surmise the struggle which raged in his mind all that night while he crouched in his waterlogged slit trench peering into the sinister darkness of the woods', wrote Jary years later. 'I do know, however, that in Hoven Woods a considerable moral triumph over stark horror was achieved by a good man, unequipped by nature for war. In my view, the bravest of the brave.'[137]

Sooner or later, any analysis of the British Army at war from 1939 to 1945 has to deal with the most important question of all. Was it any good?

The ultimate test of an army is victory, and of course the British (as they have not been slow to remind everyone for seventy years) were on the winning side in the Second World War, just as they were in the First. But this is far too crude a measure of military effectiveness to be useful. To take just the most obvious point, the British did not defeat the Germans and the Japanese alone. Even in the period from June 1940 to June 1941, they had the assistance and resources of a global empire to draw on. And during 1941, they acquired two hugely important allies, the Soviet Union and the United States of America. By the end of the war, both the USSR and the USA had built up armed forces far larger than those of the British Commonwealth and Empire. The Russian contribution to the ground war against the Nazis was particularly crucial, accounting for something like 75–80 per cent of all German combat casualties. The centre of gravity of the European war from spring 1941 onwards can fairly be said to have been located somewhere within Belarus or western Ukraine.[138] As for the war against Japan, the primary role of the Americans is indisputable.

If the British Army won most of its battles from late 1942 onwards, then, was this only because it was fighting opponents hobbled by the punishments dished out by their other, more dangerous enemies elsewhere? That was largely the view of Basil Liddell Hart, who remained an influential military historian after the war, and who devoted much of his post-1945 career to the defence of his own interwar strategic and tactical theories. The wartime British Army, he complained in 1952, had conducted itself with at best plodding competence. It had had to rely on sheer weight of materiel to compensate for the 'boldness and initiative' which the Germans had possessed and which were all too obviously missing at every level of British command.[139] In 1960 another prominent historian, Correlli Barnett, stung the pride of desert war veterans by describing the Eighth Army as a 'a cumbersome and inferior fighting instrument, capable of winning against German troops only in a carefully rehearsed, tightly controlled set-piece operation with ample margins of numerical and material superiority'.[140] Similar criticisms would later be voiced by such luminaries of military history as Sir John Keegan, Max Hastings, John Ellis and Carlo D'Este.[141] Sir Michael Howard, who had fought with distinction as a junior officer in Italy and would later write one of the official government histories of wartime grand strategy, was no less bracing in his criticism of the wartime Army just because of his personal service within it. 'We learned to be soldiers of a kind', he wrote of the young Guards Brigade officers he trained alongside, 'but not yet fighters, let alone killers. I think many of us never did . . . I was not remotely ready to command men in action against so formidable an enemy. The panache of the Brigade still camouflaged all too effectively the harsh reality of war.'[142] Indeed, he felt that 'with certain significant exceptions, the British army in the Second World War was not very good, and those of us who were fighting in it knew where its weaknesses lay'. Its problems, he thought, were numerous:

> Staff work was rigid. There was little encouragement of initiative, or devolution of responsibility. An absolute distinction was made between officers and other ranks; and as the war went on, there was an increasing reluctance to run risks and a greater reliance upon massive firepower. There were often major problems of efficiency and of discipline. It is perhaps surprising that we performed as well as we did.[143]

Any measure of an army's 'fighting power' or 'combat effectiveness' has to be made comparatively if it is to have any meaning at all. War is a contest of relative strengths and weaknesses, some of which result from decisions made within the fighting forces themselves, others of which are the product of external factors over which they have little or no control.[144] The British Army enjoyed a number of advantages over the *Wehrmacht* and the Imperial Japanese Army. It had powerful allies and colonial dependencies to absorb much of the burden of the ground fighting. It had a large and sophisticated national industrial base to furnish it with weapons and equipment, and one that, aside from a brief period in 1940–41, was mostly undisturbed by enemy bombing. It had American and Canadian-produced Lend-Lease aid to supplement whatever could not be manufactured at home. It usually enjoyed, from 1943 onwards, overwhelming naval and air support wherever it fought.

But equally, the British Army fought the war handicapped by an unusually constraining set of circumstances. It had been starved of resources for twenty years, and told to plan for a mission which proved fundamentally different from the one it was actually required to carry out in the end. With the outbreak of war, it had to absorb a huge number of raw and initially ill-equipped recruits, while at the same time providing an expeditionary force to send to France and Belgium. Then, after the German victory of 1940, it had to defend not only the home islands themselves but also to conduct operations in a number of colonial territories in the Middle East and South East Asia which lay at the end of lengthy and fragile lines of supply and communication. Moreover, it had to do all these things while the naval and air services (especially RAF Bomber Command, committed to its chimerical pursuit of victory by the Indirect Approach) siphoned off as much of the nation's war-making materiel and as many of its high-quality personnel as they could. The Army never really enjoyed the confidence of either of Britain's wartime prime ministers. Churchill ultimately burdened it with the responsibility of expediting three simultaneous land campaigns – in Italy, Burma and northwestern Europe – when it only had enough manpower for two of these, and perhaps really only one. Churchill also insisted that while the Army had to do enough ground fighting to justify his place at the three-power victory conference, it could not absorb so many casualties in the process that the public at home, unwilling to accept a slaughter on the scale of 1914–18 again, would revolt.[145] That these barely reconcilable demands were, in the end, just about met represented a great achievement on the part of Brooke and his fellow commanders.

Britain in 1939 was a liberal parliamentary democracy which took seriously the individual rights and welfare of its citizens. This placed constraints upon its military performance that were shared by the Dominions as well as the United States, but which did not exist for Germany, Japan or the Soviet Union. Britain's civilian population was neither materially nor psychologically prepared for the outbreak of war. The great majority of the country's young men had had no armed service training, and they were used to levels of personal freedom and comfort that it was neither possible nor desirable to duplicate in a wartime Army. Their assimilation into the military machine, then, was always going to take longer than it would have done had Britain been a dictatorship. The British Army could not employ the relentless propagandizing methods of the totalitarian states to stir up fanaticism in its soldiers, nor could it cow them with the threat of immediate and ruthless punishment should they fail to adopt a sufficiently self-sacrificing attitude. No reforming General Adam was required within the *Wehrmacht* or the Red Army for the simple reason that those military forces operated with an almost total disregard for the personal grievances of their men. Psychological casualties did not trouble the medical services of the Axis or Russian armies because they barely recognized their existence in the first place. As for discipline, while no soldier ever cares much for his own military policemen, Britain's mild-mannered redcaps bore little resemblance to the uniformed thugs of the *Feldgendarmerie* or *Kempeitai* or NKVD, who between them were responsible for the execution of tens, perhaps hundreds, of thousands, of their fellow soldiers. There were no punishment battalions within the British Army whereby recalcitrant troops could be sent to their deaths as a lesson to others. No British Army subaltern was allowed, as his Japanese counterpart was, to freely punch or kick or beat his men with a wooden rod as an encouragement to conform.[146]

Britain's ground war, on the whole, lacked the desperate quality of Russia's or (from 1943 onwards) Germany's or Japan's. Aside from brief moments – Dunkirk, the battle to stem Rommel's advance to the Nile in summer 1942, Kohima and Imphal – the possibility of total destruction and existential defeat was rarely something that British troops had to face. By D-Day, the German

Landser knew that he was going to end the war in one of three places: a prison camp, a hospital bed or a grave.[147] He fought on in hopeless fatalism, as much out of fear of his own side as of the enemy. His British counterpart served under very different conditions. He knew that, so long as he avoided death or a crippling injury, he would get to return home one day to pick up his life where he had left it off. It is hardly surprising, then, that his willingness to take personal risks was a good deal more circumscribed than that of the soldiers opposite him who had far less to lose.[148] Tommy rarely demonstrated the implacable ferocity that was seen in the defence of the German *Vaterland*, imperial *Nippon*, or Holy Mother Russia. But it is unreasonable to suppose that he should ever have done so.

Until very late in the war, the British Army laboured under another burden besides its civility and its relatively unprecarious situation. Most of its men had little or no combat experience. The Army's absence from the European battlefield between Dunkirk and D-Day (the small number of troops who fought in Sicily and Italy notwithstanding) left it far behind its enemies on the tactical and operational 'learning curves'. Lessons learned in North Africa from 1940–43 were not transmitted back to units in Britain efficiently, and in any case tactics that made sense when fighting across a flat and featureless desert landscape were not always relevant to preparing for war in dense European countryside. The bulk of the men of Montgomery's 21st Army Group on the eve of OVERLORD were as green as Haig's soldiers had been on the first day of the Battle of the Somme. There were plenty of deadly and humiliating mistakes for them to make along the way, especially in combat against *Wehrmacht* veterans of the Eastern Front. 'For the first two months in Normandy we lacked two things', thought platoon commander Sidney Jary, 'comprehensive and imaginative training and personal experience of battle.' Though there was little he could personally do about the first deficiency, the second he felt was quickly resolved.[149] And indeed, 21st Army Group's operational performance improved markedly as the war in northwestern Europe went on.

One of the reasons for the success of the Axis forces in close combat was the high priority they placed on putting their best quality personnel into the 'teeth' arms, notably the infantry. One historian of the wartime German Army has remarked on the 'remarkable level of intelligence and lucidity' observable in letters and diaries of *Wehrmacht* front-line combat soldiers. The typical German infantryman possessed a far greater 'descriptive power and higher degree of literacy' than his British or American counterpart.[150] This was not by chance. From the outset of the war, both the British and the US armies took a quite different approach to manpower selection than the Germans. They intentionally directed their best-educated, most intelligent men away from the infantry into the other branches of the service, especially those concerned with such vital but supplementary functions as firepower support, planning, engineering, communications, intelligence-gathering, medical care and welfare. This placed an enormous burden on Allied infantry commanders, who often seemed to receive as replacements the very men least capable of handling the tremendous mental and physical stresses of close combat. 'No account seems to have been taken of the particularly arduous role of the infantry', thought one British subaltern who fought in the Italian campaign. 'The Army medical authorities [did not] consider seriously the business of assessing mental stability. They just looked at physical characteristics, and even this was not an adequate judge of the physical strength needed in the infantry.'[151] A lieutenant in Normandy in 1944 complained, 'All I can do with my men, the sort of men I have, is to persuade them to get out of their holes in the ground, march up to the objective, dig a hole there, and get into it.'[152]

The British Army had assumed that this would not be a great problem because air and artillery firepower and armoured support would do most of the work on the battlefield anyway; the infantry would merely deliver the *coup de grâce* once the big guns had bludgeoned the enemy into submission. Yet infantry close combat remained central to ground fighting in the Second World War. Battle drill was a step in the right direction, but it could not overcome basic problems of manpower quality and inexperience. The burden of success fell, then, to the inspirational actions of NCOs and young officers. But the requirement for them to show courageous leadership under fire was inevitably costly; and they were hard to replace.[153] No other single factor was as responsible for destroying the morale and cohesion of an infantry unit as the loss of a critical mass of its junior leaders.[154] Sidney Jary believed that the men of his platoon 'were better soldiers than any we fought'; but he also acknowledged that they had a continuity of command which was highly unusual.[155] Few infantrymen were as lucky as Jary's. It was they who paid the price, in the end, for the Army's inattention to the problems of the PBI.

Having said all that, the Army's emphasis on brute mechanical force over human courage made sense given the unusual terms of engagement it was bound by. This was not 'cheating', as some admirers of the *Wehrmacht* have seemed to suggest. It was a rational response to the conditions applied by the British political class (and, ultimately, the British people). The Army did not execute its own operational model with perfect efficiency, or get its manpower distribution exactly right any more than the *Wehrmacht* did. But its personnel dispositions afforded it a depth and coherence on campaign which the logistically handicapped German Army and IJA never had. The *Wehrmacht* lived what John Buckley has called 'a hand-to-mouth existence' because of its generals' obsession with close-combat strength to the exclusion of all other functions.[156] Ultimately, its units fractured into pieces under the stresses of continual battering. Its tactical flair could win it battles, but was not sufficient to sustain it through a long and exhausting war.

Indeed, by the final months of the conflict the sense that had once haunted British troops that the Axis forces opposing them were inherently better warriors was fast wearing off. John Horsfall, who was not slow to point out his own army's deficiencies, never accepted the claim of German tactical superiority in the first place. As early as the 1940 campaign the Germans had suffered, he thought, from 'a large number of quite unnecessary casualties through incompetence, arrogant bullheadedness and lack of individual training. Their field-craft was non-existent and the tactical handling at regimental level was bad – scarcely attempted, in fact. The standard of weapon training was poor save with their machine-gunners, and their ability as marksmen was negligible.'[157] Other British soldiers took more convincing. During his wartime service Dominick Graham, who saw action in Norway, the Western Desert and the Normandy campaign as a field artillery officer, thought often about his father, who had commanded an infantry company on the Western Front twenty-five years earlier. 'It was not until the final year of the war that I felt that my army was as good as his', Graham conceded.[158] Still, by 1945 a tipping point had been reached. The German troops defending the Reich were turning out to be not the 'blond and arrogant supermen' of fearful imagination, but 'just ordinary soldiers, albeit rather scruffy ones, looking a bit archaic in their ankle-length greatcoats'.[159] 'I'm not a bit frightened', wrote Harry Wilson even as *Wehrmacht* tanks trundled towards the Channel ports during the Ardennes Offensive:

> I have respect for, but no longer any fear of, the German Army. Its strength is finished; its hands are tied and its legs hobbled . . . this stroke against the American First Army is not even a desperate gamble; it is a futile act of theatrical vanity, like that of a caught criminal jabbing a knife into his captor's arm.[160]

In the same way, by the end of the war the legendary fearlessness of the Japanese soldier had come to seem more like 'arrogant bullheadedness' and a perverse tolerance for waste than evidence of military acumen. As Slim's troops advanced towards the Irrawaddy in 1945, they discovered the rotting corpses of thousands of abandoned Japanese sick and wounded littering their route.[161] 'I never saw a Japanese defensive position that wasn't brilliantly conceived in its use of nature, and fanatically held', conceded Raymond Cooper. 'On the other hand, I never saw a Japanese attack which couldn't have been planned by a competent Boy Scout.'[162]

Given the considerable limitations that the British Army had to work within from 1939 to 1945, Sir Michael Howard's final observation seems about right: what is surprising is less that things went wrong than that the Army, in the end, performed as well as it did. Certainly, it was not alone amongst the Allied ground forces in having to go through a rapid and traumatic wartime transformation. The Army of the United States experienced much the same set of challenges and setbacks before final victory. Historian Peter Mansoor's clear-eyed but approving comments on the wartime US Army can be applied with only minor editing to Britain's Army as well:

> The great achievement of the Army was to mould a large amount of citizen-soldiers into an effective fighting force in a short time. The process did not work smoothly, and perhaps the end result was not what Army leaders had intended when they began the mobilization process ... nevertheless, [British] divisions, led by a small slice of regular cadre and filled with [conscripts and the products of OCTUs], performed competently on the battlefield once they overcame the initial shock of combat. The first battles were for the most part traumatic affairs, but [British] divisions displayed the ability to learn from their mistakes and improve their performance in future battles ... they were the building blocks upon which [British] commanders crafted their operations to destroy the *Wehrmacht* and achieve ultimate victory in the largest and most destructive war in human history.[163]

Christopher Seton-Watson had no illusions about the mixed qualities of the Army he served within. As a veteran of two chaotic evacuations, from Dunkirk and Greece, he had seen British troops at their worst moments of defeat. He knew and respected, too, the professionalism and courage of the German forces he fought against. Observing some abandoned *Wehrmacht* dugouts in Italy, he could not help but reflect on how better the enemy were at building solid defensive positions than his own side. 'The British soldier is a good digger, but he can't be induced to take war as seriously as all that', thought Seton-Watson as he examined the deep concrete walls the Germans had painstakingly constructed.

> And as for sitting in a dugout all day, well, he just gets bored and starts walking around ... I've often watched our infantry pottering round a ruined house, just exploring, or perhaps getting wood for their dinner fire, in full view of the opposite side. And they will continue to do it however well-trained.

'I suppose', he continued, 'that's the difference between a nation with war and military discipline in its bones, and a nation that can outfight and out-manoeuvre its opponents and at the same time laugh, and be careless and refuse to be crushed and dehumanised by the seriousness and starkness of it all.'

'And thank God', he added, 'for those very differences!'[164]

PART FIVE
CITIZENS

Ah, many, many times
While we dwell in sultry climes
We have dreamt and dream of you
Far away across the Blue:
Foggy Isles.

But some time there'll dawn a day
When the war-clouds roll away –
Then our cheers will smash the tiles,
Our faces wreathed in smiles,
Beer bottles stacked in piles –
When we sail across the main
And return to you again,
Foggy Isles.

Eric Murrell[1]

CHAPTER 14

THEM AND US

Poor Major Elliott. His lecture had started so well. His brief was simple enough: to talk to the men about the new government proposals for post-war welfare reform – the so-called 'Beveridge Plan' for comprehensive social insurance. What he had in mind was a peppering of vague, uplifting phrases about the future, heavy on the clichés, light on any precarious specificity, with a complete avoidance of anything smacking of party policy – reassuring, facile, benign and just the job to fill up the unit's mandatory hour of 'citizenship education'. But the men were not in the mood to behave. Elliott had not got far into his remarks before trouble broke out. Awkward questions began to be asked. Loud objections were voiced. Soon the major's anodyne monologue had dissolved into an open debate in which the soldiers in the audience – many of whom knew a great deal more about current affairs than Major Elliott himself – were steering the conversation into perilous areas. Capitalism. Socialism. *Russia*. Tugging nervously at his moustache, the major improvised a stumbling defence of the free-market principle. '*I'm all for that socialist sort of business*', he pleaded. '*But somebody with brains and foresight has to look after your money*.' After all, '*if you take away private enterprise and the resultant profits, people at the top aren't going to bother much*'. Corporal Harry Wilson, signaller, jumped to his feet. Wasn't the major's statement based more on assumption than fact? How could he be sure that standards would necessarily drop? They hadn't dropped in Russia . . .

'Elliott stroked his moustache thoughtfully', recorded Wilson in his diary that evening. 'He had to admit that Russia was doing "*jolly well*".' It was '*a great experiment, a damn fine show*'. But could they all trust the Russians? ('*What's that got to do with it?*' somebody shouted from the audience.) After all, what would happen if a reliable chap like Stalin died and '*a gang of criminals got into power and spoiled the whole business?*' If this qualified encomium to the USSR was meant to appease the crowd, it failed badly. The questions only got more pointed, the mood more heated and uncomfortable. 'The major stood there blinking and coughing', observed Wilson. 'Then he had a timely idea. "*I know!*" he exclaimed. "*I know what we want. We'll have to have a discussion on Russia. It's imperative.*" That was the end of it.' As the meeting broke up, another member of the audience approached Wilson. '*A discussion on Russia!*' he beamed. '*Let's make it as hot as mustard for him.*' 'Don't be silly', Wilson replied. 'There won't be a discussion on Russia.' And, of course, there wasn't.[1]

Freedom of expression had its limits, then. All the same, just the fact that in the summer of 1943 a British Army major was discoursing with his men on the virtues of Soviet communism, and at the behest of the War Office, no less, was a pretty remarkable development in itself. Most senior officers at the outbreak of the Second World War would have regarded such a thing as absurd and horrifying. The Army had never 'done' politics; never would; never should. Paragraph 541 of King's Regulations stated that no serving soldier was permitted to take part in political activity.[2] Army Education, such as it had existed in the pre-war years, had simply meant instruction in basic literacy and numeracy. 'Current affairs' were an anathema. Soldiers were to believe in King, Country and regiment, and do as they were told. If they were ordered to fight, they were not going to be asked what they felt about it. The British Army was not a debating society.

Which was fine so far as a professional volunteer force went. But by 1941, expecting the same political quietism from amateur citizen-soldiers was starting to seem dangerously complacent. If the *Wehrmacht*'s victory in France the previous year had demonstrated one thing, it was the matchless sense of purpose displayed by the ordinary German soldier. The *Landser* went into action with a clear sense of what he was fighting for. Nazi ideology was motivating men to die for their Führer. Couldn't a parliamentary democracy do a better job of selling *its* cause to its own troops? It was time, as Lord Croft, the undersecretary of state for war put it, to 'stimulate martial ardour in the breasts of our fighting men'.[3]

But explaining Allied war aims would be difficult so long as the common soldier lacked knowledge of even the most elementary facts about the world and Britain's place in it. A Royal Tank Regiment officer who led an early unit discussion group noted that many of his men had no idea where Poland was, what the Low Countries were, how Parliament worked, or what the term 'local government' meant.[4] In another unit, when twenty men were asked where Vienna was, nine responded 'Dorset'.[5] If the Army was ever going to persuade its soldiers that their sacrifices were necessary, some basic civics education might be in order. If it worked, it might bolster morale at a moment when little seemed to be going right for the British war effort. If it did not . . . well, it would be a way of allowing the men to let off some steam, and perhaps get to know their officers a little better. And it would make the winter months pass faster.

So in June 1941, the Army Bureau of Current Affairs (ABCA) was established with General Adam's blessing. ABCA's mandate was to produce a regular supply of pamphlets, newssheets and posters which regimental officers could use as the basis for leading a compulsory hour of current affairs education each week. An ABCA travelling theatre unit was also set up to give dramatic performances with a current affairs theme.[6] At the end of 1942, the scheme was expanded through the 'British Way and Purpose' (BWP) training programme, organized this time by the Army Education Corps (AEC). Whereas ABCA dealt largely with matters specifically concerning the war effort, the idea of BWP was to familiarize soldiers with more fundamental information about British life – the institutions of government, the Empire, the United Nations Organization, and (most provocatively of all) proposals for post-war social reform.[7]

Whether ABCA and BWP really made all that much difference to Army morale is not clear. According to a 1944 poll, about three-quarters of soldiers who took part in civics education sessions said they enjoyed them.[8] But that does not necessarily mean that they learned anything that really expanded their understanding of Britain's war aims. Civics meetings could be disheartening. AEC sergeant Anthony Burgess encountered a less than inspired attitude amongst the men he lectured in Britain and Gibraltar. '*We came in because of bloody Poland*', a group of them complained during one meeting. '*Bugger Poland. Us coming in because of Poland has meant these so-called Free Poles shoving their poles into our wives and daughters. The Jews? Bugger the Jews. Why fight for the Jews?*' It was, Burgess thought, 'a depressing session'.[9] But such grandstanding displays of cynicism did not necessarily represent soldiers' true feelings. The moral depravities of the enemy offered pretty compelling justification for the war by themselves. The gunners of Richard Hoggart's anti-aircraft regiment were hardly wide-eyed innocents. Yet all of them, in Hoggart's view, regarded it as axiomatic 'that Hitler's was an evil regime and Mussolini's comically vile'.[10] Rotterdam, Coventry, Lidice and Belsen may have provided all the evidence that British soldiers needed as to why they were participants in a noble crusade.

It was the *party* political implications of ABCA and BWP which would, in the end, generate the greatest controversy. By the end of 1942, with the Americans on the Allied side, Alamein fought and won and the German Army's martyrdom at Stalingrad well under way, the emergency period of the war had clearly come to an end. Victory over the Axis powers seemed more and more inevitable. British minds were beginning to turn to the peace that would follow that victory. As soon as the war was over, everyone knew that a parliamentary general election (delayed since 1940) would take place. Britain's servicemen and -women would be a key constituency in that election. It might matter a great deal, then, what these future voters had been told about domestic economic and social policy during their Army education sessions. Some senior officers and members of the Conservative-dominated coalition government suspected that ABCA and BWP were being used as a means of covert Labour propagandizing by left-leaning officers and NCOs. One general reportedly had 10,000 ABCA pamphlets burned, describing their contents as 'rank treason'.[11] Churchill himself made an early, though unsuccessful, attempt to close down ABCA, claiming that it would be 'prejudicial to discipline'.[12]

These Tory fears that Army education was systemically biased against them were heightened in February 1944, when a mock parliament set up by service personnel in Cairo voted in a hypothetical post-war Labour government by a large majority.[13] The group was quickly suppressed by rattled staff officers. But seventeen months later, the forecast made at the Cairo Parliament was shown to be prophetic: in a stunning reverse, Churchill was thrown out of office after an election landslide for Labour which saw the People's Party win 393 constituencies and secure an overall Commons majority of 145. Elaborate preparations had been made to allow servicemen across the world to take part in the election, and it was an open secret afterwards that the Forces vote had been overwhelmingly to Labour's benefit. Frustrated Conservatives griped that their complaints about ABCA and BWP had been confirmed. Army education had been a sneaky way of selling socialism to the troops. The Education Corps, it was said, was the only corps in the British Army that could now boast a general election as one of its battle honours.[14]

Was there anything to this? Probably not much. The Forces vote was so relatively small a slice of the overall national turnout in 1945 that it is unlikely that it did more than secure Labour a few additional seats. Attlee was going to win handsomely anyway, no matter who the men and women in uniform voted for.[15] And the idea that Army Education instructors had it in their power to brainwash large numbers of soldiers has to be taken with a considerable pinch of salt. At its peak strength in 1945 the AEC had an establishment of just 2,218 officers and NCOs, not much of a force by which to proselytize to an Army of three million.[16] Though some of its eager disciples certainly disseminated their little civics tracts 'with the fervour of the early Christian missionaries' their entreaties tended to fall flat.[17] Kingsley Martin, the *New Statesman*'s editor who served as an ABCA guest lecturer, remembered on one warm

Sunday afternoon 'discoursing upon the future of mankind' to an audience of soldiers as they slept snugly on benches.[18] If servicemen overwhelmingly voted Labour – and there is no reason to doubt that they did – it had little to do with the earnest entreaties of education officers one way or the other.

This raises a question: if too much has been made of the importance of Forces Education, what about soldering as a civics education in its own right? Being in the British Army was, after all, about the most intense crash-course in citizenship it was possible for an ordinary person to have. Army service brought men of all kinds of diverse class backgrounds and regional origins together in enforced companionship. It threw together people who otherwise would probably never have met, let alone shared any critical life experience. And it exposed them to truths about national life that in peacetime were rarely so obvious. Army service represented, in particular, an encounter with the British state at its most nakedly and unapologetically authoritarian – an unusually revealing glimpse of raw governmental power. Merely by participating in day-to-day military life, soldiers gained far more insight into the nature of their own society and its people than any number of ABCA pamphlets or serious-minded lectures on the British Way and Purpose could ever have provided. The Army would turn some men's entire mental worlds upside down. Stewart Irwin was a 'tight-arsed little Conservative' when he joined the King's Royal Rifle Corps in 1942. By the time he left the Army five years later, he 'wanted to vote Communist'.[19] To what extent did the experience of wartime soldiering change the way that the British thought about themselves and their country?

In July 1942, Lieutenant Norman Craig travelled with the rest of his battalion from Britain to the Middle East on the troopship SS *Samaria*. It was not a quick voyage. With the Mediterranean closed to most convoy traffic, the *Samaria* had no choice but to follow the convoluted 12,000-mile route down the shore of West Africa, round the Cape of Good Hope, and then northwards along the East African coastline to Aden and Port Tewfik, a journey that could take anything up to ten weeks. For Craig and his fellow officers, situated in airy and commodious above-deck cabins, it was a prolonged but not disagreeable voyage, a jaunt reminiscent of the glamour of the pre-war luxury ocean liners. Wine, cigars and excellent food were plentiful and cheap, and the mess waiters attentive. Officers had little to do apart from read, drink and gossip. In the evenings, their smoke-filled lounge reverberated to the sound of piano notes, clinking glasses and laughter, as the subalterns strolled on the open boat deck to enjoy the cool breeze of the night air and to watch the twinkling of unfamiliar constellations.

For Craig's men down below, however, things were very different:

> The only furniture in the gloomy messdecks was the long benches and rows
> of plain wooden tables, where food from the galley was dished out. At night
> hammocks were strung up side by side with hooks fixed to the low ceiling.
> They covered every spare inch of space . . . the congestion was bad enough
> in itself but in the tropics the sweltering heat and suffocating atmosphere
> turned the place into an inferno. Apart from occasional spells on the
> cramped troop deck above, the men were confined below, playing cards,
> reading or scribbling letters – clad only in shorts and canvas shoes, with
> perspiration streaming off their bodies. They had precious little sleep at
> night . . . it was a horrible journey for them.[20]

About two million British servicemen took the Cape route to Egypt or India
during the Second World War, the great majority of them rank-and-file soldiers.
It was – for the ORs anyway – an experience which rarely reflected much credit
on the Army. Harry Wilson described his troopship heading for North Africa in
1941 as 'a stinking prison', its odours including 'the maggoty, muttony smell of
the galleys, the smell of the latrines (when out of order, which often), the hot,
humid smell of the mess tables with their pots and dixies, the musty smell of the
ship's hold and lastly the smell of ourselves, our vomiting, and of our sweaty
bodies especially at night when they lie close together half-naked, on floors,
tables, and in the hammocks'.[21] All of which would have been a lot more tolerable had it not been obvious to the ORs that their officers were having an infinitely more pleasant time right above their heads.

But then receiving a commission during the Second World War gave you
access to a very different set of conditions of service than the ones you had had
to accept as a rank-and-file soldier. William Shebbeare confessed that he was
'amazed at the incredible increase in my comforts' when he became an officer.[22]
Life, agreed Anthony Cotterell in 1941, was very different in the Army once
you had a commission. You slept better, because your bed was more comfortable. You woke better too, because someone was there to hand you up a cup of
tea in the morning. Nobody shouted at you any longer. Indeed, instead of
trying to find and punish all your faults, the sergeant major was now at pains
to obscure them from sight – for so far as the Army was concerned, you were
never officially to make a mistake again. 'You wear a collar and tie', rhapsodized
Cotterell,

> and the first few days you fumble inexpertly with the stud. You wear shoes
> and they feel like plimsolls after army boots. The trousers feel soft as peach

skin. You let your hair grow and you manicure your nails. Instead of having to do everything for yourself, you don't have to do anything. In the ranks you spend a large part of your spare time getting ready for tomorrow, every little errand every little chore you have to do yourself. But now someone else scrapes the mud off your boots, someone else takes the letter to the post, someone else books the trunk call, someone else does the laundry. And as you are walking along the road, the army car pulls up and the driver asks if he can give you a lift.[23]

As an officer, ordinary soldiers saluted you and called you 'sir'. You received better pay and allowances than them. You got more clothing coupons, a higher pension if invalided out, first class rail travel, a separate mess, and a personal batman or manservant to handle your cleaning and laundry. You were awarded different, more prestigious medals if you were brave in combat; and you were rather more likely to get a medal in the first place. If captured by the enemy, the Geneva Convention said that you did not have to perform manual labour.[24] The food you received was strikingly better than anything doled out to the ORs in the cookhouse – a point that was not lost on the men themselves. A disgruntled signaller noted the stark difference between the dinner menus for the officers and Other Ranks of 48th Division Signals on one December evening near Christmas in 1939:

Officers:
   Brown Windsor; Grilled Fillet of Plaice; Roast Pheasant; Bread Sauce; Baked potatoes and Brussels sprouts; Christmas pudding; Sardine parmesan; Dessert; Coffee.

Men's mess:
   Bread; Butter; Meat paste.[25]

This does not mean that the officer–man relationship was the same in every regiment of the Army. Being in the Grenadier Guards was very different from being in the Royal Army Pay Corps. The way that officers and men regarded one another might depend a good deal on a unit's unique function and history, its peculiar traditions of peacetime recruitment and the proclivities of its commanding officer. At the outbreak of the war, Norman Smith served as a trooper in the 5th Royal Inniskilling Dragoon Guards. He complained afterwards of the 'unbridgeable gap' between the regiment's patrician officers and the ordinary soldiers. Many of the former, he thought, 'were not excessively bright and had an exaggerated idea of their gentility and an inadequate understanding of the intelligence and sensibility' of the soldiers they commanded. They would never have dreamed, for instance, of all ranks bedding down in bivouacs alongside one another. The colonel's taste for spit-and-polish was obsessive and wearying.[26] By contrast, the Territorial battalion of the Welch Regiment that novelist and newly commissioned subaltern Anthony Powell found himself posted to in 1939 had a very different mental atmosphere. Powell's fellow officers were middle-class South Walians, bankers predominantly, while the battalion's ORs were mostly miners, many of them old workmates from the local collieries who were related to one another in complex webs of kinship and marriage. There was little pretence at military formality. The officers, though better educated than their men, were tempera-mentally similar to them, and had a good understanding of how they viewed the world. The homely patterns of civilian life had been translated seamlessly from pub and pit-face to the barracks, something that smoothed but also in some ways complicated the battalion's disciplinary relationships. Though keen to do their best, few of its private soldiers had any interest in serving as NCOs, preferring to remain without rank rather than be forced into the embarrassing situation of giving orders to their cousins and 'butties'.[27]

Relations between officers and men were actually at their best when they were all facing common hardships in the face of the enemy. Fighting units tended to enjoy greater shared camaraderie across the ranks; the selfless pater-nalism that was supposed to be the foundation of all officer–man relations only really came into its own on the front line. Andrew Wilson felt it in the 'shared meals, the silent preparations for battle, the closeness of bodies in smoke-filled turrets, the jokes and obscenities' through which all soldiers hid their anxiety before combat.[28] Officers, leading from the front, were much more likely to be killed or wounded in action than their men, which made their first-class railway tickets and their occasional servings of sardine parmesan seem like rather modest compensations. At its best, the comradeship of the front expunged class division entirely – at least for a little while. 'We had complete trust in each other', thought Brian Aldiss of the West Country infantrymen that he struggled up the Manipur Road to Kohima alongside in 1944:

> We worked as a machine . . . all the training, all the ritualization of speech, had prepared us for this amazing, marvellous unity. Every fucker there loved every other fucker. The hierarchical structure of the British Army had triumphed over the class structure of the British. The difference between them came like illumination. Class divides, is meant to divide; hierarchy unites, is meant to unite. Officers, NCOs, men, from the old Brig down-wards, we were all comrades-in-arms.[29]

The intimacy forged by combat could become a platonic love that transcended rank. Writing to his mother in February 1944, Rifleman Jack Armstrong struggled to explain his feelings on the death of his company commander, Captain Strick. 'As I sit here and write you these few lines, I am broken hearted', he began:

Mother, I don't know what I shall do now. There just isn't any future for me . . . we always said to each other, we were each other's luck. There was something in that, mother, because we never left each other's side, no matter how bad the circumstances were . . . I have lost my best friend – the best in the world.[30]

But few soldiers had much experience of the sharp end's primitive solidarity. For the majority of troops encamped during the war in the UK or at a rear-area base overseas, the privileges of rank were simply a fact to be observed – conspicuous, irrelevant to the war effort, indefensible, and grotesque. Depots, thought Norman Craig, 'had a way of bringing out the worst in officers'.[31] Egyptian base life was, to Neil McCallum, the natural habitat of those 'hoary mahogany-coloured' captains and majors obsessed with 'stilted, befogged ritual' and their own creature comforts.[32] In such dreary backwaters, officers, far from being the attentive guardians of their men, often disappeared from their lives altogether. They were 'a race apart', thought Jack Garnham-Wright, 'immune from the rigours which so much dominated the lives of the other ranks'.[33] When they *were* visible, too often it was precisely when they were abusing their privileges. Officers used Army vehicles for private recreational purposes. They reserved the best local bars and hotel lounges exclusively for their own use.[34] Excessive drinking by subalterns was regarded as a serious problem. It was, thought Herbert Moran, an unedifying but common experience in 1940 and 1941 to see officers in their messes 'deliberately getting blind drunk and smashing every conceivable thing they could lay their hands on . . . telephones would be ripped off the walls, lamps torn off their fittings, chairs broken up to matchwood, tables destroyed, and the most wild extravagances and absurdities of behaviour indulged in'.[35]

The relationship between wartime officers and men could not help but be coloured by this inconsistency in the way they were treated. A survey taken in Burma and India in 1945 revealed 'extreme discontent' amongst ordinary soldiers about the 'excessive disparity in the privileges enjoyed by the higher ranks' in the theatre. 'The officers live like lords and the ORs do all the work', one man complained. 'He gets the best of everything, and we get what's left over', grumbled another.[36] Such behaviour was deeply embarrassing to Whitehall in the midst of what was supposed to be a people's war. A letter from a Black Watch private in December 1942 which reached the adjutant-general's office complained that 'remarkably few junior officers and fewer NCOs appear to have the least conception of the true meaning of leadership. It is too often interpreted as disdainful patronage; the attitude of the teacher to the infants' class; or plain bullying with a flavour of the prison warder's style.' John Sparrow's quarterly morale reports were replete with similar complaints about the 'selfishness and lack of consideration' said to be displayed by regimental officers towards their men. Sparrow worried that there was a connection between the poor behaviour of officers and British soldiers' animation about Soviet Communism. 'Russia', he warned, 'is evidently looked upon as a paradise of freedom and justice, with a benevolent government which provides unlimited scope for the individual.' Selfish officers were doing more work to produce disaffected soldiers than any number of communist agitators.[37]

We should be careful not to read too much into any of this. Some of the lauding of Russia in the barrack room may have represented genuine admiration for the feats of the Red Army. But it may also have been soldiers indulging in an opportunity to wind up their superiors. Alexander McKee thought ORs were always looking for any occasion for some 'calculated insubordination not contemplated in King's Regulations'.[38] Frustrating an earnest officer-lecturer at an ABCA session by espousing red-in-tooth-and-claw Bolshevism was too good an opportunity to pass up. It is unlikely that many of the men who harangued Major Elliott during his lecture were really all *that* passionate about communism one way or the other. What probably excited them more was the chance to tweak a commissioned officer's dignity with no danger of repercussions.

Only occasionally was British Army authority enforced with such cack-handed ineptitude that it produced any really dangerous breakdown in discipline. An example would be the SS *City of Canterbury* incident in January 1942, when over 200 servicemen refused to board a troopship in Durban harbour after they discovered that the quaters they were to be housed in were covered with coal dust, excrement, vomit and vermin. Even the senior officer sent to discipline the troops was shocked by what he found, and the War Office responded to the affair by appointing six Inspectors of Troopships whose job was to ensure that officers in transit were no longer allowed to live in luxurious isolation from the conditions their men faced.[39] But such events were exceptional. The most famous disciplinary incident of the war, the so-called 'Salerno Mutiny' of September 1943, barely simmered compared to the much more violent disturbances that broke out in France during the First World War.[40] British Army officer–man relations could be sullen at times, but they never deteriorated to the level which compromised the fighting ability of the French

Army in 1940 or the Italian Army throughout the war.[41] Some British officers were pompous and unimaginative. But they were rarely as blatantly corrupt and indifferent to the well-being of their men as the leaders of, say, Mussolini's *Regio Esercito*. The Army was wise enough to provide ways for ORs to air their grievances harmlessly – education sessions being one obvious example, but also the various Forces newspapers such as *Union Jack* and *SEAC*, slick and professionally edited periodicals with leader columns and letters pages that offered excellent opportunities for blowing off steam.[42] One night during the Anzio offensive, as the troops were moving forward for an attack, Raleigh Trevelyan overheard an officer with a public school accent shrieking 'for Heaven's sake, there, get a move on, get a *move* on' in a high-pitched nasal voice. Suddenly, a voice rang out from the ranks: '*Shut yer trap, la-di-dah.*' That was about as close to revolution as the British Army got during the Second World War.[43]

Still, the way in which the Army endorsed gaping inequalities of privilege could leave a nasty taste in the mouth. Norman Wray marked the start of his political radicalization to a freezing winter's afternoon in 1942, when he and the rest of his battalion stood for more than an hour in front of the club house on Sunningdale golf course waiting for King George VI and 'a bevy of red-tabbed staff officers' to inspect them. The men had spent days in preparation for this moment, polishing and blancoing their uniforms and kit exquisitely. 'The King', Wray recalled, 'walked by me and several hundred other poor sods. He was bored and we were bored.' Then it was all over. His Majesty went back to Buckingham Palace. They returned to their chilly and barren Nissen huts. 'The arrogance and lack of interest shown by our betters', reflected Wray, 'burnt a fire of defiance and disquiet within me whose anarchic embers still flame even after fifty years.'[44]

Harry Wilson reflected on his own political awakening after a typical Saturday morning's bull session in which 'officers who display precious little competence in action distinguish themselves prying into mugs and mess tins and looking for loose buttons'. Before the war, Wilson had 'stood in innocent awe of recognized traditions and institutions. To impugn the motives of my superiors never occurred to me'. Now he knew better. Too many officers were 'commissioned scallywags, puppy-dog officers without brains, breeding, competence or good manners, who sniff and snap and back off when faced'. One of the subalterns in his own unit was a perfect example:

> An ignorant pup, meddlesome, officious and disgustingly facetious to his subordinates . . . his idea of humour is to poke fun at defenceless men on parade . . . a wormish individual that would shrivel up under the fixed gaze of a man of character.[45]

Soldiers such as Wray and Wilson were willing to swallow such indignities for the duration of the war itself. But they left a lasting impression all the same. Army service re-emphasized the role of class in British life at a moment in history when it had seemed to be diminishing in its importance. During the 1930s, thanks to the rise in wages enjoyed by manual labourers, the convergence of working- and middle-class standards of living, and the growth of a broadly national leisure culture, class differences had become less clearly demarcated by traditional markers of dress, speech and behaviour. As the *Survey of the Social Structure of England and Wales* put it in 1937, 'All members of the community are obviously coming to resemble one another.'[46] Wartime military life was a reminder that this superficial democratization in tastes had done little to alter the fundamental hierarchies that divided up British society. Class structure 'was duplicated so grotesquely in the services', thought Anthony Burgess, that ordinary soldiers who had hitherto paid it little attention could not help but be awakened to its existence. As one Welsh sergeant said to him: '*Before the war I was red. Now I'm fucking purple.*'[47] Richard Hoggart too believed that the Forces 'reinforced, repeated, set in their own amber, the class-determined definition of British life' in a way that was too obvious to ignore and too obnoxious to defend.[48] John Sparrow worried about this, not so much for its military implications – there was little danger of any catastrophic collapse in morale – but because there was a fundamental 'lack of solidarity' within the Army, drawn along lines of class and rank, which boded ill for the British civic community after the war:

> The ordinary soldier does not fully identify himself with the Army; he looks with detachment upon it and those who control it, and thinks of those in authority, whether political or military, as his governors rather than his leaders . . .
>
> There is a regrettable tendency to think of officers, 'the authorities', and 'the Army' as an impersonal '*they*' – a body of a different caste, a large part of whose function consists in badgering the soldier about, for reasons which he does not understand.[49]

Those officers who were part of that resented 'impersonal they' saw things rather differently, of course. They did not feel themselves to be all that privileged. Leadership had its perks, to be sure, but also its penalties. The glamour of a commission was typically short-lived. Much of the officer's daily life involved dull, thankless paperwork, thanks to the Army's voracious appetite for red tape (even its list of forms was 200 pages long).[50] And being an officer was not as well compensated as it superficially seemed. A newly commissioned second lieutenant's pay rise on promotion was often more than cancelled out by the deduction of financial benefits he had previously received as an OR, especially if he had dependants at home. By 1943, the War Office was estimating that a junior married officer's expenses were typically exceeding his emoluments by £20 a year. In terms of income, he was 'probably worse off than anyone else in the Army'.[51]

Many wartime officers came from the same social backgrounds as the soldiers they commanded. Thanks to Adams's shakeup of the candidacy system, by the end of the war two-thirds of all new entrants being accepted for OCTU instruction were men who had been educated outside the public school system. One in five of them had gone to no more than an elementary school.[52] The war would produce such unlikely subalterns as Louis Heren, a former messenger boy who had grown up in the East End slums, and Alf Smith, who had left school at fourteen to go and work in an engineering firm.[53] By 1945, the rough-hewn accents of Tyneside and Liverpool and the Black Country were being heard amongst the *I-say-old-chap* hum of officer's messes throughout the world.

The officer of 'unconventional' background was often a liminal figure, neither entirely comfortable within the circle of his new peers nor welcome any longer amongst the men he had left behind. William Graham, a conscript from South Yorkshire, encountered a 'considerable gulf' between wartime subalterns like himself and the regular officers of the battalion he was commissioned into, the 1st Cameron Highlanders. 'We were much more democratic and I think less ready to be regimented', he recalled after the war. 'We did all kinds of things that were wrong, conventions that we either didn't know about or didn't care about ... in the mess you always had to stand up when a senior officer entered the room, the senior officers had their own chairs, [there were] all the silly conventions about passing the port to the left.'[54] Officers who lacked the legitimizing credential of a public school tie were suspected by their seniors of being feckless and immature. 'Beardless young OCTU products ... much too delighted with their new uniforms' were blamed for paying inadequate attention to their men.[55] The commander of one training brigade complained to the War Office that officer cadets of obscure provincial origins were bringing to their work a lack of seriousness and a cynical absence of interest in their responsibilities. Sparrow noted these criticisms in his reports to the adjutant-general's morale committee in 1942, but pointed out that much the same accusations were being made about junior Guards officers as those in other regiments – even though the Brigade of Guards had an independent officer selection process which still relied on traditional 'promising sources'.[56] In other words, if the Army's junior officers were behaving badly by 1942, it was hardly fair to single out the non-public schoolboys.

It was not easy to be a subaltern in an army more self-conscious about class than ever before. Old-fashioned aloofness towards the men was out. But overly familiar chumminess, or appearing to curry favour, was frowned on as well. Striking the right balance in how you behaved towards the ORs under your command was difficult, particularly for officers who might have little in common with them and a tin ear for small-talk. Harry Wilson's company commander Captain Stone insisted on travelling in the same carriage as some of his men on one long train journey through the Middle East. But his compassionate gesture fell flat when he began to bristle at the bad language the troops were using. 'Really, who does Captain Stone think he is!' complained Wilson in his diary. 'A clergyman in charge of a Sunday School outing? If his soul is too sensitive for strong language why does he travel with the men? If he prefers the odour of sanctity why doesn't he travel alone? We don't want him with us. We want to enjoy our naughty jokes and songs without being made self-conscious and without taking them seriously.'[57] Officers were not supposed to fraternize with ORs off duty, however intellectually simpatico they might be. Private Julian Maclaren-Ross had to hide in second lieutenant Woodrow Wyatt's digs on winter evenings as the two discussed literature, because they couldn't be seen together in public ('like a bloody courting couple', Wyatt joked).[58] Authority in the British Army was founded on tribalism, on the idea that you stuck to your own kind at all times. Mutual respect could – and indeed was supposed to – transcend the divide of rank. But friendship was out of the question. Indeed, respect and friendship were inimical to one another. After being promoted to lance-bombardier, Eric Ambler was bawled out by his sergeant for allowing an ordinary soldier to address him by his first name:

'That gunner . . . you've got on well with him, eh? He's one of your pals?'
'Yes, sergeant.'
'Not any longer he isn't. He's a gunner and you're the NCO in charge. You remember that. It's not the NCO's business to be a nice chap or a pal . . . when I hear gunners talking amongst themselves and they say '*that bastard*' about an NCO, I know I've got a good one.'[59]

Despite their complaints about unfair privileges, private soldiers were no less emotionally committed to this division than NCOs and officers. Barrack rooms were deeply conservative spaces, imbued with a powerful sense of them-and-us comradeship. Even simply accepting a 'tape' and becoming a lance-corporal, the most elementary step on the promotional ladder, could be seen as a betrayal by the rest of your mates because it placed you in a position of giving them orders.[60] No one in the Army was more despised than an OR with undisguised ambition, particularly because too many junior leaders were believed to receive their tapes unfairly. In a questionnaire given to twenty-six soldiers ranging in rank from major-general to corporal, there was consistent agreement that promotion to lance-corporal was based primarily on 'smartness in saluting', 'personal appearance' and a 'good loud voice' rather than more pertinent qualities of intelligence, technical competence or man-management skill.[61] Reg Crimp noted the change in behaviour of his section leader, Corporal Trueby, after he received his second tape and his aspirations for further promotion were aroused:

> He [used to] manage the section well, mucked in cheerfully, disclaimed all emphasis on rank (humorously professing his authority to be negligible), always undertook a lion's share of the work, and certainly didn't shirk any of the stickier jobs . . . now he fusses around to make sure everyone gets up on time, insists on our kit being laid out in perfect symmetry each morning, even though no Company orders require it, and is always inclined to take a disparagingly critical interest in the personal appearance of anyone going into Tripoli on leave. As for himself he's a paragon of scroopness [tidiness]: carefully laundered shirt and shorts, knife-edged pressed; belt blancoed to dazzling whiteness; brasses and cap-badges you can see your face in; tapes, lanyard and ribbon all in precise evidence. The trouble is he doesn't seem able to understand how any of the section can fail to share his zeal, and signs to the contrary make him very impatient.[62]

By October, 1944, Trueby had achieved his ambition of becoming battalion signals sergeant, and his zeal for punctilious correctness had become even more unbearable: 'He bustles around the parades, harrying incessantly', complained Crimp, 'with an almost fanatical gleam in his eye.'[63]

If a single tape was enough to set you apart from your mates, then a commission meant permanent exile from the cosy communality of the barrack room. Some potential subalterns baulked at this prospect. 'What the hell do I want to be an officer for?' thought Gerald Kersh after his first pre-OCTU interview:

> Where will it get me? As soon as I put a pip on my shoulder I set myself socially apart from the ordinary man in uniform. I cut myself off from intimacy with the common grousing soldier. As soon as I become an officer all the Dusties, Tugs, Knockers, Gingers and Macs will call me 'sir' and conceal their thoughts from me; put on a respectful face and stand to attention when they talk to me . . . as an officer, however earnestly I go in for hearty fraternisation and fatherly tenderness, there will be a barrier between us, and if I break down that barrier I shall be a bad officer.[64]

The Army may have been internally divided. But when it came to its relationship with civilians, it quickly closed ranks. Soldiers were united by a common disdain for everyone outside their own barrack gates. There was a peculiar cognitive dissonance to this. Wartime conscripts were emphatic that they were *not* regular soldiers, but merely citizens in temporary fancy dress. They rejected traditional Army values. They remained deeply attached to, and anxious about, the families and friends they had left behind. Yet after several years of military service, they had nonetheless acquired just the same hostility towards 'damned civvies' as the regulars. Dennis Argent was as half-hearted a conscript as you could imagine, a middle-class pacifist who registered with the greatest reluctance in the Non-Combatant Corps. But after two years in the Army, he realized to his own surprise that he had begun to acquire what he called 'the real old soldier's outlook'. The 'tawdry tarting of Luton streets on a Sunday night' drove him to fury. 'I'd like to see a bit of discipline enforced on some of Luton's noisy youth.'[65] Strikes by miners and other industrial workers back in Britain infuriated troops overseas ('try them for desertion' was a typical comment in the *Union Jack* letters column in Italy).[66] Wartime soldiers condemned the moral failures of civilians even as they insisted that they were civilians at heart themselves.

Complaints about differential scales of pay were the most obvious expression of this. No other single wartime issue prompted as many inquiries to Professor John Hilton, who offered advice to servicemen through a BBC radio programme and a *News of the World* column.[67] The British soldier had always been poorly remunerated, but by the mid-point of the war the Army's pay scale had fallen so hopelessly behind that of civilian war industry that it had become scandalous. An ordinary private soldier in early 1942 was earning 17 shillings and sixpence a week, at a time when a worker in the metal, engineering and shipbuilding trades might be bringing home almost six pounds. Even taking into account the fact that soldiers did not have to pay for their own food and lodging, this still left them with less than half the disposable income that they might have had if they had remained on civvy street. It was, thought *The Times*, hard to avoid the 'glaring contrast' between the fortunes of the nation's fighting men and those at home.[68] As one sergeant major put it, 'The soldier really begins to grouse when he goes into a pub and finds that he can only afford a single glass of beer, whilst the munition worker slaps down a £1 note and asks for whisky or gin.'[69] Not until spring 1944, however, was there any serious attempt by the government to narrow the gap between service and civilian compensation.[70] And even then, the British soldier still remained grossly underpaid compared to his American or Dominion counterpart. It is not difficult to see why he thought of himself as a member of an underappreciated 'peasant army'.[71]

The pay problem, though, was really just one expression of a deeper crisis of masculinity that beset wartime British soldiers. By 1942, many of them were overseas and haunted by worries about their families' financial plight in their absence.[72] It was important to male working-class respectability that the pater-familias visibly provide for his wife and children (one of the reasons why the dole queues of the 1930s had been so humiliating). Soldiers were left feeling insecure and embarrassed when their wives were required to leave the feminine sphere of the household and take up work in war industry. Plus, sexual jealousy was rife. Even more detested than the overpaid munitions factory lout and the indolent, pampered GI with his fat wallet and fatter mouth was the unfaithful British 'good-time girl' who slept with them both. 'Nothing did more to lower the morale of troops serving overseas than news of female infidelity, or the suspicion of it', thought Sparrow.[73] Servicewomen overseas were said – fairly or not – to be doing the reputation of their sex no favours by their flirtatious behaviour with officers and their correspondingly dismissive attitude towards the ORs. The 'prim and superior' ATS girls in Cairo in autumn 1943 were interested only in monopolizing the attention of lieutenants and above, complained Reg Crimp: 'They're at a premium, and know it. Nothing under two pips is good enough. Drinking at Shepheard's and dancing at Groppi's is just the job.'[74] Through such provocations the home front itself became thought of as an essentially feminine place, embodying in the soldier's mind all the supposed evils of women – their shallow materialism, their venality and pleasure-loving, their sexual inconstancy.[75]

The home front was also a place said to be so wrapped up in its own concerns that it had little time to listen to the soldier's. On returning to England on leave in early 1945, Norman Smith found himself alienated by the 'staggering peacetime normality' of everyday life – *why should these people be so immune*, he found himself thinking, *when at this very minute up on the Maas one of my mates in "B" Squadron may be fried to eternity or lying in a pool of his own blood?*[76] In Italy, Peter R. Hopkinson captured the Army's irritation nicely in his poem 'Neapolitan Interlude'.

My mail has just caught up with me
And that's about time too.
I'll soon find out what England thinks
And what is fresh and new . . .

'What England thinks', Hopkinson's narrator discovers, is that *it*, and not the soldier in the fighting line, is bearing the brunt of the war. Auntie Gwen in Dover lives in fear of the German guns in Calais, which she insists aim at her front door every day – even though in reality they haven't fired for months. Uncle George moans about the 30,000 aircraft off to bomb Berlin which wake him up at night. Cousin Egbert grumbles that two or three days' service a week in the Home Guard is wearing him out. At the end of the poem, Hopkinson's D-Day Dodging protagonist hunkers down in his slit trench in Campania, as the dive bombers and the anti-tank guns serenade him to sleep, and reflects ruefully how lucky he is not to be facing the 'real' war at all:

> *How proud I am of all my folk*
> *At home who bear the brunt,*
> *While I hide out in Napoli*
> *To dodge the Second Front.*[77]

Soldiers predicted that when they returned home they would be bilked of the rewards of victory by greedy civilians. There was, as one of the official military histories put it, 'a general expectation . . . that they would suffer much the same fate as their fathers, who had been glibly promised "a country fit for heroes to live in" and had subsequently spent many years drawing unemployment benefits'.[78] Civilian war workers who had enjoyed Reserved Occupation status would take all the best jobs and houses for themselves.[79] Ex-soldiers would be left to sell matches on street corners once again. Some of them predicted that violence would be the result. If his men didn't get 'jobs and homes and a modicum of comfort and leisure', worried Captain A. M. Bell MacDonald in May 1944, 'then woe betide the country. Revolution will not be far behind.' Not necessarily 'knitting bees below a guillotine or rivers of blood', he quickly added. 'But a fair sized upheaval . . .'[80]

In the end, of course, no such military Reign of Terror took place. Certainly, during the war many soldiers retreated into what journalist Frank Owen called a 'mental concentration camp' of their own making. But no organized movement of resentful veterans, trained in warfare and habituated to violence, emerged at the end of the conflict of the kind that had brought terror to Italy in the 1920s.[81] British parliamentary democracy was re-legitimated by victory. The peace settlement proved stable, even if it was guaranteed by the threat of atomic holocaust. Mosley's Blackshirts attempted to exploit the grievances of the demobbed in 1945 by the launch of an 'ex-serviceman's league', but it soon ran out of steam. Post-war Britain turned out to be unpromising territory for a demagogue. It was a land of full employment and the welfare state. The post-war labour market was tight; ex-soldiers were quickly able to take advantage of the pay gains that civilian workers had secured during the war (those same fat wage packets that had disgusted them while the fighting was on). Former servicemen who three or four years earlier were demanding that strikers be arrested were quickly won over to the possibilities of industrial action once they were back in the civilian workforce themselves. There was no army of disenchanted paupers for a would-be British Duce to manipulate.[82] The desire for a coherent and distinctive ex-service voice in public life after 1945, such as it existed, was more than adequately satisfied by sober institutions such as the British Legion, which, despite some accusations of its Tory bias in the late 1940s, remained largely aloof from partisan politics and restricted its campaigning to issues such as the plight of disabled pensioners. The bitterness that many men in uniform nursed towards civilians back in Britain was a transient emotion, born of contingent grievances that were quickly resolved once the war was over. It never intensified to the point that soldiers began to think of themselves as an entirely different, and superior, embodiment of the nation.[83]

Still, the question remains: to what extent had Army service influenced the political mood of Britain by the end of the war? There is some good evidence that working-class soldiers had had their sense of class awareness powerfully reinforced, and that the Labour Party was the primary beneficiary of this.[84] By 1944, Tom Harrisson was already predicting that the 'traditional, largely inevitable impatience of the soldier' was coming to acquire a specifically political bent that was likely to be expressed in support for a radical parliamentary agenda.[85] 'Everywhere I go', Harry Wilson had written in the Western Desert two years earlier, 'I see the same line of talk [in the Eighth Army] – there seems to be a decided socialist trend in the British ranks, a definite antagonism to the rich and privileged. If the post-war government ignores this trend it may find itself ousted by a radical socialist administration.'[86] Military life had provided a thorough schooling in 'the expression of grievance' which historian Ross McKibbin has described as the quintessential emotion which brought Labour to power in 1945.[87]

Many junior officers were caught up in this sense of grievance against the old order. After five or six years of being buggered about by the Army themselves, even propertied ex-public schoolboys who represented the Tory Party's natural voting constituency were weary of the Establishment. One of the key reasons for the scale of Attlee's victory in 1945 was the Labour Party's success in attracting middle-class voters in southern England. Disgruntled subalterns helped throw Churchill out.[88] Their flirtation with Labour was to be short lived once they were demobbed. But the experience of commanding ordinary men and of dealing with the day-to-day problems of the rank and file would have a lasting influence on the British political mood. John Sparrow noted in one of his morale reports that the war had revealed to many privileged young men just how 'the other half of the world' lived.[89] Such officers would remain Conservative by inclination, but they could never again be quite so dismissive of the problems of the working class. A generation of consensus 'wets' who would dominate the Tory leadership in the 1960s and 1970s – Edward Heath, Willie Whitelaw, Peter Carrington, Francis Pym, Ian Macleod, Anthony Barber, Ian Gilmour – would take their military sense of *noblesse oblige* with them into high office (much to the disgust of Margaret Thatcher, who, never having served in uniform during the war, remained uncontaminated by what she saw as woolly-headed sentimentality).[90]

All the same, it is important not to confuse support for Labour in 1945 with a long-term commitment to its philosophy of government. Soldiers may have voted as a bloc to kick out the Conservatives in 1945, but that does not mean that they had become deeply and permanently attached to the ideals of socialism. Duff Cooper, Ambassador to France and a former Conservative secretary of state for war, noted perceptively after the election that 'to the private soldier the government is the War Office, and the War Office is the sergeant major'. Voting was a 'brief and blessed opportunity' for the soldier to express his opinion, not of the government as such, but of the sergeant major (or, in the case of subalterns, the adjutant).[91] Of course, individual soldiers voted for Attlee in the summer of 1945 for all the same complex reasons as civilians. But Duff Cooper was surely on to something. There was a touch of the carnivalesque about the 1945 election. Voting against the government was a way of blowing a loud raspberry at 'them' and everything 'they' seemed to stand for. It was not a commitment to any clearly understood set of economic prescriptions. The British soldier, thought one 21st Army Group captain, was 'deeply distrustful of all civilian authority – parliamentary, municipal, and industrial'. He disliked the Tories – but he also had his doubts about Labour too:

> He distrusts the reforms that are brought in, either because they are too late or because they were grudgingly introduced under such pressure that he doubts whether they will ever be honourably implemented . . . in short, the British soldier is fighting for the future of the world and does not believe in that future.[92]

John Sparrow detected the same lack of confidence in the democratic system amongst the troops, and was dismayed by it. The 'narrow and uninstructed' views of many soldiers 'boded ill' for the future of the country, he wrote in autumn 1945 soon after the general election. 'While the army is becoming largely a civilian army, I do not think that it can claim to be an Army of citizens in the true sense of the word. Though most of the soldiers I met may have

voted "Socialist", few of them seemed to have any sense of social responsibility."[93] Sparrow's inclinations were Conservative and his suspicions about
Labour voters therefore far from objective. Yet many Labour Party activists
would soon be complaining themselves about just this lack of civic engagement
amongst their own supporters, the unwillingness of the working class to make
a permanent commitment to active, responsible citizenship.[94]

The citizen-soldier, as J. B. Priestley put it in his 1945 *Letter to a Returning
Serviceman*, found himself a 'sharply divided man' when it came to re-engaging
in civil life at the end of a long war. 'He faces two ways', thought Priestley:

> There is a conflict in him, and I suspect that it is this conflict that makes him
> appear less radiantly happy, far more weary and wary, than people expect him
> to be. One half of him wants to settle up, the other half wants to settle down.
> Sharing the same billet in his mind are an earnest revolutionary and a tired
> and cynical Tory ... one wants to reorganize society, and the other wants
> privacy and a domestic life. The red half cries: '*It's your duty now to fight for
> security and social justice for all*', and the blue half retorts: '*You've done enough.
> Find a job, keep quiet, and try growing tomatoes.*'[95]

Priestley, as a committed man of the left, wanted to counsel his readers not to
be 'hermits in bungalows', but rather participants in what he felt to be 'real citizenship'.[96] But his hopes were in vain. Commentators on the mood of the Army
throughout the war often remarked on the desire of most men to escape the
obligatory communitarianism of military life once the fighting was over, and
withdraw back into a life of private domesticity. 'They've had a bellyful of being
ordered about, and are not going to put up with it when the fighting is finished',
thought James Lansdale Hodson.[97] Anthony Cotterell thought that there were
very few soldiers 'who don't want to go back to exactly where they left off . . . It
all seems so cozy in retrospect. The weekends off, the mid-morning cups of tea,
the girls in the office. It all seems so friendly, another world where you weren't
shouted at or pulled out of bed in the morning.'[98]

These were not men, in other words, who were going to find the bureaucracy of Attlee's Britain – its council officials and regulators and Whitehall busy-
bodies – naturally to their taste. There was too much of the sergeant major
about them all. Noel Annan, who served in British military intelligence and
was later vice-chancellor of the University of London, thought that the
members of his intellectual generation had been won over to the idea of state
planning during the war by the success of government-funded military
projects: signals intelligence, radar, weapons development and so on.[99] But the
Army itself was a product of state planning. And the way *it* had operated during

the war had not always been a particularly encouraging advertisement for the efficacy of socialism. As Alan Wood put it in 1942:

> The Army [is] a state monopoly, and so has the natural tendency of all monopolies towards inefficiency, exploitation and nepotism. Since it had no competitors, it is free from the incentives to efficiency, economy and initiative which characterize competitive industry . . . [it has] no sale problems, no bankruptcy court, no need to maximize output, no hustle and bustle to deliver the goods, no hurry and scurry in a feverish race to keep ahead. What is the result? Waste.[100]

Such an organization might be tolerated for the purposes of defeating fascism, but could never really be taken seriously as a model of how to run things properly.

There are many reasons why Labour's victory in 1945 did not have the transformative effect that its most passionate supporters hoped for, why the short-term electoral success of Britain's progressive left could not be translated, in the end, into the creation of a permanent social democratic commonwealth. But perhaps one of them is that the whole project seemed just a little bit too familiar to ex-soldiers – that it had more than a whiff of Churchill's Army about it.

CHAPTER 15

'WHAT A COLOSSAL WASTE OF TIME WAR IS'

For the officers and men of the Sherwood Rangers Yeomanry, peace began as night visions. It was Friday, 4 May 1945, and without warning or explanation hundreds of multi-coloured Verey lights, rockets and searchlight beams were suddenly illuminating the skies over Lower Saxony. Rumours soon began to spread as to what the 'flap' might be about. Then the duty signals sergeant at regimental HQ, his face flushed with excitement, produced a hastily scribbled message from Brigade: '*No advance beyond present positions. No further harassing fire. No practical move without further orders. BBC News confirmed. German Army on 21st Army Group Front surrenders with effect from 0800 hours tomorrow 5 May 1945*.' The message was confirmed by dispatch rider an hour later. That was when the colonel ordered the drinking to start.

For Captain Stuart Hills, who had been pulled from the water off GOLD Beach on D-Day eleven months before when his amphibious tank had sunk unceremoniously into the Channel, it was a moment of painful, complicated bitter-sweetness. 'My first reaction', he wrote later, 'after the initial excitement had died down, was of indescribable relief that the killing was now over.' For the first half hour or so of peace, he was swept along with the bonhomie of champagne and back-slapping. Then the reaction started to kick in. He thought of his parents, who had been captured by the Japanese with the surrender of Hong Kong in December 1941, and were being held – assuming they were even still alive – in a civilian internment camp somewhere in East Asia. He thought, too, of his fellow officers of the regiment who had died during the campaign, including the brilliant, fearless, idiosyncratic poet and writer Keith Douglas, whose account of the battle for North Africa, *Alamein to Zem Zem*, was to become one of the literary classics of the war.

But Hills thought most of all of his best friend Denis Elmore, the young man he had first met at school in Tonbridge in 1940, and who he had enlisted alongside at the Army recruitment office in Maidstone two years later. Throughout the war, the pair had served together as junior officers in the Sherwood Rangers. 'Denis was one of those boys lucky enough to be good at everything', Hills remembered – someone clearly destined to be one of the leaders of his generation in the years to come. Elmore was a natural long-limbed athlete, a gifted intellectual, winner of multiple academic scholarships, and a man who was funny, kind and thoughtful at the same time; a great friend, and an inspiration to all. He had brought to his work as commander of a Sherman tank troop the same cheerful competence with which he did every-thing. Naturally enough, then, he had not flinched from taking the lead when, on the afternoon of 19 April 1945, he had been ordered to advance his troop along an unreconnoitred country road on the outskirts of Bremen. The rest of the men had watched Elmore's tank trundle round a corner and disappear from sight behind a hedgerow. Seconds later, there was a sharp, loud, horribly familiar percussive sound. The 88-mm anti-tank shell which had ripped through the Sherman's turret had killed Denis and two of his crew members instantly, though their blackened corpses could not be extracted from its hull until the fire had burned itself out the morning after. Elmore and his comrades had died barely two weeks before the German surrender.

'It just seemed so unfair that he was not here to see this moment', thought Hills as he watched the revelry of victory:

> He had done as much as anyone to deserve it, but instead [he] lay in the cold earth a few miles back along the road we had liberated. To be cut down so near the end, when he had so much to live for . . . quietly, I put down my glass and slipped away from the celebrations to my bed. I just wanted to be alone.[1]

The war in Europe formally came to an end on 8 May 1945. It had caused the deaths of 121,484 officers and men of the British Army. The war in the Pacific, which would not end for another three months, would, by its conclusion, be responsible for the deaths of a further 22,595 British soldiers. Total British fatalities for the war – Navy, Army, RAF, women's auxiliary services, Home Guard, merchant marine and civilian – would eventually be calculated at 357,116.[2]

That was less than half the number of Britons who had died in the First World War.[3] The Army's relative fatalities had been even lower than that. Only one soldier had died in the Second World War for every five killed in the trenches of the Western Front. This, on the face of it, represented a triumph for the government in general and the War Office in particular. Germany had been defeated once more; only this time, for a fraction of the human cost. The shadow of Colonel Blimp, of callous and incompetent old duffers massacring the nation's young men in futile massed bayonet charges, had been dispelled for good. The Army had redeemed its reputation. The generals of this war, the Montgomerys and Alexanders and Slims, had shown themselves capable and prudent leaders – strategists accomplished in the military arts, without a doubt, but more importantly, commanders who were protective of their men's lives. There would be no bitter recriminations in the pages of the war memoirs *this* time, no wrangling over who had blundered the most criminally, whose hands had the most blood on them.

Seventy years on, it is worth reflecting on how much this good fortune came down to chance rather than to astute decision-making. Churchill's strategy of Indirect Approach between June 1940 and June 1944 saved tens, perhaps hundreds of thousands of British lives.[4] But by itself it did not bring about Germany's defeat, and it never would have. Indeed, if Hitler had not decided to invade the USSR in June 1941, committing as he did the bulk of the *Wehrmacht* to a brutal and ultimately catastrophic land campaign in the east, it is hard to see how the Indirect Approach would ever have achieved anything decisive. One of the reasons that the British Army emerged from the Second World War having suffered far fewer fatalities than in the First was simply that it did not have to bear nearly the same share of the burden of defeating the Germans the second time. If, when Eisenhower's forces had crossed the English Channel on D-Day, they had had to confront not merely several dozen German divisions in the west, but several hundred, it is far from clear that Operation OVERLORD would ever have succeeded. Even if somehow it had, the necessary sacrifice in lives would have been immeasurably greater than that which actually took place. We would remember 6 June 1944 in the same horror-stricken way we remember 1 July 1916. The blunt fact is that British troops in the Second World War did not have to die in the same numbers as their fathers because Russian troops died in their place. That was not the result of strategic genius on Churchill's or anyone else's part. It was sheer bloody good luck.

But such considerations were immaterial if you were one of those people – a mother or father, a wife or sweetheart, a son or daughter, a brother or sister, a schoolmate or colleague, a fellow soldier, a comrade, a friend – who *had* lost a soldier dear to you. The fact that relatively few men had died was no consolation if one of the men who had died was a person you happened to love. Martin Lindsay was second in command, and later commander, of the 1st Gordon

Highlanders from D-Day to V-E Day. During this eleven-month expedition, seventy-five of the officers and 986 of the ORs in his battalion became casualties. One in four of them died. 'I do not believe that anyone can go through a campaign with men such as these, and watch them killed one after the other, and know that their joyous personalities were now but blackened, broken corpses tied up in a few feet of army blanket under the damp earth – and remain quite the same', he wrote after the war. 'For my part I felt that this had made a mark upon me that will never be effaced. It is as if some spring deep down inside me has run down.'[5]

For every shell that killed half a dozen soldiers, half a dozen families a world away were (as Alexander Baron put it) 'rocked with grief . . . to each of them the one dead man was their whole horizon. For each of them the world was plunged into blackness.'[6] It was a void of despair out of which some of them would never emerge. In William Woodruff's autobiographical novel *Vessel of Sadness*, he imagines a thoughtful subaltern writing to the wife of one of his men recently killed in action, a Private Allenby, to express his condolences. The lieutenant reassures her: your husband, Ronald, died a hero. Mrs Allenby writes back in thanks, but also in a kind of reproof. 'I read what you said about him having died a hero's death', she begins,

> but I didn't want my husband to die a hero's death. I wanted him to come home to me. I don't think he and I would have known what a hero was. We wanted to do what was right and proper. But we did so pray for the day when we would be together again. That's all we wanted. We only had each other. We didn't really know much about the war. Now I am alone in the world.[7]

If anything, the situation for women such as Mrs Allenby in 1945 was worse than it had been in 1918. Then, at least, there had been a national community of grief, the small consolation that your private and individual tragedy was being shared by everyone. At the end of the Second World War, sorrow was a minority experience in Britain. Those who had no one to mourn were not particularly inclined to set aside their own satisfaction at the news of victory simply in order to placate the feelings of those who did. There was sympathy, naturally – but also some impatience with those who insisted in dwelling on their private loss. The nation was in a practical mood: forward-thinking, clear-eyed, hard-headed. There were to be no massive public works projects to memorialize the dead this time, no useless 'stone monstrosities', as one commentator dismissed them in 1944. If money was available for commemorative purposes, it ought to be spent on useful things: community centres, parks and open spaces, hospital wings, swimming baths. Some villages built a bus shelter as their memorial to the dead. Others put up railings, or installed electric lighting in the parish church.

Such traditional commemoration as did take place had a postscriptual feel to it, a sense of being bolted on to the rituals of the past – as, sometimes, it literally was. Most British villages and towns already had a war memorial honouring the dead of the Great War. The number of the Fallen of 1914–18 was usually several times greater than the number of local people who had been killed in the war just ended. So the new names were just added to the bottom of the existing memorial, rather than afforded one of their own. Sometimes a bronze plaque was affixed, to save money. In the same way, rather than a wholly new site of national mourning being placed alongside the existing Cenotaph in Whitehall, its sides were simply appended with *MCMXXXIX* and *MCMXLV*. The commemoration of both wars was rolled into something dubbed 'Remembrance Sunday' – not identical with, but closely anchored to, the old Armistice Day of 11 November.[8] It was all done in a very tasteful, thoroughly British way. But there was something of the footnote about it all the same. No one but the bravest would quite come out and say so openly, but there was a widely shared sense in 1945 that the First World War had been, and always would be, the 'real' war, and that this more recent conflict, nobly fought to be sure, simply could never measure up to its tragic profundity.[9]

Indeed, when the Imperial (later Commonwealth) War Graves Commission was first considering its commemorative strategy for the Second World War, some of its members suggested that it would be inappropriate to honour the dead of this lesser conflict with the same grandeur that had been lavished on the Fallen of Flanders and Picardy.[10] In the end the Commission rejected this line of thought and committed itself to building a second international network of cemeteries – 559 were eventually agreed upon – to parallel those it had constructed after 1918.[11] Rising construction costs, manpower shortages and political instability in some of the former theatres of war made the building process much slower than it had been after the Armistice, however. Many of the largest cemeteries would not be completed until the late 1950s.[12] It was decided that, once again, no repatriation of bodies would be permitted. Men were to be buried in the region of the world in which they had died – even if that meant that they would be laid to rest in former enemy territory, a prospect that provoked no small amount of anger in the immediate aftermath of the war, when feelings towards Germany and Japan were at their most bitter. In theory, the decision against repatriation maintained an admirable principle of equality. In practice, it also brought with it a certain amount of class favouritism. The less geographically concentrated nature of the Second World War meant that the graves of the dead were often located far away from Britain: in the southern Mediterranean, in North Africa, the Middle East, India, Burma, Malaya. The government was willing to provide free passage to next-of-kin to visit cemeteries on the Continent, but no further than that.[13] Civilians whose relatives had died outside of Europe, and who did not have the means to finance an expensive trip halfway around the world, were out of luck. For many who had lost a son or a husband or a father on the Mareth Line or at Kohima, a photograph of a distant gravestone was all that they would ever see.

The new cemeteries were built to much the same model and with the same fierce, prescriptive rigour as the grand cities of the dead constructed by Baker, Blomfield and Lutyens. The CWGC sites near old battlefields such as Bayeux and El Alamein and Anzio remain as moving today as they were half a century ago. Still, some soldiers retained mixed feelings about these immaculate parade-ground resting places. As Martin Lindsay oversaw the burial of some of his Highlanders in the grounds of a Normandy chateau in summer 1944, he already foresaw with regret how they would one day be exhumed and removed to a more formal site of commemoration. 'I wished they could all be left to lie where they had been so tenderly placed by those who loved them, near where they fell', he wrote. He knew that the local people, who had seen for themselves how these men had sacrificed all for the liberty of France, would take good care of the graves. Why, then, move them at all? Why dig them up and take them to some vast and forbidding military cantonment, where they would be dressed by the right amongst strangers, regimented in death as they had been in life, forever and ever?[14]

For Anthony Babington, peace began as a 'frenzied screech – a searing of the air all round'. It was 31 October 1944, and he and two men of his company were reconnoitring a small field in southern Holland. Suddenly Babington felt a 'fearful, crushing nothingness' overwhelm him as he fell to the ground. 'I opened my eyes and tried to reorientate my swimming senses', he wrote later:

> There was a loud, continuous buzzing in my head. I fought hard to come to but I seemed to be wedged in the first fleeting phase of returning consciousness . . . at first I thought I had merely been stunned by the blast of an exploding shell which had landed close to me, but I soon realized that it was something far more serious, something the like of which I had never experienced before. I was not aware of any pain, nor even of any definite areas of physical discomfort: it was far worse than that, and far more frightening. I seemed to be drifting in a plane beyond the manifest limits of suffering.[15]

Babington's head wound was so severe that there was some debate at the regimental aid post about whether it was worth wasting an ambulance to send him back to a casualty clearing station – he would surely die on the journey anyway. In the end, they decided to chance it. Within a few hours, he was in a hospital in Brussels; some time later, in a transport plane returning to England. Though intermittently conscious, he had no idea what had happened to him. He could neither move nor speak. His brain, he thought, 'seemed to have lost all contact with my body'.[16] Over the course of several surgeries and many months of excruciating recuperation, some of his faculties began to recover. He was going to live. But his long-term prognosis was grim. The exploding shell had caused major brain damage. The entire right side of his body was apparently paralysed. He had lost the ability to talk, to read and to write. Watching the celebrations on the night the Germans surrendered, Babington felt utterly disengaged from the mood of excitement around him. 'These people were rejoicing, I thought, because their present tribulations were at an end ... for some of us, however, the future would be a barren ordeal which would probably last us the rest of our lives.'[17]

Shortly after V-E Day, he received a medical board inspection and was granted an immediate discharge with a 100 per cent disability pension. 'They told me formally that I was permanently unfit for any form of service whatsoever; that I was no longer required', he wrote in his first memoir, *No Memorial*. The decision was expected, indeed inevitable; but came tinged with grief all the same. 'I had never intended to make the Army my career', he acknowledged. Still:

> There was an inexpressible sadness about the finality of the Board's decision; the fundamental sorrow which always casts its melancholy shadow over any parting of the ways. I seemed to realize for the first time what they were taking away from me; my uniform, my commission, and my job. I was to be a civilian, an ex-serviceman; from now on I was no longer a 'brother officer' to my friends; I was an 'old comrade'; a relationship of the past rather than of the present.[18]

Babington would, as it turned out, make a remarkable recovery from his injuries. As sensation in his right leg slowly returned he was able to re-learn to walk. He recovered the ability to read, to speak and to write with his left hand. Refusing to abandon his pre-war ambition to pursue a legal career, he studied for his bar exams with financial assistance from a government Further Education and Training Scheme, and was called to the Middle Temple in 1948. Later, he became a circuit judge and the author of a number of military histories. He lived, against the odds, to the age of eighty-four.

But his life was irrevocably altered by his injuries. Babington's right arm was permanently paralysed, and so he had to learn many of the basic functions of life – bathing, shaving, dressing, putting on a tie, tying shoelaces, cutting food, spreading butter – from scratch. He had difficulty handling coins, opening envelopes, unscrewing jars. Carrying an umbrella or a briefcase was as encumbering to him as a large parcel would have been for a man with two healthy arms. His handwriting was never easy to read again. He spoke with a pronounced stammer. His balance remained precarious. He suffered from headaches and insomnia. He developed tuberculosis as a complication of his wounds. And his fiancée Emma broke up with him shortly after he returned to England. All her hopes for the future, she explained to him in a letter she sent while he was recuperating in hospital, had been centred around the life that the two of them would share after the war. But that vision had been shattered for ever. They would never be the same people again because of what had happened. She could not bear to see him in the condition he was in. They never spoke to one another again. Emma left England to marry a Rhodesian farmer, Babington learned many years later. It was an unhappy marriage, and she died, alone, of cancer sometime in the 1950s. Until her death, she had kept Babington's photograph by her bedside. He himself never married. 'On that morning in Holland a part of me had died and a part had been reborn', he wrote towards the end of his life. 'I was now a different person, destined to a vastly different experience.'[19]

All told, 239,617 officers and men of the British Army were recorded as having been non-fatally wounded in action during the Second World War.[20] Many were able to make a full recovery and eventually to return to their units. Others, like Anthony Babington, were not. The human body was a frail thing to expose to fire and steel, shrapnel and high explosive, flying concrete and glass. Soldiers were shot, punctured with shell fragments, lacerated by shards of debris. They had their backs broken, their hands and feet scythed off, their limbs pulverized, their eardrums permanently shattered by concussive explosions, their eyes burned out of their sockets. Eric de Mauny described the surgeons at a casualty clearing station during the Battle of Alamein, 'their eyes dark with fatigue, cutting away sections of blood-soaked uniform, trimming, probing and sewing up the gaping flesh with calm and studious concentration'. One young German soldier was wheeled into the operating tent with multiple stomach wounds:

Yards of intestine were hauled out on a metal side tray, each perforation neatly sutured, then the whole lot unceremoniously shoved back into the open space of the abdomen. It was like watching a seemingly impossible repair of a badly punctured bicycle tyre.

Yet somehow, it worked. The German lived.[21] Advances in military medicine – the widespread availability of penicillin and sulphonamides to ward off infection, blood transfusions to resuscitate men in shock, motor and air ambulances to get the critically wounded to rear-area hospitals quickly – meant that survival rates in the Second World War were much better than they had been in the First. By one estimate, a British soldier was twenty-five times more likely to survive a battle wound from 1939 to 1945 than his father had from 1914 to 1918.[22] Over half of all casualties with chest wounds died in the First World War. Only one in twenty did in the Second.[23] This meant that a great many more wounded soldiers survived the war to return home. It also meant that more ex-servicemen had to come to terms with a life-altering disability – blindness, deafness, paralysis, dismemberment, nerve damage, mental impairment, chronic pain – which in the earlier war would have simply killed them off. It meant that more families that had sent their healthy young sons and husbands off to war had afterwards to care for men who might no longer be able to walk or read or pour themselves a glass of water, let alone go out to work.

Given the higher rate of survival from traumatic injury, it is surprising that by the end of 1946 only 412,000 surviving veterans of the Second World War were receiving a disability pension compared to the more than 2.4 million ex-servicemen – about two in five of those who had served – who were granted one after the Great War.[24] But the discrepancy may reflect the parsimony of the Ministry of Pensions as much as any difference in actual war experience. In some respects, the state's treatment of the war disabled was much better in 1945 than it had been in 1918. The rehabilitative therapy it had to offer was more advanced, the prosthetic limbs it could equip amputees with sturdier and more sophisticated.[25] An Employment Act passed in March 1944 required all but the smallest businesses to set aside at least 3 per cent of places in their workforce for the legally disabled. Certain jobs – lift and car park attendants, for instance – were reserved exclusively for disabled employees, principally ex-servicemen. The Ministry of Labour established ninety REMPLOY factories (still operating today) to provide work opportunities for 6,000 men too seriously injured to enter the regular workforce.[26] Blind and crippled ex-soldiers were no longer reduced to begging or selling trinkets on street corners.

But accompanying such enlightened reforms were also fierce battles over pension rights. At the very outset of the war, payment rates for new war disability claimants were dramatically slashed, so that a man who had lost a leg at Dunkirk would be paid less than half the weekly pension of someone who had received a similar injury at Passchendaele a quarter century before. By 1945, the 100 per cent disability pension had risen to 45 shillings a week. But this still represented only a one-shilling increase on the 1918 rate.[27] Many disabled men found themselves in a long and distressing battle of attrition with the Ministry over attempts to downgrade their medical category, and thus their eligibility for pension benefits. 'It was old fogies sitting behind a desk, and there were times when I could have shoved them and their desk through the wall', remembered Jockie Bell, a former prisoner of the Japanese in the Far East. 'It was cruel.'[28] Fred Goddard had been badly wounded in the legs, back and head at Tobruk in June 1941 before being captured by the Italians. He survived his terrible injuries and two years of captivity in Italy before being repatriated home on compassionate grounds. Initially, after his medical discharge from the Army, he was awarded a 30 per cent disability pension. In November 1946, however, he received word that this was going to be reduced to 20 per cent. The reduction would not only mean an immediate cut in his weekly income, but after a year permanent removal from the pension list. As it happened, on the day he was scheduled to go before a tribunal to appeal the decision he was in hospital recovering from one of the many operations he had to undergo to remove shrapnel from his leg. The tribunal was informed that Goddard would be attending the hearing on a stretcher. It was a prospect that was sufficiently embarrassing to sway the minds of the men from the Ministry. A tribunal member immediately phoned back to say not to bother: the appeal had been automatically granted.[29] Such penny-pinching was not exceptional. 'It is the state's plain duty to do all that is just and fitting for war pensioners', suggested *The Times* in August 1948. 'Clearly there is now a widespread belief that this duty is not being fully discharged.'[30]

Worst-off of all were ex-soldiers suffering from psychiatric injuries. By July 1946, around 33,000 financial awards had been made to Second World War servicemen and women experiencing what were officially recognized as psychoneurotic symptoms.[31] They represented only a fraction of the 118,000 ex-soldiers who had been discharged on mental health grounds from the Army at some point or other during the war.[32] But then, the whole approach to military psychiatric care between 1939 and 1945 had been organized around a desire to keep the number of post-war pension payments as few as possible. The government wanted to avoid a commitment of the kind it had had to take on after the Great War, when 120,000 ex-servicemen had been declared eligible for a pension for a 'primarily psychiatric disability'.[33] Hence the state's enthusiasm for the theory fashionable amongst psychiatrists in 1945: that soldiers were only liable to suffer long-term mental trauma if they had entered military service predisposed to such problems already by heredity or some distressing childhood experience. Normal men might get temporarily 'exhausted' in battle, to be sure. But they would always recover quickly enough with the right treatment. Only the truly abnormal would experience permanent trauma. And since the onset of their abnormality had long preceded their entry into the Army, the government had not caused their suffering and had no responsibility to compensate them for it. Only in truly 'exceptional circumstances' was any ex-servicemen supposed to receive payment for his wartime mental injuries.[34] There was little patience for the idea that symptoms of psychoneurotic injury might not manifest themselves for months, or even years, after demobilization – the condition then known as 'delayed shell shock', and which we would call today post-traumatic stress disorder (PTSD). Anyone experiencing traumatic 'flashbacks' (that term would not enter the medical lexicon for another half-century) had clearly been mentally ill long before the war began. His problems were his own – and certainly not the concern of the Ministry of Pensions.[35]

So men such as Fred Eggleton, a trooper of the Normandy campaign who became a travelling salesman after the war, were left to battle their inner demons by themselves. Nine years after his demobilization, Fred seemed to most casual acquaintances a man of bottomless sociability. Only those who took the time to watch him more closely could see glimpses of the grief and pain hidden behind his hail-fellow-well-met performance – the jerky movements of the body, the tightly strung nerves, the fear of being alone, the nausea at the odour of roast beef (so distressingly similar to the smell of a burned-out tank), the reliance on pint after pint of beer to get him through the day.[36] Another ex-soldier, Stanley Whitehouse, endured years of 'horrible and realistic nightmares, waking up lathered in sweat and shouting hysterically'. Even in daylight he was haunted by the feeling that what looked like an innocent English bush or hedge might contain a well-camouflaged German machine-gun nest.[37] Such men could be found throughout mid-century Britain, if one cared to look. Few people did. The traumatized lived within a culture in which the disclosure of psychological vulnerability was considered unhealthy.[38] So thousands of men such as Eggleton and Whitehouse shambled through their post-war lives as best they could, drawing on the assistance of alcohol, sex, gambling, or whatever other palliative drug they could find; not understanding their own condition, perhaps secretly feeling ashamed of it, falling apart in full public view, but without fuss. They were the 'men who didn't come back the same from the war' – eccentric, but harmlessly so, cheerful enough in fact so long as you caught them in the right mood. There to be gently humoured. And eventually, when the laughter stopped, as it always did in the end, quietly forgotten about.

For John Masters, peace began as a throwaway remark by a stranger. It was the early autumn of 1945, and he and his wife were emerging on to the foothills of the Himalayas in India after having spent most of the summer on a long mountain hiking trek, far from news of the war. As they were on the return leg of their journey, a passing traveller hailed them. He had a remarkable story to tell. A few weeks before, the Americans had dropped a special new bomb on Japan, a weapon powerful enough to wipe out an entire city in a single explosion. It had been enough to convince the Japanese government to surrender. The war was over. 'I felt a physical shock, as though a stranger met in the path, a man with whom I had been passing the time, no more, had shot me', Masters recalled. '*The war is over, finished. . .*' His relief at the news was mixed with an embarrassed indignation at the off-handedness of it all, that he, a professional soldier, 'dedicated to war', should be one of the last people in the world to find out. There was also, he confessed, 'a sense of loss' at the sudden cessation of a conflict to which he had devoted the last six years of his life, and to which he had been steeling himself to return at the end of his Army leave:

> Not [a sense] of regret but of loss, as when a factory that has hammered and clanked outside your window for six years is suddenly, one morning, vanished. For a moment I could only see what would be gone – the sense of purpose, unselfishness, comradeship, sacrifice, courage. There was no reason why these qualities should not be devoted to peace in and between peoples – but they had not been after 1918 and I did not think they would be now.[39]

Though most British soldiers received the news of victory a good deal less belatedly than Masters, that vague sense of anti-climax was not at all unusual. 'Never was anything such a flop for me', John Guest wrote shortly after the German surrender. 'I've been winding myself up daily for five years, and now that it is all over I'm just incapable of further action.'[40] Everyone in Jocelyn Pereira's unit seemed 'flat, tired, uncomprehending' on V-E Day, 'as though it would take us many days to realize what had happened'. After so many years of war, peace now seemed something 'fantastically remote and unreal', an artefact from a long-lost childhood, a state of existence both utterly unfamiliar and perhaps even mildly threatening. As Pereira put it:

> I had lived whole lifetimes since then, so that I had become a quite different person. Presumably life was about to blossom out into security, plenty, freedom, happiness, and all the things that we had been told we were fighting for, but the notion was as remotely obscure as if one had been announced as the next Dalai Lama. Whatever life might hold in the future, nothing would ever matter so much as what was past. I might live to a great age or I might be run over by a bus in Piccadilly, but whatever occurred

would be curiously trivial in comparison. It would be wonderful never again to know fear and fatigue and discomfort, as we had known them in the days that it seemed were over, and yet there was something missing.[41]

Part of the reason for this lack of enthusiasm amongst these men may have been that while their war was over, their soldiering was not. The broad outlines of what was to be the British military demobilization plan had been announced in September 1944, and had been met with general approval throughout the Forces. Release priority was to be decided for the vast majority of soldiers by a simple combination of age and years of service, with very few exceptions made for 'key men' with special skills needed at home (so no grousing about favouritism or loopholes). No one's demob was to be delayed just because of their being overseas. The mechanism was fine. The problem was that no one knew when the key would be turned to start the whole thing off. Just as Chamberlain had wanted to avoid chaos in 1939 by mobilizing too quickly, so his successors six years later – first Churchill, and then, following his victory at the general election in July 1945, Clement Attlee – wanted to keep the process of demobilization as stately and predictable as possible. Fears of a post-war economic slump similar to that which had taken place in 1920 were still high on V-E Day. No one wanted to watch servicemen coming out of the Forces and immediately lining up in the dole queue. Plus, there was a world for the British Army to police: vanquished enemies to control, reconquered imperial territories (some of which were in no mood to be 'liberated' by their old colonial oppressors) to garrison. So for many months following the formal end of hostilities, the majority of soldiers would be staying right where they were. The British state had taken its sweet time getting them into uniform. It was going to take its sweet time getting them out of it.[42]

This was depressing enough by itself. But peace also meant a return to all the bullshit of 'proper' regular soldiering. When he heard news of the German surrender in northern Italy, Reg Crimp's pleasure was sharply attenuated by the thought of what was surely going to follow: 'the barren ugliness of the barrack buildings . . . the minor irritating fatigues, queues for meals, snores at night, and the pervasive reek of diesel oil.'[43] While the fighting was on, combat service had offered a sanctuary from the worst types of officious drill and spit-and-polish found back in the UK. Now, the spirit of the Regular Army at its most tedious and peremptory was going to reassert itself from Catterick to Calcutta. For Andrew Wilson, all that the announcement of Hitler's death seemed to portend was an unlovely vision of peacetime military existence: 'offices with In and Out trays, training programmes, dinner nights in mess, fatigues for the men and dismal queues at the cookhouse.'[44]

After three years of fighting in Sicily, Italy and northwest Europe, Jack Swaab had as much reason as any soldier to welcome the end of the war. But by the summer of 1945, he was finding that peacetime Army life in Germany, though infinitely less dangerous than before the German surrender, was also far more dreary. 'The prospect of another year or even longer in these conditions depresses everybody', he wrote in his diary. Swaab's commanding officer, in a display of 'absolute pig-headedness', had insisted on creating a full-dress regimental mess, with wine and catering secretaries and waiters with starched white jackets and brilliantly polished buttons. Every other officer in the regiment had opposed it as an unnecessary waste of time. But the colonel's will had prevailed. 'Not that one really expects or even necessarily wants democracy in an Army', acknowledged Swaab. 'But common sense at least would be welcome.' As for the ORs, they were being treated to rounds of blancoing and a new order that, in addition to merely being immaculately cleaned, all unit vehicles were henceforth to be varnished too. '*Varnished!*' Swaab despaired. '*The army in peace time. . .*'[45]

And so the routine went on through summer 1945; autumn 1945; Christmas 1945; New Year's Day 1946; spring 1946 . . . For hundreds of thousands of soldiers, the arrival of 1946 was merely the beginning of an eighth year in uniform, complete with more drill, more polishing, more sentry duty, more paperwork. But with 1946 came, at last, a speed-up in demob. Groups 25, 26 and 27, the biggest age-and-service groups of the lot, finally got their tickets home. And so home they went, re-enacting in reverse that long journey they had taken to war all the way back in 1939 and 1940 and 1941. Decked out once again in civvy vestments (how strange and ill-fitting they seemed after battle-dress!), clutching the same kinds of cardboard suitcases and packages wrapped in manila paper they had taken with them to their training depots, they assembled on railway platforms and at bus stops, passing kitbags and typed RTO notices and loudspeakers blaring out the same unintelligible orders that had greeted them at their mobilization so long ago. John Guest, in transit through Victoria station en route home, felt an identical 'bewilderment and fear' to that which he had experienced at the beginning of the war.[46] Marching in smart military cadence now, where once, as callow and untrained recruits, they had stumbled and shuffled, they made their way along main streets, up side streets, through garden gates, up to front doors. And then. . .

And then . . . what? A world of possibilities. Just as there had been no single wartime soldiering experience, so there would be no single post-war demob experience either. Most men would be greeted by their families with unconditional delight. Some would be received with polite but lukewarm indifference. A few would encounter unalloyed hostility. For many ex-soldiers, demob would mean a swift and relatively painless picking up of a life lightly laid aside at the beginning of the war, with few doubts or hesitations or false starts. For others, there would be a more complicated and ambivalent transition back to normality – successful in the end, but punctuated along the way with moments of anxiety and frustration. And for an unfortunate few with 'no house, no job, no prospects, little money' – what lay ahead were years of disenchantment, anger, grief and failure, ending perhaps in the divorce court, the doss-house, the prison cell or the pauper's grave.[47] Most ex-soldiers would be alright in the end. A small number, though, would be crushed by the trauma of peace.

The return to civvy street would mean a resumption of the quotidian concerns of life – the job, the rent payments, the evening classes, the bills for the kids' shoes. For those who had been overseas for many years, it would mean adjusting to a country very different from the one they had left behind at embarkation, a Britain now of ration books and rubble-strewn streets and drab utility garments. It might mean adjusting to a spouse and children who were virtual strangers. At one war factory visited by James Lansdale Hodson, thirty-eight out of forty women had married a serviceman during the war, and had spent barely a few weeks of matrimonial bliss with him before they had been parted. 'What sort of life will they build together?' wondered Hodson.[48] Delicate negotiations would have to take place within families unsettled by the welcome but disruptive intrusion of a long-lost husband and father. In some cases, relationships would not be able to withstand the transition. Leslie Phillips' fiancée had enjoyed the thought of marrying a smart young Army officer. After his demob, she was less enamoured of the prospect of being the wife of a theatre box office attendant on £5 a week. She dumped him shortly after his departure from the Army for the more consistently martial attentions of a regular major.[49]

The men themselves would be different on their return, too – taller, in some cases; certainly heavier; fitter; bronzed from the tropical sun, perhaps; and in many cases more confident and self-reliant. 'He has *greatly* improved since he joined the Army', commented one soldier on his brother, who had also recently joined up. 'A lot of the coltish edges of adolescence have been knocked off . . . the necessity of meeting and accommodating himself to all sorts of people, the necessity of living independently and having to think and get along for himself, have done him a hell of a lot of good.'[50] But with loss of youthful exuberance might come a certain coarseness and impatience and listlessness. 'My long absence had so separated me from the life I had known before that I never really adjusted to the comforts and freedom it offered', thought Gordon Nisbett upon his homecoming. 'Virtually a boy when I left home, I returned a man. The vicissitudes of warfare had dulled my sensitivity and hardened me physically. At night, my body took unkindly to the mattress and sheets. I slept less well than I had done when lying on the earth wrapped in a single blanket between the coverings of my groundsheet and gas cape.'[51] Geoffrey Picot felt 'emotionally punch-drunk' on his arrival back in civilian life. 'Six years of fearful danger, limitless thrills, bleak disaster, unqualified triumph, of living life at the extremity, had drained from me the ability to savour the moments.'[52] David Holbrook, demobbed and walking round a northern city in late 1945 with nowhere particularly to go and nothing to do, realized that he had ceased to be a member of the uniformed tribe that took him seriously, saluted him, recognized his right of command and obeyed his orders without question. 'He noticed that people no longer looked at him, or only looked with indifference. He walked on a little and looked at himself in a shop window. Whoever was that? Who was this unknown civilian man, in such very ordinary factory clothes?' Holbrook wondered:

> For a moment of terror he wanted to go back – to claim his lieutenancy, his functions, his number, his rank, his qualifications, pay, board, and mess . . . there was no organization to back him up in authority, or in dealings with others. No woman would respond to him in the role of a young officer, bearing the insignia of units with a bloody history. He was nothing, nobody.[53]

For some soldiers, demob would be the point at which it all started to go wrong, the moment at which the confidence and satisfaction that had welled up inside them during the war years would begin to haemorrhage out, never to be replaced. Whether through lack of the right connections, snobbery or simply just bad luck, they would never be able to replicate in civvy street the triumph they had made of the Army. Approaching his own demob shortly after the war's end, George Greenfield fell into company with a lieutenant-colonel who had won the DSO with two bars for the superlative leadership of his battalion in Sicily and Italy. The colonel had requested a permanent commission in the Army, but this had been turned down: after all, he had not, as Greenfield noted, 'been to the 'right' school, nor to Sandhurst. His vowel sounds were broad, not clipped as befitted a real officer.' 'So you see', he told Greenfield, 'it's back to the bank.' They had had to keep his job open for him by law. But all the same:

> It won't be the kind of job I'd now have if I'd stayed on these past four or five years. Like deputy manager, even manager maybe. 'Sorry, Mr. Kelly: Miss Snooks or this fellow with a bad heart filled your vacancy. Lots o' things have changed since you went away. 'Course, we appreciate what you done, but you will admit there's a lot of catching up to do. So we'll give you a refresher course an' then you can go back to being a cashier.'

Kelly, thought Greenfield, was a man 'whose tragedy was that he was more at home in war than in a world at peace'.[54]

In his 1948 book *Labour, Life and Poverty*, the sociologist Ferdinand Zweig chronicled the stories of many ex-soldiers who, for one reason or another, were finding it impossible to readjust satisfactorily to civilian life. Zweig was struck by the number of former servicemen who had served with distinction during the war, but who now 'found a void within themselves . . . a psychological and moral vacuum'. In the Forces, they had been given an important purpose to their lives, 'a strong moral framework'. But now 'the purpose has vanished, they feel stranded in no-man's-land, not knowing what to do next. And they are in desperate need of substituting something for their lost endeavour and purpose'.[55] John Mulgan recognized the same problem in himself. 'In war, when you are working well together, you find the sober pleasure of working in concert with friends and companions and at the same time feel pride in yourself for the part you can play as an individual', he wrote in his memoir *Report on Experience*, completed in late April 1945, just a few weeks short of V-E Day:

> This takes place in war against a background of issues which are large enough to be impressed in your mind as life and death, and victory and defeat . . . honest men will admit that they have been happy in war-time and some of them have afterwards tried to find the same things in peace and always failed.[56]

Mulgan was speaking from the heart. On finishing *Report on Experience*, he posted the manuscript to his wife back in New Zealand, and then returned to his Cairo hotel bedroom where he took an overdose of morphine and killed himself. He was thirty-three years old.

For most soldiers, though, the war, and their Army service with it, simply ended, with neither a great deal of fuss, nor any particular regret. What had it all amounted to? wondered Norman Wray, called up in April 1941 and demobilized in December 1946. Mostly, he reflected, a lot of waiting around – waiting for something to happen, waiting for something to do, waiting for someone in charge to make their mind up:

> Waiting at Liverpool Docks to board MV *Duchess of Bedford* bound for Algiers. On board a bobbing LST to beach at Salerno. Wet, worried, waiting to wade across the River Volturno. Prostrate and helpless under a German mortar barrage waiting for it to stop. Wretched, waiting on high cold mountains, for Jerry to counterattack. Waiting for orders to scurry back from a

patrol to our lines and the comfort of our slit trenches. In action, always waiting for something to happen. Shit scared, and when it did, waiting for it to stop. Waiting, waiting, waiting for the war to end.[57]

No Army song captured the essence of soldiering quite so well as *Why Are We Waiting?*, sung to the tune of *Adeste Fideles*.[58] 'So much has been written of the horror of war – so little of the boredom', thought John Guest.[59] And indeed, for many ex-soldiers in the years immediately after the Second World War, their overall impression of their military service seems to have been that it was neither especially traumatizing, nor all that rejuvenating, but simply *tiresome* – a distraction from altogether more important things, a squandering of years that could otherwise have been spent doing something altogether more constructive. Getting married. Raising a family. Building a career. 'What a colossal waste of time war is!' complained Harry Wilson as he reflected on another year spent in thankless exile from Britain.[60] A soldier in Geoffrey Picot's platoon remarked that the military locusts had eaten five irreplaceable years of his life and youth.[61] Had the war been necessary? Certainly. Justly fought? To be sure. But it was now time to move on and forget about it all. 'We put up with [the Army] in a marking-time sort of way', thought Richard Hoggart, 'as if disconnected from real life. That was to start afterwards.'[62]

And indeed, the decades immediately following the war would be marked by a wholesale forgetting amongst former citizen-soldiers, as they shed their military identities and returned as briskly as possible to the lives they had left behind. Few men regretted their service, but few also saw much point in clinging to the past. By 1954, after a brief post-war surge in numbers, the British Legion was down to just 847,000 members, and of those 400,000 were veterans of the Great War.[63] Former soldiers, explained a Legion representative, were 'sick with everything connected with the war service'.[64] Little fuss was made about the early commemorative milestones of the war. The tenth and twentieth anniversaries of D-Day barely rated a mention in *The Times*. But then harping on your old wartime experiences, clinging to your faded military identity, was seen as a little odd or suspicious in the immediate post-war years, a sign of immaturity or charlatanry. Those ex-soldier bores who propped up provincial bars, 'their flow of reminiscence recalling some-times the Baron Münchhausen, sometimes the Ancient Mariner' were to be avoided.[65] Wartime comradeships rarely felt the same afterwards. Rupert Croft-Cooke thought that there was an intensity to Army friendship which was wholly a product of the peculiar circumstances in which men found themselves intimately thrown together, and which usually did not last after-wards.[66] In 1957, *The Times* suggested that 'the marks of the demobilized man have almost faded away. He is no longer ex-service, he is just a man again. Perhaps it is for the best.'[67]

This is not to say that Churchill's Army had made no imprint on post-war national life. The experience of military service insinuated its way into British popular culture in the 1950s and 1960s through literature, comedy, drama and music. The most obvious expression of this was the conventional, serious war film, a staple of 1950s British entertainment. Through earnest celebrations of imperial pluck such as *The Cockleshell Heroes* (1955) or *Ice Cold in Alex* (1958), domesticated ex-servicemen could vicariously enjoy the bonding of the all-male wartime mob once more.[68] But the Army's influence did not end with heroic derring-do. Military songs, doggerel, mythmaking and rumour-mongering were fondly remembered too; and the private jokes of the Army's rude but vital culture informed much post-war British comedy writing, both for the printed page and for radio, television and cinema. A dollop of parade-ground belly-aching and wit informed the work of many of the so-called 'Movement' writers of the 1950s, a circle which included Kingsley Amis (formerly of the Royal Corps of Signals), John Holloway (Royal Artillery), Robert Conquest (Ox and Bucks Light Infantry) and John Braine (Royal Navy). Amis's 'Lucky' Jim Dixon, perhaps the quintessential protagonist of the early 1950s British novel, is a recognizable ex-Forces type: a temporary gentleman subaltern, raised from his lower-middle class provincial origins to a position of much responsibility but little honour or dignity, the beneficiary of a bit of 'egalitarian window dressing' who during the war was never allowed to forget how little he belonged in the regimental mess, and who still does not belong in the senior common room.[69] The anti-hero Joe Lampton of John Braine's 1957 novel *Room at the Top* – a coarse, lusty, bloody-minded, self-consciously 'tough' ex-POW – is marked by his military past every bit as much as Dixon. Even John Osborne's Jimmy Porter, though a bit too young to look back in anger on the war years himself, possesses a chip on his shoulder and a taste for sardonic wordplay which could easily have been acquired from an older brother who had done his time in uniform.

An entire generation of British light entertainment performers and writers drafted their acts on the stages of wartime ENSA touring troupes and regimental concert parties, or in front of impromptu barracks audiences. These included ex-soldiers Tommy Cooper, Charlie Chester, Frankie Howerd, Kenneth Williams, Kenneth Connor, Terry-Thomas and Alfie Bass.[70] The result was a string of service comedies that began on BBC Radio with *Much-Binding-in-the-Marsh* and *The Navy Lark*, and continued on to the small screen with *The Army Game* before transferring to film via *Reluctant Heroes* (1951), *Private's Progress* (1956), *I Only Arsked!* (1958), and *Carry on Sergeant* (1958). Fictional sites such as *The Army Game*'s transit and supply ordnance depot at

Nether Hopping represented the military life as most wartime ex-soldiers remembered it, a mixture of boredom and bullshit enlivened by occasional subversive outbreaks of the carnivalesque.[71] Even many comedies which had no ostensible connection with the armed forces were solidly rooted in service humour. Much of *The Goon Show*'s appeal lay in its recycling of the verbal perambulations, running jokes, catchphrases and stock characters (the scrim-shanker, the ferocious sergeant major, the nice-but-dim subaltern, the pompous gin-swilling colonel) which Spike Milligan and Harry Secombe had encountered in the Royal Artillery and Peter Sellers and Michael Bentine in the RAF. Figures such as Major Bloodnok (Colonel Blimp for a younger generation) were instantly familiar to legions of ex-servicemen in the Goons' audience. As John Cleese later put it, the humour of the series was that of 'very clever NCOs making jokes that the officers wouldn't quite have understood'.[72]

Still, it was not until the 1960s that wartime soldiers really started to become self-conscious about their status as ex-servicemen. The winding up of National Service in 1963 must have played some part in this. Peacetime conscription had, in its way, artificially extended the mental atmosphere of the Second World War well into the post-war years. Through spending up to two years in the Forces, young British men in the pre-Beatles era had shared an experience with the older wartime cohort which gave them a set of common cultural reference points. The end of conscription brought to a close a period extending back fifty years in which the majority of able-bodied British men had, at some time or other in their lives, undergone military service. Though the armed forces had never been particularly interested in using the call-up as a socio-logical tool – British conscription was never consciously about nation-building or turning 'peasants into Englishmen' on the French model – the ending of military service as a collective rite of passage would, all the same, widen the experiential gap between those men born before 1940 and those after it. Never again would British male teenagers undergo a mass initiation on the barrack square which would link them with the older generations that had trodden the same parade grounds.[73] It would be harder than ever for the young to understand the old, and vice versa.

Plus, the end of National Service came at the same time as a dramatic retreat from Britain's status as an imperial Great Power. Wartime soldiers had belonged to an Army which had garrisoned one quarter of the world's land surface. However much they may have disliked their personal encounters with Egypt and India between 1939 and 1945, they had never doubted for a moment that their country would always police and occupy such scattered global territories. The existence of the British Empire was something they had taken as an unal-terable fact. The withdrawals from India in 1947 and Palestine, Ceylon and

Burma the following year did not really shake this assumption; these could be rationalized, after all, as necessary retrenchments. It was the Suez debacle in 1956 and the rapid abandonment of tropical Africa that followed shortly afterwards which really drove home the point that Britain was an imperial nation no longer. It was hard for a generation of ex-soldiers that had grown up celebrating Empire Day and gazing at the 'pink bits' on the world map to understand why Britain had suddenly shrunk to the status of just another middle-ranking European power. Hard not to feel, too, that decolonization represented a personal rebuke: that their sacrifices on behalf of the Empire had all been for nothing.

The end of National Service and the collapse of the Empire coincided with spectacular changes in youth culture which would be a source of puzzlement and distress to many older Britons. The wartime generation had found it tough enough to deal with Angry Young Men and Teddy Boys in the 1950s. They were now to be alternately baffled and outraged by waves of mods, rockers and hippies. The contrast between the austere, self-denying 1940s and the affluent, self-indulgent 1960s was striking – and while Britons of all ages enjoyed the material benefits of full employment and cheap consumer goods, those who had lived through the war as adults were appalled by the casual irreverence that young people now seemed to show to institutions and values that they themselves had, if not always loved, then at least taken completely for granted.

All this was happening at exactly the moment that the British wartime generation was reaching middle age, and as a result coming to reflect more sentimentally than before on its own past. Few ex-soldiers had experienced anything since the war that had been nearly as dramatic or exciting as their Army days. Post-war routine had lacked the passionate intensity of the 1940s. The comradeship of the barrack room had never been adequately replicated on the factory floor or in the office canteen. As former boy soldiers saw their hair-lines recede and their waistlines expand, so they began to look back on their service days with more and more indulgence. Memories of the martinet sergeant major softened. Incidents which, at the time, had been loathsome or infuriating – that dreadful cookhouse meal, the interminable parade, those gruelling punishment details – now seemed harmless enough; moments of nostalgic pride and affection, in fact. As ex-soldiers looked in mystified disapproval at their own children – so lazy, impertinent, over-privileged, self-absorbed! – and the dilapidated condition of the once-mighty British Empire they had fought to save, their values became more conservative. They forgot that not so very long before they, too, had been dismissed by *their* elders as impudent spoon-fed idlers. They forgot, too, that while military service had been a fact of life it had not been seen as the answer to the nation's problems at all – indeed, it had been blamed for destroying the character of the young. In 1946, one columnist for the conservative *Spectator* magazine had condemned the 'curious dictum' that Army life was good for teenagers:

> Consider what actually happens. At 18 – the pinnacle of golden youth – these boys are removed from school, from college, from jobs; they are sepa-rated from their homes, their families, their friends, and their personal interests and activities. They are put into uniform, given a 'protective packet' against venereal disease, subjected – subjected is the accurate word – to the dubious educational attentions of the typical sergeant-major, and carefully instructed in the arts of destruction. They sleep eight to 10 in a hut – bad, good, and indifferent, foul-mouthed and fastidious – without privacy or solitude. They are compelled to expend the major part of their surging vitality in uncreative and usually uninteresting activity, and their leisure, such as it is, in equally uncreative time-killing, or in bought pleasure – drinks, cinemas, women . . . where do the police go immediately an investi-gation starts? To the nearest military camp.[74]

But by the 1960s, as the phenomenon of mass Army service receded into the national past, such old concerns were being slowly forgotten. As ageing ex-soldiers reflected on the state of a country that resembled less and less the Britain they had known in their youth, they concluded that it was the absence of those same military virtues which they had so heartily disliked during the war – obedience, punctilious attention to tidiness and cleanliness, deference to superiors – that was causing the country to go to the dogs. Colonel Blimp, wherever he was, might have been forgiven for raising a rueful smile at this.

Such selective recollection was understandable enough. No one should be blamed for looking back on the exquisite simplicity of their youth with a sense of affection and regret. Least of all a soldier from a war long ended.

One late afternoon in Italy sometime in 1944, the men of rifleman Alex Bowlby's platoon were driving back to their camp after a day spent practising an opposed river crossing when they began to sing *Lili Marlene*, that old soldier's favourite appropriated from the Afrika Korps back in the Western Desert. It was a tremendous cock-a-hoop rendition of *Lili*, proud, defiant and joyous. 'We'd pinched the enemy's song, pinched his girl in a way, and we flung her back at him like a gauntlet', remembered Bowlby many years later. Then, as they reached the second verse, something unexpected and wonderful happened. 'The song got out of control':

One moment we were singing it, the next *it* was singing *us*. It took over like an automatic pilot. For the first time in my life I lost all sense of self. I was inextricably part of the platoon and they were part of me. We were all one. Nothing else mattered. I grinned hugely at my neighbours and they grinned back. In triumph. They'd felt it too. After we'd stopped singing we marched the last hundred yards to the camp in silence. On a route-march we sang and talked and sang again, but not on this one. Everyone had sensed an inexplicable happiness and no-one wanted to break the spell.

At the time it was a mystery, but a few post-war years of a family *grand-guignol* helped me to unravel it. As I discovered that peace can be a much more disturbing process than war and that the near-loss of one's own sense of self under pressure more terrifying than fear of death in battle, I began to retreat to memories of the war, and the happiness and security it had brought me. It was then that I suddenly felt I understood what had happened on that march. All of us knew that within a few days we would be in action. Any one of us might be killed. Yet none of us gave it a thought. And because we didn't, because in those great, triumphant shouts we challenged not only the Germans, but the death they stood for, we lost, if only for a moment, the need to protect ourselves.

We had let go.[75]

APPENDIX

Notes on the Organization and Structure of the British Army in the Second World War

(These notes are intended to be broadly illustrative, *not* exhaustive. To document fully all the rococo variations on the basic patterns of organization and structure within the wartime British Army would take a book at least as long as this one already is. Readers interested in more details are directed towards George Forty's *British Army Handbook 1939–1945*. Stroud: Sutton, 1998, which is the source of much of the information below.)

Other than the symbolic figure of His Majesty King George VI, the British Army during the Second World War had no single commander-in-chief. Supreme command was vested instead in a committee called the Army Council, which had been created before the First World War in imitation of the Admiralty Board. Its membership fluctuated in size and composition during the war, but it always reflected the traditional division of responsibility between the civilian government of the day and the Army's permanent professional officer class. Its most senior political figure, and its chairman, was the secretary of state for war, who was in overall charge of the War Office and who represented the Army's interests in Cabinet. He was advised by a coterie of officers led by the chief of the Imperial General Staff (CIGS) and seconded by the adjutant-general to the Forces (AG), the latter of whom was responsible for personnel matters.

When Winston Churchill became prime minister in May 1940, he assumed the role of 'minister of defence', a title giving him broad undefined power to make military policy over the heads of his traditional secretaries of state. As the war went on, Churchill increasingly confined decisions about grand strategy and operations to himself, advised by a Chiefs of Staff Committee (COS) representing the three armed services. From March 1942 this was permanently chaired by the CIGS. As a result, the Army Council's importance as a decision-making body was much reduced, and its mostly administrative duties were usually handled by an executive subcommittee led by the permanent undersecretary of state for war.

Secretary of State for War

Leslie Hore-Belisha (May 1937–January 1940)
Oliver Stanley (January 1940–May 1940)
Anthony Eden (May 1940–December 1940)
David Margesson (December 1940–February 1942)
Sir P. J. (Percy James) Grigg (February 1942–July 1945)
Jack Lawson (August 1945–October 1946)

Chief of the Imperial General Staff (CIGS)

Field Marshal Sir Cyril Deverell (February 1936–December 1937)
General Viscount Gort (December 1937–September 1939)
General Sir Edmund Ironside (September 1939–May 1940)
Field Marshal Sir John Dill (May 1940–December 1941)
Field Marshal Sir Alan Brooke (December 1941–June 1946)

Adjutant-General to the Forces (AG)

General Robert Gordon-Finlayson (July 1939–June 1940)
General Sir Henry Colville Wemyss (June 1940–June 1941)
General Sir Ronald Forbes Adam (June 1941–July 1946)

Before the outbreak of war, the Army was formally divided into the Regular Army and a part-time auxiliary arm known as the Territorial Army (TA).[1] Peacetime recruits joining these two forces attested under different conditions of service. In the winter of 1939, however, both the regular and TA forces were merged into a single 'national' Army that existed for the remainder of the war, and so for all practical purposes the distinction between the two disappeared. Some individual battalions, brigades and divisions continued to be described as 'Territorial' because of their origins, but this was a purely symbolic distinction.

As the metropolitan centre of a worldwide empire, Britain also maintained a number of colonial armies, the largest and most important of which was the Indian Army. Although at the start of the war most of the Indian Army's officers were British (it subsequently went through a rapid process of

'Indianization') it was administratively distinct from the British Army, answering to the viceroy in New Delhi rather than the War Office. The term 'Army of India' was sometimes used to describe the mixture of British Army and Indian Army units within the subcontinent at any given time. British and Indian Army units were usually combined in the same Army of India field formations. An Indian Infantry division, for instance, typically had nine infantry battalions, three of which would be British.

Wartime British Army units also often served alongside formations belonging to the Dominion forces of Canada, Australia, New Zealand and South Africa. For operational purposes these 'colonial' forces were led by whoever was the local theatre commander (usually a British general officer), but they maintained their own personnel and disciplinary structures.

Functionally, the British Army was organized into corps. Note that the term 'corps' was also used in a distinct operational sense to describe a field force of two or more divisions commanded by a lieutenant general (for which see below). The functional corps were divided into *the Arms*, or fighting branches, popularly known as the 'teeth', and *the Services*, or support branches, known as the 'tail'.

The functional corps of the British Army in 1945 were, in official order of precedence:

THE ARMS:
The Household Cavalry
The Royal Armoured Corps (RAC)
The Royal Regiment of Artillery (RA)
The Corps of Royal Engineers (RE)
The Royal Corps of Signals (R Sigs)
The Infantry
The Reconnaissance Corps
The Army Air Corps (AAC)

THE SERVICES:
The Royal Army Chaplains' Department
The Royal Army Service Corps (RASC)
The Royal Army Medical Corps (RAMC)
The Royal Army Ordnance Corps (RAOC)
The Royal Electrical and Mechanical Engineers (REME)
The Royal Army Pay Corps
The Royal Army Veterinary Corps
The Army Educational Corps
The Army Dental Corps

The Pioneer Corps
The Intelligence Corps
The Army Catering Corps
The Army Physical Training Corps
The Corps of Military Police
The Military Provost Staff Corps
The Queen Alexandra's Imperial Nursing Service
The Auxiliary Territorial Service (ATS)
The Officer's Training Corps (OTC)
The General Service Corps (GSC)

The RAC and the Infantry were really loose associations of regiments. The wartime RAC was a union of three distinct types of units: the old mounted cavalry and yeomanry regiments which had been mechanized after 1918; the Royal Tank Regiment (RTR), which had been created during the Great War (originally known as the Tank Corps); and from 1941 onwards, a number of infantry battalions that had been temporarily converted to armour. The Infantry was composed of the five Foot Guards regiments that collectively made up the Brigade of Guards, and the sixty-four regiments of the infantry of the line. The Brigade of Guards regarded itself as a *corps d'élite*, and along with the Household Cavalry maintained its own recruitment and training system distinct from the rest of the Army.

The term *regiment* had (and continues to have) a large number of possible meanings within the British Army, depending on context. For instance, the Royal Regiment of Artillery was a functional corps which also fielded operational units called regiments (as did the RAC and Royal Corps of Signals). In the infantry, however, the regiment was an administrative entity. Each infantry regiment was composed of a central recruitment and training depot which fed drafts of replacements to several numbered battalions (1st, 2nd, 3rd, etc.) which were the regiment's operational field units. In peacetime, most infantry regiments had two Regular Army battalions and one or more associated TA battalions. In 1939, the decision was made to follow the precedent of the Great War and expand the line infantry, not by raising entirely new regiments but by simply adding new battalions to existing regiments. Battalions of the same regiment did not necessarily serve together in the same brigades; indeed, this was uncommon. But they bore the same cap badges and insignia, shared the same idiosyncratic traditions and regarded themselves as members of a single regimental family, even if they rarely if ever encountered one another across the theatres of war. Officers and men seconded from their regiment to serve in other formations during the war (for example, in the Special Service or 'commando' battalions) remained for administrative purposes members of their home regiment, and continued to wear its cap badge. Such cross-posting became increasingly common as the war went on.

The Army Air Corps, formed in 1942, consisted of three wartime creations: the Parachute Regiment, the Glider Pilot Regiment and the Special Air Service (SAS) Regiment.

The army units of 'Home Forces' stationed in the United Kingdom were organized into geographical commands, each answering to a central General Headquarters (GHQ). Home Forces also consisted of AA (Anti-Aircraft) Command and the part-time Home Guard, composed of men otherwise unable to serve in the Army for reasons of age, occupation or infirmity.

The original field force sent across the English Channel in September 1939 was called the British Expeditionary Force (BEF), in imitation of the army of the same name that had served in France and Belgium during the First World War. After its defeat and evacuation back to the United Kingdom in spring 1940, the BEF was disbanded.

Several other overseas commands were created during the war with their own local GHQs. Their responsibilities expanded and contracted as circumstances demanded. Middle East Command, for instance, was at different periods of the war responsible for British forces in Egypt (its GHQ was in Cairo), Libya, the Sudan, Palestine, Transjordan, Cyprus, Malta, Aden, Iraq, Persia (Iran), British Somaliland, Ethiopia and Greece. Other important commands included the British North Africa Force (BNAF), responsible for troops in Algeria and Tunisia; the Central Mediterranean Force (CMF) in Italy and Greece; and South East Asia Command (SEAC) in India and Burma.

As Britain's war became an increasingly coalition effort, so its army units began to serve under multinational, especially Anglo-Canadian-American, commands. During the liberation of northwestern Europe from 1944 to 1945, for instance, British forces in the theatre answered to Supreme Headquarters Allied Expeditionary Force (SHAEF), commanded by General Eisenhower. The largest headquarters formation below SHAEF was Field Marshal Montgomery's 21st Army Group, which consisted of one British field army (the 2nd) and one Canadian army (the 1st).[2] For administrative purposes, British troops in northwestern Europe were also counted as members of the 'British Liberation Army', or BLA.

The largest exclusively British Commonwealth/Empire land formation during the war was the *field army*, usually commanded by a general or lieutenant general. By the end of the war, seven British field armies had been created, of which probably the most famous were the Eighth, which fought in the Western Desert, Tunisia, Sicily and Italy, and the 14th, the so-called 'forgotten army' of Burma.

In addition to the reserve and line-of-communication troops under the direct control of its own headquarters, a field army consisted of two or more *corps*, each of which was usually commanded by a lieutenant general. In all, thirteen regular corps were created during the war, plus one airborne corps and three anti-aircraft corps.

A corps consisted of two or more *divisions*, each of which was usually commanded by a major general. Divisions were designated as infantry, armoured or airborne. A late-war infantry division's establishment strength was approximately 18,400 men, an armoured division's 15,000, and an airborne division's 12,000.

A division consisted of three or more infantry or armoured/tank *brigades*, each of which was usually commanded by a brigadier.[3] In support of its brigades, a late-war infantry division also possessed three regiments of field artillery, an anti-tank regiment, a light anti-aircraft (LAA) regiment, a reconnaissance regiment, four field companies of Royal Engineers and a machine-gun (MG) battalion.

A 1944 infantry brigade consisted of three infantry *battalions*, each of which was usually commanded by a lieutenant colonel and consisted at full strength of approximately thirty-six officers and 800 men. A battalion was divided into four rifle *companies* of five officers and 122 men, each of which was usually commanded by a major or captain, with an additional HQ company and a support company. A rifle company was divided into three rifle *platoons* of thirty-seven men, each of which was usually commanded by a lieutenant, plus an HQ platoon. A rifle platoon was divided into a three-man platoon HQ, a three-man light mortar section and three rifle *sections* of ten men each, each of which was usually commanded by a corporal.

A 1944 armoured brigade consisted of a motorized infantry battalion and three armoured *regiments*, each of which possessed about 37 officers, 655 men and 70 tanks. In addition to supporting arms, each of these regiments was divided into three *squadrons* which were, in turn, divided into five *troops* of three or four tanks apiece, each troop being usually commanded by a lieutenant. An individual tank had four or five crew members and (if not the troop commander's own vehicle) was usually commanded by a sergeant or corporal.

A Royal Artillery field regiment consisted of three *batteries* of 200 officers and men, each of which was divided into two *troops* of four guns apiece. An individual 25-pounder field gun had five or six crew members and was usually commanded by a sergeant.

The basic distinction in rank in the British Army was between *Officers* and *Other Ranks* (ORs, also 'British Other Ranks' or BORs). The terms 'rank and file' and 'men' (as in, 'officers and men') were sometimes used in place of Other Ranks.

Officers held the King's Commission, which put them under different disciplinary conditions than other soldiers, and gave them the unique responsibility for exercising *command* over their subordinates (thus being accountable for their behaviour while on active service, for instance).

British Army officers in the Second World War were ranked as follows:

Field marshal (only nine men were promoted to this rank during the war)
General
Lieutenant general
Major general
Brigadier
Colonel (usually a staff rather than a field appointment)
Lieutenant-colonel
Major
Captain
Lieutenant
Second lieutenant

Lieutenants and second lieutenants were also known as 'subalterns', and were usually addressed by all ranks as 'Mr'. The Household Division had its own peculiar terminology. Second lieutenants in the Foot Guards were known as 'ensigns', and in the Household Cavalry as 'cornets'.

British Army Other Ranks were subdivided into *warrant officers* (WOs), *non-commissioned officers* (NCOs) and ordinary private soldiers.

Warrant officers did not hold the King's Commission and were not saluted. But like commissioned officers (and unlike NCOs), they were addressed as 'sir' by those of inferior rank. In ascending order of seniority they were ranked Class II and Class I.[4] Warrant officers were addressed by their functional titles. The most important WOI was the regimental sergeant major (RSM), the most senior OR in a unit, and in many respects second only to its commander in authority. Each infantry company had a company sergeant major (CSM), a WOII position.

Directly below warrant officers were NCOs, who were ranked as follows:

Staff sergeant
Sergeant
Corporal ('bombardier' in the Royal Artillery)
Lance-corporal/lance-bombardier (technically an unpaid appointment rather
than a rank)

Ordinary soldiers without rank were either known as 'private' or by a title
traditional to their particular unit or arm of the service. For instance, Royal
Engineers were known as 'sappers' and Royal Artillerymen as 'gunners', whilst
privates in the Foot Guards were called 'guardsmen', in the rifle regiments
'riflemen' and in the Royal Armoured Corps 'troopers'.

NOTES

Introduction

1. James Smith, *British Writers and MI5 Surveillance, 1930–1960*. Cambridge: Cambridge University Press, 2012, 97.
2. *LFC History*: www.lfchistory.net/SeasonArchive/Game/4908. Accessed 31 March 2014. This was the last First Division game either team would play until 1946.
3. Douglas Arthur, *Desert Watch: A Story of the Battle of Beda Fomm – And What Went on Before – As Seen Through the Eyes of Driver D. Arthur (Young Doug), No. 1 Battery, 106th Lancashire Hussars (Yeomanry) Regiment, Royal Horse Artillery*. Bedale: Blaisdon Publishing, 2000, 7–31.
4. Richard Hoggart, *A Sort of Clowning: Life and Times, Vol. 2: 1940–1959*. Oxford: Oxford University Press, 1991, 5. Amongst the few earlier attempts at such an engagement are David Englander and Tony Mason, *The British Soldier in World War II*. Warwick: Warwick University Working Papers in Social History, *c.*1984; Jeremy Crang, *The British Army and the People's War 1939–1945*. Manchester: Manchester University Press, 2000; and the chapter on the armed forces in Geoffrey Field, *Blood, Sweat, and Toil: Remaking the British Working Class, 1939–1945*. Oxford: Oxford University Press, 2011. The best operational history of the British Army during the Second World War is David Fraser, *And We Shall Shock Them: The British Army in the Second World War*. London: Cassell, 2002.
5. NA WO 259/44.
6. Gerard De Groot, "'I Love the Scent of Cordite in Your Hair": Gender Dynamics in Mixed Antiaircraft Batteries during the Second World War' in *History* 82:265 (2002); Jeremy Crang, 'The Revival of the British Women's Auxiliary Services in the Late Nineteen-thirties' in *Historical Research* 83:220 (2010); Lucy Noakes, *Women in the British Army: War and the Gentle Sex, 1907–1948*. London: Routledge, 2006.
7. For example, see Tom Harrisson, *Living Through the Blitz*. London: Collins, 1976, 324–30; Sally Sokoloff, 'Soldiers or Civilians? The Impact of Army Service in World War Two on Birmingham Men' in *Oral History* 25 (Autumn 1997).
8. Also, in this world war, unlike the First, almost all officers serving 'for the duration' spent at least some time in the ranks before they were commissioned, and thus they experienced the point of view, however brief, of being led as well as leading.
9. *Strength and Casualties of the Armed Forces and Auxiliary Services of the United Kingdom 1939–1945*. Cmnd. 6832. London: HMSO, 1946.
10. Peter Howlett, *Fighting with Figures: A Statistical Digest of the Second World War*. Cmnd. 6832. London: HMSO, 1995.
11. Cmnd. 6832.
12. David French, *Raising Churchill's Army: The British Army and the War against Germany, 1919–1945*. Oxford: Oxford University Press, 2000, 63. This figure includes 224,000 regulars and 34,000 conscripted 'militiamen', but does not include the Territorial Army or reservists.

13. J. M. Winter, *The Great War and the British People*. Houndmills: Macmillan, 1985, 73. Another 90,000 British citizens served in the various women's auxiliary forces during the First World War.

14. Ibid., 73; *Statistics of the Military Effort of the British Empire During the Great War, 1914–1920*. London: HMSO, 1922, 243, gives an Army fatality figure of 574,889, including 512,564 for the British Expeditionary Force in France and Belgium.

15. Cmnd. 6832. These figures include 5,696 servicemen (of whom 2,267 were soldiers) still officially listed as missing on 28 February 1946.

16. John Robert Peaty, British Army Manpower Crisis 1944. Unpublished thesis, King's College University of London, 2000, 244, 247.

17. James Lansdale Hodson, *Through the Dark Night; Being some Account of a War Correspondent's Journeys, Meetings and what was said to Him, in France, Britain, and Flanders during 1939–1940*. London: Gollancz, 1941, 9, 20.

18. Anthony Cotterell, *What! No Morning Tea?* London: Gollancz, 1941, 9–10.

19. David French, *Military Identities: The Regimental System, the British Army, and the British People, c.1870–2000*. Oxford: Oxford University Press, 2005, 257.

20. Ian Hay, *The King's Service: An Informal History of the British Infantry Soldier*. London: Methuen, 1938, 306.

21. D. Evans, Imperial War Museum Department of Documents IWM:D 2028 92/37/1.

22. Simon Garfield, *We Are at War: The Remarkable Diaries of Five Ordinary People in Extraordinary Times*. London: Ebury, 2005, 213.

23. General Sir Ronald Adam. Liddell Hart Centre for Military Archives, LHCMA 3-13.

24. Michael Carver, *The Seven Ages of the British Army*. New York: Beaufort Books, c.1984, 201.

25. Eric Ambler, *Here Lies: An Autobiography*. London: Weidenfeld & Nicolson, 1986, 159.

26. Harry Wilson, 731. IWM:D 4709 80/5/1.

27. John Atkins, 'On Guard', *The Adelphi*, January–March 1945, 73.

28. Norman Smith, *Tank Soldier*. Lewes: Book Guild, 1989, 25.

29. Anthony Burgess, *Little Wilson and Big God, Being the First Part of the Confessions of Anthony Burgess*. London: Heinemann, 1987, 242.

30. J. L. Hunt, A. G. Pringle and C. Morgan, *Service Slang*. London: Faber and Faber, 2008, 17–18.

31. Julian Maclaren-Ross, *Collected Memoirs*. London: Black Spring Press, 2004, 254.

32. David Cooper. IWM:D 202 90/6/1.

33. George MacDonald Fraser, *Quartered Safe Out Here: A Recollection of the War in Burma with a New Epilogue: Fifty Years On*. HarperCollins, 2000, 276.

34. Geoffrey Picot, *Accidental Warrior: In the Front Line from Normandy till Victory*. Lewes: Book Guild, 1993, 9.

35. Max Hastings, *Winston's War: Churchill, 1940–1945*. New York: Alfred A. Knopf, 2009, 217.

36. *Ex-Services Review*, January–February 1945, 4.

37. E. P. Danger. IWM:D 4465 82/37/1.

38. Sydney Jary, *18 Platoon*. Carshalton Beeches: Sydney Jary, c.1987, 133.

39. Peter Ustinov, *Dear Me*. London: Little, Brown, 1977, 172.

40. Ibid., 210.

Part One: Regulars

1. Anthony Babington, *Military Intervention in Britain: From the Gordon Riots to the Gibraltar Incident*. London: Routledge, 1990, 121.

1 Colonel Lawrence and Colonel Blimp

1. John Masters, *Bugles and a Tiger: A Volume of Autobiography*. New York: Viking, 1956, 5.

2. Ibid., 11.

3. *The Times*, 31 May 1934, 13; *The Times*, 6 November 1935, 13. The calm in Waziristan would not last much longer. In 1936, a religious zealot known as the Faqir of Ipi encouraged a general uprising of the Pathan tribes. For the next three years the British would fight a mountain campaign against the insurgents, drawing on as many as 30,000 regular and native troops to suppress the uprising.

4. Masters, *Bugles and a Tiger*, 11.

5. Two additional regular infantry divisions were held back in England until late August and early September.

6. John Keegan, *The Face of Battle: A Study of Agincourt, Waterloo, and the Somme*. London: Pimlico, 2004, 216.

7. Martin Middlebrook, *The First Day on the Somme: 1 July 1916*. London: Penguin, 2001, 97.

8. Robin Prior and Trevor Wilson, *The Somme*. New Haven: Yale University Press, 2006, 114–15.

9. Only one of the battalion's four companies was actually from Accrington. The rest were from other small towns in East Lancashire.

10. William James Philpott, *Bloody Victory: The Sacrifice on the Somme and the Making of the Twentieth Century*. London: Little, Brown, 2009, 192; William Turner, *Pals: The 11th (Service) Battalion (Accrington) East Lancashire Regiment*. Barnsley: Wharncliffe Publishing, 1991, 160.

11. Keegan, *Face of Battle*, 285.

12. J. M. Winter, *The Great War and the British People*. Houndmills: Macmillan, 1985, 73.

13. David Cannadine, 'War and Death, Grief and Mourning in Modern Britain' in Joachim Whaley, ed., *Mirrors of Mortality: Studies in the Social History of Death*. London: Europa, 1981.

14. Robert C. Self, *Neville Chamberlain: A Biography*. Aldershot: Ashgate, 2006, 71–2.

15. John Terraine, *The Right of the Line: The Royal Air Force in the European War, 1939–1945*. London: Hodder & Stoughton, 1985, 60.

16. Winston Churchill, *The World Crisis*. New York: Free Press, 2005, 667.

17. David Lloyd George, *War Memoirs of David Lloyd George*. New York: AMS Press, 1982, 2014, 2033.

18. Carlo D'Este, *Warlord: A Life of Winston Churchill at War, 1874–1945*. New York: HarperPerennial, 2008, 296.

19. C. S. Forester, *The General*. Annapolis, MD: Nautical & Aviation Publishing, 1982, 195–6.

20. Daniel Todman, *The Great War: Myth and Memory*. London: Hambledon Continuum, 2005, 82.

21. For some of the literature on the British 'learning curve' and the victories of 1918, see Paddy Griffith, *Battle Tactics of the Western Front: The British Army's Art of Attack, 1916–18*. New Haven: Yale University Press, 1996; Gary Sheffield, *Forgotten Victory: The First World War: Myths and Realities*. London: Headline, 2001; Tim Travers, *The Killing Ground: The British Army, the Western Front and the Emergence of Modern Warfare, 1900–1918*. Barnsley: Pen & Sword, 2003.

22. Michael Heffernan, 'For Ever England: The Western Front and the Politics of Remembrance in Britain' in *Cultural Geographies* 2:293 (1995).

23. Brian Reid, 'T. E. Lawrence and Liddell Hart' in *History* 70:229 (1985).

24. John D. Clare, *Interpretations of Haig*: www.johndclare.net/wwi3_HaigHistoriography.html. Accessed 1 April 2014.

25. *The Times*, 26 October 1937, 15.

26. Nicholas Rankin, *A Genius for Deception: How Cunning Helped the British Win Two World Wars*. Oxford: Oxford University Press, 2009, 123.

27. B. H. Liddell Hart, *The Decisive Wars of History: A Study in Strategy*. London: G. Bell & Sons, 1929, 5. To what extent Liddell Hart's theory of land warfare, which he called the 'expanding torrent' strategy, influenced the development of German Blitzkrieg tactics in the Second World War remains controversial. See Brian Bond, *Liddell Hart: A Study of his Military Thought*. London: Cassell, 1977; John J. Mearsheimer, *Liddell Hart and the Weight of History*. Ithaca: Cornell University Press, 1988.

28. Terraine, *The Right of the Line*, 10.

29. B. H. Liddell Hart, *Paris: Or, the Future of War*. London: Kegan Paul, 1925, 36–7.

30. Ibid., 41.

31. David Edgerton, *England and the Aeroplane: Militarism, Modernity and Machines*. Houndmills: Macmillan, 1991, 46.

32. David French, 'Doctrine and Organization in the British Army, 1919–1932' in *Historical Journal* 44:2 (2001).

33. LHCMA Adam 3-13.

34. Keith Jeffrey, 'The Post-War Army' in Ian F. W. Beckett and Keith Simpson, eds., *A Nation in Arms: A Social Study of the British Army in the First World War*. Manchester: Manchester University Press, 1985, 214.

35. *General Annual Report on the British Army*. Cmnd. 4821. London: HMSO, 1934.

36. The phrase comes from Colonel G. F. R. Henderson, a leading critic of British defence policy in the 1890s. Quoted in Brian Bond, *British Military Policy Between the Two World Wars*. Oxford: Clarendon Press, 1980, 100.
37. Robin Higham, *Armed Forces in Peacetime: Britain, 1918–1940*. Hamden, CT: Archon Books, 1962, 326.
38. Bond, *British Military Policy*, 75.
39. Terraine, *The Right of the Line*, 61.

2 Gentlemen and Old Sweats

1. Victor Gregg, *Rifleman: A Front Line Life from Alamein and Dresden to the Fall of the Berlin Wall*. London: Bloomsbury, 2011, 23–4.
2. Richard Cartwright. IWM:D 3168 95/23/1.
3. Frederick Cottier. IWM:S 10601.
4. J. E. Bowman, *Three Stripes and a Gun: A Young Man's Journey Towards Maturity*. Braunton: Merlin, 1987, 21.
5. *The Times*, 8 January 1937, 13.
6. *General Annual Report on the British Army*. Cmnd. 5950. London: HMSO, 1938, 68.
7. Bowman, *Three Stripes and a Gun*, 22.
8. David French, *Military Identities: The Regimental System, the British Army, and the British People, c.1870–2000*. Oxford: Oxford University Press, 2005, 36.
9. *General Annual Report* 1938, 77.
10. Ian Hay, *The King's Service: An Informal History of the British Infantry Soldier*. London: Methuen, 1938, 338.
11. *The Times*, 8 January 1937, 13.
12. Robert Green. IWM:S 6226.
13. Frank Griffin ['Private XYZ'], *I Joined the Army*. London: Fact, 1937, 66.
14. Ibid., 82.
15. Hay, *The King's Service*, 333.
16. Captain J. R. J. MacNamara, 'The Army To-Day' in *The Nineteenth Century*, September 1937, 278.
17. Anthony Babington, *Military Intervention in Britain: From the Gordon Riots to the Gibraltar Incident*. London: Routledge, 1990, 144–7.
18. Anthony Clayton, *The British Officer: Leading the Army from 1660 to the Present*. Harlow: Longman, 2005, 150.
19. *The Times*, 5 April 1937, 10.
20. *The Times*, 12 March 1937, 17.
21. Martin van Creveld, *Fighting Power: German and US Army Performance, 1939–1945*. Westport, CT: Greenwood Press, 1982, 20; David French, *Raising Churchill's Army: The British Army and the War against Germany, 1919–1945*. Oxford: Oxford University Press, 2000, 49.
22. John Masters, *Bugles and a Tiger: A Volume of Autobiography*. New York: Viking, 1956, 27–8.
23. David Hunt, *A Don at War*. London: Cass, 1990, 11.
24. Peter Carrington, *Reflecting on Things Past: The Memoirs of Peter Lord Carrington*. New York: Harper & Row, 1989, 31.
25. Many numbered regiments of foot had in fact been given county designations during the eighteenth century, but these had little relevance to recruiting, and in practice most soldiers prior to the Cardwell-Childers reforms still referred to their regiments by their number rather than their name.
26. William Lloyd McElwee, *The Art of War: Waterloo to Mons*. Bloomington: Indiana University Press, 1975, 79–80.
27. The 108th was one of the former regiments of the privately owned East India Company, taken under British state control in 1858.
28. French, *Military Identities*, 77–8.
29. Ibid., 26.
30. Masters was not in fact an officer of the DCLI but a newly commissioned Indian Army subaltern. He had, as custom dictated, been temporarily posted to a British Army battalion in order to 'learn the ropes' before he joined his own Indian regiment.
31. Masters, *Bugles and a Tiger*, 18.

32. Captain James Russell Kennedy, *This, Our Army*. London: Hutchinson, 1935, 116.
33. Michael L. Waller, The Conservatism of the British Cavalry and its Effects on the British Army of WWII. Unpublished thesis, Drew University, 2009, 159. The figure for the cavalry includes Territorial Yeomanry and Indian Army regiments.
34. Brian Bond, *British Military Policy Between the Two World Wars*. Oxford: Clarendon Press, 1980, 127.
35. J. F. C. Fuller, *Memoirs of an Unconventional Soldier*. London: Nicholson and Watson, 1936, 363.
36. Tim Bishop and Bruce Shand, *One Young Soldier: The Memoirs of a Cavalryman*. Norwich: M. Russell, 1993, 2.
37. Ibid., 5–6, 14.
38. Robert Larson, *The British Army and the Theory of Armored Warfare, 1918–1940*. Newark, DE: University of Delaware Press, 1984, 29–30.
39. Waller, *The Conservatism of the British Cavalry*, 176.
40. Shelford Bidwell and Dominick Graham, *Fire-Power: British Army Weapons and Theories of War, 1904–1945*. London: Allen & Unwin, 1982, 156.
41. French, *Raising Churchill's Army*, 82.
42. David French, 'The Mechanization of the British Cavalry between the World Wars' in *War in History* 10:3 (2003).
43. Gordon Patrick Armstrong, *The Controversy over Tanks in the British Army 1919 to 1933*. Unpublished thesis, King's College, University of London, 1976, 70–1.
44. Bishop and Shand, *One Young Soldier*, 28.
45. Robert ffrench-Blake. IWM:S 106.
46. French, 'Mechanization', 316.
47. Bishop and Shand, *One Young Soldier*, 27.
48. Philip Ziegler, *Soldiers: Fighting Men's Lives, 1901–2001*. London: Chatto & Windus, 2001, 149–53.
49. John Boyd Orr, *Food, Health and Income*. London: Garland, 1985, 49.
50. RMA Woolwich trained artillery and engineering officers.
51. C. B. Otley, 'The Social Origins of British Army Officers' in *Sociological Review* 18:2 (1970), 225; van Creveld, *Fighting Power*, 22.
52. Many thanks to Diane Flanagan for her assistance on this point.
53. French, *Military Identities*, 52.
54. For more on service families, see P. J. Cain and A. G. Hopkins, *British Imperialism 1688–2000*. Harlow: Longman, 2002, 421–4.
55. Bernard Crick, *George Orwell: A Life*. Harmondsworth: Penguin, 1980, 53.
56. Philip Warner, *Auchinleck: The Lonely Soldier*. Bel Air, CA: Buchan & Enright, 1981, 8–9.
57. Nigel Hamilton, *Monty: The Making of a General, 1887–1942*. London: Hamilton, 1981, 36–51; Bernard Law Montgomery, *The Memoirs of Field-Marshal the Viscount Montgomery of Alamein*. Cleveland: World Publishing Co., 1958, 23–4.
58. Michael Carver, *The Seven Ages of the British Army*. New York: Beaufort Books, c.1984, 201.
59. MacNamara, 'The Army To-Day', 276.
60. David Niven, *The Moon's a Balloon*. New York: Putnam, 1971, 75, 92.
61. Ibid., 85.
62. David Scourfield. IWM:S 6367.
63. John Watson. IWM:S 18372.
64. Bidwell and Graham, *Fire-Power*, 157.
65. E. B. Thornhill. IWM:D 8419 99/36/1.
66. John Keegan, 'Regimental Ideology' in G. Best and A. Wheatcroft, eds, *War, Economy, and the Military Mind*. London: Croom Helm, 1976, 9–11.
67. J. M. Brereton, *The British Soldier: A Social History from 1661 to the Present Day*. London: Bodley Head, 1986, 141.
68. Bowman, *Three Stripes and a Gun*, 22.
69. Richard Cartwright. IWM:D 3168 95/23/1.
70. Carver, *The Seven Ages*, 201.
71. Griffin, *I Joined the Army*, 15.
72. *General Annual Report on the British Army*. Cmnd. 4821. London: HMSO, 1934, 13.
73. Griffin, *I Joined the Army*, 19.
74. Ziegler, *Soldiers*, 153.
75. Ibid., 81–7.

76. Bishop and Shand, *One Young Soldier*, 7.
77. Benedict Anderson, *Imagined Communities: Reflections on the Origin and Spread of Nationalism*. London: Verso, 1991.
78. Masters, *Bugles and a Tiger*, 16.
79. William Graham. IWM:S 19673.
80. Philip Pardoe. IWM:S 6465.
81. French, *Raising Churchill's Army*, 125.
82. Hay, *The King's Service*, 328.
83. Richard Cartwright. IWM:D 3168 95/23/1.
84. Griffin, *I Joined the Army*, 59.
85. *General Annual Report* 1934, 32–3. The British Army defined a 'unit' as an infantry or tank battalion, a cavalry regiment, an artillery brigade (renamed a regiment in 1938), or an engineering company.
86. David French, 'Big Wars and Small Wars between the Wars, 1919–1939' in Hew Strachan, ed., *Big Wars and Small Wars: The British Army and the Lessons of War in the 20th Century*. London: Routledge, 2006, 46.
87. Ziegler, *Soldiers*, 218.
88. Albert Chapman. IWM:S 17978.
89. Alec Lewis. IWM:D 13428 05/45/1.
90. Robert Green. IWM:S 6226.
91. French, *Military Identities*, 136, 143.
92. Bond, *British Military Policy*, 68.
93. Max Hastings, *Winston's War: Churchill, 1940–1945*. New York: Alfred A. Knopf, 2009, 223.
94. French, *Raising Churchill's Army*, 58.
95. French, *Military Identities*, 71.
96. Bidwell and Graham, *Fire-Power*, 162–3.
97. Bishop and Shand, *One Young Soldier*, 24.
98. MacNamara, 'The Army To-Day', 277.
99. Niven, *The Moon's a Balloon*, 84.
100. Philip Pardoe. IWM:S 6465.
101. French, *Military Identities*, 154.
102. Carrington, *Reflecting*, 24, 32. See also Masters, *Bugles and a Tiger*, 32.

3 Strange Defeat

1. E. J. Manley. IWM:D 12308 P284.
2. John Horsfall, *Say Not the Struggle*. Kineton: Roundwood Press, 1977, 12.
3. Viscount Alanbrooke, *War Diaries, 1939–1945*. London: Weidenfeld & Nicolson, 2001, 24.
4. John Terraine, *The Right of the Line: The Royal Air Force in the European War, 1939–1945*. London: Hodder & Stoughton, 1985, 48.
5. Richard Overy, *The Morbid Age: Britain and the Crisis of Civilisation, 1919–1939*. London: Allen Lane, 2009, 177.
6. James P. Levy, *Appeasement and Rearmament: Britain, 1936–1939*. Lanham, MD: Rowman & Littlefield, 2006, 69.
7. Corelli Barnett, *Strategy and Society*. Manchester: Manchester University Press, 1976, 6.
8. Michael Howard, *The Continental Commitment*. London: Ashfield Press, 1989, 115.
9. Daniel Hucker, 'Franco-British Relations and the Question of Conscription in Britain, 1938–1939' in *Contemporary European History* 17:4 (2008), 441.
10. David Reynolds, *In Command of History: Churchill Fighting and Writing the Second World War*. London: Allen Lane, 2004, 99–100.
11. B. H. Liddell Hart, *Paris: Or, the Future of War*. London: Kegan Paul, 1925, 43–4.
12. Levy, *Appeasement and Rearmament*, 69.
13. *The Times*, 11 March 1938, 9.
14. Brian Bond, *British Military Policy Between the Two World Wars*. Oxford: Clarendon Press, 1980, 234.
15. Unlike Chamberlain, Hitler was unconvinced of the power of strategic bombing. 'A country cannot be brought to defeat by an air force', he is supposed to have remarked after Munich. Uri Bialer, *The Shadow of the Bomber: The Fear of Air Attack and British Politics, 1932–1939*. London: Royal Historical Society, 1980, 133.

16. Howard, *The Continental Commitment*, 126.

17. Bond, *British Military Policy*, 289.

18. *General Annual Report on the British Army*. Cmnd. 5950. London: HMSO, 1938, 5.

19. *Daily Express*, 27 June 1938, 13; Daniel Hucker, *Public Opinion and the End of Appeasement in Britain and France*. Farnham: Ashgate, 2011. 66.

20. Lothar Kettenacker, 'Great Britain: Declaring War as a Matter of Honor' in Lothar Kettenacker and Torsten Riotted, eds, *The Legacies of Two World Wars*. New York: Berghahn Books, 2011.

21. Bond, *British Military Policy*, 305.

22. Henry Pownall, *Chief of Staff: The Diaries of Lieutenant-General Sir Henry Pownall: Volume 1, 1933–1940*. London: Leo Cooper, 1972, 201.

23. Donald Callander. IWM:S 7166.

24. Horsfall, *Say Not the Struggle*, 7.

25. L. F. Ellis, *The War in France and Flanders, 1939–1940*. London: HMSO, 1953, 17.

26. Cyril Falls, 'Vereker, John Standish Surtees Prendergast, Sixth Viscount Gort (1886–1946)', rev. Brian Bond, *Oxford Dictionary of National Biography*: www.oxforddnb.com/view/article/36642. Accessed 1 April 2014; Ellis, *The War in France and Flanders*, 323; Pownall, *Chief of Staff*, 203; Alanbrooke, *War Diaries*, 18, 36.

27. Colin Bruce, *War on the Ground*. London: Constable, 1995, 65.

28. Wilfred Leonard Saunders, *Dunkirk Diary of a Very Young Soldier*. Birmingham: Birmingham City Council, Public Libraries Dept., 1989, 34–9.

29. James Lansdale Hodson, *Through the Dark Night; Being some Account of a War Correspondent's Journeys, Meetings and what was said to Him, in France, Britain, and Flanders during 1939–1940*. London: Gollancz, 1941, 26.

30. Horsfall, *Say Not the Struggle*, 12.

31. Ibid., 22.

32. Hugh Sebag-Montefiore, *Dunkirk: Fight to the Last Man*. London: Penguin, 2007, 21–3.

33. Saunders, *Dunkirk Diary*, 33–6.

34. Donald Callander. IWM:S 7166.

35. Saunders, *Dunkirk Diary*, 37–41.

36. Robert Green. IWM:S 6226.

37. Quoted in Angus Calder, *The People's War: Britain, 1939–1945*. London: Pimlico, 2008, 59.

38. Alanbrooke, *War Diaries*, 20.

39. Ibid., 47.

40. Ibid., 20; E. K. G. Sixsmith, 'The British Army in May 1940 – A Comparison with the BEF 1914' in *RUSI Journal* 127:3 (1982).

41. Bernard Law Montgomery, *The Memoirs of Field-Marshal the Viscount Montgomery of Alamein*. Cleveland: World Publishing Co., 1958, 47.

42. Donald Callander. IWM:S 7166.

43. Brian Bond, 'Preparing the Field Force, February 1939–May 1940' in Brian Bond and Michael Taylor, eds, *The Battle of France and Flanders, 1940: Sixty Years On*. London: Leo Cooper, 2001, 5.

44. David Fletcher, *Matilda Infantry Tank, 1938–1945*. Oxford: Osprey, 1994, 9–10; Robert Larson, *The British Army and the Theory of Armored Warfare, 1918–1940*. Newark, DE: University of Delaware Press, 1984, 223.

45. Peter Dennis, *The Territorial Army, 1906–1940*. Woodbridge: Royal Historical Society, 1987, 152.

46. According to Montgomery, the first that the CIGS Lord Gort knew of this decision was when he read about it in the newspaper. Montgomery, *Memoirs*, 48.

47. Hew Strachan, 'The Territorial Army and National Defence' in Keith Neilson and Greg Kennedy, eds, *The British Way in Warfare: Power and the International System, 1856–1956*. Farnham: Ashgate, 2010, 172.

48. Francis Docketty. IWM:S 4822.

49. Ibid.; Strachan, 'Territorial Army', 172.

50. Bill Cheall, *Fighting Through From Dunkirk to Hamburg: A Green Howards Wartime Memoir*. Barnsley: Pen & Sword, 2011. Kindle locations 310–11.

51. David French, *Raising Churchill's Army: The British Army and the War against Germany, 1919–1945*. Oxford: Oxford University Press, 2000, 158.

52. T. K. Derry, *The Campaign in Norway*. London: HMSO, 1952, 85.

53. Ibid., 168.
54. Henrik O. Lunde, *Hitler's Preemptive War: The Battle for Norway, 1940*. Havertown: Casemate, 2010, 323.
55. Max Hastings, *All Hell Let Loose: The World at War 1939–45*. London: HarperPress, 2011, Kindle locations 1067–9.
56. Derry, *The Campaign in Norway*, 111.
57. Ibid., 98–9; Lunde, *Hitler's Preemptive War*, 231.
58. Lunde, *Hitler's Preemptive War*, 328.
59. Derry, *The Campaign in Norway*, 235.
60. Winston Churchill, *The Gathering Storm*. London: Penguin, 2005, 608.
61. NA WO 217/24.
62. Christopher Seton-Watson, *Dunkirk, Alamein, Bologna: Letters and Diaries of an Artilleryman, 1939–1945*. London: Buckland, 1993, 26–8.
63. Horsfall, *Say Not the Struggle*, 25.
64. There were significant problems with Army communications as a whole throughout the campaign, caused by a lack of equipment and training. See Simon Godfrey, *British Army Communications in the Second World War*. London: Bloomsbury, 2013, 45–69.
65. E. J. Manley. IWM:D 12308 P284.
66. Horsfall, *Say Not the Struggle*, 140–1.
67. Doug Dildy, *Dunkirk, 1940: Operation Dynamo*. Oxford: Osprey, 2010, 86. Of the evacuated troops, around 13 per cent (48,474) were transported by French vessels. A further 27,900 British troops not included in these figures had already been evacuated from France prior to the formal start of the Dunkirk evacuation.
68. Ibid., 88.
69. Max Hastings, *Winston's War: Churchill, 1940–1945*. New York: Alfred A. Knopf, 2009, 46, 53; *Lancastria Association of Scotland*: www.lancastria.org.uk/victim-list/. Accessed 1 April 2014.
70. Seton-Watson, *Dunkirk, Alamein, Bologna*, 42–3.
71. Ian Beckett, *The Amateur Military Tradition: 1558–1945*. Manchester: Manchester University Press, 1991, 259; Peter Caddick-Adams, 'Phoney War and Blitzkrieg: The Territorial Army in 1939–1940' in *RUSI Journal* 143:2 (1998).
72. Charles More, *The Road to Dunkirk: The British Expeditionary Force and the Battle of the Ypres-Comines Canal, 1940*. London: Frontline Books, 2013.
73. Ben Shephard, *A War of Nerves: Soldiers and Psychiatrists in the Twentieth Century*. Cambridge, MA: Harvard University Press, 2001, 170.
74. Ellis, *The War in France and Flanders*, 326.
75. *Daily Mirror*, 4 June 1940, 6.
76. *Daily Mirror*, 1 June 1940, 8–9.
77. *Daily Mirror*, 1 June 1940, 7.
78. Robert Green. IWM:S 6226.
79. Calder, *The People's War*, 126.
80. Shephard, *War of Nerves*, 171.
81. Lionel G. Baylis. IWM:D 7969 98/23/1.
82. Horsfall, *Say Not the Struggle*, 160, 57.
83. Sebag-Montefiore, *Dunkirk*, 506.
84. Ellis, *The War in France and Flanders*, 327.
85. Dildy, *Dunkirk, 1940*, 89.
86. Hastings, *Winston's War*, 21.

Part Two: Civvies

1. Mass-Observation Archive, University of Sussex, TC29 Box 2.

4 Army of Shopkeepers

1. David Holbrook, *Flesh Wounds*. Stroud: Tempus, 2007, 33–55.
2. Spike Mays, *Fall Out the Officers*. London: Eyre & Spottiswoode, 1969, 59–60.
3. Kingsley Amis, *Memoirs*. London: Vintage, 2004, 78.
4. Rupert Croft-Cooke, *The Licentious Soldiery*. W.H. Allen, 1971, 34.

5. John Guest, *Broken Images: A Journal*. London: Leo Cooper, 1970, 30.

6. Conscription was not introduced in Northern Ireland. In December 1941, the National Service Act was amended to permit conscription of men up to age fifty-one.

7. Simon Garfield, *We Are at War: The Remarkable Diaries of Five Ordinary People in Extraordinary Times*. London: Ebury, 2005, 208.

8. 'Repercussions of Conscription', *US*, 17 February 1940. Mass-Observation Archive, University of Sussex, File Report 31.

9. Part of the reason for the unfavourable comparison with 1914 was that the outbreak of the First World War was not remembered in 1939 as accurately as people supposed. The response to Kitchener's call for volunteers had in fact been more complex than they remembered. See Peter Simkins, *Kitchener's Army: The Raising of the New Armies, 1914–16*. Manchester: Manchester University Press, 1988; David Silbey, *The British Working Class and Enthusiasm for War, 1914–1916*. New York: Frank Cass, 2005.

10. Robert Graves and Alan Hodge, *The Long Week-end: A Social History of Great Britain, 1918–1939*. New York: Norton, 1994, 446.

11. *The Observer*, 15 August 1937, 12.

12. Ian Hay, *The King's Service: An Informal History of the British Infantry Soldier*. London: Methuen, 1938, 306.

13. Robert Mackay, *Half the Battle: Civilian Morale in Britain during the Second World War*. Manchester: Manchester University Press, 2002, 22–6.

14. James Lansdale Hodson, *The Home Front: Being some Account of Journeys, Meetings and what was said to Me in and about England during 1942–1943*. London: Gollancz, 1944, 302–3.

15. Andrew Wilson, *Flame Thrower*. New York: Bantam, 1984, 143.

16. Richard Terrell, *Civilians in Uniform: A Memoir, 1937–1945*. London: Radcliffe Press, 1998, 16.

17. Ross McKibbin, *Classes and Cultures: England 1918–1951*. Oxford: Oxford University Press, 1998, 533–4.

18. Martin Ceadel, *Pacifism in Britain, 1914–1945: The Defining of a Faith*. Oxford: Oxford University Press, 1980, 283.

19. Daniel Todman, *The Great War: Myth and Memory*. London: Hambledon Continuum, 2005, 129–35.

20. Michael Paris, *Over the Top: The Great War and Juvenile Literature in Britain*. Westport, CT: Praeger, 2004, 154–61.

21. See, for example, Denis Hayes, *Challenge of Conscience: The Story of the Conscientious Objectors of 1939–1945*. London: Allen & Unwin, 1949; Rachel Barker, *Conscience, Government and War*. London: Routledge & Kegan Paul, 1982; Felicity Goodall, *A Question of Conscience: Conscientious Objection in Two World Wars*. Stroud: Sutton, 1997.

22. H. M. D. Parker, *Manpower: A Study of Wartime Policy and Administration*. London: HMSO, 1957, 488. This is not to deny that some COs suffered physical and mental abuse. For instance, an officer and six NCOs at a Liverpool detention barracks were convicted in 1940 of cruelty towards conscripted men who had declared themselves conscientious objectors. See Geoffrey Field, *Blood, Sweat, and Toil: Remaking the British Working Class, 1939–1945*. Oxford: Oxford University Press, 2011, 270. During the war, about 6,000 men joined the Army's 'Non-Combatant Corps' (NCC), which was created to allow conscientious objectors to perform military service without being trained or equipped with weapons. See Michael Snape, *God and the British Soldier: Religion and the British Army in the First and Second World Wars*. London: Routledge, 2005, 193.

23. R. F. Songhurst. IWM:D 2373 86/24/1.

24. Anthony Babington, *An Uncertain Voyage*. Chichester: Barry Rose Law, 2000, 111. His depression might have been influenced by the fact that he had had to cut short his holiday in Paris with a chorus-girl.

25. J. Herbert Parker-Jones. IWM:D 9078 01/10/1.

26. Philip Larkin, 'MCMIX' in *Collected Poems*. London: Faber and Faber, 1990, 127.

27. *The Times*, 5 September 1939, 10.

28. Simon Heffer, *Like the Roman: The Life of Enoch Powell*. London: Weidenfeld & Nicolson, 1998, 56.

29. Almost the whole Oxford undergraduate body did the same, including the members of the same Union which had so dramatically declined to fight for King and Country six years earlier. See Paul Addison, 'Oxford and the Second World War' in Brian Harrison, ed., *The*

History of the University of Oxford: The Twentieth-century. Volume 8. Oxford: Oxford University Press, 1994, 167; R. B. McCallum, *Public Opinion and the Last Peace*. Oxford: Oxford University Press, 1944, 177–80.

30. Peter J. Conradi, *A Very English Hero: The Making of Frank Thompson*. London: Bloomsbury, 2012, 143. Thompson was captured serving as an SOE agent in Bulgaria in 1944 and executed. His brother, the historian Edward Palmer (E. P.) Thompson, was also a Communist Party member who served as a junior officer in the Royal Armoured Corps in Italy.

31. Richard Doherty, *Irish Volunteers in the Second World War*. Dublin: Four Courts Press, 2002, 25.

32. Ibid., 42.

33. Keith Jeffery, 'The British Army and Ireland since 1922' in T. Bartlett and K. Jefferey, eds, *A Military History of Ireland*. Cambridge: Cambridge University Press, 1996, 438.

34. Ian S. Wood, "Twas England Bade our Wild Geese Go: Soldiers of Ireland in the Second World War' in Paul Addison and Angus Calder, eds, *Time to Kill: The Soldier's Experience of War in the West, 1939–1945*. London: Pimlico, 1997, 80; Bernard Kelly, '"True Citizens" and "Pariah Dogs": Demobilisation, Deserters, and the De Valera Government, 1945', in the *Irish Sword* 28:114 (2011).

35. Doherty, *Irish Volunteers*, 29–35.

36. Ernest Sanger, *Letters from the Two World Wars*. Stroud: Sutton, 1993, 182.

37. Richard Buckle, *The Most Upsetting Woman*. London: Collins, 1981, 181.

38. *The Times*, 23 October 1939, 9.

39. Parker, *Manpower*, 485.

40. In fact, it was to take far longer than anyone initially supposed. By the end of 1939, only 727,000 men had been required to register out of an available pool of over eight million; and of those, barely 113,000 had actually been called up into the Army. Ibid., 485–8; Peter Howlett, *Fighting with Figures: A Statistical Digest of the Second World War*. London: HMSO, 1995, 5.

41. LHCMA Adam 3-2; Parker, *Manpower*, 484.

42. Mass-Observation Archive, University of Sussex, File Report 274.

43. NA WO 365/216; Howlett, *Fighting With Figures*, 5.

44. Winston Churchill, *The Churchill War Papers. Vol. 2. Never Surrender, May 1940–December 1940*. New York: W.W. Norton, 1995, 518.

45. A. J. K. Piggott, *Manpower Problems*. London: The War Office, 1949, 15–16; NA WO 277/12.

46. David French, *Raising Churchill's Army: The British Army and the War against Germany, 1919–1945*. Oxford: Oxford University Press, 2000, 185.

47. LHCMA Adam 3-2.

48. M. M. Postan, *British War Production*. London: HMSO, 1952, 117.

49. David Edgerton, *Britain's War Machine: Weapons, Resources and Experts in the Second World War*. London: Allen Lane, 2011, 59–61.

50. Viscount Alanbrooke, *War Diaries, 1939–1945*. London: Weidenfeld & Nicolson, 2001, 106.

51. Ibid., 90.

52. T. E. B. Howarth. IWM:D 2924 84/7/1.

53. Guest, *Broken Images*, 11–12.

54. Parker, *Manpower*, 485. Not including reservists and TAs.

55. Richard Holborow. IWM:D 15631 07/23/1.

56. A. G. Herbert. IWM:D 7625 98/16/1.

57. Parker, *Manpower*, 174.

58. Piggott, *Manpower Problems*, 63.

59. Gerald Kersh, *Clean, Bright, and Slightly Oiled*. London: Heinemann, 1946, 62.

60. Glyn Prysor, *Citizen Sailors: The Royal Navy in the Second World War*. London: Viking, 2011, 109; David Englander and James Osborne, 'Jack, Tommy, and Henry Dubb: The Armed Forces and the Working Class' in *Historical Journal* 21:3 (1978).

61. Martin Francis, *The Flyer: British Culture and the Royal Air Force 1939–1945*. Oxford: Oxford University Press, 2008, 14.

62. John James, *The Paladins: A Social History of the RAF up to the Outbreak of World War II*. London: Macdonald & Co., 1990, 108–13.

63. *The Times*, 8 January 1937, 13.

64. Mass-Observation Archive, University of Sussex, TC29 Box 1.

65. Arthur Kellas, *Down to Earth, or, Another Bloody Cock-Up: A Parachute Subaltern's Story*. Edinburgh: Pentland Place, 1990, 93–4.

66. Croft-Cooke, *Licentious Soldiery*, 33.
67. Alan Wood, *Bless 'Em All: An Analysis of the British Army, its Morale, Efficiency and Leadership*. London: Secker & Warburg, 1942, 12.
68. Anthony Cotterell, *What! No Morning Tea?* London: Gollancz, 1941, 14.
69. Maurice Merritt, *Eighth Army Driver*. Tunbridge Wells, Kent: Midas Books, 1981, 4.
70. S. C. Procter. IWM:D 5636 96/1/1.
71. Sandra Koa Wing, ed., *Our Longest Days: A People's History of the Second World War*. London: Profile Books, 2008, 56.
72. R. H. Lloyd-Jones. IWM:D 125 89/1/1.
73. Cotterell, *What! No Morning Tea?*, 18–19.
74. Geoffrey Cotterell, *Then a Soldier*. London: Eyre & Spottiswoode, 1944, 11.
75. John Coldstream, *Dirk Bogarde: The Authorised Biography*. London: Phoenix, 2005, 117–18.
76. Snape, *God and the British Soldier*, 146.
77. This estimate is based on the 6 per cent of the British male population in the 1990s who acknowledged having had at least one homosexual experience during their lifetime. See Emma Vickers, *Queen and Country: Same Sex Desire in the British Armed Forces, 1939–1945*. Manchester: Manchester University Press, 2013, 4.
78. Postan, *British War Production*, 96; Howlett, *Fighting with Figures*, 38.
79. NA WO 32/9680. These figures do not include officers.
80. Terrell, *Civilians in Uniform*, 1.
81. Mays, *Fall Out the Officers*, 23.
82. NA WO 365/216.
83. B. Ungerson, *Personnel Selection*. London: The War Office, 1953, 47–8; NA WO 277/19; French, *Raising Churchill's Army*, 65.
84. Sheila Ferguson and Hilde Fitzgerald, *Studies in the Social Services*. London: HMSO, 1954, 3.
85. Croft-Cooke, *Licentious Soldiery*, 25, 28.
86. Cotterell, *What! No Morning Tea?* 28.
87. Norman Craig, *The Broken Plume: A Platoon Commander's Story, 1940–45*. London: Imperial War Museum, 1982, 17.
88. Anthony Burgess, *Little Wilson and Big God, Being the First Part of the Confessions of Anthony Burgess*. London: Heinemann, 1987, 240.
89. John Foley, *Mailed Fist*. St Albans: Mayflower, 1975, 9.
90. T. E. B. Howarth. IWM:D 2924 84/7/1.
91. Ian Hay, *Arms and the Men*. London: HMSO, 1977, 321.
92. Stephen Constantine, *Social Conditions in Britain, 1918–1939*. London: Methuen, 1983, 34.
93. Ina Zweiniger-Bargiowoska, 'Building a British Superman: Physical Culture in Interwar Britain' in *Journal of Contemporary History* 41:4 (2006).
94. Anthony Cotterell, *Oh, It's Nice to be in the Army!* London: Gollancz, 1941, 10.
95. Melanie Tebbutt, *Being Boys: Youth, Leisure and Identity in the Inter-war Years*. Manchester: Manchester University Press, 2012, 109.
96. John Boyd Orr, *Food, Health and Income*. London: Garland, 1985, 18.
97. LHCMA Adam 3-13.
98. Julie Anderson, *War, Disability and Rehabilitation: 'Soul of a Nation'*. Manchester: Manchester University Press, 2011, 77–8.
99. Emma Reilly, Civilians into Soldiers: The British Male Military Body in the Second World War. Unpublished thesis, University of Strathclyde, 2010, 91.
100. J. M. Winter, *The Great War and the British People*. Houndmills: Macmillan, 1985, 57.
101. Robert Ahrenfeldt, *Psychiatry in the British Army in the Second World War*. London: Routledge & Kegan Paul, 1958, 278.
102. Ben Shephard, *A War of Nerves: Soldiers and Psychiatrists in the Twentieth Century*. Cambridge, MA: Harvard University Press, 2001, 172.
103. A detailed analysis of one German wartime infantry division suggests that over one in three of its men had served in the pre-war German Army at some time or other, and more than half had, at the very least, been in one of Nazi Germany's various paramilitary forces (such as the RAD or Reich Labour Service) prior to their wartime call-up. See Christoph Rass, 'The Social Profile of the German Army's Combat Units, 1939–1945' in Jörg Echternkamp, ed., *Germany and the Second World War Volume XI/I: German Wartime Society 1939–1945*. Oxford: Oxford University Press, 2008, 719–20.

104. During the war itself, the British Home Guard was to serve a similar (if altogether more benign) acculturating function as the Hitler Youth did in Germany. By 1944 and 1945, it was increasingly normal for Army recruits to have spent a year or two before their call-up as Home Guardsmen, and thus to have already learned some of the rudimentary elements of Army life – drill, saluting, mounting sentry, stripping and cleaning a rifle, and so on. But the bulk of wartime soldiers joined the Army between 1939 and 1941, and so missed this late-war innovation.

105. David Fowler, *The First Teenagers: The Lifestyle of Young Wage-Earners in Interwar Britain*. London: Woburn Press, 1995, 144–53; Tammy Proctor, *On My Honour: Guides and Scouts in Interwar Britain*. Philadelphia: American Philosophical Society, 2002, 101. For the militaristic culture of boys' clubs and societies before 1914, see Gary Sheffield, *Leadership in the Trenches: Officer-Man Relations, Morale, and Discipline in the British Army in the Era of the First World War*. New York: St Martin's Place, 2000, 69.

106. Fowler, *The First Teenagers*, 141, 153–6.

107. R. E. Urquhart, 'The History and Aims of the Army Cadet Force' in *Journal of the Royal Society of Arts* 91:4740 (April, 1947), 322.

108. Winter, *The Great War and the British People*, 63; P. E. Dewey, 'Military Recruiting and the British Labour Force during the First World War', in *Historical Journal* 27:1 (1984).

109. Sheffield, *Leadership in the Trenches*, 69, 71.

110. Andrew August, *The British Working Class 1832–1940*. Harlow: Pearson, 2007, 112, 110.

111. John Bourne, 'The British Working Man in Arms' in Hugh Cecil and Peter H. Liddle, eds, *Facing Armageddon: The First World War Experienced*. Barnsley: Pen & Sword Books, 1996, 348-9. See also Sheffield, *Leadership in the Trenches*, 72.

112. Tony Mason, '"Hunger . . . Is a Very Good Thing": Britain in the 1930s' in Nick Tiratsoo, ed., *From Blitz to Blair*. London: Weidenfeld & Nicolson, 1997, 2.

113. J. B. Priestley, *English Journey*. London: Harper & Brothers, 1934, 249.

114. Roy Close, *In Action with the SAS: A Soldier's Odyssey from Dunkirk to Berlin*. Barnsley: Pen & Sword, 2005. Kindle locations 181–184.

115. Joanna Bourke, *Working Class Cultures in Britain, 1890–1960: Gender, Class, and Ethnicity*. London: Routledge, 1994, 6.

116. Priestley, *English Journey*, 319.

117. Selina Todd, 'Flappers and Factory Lads: Youth and Youth Culture in Interwar Britain' in *History Compass* 4:4 (2006).

118. Bourke, *Working Class Cultures in Britain*, 5–15; Peter Scott, *The Making of the Modern British Home*. Oxford: Oxford University Press, 2013, 1.

119. Bourke, *Working Class Cultures in Britain*, 58.

120. Tebbutt, *Being Boys*, 26.

121. Fowler, *The First Teenagers*, 145, Stephen G. Jones, *Workers at Play: A Social and Economic History of Leisure, 1918–1939*. London: Routledge & Kegan Paul, 1986, 55.

122. Tebbutt, *Being Boys*, 207.

123. Selina Todd, *The People: The Rise and Fall of the Working Class, 1910–2010*. London: John Murray, 2014, 99.

124. George Orwell, *Facing Unpleasant Facts: Narrative Essays*. New York: Houghton Mifflin, 2009, 136–7.

125. Edward Heath, *The Course of My Life: An Autobiography*. London: Hodder & Stoughton, 1998, 86.

126. Foley, *Mailed Fist*, 7; J. H. Witte. IWM:D 1279 87/12/1.

127. NA WO 163/161.

128. J. M. Brereton, *The British Soldier: A Social History from 1661 to the Present Day*. London: Bodley Head, 1986, 163.

129. Reginald Crimp, 10 November 1943. IWM:D 5659 96/50/1.

130. Reilly, *Civilians into Soldiers*, 37.

131. Holbrook, *Flesh Wounds*, 35.

132. Wood, *Bless 'Em All*, 26.

133. Guest, *Broken Images*, 24.

134. Kersh, *Clean, Bright, and Slightly Oiled*, 55.

135. Neil Barber, ed., *Fighting with the Commandos: Recollections of Stan Scott, No. 3 Commando*. Barnsley: Pen & Sword, 2008. Kindle locations 971–2.

136. L. R. F. Kenyon. IWM:D 3868 84/83/3.

137. Burgess, *Little Wilson and Big God*, 241–2.
138. Cotterell, *Oh, It's Nice to be in the Army!*, 7, 13.
139. Brian Aldiss, *A Soldier Erect: or Further Adventures of the Hand-Reared Boy*. London: Weidenfeld & Nicolson, 1971, Kindle location 361.
140. Terrell, *Civilians in Uniform*, 33–4.
141. Wood, *Bless 'Em All*, 25.
142. V. M. Sissons. IWM:D 1249 87/6/1. Brian Aldiss thought the main difference between school and the Army was that in the latter there was greater freedom and less swearing. Aldiss, *A Soldier Erect*, Kindle locations 812–14.
143. Croft-Cooke, *Licentious Soldiery*, 27, 37.

5 Britain Blancoes while Russia Bleeds

1. Max Hastings, *All Hell Let Loose: The World at War 1939–45*. London: HarperPress, 2011, Kindle locations 4142–4.
2. John Ferris, 'Worthy of Some Better Enemy? The British Estimate of the Imperial Japanese Army, 1919–1941, and the Fall of Singapore' in *Canadian Journal of History* 28:2 (1993).
3. Christopher Bayly and Tim Harper, *Forgotten Armies: The Fall of British Asia, 1941–1945*. Cambridge, MA: Belknap, 2005, 142.
4. NA CAB 66/24/7.
5. Ernest Sanger, *Letters from the Two World Wars*. Stroud: Sutton, 1993, 197.
6. Mass-Observation Archive, University of Sussex, TC29 Box 1.
7. In June 1940, Benito Mussolini made an opportunistic declaration of war against Britain in the hopes of scooping up territory for his new Mediterranean empire.
8. This partly reflects the greater German skill at recovering their tanks from the battlefield of North Africa and repairing them for redeployment.
9. Technically, Auchinleck was overall commander-in-chief for Middle East Command. Eighth Army's commander was Alan Cunningham from September to mid-November 1941, when Auchinleck relieved him of his office in the middle of the CRUSADER offensive and replaced him with General Neil Ritchie. Ritchie was sacked in his turn the following June during the battle for Gazala, and Auchinleck took personal command until mid-August 1942, when Churchill appointed General Alexander commander-in-chief and General Montgomery commander of Eighth Army.
10. Tim Moreman, *Desert Rats: British 8th Army in North Africa 1941–1943*. Oxford: Osprey, 2007, 34.
11. Louis Allen, *Burma: The Longest War 1941–45*. New York: St Martin's Press, 1984, 90.
12. Viscount Alanbrooke, *War Diaries, 1939–1945*. London: Weidenfeld & Nicolson, 2001, 231.
13. James Ambrose Brown, *Retreat to Victory: A Springbok's Diary in North Africa: Gazala to El Alamein 1942*. Johannesburg: Ashanti Publishing, 1991, 159; Niall Barr, *Pendulum of War: The Three Battles of El Alamein*. London: Jonathan Cape, 2004, 35; Artemis Cooper, *Cairo in the War: 1939–1945*.London: H. Hamilton, 1989, 189.
14. Alanbrooke, *War Diaries*, 269.
15. H. P. Samwell, *Fighting with the Desert Rats: An infantry Officer's War with the Eighth Army*. Barnsley: Pen & Sword, 2012, 21.
16. Jonathan Fennell, *Combat and Morale in the North African Campaign: The Eighth Army and the Path to El Alamein*. Cambridge: Cambridge University Press, 2010, 283.
17. Cyril Joly, *Take These Men*. London: Buchan & Enright, 1985, 325.
18. *Tribune*, 20 March 1942.
19. *Daily Express*, 23 June 1942, 2.
20. *Daily Mirror*, 23 June 1942, 1.
21. Arthur Kellas, *Down to Earth, or, Another Bloody Cock-Up: A Parachute Subaltern's Story*. Edinburgh: Pentland Place, 1990, 76–7.
22. Ibid., 20.
23. An absentee is believed to have been planning to return to his unit eventually, while a deserter, according to the *Manual of Military Law*, has 'an intention . . . either not to return to His Majesty's service at all, or to escape some particular important service'. Given that the culprit's original intentions are extremely hard to judge at a court martial, the decision to downgrade a charge to AWL rather than desertion was and is often simply a matter of ameliorating the punishment. See Mark Connelly and Walter Miller, 'British Courts Martial in North Africa 1940–3' in *Twentieth Century British History* 15:3 (2004).

24. J. H. A. Sparrow, *Morale*. London: The War Office, 1949, 6; NA WO 277/16.

25. A. B. McPherson, *Discipline*. London: The War Office, 1950, Appendix V; NA WO 277/7.

26. John Guest, *Broken Images: A Journal*. London: Leo Cooper, 1970, 14.

27. Ibid., 42.

28. NA WO 259/62.

29. NA WO 163/161.

30. Frank Owen, Preface, in Alan Wood, *Bless 'Em All: An Analysis of the British Army, its Morale, Efficiency and Leadership*. London: Secker & Warburg, 1942, 16.

31. *The Spectator*, 10 April 1942, 355.

32. Geoffrey Field, *Blood, Sweat, and Toil: Remaking the British Working Class, 1939–1945*. Oxford: Oxford University Press, 2011, 262; *Daily Express*, 13 April 1942, 2.

33. Wood, *Bless 'Em All*, 27, 29. The complaint was not a new one. In 1937, Captain J. R. J. MacNamara had bemoaned the fact that the new recruit became a 'skivvy' as soon as he put on uniform. 'Expecting to be ennobled, he becomes debased. He is given a bucket and a rag and put on washing the dank passages of an officer's mess.' Captain J. R. J. MacNamara, 'The Army To-Day', in *The Nineteenth Century*, September 1937, 270.

34. *The Listener*, 14 March 1940, 527.

35. Roy Close, *In Action with the SAS: A Soldier's Odyssey from Dunkirk to Berlin*. Barnsley: Pen & Sword, 2005. Kindle locations 1013–15.

36. Peter Carrington, *Reflecting on Things Past: The Memoirs of Peter Lord Carrington*. New York: Harper & Row, 1989, 31.

37. C. W. Valentine, *The Human Factor in the Army*. Aldershot: Gate & Polden, 1943, 60–3.

38. L. R. F. Kenyon. IWM:D 3868 84/8/3.

39. Harry Wilson, 39. IWM:D 4709 80/5/1.

40. John Mulgan, *Report on Experience*. Oxford: Oxford University Press, 1984, 47.

41. Bill Cheall, *Fighting Through from Dunkirk to Hamburg: A Green Howards Wartime Memoir*. Barnsley: Pen & Sword, 2011, Kindle locations 207–10.

42. Reginald Crimp, *The Diary of a Desert Rat*. London: Cooper, 1971, 27.

43. David French, *Military Identities: The Regimental System, the British Army, and the British People, c.1870–2000*. Oxford: Oxford University Press, 2005, 68.

44. Peter Ustinov, *Dear Me*. London: Little, Brown, 1977, 130.

45. Valentine, *The Human Factor*, 33.

46. Norman Craig, *The Broken Plume: A Platoon Commander's Story, 1940–45*. London: Imperial War Museum, 1982, 21.

47. Dennis Newland. IWM:D 12197 03/22/1.

48. Kellas, *Down to Earth*, 93–4.

49. Wood, *Bless 'Em All*, 7–8.

50. Richard Holmes, *Soldiers: Army Lives and Loyalties from Redcoats to Dusty Warriors*. London: HarperPress, 2011, 210.

51. LHCMA Adam 3-1, 3-13.

52. E. S. Turner, *Gallant Gentlemen: A Portrait of the British Officer 1600–1956*. London: Michael Joseph, 1956, 299.

53. LHCMA Adam 3–13.

54. Holmes, *Soldiers*, 196.

55. Charles Messenger, *Call to Arms: The British Army 1914–18*. London: Weidenfeld & Nicolson, 2005, 333.

56. Holmes, *Soldiers*, 201.

57. G. Salaman and K. Thompson, 'Class Culture and the Persistence of an Elite: The Case of Army Officer Selection' in *Sociological Review* 26:2 (1978), 287.

58. J. M. Brereton, *The British Soldier: A Social History from 1661 to the Present Day*. London: Bodley Head, 1986, 142–3; Keith Simpson, 'The Officers' in Ian F. W. Beckett and Keith Simpson, eds, *A Nation in Arms: A Social Study of the British Army in the First World War*. Manchester: Manchester University Press, 1985, 64. By tradition, the niche ranks of quartermaster and riding master had always been appointments given to long-serving Warrant Officers.

59. Jeremy Crang, *The British Army and the People's War 1939–1945*. Manchester: Manchester University Press, 2000, 21.

60. Gary Sheffield, *Leadership in the Trenches: Officer-Man Relations, Morale, and Discipline in the British Army in the Era of the First World War*. New York: St Martin's Place, 2000, 99.

61. M. Petter, "'Temporary Gentlemen'" in the Aftermath of the Great War: Rank, Status and the Ex-Officer Problem', in *Historical Journal* 37:1 (2009).
62. LHCMA Adam 3-13.
63. Crang, *The British Army*, 23.
64. Holmes, *Soldiers*, 211; David French, *Raising Churchill's Army: The British Army and the War against Germany, 1919–1945*. Oxford: Oxford University Press, 2000, 73.
65. L. R. F. Kenyon. IWM:D 3868 84/83/3.
66. Anthony Babington, *An Uncertain Voyage*. Chichester: Barry Rose Law, 2000, 141.
67. French, *Raising Churchill's Army*, 74.
68. Eric Ambler, *Here Lies: An Autobiography*. London: Weidenfeld & Nicolson, 1986, 169.
69. Craig, *The Broken Plume*, 24.
70. Gerald Kersh, *Clean, Bright, and Slightly Oiled*. London: Heinemann, 1946, 59–60.
71. Julian Maclaren-Ross, *Collected Memoirs*. London: Black Spring Press, 2004, 259.
72. Leslie Phillips, *Hello: The Autobiography*. London: Orion, 2006, 69.
73. Jack Garnham-Wright. IWM:D 6910 97/19/1.
74. Field, *Blood, Sweat, and Toil*, 262.
75. *Daily Mirror*, 6 March 1942, 3.
76. *Daily Mirror*, 23 June 1942, 1.
77. *The Times*, 15 January 1941, 5.
78. NA WO 163/161.
79. Crang, *The British Army*, 36.
80. NA WO 163/161.
81. R. A. C. Radcliffe, 'Officer-Man Relationships' in *Army Quarterly* 46:1 (May 1943).
82. Melanie Tebbutt, *Being Boys: Youth, Leisure and Identity in the Inter-war Years*. Manchester: Manchester University Press, 2012, 108.
83. F. G. Poole, 'Youth and National Defence', in *RUSI Journal* 83:532 (1938), 722.
84. Tebbutt, *Being Boys*, 93.
85. Herbert Moran, *In My Fashion*. London: Peter Davies, 1946, 51–143.
86. Henrik Lunde, *Hitler's Preemptive War: The Battle for Norway, 1940*. Havertown: Casemate, 2010, 549.
87. Edmund Ironside, *Time Unguarded: The Ironside Diaries, 1937–1940*. New York: McKay, 1963, 352.
88. Henry Pownall, *Chief of Staff: The Diaries of Lieutenant-General Sir Henry Pownall: Volume 1, 1933–1940*. London: Leo Cooper, 1972, 369.
89. Henry Pownall, *Chief of Staff: The Diaries of Lieutenant-General Sir Henry Pownall: Volume 2, 1940–1944*. London: Leo Cooper, 1974, 97–9.
90. NA WO 259/62.
91. NA WO 259/62.
92. NA WO 259/64.
93. Alanbrooke, *War Diaries*, 188.
94. Andrew Roberts, *Masters and Commanders How Four Titans Won the War in the West, 1941–1945*. New York: HarperCollins, 2009, 125.
95. French, *Raising Churchill's Army*, 1.
96. George Lauer, Perspectives on Infantry: Quality and Cohesion: Comparison of American, British, and German Army Manpower Policies and Effects on the Infantry Small Unit during the Second World War, 1939–1945. Unpublished thesis. Florida State University, 2010, 287.
97. Raymond Callahan, *Churchill and his Generals*. Lawrence, KS: University Press of Kansas, 2007, 2.
98. Alanbrooke, *War Diaries*, 226.
99. Carlo D'Este, *Warlord: A Life of Winston Churchill at War, 1874–1945*. New York: Harper, 2008, 567–8.
100. Roberts, *Masters and Commanders*, 181.
101. E. Y. Whittle, British Casualties on the Western Front 1914–1918 and their Influence on the Military Conduct of the Second World War. Unpublished thesis. University of Leicester, 1991, 155.
102. But cf. the account of 'temperate heroes' in Sonya Rose, *Which People's War? National Identity and Citizenship in Wartime Britain 1939–1945*. Oxford: Oxford University Press, 2004, 151–96.

6 Get Some Service In

1. LHCMA Adam 3-10.
2. LHCMA Adam 3-13.
3. Roger Broad, *The Radical General: Sir Ronald Adam and Britain's New Model Army 1941–1946*. Stroud: History, 2013, Kindle locations 3834–5.
4. Jeremy Crang, 'The Defence of the Dunkirk Perimeter' in Brian Bond and Michael Taylor, eds, *The Battle of France and Flanders, 1940: Sixty Years On*. London: Leo Cooper, 2001.
5. LHCMA Adam 313.
6. Jeremy Crang, 'The British Soldier on the Home Front: Army Morale Reports 1940–45' in Paul Addison and Angus Calder, eds, *Time to Kill: The Soldier's Experience of War in the West, 1939–1945*. London: Pimlico, 1997.
7. John Lowe, *The Warden: A Portrait of John Sparrow*. London: HarperCollins, 1999, 108.
8. *The Times*, 5 January 1983, 12.
9. Lowe, *The Warden*, 13.
10. Viscount Alanbrooke, *War Diaries, 1939–1945*. London: Weidenfeld & Nicolson, 2001, 558.
11. Ronald Adam, correspondence with Sir Henry Maitland Wilson, 14 March 1944, NA WO 214/62. Adam does not refer to this advocacy in his draft memoirs, but notes that it was fortunate in hindsight that the Army never, in the end, reintroduced the death penalty. LHCMA Adam 3-13.
12. Victor Scannell, *The Tiger and the Rose: An Autobiography*. London: Hamilton, 1971, 3.
13. Leo Page, *The Young Lag*. London: Faber and Faber, 1950, 158–9.
14. Scannell, *The Tiger and the Rose*, 56.
15. For a recent treatment that takes this approach, see Charles Glass, *Deserter: The Last Untold Story of the Second World War*. London: HarperPress, 2013.
16. A. B. McPherson, *Discipline*. London: The War Office, 1950, Appendix I; NA WO 277/7.
17. LHCMA Adam 3-13.
18. LHCMA Adam 3-4-6.
19. Nafsika Thalassis, 'Useless Soldiers: The Dilemma of Discharging Mentally Unfit Soldiers During the Second World War' in *Social History of Medicine* 23:1 (2010); Elizabeth Roberts-Pedersen, 'A Weak Spot in the Personality? Conceptualizing "War Neurosis" in British Medical Literature of the Second World War' in *Australian Journal of Politics and History* 58:3 (2012).
20. Robert Ahrenfeldt, *Psychiatry in the British Army in the Second World War*. London: Routledge & Kegan Paul, 1958, 123. The number of deserters who were originally volunteers (such as Scannell) rather than conscripts was also disproportionately high, suggesting that the very act of volunteering might be indicative of a dangerous level of immaturity or emotional fragility rather than a positive sign of patriotism.
21. Ibid., 23. Such men were usually placed in the Pioneer Corps, formed in autumn 1939 to perform manual labouring work. At the start of the war it was also the only one of the Army's corps which would accept recruits of German or Austrian nationality, and so it included some of the most educationally accomplished soldiers in the British Army as well as the least. The writer Arthur Koestler, the artist Johannes Koelz and Sigmund Freud's son Martin were amongst its recruits; the Pioneer Corps was said to possess one of the best classical orchestras in the country at the time. See Helen Fry, *The King's Most Loyal Enemy Aliens: Germans Who Fought for Britain in the Second World War*. Stroud: Sutton Publishing, 2008.
22. Ben Shephard, *A War of Nerves: Soldiers and Psychiatrists in the Twentieth Century*. Cambridge, MA: Harvard University Press, 2001, 188. Some 4,000 young soldiers who were not necessarily considered to be lost causes, but whose immaturity was deemed to put them at risk of becoming deserters, were placed by the DSP in Special Training Units where they were given close attention by Army psychologists. Labour companies were created which attempted to rehabilitate older men with poor disciplinary records. McPherson, *Discipline*, 63–71.
23. Jeremy Crang, *The British Army and the People's War 1939–1945*. Manchester: Manchester University Press, 2000, 100–6; J. H. A. Sparrow, *Morale*. London: The War Office, 1949, 6–7; NA WO 277/16.
24. J. B. Tomlinson. IWM:D 613 90/29/1. See also Lizzie Collingham, *The Taste of War: World War II and the Battle for Food*. London: Penguin, 2012, 399–403.
25. M. C. Morgan, *Welfare*. London: The War Office, 1953; NA WO 277/4.

26. Anthony Burgess, *Little Wilson and Big God, Being the First Part of the Confessions of Anthony Burgess*. Heinemann, 1987, 267.

27. Crang, *The British Army*, 5–15.

28. Broad, *The Radical General*, Kindle locations 2056–8.

29. B. Ungerson, *Personnel Selection*. London: The War Office, 1953, 39–45; NA WO 277/19; Broad, *The Radical General*, Kindle location 2370; Georgina Natzio, 'British Army Servicemen and Women 1939–45: Their Selection, Care and Management' in *RUSI Journal* 138:1 (1993).

30. David French, *Raising Churchill's Army: The British Army and the War against Germany, 1919–1945*. Oxford: Oxford University Press, 2000, 74.

31. NA WO 216/61.

32. Crang, *The British Army*, 31–3.

33. LHCMA Adam 3-13.

34. Crang, *The British Army*, 33–4.

35. Ibid., 15.

36. Ibid., 34.

37. Broad, *The Radical General*, Kindle locations 2767–9.

38. McPherson, *Discipline*, 117.

39. Mass-Observation Archive, University of Sussex, TC29 Box 2.

40. Mass-Observation Archive, University of Sussex, File Report 1942.

41. Neil Barber, ed., *Fighting with the Commandos: Recollections of Stan Scott, No. 3 Commando*. Barnsley: Pen & Sword, 2008. Kindle locations 526–30.

42. Reginald Crimp, *The Diary of a Desert Rat*. London: Cooper, 1971, 171.

43. John Guest, *Broken Images: A Journal*. London: Leo Cooper, 1970, 52.

44. Anthony Cotterell, *Oh, It's Nice to be in the Army!*, London: Gollancz, 1941, 22.

45. Alan Wood, *Bless 'Em All: An Analysis of the British Army, its Morale, Efficiency and Leadership*. London: Secker & Warburg, 1942, 25–6.

46. Colin MacInnes, *To The Victors the Spoils*. London: Allison & Busby, 1986, 82–3.

47. Arthur Calder-Marshall ('A Private'), 'Ours Not to Reason Why' in *Horizon*, March 1941, 185–6.

48. David Cooper. IWM:D 202 90/6/1.

49. Burgess, *Little Wilson and Big God*, 244.

50. Mass-Observation Archive, University of Sussex, File Report 1941.

51. Crimp, *The Diary of a Desert Rat*, 135.

52. Burgess, *Little Wilson and Big God*, 244–5.

53. Douglas Arthur, *Desert Watch: A Story of the Battle of Beda Fomm – And What Went on Before – As Seen Through the Eyes of Driver D. Arthur (Young Doug), No. 1 Battery, 106th Lancashire Hussars (Yeomanry) Regiment, Royal Horse Artillery*. Bedale: Blaisdon Publishing, 2000, 43–7.

54. Rupert Croft-Cooke, *The Licentious Soldiery*. London: W. H. Allen, 1971, 25, 34, 37.

55. Guest, *Broken Images*, 7.

56. Denis Argent, *A Soldier in Bedfordshire, 1941–1942: The Diary of Private Denis Argent, Royal Engineers*. Woodbridge: Boydell Press, 2009, 66.

57. Harry Wilson, Introduction. IWM:D 4709 80/5/1.

58. Maurice Merritt, *Eighth Army Driver*. Tunbridge Wells, Kent: Midas Books, 1981, 13.

59. Tom Harrisson, 'The British Soldier: Changing Attitudes and Ideas' in *British Journal of Psychology* 35:2 (1945), 38.

60. Merritt, *Eighth Army Driver*, 22.

61. Calder-Marshall, 'Ours Not to Reason Why', 179.

62. Norman Craig, *The Broken Plume: A Platoon Commander's Story, 1940–45*. London: Imperial War Museum, 1982, 17.

63. Sandra Koa Wing, ed., *Our Longest Days: A People's History of the Second World War*. London: Profile Books, 2008, 59.

64. Anthony Cotterell, *What! No Morning Tea?* London: Gollancz, 1941, 47.

65. Brian Aldiss, *A Soldier Erect: or Further Adventures of the Hand-Reared Boy*. London: Weidenfeld & Nicolson, 1971, Kindle locations 1069–89.

66. Ibid., Kindle locations 1477–83.

67. The Army's willingness to encourage the open discussion of sexual matters distinguished it from the 'institutionalised culture of public silence and euphemism' more typical of Britain at the time. See Simon Szreter and Kate Fisher, *Sex Before the Sexual Revolution: Intimate Life in England 1918–1963*. Cambridge: Cambridge University Press, 2010, 74.

68. Geoffrey Picot, *Accidental Warrior: In the Front Line from Normandy till Victory*. Lewes: Book Guild, 1993, 18.

69. Claire Langhamer, *The English in Love: The Intimate Story of an Emotional Revolution*. Oxford: Oxford University Press, 2013, 102.

70. Gerard De Groot, '"I Love the Scent of Cordite in Your Hair": Gender Dynamics in Mixed Anti-aircraft Batteries during the Second World War' in *History* 82:265 (2002).

71. Koa Wing, ed., *Our Longest Days*, 67.

72. Norman Smith, *Tank Soldier*. Lewes: Book Guild, 1989, 104.

73. Picot, *Accidental Warrior*, 19.

74. Koa Wing, ed., *Our Longest Days*, 66–7.

75. S. C. Proctor. IWM:D 5636 91/1/1.

76. R. H. Lloyd Jones. IWM:D 125 89/1/1.

77. *The Times*, 24 September, 1941, 2.

78. Emma Vickers, *Queen and Country: Same Sex Desire in the British Armed Forces, 1939–1945*. Manchester: Manchester University Press, 2013, 108–12.

79. Emma Reilly, Civilians into Soldiers: The British Male Military Body in the Second World War. Unpublished thesis, University of Strathclyde, 2010, 105–7.

80. Lowe, *The Warden*, 93–5.

81. It was not unknown in some regular units posted for long periods overseas for at least one soldier to advertise himself as sexually available to the others for payment. Anthony Babington, *An Uncertain Voyage*. Chichester: Barry Rose Law, 2000, 134.

82. C. Macdonald Hull, *A Man from Alamein*. London: Corgi, 1973, 272–4.

83. Raleigh Trevelyan, *The Fortress: A Diary of Anzio and After*. London: Leo Cooper, 1972, 90.

84. Sex between officers and men was punished much more severely than that between men of equivalent rank, because it was perceived as breaking a disciplinary taboo. See Herbert Moran, *In My Fashion*. London: Peter Davies, 1946, 128.

85. Patrick Higgins, *Heterosexual Dictatorship: Male Homosexuality in Postwar Britain*. London: Fourth Estate, 1996.

86. J. B. Tomlinson. IWM:D 613 90/29/1.

87. John Coldstream, *Dirk Bogarde: The Authorised Biography*. London: Phoenix, 2005, 158–9.

88. Julian Maclaren-Ross, *Collected Memoirs*. London: Black Spring Press, 2004, 268.

89. Gerald Kersh, *Clean, Bright, and Slightly Oiled*. London: Heinemann, 1946, 55–6.

90. Wood, *Bless 'Em All*, 30.

91. Reilly, *Civilians into Soldiers*, 110.

92. Craig, *The Broken Plume*, 16.

93. Simon Heffer, *Like the Roman: The Life of Enoch Powell*. Weidenfeld & Nicolson, 1998, 57.

94. David Holbrook, *Flesh Wounds*. Tempus, 2007, 68–9.

95. Craig, *The Broken Plume*, 24.

96. Vincent Porter and Chaim Letewski, 'The Way Ahead: Case History of a Propaganda Film' in *Sight and Sound* 50 (1981).

97. Calder-Marshall, 'Ours Not to Reason Why', 177.

98. Eric Ambler, *Here Lies: An Autobiography*. London: Weidenfeld & Nicolson, 1986, 184–5.

99. Ibid.

100. Craig, *The Broken Plume*, 35.

Part Three: Crusaders

1. Spike Mays, *Fall Out the Officers*. London: Eyre & Spottiswoode, 1969, 160–1.

7 Into the Blue

1. John Hudson, *Sunset in the East: Fighting Against the Japanese through the Siege of Imphal and Alongside Them in Java, 1943–1946*. Barnsley: Leo Cooper, 2002, 8–9.

2. John Ellis, *The Sharp End: The Fighting Man in World War II*. London: Aurum, 2011, 364.

3. Sheila Ferguson and Hilde Fitzgerald, *Studies in the Social Services*. London: HMSO, 1954, 3. This figure does not take into account the 40,000 British POWs who were held in captivity for more than five years.

4. J. H. A. Sparrow, *Morale*. London: The War Office, 1949, 8–9.

5. Ben Shephard, *A War of Nerves: Soldiers and Psychiatrists in the Twentieth Century*. Cambridge, MA: Harvard University Press, 2001, 243.

6. J. H. A. Sparrow, *Tour of India and South East Asia Command, 28th June 1945–15th October 1945*. Imperial War Museum Department of Printed Books IWM:PB 02(41).13 [South East Asia Command]/6.

7. CQMS Bill Points, letter to Mrs Mary Jones, 22 August 22, 1945. IWM:D 6902 78/55/1; LHCMA Adam 3-6-3.

8. Jack Swaab, *Field of Fire: Diary of a Gunner Officer*. Stroud: Sutton, 2005, 352.

9. According to the May–July 1942 Morale Report from Egypt, the BBC's Richard Dimbleby was 'far more unpopular than Rommel' amongst the men of the Eighth Army because of broadcast comments he had made during the retreat from Gazala. NA WO 163/161.

10. W. G. Holloway, '1st Army Soldier' in Victor Selwyn, *From Oasis into Italy: War Poems and Diaries from Africa and Italy, 1940–1946*. London: Shepheard-Walwyn, 1983, 84–5.

11. LHCMA Adam 3-6-4.

12. Brian Aldiss, *A Soldier Erect: or Further Adventures of the Hand-Reared Boy*. London: Weidenfeld & Nicolson, 1971, Kindle locations 1992–3.

13. Clive Branson, *British Soldier in India: The Letters of Clive Branson*. London: The Communist Party, 1944, 72.

14. Dan Billany, *The Trap*. London: Faber and Faber, 1986, 191–2. Billany served as a subaltern in the North African campaign and was captured during the retreat from Gazala in June 1942. He wrote *The Trap* while a prisoner-of-war in Italy. After the Italian surrender in 1943 he escaped from his camp and deposited the manuscript with an Italian farmer, who sent it along to his next-of-kin in Britain after the war. Billany died in mysterious circumstances before reaching Allied lines.

15. NA WO 277/4.

16. Harry Wilson, 536. IWM:D 4709 80/5/1.

17. Reginald Crimp, 26 April 1944. IWM:D 5659 96/50/1.

18. A. M. Bell MacDonald. IWM:D 10786 Con Shelf.

19. Robert Lees, 'Venereal Diseases in the Armed Forces Overseas (1)' in *British Journal of Venereal Diseases* 22:4 (1946), 150.

20. Tim Bishop and Bruce Shand, *One Young Soldier: The Memoirs of a Cavalryman*. Norwich: M. Russell, 1993, 142.

21. Cecil Beaton, 'Libyan Diary – II' in *Horizon*, February 1943, 104.

22. Christopher Seton-Watson, *Dunkirk, Alamein, Bologna: Letters and Diaries of an Artilleryman, 1939–1945*. London: Buckland, 1993, 161.

23. H. J. Griffin, *An Eighth Army Odyssey*. Edinburgh: Pentland Press, 1997, 107.

24. Seton-Watson, *Dunkirk, Alamein, Bologna*, 88.

25. John Guest, *Broken Images: A Journal*. London: Leo Cooper, 1970, 105.

26. Douglas Arthur, *Desert Watch: A Story of the Battle of Beda Fomm – And What Went on Before – As Seen Through the Eyes of Driver D. Arthur (Young Doug), No. 1 Battery, 106th Lancashire Hussars (Yeomanry) Regiment, Royal Horse Artillery*. Bedale: Blaisdon Publishing, 2000, 155.

27. Reginald Crimp, 10 May, 1944. IWM:D 5659 96/50/1.

28. Hudson, *Sunset in the East*, 94.

29. George Orwell, *All Art is Propaganda: Critical Essays*. New York: Houghton Mifflin, 2009, 77–8.

30. Ian R. G. Spencer, *British Immigration Policy Since 1939: The Making of Multi-Racial Britain*. New York: Routledge, 1997, 3. Some Indian sailors or 'lascars' lived a quasi-legal life in Britain, effectively excluded from permanent settlement by discriminatory legislation. See George Wemyss in Rehana Ahmed and Sumita Mukherjee, eds, *South Asian Resistances in Britain 1858–1947*. London: Continuum, 2012.

31. By October 1942, the secretary of state for war would be suggesting that British troops ought to be 'educated' to adopt the same attitude towards blacks as white American troops. Richard Toye, *Churchill's Empire: The World That Made Him and the World He Made*. New York: Henry Holt & Co., 2010, 248.

32. Hundreds of thousands of non-Europeans did, of course, serve the British Crown outside the United Kingdom in the Indian Army and other colonial forces such as the King's African Rifles and the Royal West African Frontier Force. But these were institutionally distinct from the British Army.

33. Stephen Bourne, *The Motherland Calls: Britain's Black Servicemen and Women, 1939–45*. Stroud: The History Press, 2012, 23–5; David Killingray, 'Race and Rank in the British Army

in the Twentieth Century' in *Ethnic and Racial Studies* 10:3 (1987), 280–1. Moody ended the war a major. He had been preceded by Walter Tull, who had commanded a platoon of the 17th Middlesex Regiment during the First World War and had been killed in action in spring 1918. The RAF was rather more open to the commissioning of non-European men during the Second World War, particularly from the West Indies, and by 1945 it had made over seventy of them officers.

34. Branson, *British Soldier in India*, 43.
35. Peter Schrijvers, *Liberators: The Allies and Belgian Society 1944–45*. Cambridge: Cambridge University Press, 2009; Mary Louise Roberts, *What Soldiers Do: Sex and the American GI in World War II France*. Chicago: University of Chicago Press, 2013.
36. Colin MacInnes, *To the Victors the Spoils*. London: Allison & Busby, 1986, 27.
37. Branson, *British Soldier in India*, 29.
38. Brian Aldiss, *Trillion Year Spree: The History of Science Fiction*. London: Paladin, 1988, 280.
39. Reginald Crimp, *The Diary of a Desert Rat*. London: Cooper, 1971, 2–3.
40. I. S. O. Playfair, *The Mediterranean and Middle East*. Vol. 2. London: HMSO, 1974, 223.
41. Alan Moorehead, *The Desert War*. London: Aurum, 2009, 576.
42. Ibid., 531; Peter Cochrane, *Charlie Company: In Service with C Company 2nd Queen's Own Cameron Highlanders, 1940–44*. Stroud: Spellmount, 2007, 9, 13.
43. Neil McCallum, *Journey with a Pistol: A Diary of War*. London: Gollancz, 1959, 37.
44. Norman Craig, *The Broken Plume: A Platoon Commander's Story, 1940–45*. London: Imperial War Museum, 1982, 51.
45. Ibid., 44.
46. David French, *The British Way in Warfare: 1688–2000*. London: Unwin Hyman, 1990, 198.
47. Moorehead, *The Desert War*, 579.
48. Ellis, *The Sharp End*, 309.
49. Reginald Crimp, 21 March 1945. IWM:D 5659 96/50/1.
50. Moorehead, *The Desert War*, 578–80.
51. Ibid., 579. Technically it is not quite right to call the Eighth Army the Desert Rats. It was the men of the 7th Armoured Division, *in situ* in Egypt at the outbreak of the war, who bore a jerboa as the identifying flash on their vehicles. Later the name began to be applied more broadly to all soldiers of the Eighth Army, a dilution in its meaning which became commonplace, but which was much resented by the 7th Armoured's soldiers.
52. Harry Wilson, 94. IWM:D 4709 80/5/1.
53. Philip Warner, *Auchinleck: The Lonely Soldier*. London: Buchan & Enright, 1981, 85.
54. Harry K. Gaunt, IWM:D 1544 92/1/1.
55. Crimp, *The Diary of a Desert Rat*, 30.
56. Harry K. Gaunt, IWM:D 1544 92/1/1.
57. Warner, *Auchinleck*, 84.
58. Craig, *The Broken Plume*, 116.
59. J. Herbert Parker-Jones. IWM:D 9078 01/10/1.
60. Bishop and Shand, *One Young Soldier*, 82.
61. McCallum, *Journey with a Pistol*, 41.
62. Craig, *The Broken Plume*, 47.
63. Arthur, *Desert Watch*, 87; Seton-Watson, *Dunkirk, Alamein, Bologna*, 96.
64. Beaton, 'Libyan Diary I', 29.
65. Seton-Watson, *Dunkirk, Alamein, Bologna*, 154.
66. Harry Wilson, 122. IWM:D 4709 80/5/1.
67. E. P. Danger. IWM:D 4465 82/37/1.
68. Robert Metcalfe, *No Time for Dreams: A Soldier's Six-year Journey through World War II*. Burnstown: General Store Publishing House, 1997, 69; Harry Wilson, 287. IWM:D 4709 80/5/1.
69. Harry K. Gaunt, IWM:D 1544 92/1/1.
70. Seton-Watson, *Dunkirk, Alamein, Bologna*, 92.
71. Craig, *The Broken Plume*, 48.
72. Billany, *The Trap*, 244–5.
73. Moorehead, *The Desert War*, 10; Bishop and Shand, *One Young Soldier*, 73; Billany, *The Trap*, 313.
74. Crimp, *The Diary of a Desert Rat*, 33; Beaton, 'Libyan Diary II', 88.
75. Cochrane, *Charlie Company*, 8.

76. A. J. Mills. IWM:D 4269 83/24/1.
77. Jonathan Fennell, *Combat and Morale in the North African Campaign: The Eighth Army and the Path to El Alamein.* Cambridge: Cambridge University Press, 2010, 128.
78. Crimp, *The Diary of a Desert Rat,* 23–4.
79. Seton-Watson, *Dunkirk, Alamein, Bologna,* 92, 58, 96.
80. Beaton, 'Libyan Diary II', 108; Beaton, 'Libyan Diary I', 35.
81. Seton-Watson, *Dunkirk, Alamein, Bologna,* 92.
82. Ken Ford, *Battleaxe Division: From Africa to Italy with the 78th Division 1942–45.* Stroud: Sutton, 2003, 246–7.
83. Beaton, 'Libyan Diary II', 108.
84. McCallum, *Journey With a Pistol,* 35.
85. Craig, *The Broken Plume,* 43, 121; Seton-Watson, *Dunkirk, Alamein, Bologna,* 90.
86. Reginald Crimp, 5 August 1943. IWM:D 5659 96/50/1; Artemis Cooper, *Cairo in the War: 1939–1945.* London: H. Hamilton, 1989, 114.
87. Craig, *The Broken Plume,* 120.
88. McCallum, *Journey with a Pistol,* 61.
89. Mark Harrison, *Medicine and Victory: British Military Medicine in the Second World War.* Oxford: Oxford University Press, 2008, 105; Cooper, *Cairo in the War,* 115.
90. J. H. Witte. IWM:D 1279 87/12/1.
91. Arthur, *Desert Watch,* 136.
92. Harry Wilson, 102. IWM:D 4709 80/5/1.
93. Guest, *Broken Images,* 104.
94. Arthur, *Desert Watch,* 152.
95. Spike Mays, *Fall Out the Officers.* London: Eyre & Spottiswoode, 1969, 106.
96. Harry Wilson, 113. IWM:D 4709 80/5/1.
97. A. J. Mills. IWM:D 4269 83/24/1.
98. Craig, *The Broken Plume,* 42; A. J. Mills. IWM:D 4269 83/24/1.
99. Patrick Hynes, *The Militiaman.* London: Avon, 1994, 44–5.
100. McCallum, *Journey with a Pistol,* 35, 59. The British were not alone in this. 'Everywhere Australian soldiers went [in the Middle East], some of them behaved like bullies and savages, frightening or robbing or hurting others to satisfy their own selfish ends.' Mark Johnston, *Anzacs in the Middle East: Australian Soldiers, Their Allies, and the Local People in World War II.* Cambridge: Cambridge University Press, 2013, 205.
101. Hynes, *The Militiaman,* 26.
102. Metcalfe, *No Time for Dreams,* 58.
103. Harry Wilson, 96. IWM:D 4709 80/5/1.
104. Seton-Watson, *Dunkirk, Alamein, Bologna,* 56.
105. Billany, *The Trap,* 234–5.
106. Richard Weight, *Patriots: National Identity in Britain, 1940–2000.* London: Macmillan, 2002, 79.

8 Come to Sunny Italy

1. Reginald Crimp, 10 May 1944. IWM:D 5659 96/50/1.
2. Alan Moorehead, *Eclipse.* New York: Harper & Row, 1968, 6.
3. Harry Wilson, 468. IWM:D 4709 80/5/1.
4. Reginald Crimp, 16 May 1944. IWM:D 5659 96/50/1.
5. Ibid., 8 May 1944.
6. Christopher Seton-Watson, *Dunkirk, Alamein, Bologna: Letters and Diaries of an Artilleryman, 1939–1945.* London: Buckland, 1993, 233.
7. John Guest, *Broken Images: A Journal.* London: Leo Cooper, 1970, 162.
8. Ibid., 207.
9. Walter Elliott, *Esprit de Corps: A Scots Guards Officer on Active Service, 1943–1945.* Norwich: M. Russell, 1996, 62.
10. Victor Selwyn, *From Oasis into Italy: War Poems and Diaries from Africa and Italy, 1940–1946.* London: Shepheard-Walwyn, 1983, 98–9.
11. Norman Lewis, *Naples '44.* New York: Pantheon Books, 1978, 93.
12. Richard Hoggart, *A Sort of Clowning: Life and Times, Vol. 2: 1940–1959.* Oxford: Oxford University Press, 1991, 49; Selwyn, *From Oasis into Italy,* 98–9.

13. H. P. Samwell, *Fighting with the Desert Rats: An infantry Officer's War with the Eighth Army.* Barnsley: Pen & Sword, 2012, 187.
14. Neil McCallum, *Journey with a Pistol: A Diary of War.* London: Gollancz, 1959, 154.
15. Moorehead, *Eclipse*, 66.
16. Harry Wilson, 465. IWM:D 4709 80/5/1.
17. Reginald Crimp, 4–8 May 1944. IWM:D 5659 96/50/1.
18. Michael Howard, *Grand Strategy. Vol. 4, August 1942–September 1943.* London: HMSO, 1970, 419, 644–5; Max Hastings, *All Hell Let Loose: The World at War 1939–45.* London: HarperPress, 2011, Kindle location 8390; Rick Atkinson, *The Day of Battle: The War in Sicily and Italy, 1943–1944.* New York: Henry Holt, 2007, 15.
19. Lieutenant-Colonel Lionel Wigram, one of the founders of the War Office School of Infantry who accompanied the Sicilian expedition as an observer, wrote a report on the campaign criticizing British tactical methods. 'The Germans have undoubtedly in one way scored a decisive success . . . they have been able to evacuate their forces almost intact having suffered very few casualties [while] they have inflicted heavy casualties on us.' Montgomery was so furious when he heard of the report that he summoned Wigram to his headquarters for a personal dressing-down and subsequently had him demoted. Wigram was killed in action in Italy. See Denis Forman, *To Reason Why.* Barnsley: Pen & Sword Military, 2008.
20. Selwyn, *From Oasis into Italy*, 189.
21. Moorehead, *Eclipse*, 61.
22. Guest, *Broken Images*, 160.
23. Reginald Crimp, 20 July 1944. IWM:D 5659 96/50/1.
24. Raleigh Trevelyan, *The Fortress: A Diary of Anzio and After.* London: Leo Cooper, 1972, 20–6.
25. Ibid., 81.
26. Tom Roe, *Anzio Beachhead: Diary of a Signaller.* Derby: Higham Press, 1988, 79.
27. Ian Gooderson, *A Hard Way to Make a War: The Italian Campaign in the Second World War.* London: Conway, 2008, 327. Another five German divisions were in northern Italy engaged in anti-partisan activities.
28. LHCMA Adam 3-6-4.
29. Reginald Crimp, 3 December 1944. IWM:D 5659 96/50/1.
30. According to Astor's own account, in December 1944 she received an airgraph from a group of soldiers in Italy which was signed 'D-Day Dodgers'. Thinking that this was the nickname that the unit had chosen for itself, she responded to them '*Dear D-Day Dodgers. . .*' and there the story began. The allegations pained her deeply, and she asked the Ministry of Information, without success, to refute them. Astor was a popular hate figure amongst British troops, and there was a whiff of misogyny to her notoriety: she was one of the few prominent women in British political life at the time. She was said to have demanded that troops returning from overseas be required to wear yellow armbands or badges to indicate that they might be carriers of VD. See *Daily Mirror*, 27 February 1945, 6; David Martin, 'Nancy Astor and Hamish Henderson's "The Ballad of the D-Day Dodgers"' in *History Teaching Review* 22 (2008); Selwyn, *From Oasis into Italy*, xx.
31. Seton-Watson, *Dunkirk, Alamein, Bologna*, 240.
32. Guest, *Broken Images*, 200.
33. Elliott, *Esprit de Corps*, 94.
34. Ibid., 68.
35. John Peaty, 'The Desertion Crisis in Italy, 1944' in *RUSI Journal* 147:3 (2002), 78.
36. Ben Shephard, *A War of Nerves: Soldiers and Psychiatrists in the Twentieth Century.* Cambridge, MA: Harvard University Press, 2001, 240.
37. Anonymous, 'The Desertion Crisis in Italy' in *RUSI Journal* 147:5 (2002), 84.
38. 'Sod's Opera', *Onward 15 Army Group*. Beautiful Jo Records, 2000. The song refers to a reshuffle of command between December 1944 and January 1945. General Henry 'Jumbo' Wilson stepped down as supreme allied commander in the Mediterranean to become chief of the British Joint Staff Mission in Washington DC. His position was taken by General Harold Alexander, former commander-in-chief of 15th Army Group (otherwise known as Allied Armies in Italy or AAI). Alexander was in turn replaced by the American General Mark Clark.
39. David Hunt, *A Don at War.* London: Cass, 1990, 237.
40. Gregory Blaxland, *Alexander's Generals: The Italian Campaign 1944–45.* London: William Kimber, 1979, 11; Ian Hay, *Arms and the Men.* London: HMSO, 1977, 195. For a judicious

discussion of the strategic importance of the Italian campaign, see Gooderson, *A Hard Way to Make a War*, 319–28.

41. Seton-Watson, *Dunkirk, Alamein, Bologna*, 227.
42. Reginald Crimp, 9 May 1944. IWM:D 5659 96/50/1.
43. Robert Edsel, *Saving Italy: The Race to Rescue a Nation's Treasures from the Nazis*. New York: W.W. Norton, 2013.
44. Wynford Vaughan-Thomas, *Trust to Talk*. London: Hutchinson, 1980, 167.
45. Alex Bowlby, *The Recollections of Rifleman Bowlby*. London: Cassell, 1999, 120.
46. Moorehead, *Eclipse*, 36.
47. Leonard Melling, *With the Eighth in Italy*. Manchester: Torch, 1955, 45–6.
48. Hoggart, *A Sort of Clowning*, 49.
49. Robert Metcalfe, *No Time for Dreams: A Soldier's Six-year Journey through World War II*. Burnstown: General Store Publishing House, 1997, 128.
50. Melling, *With the Eighth in Italy*, 80.
51. Lewis, *Naples '44*, 155, 47, 99, 28, 138, 155, 43.
52. Ben Shephard, *The Long Road Home: The Aftermath of the Second World War*. New York: Knopf, 2011, 45.
53. Lewis, *Naples '44*, 28–9.
54. Trevelyan, *The Fortress*, 134–5.
55. Harry Wilson, 590. IWM:D 4709 80/5/1.
56. Lewis, *Naples '44*, 105.
57. Guest, *Broken Images*, 163.
58. Moorehead, *Eclipse*, 67.
59. Hoggart, *A Sort of Clowning*, 49.
60. Maurice Merritt, *Eighth Army Driver*. Tunbridge Wells, Kent: Midas Books, 1981, 116.
61. Trevelyan, *The Fortress*, 136.
62. Lewis, *Naples '44*, 78.
63. Spiller, B. F. IWM:D 11941 02/52/1.
64. Norman Craig, *The Broken Plume: A Platoon Commander's Story, 1940–45*. London: Imperial War Museum, 1982, 153.
65. Moorehead, *Eclipse*, 52.
66. Seton-Watson, *Dunkirk, Alamein, Bologna*, 231.
67. Donald Thomas, *An Underworld at War: Spivs, Deserters, Racketeers & Civilians in the Second World War*. London: John Murray, 2003, 189; Clive Emsley, *Soldier, Sailor, Beggarman, Thief: Crime and the British Armed Services since 1914*. Oxford: Oxford University Press, 2013, 105.
68. Ibid., 92.
69. William Woodruff, *Vessel of Sadness*. Bath: Paragon, 2005, 60–2.

9 Fighting Bloody Nature

1. John Masters, *The Road Past Mandalay*. London: Cassell, 2002, 212.
2. Raymond Cooper, *'B' Company, 9th Battalion, the Border Regiment, 48 Brigade, 17 Indian (Light) Division, IV Corps, 14th Army, South East Asia Command: One Man's War in Burma, 1942–1944, Recalled in Hospital in 1945*. London: Dobson, 1978, 63.
3. George MacDonald Fraser, *Quartered Safe Out Here: A Recollection of the War in Burma with a New Epilogue: Fifty Years On*. London: HarperCollins, 2000, 38–9.
4. Eric Murrell, *For Your Tomorrow: A Cipher-Sergeant's Diary, 1941–1945*. Dorchester: Plush, 1999, 54.
5. Julian Thompson, *Forgotten Voices of Burma*. London: Ebury, 2010, 114.
6. William Cochrane, *Chindit: Special Force, Burma, 1944*. Philadelphia: Xlibris, 2000, 44.
7. Robin Painter, *A Signal Honour: With the Chindits and the XIV Army in Burma*. London: Leo Cooper, 1999, 119.
8. NA WO 214/62.
9. Reginald Crimp, 17 October 1943. IWM:D 5659 96/50/1.
10. James Lunt, seconded to the Burma Rifles in 1939, noted that in two-and-a-half years of peacetime training prior to the Japanese invasion his unit only ever performed one jungle exercise. James Lunt, 'A Hell of a Licking: Some Reflections on the Retreat from Burma, December 1941–May 1942' in *RUSI Journal* 130:3 (1985), 55.

11. Louis Allen, *Burma: The Longest War 1941–45*. New York: St Martin's Press, 1984, 109.

12. Frank McLynn, *The Burma Campaign: Disaster into Triumph 1942–1945*. New Haven: Yale University Press, 2011, 103.

13. Cooper, *'B' Company*, 33.

14. Christopher M. Bell, *Churchill and Sea Power*. Oxford: Oxford University Press, 2013, 300.

15. Viscount Alanbrooke, *War Diaries, 1939–1945*. London: Weidenfeld & Nicolson, 2001, 394.

16. Allen, *Burma: The Longest War*, 630–32.

17. Christopher Bayly and Tim Harper, *Forgotten Armies: The Fall of British Asia, 1941–1945*. Cambridge, MA: Belknap, 2005, 275.

18. Mark Harrison, *Medicine and Victory: British Military Medicine in the Second World War*. Oxford: Oxford University Press, 2008, 195.

19. Ibid., 276.

20. Fraser, *Quartered Safe Out Here*, 45.

21. Allen, *Burma: The Longest War*, 114–16; McLynn, *The Burma Campaign*, 99–100.

22. Tim Moreman, *The Jungle, The Japanese and the British Commonwealth Armies at War 1941–1945*. New York: Frank Cass, 2005.

23. John Hudson, *Sunset in the East: Fighting Against the Japanese through the Siege of Imphal and Alongside Them in Java, 1943–1946*. Barnsley: Leo Cooper, 2002, 64.

24. M. C. Morgan, *Welfare*. London: The War Office, 1953, 154–8; Alan Jeffreys, *British Infantryman in the Far East, 1941–45*. Oxford: Osprey, 2003; N. R. M. Borton, 'The 14th Army in Burma: A Case Study in Delivering Fighting Power' in *Defence Studies* 2:3 (2002); Robert Lyman, *Slim, Master of War*. London: Constable, 2004, 136–45.

25. Bernard Porter, *The Absent-minded Imperialists: Empire, Society, and Culture in Britain*. Oxford: Oxford University Press, 2004, 318. On the other hand, as Raymond Callaghan put it, 'Slim's great victory helped the British, unlike the French, Dutch, or later the Americans, to leave Asia with some dignity. That, perhaps, is no small thing.' Allen, *Burma: The Longest War*, 633.

26. Brian Aldiss, *A Soldier Erect: or Further Adventures of the Hand-Reared Boy*. London: Weidenfeld & Nicolson, 1971, Kindle locations 368–424.

27. J. M. Brereton, *The British Soldier: A Social History from 1661 to the Present Day*. London: Bodley Head, 1986, 152–3.

28. Richard Cartwright. IWM:D 3168 95/23/1.

29. Hudson, *Sunset in the East*, 13.

30. Masters, *The Road Past Mandalay*, 23.

31. Painter, *A Signal Honour*, 21.

32. Hudson, *Sunset in the East*, 10–11. Tension between the pre-war colonial elite and wartime visitors from Britain was not confined to India. In East Africa, troops complained that the settler population treated them like 'white natives'. (NA WO 163/161).

33. Cooper, *'B' Company*, 29.

34. Porter, *The Absent-minded Imperialists*, 264–73.

35. Fraser, *Quartered Safe Out Here*, 266.

36. J. H. A. Sparrow, *Tour of India and South East Asia Command, 28th June 1945–15th October 1945*. IWM:PB 02(41).13 [South East Asia Command]/6.

37. Aldiss, *A Soldier Erect*, Kindle locations 605–9.

38. Cochrane, *Chindit*, 25.

39. Rupert Croft-Cooke, *The Gorgeous East*. London: W.H. Allen, 1965, 3.

40. Richard Terrell, *Civilians in Uniform: A Memoir, 1937–1945*. London: Radcliffe Press, 1998, 112.

41. Murrell, *For Your Tomorrow*, 153–4.

42. Sparrow, *Tour of India*.

43. Cooper, *'B' Company*, 29.

44. Ibid., 56.

45. Aldiss, *A Soldier Erect*, Kindle locations 3227–32.

46. Ibid., Kindle locations 3294–301.

47. Masters, *The Road Past Mandalay*, 234.

48. Ernest Sanger, *Letters from the Two World Wars*. Stroud: Sutton, 1993, 204.

49. Cooper, *'B' Company*, 59.

50. Murrell, *For Your Tomorrow*, 145.

51. Aldiss, *A Soldier Erect*, Kindle locations 3311–16.

52. Thompson, *Forgotten Voices of Burma*, 181.
53. Richard Rhodes James, *Chindit*. London: J. Murray, 1980, 15.
54. Masters, *The Road Past Mandalay*, 225.
55. McLynn, *The Burma Campaign*, 9–12.
56. Masters, *The Road Past Mandalay*, 269; Mike Lowry, *Fighting Through to Kohima: A Memoir of War in India and Burma*. Barnsley: Pen & Sword, 2008, 72.
57. Ibid., 71.
58. Fraser, *Quartered Safe Out Here*, 232.
59. Hudson, *Sunset in the East*, 27.
60. Aldiss, *A Soldier Erect*, Kindle locations 3733–4.
61. Masters, *The Road Past Mandalay*, 268, 276.
62. Ibid., 281.
63. Painter, *A Signal Honour*, 150.
64. NA WO 162/299.
65. McLynn, *The Burma Campaign*, 1.
66. Cooper, *'B' Company*, 86.
67. Murrell, *For Your Tomorrow*, 61.
68. Hudson, *Sunset in the East*, 70–1.

10 Second Front

1. Jack Swaab, *Field of Fire: Diary of a Gunner Officer*. Stroud: Sutton, 2005, 192.
2. Jocelyn Pereira, *A Distant Drum: War Memories of the Intelligence Officer of the 5th Bn. Coldstream Guards, 1944–45*. Wakefield: S.R. Publishers, 1972, 2.
3. Swaab, *Field of Fire*, 177.
4. Pereira, *A Distant Drum*, 2.
5. Swaab, *Field of Fire*, 187.
6. This was a reconstituted version of the same 51st (Highland) Infantry Division that had been forced to surrender at Saint-Valery-en-Caux in June 1940.
7. The 1st Airborne Division also returned to the UK, though this was a recently constituted formation that had only been in the Mediterranean theatre for a few months.
8. Stephen Hart, *Colossal Cracks: Montgomery's 21st Army Group in Northwest Europe, 1944–45*. Mechanicsburg, PA: Stackpole Books, 2007, 29.
9. Allan Converse, *Armies of Empire: The 9th Australian and 50th British Divisions in Battle, 1939–1945*. Cambridge: Cambridge University Press, 2011, 181, 191–2.
10. Max Hastings, *All Hell Let Loose: The World at War 1939–45*. London: HarperPress, 2011, Kindle location 10036.
11. Swaab, *Field of Fire*, 185.
12. H. F. Joslen, *Orders of Battle: United Kingdom and Colonial Formations and Units in the Second World War, 1939–1945*. London: HMSO, 1960.
13. David Holbrook, *Flesh Wounds*. Stroud: Tempus, 2007, 97.
14. Robert Woollcombe, *Lion Rampant*. London: Leo Cooper, 1970, 42.
15. Pereira, *A Distant Drum*, 2–3.
16. Ken Tout, *By Tank: D to VE Days*. London: R. Hale, 2007, 10.
17. Woollcombe, *Lion Rampant*, 11, 15.
18. When Churchill heard that Gort's counterattack towards Arras had fizzled out on 24 May he had commented acidly to his personal chief of staff 'Pug' Ismay: 'If one side fights and the other does not, the war is apt to become somewhat unequal.' Max Hastings, *Winston's War: Churchill, 1940–1945*. New York: Alfred A. Knopf, 2009, 30.
19. J. M. A. Gwyer and James Ramsay Montagu Butler, *Grand Strategy. Vol. 3 Part I, June 1941–August 1942*. London: HMSO, 1964, 40.
20. Winston Churchill, *The Churchill War Papers. Vol. 3. The Ever-widening War, 1941*. New York: W.W. Norton, 2000, 1273.
21. *Naval History and Heritage Command*: www.history.navy.mil/library/online/comnaveu/comnaveu-2.htm. Accessed 6 May 2014.
22. John Robert Peaty, British Army Manpower Crisis 1944. Unpublished thesis, King's College University of London, 2000, 334. Of the remainder, 192,000 were garrisoning the Middle East and 64,000 were in traditional colonial stations such as Malta and Gibraltar. Just over one million British soldiers were in the UK.

23. John Ellis, *The World War II Databook: The Essential Facts and Figures for all the Combatants*. London: Aurum, 1993, 256; *Strength and Casualties of the Armed Forces and Auxiliary Services of the United Kingdom 1939–1945*. Cmnd. 6832. HMSO, 1946.
24. NA WO 163/163.
25. Walter Elliott, *Esprit de Corps: A Scots Guards Officer on Active Service, 1943–1945*. Norwich: M. Russell, 1996, 126.
26. Ken Ford, *El Alamein 1942: The Turning of the Tide*. Oxford: Osprey, 2005, 26–8, 65; Ken Ford, *Caen 1944*. Oxford: Osprey, 2004, 87. At El Alamein, Rommel also commanded nine Italian divisions with 298 tanks, though these were generally of low quality.
27. Bernard Law Montgomery, *The Memoirs of Field-Marshal the Viscount Montgomery of Alamein*. Cleveland: World Publishing Co., 1958, 231; Niall Barr, *Pendulum of War: The Three Battles of El Alamein*. London: Jonathan Cape, 2004, 404.
28. John Buckley, *Monty's Men: The British Army and the Liberation of Europe, 1944–5*. New Haven: Yale University Press, 2013, 4.
29. Max Hastings, *Overlord: D-Day and the Battle for Normandy 1944*. London: Pan, 1999, 211.
30. John Ellis, *The Sharp End: The Fighting Man in World War II*. London: Aurum, 2011, 162.
31. Stanley Whitehouse, *Fear is the Foe: A Footslogger from Normandy to the Rhine*. London: Hale, 1995, 141.
32. Richard Overy, *The Bombing War: Europe, 1939–1945*. London: Allen Lane, 2013, 313.
33. Woollcombe, *Lion Rampant*, 120.
34. Pereira, *A Distant Drum*, 7.
35. John Foley, *Mailed Fist*. St Albans: Mayflower, 1975, 72.
36. Ernest Sanger, *Letters from the Two World Wars*. Stroud: Sutton, 1993, 180; Tout, *By Tank*, 15.
37. Trevor Greenwood, *D-Day to Victory: The Diaries of a British Tank Commander*. London: Simon & Schuster, 2012, 69.
38. Pereira, *A Distant Drum*, 9.
39. Stephen Badsey, *Normandy 1944: Allied Landings and Breakout*. Oxford: Osprey, 1990, 84–5.
40. Anthony Beevor, *D-Day: The Battle for Normandy*. New York: Viking, 2009, 252.
41. Holbrook, *Flesh Wounds*, 151.
42. Geoffrey Picot, *Accidental Warrior: In the Front Line from Normandy till Victory*. Lewes: Book Guild, 1993, 116–17.
43. Greenwood, *D-Day to Victory*, 80, 109.
44. Pereira, *A Distant Drum*, 9.
45. Kingsley Amis, *Memoirs*. London: Vintage, 2004, 86.
46. Whitehouse, *Fear is the Foe*, 35; Andrew Wilson, *Flame Thrower*. New York: Bantam, 1984, 76.
47. John Smith, *In at the Finish*. London: Minerva, 1995, 139.
48. Picot, *Accidental Warrior*, 164.
49. Smith, *In at the Finish*, 25.
50. Beevor, *D-Day*, 519.
51. Alexander McKee, *Caen: Anvil of Victory*. London: Souvenir, 2000, 214–15.
52. Woodrow Wyatt, 'Letter from France' in *Horizon*, October 1944, 229.
53. Whitehouse, *Fear is the Foe*, 51.
54. Badsey, *Normandy 1944*, 85.
55. Smith, *In at the Finish*, 25.
56. Picot, *Accidental Warrior*, 158.
57. Alan Moorehead, *Eclipse*. New York: Harper & Row, 1968, 159–60.
58. Peter Schrijvers, *Liberators: The Allies and Belgian Society 1944–45*. Cambridge: Cambridge University Press, 2009, 49–68.
59. Colin MacInnes, *To the Victors the Spoils*. London: Allison & Busby, 1986, 23.
60. Greenwood, *D-Day to Victory*, 207.
61. Ibid., 211; Pereira, *A Distant Drum*, 103.
62. Picot, *Accidental Warrior*, 198.
63. Greenwood, *D-Day to Victory*, 159.
64. Swaab, *Field of Fire*, 229.
65. Pereira, *A Distant Drum*, 118.
66. Ellis, *The Sharp End*, 186.
67. Pereira, *A Distant Drum*, 121.

68. Sydney Jary, *18 Platoon*. Carshalton Beeches: Sydney Jary, *c*.1987, 93; Whitehouse, *Fear is the Foe*, 134; Swaab, *Field of Fire*, 298–9.
69. Ibid., 300.
70. Smith, *In at the Finish*, 182.
71. Ibid., 243.
72. *Daily Telegraph*, 8 January 2009.
73. Moorehead, *Eclipse*, 230.
74. MacInnes, *To the Victors the Spoils*, 146.
75. Moorehead, *Eclipse*, 230.
76. Peter White, *With the Jocks: A Soldier's Struggle for Europe, 1944–45*. Stroud: Sutton, 2003, 474–5.
77. Bill Bellamy, *Troop Leader: A Tank Commander's Story*. Stroud: Sutton, 2007, 168.
78. Elliott, *Esprit de Corps*, 135.
79. Moorehead, *Eclipse*, 231.
80. Martin Lindsay, *So Few Got Through: The Personal Diary of Lieut-Col. Martin Lindsay, D.S.O., M.P., Who Served with the Gordon Highlanders in the 51st Highland Division from July, 1944, to May, 1945*. London: Collins, 1968, 203.
81. NA WO 163/161.
82. Norman Lewis, *Naples '44*. New York: Pantheon Books, 1978, 31.
83. Hastings, *All Hell Let Loose*, Kindle locations 10120–2.
84. Sean Longden, *To the Victor the Spoils: D-Day and VE Day, The Reality Behind the Heroism*. London: Robinson, 2007, 329; Beevor, *D-Day*, 452.
85. Longden, *To the Victor the Spoils*, 337.
86. Lindsay, *So Few Got Through*, 148.
87. MacInnes, *To the Victors the Spoils*, 183–4.
88. Bill Deedes, *Dear Bill: W. F. Deedes Reports*. London: Macmillan, 2005, 87.
89. A. J. Forrest. IWM:D 310 91/13/1.
90. Moorehead, *Eclipse*, 253–4.
91. Longden, *To the Victor the Spoils*, 339.
92. Buckley, *Monty's Men*, 279.
93. *Germany 1944: The British Soldier's Pocketbook*. Kew: National Archives, 2006, 4–5.
94. Ibid., 18–21.
95. Lindsay, *So Few Got Through*, 249.
96. Swaab, *Field of Fire*, 347, 352.
97. White, *With the Jocks*, 22–3.
98. Ibid., 531–2.
99. Adrian Smith, *The City of Coventry: A Twentieth Century Icon*. London: I.B. Tauris, 2006, 55–6.
100. Rupert Croft-Cooke, *The Gorgeous East*. London: W.H. Allen, 1965, 2.
101. Denis Healey, *The Time of My Life*. New York: W.W. Norton, 1990, 61.
102. Richard Weight, *Patriots: National Identity in Britain, 1940–2000*. London: Macmillan, 2002, 27; Malcolm Smith, *Britain and 1940: History, Myth, and Popular Memory*. London: Routledge, 2000, 130–48; Mark Connelly, *We Can Take It! Britain and the Memory of the Second World War*. London: Pearson Longman, 2004, 280–94.
103. Richard Hoggart, *A Sort of Clowning: Life and Times, Vol. 2: 1940–1959*. Oxford: Oxford University Press, 1991, 60.
104. Weight, *Patriots*, 62.

Part Four: Killers

1. Tim Kendall, ed., *The Oxford Handbook of British and Irish War Poetry*. Oxford: Oxford University Press, 2009, 374.

11 Teeth and Tail

1. William Cochrane, *Chindit: Special Force, Burma, 1944*. Philadelphia: Xlibris, 2000, 63–5.
2. David Holbrook, *Flesh Wounds*. Stroud: Tempus, 2007, 96–8.
3. Alexander Baron, *From the City, From the Plough*. New York: Washburn, 1949, 128.
4. *The Spectator*, 10 September 1942, 9.

5. B. Ungerson, *Personnel Selection*. London: The War Office, 1953, 48; NA WO 277/19.

6. Ben Shephard, *A War of Nerves: Soldiers and Psychiatrists in the Twentieth Century*. Cambridge, MA: Harvard University Press, 2001, 194.

7. Dudley Anderson, *Three Cheers for the Next Man to Die*. Oxford: Isis, 2003, 50.

8. Raleigh Trevelyan, *The Fortress: A Diary of Anzio and After*. London: Leo Cooper, 1972, 125.

9. Stanley Whitehouse, *Fear is the Foe: A Footslogger from Normandy to the Rhine*. London: Hale, 1995, 39.

10. Colin MacInnes, *To the Victors the Spoils*. London: Allison & Busby, 1986, 18.

11. R. M. Wingfield, *The Only Way Out*. London: Hutchinson, 1955, 94.

12. Ibid., 18.

13. *General Annual Report on the British Army*. Cmnd. 5950. London: HMSO, 1938, 23.

14. John Robert Peaty, British Army Manpower Crisis 1944. Unpublished thesis, King's College University of London, 2000, 333.

15. Neil McCallum, *Journey With a Pistol: A Diary of War*. London: Gollancz, 1959, 54.

16. NA WO 163/163.

17. *Soldier*, October 1946, 6.

18. *General Annual Report on the British Army*. Cmnd. 5950. London: HMSO, 1938, 23; Peaty, *British Army Manpower Crisis 1944*, 333.

19. Kingsley Amis, *Memoirs*. London: Vintage, 2004, 80.

20. NA WO 162/299. These figures exclude deaths from non-combat causes (illness and injuries brought on by accidents) which were more evenly distributed across the corps of service.

21. Martin Lindsay, *So Few Got Through: The Personal Diary of Lieut-Col. Martin Lindsay, D.S.O., M.P., Who Served with the Gordon Highlanders in the 51st Highland Division from July, 1944, to May, 1945*. London: Collins, 1968, 248.

22. Figures derived from Peaty, *British Army Manpower Crisis 1944*, 333 and NA WO 162/299.

23. Charles Farrell, *Reflections 1939–1945: A Scots Guards Officer in Training and War*. Edinburgh: Pentland Press, 2000, 112.

24. Norman Craig, *The Broken Plume: A Platoon Commander's Story, 1940–45*. London: Imperial War Museum, 1982, 66.

25. Ibid., 162.

26. Robert Woollcombe, *Lion Rampant*. London: Leo Cooper, 1970, 41.

27. John Hudson, *Sunset in the East: Fighting Against the Japanese through the Siege of Imphal and Alongside Them in Java, 1943–1946*. Barnsley: Leo Cooper, 2002, 81.

28. Craig, *The Broken Plume*, 176.

29. Wingfield, *The Only Way Out*, 79.

30. Trevor Greenwood, *D-Day to Victory: The Diaries of a British Tank Commander*. London: Simon & Schuster, 2012, 74.

31. Peaty, *British Army Manpower Crisis 1944*, 333; NA WO 162/299.

32. Jocelyn Pereira, *A Distant Drum: War Memories of the Intelligence Officer of the 5th Bn. Coldstream Guards, 1944–45*. Wakefield: S.R. Publishers, 1972, 160.

33. Quoted in John Ellis, *The Sharp End: The Fighting Man in World War II*. London: Aurum, 2011, 303.

34. Jack Swaab, *Slouching in the Undergrowth: The Long Life of a Gunner Officer*. Stroud: Fonthill Media, 2012, 59.

35. Reginald Crimp, *The Diary of a Desert Rat*. London: Cooper, 1971, 117–18.

36. Reginald Crimp, 7 April 1944. IWM:D 5659 96/50/1. The standing of the 'Red Caps' in the eyes of the infantry did improve somewhat in Normandy, where they were routinely exposed to German artillery fire while serving as traffic police at crossroads. See Alexander McKee, *Caen: Anvil of Victory*. London: Souvenir, 2000, 115.

37. McCallum, *Journey With a Pistol*, 136, 99.

38. Douglas Arthur, *Desert Watch: A Story of the Battle of Beda Fomm – And What Went on Before – As Seen Through the Eyes of Driver D. Arthur (Young Doug), No. 1 Battery, 106th Lancashire Hussars (Yeomanry) Regiment, Royal Horse Artillery*. Bedale: Blaisdon Publishing, 2000, 153.

39. Christopher Seton-Watson, *Dunkirk, Alamein, Bologna: Letters and Diaries of an Artilleryman, 1939–1945*. London: Buckland, 1993, 99.

40. John Strawson, *Gentlemen in Khaki: The British Army 1890–1990*. London: Secker & Warburg, 1989, 168.

41. Reginald Crimp, 23 December 1943. IWM:D 5659 96/50/1.

42. B. F. Spiller. IWM:D 11941 02/52/1.

43. Norman Smith, *Tank Soldier*. Lewes: Book Guild, 1989, 69.
44. J. H. A. Sparrow, *Tour of India and South East Asia Command, 28th June 1945–15th October 1945*. IWM:PB 02(41).13 [South East Asia Command]/6, 33.
45. Hudson, *Sunset in the East*, 91.
46. Joanna Bourke, *An Intimate History of Killing: Face-to-face Killing in Twentieth-Century Warfare*. New York: Basic Books, 1999, 120.
47. Mass-Observation Archive, University of Sussex, File Report 1262.
48. Denis Argent, *A Soldier in Bedfordshire, 1941–1942: The Diary of Private Denis Argent, Royal Engineers*. Woodbridge: Boydell Press, 2009, 81.
49. Shephard, *A War of Nerves*, 184.
50. NA WO 162/299.
51. Geoffrey Picot, *Accidental Warrior: In the Front Line from Normandy till Victory*. Lewes: Book Guild, 1993, 105.
52. Whitehouse, *Fear is the Foe*, 185.
53. George MacDonald Fraser, *Quartered Safe Out Here: A Recollection of the War in Burma with a New Epilogue: Fifty Years On*. London: HarperCollins, 2000, 46.
54. Pereira, *A Distant Drum*, 48.
55. Whitehouse, *Fear is the Foe*, 128.
56. Craig, *The Broken Plume*, 162.
57. David French, *Military Identities: The Regimental System, the British Army, and the British People, c.1870–2000*. Oxford University Press, 2005, 37.
58. Christopher Bayly and Tim Harper, *Forgotten Armies: The Fall of British Asia, 1941–1945*. Belknap, 2005, 274.
59. David French, *Raising Churchill's Army: The British Army and the War against Germany, 1919–1945*. Oxford: Oxford University Press, 2000, 70.
60. Janie Corley, Jeremy Crang and Ian Deary, 'Childhood IQ and In-Service Mortality in Scottish Army Personnel during World War II' in *Intelligence* 37 (2009), 240.
61. Leslie Phillips, *Hello: The Autobiography*. London: Orion, 2006, 74.
62. Robert Ahrenfeldt, *Psychiatry in the British Army in the Second World War*. London: Routledge & Kegan Paul, 1958, 205–6.
63. George Lauer, Perspectives on Infantry: Quality and Cohesion: Comparison of American, British, and German Army Manpower Policies and Effects on the Infantry Small Unit during the Second World War, 1939–1945. Unpublished thesis, Florida State University, 2010, 48.
64. Timothy Harrison Place, 'Lionel Wigram, Battle Drill and the British Army in the Second World War' in *War in History* 7:4 (2000), 445.
65. Lauer, *Perspectives on Infantry*, 118.
66. Wingfield, *The Only Way Out*, 165.
67. Timothy Harrison Place, *Military Training in the British Army, 1940–1944: from Dunkirk to D-Day*. London: Frank Cass, 2000, 130. The German victory in 1940 revived the firepower- and technology-intensive mantra of the War Office's *Field Service Regulations* of the 1920s which had hitherto made little practical impression on Army doctrine. See David French, 'Doctrine and Organization in the British Army, 1919–1932' in *Historical Journal* 44:2 (2001).
68. F. W. Perry, *The Commonwealth Armies: Manpower and Organisation in Two World Wars*. Manchester: Manchester University Press, 1988, 54.
69. Winston Churchill, *The Churchill War Papers. Vol. 2. Never Surrender, May 1940–December 1940*. New York: W.W. Norton, 1995, 948.
70. Peaty, *British Army Manpower Crisis 1944*, 26; David Edgerton, *Britain's War Machine: Weapons, Resources and Experts in the Second World War*. London: Allen Lane, 2011, 219. The actual count was six armoured divisions and twelve independent armoured and tank brigades. The Army distinguished between 'tank' brigades equipped with infantry-support vehicles and 'armoured' brigades equipped with lighter and faster pursuit vehicles, although by the end of the war the distinction was becoming increasingly meaningless. See Perry, *The Commonwealth Armies*, 76 for comparative figures from other WWII armies.
71. Peaty, *British Army Manpower Crisis 1944*, 145. The division originally consisted of two Guards armoured brigades, the 5th and 6th. In 1942 the latter, renamed the 6th Guards Tank Brigade, became an independent formation.
72. Shortly before D-Day, Brooke, Grigg and Montgomery tried, unsuccessfully in the face of opposition from Churchill, to have the 6th Guards Tank Brigade broken up and its men made available as replacement infantry.

73. Peter Carrington, *Reflecting on Things Past: The Memoirs of Peter Lord Carrington*. New York: Harper & Row, 1989, 39–41. See also Farrell, *Reflections 1939–1945*, 42.

74. Peaty, *British Army Manpower Crisis 1944*, 86–93. According to Peaty, there is little evidence to show that any of the large number of British anti-tank and light anti-aircraft (LAA) regiments attached to corps and divisional formations of 21AG played a significant role in the fighting in Normandy, at least in their putative role (some were repurposed for other ground-support functions).

75. Ken Tout, *By Tank: D to VE Days*. R. Hale, 2007, 28–9. A post-war War Office analysis of Allied tank losses showed that, while in North Africa 40 per cent of tanks were damaged or destroyed by towed enemy anti-tank guns, by the time of the campaign in northwestern Europe that figure had fallen to just 23 per cent. Mines and various models of hand-held German anti-tank weapons accounted for 36 per cent of Allied tank losses in France and Germany in 1944–5. See NA WO 291/1186.

76. Craig, *The Broken Plume*, 176.

77. Stephen Hart, *Colossal Cracks: Montgomery's 21st Army Group in Northwest Europe, 1944–45*. Mechanicsburg, PA: Stackpole Books, 2007, 46.

78. Peaty, *British Army Manpower Crisis 1944*, 170.

79. Perry, *The Commonwealth Armies*, 69–74.

80. Shephard, *A War of Nerves*, 240–41.

81. Churchill, *The Churchill War Papers. Vol. 2*, 1207–9.

82. Winston Churchill, *The Churchill War Papers. Vol. 3. The Ever-widening War, 1941*. New York: W.W. Norton, 2000, 37–8. See also Dave Palmer, 'Teeth and Tail in the British Army: Churchill and Wavell' in *Army* 24 (1974).

83. Winston Churchill, *The Hinge of Fate*. London: Penguin, 2005, 925–6.

84. Lauer, *Perspectives on Infantry*, 372.

85. French, *Raising Churchill's Army*, 110.

86. Peaty, *British Army Manpower Crisis 1944*, 26–7, 104. These figures do not include six brigades of additional Special Forces units manned by colonial and Allied troops.

87. Simon Anglim, *Orde Wingate and the British Army, 1922–1944*. London: Pickering & Chatto, 2010, 37–9, 103–5.

88. Carlo D'Este, *Warlord: A Life of Winston Churchill at War, 1874–1945*. New York: Harper, 2008, 297.

89. It was often said by Wingate himself and his supporters that Chindit Force was not an 'elite' formation at all, but rather that it was composed of ordinary rifle battalions made up of run-of-the-mill British soldiers, some of them far from young. This may have been true of Operation LONGCLOTH, but it was not so of the larger follow-up expedition, Operation THURSDAY, which was preceded by a thorough winnowing-out process. After 70th Division was broken up to join the Chindits, for instance, four in ten of its men were dismissed from the new force and returned to the general army pool (Peaty, *British Army Manpower Crisis 1944*, 130). Even men who wore glasses were thrown out of the THURSDAY force.

90. Anglim, *Orde Wingate and the British Army*, 178.

91. The soldier and diplomat Sir David Hunt believed that the generals of the Second World War over-indulged the advocates of Special Forces operations because they feared that otherwise they would be accused of seeming old-fashioned. See Shelford Bidwell, 'Five Armies 1920–1970' in *Army Quarterly* 99 (October 1969), 174.

92. Ibid., 118. Of the seventeen commandos by April 1944, seven belonged to the Army, nine to the Royal Marines, and one was composed of a mixture of French, Dutch, Belgian and other allied soldiers.

93. See Alan Allport, *Demobbed: Coming Home after the Second World War*. New Haven: Yale University Press, 2009, 177–8.

94. James Owen, *Commando: Winning World War II Behind Enemy Lines*. London: Little, Brown, 2012, xxix–xxx.

95. Ibid., 369–71.

96. John Greenacre, *Churchill's Spearhead: The Development of Britain's Airborne Forces during World War II*. Barnsley: Pen & Sword, 2010, Kindle locations 2972–3.

97. In Sicily in July 1943, almost half the gliders carrying the first wave of assault troops crashed into the sea, drowning hundreds of men, whilst a few days later the Allied transport planes carrying the second-wave paratrooper force were so shot up on their approach to the drop zone by their own as well as Axis anti-aircraft fire that the few troops who made it to the ground

were quickly overwhelmed by the Germans. Operation MARKET-GARDEN's failure is well known. The final major drop of the war took place at Wesel in northwestern Germany in March 1945, its goal to establish a bridgehead on the eastern bank of the Rhine. Operation VARSITY, as it was known, was technically a success. But given the modest accomplishments of the mission – the crossing of the Rhine in spring 1945 was a foregone conclusion – and the meagre German defences that 6th Airborne Division faced, the human cost of the operation (1,434 casualties in three days of fighting out of an initial divisional strength of 12,000 men) was arguably excessive. VARSITY may have been mounted more as a way of giving the airborne forces something to do than because of any pressing military need.

98. Farrell, *Reflections 1939–1945*, 106.
99. Robin Painter, *A Signal Honour: With the Chindits and the XIV Army in Burma*. London: Leo Cooper, 1999, 58.
100. Richard Rhodes James, *Chindit*. London: J. Murray, 1980, 8; Anglim, *Orde Wingate and the British Army*, 176.
101. John Masters, *The Road Past Mandalay*. London: Cassell, 2002, 140. For discussion of THURSDAY's effectiveness, see Anglim, *Orde Wingate and the British Army*, 202–12; Robert Lyman, *Slim, Master of War*. London: Constable, 2004, 210–15.
102. Julian Thompson, *Forgotten Voices of Burma*. London: Ebury, 2010, 367.
103. Greenacre, *Churchill's Spearhead*, Kindle locations 2976–7.
104. J. H. A. Sparrow, *Morale*. London: The War Office, 1949, 22; NA WO 277/16.
105. This was a mistake the *Wehrmacht* avoided, which meant that the overall quality of its NCOs in its line infantry regiments was generally superior. See Dominick Graham and Shelford Bidwell, *Tug of War: The Battle for Italy, 1943–1945*. Barnsley: Pen & Sword, 2004, 107.
106. Lloyd Clark, *Arnhem: Jumping the Rhine 1944 and 1945*. London: Headline Review, 2008, 94. Julian Thompson has argued that while some very small special forces units (the Special Air Service and the Long Range Desert Group in particular) were probably cost-effective, with most of the others that Britain raised during the war 'one finds [it] hard to see how they contributed to Allied victory in any quantifiable way'. Julian Thompson, *The Imperial War Museum Book of War Behind Enemy Lines*. London: Sidgwick & Jackson, 1999, 420–2.

12 The Grammar of War

1. Norman Smith, *Tank Soldier*. Lewes: Book Guild, 1989, 111.
2. John Smith, *In at the Finish*. London: Minerva, 1995, 196.
3. John Hudson, *Sunset in the East: Fighting Against the Japanese through the Siege of Imphal and Alongside Them in Java, 1943–1946*. Barnsley: Leo Cooper, 2002, 96.
4. Ken Tout, *By Tank: D to VE Days*. London: R. Hale, 2007, 43.
5. David Holbrook, *Flesh Wounds*. Stroud: Tempus, 2007, 115–16.
6. Peter Elstob, *Warriors for the Working Day*. London: Corgi, 1974, 268.
7. Tout, *By Tank*, 43–56.
8. Trevor Greenwood, *D-Day to Victory: The Diaries of a British Tank Commander*. London: Simon & Schuster, 2012, 85–6.
9. Vernon Scannell, *Argument of Kings*. London: Robson, 1987, 152.
10. Neil McCallum, *Journey with a Pistol: A Diary of War*. London: Gollancz, 1959, 50.
11. William Cochrane, *Chindit: Special Force, Burma, 1944*. Philadelphia: Xlibris, 2000, 95–6.
12. R. M. Wingfield, *The Only Way Out*. London: Hutchinson, 1955, 173.
13. Jocelyn Pereira, *A Distant Drum: War Memories of the Intelligence Officer of the 5th Bn. Coldstream Guards, 1944–45*. Wakefield: S.R. Publishers, 1972, 38.
14. John Foley, *Mailed Fist*. St Albans: Mayflower, 1975, 44; Sydney Jary, *18 Platoon*. Carshalton Beeches: Sydney Jary, *c*.1987, 131; Smith, *In at the Finish*, 131; Holbrook, *Flesh Wounds*, 140.
15. John Ellis, *The Sharp End: The Fighting Man in World War II*. London: Aurum, 2011, 68.
16. Robert Woollcombe, *Lion Rampant*. London: Leo Cooper, 1970, 53–4.
17. Christopher Seton-Watson, *Dunkirk, Alamein, Bologna: Letters and Diaries of an Artilleryman, 1939–1945*. London: Buckland, 1993, 144.
18. Victor Selwyn, *From Oasis into Italy: War Poems and Diaries from Africa and Italy, I 940–1946*. London: Shepheard-Walwyn, 1983, 17.
19. Norman Craig, *The Broken Plume: A Platoon Commander's Story, 1940–45*. London: Imperial War Museum, 1982, 60; Jake Wardrop, *Tanks Across the Desert: The War Diary of Jake Wardrop*. London: W. Kimber, 1981, 87.

20. Raleigh Trevelyan, *The Fortress: A Diary of Anzio and After*. London: Leo Cooper, 1972, 72.
21. McCallum, *Journey with a Pistol*, 116.
22. Smith, *In at the Finish*, 139.
23. Holbrook, *Flesh Wounds*, 108; Tout, *By Tank*, 17.
24. Foley, *Mailed Fist*, 67.
25. Wingfield, *The Only Way Out*, 92, 131; Smith, *Tank Soldier*, 20; Alexander McKee, *Caen: Anvil of Victory*. London: Souvenir, 2000, 313.
26. George MacDonald Fraser, *Quartered Safe Out Here: A Recollection of the War in Burma with a New Epilogue: Fifty Years On*. London: HarperCollins, 2000, 3.
27. Craig, *The Broken Plume*, 56.
28. Smith, *In at the Finish*, 34; Holbrook, *Flesh Wounds*, 130.
29. Ibid., 121.
30. Tout, *By Tank*, 18.
31. Cochrane, *Chindit*, 79.
32. Foley, *Mailed Fist*, 159.
33. Fraser, *Quartered Safe Out Here*, 123–4.
34. Scannell, *Argument of Kings*, 166.
35. Alex Bowlby, *The Recollections of Rifleman Bowlby*. London: Cassell, 1999, 182.
36. Pereira, *A Distant Drum*, 9.
37. Foley, *Mailed Fist*, 48.
38. Greenwood, *D-Day to Victory*, 238–9.
39. John Mulgan, *Report on Experience*. Oxford: Oxford University Press, 1984, 33.
40. Wilfred Leonard Saunders, *Dunkirk Diary of a Very Young Soldier*. Birmingham: Birmingham City Council, Public Libraries Dept. 1989, 1.
41. Hudson, *Sunset in the East*, 69–70, 7.
42. Richard W. Holborow. IWM:D 15631 07/23/1.
43. Quoted in Gary Sheffield, 'The Shadow of the Somme: The Influence of the First World War on British Soldiers' Perceptions and Behaviour in the Second World War' in Paul Addison and Angus Calder, eds, *Time To Kill: The Soldier's Experience of War in the West, 1939–1945*. London: Pimlico, 1997, 30.
44. George Orwell, *Facing Unpleasant Facts: Narrative Essays*. New York: Houghton Mifflin, 2009, 55.
45. Ronald Elliott. IWM:S 10167.
46. A. J. Mills. IWM:D 4269 83/24/1.
47. For the reinforcement of this idea through children's fiction of the interwar years, see Michael Paris, *Over the Top: The Great War and Juvenile Literature in Britain*. Westport, CT: Praeger, 2004, 154–61.
48. Orwell, *Facing Unpleasant Facts*, 55.
49. Arthur Kellas, *Down to Earth, or, Another Bloody Cock-Up: A Parachute Subaltern's Story*. Edinburgh: Pentland Place, 1990, 51.
50. Bill Bellamy, *Troop Leader: A Tank Commander's Story*. Stroud: Sutton, 2007, 1.
51. Alfred Baldwin. IWM:S 6491.
52. Jon Lawrence, 'Forging a Peaceable Kingdom: War, Violence, and Fear of Brutalization in Post-First World War Britain' in *Journal of Modern History* 75:3 (2003).
53. Adrian Gregory, 'Peculiarities of the English: War, Violence and Politics: 1900–1939' in *Journal of Modern European History* 1:1 (2003).
54. Hugh Cunningham, *The Invention of Childhood*. London: BBC Books, 2006, 201.
55. Joanna Bourke, 'Fear and the British and American Military, 1914–45' in *Historical Research* 74:185 (2001), 320–1.
56. NA WO 231/8.
57. David French, *Raising Churchill's Army: The British Army and the War against Germany, 1919–1945*. Oxford: Oxford University Press, 2000, 152.
58. Kellas, *Down to Earth*, 31.
59. Ibid., 105.
60. Colin MacInnes, *To the Victors the Spoils*. London: Allison & Busby, 1986, 65–6.
61. Tim Bishop and Bruce Shand, *One Young Soldier: The Memoirs of a Cavalryman*. Norwich: M. Russell, 1993, 150.
62. Wingfield, *The Only Way Out*, 25.

63. Stanley Whitehouse, *Fear is the Foe: A Footslogger from Normandy to the Rhine*. London: Hale, 1995, 104.

64. Andrew Wilson, *Flame Thrower*. New York: Bantam, 1984, 59.

65. Robin Painter, *A Signal Honour: With the Chindits and the XIV Army in Burma*. London: Leo Cooper, 1999, 119; Brian Aldiss, *A Soldier Erect: or Further Adventures of the Hand-Reared Boy*. London: Weidenfeld & Nicolson, 1971, Kindle locations 851–3.

66. John Masters, *The Road Past Mandalay*. London: Cassell, 2002, 163.

67. Reginald Crimp, 15 January 1945. IWM:D 5659 96/50/1.

68. George Lauer, Perspectives on Infantry: Quality and Cohesion: Comparison of American, British, and German Army Manpower Policies and Effects on the Infantry Small Unit during the Second World War, 1939–1945. Unpublished thesis, Florida State University, 2010, 288–9.

69. Bowlby, *The Recollections*, 70. The British Army had considered the possibility of switching to a semi-automatic rifle between the wars and of issuing weapons with a greater volume of fire more generally, but had decided against this for reasons of cost and the logistical and political complexities of imperial policing duties. See French, *Raising Churchill's Army*, 81–9.

70. Reginald Crimp, 18 July 1944. IWM:D 5659 96/50/1.

71. Denis Forman, *To Reason Why*. Barnsley: Pen & Sword Military, 2008, 18.

72. Trevelyan, *The Fortress*, 92.

73. Craig, *The Broken Plume*, 69.

74. Whitehouse, *Fear is the Foe*, 94.

75. Jary, *18 Platoon*, 104; Dudley Anderson, *Three Cheers for the Next Man to Die*. Oxford: Isis, 2003, 35; Walter Elliott, *Esprit de Corps: A Scots Guards Officer on Active Service, 1943–1945*. Norwich: M. Russell, 1996, 132.

76. Jary, *18 Platoon*, 5; McKee, *Caen: Anvil of Victory*, 316.

77. Whitehouse, *Fear is the Foe*, 82.

78. NA WO291/491; French, *Raising Churchill's Army*, 88.

79. Bishop and Shand, *One Young Soldier*, 59.

80. Trevelyan, *The Fortress*, 78.

81. French, *Raising Churchill's Army*, 88–9.

82. Martin Lindsay, *So Few Got Through: The Personal Diary of Lieut-Col. Martin Lindsay, D.S.O., M.P., Who Served with the Gordon Highlanders in the 51st Highland Division from July, 1944, to May, 1945*. London: Collins, 1968, 35. See also Robert Boscawen, *Armoured Guardsman*. London: Leo Cooper, 2000, 40–1.

83. Elstob, *Warriors for the Working Day*, 224.

84. McKee, *Caen: Anvil of Victory*, 101.

85. Holbrook, *Flesh Wounds*, 164–5.

86. Smith, *In at the Finish*, 46.

87. Foley, *Mailed Fist*, 80–7.

88. John Buckley, *British Armour in the Normandy Campaign, 1944*. London: Routledge, 2004, 105–34. See also French, *Raising Churchill's Army*, 96–106. For a defence of British wartime tank quality, see David Edgerton, *Britain's War Machine: Weapons, Resources and Experts in the Second World War*. London: Allen Lane, 2011.

89. Jary, *18 Platoon*, 53–4; Anthony King, *The Combat Soldier: Infantry Tactics and Cohesion in the Twentieth and Twenty-first Centuries*. Oxford: Oxford University Press, 2013, 187–98.

90. Bowlby, *The Recollections*, 166; Jary, *18 Platoon*, 16–17.

91. Holbrook, *Flesh Wounds*, 116.

92. NA WO 222/124.

93. John Buckley, *Monty's Men: The British Army and the Liberation of Europe, 1944–5*. New Haven: Yale University Press, 2013, 41.

94. Peter White, *With the Jocks: A Soldier's Struggle for Europe, 1944–45*. Stroud: Sutton, 2003, 429–30. For a German account of a 'Jabo' attack, see McKee, *Caen: Anvil of Victory*, 105–6.

95. Craig, *The Broken Plume*, 56.

96. Elliott, *Esprit de Corps*, 62.

97. Woollcombe, *Lion Rampant*, 53–4.

98. McKee, *Caen: Anvil of Victory*, 329.

99. Ernest Sanger, *Letters from the Two World Wars*. Stroud: Sutton, 1993, 186.

100. French, *Raising Churchill's Army*, 56–60.

101. Ibid., 205–7.
102. Jary, *18 Platoon*, 18–19.
103. King, *The Combat Soldier*, 201.
104. Hew Strachan, 'Training, Morale and Modern War', in *Journal of Contemporary History* 41:2 (2006); Dave Grossman, *On Killing*. London: Little, Brown, 2009, 253–61.
105. Timothy Harrison Place, *Military Training in the British Army, 1940–1944: from Dunkirk to D-Day*. London: Frank Cass, 2000, 168–75.
106. Forman, *To Reason Why*, 199.
107. Max Hastings, *All Hell Let Loose: The World at War 1939–45*. London: HarperPress, 2011, Kindle locations 10248–50.
108. King, *The Combat Soldier*, 40–61.
109. Forman, *To Reason Why*, 200.
110. Tim Moreman, *The Jungle, The Japanese and the British Commonwealth Armies at War 1941–1945*. New York: Frank Cass, 2005; Jonathan Fennell, *Combat and Morale in the North African Campaign: The Eighth Army and the Path to El Alamein*. Cambridge: Cambridge University Press, 2010.
111. John Horsfall, *Say Not the Struggle*. Kineton: Roundwood Press, 1977, 41.
112. Craig, *The Broken Plume*, 67.
113. Holbrook, *Flesh Wounds*, 218–19.
114. Ibid., 140–1.
115. Greenwood, *D-Day to Victory*, 248.
116. Tout, *By Tank*, 55.
117. Ellis, *The Sharp End*, 71.
118. Simon Wessely, 'Twentieth-century Theories on Combat Motivation and Breakdown' in *Journal of Contemporary History* 41:2 (2006). The classic account from the period is Edward Shils and Morris Janowitz, 'Cohesion and Disintegration in the Wehrmacht in World War II', in *Public Opinion Quarterly* 12:2 (1948).
119. Craig, *The Broken Plume*, 75.
120. King, *The Combat Soldier*, 32.
121. Lindsay, *So Few Got Through*, 118.
122. Tout, *By Tank*, 37.
123. Cochrane, *Chindit*, 171; Jary, *18 Platoon*, 7.
124. Dan Billany, *The Trap*. London: Faber and Faber, 1986, 339.
125. Geoffrey Picot, *Accidental Warrior: In the Front Line from Normandy till Victory*. Lewes: Book Guild, 1993, 101.
126. Max Hastings, *Overlord: D-Day and the Battle for Normandy 1944*. London: Pan, 1999, 149.
127. Hudson, *Sunset in the East*, 75.
128. Bowlby, *The Recollections*, 171.
129. Picot, *Accidental Warrior*, 97.
130. Trevelyan, *The Fortress*, 89.
131. Strome Galloway, *With the Irish Against Rommel: A Diary of 1943*. Langley, BC: Battleline Books, *c.*1984, 174.
132. Craig, *The Broken Plume*, 75.
133. Bowlby, *The Recollections*, 115.
134. Cochrane, *Chindit*, 96–8.
135. Jack Swaab, *Field of Fire: Diary of a Gunner Officer*. Stroud: Sutton, 2005, 258.
136. Richard Buckle, *The Most Upsetting Woman*. London: Collins, 1981, 211.
137. Ibid., 234; Michael Howard, *Captain Professor: The Memoirs of Sir Michael Howard*. London: Continuum, 2006, 87–8.
138. Pereira, *A Distant Drum*, 159.
139. Reginald Crimp, 15 December 1943. IWM:D 5659 96/50/1.
140. Elliott, *Esprit de Corps*, 139.
141. Howard, *Captain Professor*, 75.
142. Elstob, *Warriors for the Working Day*, 210; Bowlby, *The Recollections*, 134.
143. Whitehouse, *Fear is the Foe*, 139.
144. Reginald Crimp, 7–31 July 1944. IWM:D 5659 96/50/1.
145. Jary, *18 Platoon*, xv–xvii, 76.
146. Ibid., 81.

13 Categories of Courage

1. Walter Elliott, *Esprit de Corps: A Scots Guards Officer on Active Service, 1943–1945*. Norwich: M. Russell, 1996, 73.
2. Arthur Kellas, *Down to Earth, or, Another Bloody Cock-Up: A Parachute Subaltern's Story*. Edinburgh: Pentland Place; 1990, 117.
3. Stanley Whitehouse, *Fear is the Foe: A Footslogger from Normandy to the Rhine*. London: Hale, 1995, 114.
4. Frank Baines, *Chindit Affair: A Memoir of the War in Burma*. Barnsley: Pen & Sword, 2011, 148–9.
5. Ibid., 127.
6. Geoffrey Picot, *Accidental Warrior: In the Front Line from Normandy till Victory*. Lewes: Book Guild, 1993, 300–1.
7. John Kenneally, *The Honour and the Shame*. London: Headline Review, 2007, 92.
8. E. P. Danger. IWM:D 4465 82/37/1.
9. Martin Lindsay, *So Few Got Through: The Personal Diary of Lieut-Col. Martin Lindsay, D.S.O., M.P., Who Served with the Gordon Highlanders in the 51st Highland Division from July, 1944, to May, 1945*. London: Collins, 1968, 71.
10. Ibid., 104.
11. John Masters, *The Road Past Mandalay*. London: Cassell, 2002, 278.
12. E. P. Danger. IWM:D 4465 82/37/1.
13. Whitehouse, *Fear is the Foe*, 56, 98.
14. Ibid., 164.
15. Norman Craig, *The Broken Plume: A Platoon Commander's Story, 1940–45*. London: Imperial War Museum, 1982, 101.
16. Christopher Seton-Watson, *Dunkirk, Alamein, Bologna: Letters and Diaries of an Artilleryman, 1939–1945*. London: Buckland, 1993, 167.
17. Michael Howard, *Captain Professor: The Memoirs of Sir Michael Howard*. London: Continuum, 2006, 73.
18. Richard Hoggart, *A Sort of Clowning: Life and Times, Vol. 2: 1940–1959*. Oxford: Oxford University Press, 1991, 41.
19. Robert Woollcombe, *Lion Rampant*. London: Leo Cooper, 1970, 69.
20. John Hudson, *Sunset in the East: Fighting Against the Japanese through the Siege of Imphal and Alongside Them in Java, 1943–1946*. Barnsley: Leo Cooper, 2002, 61–2.
21. Peter Cochrane, *Charlie Company: In Service with C Company 2nd Queen's Own Cameron Highlanders, 1940–44*. Stroud: Spellmount, 2007, 32.
22. Geoffrey Druitt. IWM:D 5600 96/38/1.
23. Norman Lewis, *Naples '44*. New York: Pantheon Books, 1978, 20.
24. Andrew Wilson, *Flame Thrower*. New York: Bantam, 1984, xiii, 111–12.
25. Anthony Babington, *An Uncertain Voyage*. Chichester: Barry Rose Law, 2000, 149.
26. John Ellis, *The Sharp End: The Fighting Man in World War II*. London: Aurum, 2011, 177.
27. Raleigh Trevelyan, *The Fortress: A Diary of Anzio and After*. London: Leo Cooper, 1972, 66; Joanna Bourke, 'Fear and the British and American Military, 1914–45' in *Historical Research* 74:185 (2001); Alexander Watson, *Enduring the Great War: Combat, Morale and Collapse in the German and British Armies, 1914–1918*. Cambridge: Cambridge University Press, 2008, 28–9.
28. Ellis, *The Sharp End*, 70.
29. NA WO 222/124. Some anti-aircraft gunners requested that they be allowed to man their guns rather than to take cover during dive-bombing raids, even though their weapons had little appreciable chance of hitting the enemy; the feverish activity of manning a gun was more reassuring than waiting passively to be hit in a slit-trench. See NA WO 222/66.
30. R. M. Wingfield, *The Only Way Out*. London: Hutchinson, 1955, 44; Edgar Jones and Simon Wessely, 'Psychiatric Battle Casualties: An Intra- and Interwar Comparison', in *British Journal of Psychiatry* 178 (2001), 244. For the effects of a Nebelwerfer attack, see Whitehouse, *Fear is the Foe*, 164; Woollcombe, *Lion Rampant*, 90.
31. Ellis, *The Sharp End*, 72.
32. Howard, *Captain Professor*, 82.
33. Carlo D'Este, *Decision in Normandy*. New York: HarperPerennial, 1994, 289.
34. Lindsay, *So Few Got Through*, 101.

35. Ibid., 200.
36. Jocelyn Pereira, *A Distant Drum: War Memories of the Intelligence Officer of the 5th Bn. Coldstream Guards, 1944–45*. Wakefield: S.R. Publishers, 1972, 11.
37. Charles Moran, *The Anatomy of Courage*. Boston: Houghton Mifflin, 1967, 64.
38. Wingfield, *The Only Way Out*, 125.
39. Babington, *An Uncertain Voyage*, 189–90.
40. Alexander Baron, *From the City, From the Plough*. New York: Washburn, 1949, 128.
41. Ernest Sanger, *Letters from the Two World Wars*. Stroud: Sutton, 1993, 214–15.
42. Whitehouse, *Fear is the Foe*, 50.
43. David Holbrook, *Flesh Wounds*. Stroud: Tempus, 2007, 164.
44. Woollcombe, *Lion Rampant*, 206–9.
45. Denis Forman, *To Reason Why*. Barnsley: Pen & Sword Military, 2008, 204.
46. Alexander McKee, *Caen: Anvil of Victory*. London: Souvenir, 2000, 326.
47. Whitehouse, *Fear is the Foe*, 132, 156.
48. A. B. McPherson, *Discipline*. London: The War Office, 1950, Appendix I(c); NA WO 277/7.
49. John Peaty, 'The Desertion Crisis in Italy, 1944' in *RUSI Journal* 147:3 (2002), 76.
50. Robert Ahrenfeldt, *Psychiatry in the British Army in the Second World War*. London: Routledge & Kegan Paul, 1958, 271.
51. David French, 'Discipline and the Death Penalty in the British Army in the War against Germany during the Second World War', in *Journal of Contemporary History* 33:4 (1998), 539.
52. Mark Connelly and Walter Miller, 'British Courts Martial in North Africa 1940–3' in *Twentieth Century British History* 15:3 (2004).
53. McPherson, *Discipline*, 54–8.
54. NA WO163/163.
55. Anonymous, 'The Desertion Crisis in Italy' in *RUSI Journal* 147:5 (2002), 86.
56. [missing notes text]
57. Alex Bowlby, *The Recollections of Rifleman Bowlby*. London: Cassell, 1999, 58.
58. Reginal Crimp, 9 July 1944. IWM: D5659, 96/50/1.
59. Ben Shephard, '"Pitiless Psychology": The Role of Prevention in British Military Psychiatry in the Second World War' in *History of Psychiatry* 10 (1999), 34–5.
60. Neil McCallum, *Journey With a Pistol: A Diary of War*. London: Gollancz, 1959, 94.
61. Edgar Jones and Simon Wessely, 'A Paradigm Shift in the Conceptualization of Psychological Trauma in the 20th Century', in *Journal of Anxiety Disorders* 21 (2007), 169.
62. Edgar Jones and Simon Wessely, *Shell Shock to PTSD: Military Psychiatry from 1900 to the Gulf War*. New York: Psychology Press, 2005, 78.
63. NATO forces, for instance, today use a variation on PIE known as BICEPS (Brevity, Immediacy, Centrality, Expectancy, Proximity, Simplicity).
64. The RAMC also used the vaguer term 'Not Yet Diagnosed (Nervous)', or NYD(N).
65. Ben Shephard, *A War of Nerves: Soldiers and Psychiatrists in the Twentieth Century*. Cambridge, MA: Harvard University Press, 2001, 255.
66. Sydney Jary, *18 Platoon*. Carshalton Beeches: Sydney Jary, c.1987, 70–1.
67. Craig, *The Broken Plume*, 90.
68. Ahrenfeldt, *Psychiatry in the British Army*, 173.
69. Edgar Jones, 'War and the Practice of Psychotherapy: The UK Experience 1939–1960' in *Medical History* 48:4 (2004).
70. McPherson, *Discipline*, Appendix I(a).
71. Jeremy Crang, *The British Army and the People's War 1939–1945*. Manchester: Manchester University Press, 2000, 144–5.
72. During approximately the same twelve-month period at the end of the First World War, around 37,000 British ORs were convicted of court-martial offences overseas. Given that the strength of the British Army outside the UK was about 2.1 million by the time of the Armistice, that means that the conviction rate per 1,000 soldiers was almost identical to that of 1944–45. *Statistics of the Military Effort of the British Empire during the Great War, 1914–1920*. London: HMSO, 1922.
73. Harry Wilson, Introduction. IWM:D 4709 80/5/1.
74. Jeremy Crang, 'The Abolition of Compulsory Church Parades in the British Army', in *Journal of Ecclesiastical History* 56:1 (2005).
75. J. E. Bowman, *Three Stripes and a Gun: A Young Man's Journey Towards Maturity*. Braunton: Merlin, 1987, 224.

76. Michael Snape, *God and the British Soldier: Religion and the British Army in the First and Second World Wars*. London: Routledge, 2005, 1.
77. Ibid., 51.
78. Bowman, *Three Stripes and a Gun*, 224.
79. Edward M. Spiers, 'The Regular Army in 1914' in Ian F. W. Beckett and Keith Simpson, eds, *A Nation in Arms: A Social Study of the British Army in the First World War*. Manchester: Manchester University Press, 1985, 43–4.
80. John Horsfall, *Say Not the Struggle*. Kineton: Roundwood Press, 1977, 9.
81. Jary, *18 Platoon*, 86.
82. McCallum, *Journey With a Pistol*, 48.
83. Ibid., 80.
84. David French, *Military Identities: The Regimental System, the British Army, and the British People, c.1870–2000*. Oxford University Press, 2005, 281.
85. Allan Converse, *Armies of Empire: The 9th Australian and 50th British Divisions in Battle, 1939–1945*. Cambridge: Cambridge University Press, 2011, 154.
86. Peter Caddick-Adams, *Monte Cassino: Ten Armies in Hell*. Oxford: Oxford University Press, 2010, 75.
87. Anthony Burgess, *Little Wilson and Big God, Being the First Part of the Confessions of Anthony Burgess*. London: Heinemann, 1987, 280.
88. Roger Broad, *The Radical General: Sir Ronald Adam and Britain's New Model Army 1941–1946*. Stroud: History, 2013, Kindle location 2116.
89. Craig C. French, 'The Fashioning of *Esprit de Corps* in the 51st Highland Division from St Valery to El Alamein' in *Journal of the Society for Army Historical Research* 77:312 (1999).
90. Trevelyan, *The Fortress*, 48.
91. Jonathan Fennell, *Combat and Morale in the North African Campaign: The Eighth Army and the Path to El Alamein*. Cambridge: Cambridge University Press, 2010, 262.
92. Vernon Scannell, *Argument of Kings*. London: Robson, 1987, 118–19.
93. Fennell, *Combat and Morale in the North African Campaign*, 287; Niall Barr, *Pendulum of War: The Three Battles of El Alamein*. London: Jonathan Cape, 2004, xxxviii.
94. Bernard Law Montgomery, *The Memoirs of Field-Marshal the Viscount Montgomery of Alamein*. Cleveland: World Publishing Co., 1958, 101.
95. NA WO 163/161.
96. Haig's supposed detachment from the experience of the ordinary soldiers who served under him on the Western Front has been challenged; see S. P. MacKenzie, 'Morale and the Cause: The Campaign to Shape the Outlook of Soldiers in the British Expeditionary Force, 1914–1918', in *Canadian Journal of History* 25:2 (1990).
97. D. Evans. IWM:D 2028 92/37/1.
98. Jary, *18 Platoon*, 73.
99. Anthony Powell, *To Keep the Ball Rolling: The Memoirs of Anthony Powell*. Chicago: University of Chicago Press, 2001, 301.
100. Craig, *The Broken Plume*, 100.
101. Norman Smith, *Tank Soldier*. Lewes: Book Guild, 1989, 53–4.
102. Converse, *Armies of Empire*, 126, 191.
103. George MacDonald Fraser, *Quartered Safe Out Here: A Recollection of the War in Burma with a New Epilogue: Fifty Years On*. London: HarperCollins, 2000, 35–6.
104. Robert Lyman, *Slim, Master of War*. London: Constable, 2004.
105. E. P. Danger. IWM:D 4465 82/37/1.
106. Howard, *Captain Professor*, 58.
107. Ibid., 85.
108. Craig, *The Broken Plume*, 77.
109. Woollcombe, *Lion Rampant*, 206–9, 214.
110. Trevelyan, *The Fortress*, 93.
111. Reginald Crimp, *The Diary of a Desert Rat*. London: Cooper, 1971, 154.
112. Baines, *Chindit Affair*, 127.
113. McKee, *Caen: Anvil of Victory*, 118–19.
114. Bryn Hammond, *El Alamein: The Battle that Turned the Tide of the Second World War*. Oxford: Osprey, 2012, 275–6.
115. McKee, *Caen: Anvil of Victory*. 200–2.
116. Woollcombe, *Lion Rampant*, 225.

117. Whitehouse, *Fear is the Foe*, 113.
118. Dudley Anderson, *Three Cheers for the Next Man to Die*. Oxford: Isis, 2003, 66.
119. Whitehouse, *Fear is the Foe*, 49.
120. Jary, *18 Platoon*, 61. See also Wingfield, *The Only Way Out*, 62.
121. Kenneally, *The Honour and the Shame*, 93.
122. Craig, *The Broken Plume*, 84.
123. Wingfield, *The Only Way Out*, 73.
124. Whitehouse, *Fear is the Foe*, 120.
125. Baines, *Chindit Affair*, 119.
126. John Shipster, *Mist on the Rice-fields: A Soldier's Story of the Burma Campaign and the Korean War*. London: Leo Cooper, 2000, 34.
127. McCallum, *Journey with a Pistol*, 105. It has been suggested that only about one in fifty combat soldiers has the 'aggressively psychopathic' personality that allows him to genuinely enjoy killing without the need for preconditioning. See Dave Grossman, *On Killing*. London: Little, Brown, 2009, 180-5.
128. Bill Bellamy, *Troop Leader: A Tank Commander's Story*. Stroud: Sutton, 2007, 150.
129. Trevelyan, *The Fortress*, 94.
130. Babington, *An Uncertain Voyage*, 151. For other examples of 'midrange denial', see Grossman, *On Killing*, 111.
131. NA CAB 106/200.
132. Ahrenfeldt, *Psychiatry in the British Army*, 198-201; Shephard, *A War of Nerves*, 233.
133. Masters, *The Road Past Mandalay*, 55.
134. Horsfall, *Say Not the Struggle*, 15.
135. Jary, *18 Platoon*, 117.
136. Ibid., 89.
137. Ibid., 83-6.
138. Norman Davies, *Europe at War 1939-1945*. London: Pan, 2007, 19-25.
139. John Buckley, *Monty's Men: The British Army and the Liberation of Europe, 1944-5*. New Haven: Yale University Press, 2013, 300.
140. Corelli Barnett, *The Desert Generals*. Edison, NJ: Castle Books, 2004, 313.
141. Chester Wilmot, *The Struggle for Europe*. New York: Harper, 1952; John Keegan, *Six Armies in Normandy*. New York: Penguin, 1994; Max Hastings, *Overlord: D-Day and the Battle for Normandy 1944*. London: Pan, 1999; Max Hastings, *Winston's War: Churchill, 1940-1945*. New York: Alfred A. Knopf, 2009; John Ellis, *Brute Force: Allied Strategy and Tactics in the Second World War*. New York: Viking, 1990; D'Este, *Decision in Normandy*.
142. Howard, *Captain Professor*, 56.
143. Quoted in Richard Kohn, 'Scholarship on World War II: Present and Future', in *Journal of Military History* 55:3 (1991).
144. For a discussion of these terms, see Martin van Crevald, *Fighting Power: German and US Army Performance, 1939-1945*. Westport, CT: Greenwood Press, 1982, 3; Peter Mansoor, *The GI Offensive in Europe*. Lawrence, KS: University Press of Kansas, 1999, 2-4.
145. Buckley, *Monty's Men*, 296; Stephen Hart, *Colossal Cracks: Montgomery's 21st Army Group in Northwest Europe, 1944-45*. Mechanicsburg, PA: Stackpole Books, 2007.
146. Shephard, *War of Nerves*, 303-11; Catherine Merridale, *Ivan's War: Life and Death in the Red Army, 1939-1945*. London: Picador, 2006, 268; Meirion Harries, *Soldiers of the Sun: The Rise and Fall of the Imperial Japanese Army*. New York: Random House, 1992, 421-2.
147. McKee, *Caen: Anvil of Victory*. 113.
148. Based upon the experience of the First World War, British troops in 1939 assumed that if they surrendered to the enemy then the experience of captivity would be relatively benign – something that was broadly true in the case of the Germans and Italians, and cruelly mistaken in the case of the Japanese. Had the men garrisoning Singapore appreciated what being a POW in the Far East was going to be like, it is reasonable to assume that their resistance would have been a good deal more formidable in February 1942.
149. Jary, *18 Platoon*, 16-17.
150. Stephen G. Fritz, *Frontsoldaten*. Lexington: University Press of Kentucky, 1997, 8. See also George Lauer, Perspectives on Infantry: Quality and Cohesion: Comparison of American, British, and German Army Manpower Policies and Effects on the Infantry Small Unit during the Second World War, 1939-1945. Unpublished thesis, Florida State University, 2010.
151. Anonymous, 'The Desertion Crisis in Italy'.

152. D'Este, *Decision in Normandy*, 283.
153. Ibid., 279.
154. Picot, *Accidental Warrior*, 76. As an example, the 7th Hampshire battalion, which made up a sizeable portion of all the psychiatric casualties in 21st Army Group from 10–17 July 1944, had seen only a fairly normal level of combat. But during that period they had lost their commanding officer twice, their second-in-command, their medical officer, their forward observation officer and many subalterns. See Shephard, *A War of Nerves*, 254.
155. Jary, *18 Platoon*, 34–6. Jary calculated that the chance of his survival and that of his three most experienced NCOs was 45-1.
156. Buckley, *Monty's Men*, 15.
157. Horsfall, *Say Not the Struggle*, 166.
158. Dominick Graham, *Against Odds: Reflections on the Experiences of the British Army, 1914–45*. New York: St Martin's Press, 1999, 49.
159. John Foley, *Mailed Fist*. St Albans: Mayflower, 1975, 44.
160. Harry Wilson, 700. IWM:D 4709 80/5/1.
161. Robin Painter, *A Signal Honour: With the Chindits and the XIV Army in Burma*. London: Leo Cooper, 1999, 119.
162. Raymond Cooper, *'B' Company, 9th Battalion, the Border Regiment, 48 Brigade, 17 Indian (Light) Division, JV Corps, 14th Army, South East Asia Command: One Man's War in Burma, 1942–1944, Recalled in Hospital in 1945*. London: Dobson, 1978, 130.
163. Adapted from Mansoor, *The GI Offensive*, 226–67.
164. Seton-Watson, *Dunkirk, Alamein, Bologna*, 204.

Part Five: Citizens

1. Eric Murrell, *For Your Tomorrow: A Cipher-Sergeant's Diary, 1941–1945*. Doncaster: Plush, 1999, 187.

14 Them and Us

1. Harry Wilson, 6 August, 1943. IWM:D 4709 80/5/1.
2. S. P. MacKenzie, *Politics and Military Morale: Current-Affairs and Citizenship Education in the British Army, 1914–1950*. Oxford: Oxford University Press, 1992, 103.
3. Roger Broad, *The Radical General: Sir Ronald Adam and Britain's New Model Army 1941–1946*. Stroud: History, 2013, Kindle locations 2915–16.
4. MacKenzie, *Politics and Military Morale*, 87.
5. James Lansdale Hodson, *The Home Front: Being some Account of Journeys, Meetings and what was said to Me in and about England during 1942–1943*. London: Gollancz, 1944, 299.
6. Don Watson, '"Where Do We Go From Here?" Education, Theatre and Politics in the British Army, 1942–1945' in *Labour History Review* 59:3 (1994).
7. Penelope Summerfield, 'Education and Politics in the British Armed Forces in the Second World War' in the *International Review of Social History* 26:2 (1981); Neil Grant, 'Citizen Soldiers: Army Education in World War II' in Formations Editorial Collective, eds, *Formations of Nation and People*. London: Routledge & Kegan Paul, 1984; Jeremy Crang, *The British Army and the People's War 1939–1945*. Manchester: Manchester University Press, 2000, 114–38.
8. MacKenzie, *Politics and Military Morale*, 185.
9. Anthony Burgess, *Little Wilson and Big God, Being the First Part of the Confessions of Anthony Burgess*. London: Heinemann, 1987, 272.
10. Richard Hoggart, *A Sort of Clowning: Life and Times, Vol. 2: 1940–1959*. Oxford: Oxford University Press, 1991, 17.
11. MacKenzie, *Politics and Military Morale*, 97.
12. Ibid., 100.
13. Ibid.,166–8.
14. Margaret Thatcher, *The Path to Power*. London: HarperCollins, 1995, 44.
15. Jeremy Crang, 'Politics on Parade: Army Education and the 1945 General Election' in *History* 81:262 (1996).
16. MacKenzie, *Politics and Military Morale*, 179.
17. William Woodruff, *Vessel of Sadness*. Bath: Paragon, 2005, 116.

18. MacKenzie, *Politics and Military Morale*, 190.

19. Stewart Irwin. IWM:S 18210.

20. Norman Craig, *The Broken Plume: A Platoon Commander's Story, 1940–45*. London: Imperial War Museum, 1982, 38–9.

21. Harry Wilson, 47. IWM:D 4709 80/5/1.

22. William Shebbeare ['Captain X'], *A Soldier Looks Ahead*. London: Labour Book Service, 1944, 51.

23. Anthony Cotterell, *Oh, It's Nice to be in the Army!* London: Gollancz, 1941, 76.

24. Geoffrey Field, *Blood, Sweat, and Toil: Remaking the British Working Class, 1939–1945*. Oxford: Oxford University Press, 2011, 261.

25. Wilfred Leonard Saunders, *Dunkirk Diary of a Very Young Soldier*. Birmingham: Birmingham City Council, Public Libraries Dept, 1989, 28.

26. Norman Smith, *Tank Soldier*. Lewes: Book Guild, 1989, 39.

27. Anthony Powell, *To Keep the Ball Rolling: The Memoirs of Anthony Powell*. Chicago: University of Chicago Press, 2001, 270.

28. Andrew Wilson, *Flame Thrower*. New York: Bantam, 1984, 157.

29. Brian Aldiss, *A Soldier Erect: or Further Adventures of the Hand-Reared Boy*. London: Weidenfeld & Nicolson, 1971, Kindle locations 3585–8.

30. Victor Selwyn, *From Oasis into Italy: War Poems and Diaries from Africa and Italy, 1940–1946*. London: Shepheard-Walwyn, 1983, 223.

31. Craig, *The Broken Plume*, 41.

32. Neil McCallum, *Journey with a Pistol: A Diary of War*. London: Gollancz, 1959, 41.

33. Jack Garnham-Wright. IWM:D 6910 97/19/1.

34. Crang, *The British Army*, 58–67.

35. Herbert Moran, *In My Fashion*. London: Peter Davies, 1946, 167.

36. E. W. Browne et al., *The Soldier and the Army: Opinions on Some Aspects of Army Life*. Calcutta: SEAC, 1946, 26–8.

37. NA WO 163/161.

38. Alexander McKee, *Caen: Anvil of Victory*. London: Souvenir, 2000, 19.

39. Gerry Rubin, *Murder, Mutiny and the Military: British Court Martial Cases, 1940–1966*. London: Francis Boutle, 2005, 59–73; NA WO 163/161. See also Howard Jackson's account on the BBC *People's War* site: www.bbc.co.uk/history/ww2peopleswar/stories/30/a4145230. shtml. Accessed 12 May 2014. The mutineers were court-martialled, but ultimately their punishments were suspended. For those roughly 1,000 soldiers and airmen who had chosen not to participate in the insubordination, the consequences of loyalty were grim. The *City of Canterbury* arrived in Singapore just before its besieged garrison capitulated, and they spent the rest of the war in Japanese captivity.

40. About 1,500 men refused to obey orders when they were landed at the Salerno invasion beach in September 1943 and told that they were to be disbursed as replacements across British units attached to the US 5th Army, rather than joining the 50th and 51st infantry divisions in Sicily as they had originally expected. Most of the original 1,500 were eventually persuaded to accept their new draft orders, but 191 especially recalcitrant soldiers were taken to North Africa and charged with mutiny. All were found guilty and three were sentenced to death, though this was subsequently reduced to twelve years' hard labour. General Adam, who believed that the whole affair had been the product of clumsy and insensitive man-management, was appalled at the dubious legal character of the court martial and the severity of its punishments. He was successful in having all the convictions subsequently suspended. See Clive Emsley, *Soldier, Sailor, Beggarman, Thief: Crime and the British Armed Services since 1914*. Oxford: Oxford University Press, 2013, 118. There was no repeat in the Second World War of the bacchanalian riot that erupted at the British Army training centre near Étaples in France in 1917, during which over a thousand men, provoked by harsh discipline and the shooting of one of their comrades by the Military Police, broke out of camp and raucously occupied the town itself for several days.

41. Karl-Heinz Frieser, *The Blitzkrieg Legend: The 1940 Campaign in the West*. Annapolis, MD: Naval Institute Press, 2005, 320–6; Pier Paolo Battistelli, *Italian Soldier in North Africa 1941–43*. Oxford: Osprey, 2013, 53–7.

42. S. P. MacKenzie, 'Vox Populi: British Army Newspapers in the Second World War' in *Journal of Contemporary History* 24:4 (1989).

43. Raleigh Trevelyan, *The Fortress: A Diary of Anzio and After*. London: Leo Cooper, 1972, 84.

44. Norman Wray. IWM:D 9365 99/85/1. The prime minister did not always impress in person either. E. P. Danger's Grenadier Guards battalion was paraded for Churchill's inspection in Tunis in June 1943. He thought the Great Man 'a shapeless mass of dough, terribly pasty-faced and ill . . . [he] gave a very weak and wobbly V-sign. The lads were disgusted that he did not say anything to them.' E. P. Danger. IWM:D 4465 82/37/1.

45. Harry Wilson, 731. IWM:D 4709 80/5/1.

46. David Cannadine, *The Rise and Fall of Class in Britain*. New York: Columbia University Press, 2000, 134.

47. Burgess, *Little Wilson and Big God*, 268.

48. Hoggart, *A Sort of Clowning*, 5.

49. NA WO 163/161.

50. Cotterell, *Oh, It's Nice to be in the Army!*, 50.

51. NA WO 163/161.

52. J. H. A. Sparrow, *Morale*. London: The War Office, 1949, 22.

53. Louis Heren, *Growing Up Poor in London*. London: Hamilton, 1973; Adrian Smith, *The City of Coventry: A Twentieth Century Icon*. London: I.B. Tauris, 2006.

54. William Graham. IWM:S 19673.

55. Crang, *The British Army*, 62.

56. NA WO 163/161.

57. Harry Wilson, 301. IWM:D 4709 80/5/1.

58. Julian Maclaren-Ross, *Collected Memoirs*. London: Black Spring Press, 2004, 256. See also John Guest, *Broken Images: A Journal*. London: Leo Cooper, 1970, 47.

59. Eric Ambler, *Here Lies: An Autobiography*. London: Weidenfeld & Nicolson, 1986, 167.

60. Rupert Croft-Cooke, *The Licentious Soldiery*. London: W.H. Allen, 1971, 73. See also Julian Maclaren-Ross's 1944 short story 'The Tape', in Julian Maclaren-Ross, *Selected Stories*. Stockport: Dewi Lewis, 2004.

61. C. W. Valentine, *The Human Factor in the Army*. Aldershot: Gate & Polden, 1943, 21–2.

62. Reginald Crimp,18 June 1944. IWM:D 5659 96/50/1.

63. Ibid., 14 October 1944.

64. Gerald Kersh, *Clean, Bright, and Slightly Oiled*. London: Heinemann, 1946, 61.

65. Denis Argent, *A Soldier in Bedfordshire, 1941–1942: The Diary of Private Denis Argent, Royal Engineers*. Woodbridge: Boydell Press, 2009, 159.

66. James Lansdale Hodson, *The Sea and the Land: Being Some Account of Journeys, Meetings, and what was said to Me in Britain, France, Italy, Germany and Holland between March 1943 and May 1945*. London: Gollancz, 1945, 216–18.

67. David Englander and Tony Mason, *The British Soldier in World War II*. Warwick: Warwick University Working Papers in Social History, c.1984, 13.

68. *The Times*, 14 August 1942, 5.

69. NA WO 163/161.

70. Sparrow, *Morale*, 14.

71. Norman Lewis, *Naples '44*. New York: Pantheon Books, 1978, 46.

72. Sally Sokoloff, '"How Are They at Home?" Community, State and Servicemen's Wives in England, 1939–45' in *Women's History Review* 8:1 (1999).

73. Sparrow, *Morale*, 9; Alan Allport, *Demobbed: Coming Home after the Second World War*. New Haven: Yale University Press, 2009, 81–106.

74. Reginald Crimp, 27 October 1943. IWM:D 5659 96/50/1.

75. Sonya Rose, 'Sex, Citizenship, and the Nation in World War II Britain', in *American Historical Review* 103:4 (1998).

76. Smith, *Tank Soldier*, 175. See also Jocelyn Pereira, *A Distant Drum: War Memories of the Intelligence Officer of the 5th Bn. Coldstream Guards, 1944-45*. Wakefield: S.R. Publishers, 1972, 135.

77. Selwyn, *From Oasis into Italy*, 147.

78. Quoted in John Ellis, *The Sharp End: The Fighting Man in World War II*. London: Aurum, 2011, 255–6.

79. NA WO 163/164.

80. A. M. Bell MacDonald. IWM:D 10786 Con Shelf. See also Allport, *Demobbed*, 6–7.

81. Hodson, *The Home Front*, 144.

82. Indeed, the majority of veterans who had joined the Forces before 1942 would end up having a somewhat better lifetime earnings outcome than those who immediately followed them

into the armed services. See Robert A. Hart, 'Above and Beyond the Call: Long-Term Real Earning Effects of British Male Military Conscription during WWII and the Post-war Years', *Discussion Paper No. 4118*, Institute for the Study of Labor (2009). http://ftp.iza.org/dp4118.pdf.

83. Sally Sokoloff, 'Soldiers or Civilians? The Impact of Army Service in World War Two on Birmingham Men' in *Oral History* 25 (Autumn, 1997). See also David Englander, 'Soldiering and Identity: Reflections on the Great War' in *War in History* 1:3 (1994).

84. Field, *Blood, Sweat, and Toil*, 296.

85. Tom Harrisson, 'The British Soldier: Changing Attitudes and Ideas' in *British Journal of Psychology* 35:2 (1945), 38.

86. Harry Wilson, 266. IWM:D 4709 80/5/1.

87. Ross McKibbin, *Classes and Cultures: England 1918–1951*. Oxford: Oxford University Press, 1998, 531–2.

88. Steven Fielding, 'What Did "The People" Want? The Meaning of the 1945 General Election' in *Historical Journal* 35:3 (1992), 636–7.

89. NA WO 163/161.

90. Thatcher, *The Path to Power*, 43. Thomas Bruscino has made a somewhat analogous argument about the Army of the United States, proposing that the mixing of soldiers of different ethnic and religious backgrounds during the war (with the notable exception of African-Americans) made post-war US society more tolerant of diversity. See Thomas Bruscino, *A Nation Forged in War: How World War II Taught Americans to Get Along*. Knoxville, TN: University of Tennessee Press, 2010.

91. MacKenzie, *Politics and Military Morale*, 188.

92. *The Spectator*, 24 November 1944, 475.

93. J. H. A. Sparrow, *Tour of India and South East Asia Command, 28th June 1945–15th October 1945*. IWM:PB 02(41).13 [South East Asia Command]/6, 10–11.

94. Steven Fielding, Peter Thompson and Nick Tiratsoo, *'England Arise!' The Labour Party and Popular Politics in 1940s Britain*. Manchester: Manchester University Press, 1995, 213; Steven Fielding, '"Don't Know and Don't Care": Popular Political Attitudes in Labour's Britain, 1945–1951' in Nick Tiratsoo, ed., *The Attlee Years*. London: Pinter, 1991.

95. J. B. Priestley, *Letter to a Returning Serviceman*. London: Home and Van Thal, 1945, 3–4.

96. Ibid., 31.

97. Hodson, *The Sea and the Land*, 140.

98. Cotterell, *Oh, It's Nice to be in the Army!*, 102.

99. Noel Annan, *Our Age: English Intellectuals between the World Wars: Portrait of a Generation*. New York: Random House, 1990, 208.

100. Alan Wood, *Bless 'Em All: An Analysis of the British Army, its Morale, Efficiency and Leadership*. London: Secker & Warburg, 1942, 38.

15 'What a Colossal Waste of Time War Is'

1. Stuart Hills, *By Tank into Normandy*. London: Cassell, 2002, 236–42.

2. *Strength and Casualties of the Armed Forces and Auxiliary Services of the United Kingdom 1939–1945*. Cmnd. 6832. London: HMSO, 1946.

3. J. M. Winter, *The Great War and the British People*. Houndmills: Macmillan, 1985, 71.

4. Although it should be noted that while 38,384 British officers were killed in the First World War, the RAF lost 70,253 aircrew on operations between 1939 and 1945 – 55,573 in Bomber Command alone. John Terraine, *The Right of the Line: The Royal Air Force in the European War, 1939–1945*. Hodder and Stoughton, 1985, 682.

5. Martin Lindsay, *So Few Got Through: The Personal Diary of Lieut-Col. Martin Lindsay, D.S.O., M.P., Who Served with the Gordon Highlanders in the 51st Highland Division from July, 1944, to May, 1945*. London: Collins, 1968, 254–5.

6. Alexander Baron, *From the City, From the Plough*. New York: Washburn, 1949, 198.

7. William Woodruff, *Vessel of Sadness*. Bath: Paragon, 2005, 152.

8. Alternative dates for the commemoration of the Second World War were considered (including 8 May and 15 August), but none could be found that was both comprehensive and emotionally resonant. Keith Robbins, 'Commemorating the Second World War in Britain: Problems of Definition', in *History Teacher* 29:2 (1996); Adrian Gregory, *The Silence of Memory: Armistice Day 1919–1946*. Oxford: Oxford University Press, 1994, 215–21.

9. Nick Hewitt, 'A Sceptical Generation? War Memorials and the Collective Memory of the Second World War in Britain, 1945–2000' in Dominik Geppert, ed., *The Postwar Challenge: Cultural, Social, and Political Change in Western Europe, 1945–58*. Oxford: Oxford University Press, 2003.

10. Philip Longworth, *The Unending Vigil: A History of the Commonwealth War Graves Commission, 1917–1984*. London: Leo Cooper, 1985, 162. The Commission replaced 'Imperial' with 'Commonwealth' in 1960.

11. Ibid., 206.

12. Ibid., 204.

13. Ibid., 209. The British Legion and regimental associations were sometimes able to subsidize further travel.

14. Lindsay, *So Few Got Through*, 43. For a similar sentiment, see Alexander McKee, *Caen: Anvil of Victory*. London: Souvenir, 2000, 114.

15. Anthony Babington, *An Uncertain Voyage*. Chichester: Barry Rose Law, 2000, 199–200.

16. Ibid., 200.

17. Ibid., 234.

18. Anthony Babington, *No Memorial*. London: Heinemann, 1954, 59.

19. Babington, *An Uncertain Voyage*, 209.

20. NA WO 162/299. Cmnd. 6832 gives a figure of 239,575. These aggregate figures presumably include soldiers who were wounded more than once.

21. Victor Selwyn, *From Oasis into Italy: War Poems and Diaries from Africa and Italy, 1940–1946*. London: Shepheard-Walwyn, 1983, 24–5.

22. Mark Harrison, *Medicine and Victory: British Military Medicine in the Second World War*. Oxford: Oxford University Press, 2008, 275.

23. John Ellis, *The Sharp End: The Fighting Man in World War II*. London: Aurum, 2011, 169.

24. Ena Elsey, The Rehabilitation and Employment of Disabled Ex-Servicemen after the Two World Wars. Unpublished thesis. University of Teeside, 1994, 3.

25. Julie Anderson, *War, Disability and Rehabilitation: 'Soul of a Nation'*. Manchester: Manchester University Press, 2011, 77.

26. Peter Reese, *Homecoming Heroes: An Account of the Reassimilation of British Military Personnel into Civilian Life*. London: Leo Cooper, 1992, 196–7; Anderson, *War, Disability and Rehabilitation*, 183.

27. Reese, *Homecoming Heroes*, 201.

28. Jonathan Moffat, *Moon Over Malaya: A Tale of Argylles and Marines*. Stroud: Tempus, 2002, 344.

29. Fred Goddard, *Battlefields of Life*. Lewes: Book Guild, 1999, 121.

30. *The Times*, 11 August 1948, 5.

31. *House of Commons Debates* 18 July 1946: http://hansard.millbanksystems.com/written_answers/1946/jul/18/psychoneurosis. Accessed 13 May 2014.

32. Tom Harrison, *Bion, Rickman, Foulkes and the Northfield Experiments: Advancing on a Different Front*. London: Jessica Kingsley, 2000, 105.

33. Anthony Babington, *Shell-Shock: A History of the Changing Attitudes to War Neurosis*. London: Leo Cooper, 1997, 121.

34. Elizabeth Roberts-Pedersen, 'A Weak Spot in the Personality? Conceptualizing "War Neurosis" in British Medical Literature of the Second World War' in *Australian Journal of Politics and History* 58:3 (2012), 416; Edgar Jones and Simon Wessely, *Shell Shock to PTSD: Military Psychiatry from 1900 to the Gulf War*. New York: Psychology Press, 2005, 105–7; Ben Shephard, *A War of Nerves: Soldiers and Psychiatrists in the Twentieth Century*. Cambridge, MA: Harvard University Press, 2001, 166–8. Initially, at the outbreak of war the government had announced that *no* war pensions would be granted for psychiatric injuries whatsoever, though by June 1941 it had been forced to abandon this uncompromising position. See Edgar Jones and Simon Wessely, 'A Paradigm Shift in the Conceptualization of Psychological Trauma in the 20th Century' in *Journal of Anxiety Disorders* 21 (2007), 169.

35. Ibid., 170; Ben Shephard, '"Pitiless Psychology": The Role of Prevention in British Military Psychiatry in the Second World War' in *History of Psychiatry* 10 (1999), 499.

36. Reese, *Homecoming Heroes*, 203.

37. Stanley Whitehouse, *Fear is the Foe: A Footslogger from Normandy to the Rhine*. London: Hale, 1995, 119.

38. Jones and Wessely, *Shell Shock to PTSD*, 98–9.

39. John Masters, *The Road Past Mandalay*. London: Cassell, 2002, 334.

40. John Guest, *Broken Images: A Journal*. London: Leo Cooper, 1970, 209.

41. Jocelyn Pereira, *A Distant Drum: War Memories of the Intelligence Officer of the 5th Bn. Coldstream Guards, 1944–45*. Wakefield: S.R. Publishers, 1972, 177.

42. Alan Allport, *Demobbed: Coming Home after the Second World War*. New Haven: Yale University Press, 2009, 26–33.

43. Reginald Crimp, 4 May 1945. IWM:D 5659 96/50/1.

44. Andrew Wilson, *Flame Thrower*. New York: Bantam, 1984, 186.

45. Jack Swaab, *Field of Fire: Diary of a Gunner Officer*. Stroud: Sutton, 2005, 373–8.

46. Guest, *Broken Images*, 225.

47. Swaab, *Field of Fire*, 395.

48. James Lansdale Hodson, *The Sea and the Land: Being Some Account of Journeys, Meetings, and what was said to Me in Britain, France, Italy, Germany and Holland between March 1943 and May 1945*. London: Gollancz, 1945, 104.

49. Leslie Phillips, *Hello: The Autobiography*. London: Orion, 2006, 106.

50. B. F. Spiller. IWM:D 11941 02/52/1.

51. Gordon Nisbett, *For the Duration: The Journal of a Conscript, 1941 to 1946*. Edinburgh: Pentland Place, 1996, 159–60.

52. Geoffrey Picot, *Accidental Warrior: In the Front Line from Normandy till Victory*. Lewes: Book Guild, 1993, 305.

53. David Holbrook, *Flesh Wounds*. Stroud: Tempus, 2007, 243–4.

54. George Greenfield, *Chasing the Beast: One Man's War*. London: Richard Cohen, 1998, 188–9. The 1960 melodrama *Tunes of Glory* starring John Mills and Alec Guinness (two stalwarts of the traditional 1950s war film) is an analysis of the way in which 'upstart' temporary officers such as Kelly, who had thrived in the unique conditions of wartime, could not be successfully assimilated into the class-bound peacetime regular Army. See Andrew Spicer, 'Echoes of War: *Tunes of Glory* and the Demise of the Officer Class in British Cinema' in Danielle Hipkins and Gill Plain, eds, *War-torn Tales: Literature, Film and Gender in the Aftermath of World War II*. Oxford: Peter Lang, 1997.

55. Ferdinand Zweig, *Labour, Life and Poverty*. London: Gollanz, 1948, 50.

56. John Mulgan, *Report on Experience*. Oxford: Oxford University Press, 1984, 76–7.

57. Norman Wray. IWM:D 9365 99/85/1.

58. Rupert Croft-Cooke, *The Licentious Soldiery*. London: W. H. Allen, 1971, 74.

59. Guest, *Broken Images*, 110.

60. Harry Wilson, 731. IWM:D 4709 80/5/1.

61. Picot, *Accidental Warrior*, 103.

62. Richard Hoggart, *A Sort of Clowning: Life and Times, Vol. 2: 1940–1959*. Oxford: Oxford University Press, 1991, 69.

63. Graham Wootton, *The Official History of the British Legion*. London: MacDonald & Evans, 1956, 305.

64. Toby Haggith, 'Great Britain: Remembering a Just War' in Lothar Kettenacker and Torsten Riotte, *The Legacies of the Two World Wars: European Societies in the Twentieth Century*. New York: Berghahn Books, 2011, 239.

65. T. E. B. Howarth, *Prospect and Reality: Britain 1945–1955*. London: Collins, 1985, 43.

66. Croft-Cooke, *The Licentious Soldiery*, 43.

67. *The Times*, 12 November 1957, 9.

68. John Ramsden, 'Refocussing "The People's War": British War Films of the 1950s' in *Journal of Contemporary History* 33:1 (1998); Martin Francis, 'A Flight from Commitment? Domesticity, Adventure and the Masculine Imaginary in Britain after the Second World War' in *Gender and History* 19:1 (2007). It ought to be noted, however, that middle-aged men only represented a small proportion of the total cinema audience during the golden age of the British war film. In 1958, almost half of homeowners didn't go to see a film at all, whereas 38 per cent of young people living with their parents saw one a week. See David Docherty, David Morrison and Michael Tracey, *The Last Picture Show? Britain's Changing Film Audience*. London: British Film Institute, 1987, 26.

69. Blake Morrison, *The Movement: English Poetry and Fiction of the 1950s*. Oxford: Oxford University Press, 1980, 75.

70. Also Kenneth Horne, Tony Hancock, Jimmy Edwards, Frank Muir and Denis Norden for the RAF, and John Pertwee for the RN.

71. Andrew Spicer, 'The "Other War": Images of the Second World War in Service Comedies', in S. Bennett et al., eds, *Relocating Britishness*. Manchester: Manchester University Press, 2004.

72. Brian Harrison, *Seeking a Role: The United Kingdom, 1951-1970*. Oxford: Oxford University Press, 2009, 400.

73. Richard Vinen, *National Service: Conscription in Britain, 1945-1963*. London: Allen Lane, 2014.

74. *The Spectator*, 15 March 1946, 266.

75. Alex Bowlby, *The Recollections of Rifleman Bowlby*. London: Cassell, 1999, 12-13.

Appendix

1. For a few months in the summer of 1939, the conscripted 'militiamen' formed a third component of the Army. They were absorbed into the national Army after the outbreak of war.

2. Though it should be noted that one of the two corps attached to First Canadian Army throughout the whole of the northwestern European campaign was in fact British (I Corps).

3. The Army maintained a functional distinction between tank and armoured brigades. Tank brigades, which were intended to support infantry formations, were equipped with heavier infantry or 'I' tanks rather than the lighter 'cruiser' tanks of the armoured brigades, which were intended for rapid pursuit and exploitation.

4. At the start of the war a rank of WO Class III also existed, but its use was discontinued after 1940.

BIBLIOGRAPHY

Archival Materials

Imperial War Museum Department of Documents, Southwark, London SEl 6HZ

Baylis, Lionel G. 7969 98/23/1
Bell MacDonald, A. M. 10786 Con Shelf
Cartwright, Richard 3168 95/23/1
Cooper, David 202 90/6/1
Crimp, Reginald 5659 96/50/1
Danger, E. P. 4465 82/37/1
Druitt, Geoffrey P. 5600 96/38/1
Evans, D. 2028 92/37/1
Forrest, A. J. 310 91/13/1
Garnham-Wright, Jack 6910 97/19/1
Gaunt, Harry K. 1544 92/1/1
Herbert, A. G. 7625 98/16/1
Holborow, Richard 15631 07/23/ l
Howarth, T. E. B. 2924 84/7/1
Jones, Mary 6902 78/55/1
Kenyon, L. R. F. 3868 84/83/3
Lewis, Alec 13428 05/45/1
Lloyd-Jones, R. H. 125 89/1/1
Manley, E. J. 12308 P284
Mills, A. J. 4269 83/24/1
Newland, Dennis 12197 03/22/1
Parker-Jones, J. Herbert 9078 01/10/1
Procter, S. C. 5636 96/1/1
Sissons, V. M. 1249 87/6/1
Songhurst, R. F. 2373 86/24/1
Spiller, B. F. 11941 02/52/1
Thornhill, E. B. 8419 99/36/1
Tomlinson, J. B. 613 90/29/1
Wilson, Harry 4709 80/5/1
Witte, J. H. 1279 87/12/1
Wray, Norman 9365 99/85/1

Imperial War Museum Department of Printed Books, Southwark, London SE1 6HZ

Sparrow, J. H. A., *Tour of India and South East Asia Command, 28th June 1945–15th October 1945.* 02(41).13 [South East Asia Command]/6

Imperial War Museum Department of Sound Records, Southwark, London SE1 6HZ

Baldwin, Alfred 6491
Callander, Donald 7166
Chapman, Albert 17978
Cottier, Frederick 10601
Docketty, Francis 4822
Elliott, Ronald 10167
ffrench-Blake, Robert 106
Graham, William 19673
Green, Robert 6226
Irwin, Stewart 18210
Pardoe, Philip 6465
Scourfield, David 6367
Watson, John 18372

Liddell Hart Centre for Military Archives, King's College University of London, London WC2R 2LS

Adam, Gen Sir Ronald, 2nd Bt (1885–1982) 3-1, 3-2, 3-4-6, 3-6-3, 3-6-4, 3-10, 3-13

Mass-Observation Archive, University of Sussex, Brighton BN1 9QL

File Reports 31, 274, 1262, 1941, 1942
Topic Collection TC29 Boxes 1 & 2

The National Archives, Kew, Richmond, Surrey TW9 4DU

CAB Series 66/24/7, 106/200
WO Series 32/9680, 162/299, 163/161, 163/163, 163/164, 214/62, 216/61, 217/24, 222/66, 222/124, 231/8, 259/44, 259/62, 259/64, 277/4, 277/7, 277/12, 277/16, 277/19, 291/491, 291/1186, 365/216

Government Publications

Browne, E. W. et al., *The Soldier and the Army: Opinions on Some Aspects of Army Life.* Calcutta: SEAC, 1946
Derry, T. K., *The Campaign in Norway.* London: HMSO, 1952
Ellis, L. F., *The War in France and Flanders, 1939–1940.* London: HMSO, 1953
Ferguson, Sheila and Hilde Fitzgerald, *Studies in the Social Services.* London: HMSO, 1954
General Annual Report on the British Army, Cmnd. 4821. London: HMSO, 1934
—, Cmnd. 5950. London: HMSO, 1938
Germany 1944: The British Soldier's Pocketbook. Kew: National Archives, 2006
Gwyer, J.M.A, and James Ramsay Montagu Butler, *Grand Strategy. Vol. 3 Part I, June 1941–August 1942.* London: HMSO, 1964
Hay, Ian, *Arms and the Men.* London: HMSO, 1977
Howard, Michael, *Grand Strategy. Vol. 4, August 1942–September 1943.* London: HMSO, 1970
Howlett, Peter, *Fighting with Figures: A Statistical Digest of the Second World War.* London: HMSO, 1995
Joslen, H. F., *Orders of Battle: United Kingdom and Colonial Formations and Units in the Second World War, 1939–1945.* London: HMSO, 1960
McPherson, A. B., *Discipline.* London: The War Office, 1950
Morgan, M. C., *Welfare.* London: The War Office, 1953
Parker, H. M. D., *Manpower: A Study of Wartime Policy and Administration.* London: HMSO, 1957

Piggott, A. J. K., *Manpower Problems*. London: The War Office, 1949

Playfair, I. S. O., *The Mediterranean and Middle East. Vol. 2*. London: HMSO, 1974

Postan, M. M., *British War Production*. London: HMSO, 1952

Sparrow, J. H. A., *Morale*. London: The War Office, 1949

Statistics of the Military Effort of the British Empire During the Great War, 1914–1920. London: HMSO, 1922

Strength and Casualties of the Armed Forces and Auxiliary Services of the United Kingdom 1939–1945. Cmnd. 6832. London: HMSO, 1946

Ungerson, B., *Personnel Selection*. London: The War Office, 1953

Newspapers and Magazines

The Adelphi
Daily Express
Daily Mirror
Daily Telegraph
Ex-Services Review
Horizon
The Listener
The Nineteenth Century
The Observer
Soldier
The Spectator
The Times
Tribune

Books and Book Chapters

Addison, Paul, 'Oxford and the Second World War' in Brian Harrison, ed., *The History of the University of Oxford: The Twentieth-century. Volume 8*. Oxford: Oxford University Press, 1994

Ahrenfeldt, Robert, *Psychiatry in the British Army in the Second World War*. London: Routledge & Kegan Paul, 1958

Alanbrooke, Viscount, *War Diaries, 1939–1945*. London: Weidenfeld & Nicolson, 2001

Aldiss, Brian, *A Soldier Erect: or Further Adventures of the Hand-Reared Boy*. London: Weidenfeld & Nicolson, 1971. Kindle edition

—, *Trillion Year Spree: The History of Science Fiction*. London: Paladin, 1988

Allen, Louis, *Burma: The Longest War 1941–45*. New York: St Martin's Press, 1984

Allport, Alan, *Demobbed: Coming Home after the Second World War*. New Haven: Yale University Press, 2009

Ambler, Eric, *Here Lies: An Autobiography*. London: Weidenfeld & Nicolson, 1986

Amis, Kingsley, *Memoirs*. London: Vintage, 2004

Anderson, Benedict, *Imagined Communities: Reflections on the Origin and Spread of Nationalism*. London: Verso, 1991

Anderson, Dudley, *Three Cheers for the Next Man to Die*. Oxford: Isis, 2003

Anderson, Julie, *War, Disability and Rehabilitation: 'Soul of a Nation'*. Manchester: Manchester University Press, 2011

Anglim, Simon, *Orde Wingate and the British Army, 1922–1944*. London: Pickering & Chatto, 2010

Annan, Noel, *Our Age: English Intellectuals between the World Wars: Portrait of a Generation*. New York: Random House, 1990

Argent, Denis, *A Soldier in Bedfordshire, 1941–1942: The Diary of Private Denis Argent, Royal Engineers*. Woodbridge: Boydell Press, 2009

Arthur, Douglas, *Desert Watch: A Story of the Battle of Beda Fomm – And What Went on Before – As Seen Through the Eyes of Driver D. Arthur (Young Doug), No. 1 Battery, 106th Lancashire Hussars (Yeomanry) Regiment, Royal Horse Artillery*. Bedale: Blaisdon Publishing, 2000

Atkinson, Rick, *The Day of Battle: The War in Sicily and Italy, 1943–1944*. New York: Henry Holt, 2007

August, Andrew, *The British Working Class 1832–1940*. Harlow: Pearson, 2007

Babington, Anthony, *No Memorial*. London: Heinemann, 1954

—, *Military Intervention in Britain: From the Gordon Riots to the Gibraltar Incident*. London: Routledge, 1990

—, *Shell-Shock: A History of the Changing Attitudes to War Neurosis*. London: Leo Cooper, 1997

—, *An Uncertain Voyage*. Chichester: Barry Rose Law, 2000

Badsey, Stephen, *Normandy 1944: Allied Landings and Breakout*. Oxford: Osprey, 1990

Baines, Frank, *Chindit Affair: A Memoir of the War in Burma*. Barnsley: Pen & Sword, 2011

Barber, Neil, ed., *Fighting with the Commandos: Recollections of Stan Scott, No. 3 Commando*. Barnsley: Pen & Sword, 2008. Kindle edition

Barker, Rachel, *Conscience, Government and War*. London: Routledge & Kegan Paul, 1982

Barnett, Corelli, *Strategy and Society*. Manchester: Manchester University Press, 1976

—, *The Desert Generals*. Edison, NJ: Castle Books, 2004

Baron, Alexander, *From the City, From the Plough*. New York: Washburn, 1949

Barr, Niall, *Pendulum of War: The Three Battles of El Alamein*. London: Jonathan Cape, 2004

Battistelli, Pier Paolo, *Italian Soldier in North Africa 1941–43*. Oxford: Osprey, 2013

Bayly, Christopher and Tim Harper, *Forgotten Armies: The Fall of British Asia, 1941–1945*. Cambridge, MA: Belknap, 2005

Beckett, Ian, *The Amateur Military Tradition: 1558–1945*. Manchester: Manchester University Press, 1991

Beevor, Anthony, *D-Day: The Battle for Normandy*. New York: Viking, 2009

Bell, Christopher M., *Churchill and Sea Power*. Oxford: Oxford University Press, 2013

Bellamy, Bill, *Troop Leader: A Tank Commander's Story*. Stroud: Sutton, 2007

Bialer, Uri, *The Shadow of the Bomber: The Fear of Air Attack and British Politics, 1932–1939*. London: Royal Historical Society, 1980

Bidwell, Shelford and Dominick Graham, *Fire-Power: British Army Weapons and Theories of War, 1904–1945*. London: Allen & Unwin, 1982

Billany, Dan, *The Trap*. London: Faber and Faber, 1986

Bishop, Tim and Bruce Shand, *One Young Soldier: The Memoirs of a Cavalryman*. Norwich: M. Russell, 1993

Blaxland, Gregory, *Alexander's Generals: The Italian Campaign 1944–45*. London: William Kimber, 1979

Bond, Brian, *Liddell Hart: A Study of his Military Thought*. London: Cassell, 1977

—, *British Military Policy Between the Two World Wars*. Oxford: Clarendon Press, 1980

—, 'Preparing the Field Force, February 1939–May 1940' in Brian Bond and Michael Taylor, eds, *The Battle of France and Flanders, 1940: Sixty Years On*. London: Leo Cooper, 2001

Boscawen, Robert, *Armoured Guardsman*. London: Leo Cooper, 2000

Bourke, Joanna, *Working Class Cultures in Britain, 1890–1960: Gender, Class, and Ethnicity*. London: Routledge, 1994

—, *An Intimate History of Killing: Face-to-face Killing in Twentieth-century Warfare*. New York: Basic Books, 1999

Bourne, John, 'The British Working Man in Arms' in Hugh Cecil and Peter H. Liddle, eds, *Facing Armageddon: The First World War Experienced*. Barnsley: Pen & Sword Books, 1996

Bourne, Stephen, *The Motherland Calls: Britain's Black Servicemen and Women, 1939–45*. Stroud: The History Press, 2012

Bowlby, Alex, *The Recollections of Rifleman Bowlby*. London: Cassell, 1999

Bowman, J. E., *Three Stripes and a Gun: A Young Man's Journey Towards Maturity*. Braunton: Merlin, 1987

Branson, Clive, *British Soldier in India: The Letters of Clive Branson*. London: The Communist Party, 1944

Brereton, J. M., *The British Soldier: A Social History from 1661 to the Present Day*. London: Bodley Head, 1986

Broad, Roger, *The Radical General: Sir Ronald Adam and Britain's New Model Army 1941–1946*. Stroud: History, 2013. Kindle edition

Brown, James Ambrose, *Retreat to Victory: A Springbok's Diary in North Africa: Gazala to El Alamein 1942*. Johannesburg: Ashanti Publishing, 1991

Bruce, Colin, *War on the Ground*. London: Constable, 1995

Bruscino, Thomas, *A Nation Forged in War: How World War II Taught Americans to Get Along*. Knoxville, TN: University of Tennessee Press, 2010

Buckle, Richard, *The Most Upsetting Woman*. London: Collins, 1981

Buckley, John, *British Armour in the Normandy Campaign, 1944*. London: Routledge, 2004

—, *Monty's Men: The British Army and the Liberation of Europe, 1944–5*. New Haven: Yale University Press, 2013

Burgess, Anthony, *Little Wilson and Big God, Being the First Part of the Confessions of Anthony Burgess*. London: Heinemann, 1987

Caddick-Adams, Peter, *Monte Cassino: Ten Armies in Hell*. Oxford: Oxford University Press, 2010

Cain, P. J. and A. G. Hopkins, *British Imperialism 1688–2000*. Harlow: Longman, 2002

Calder, Angus, *The People's War: Britain, 1939–1945*. London: Pimlico, 2008

Callahan, Raymond, *Churchill and his Generals*. Lawrence, KS: University Press of Kansas, 2007

Cannadine, David, 'War and Death, Grief and Mourning in Modern Britain' in Joachim Whaley, ed., *Mirrors of Mortality: Studies in the Social History of Death*. London: Europa, 1981

—, *The Rise and Fall of Class in Britain*. New York: Columbia University Press, 2000

Carrington, Peter, *Reflecting on Things Past: The Memoirs of Peter Lord Carrington*. New York: Harper & Row, 1989

Carver, Michael, *The Seven Ages of the British Army*. New York: Beaufort Books, *c.*1984

Ceadel, Martin, *Pacifism in Britain, 1914–1945: The Defining of a Faith*. Oxford: Oxford University Press, 1980

Cheall, Bill, *Fighting Through from Dunkirk to Hamburg: A Green Howards Wartime Memoir*. Barnsley: Pen & Sword, 2011. Kindle edition

Churchill, Winston, *The Churchill War Papers. Vol. 2. Never Surrender, May 1940–December 1940*. New York: W.W. Norton, 1995

—, *The Churchill War Papers. Vol. 3. The Ever-widening War, 1941*. New York: W.W. Norton, 2000

—, *The Gathering Storm*. London: Penguin, 2005

—, *The Hinge of Fate*. London: Penguin, 2005

—, *The World Crisis*. New York: Free Press, 2005

Clark, Lloyd, *Arnhem: Jumping the Rhine 1944 and 1945*. London: Headline Review, 2008

Clayton, Anthony, *The British Officer: Leading the Army from 1660 to the Present*. Harlow: Longman, 2005

Close, Roy, *In Action with the SAS: A Soldier's Odyssey from Dunkirk to Berlin*. Barnsley: Pen & Sword, 2005. Kindle edition

Cochrane, Peter, *Charlie Company: In Service with C Company 2nd Queen's Own Cameron Highlanders, 1940–44*. Stroud: Spellmount, 2007

Cochrane, William, *Chindit: Special Force, Burma, 1944*. Philadelphia: Xlibris, 2000

Coldstream, John, *Dirk Bogarde: The Authorised Biography*. London: Phoenix, 2005

Collingham, Lizzie, *The Taste of War: World War II and the Battle for Food*. London: Penguin, 2012

Connelly, Mark, *We Can Take It! Britain and the Memory of the Second World War*. London: Pearson Longman, 2004

Conradi, Peter J., *A Very English Hero: The Making of Frank Thompson*. London: Bloomsbury, 2012

Constantine, Stephen, *Social Conditions in Britain, 1918–1939*. London: Methuen, 1983

Converse, Allan, *Armies of Empire: The 9th Australian and 50th British Divisions in Battle, 1939–1945*. Cambridge: Cambridge University Press, 2011

Cooper, Artemis, *Cairo in the War: 1939–1945*. London: H. Hamilton, 1989

Cooper, Raymond, *'B' Company, 9th Battalion, the Border Regiment, 48 Brigade, 17 Indian (Light) Division, IV Corps, 14th Army, South East Asia Command: One Man's War in Burma, 1942–1944, Recalled in Hospital in 1945*. London: Dobson, 1978

Cotterell, Anthony, *Oh, It's Nice to be in the Army!* London: Gollancz, 1941

—, *What! No Morning Tea?* London: Gollancz, 1941

Cotterell, Geoffrey, *Then a Soldier*. London: Eyre & Spottiswoode, 1944

Craig, Norman, *The Broken Plume: A Platoon Commander's Story, 1940–45*. London: Imperial War Museum, 1982

Crang, Jeremy, 'The British Soldier on the Home Front: Army Morale Reports 1940–45' in Paul Addison and Angus Calder, eds, *Time to Kill: The Soldier's Experience of War in the West, 1939–1945*. London: Pimlico, 1997

—, *The British Army and the People's War 1939–1945*. Manchester: Manchester University Press, 2000

—, 'The Defence of the Dunkirk Perimeter' in Brian Bond and Michael Taylor, eds, *The Battle of France and Flanders, 1940: Sixty Years On*. London: Leo Cooper, 2001

Crick, Bernard, *George Orwell: A Life*. London: Penguin, 1980

Crimp, Reginald, *The Diary of a Desert Rat*. London: Cooper, 1971

Croft-Cooke, Rupert, *The Gorgeous East*. London: W.H. Allen, 1965

—, *The Licentious Soldiery*. London: W.H. Allen, 1971

Cunningham, Hugh, *The Invention of Childhood*. London: BBC Books, 2006

Davies, Norman, *Europe at War 1939–1945*. London: Pan, 2007

Deedes, William, *Dear Bill: W.F. Deedes Reports*. London: Macmillan, 2005

Dennis, Peter, *The Territorial Army, 1906–1940*. Woodbridge: Royal Historical Society, 1987

D'Este, Carlo, *Decision in Normandy*. New York: HarperPerennial, 1994

—, *Warlord: A Life of Winston Churchill at War, 1874–1945*. New York: Harper, 2008

Dildy, Doug, *Dunkirk, 1940: Operation Dynamo*. Oxford: Osprey, 2010

Docherty, David, David Morrison and Michael Tracey, *The Last Picture Show? Britain's Changing Film Audience*. London: British Film Institute, 1987

Doherty, Richard, *Irish Volunteers in the Second World War*. Dublin: Four Courts Press, 2002

Edgerton, David, *England and the Aeroplane: Militarism, Modernity and Machines*. Houndmills: Macmillan, 1991

—, *Britain's War Machine: Weapons, Resources and Experts in the Second World War*. London: Allen Lane, 2011

Edsel, Robert, *Saving Italy: The Race to Rescue a Nation's Treasures from the Nazis*. New York: W.W. Norton, 2013

Elliott, Walter, *Esprit de Corps: A Scots Guards Officer on Active Service, 1943–1945*. Norwich: M. Russell, 1996

Ellis, John, *Brute Force: Allied Strategy and Tactics in the Second World War*. New York: Viking, 1990

—, *The World War II Databook: The Essential Facts and Figures for all the Combatants*. London: Aurum, 1993

—, *The Sharp End: The Fighting Man in World War II*. London: Aurum, 2011

Elstob, Peter, *Warriors for the Working Day*. London: Corgi, 1974

Emsley, Clive, *Soldier, Sailor, Beggarman, Thief: Crime and the British Armed Services since 1914*. Oxford: Oxford University Press, 2013

Englander, David and Tony Mason, *The British Soldier in World War II*. Warwick: Warwick University Working Papers in Social History, c.1984

Farrell, Charles, *Reflections 1939–1945: A Scots Guards Officer in Training and War*. Edinburgh: Pentland Press, 2000

Fennell, Jonathan, *Combat and Morale in the North African Campaign: The Eighth Army and the Path to El Alamein*. Cambridge: Cambridge University Press, 2010

Field, Geoffrey, *Blood, Sweat, and Toil: Remaking the British Working Class, 1939–1945*. Oxford: Oxford University Press, 2011

Fielding, Steven, '"Don't Know and Don't Care": Popular Political Attitudes in Labour's Britain, 1945–1951' in Nick Tiratsoo, ed., *The Attlee Years*. London: Pinter, 1991

Fielding, Steven, Peter Thompson and Nick Tiratsoo, *'England Arise!' The Labour Party and Popular Politics in 1940s Britain*. Manchester: Manchester University Press, 1995

Fletcher, David, *Matilda Infantry Tank, 1938–1945*. Oxford: Osprey, 1994

Foley, John, *Mailed Fist*. St Albans: Mayflower, 1975

Ford, Ken, *Battleaxe Division: From Africa to Italy with the 78th Division 1942–45*. Stroud: Sutton, 2003

—, *Caen 1944*. Oxford: Osprey, 2004

—, *El Alamein 1942: The Turning of the Tide*. Oxford: Osprey, 2005

Forester, C. S., *The General*. Annapolis, MD: Nautical & Aviation Publishing, 1982

Forman, Denis, *To Reason Why*. Barnsley: Pen & Sword Military, 2008

Fowler, David, *The First Teenagers: The Lifestyle of Young Wage-Earners in Interwar Britain*. London: Woburn Press, 1995

Francis, Martin, *The Flyer: British Culture and the Royal Air Force 1939–1945*. Oxford: Oxford University Press, 2008

Fraser, David, *And We Shall Shock Them: The British Army in the Second World War*. London: Cassell, 2002

Fraser, George MacDonald, *Quartered Safe Out Here: A Recollection of the War in Burma with a New Epilogue: Fifty Years On*. London: HarperCollins, 2000

French, David, *The British Way in Warfare: 1688–2000*. London: Unwin Hyman, 1990

—, *Raising Churchill's Army: The British Army and the War against Germany, 1919–1945*. Oxford: Oxford University Press, 2000

—, *Military Identities: The Regimental System, the British Army, and the British People, c.1870–2000*. Oxford: Oxford University Press, 2005

—, 'Big Wars and Small Wars between the Wars, 1919–1939' in Hew Strachan, ed., *Big Wars and Small Wars: The British Army and the Lessons of War in the 20th Century*. London: Routledge, 2006

Frieser, Karl-Heinz, *The Blitzkrieg Legend: The 1940 Campaign in the West*. Annapolis, MD: Naval Institute Press, 2005

Fritz, Stephen G., *Frontsoldaten*. Lexington: University Press of Kentucky, 1997

Fry, Helen, *The King's Most Loyal Enemy Aliens: Germans Who Fought for Britain in the Second World War*. Stroud: Sutton Publishing, 2008

Fuller, J. F. C., *Memoirs of an Unconventional Soldier*. London: Nicholson and Watson, 1936

Galloway, Strome, *With the Irish Against Rommel: A Diary of 1943*. Langley, BC: Battleline Books, c.1984

Garfield, Simon, *We Are at War: The Remarkable Diaries of Five Ordinary People in Extraordinary Times*. London: Ebury, 2005

Glass, Charles, *Deserter: The Last Untold Story of the Second World War*. London: HarperPress, 2013

Goddard, Fred, *Battlefields of Life*. Lewes: Book Guild, 1999

Godfrey, Simon, *British Army Communications in the Second World War*. London: Bloomsbury, 2013

Goodall, Felicity, *A Question of Conscience: Conscientious Objection in Two World Wars*. Stroud: Sutton, 1997

Gooderson, Ian, *A Hard Way to Make a War: The Italian Campaign in the Second World War*. London: Conway, 2008

Graham, Dominick, *Against Odds: Reflections on the Experiences of the British Army, 1914–45*. New York: St Martin's Press, 1999

Graham, Dominick and Shelford Bidwell, *Tug of War: The Battle for Italy, 1943–1945*. Barnsley: Pen & Sword, 2004

Grant, Neil, 'Citizen Soldiers: Army Education in World War II' in Formations Editorial Collective, eds, *Formations of Nation and People*. London: Routledge & Kegan Paul, 1984

Graves, Robert and Alan Hodge, *The Long Week-end: A Social History of Great Britain, 1918–1939*. New York: Norton, 1994

Greenacre, John, *Churchill's Spearhead: The Development of Britain's Airborne Forces during World War II*. Barnsley: Pen & Sword, 2010. Kindle edition

Greenfield, George, *Chasing the Beast: One Man's War*. London: Richard Cohen, 1998

Greenwood, Trevor, *D-Day to Victory: The Diaries of a British Tank Commander*. London: Simon & Schuster, 2012

Gregory, Adrian, *The Silence of Memory: Armistice Day 1919–1946*. Oxford: Oxford University Press, 1994

Gregg, Victor, *Rifleman: A Front Line Life from Alamein and Dresden to the Fall of the Berlin Wall*. London: Bloomsbury, 2011

Griffin, Frank ['Private XYZ'], *I Joined the Army*. London: Fact, 1937

Griffin, H. J., *An Eighth Army Odyssey*. Edinburgh: Pentland Press, 1997

Griffith, Paddy, *Battle Tactics of the Western Front: The British Army's Art of Attack, 1916–18*. New Haven: Yale, 1996

Grossman, Dave, *On Killing*. London: Little, Brown, 2009

Guest, John, *Broken Images: A Journal*. London: Leo Cooper, 1970

Haggith, Toby, 'Great Britain: Remembering a Just War' in Lothar Kettenacker and Torsten Riotte, *The Legacies of the Two World Wars: European Societies in the Twentieth Century*. New York: Berghahn Books, 2011

Hamilton, Nigel, *Monty: The Making of a General, 1887–1942*. London: Hamilton, 1981

Hammond, Bryn, *El Alamein: The Battle that Turned the Tide of the Second World War*. Oxford: Osprey, 2012

Harries, Meirion, *Soldiers of the Sun: The Rise and Fall of the Imperial Japanese Army*. New York: Random House, 1992

Harrison, Brian, *Seeking a Role: The United Kingdom, 1951-1970*. Oxford: Oxford University Press, 2009

Harrison, Mark, *Medicine and Victory: British Military Medicine in the Second World War*. Oxford: Oxford University Press, 2008

Harrison, Tom, *Bion, Rickman, Foulkes and the Northfield Experiments: Advancing on a Different Front*. London: Jessica Kingsley, 2000

Harrisson, Tom, *Living Through the Blitz*. London: Collins, 1976

Hart, Stephen, *Colossal Cracks: Montgomery's 21st Army Group in Northwest Europe, 1944–45*. Mechanicsburg, PA: Stackpole Books, 2007

Hastings, Max, *Overlord: D-Day and the Battle for Normandy 1944*. London: Pan, 1999

—, *Winston's War: Churchill, 1940–1945*. New York: Alfred A. Knopf, 2009

—, *All Hell Let Loose: The World at War 1939–45*. London: HarperPress, 2011. Kindle edition

Hay, Ian, *The King's Service: An Informal History of the British Infantry Soldier*. London: Methuen, 1938

Hayes, Denis, *Challenge of Conscience: The Story of the Conscientious Objectors of 1939–1945*. London: Allen & Unwin, 1949

Healey, Denis, *The Time of My Life*. New York: W.W. Norton, 1990

Heath, Edward, *The Course of My Life: An Autobiography*. London: Hodder & Stoughton, 1998

Heffer, Simon, *Like the Roman: The Life of Enoch Powell*. London: Weidenfeld & Nicolson, 1998

Heren, Louis, *Growing Up Poor in London*. London: Hamilton, 1973

Hewitt, Nick, 'A Sceptical Generation? War Memorials and the Collective Memory of the Second World War in Britain, 1945–2000' in Dominik Geppert, ed., *The Postwar Challenge: Cultural, Social, and Political Change in Western Europe, 1945–58*. Oxford: Oxford University Press, 2003

Higgins, Patrick, *Heterosexual Dictatorship: Male Homosexuality in Postwar Britain*. London: Fourth Estate, 1996

Higham, Robin, *Armed Forces in Peacetime: Britain, 1918–1940*. Hamden, CT: Archon Books, 1962

Hills, Stuart, *By Tank into Normandy*. London: Cassell, 2002

Hodson, James Lansdale, *Through the Dark Night; Being some Account of a War Correspondent's Journeys, Meetings and what was said to Him, in France, Britain, and Flanders during 1939–1940*. London, Gollancz, 1941

—, *The Home Front: Being some Account of Journeys, Meetings and what was said to Me in and about England during 1942–1943*. London: Gollancz, 1944

—, *The Sea and the Land: Being Some Account of Journeys, Meetings, and what was said to Me in Britain, France, Italy, Germany and Holland between March 1943 and May 1945*. London: Gollancz, 1945

Hoggart, Richard, *A Sort of Clowning: Life and Times, Vol. 2: 1940–1959*. Oxford: Oxford University Press, 1991

Holbrook, David, *Flesh Wounds*. Stroud: Tempus, 2007

Holmes, Richard, *Soldiers: Army Lives and Loyalties from Redcoats to Dusty Warriors*. London: HarperPress, 2011

Horsfall, John, *Say Not the Struggle*. Kineton: Roundwood Press, 1977

Howard, Michael, *The Continental Commitment*. London: Ashfield Press, 1989

—, *Captain Professor: The Memoirs of Sir Michael Howard*. London: Continuum, 2006

Howarth, T. E. B., *Prospect and Reality: Britain 1945–1955*. London: Collins, 1985

Hucker, Daniel, *Public Opinion and the End of Appeasement in Britain and France*. Farnham: Ashgate, 2011

Hudson, John: *Sunset in the East: Fighting Against the Japanese through the Siege of Imphal and Alongside Them in Java, 1943–1946*. Barnsley: Leo Cooper, 2002

Hunt, David, *A Don at War*. London: Cass, 1990

Hunt, J. L., A. G. Pringle and C. Morgan, *Service Slang*. London: Faber and Faber, 2008

Hynes, Patrick, *The Militiaman*. London: Avon, 1994

Ironside, Edmund, *Time Unguarded: The Ironside Diaries, 1937–1940*. New York: McKay, 1963

James, John, *The Paladins: A Social History of the RAF up to the Outbreak of World War II*. London: Macdonald & Co., 1990

James, Richard Rhodes, *Chindit*. London: J. Murray, 1980

Jary, Sydney, *18 Platoon*. Carshalton Beeches: Sydney Jary, *c*.1987

Jeffrey, Keith, 'The Post-War Army' in Ian F. W. Beckett and Keith Simpson, eds, *A Nation in Arms: A Social Study of the British Army in the First World War*. Manchester: Manchester University Press, 1985

—, 'The British Army and Ireland since 1922' in T. Bartlett and K. Jefferey, eds, *A Military History of Ireland*. Cambridge: Cambridge University Press, 1996

Jeffreys, Alan, *British Infantryman in the Far East, 1941–45*. Oxford: Osprey, 2003

Johnston, Mark, *Anzacs in the Middle East: Australian Soldiers, Their Allies, and the Local People in World War II*. Cambridge: Cambridge University Press, 2013

Joly, Cyril, *Take These Men*. London: Buchan & Enright, 1985

Jones, Edgar, and Wessely, Simon, *Shell Shock to PTSD: Military Psychiatry from 1900 to the Gulf War*. New York: Psychology Press, 2005

Jones, Stephen G., *Workers at Play: A Social and Economic History of Leisure, 1918–1939*. London: Routledge & Kegan Paul, 1986

Keegan, John, 'Regimental Ideology' in G. Best and A. Wheatcroft, eds, *War, Economy, and the Military Mind*. London: Croom Helm, 1976

—, *Six Armies in Normandy*. New York: Penguin, 1994

—, *The Face of Battle: A Study of Agincourt, Waterloo, and the Somme*. London: Pimlico, 2004

Kellas, Arthur, *Down to Earth, or, Another Bloody Cock-Up: A Parachute Subaltern's Story*. Edinburgh: Pentland Place, 1990

Kendall, Tim, ed., *The Oxford Handbook of British and Irish War Poetry*. Oxford: Oxford University Press, 2009

Kenneally, John, *The Honour and the Shame*. London: Headline Review, 2007

Kennedy, Captain James Russell, *This, Our Army*. London: Hutchinson, 1935

Kersh, Gerald, *Clean, Bright, and Slightly Oiled*. London: Heinemann, 1946

Kettenacker, Lothar, 'Great Britain: Declaring War as a Matter of Honor' in Lothar Kettenacker and Torsten Riotted, eds, *The Legacies of Two World Wars*. New York: Berghahn Books, 2011

King, Anthony, *The Combat Soldier: Infantry Tactics and Cohesion in the Twentieth and Twenty-first Centuries*. Oxford: Oxford University Press, 2013

Koa Wing, Sandra, ed., *Our Longest Days: A People's History of the Second World War*. London: Profile Books, 2008

Langhamer, Claire, *The English in Love: The Intimate Story of an Emotional Revolution*. Oxford: Oxford University Press, 2013

Larkin, Philip, *Collected Poems*. London: Faber and Faber, 1990

Larson, Robert, *The British Army and the Theory of Armored Warfare, 1918–1940*. Newark, DE: University of Delaware Press, 1984

Levy, James P., *Appeasement and Rearmament: Britain, 1936–1939*. Lanham, MD: Rowman & Littlefield, 2006

Lewis, Norman, *Naples '44*. New York: Pantheon Books, 1978

Liddell Hart, B. H., *Paris: Or, the Future of War*. London: Kegan Paul, 1925

—, *The Decisive Wars of History: A Study in Strategy*. London: G. Bell & Sons, 1929

Lindsay, Martin, *So Few Got Through: The Personal Diary of Lieut-Col. Martin Lindsay, D.S.O., M.P., Who Served with the Gordon Highlanders in the 51st Highland Division from July, 1944, to May, 1945*. London: Collins, 1968

Lloyd George, David, *War Memoirs of David Lloyd George*. New York: AMS Press, 1982

Longden, Sean, *To the Victor the Spoils: D-Day and VE Day, The Reality Behind the Heroism*. London: Robinson, 2007

Longworth, Philip, *The Unending Vigil: A History of the Commonwealth War Graves Commission, 1917–1984*. London: Leo Cooper, 1985

Lowe, John, *The Warden: A Portrait of John Sparrow*. London: HarperCollins, 1999

Lowry, Mike, *Fighting Through to Kohima: A Memoir of War in India and Burma*. Barnsley: Pen & Sword, 2008

Lunde, Henrik, *Hitler's Preemptive War: The Battle for Norway, 1940*. Havertown: Casemate, 2010

Lyman, Robert, *Slim, Master of War*. London: Constable, 2004

McCallum, Neil, *Journey with a Pistol: A Diary of War*. London: Gollancz, 1959

McCallum, R. B., *Public Opinion and the Last Peace*. Oxford: Oxford University Press, 1944

Macdonald Hull, C., *A Man from Alamein*. London: Corgi, 1973

McElwee, William Lloyd, *The Art of War: Waterloo to Mons*. Bloomington: Indiana University Press, 1975

MacInnes, Colin, *To the Victors the Spoils*. London: Allison & Busby, 1986

Mackay, Robert, *Half the Battle: Civilian Morale in Britain during the Second World War*. Manchester: Manchester University Press, 2002

McKee, Alexander, *Caen: Anvil of Victory*. London: Souvenir, 2000

MacKenzie, S. P., *Politics and Military Morale: Current-Affairs and Citizenship Education in the British Army, 1914–1950*. Oxford: Oxford University Press, 1992

McKibbin, Ross, *Classes and Cultures: England 1918–1951*. Oxford: Oxford University Press, 1998

Maclaren-Ross, Julian, *Collected Memoirs*. London: Black Spring Press, 2004

—, *Selected Stories*. Stockport: Dewi Lewis, 2004

McLynn, Frank, *The Burma Campaign: Disaster into Triumph 1942–1945*. New Haven: Yale University Press, 2011

Mansoor, Peter, *The GI Offensive in Europe*. Lawrence, KS: University Press of Kansas, 1999

Mason, Tony, '"Hunger . . . Is a Very Good Thing": Britain in the 1930s' in Nick Tiratsoo, ed., *From Blitz to Blair*. London: Weidenfeld & Nicolson, 1997

Masters, John, *Bugles and a Tiger: A Volume of Autobiography*. New York: Viking, 1956

—, *The Road Past Mandalay*. London: Cassell, 2002

Mays, Spike, *Fall Out the Officers*. London: Eyre & Spottiswoode, 1969

Mearsheimer, John J., *Liddell Hart and the Weight of History*. Ithaca: Cornell University Press, 1988

Melling, Leonard, *With the Eighth in Italy*. Manchester: Torch, 1955

Merridale, Catherine, *Ivan's War: Life and Death in the Red Army, 1939–1945*. London: Picador, 2006

Merritt, Maurice, *Eighth Army Driver*. Tunbridge Wells, Kent: Midas Books, 1981

Messenger, Charles, *Call to Arms: The British Army 1914–18*. London: Weidenfeld & Nicolson, 2005

Metcalfe, Robert, *No Time for Dreams: A Soldier's Six-year Journey through World War II*. Burnstown: General Store Publishing House, 1997

Middlebrook, Martin, *The First Day on the Somme: 1 July 1916*. London: Penguin, 2001

Moffat, Jonathan, *Moon Over Malaya: A Tale of Argylles and Marines*. Stroud: Tempus, 2002

Montgomery, Bernard Law, *The Memoirs of Field-Marshal the Viscount Montgomery of Alamein*. Cleveland: World Publishing Co., 1958

Moorehead, Alan, *Eclipse*. New York: Harper & Row, 1968

—, *The Desert War*. London: Aurum, 2009

Moran, Charles, *The Anatomy of Courage*. Boston: Houghton Mifflin, 1967

Moran, Herbert, *In My Fashion*. London: Peter Davies, 1946

More, Charles, *The Road to Dunkirk: The British Expeditionary Force and the Battle of the Ypres-Comines Canal, 1940*. London: Frontline Books, 2013

Moreman, Tim, *The Jungle, The Japanese and the British Commonwealth Armies at War 1941–1945*. New York: Frank Cass, 2005

—, *Desert Rats: British 8th Army in North Africa 1941–1943*. Oxford: Osprey, 2007

Morrison, Blake, *The Movement: English Poetry and Fiction of the 1950s*. Oxford: Oxford University Press, 1980

Mulgan, John, *Report on Experience*. Oxford: Oxford University Press, 1984

Murrell, Eric, *For Your Tomorrow: A Cipher-Sergeant's Diary, 1941–1945*. Dorchester: Plush, 1999

Nisbett, Gordon, *For the Duration: The Journal of a Conscript, 1941 to 1946*. Edinburgh: Pentland Place, 1996

Niven, David, *The Moon's a Balloon*. New York: Putnam, 1971

Noakes, Lucy, *Women in the British Army: War and the Gentle Sex, 1907–1948*. London: Routledge, 2006

Orr, John Boyd, *Food, Health and Income*. London: Garland, 1985

Orwell, George, *Facing Unpleasant Facts: Narrative Essays*. New York: Houghton Mifflin, 2009

—, *All Art is Propaganda: Critical Essays*. New York: Houghton Mifflin, 2009

Overy, Richard, *The Morbid Age: Britain and the Crisis of Civilisation, 1919–1939*. London: Allen Lane, 2009

—, *The Bombing War: Europe, 1939–1945*. London: Allen Lane, 2013

Owen, James, *Commando: Winning World War II Behind Enemy Lines*. London: Little, Brown, 2012

Page, Leo, *The Young Lag*. London: Faber and Faber, 1950

Painter, Robin, *A Signal Honour: With the Chindits and the XIV Army in Burma*. London: Leo Cooper, 1999

Paris, Michael, *Over the Top: The Great War and Juvenile Literature in Britain*. Westport, CT: Praeger, 2004

Pereira, Jocelyn, *A Distant Drum: War Memories of the Intelligence Officer of the 5th Bn. Coldstream Guards, 1944–45*. Wakefield: S.R. Publishers, 1972

Perry, F. W., *The Commonwealth Armies: Manpower and Organisation in Two World Wars*. Manchester: Manchester University Press, 1988

Phillips, Leslie, *Hello: The Autobiography*. London: Orion, 2006

Philpott, William James, *Bloody Victory: The Sacrifice on the Somme and the Making of the Twentieth Century*. London: Little, Brown, 2009

Picot, Geoffrey, *Accidental Warrior: In the Front Line from Normandy till Victory*. Lewes: Book Guild, 1993

Place, Timothy Harrison, *Military Training in the British Army, 1940–1944: from Dunkirk to D-Day*. London: Frank Cass, 2000

Porter, Bernard, *The Absent-minded Imperialists: Empire, Society, and Culture in Britain*. Oxford: Oxford University Press, 2004

Powell, Anthony, *To Keep the Ball Rolling: The Memoirs of Anthony Powell*. Chicago: University of Chicago Press, 2001

Pownall, Henry, *Chief of Staff: The Diaries of Lieutenant-General Sir Henry Pownall: Volume 1, 1933–1940*. London: Leo Cooper, 1972

—, *Chief of Staff: The Diaries of Lieutenant-General Sir Henry Pownall: Volume 2, 1940–1944*. London: Leo Cooper, 1974

Priestley, J. B., *English Journey*. London: Harper & Brothers, 1934

—, *Letter to a Returning Serviceman*. London: Home and Van Thal, 1945

Prior, Robin and Trevor Wilson, *The Somme*. New Haven: Yale University Press, 2006

Proctor, Tammy, *On My Honour: Guides and Scouts in Interwar Britain*. Philadelphia: American Philosophical Society, 2002

Prysor, Glyn, *Citizen Sailors: The Royal Navy in the Second World War*. London: Viking, 2011

Rankin, Nicholas, *A Genius for Deception: How Cunning Helped the British Win Two World Wars*. Oxford: Oxford University Press, 2009

Rass, Christoph, 'The Social Profile of the German Army's Combat Units, 1939–1945' in Jörg Echternkamp, ed., *Germany and the Second World War Volume XI/I: German Wartime Society 1939–1945*. Oxford: Oxford University Press, 2008

Reese, Peter, *Homecoming Heroes: An Account of the Reassimilation of British Military Personnel into Civilian Life*. London: Leo Cooper, 1992

Reynolds, David, *In Command of History: Churchill Fighting and Writing the Second World War*. London: Allen Lane, 2004

Roberts, Andrew, *Masters and Commanders How Four Titans Won the War in the West, 1941–1945*. New York: HarperCollins, 2009

Roberts, Mary Louise, *What Soldiers Do: Sex and the American GI in World War II France*. Chicago: University of Chicago Press, 2013

Roe, Tom, *Anzio Beachhead: Diary of a Signaller*. Derby: Higham Press, 1988

Rose, Sonya, *Which People's War? National Identity and Citizenship in Wartime Britain 1939–1945*. Oxford: Oxford University Press, 2004

Rubin, Gerry, *Murder, Mutiny and the Military: British Court Martial Cases, 1940–1966*. London: Francis Boutle, 2005

Samwell, H. P., *Fighting with the Desert Rats: An infantry Officer's War with the Eighth Army*. Barnsley: Pen & Sword, 2012

Sanger, Ernest, *Letters from the Two World Wars*. Stroud: Sutton, 1993

Saunders, Wilfred Leonard, *Dunkirk Diary of a Very Young Soldier*. Birmingham: Birmingham City Council, Public Libraries Dept, 1989

Scannell, Vernon, *The Tiger and the Rose: An Autobiography*. London: Hamilton, 1971

—, *Argument of Kings*. London: Robson, 1987

Schrijvers, Peter, *Liberators: The Allies and Belgian Society 1944–45*. Cambridge: Cambridge University Press, 2009

Scott, Peter, *The Making of the Modern British Home*. Oxford: Oxford University Press, 2013

Sebag-Montefiore, Hugh, *Dunkirk: Fight to the Last Man*. London: Penguin, 2007

Self, Robert C., *Neville Chamberlain: A Biography*. Aldershot: Ashgate, 2006

Selwyn, Victor, *From Oasis into Italy: War Poems and Diaries from Africa and Italy, 1940–1946*. London: Shepheard-Walwyn, 1983

Seton-Watson, Christopher, *Dunkirk, Alamein, Bologna: Letters and Diaries of an Artilleryman, 1939–1945*. London: Buckland, 1993

Shebbeare, William ['Captain X'], *A Soldier Looks Ahead*. London: Labour Book Service, 1944

Sheffield, Gary, 'The Shadow of the Somme: The Influence of the First World War on British Soldiers' Perceptions and Behaviour in the Second World War' in Paul Addison and Angus Calder, eds, *Time To Kill: The Soldier's Experience of War in the West, 1939–1945*. London: Pimlico, 1997

—, *Leadership in the Trenches: Officer-Man Relations, Morale, and Discipline in the British Army in the Era of the First World War*. New York: St Martin's Place, 2000

—, *Forgotten Victory: The First World War: Myths and Realities*. London: Headline, 2001

Shephard, Ben, *A War of Nerves: Soldiers and Psychiatrists in the Twentieth Century*. Cambridge, MA: Harvard University Press, 2001

—, *The Long Road Home: The Aftermath of the Second World War*. New York: Knopf, 2011

Shipster, John, *Mist on the Rice-fields: A Soldier's Story of the Burma Campaign and the Korean War*. London: Leo Cooper, 2000

Silbey, David, *The British Working Class and Enthusiasm for War, 1914–1916*. New York: Frank Cass, 2005

Simkins, Peter, *Kitchener's Army: The Raising of the New Armies, 1914–16*. Manchester: Manchester University Press, 1988

Simpson, Keith, 'The Officers' in Ian F. W. Beckett and Keith Simpson, eds, *A Nation in Arms: A Social Study of the British Army in the First World War*. Manchester: Manchester University Press, 1985

Smith, Adrian, *The City of Coventry: A Twentieth Century Icon*. London: I.B. Tauris, 2006

Smith, James, *British Writers and MI5 Surveillance, 1930–1960*. Cambridge: Cambridge University Press, 2012

Smith, John, *In at the Finish*. London: Minerva, 1995

Smith, Malcolm, *Britain and 1940: History, Myth, and Popular Memory*. London: Routledge, 2000

Smith, Norman, *Tank Soldier*. Lewes: Book Guild, 1989

Snape, Michael, *God and the British Soldier: Religion and the British Army in the First and Second World Wars*. London: Routledge, 2005

Spencer, Ian R. G., *British Immigration Policy since 1939: The Making of Multi-Racial Britain*. New York: Routledge, 1997

Spicer, Andrew, 'Echoes of War: *Tunes of Glory* and the Demise of the Officer Class in British Cinema' in Danielle Hipkins and Gill Plain, eds, *War-torn Tales: Literature, Film and Gender in the Aftermath of World War II*. Oxford: Peter Lang, 1997

—, 'The "Other War": Images of the Second World War in Service Comedies', in S. Bennett et al., eds, *Relocating Britishness*. Manchester: Manchester University Press, 2004

Spiers, Edward M., 'The Regular Army in 1914' in Ian F. W. Beckett and Keith Simpson, eds, *A Nation in Arms: A Social Study of the British Army in the First World War*. Manchester: Manchester University Press, 1985

Strachan, Hew, 'The Territorial Army and National Defence' in Keith Neilson and Greg Kennedy, eds, *The British Way in Warfare: Power and the International System, 1856–1956*. Farnham: Ashgate, 2010

Strawson, John, *Gentlemen in Khaki: The British Army 1890–1990*. London: Secker & Warburg, 1989

Swaab, Jack, *Field of Fire: Diary of a Gunner Officer*. Stroud: Sutton, 2005

—, *Slouching in the Undergrowth: The Long Life of a Gunner Officer*. Stroud: Fonthill Media, 2012

Szreter, Simon and Kate Fisher, *Sex Before the Sexual Revolution: Intimate Life in England 1918–1963*. Cambridge: Cambridge University Press, 2010

Tebbutt, Melanie, *Being Boys: Youth, Leisure and Identity in the Inter-war Years*. Manchester: Manchester University Press, 2012

Terraine, John, *The Right of the Line: The Royal Air Force in the European War, 1939–1945*. London: Hodder & Stoughton, 1985

Terrell, Richard, *Civilians in Uniform: A Memoir, 1937–1945*. London: Radcliffe Press, 1998

Thatcher, Margaret, *The Path to Power*. London: HarperCollins, 1995

Thomas, Donald, *An Underworld at War: Spivs, Deserters, Racketeers & Civilians in the Second World War*. London: John Murray, 2003

Thompson, Julian, *The Imperial War Museum Book of War Behind Enemy Lines*. London: Sidgwick & Jackson, 1999

—, *Forgotten Voices of Burma*. London: Ebury, 2010

Todd, Selina, *The People: The Rise and Fall of the Working Class, 1910–2010*. London: John Murray, 2014

Todman, Daniel; *The Great War: Myth and Memory*. London: Hambledon Continuum, 2005

Tout, Ken, *By Tank: D to VE Days*. London: R. Hale, 2007

Toye, Richard, *Churchill's Empire: The World That Made Him and the World He Made*. New York: Henry Holt & Co., 2010

Travers, Tim, *The Killing Ground: The British Army, the Western Front and the Emergence of Modern Warfare, 1900–1918*. Barnsley: Pen & Sword, 2003

Trevelyan, Raleigh, *The Fortress: A Diary of Anzio and After*. London: Leo Cooper, 1972

Turner, E. S., *Gallant Gentlemen: A Portrait of the British Officer 1600–1956*. London: Michael Joseph, 1956

Turner, William, *Pals: The 11th (Service) Battalion (Accrington) East Lancashire Regiment*. Barnsley: Wharncliffe Publishing, 1991

Ustinov, Peter, *Dear Me*. London: Little, Brown, 1977

Valentine, C. W., *The Human Factor in the Army*. Aldershot: Gate & Polden, 1943

van Creveld, Martin, *Fighting Power: German and US Army Performance, 1939–1945*. Westport, CT: Greenwood Press, 1982

Vaughan-Thomas, Wynford, *Trust to Talk*. London: Hutchinson, 1980

Vickers, Emma, *Queen and Country: Same Sex Desire in the British Armed Forces, 1939–1945*. Manchester: Manchester University Press, 2013

Vinen, Richard, *National Service: Conscription in Britain, 1945–1963*. London: Allen Lane, 2014

Wardrop, Jake, *Tanks Across the Desert: The War Diary of Jake Wardrop*. London: W. Kimber, 1981

Warner, Philip, *Auchinleck: The Lonely Soldier*. London: Buchan & Enright, 1981

Watson, Alexander, *Enduring the Great War: Combat, Morale and Collapse in the German and British Armies, 1914–1918*. Cambridge: Cambridge University Press, 2008

Weight, Richard, *Patriots: National Identity in Britain, 1940–2000*. London: Macmillan, 2002

Wemyss, George, 'Littoral Struggles, Liminal Lives: Indian Merchant Seafarers' Resistances' in Rehana Ahmed and Sumita Mukherjee, eds, *South Asian Resistances in Britain 1858–1947*. London: Continuum, 2012

White, Peter, *With the Jocks: A Soldier's Struggle for Europe, 1944–45*. Stroud: Sutton, 2003

Whitehouse, Stanley, *Fear is the Foe: A Footslogger from Normandy to the Rhine*. London: Hale, 1995

Wilmot, Chester, *The Struggle for Europe*. New York: Harper, 1952

Wilson, Andrew, *Flame Thrower*. New York: Bantam, 1984

Wingfield, R. M., *The Only Way Out*. London: Hutchinson, 1955

Winter, J. M., *The Great War and the British People*. Houndmills: Macmillan, 1985

Wood, Alan ['Boomerang'], *Bless 'Em All: An Analysis of the British Army, its Morale, Efficiency and Leadership*. London: Secker & Warburg, 1942

Wood, Ian S., ''Twas England Bade our Wild Geese Go: Soldiers of Ireland in the Second World War' in Paul Addison and Angus Calder, eds, *Time to Kill: The Soldier's Experience of War in the West, 1939–1945*. London: Pimlico, 1997

Woodruff, William, *Vessel of Sadness*. Bath: Paragon, 2005

Woollcombe, Robert, *Lion Rampant*. London: Leo Cooper, 1970

Wootton, Graham, *The Official History of the British Legion*. London: MacDonald & Evans, 1956

Ziegler, Philip, *Soldiers: Fighting Men's Lives, 1901–2001*. London: Chatto & Windus, 2001

Zweig, Ferdinand, *Labour, Life and Poverty*. London: Gollancz, 1948

Scholarly Journal Articles

Anonymous, 'The Desertion Crisis in Italy' in *RUSI Journal* 147:5 (2002)

Bidwell, Shelford, 'Five Armies 1920–1970' in *Army Quarterly* 99 (October 1969)

Borton, N. R. M., 'The 14th Army in Burma: A Case Study in Delivering Fighting Power' in *Defence Studies* 2:3 (2002)

Bourke, Joanna, 'Fear and the British and American Military, 1914–45' in *Historical Research* 74:185 (2001)

Caddick-Adams, Peter, 'Phoney War and Blitzkrieg: The Territorial Army in 1939–1940' in *RUSI Journal* 143:2 (1998)

Connelly, Mark and Walter Miller, 'British Courts Martial in North Africa 1940–3' in *Twentieth Century British History* 15:3 (2004)

Corley, Janie, Jeremy Crang and Ian Deary, 'Childhood IQ and In-Service Mortality in Scottish Army Personnel during World War II' in *Intelligence* 37 (2009)

Crang, Jeremy, 'Politics on Parade: Army Education and the 1945 General Election' in *History* 81:262 (1996)

—, 'The Abolition of Compulsory Church Parades in the British Army' in *Journal of Ecclesiastical History* 56:1 (2005)

—, 'The Revival of the British Women's Auxiliary Services in the Late Nineteen-thirties' in *Historical Research* 83:220 (2010)

De Groot, Gerard, '"I Love the Scent of Cordite in Your Hair": Gender Dynamics in Mixed Antiaircraft Batteries during the Second World War' in *History* 82:265 (2002)

Dewey, P. E., 'Military Recruiting and the British Labour Force during the First World War' in *Historical Journal* 27:1 (1984)

Englander, David, 'Soldiering and Identity: Reflections on the Great War' in *War in History* 1:3 (1994)

Englander, David and James Osborne, 'Jack, Tommy, and Henry Dubb: The Armed Forces and the Working Class' in *Historical Journal* 21:3 (1978)

Falls, Cyril, 'Vereker, John Standish Surtees Prendergast, Sixth Viscount Gort (1886–1946)', rev. Brian Bond, *Oxford Dictionary of National Biography*: www.oxforddnb.com/view/ article/36642. Accessed 1 April 2014

Ferris, John, 'Worthy of Some Better Enemy? The British Estimate of the Imperial Japanese Army, 1919–1941, and the Fall of Singapore' in *Canadian Journal of History* 28:2 (1993)

Fielding, Steven, 'What Did "The People" Want? The Meaning of the 1945 General Election' in *Historical Journal* 35:3 (1992)

Francis, Martin, 'A Flight from Commitment? Domesticity, Adventure and the Masculine Imaginary in Britain after the Second World War' in *Gender and History* 19:1 (2007)

French, Craig C., 'The Fashioning of *Esprit de Corps* in the 51st Highland Division from St Valery to El Alamein' in *Journal of the Society for Army Historical Research* 77:312 (1999)

French, 'Discipline and the Death Penalty in the British Army in the War against Germany during the Second World War' in *Journal of Contemporary History* 33:4 (1998)

—, 'The Mechanization of the British Cavalry between the World Wars' in *War in History* 10:3 (2003)

—, David, 'Doctrine and Organization in the British Army, 1919–1932' in *Historical Journal* 44:2 (2001)

Gregory, Adrian, 'Peculiarities of the English: War, Violence and Politics: 1900–1939' in *Journal of Modern European History* 1:1 (2003)

Harrisson, Tom, 'The British Soldier: Changing Attitudes and Ideas' in *British Journal of Psychology* 35:2 (1945)

Hart, Robert A., 'Above and Beyond the Call: Long-term Real Earning Effects of British Male Military Conscription during WWII and the Post-war Years', *Discussion Paper No. 4118*, Institute for the Study of Labor (2009): http://ftp.iza.org/dp4118.pdf

Heffernan, Michael, 'For Ever England: The Western Front and the Politics of Remembrance in Britain' in *Cultural Geographies* 2:293 (1995)

Hucker, Daniel, 'Franco-British Relations and the Question of Conscription in Britain, 1938–1939' in *Contemporary European History* 17:4 (2008)

Jones, Edgar, 'War and the Practice of Psychotherapy: The UK Experience 1939–1960' in *Medical History* 48:4 (2004)

Jones, Edgar and Simon Wessely, 'Psychiatric Battle Casualties: An Intra- and Interwar Comparison' in *British Journal of Psychiatry* 178 (2001)

—, 'A Paradigm Shift in the Conceptualization of Psychological Trauma in the 20th Century' in *Journal of Anxiety Disorders* 21 (2007)

Kelly, Bernard, '"True Citizens" and "Pariah Dogs": Demobilisation, Deserters, and the De Valera Government, 1945' in the *Irish Sword* 28:114 (2011)

Killingray, David, 'Race and Rank in the British Army in the Twentieth Century' in *Ethnic and Racial Studies* 10:3 (1987)

Kohn, Richard, 'Scholarship on World War II: Present and Future' in *Journal of Military History* 55:3 (1991)

Lawrence, Jon, 'Forging a Peaceable Kingdom: War, Violence, and Fear of Brutalization in Post-First World War Britain' in *Journal of Modern History* 75:3 (2003)

Lees, Robert, 'Venereal Diseases in the Armed Forces Overseas (1)' in *British Journal of Venereal Diseases* 22:4 (1946)

Lunt, James, 'A Hell of a Licking: Some Reflections on the Retreat from Burma, December 1941–May 1942' in *RUSI Journal* 130:3 (1985)

MacKenzie, S. R., 'Vox Populi: British Army Newspapers in the Second World War' in *Journal of Contemporary History* 24:4 (1989)

—, 'Morale and the Cause: The Campaign to Shape the Outlook of Soldiers in the British Expeditionary Force, 1914–1918' in *Canadian Journal of History* 25:2 (1990)

Martin, David, 'Nancy Astor and Hamish Henderson's "The Ballad of the D-Day Dodgers"' in *History Teaching Review* 22 (2008)

Natzio, Georgina, 'British Army Servicemen and Women 1939–45: Their Selection, Care and Management' in *RUSI Journal* 138:1 (1993)

Otley, C. B., 'The Social Origins of British Army Officers' in *Sociological Review* 18:2 (1970)

Palmer, Dave, 'Teeth and Tail in the British Army: Churchill and Wavell' in *Army* 24 (1974)

Peaty, John, 'The Desertion Crisis in Italy, 1944' in *RUSI Journal* 147:3 (2002)

Petter, M., '"Temporary Gentlemen" in the Aftermath of the Great War: Rank, Status and the Ex-Officer Problem' in *Historical Journal* 37:1 (2009)

Place, Timothy Harrison, 'Lionel Wigram, Battle Drill and the British Army in the Second World War' in *War in History* 7:4 (2000)

Poole, F. G., 'Youth and National Defence' in *RUSI Journal* 83:532 (1938)

Porter, Vincent and Chaim Letewski, 'The Way Ahead: Case History of a Propaganda Film' in *Sight and Sound* 50 (1981)

Radcliffe, R.A.C., 'Officer-Man Relationships' in *Army Quarterly* 46:1 (May 1943)

Ramsden, John, 'Refocussing "the People's War": British War Films of the 1950s' in *Journal of Contemporary History* 33:1 (1998)

Reid, Brian, 'T. E. Lawrence and Liddell Hart' in *History* 70:229 (1985)

Robbins, Keith, 'Commemorating the Second World War in Britain: Problems of Definition' in *History Teacher* 29:2 (1996)

Roberts-Pedersen, Elizabeth, 'A Weak Spot in the Personality? Conceptualizing "War Neurosis" in British Medical Literature of the Second World War' in *Australian Journal of Politics and History* 58:3 (2012)

Rose, Sonya, 'Sex, Citizenship, and the Nation in World War II Britain' in *American Historical Review* 103:4 (1998)

Salaman, G., and Thompson, K., 'Class Culture and the Persistence of an Elite: The Case of Army Officer Selection' in *Sociological Review* 26:2 (1978)

Shephard, Ben, '"Pitiless Psychology": The Role of Prevention in British Military Psychiatry in the Second World War' in *History of Psychiatry* 10 (1999)

Shils, Edward and Morris Janowitz, 'Cohesion and Disintegration in the Wehrmacht in World War II' in *Public Opinion Quarterly* 12:2 (1948)

Sixsmith, E. K. G., 'The British Army in May 1940 – A Comparison with the BEF 1914' in *RUSI Journal* 127:3 (1982)

Sokoloff, Sally, 'Soldiers or Civilians? The Impact of Army Service in World War Two on Birmingham Men' in *Oral History* 25 (Autumn 1997)

—, '"How Are They at Home?" Community, State and Servicemen's Wives in England, 1939–45' in *Women's History Review* 8:1 (1999)

Strachan, Hew, 'Training, Morale and Modern War' in *Journal of Contemporary History* 41:2 (2006)

Summerfield, Penelope, 'Education and Politics in the British Armed Forces in the Second World War' in the *International Review of Social History* 26:2 (1981)

Thalassis, Nafsika, 'Useless Soldiers: The Dilemma of Discharging Mentally Unfit Soldiers During the Second World War' in *Social History of Medicine* 23:1 (2010)

Todd, Selina, 'Flappers and Factory Lads: Youth and Youth Culture in Interwar Britain' in *History Compass* 4:4 (2006)

Urquhart, R. E., 'The History and Aims of the Army Cadet Force' in *Journal of the Royal Society of Arts* 91:4740 (April 1947)

Watson, Don, '"Where Do We Go From Here?": Education, Theatre and Politics in the British Army, 1942–1945' in *Labour History Review* 59:3 (1994)

Wessely, Simon, 'Twentieth-century Theories on Combat Motivation and Breakdown' in *Journal of Contemporary History* 41:2 (2006)

Zweiniger-Bargiowoska, Ina, 'Building a British Superman: Physical Culture in Interwar Britain' in *Journal of Contemporary History* 41:4 (2006)

Unpublished Theses

Armstrong, Gordon Patrick, The Controversy over Tanks in the British Army 1919 to 1933. King's College University of London, 1976

Elsey, Ena, The Rehabilitation and Employment of Disabled Ex-Servicemen after the Two World Wars. University of Teeside, 1994

Lauer, George, Perspectives on Infantry: Quality and Cohesion: Comparison of American, British, and German Army Manpower Policies and Effects on the Infantry Small Unit during the Second World War, 1939–1945. Florida State University, 2010

Peaty, John Robert, British Army Manpower Crisis 1944. King's College, University of London, 2000

Reilly, Emma, Civilians into Soldiers: The British Male Military Body in the Second World War. University of Strathclyde, 2010

Waller, Michael L., The Conservatism of the British Cavalry and its Effects on the British Army of WWII. Drew University, 2009

Whittle, E. Y., British Casualties on the Western Front 1914–1918 and their Influence on the Military Conduct of the Second World War. University of Leicester, 1991

Music

'Sod's Opera', *Onward 15 Army Group*. Beautiful Jo Records, 2000

Websites

BBC People's War (www.bbc.co.uk/history/ww2peopleswar)
Hansard (http://hansard.millbanksystems.com)
John D. Clare (www.johndclare.net)
Lancastria Association of Scotland (www.lancastria.org.uk)
LFC History (www.lfchistory.net)
Naval History and Heritage Command (www.history.navy.mil)

INDEX